Lecture Notes in Artificial Intelligence   9736

Subseries of Lecture Notes in Computer Science

LNAI Series Editors

Randy Goebel
  University of Alberta, Edmonton, Canada
Yuzuru Tanaka
  Hokkaido University, Sapporo, Japan
Wolfgang Wahlster
  DFKI and Saarland University, Saarbrücken, Germany

LNAI Founding Series Editor

Joerg Siekmann
  DFKI and Saarland University, Saarbrücken, Germany

More information about this series at http://www.springer.com/series/1244

Don Harris (Ed.)

Engineering Psychology and Cognitive Ergonomics

13th International Conference, EPCE 2016
Held as Part of HCI International 2016
Toronto, ON, Canada, July 17–22, 2016
Proceedings

 Springer

Editor
Don Harris
Coventry University
Coventry
UK

ISSN 0302-9743 ISSN 1611-3349 (electronic)
Lecture Notes in Artificial Intelligence
ISBN 978-3-319-40029-7 ISBN 978-3-319-40030-3 (eBook)
DOI 10.1007/978-3-319-40030-3

Library of Congress Control Number: 2016940357

LNCS Sublibrary: SL7 – Artificial Intelligence

Printed on acid-free paper

This Springer imprint is published by Springer Nature
The registered company is Springer International Publishing AG Switzerland

Foreword

The 18th International Conference on Human-Computer Interaction, HCI International 2016, was held in Toronto, Canada, during July 17–22, 2016. The event incorporated the 15 conferences/thematic areas listed on the following page.

A total of 4,354 individuals from academia, research institutes, industry, and governmental agencies from 74 countries submitted contributions, and 1,287 papers and 186 posters have been included in the proceedings. These papers address the latest research and development efforts and highlight the human aspects of the design and use of computing systems. The papers thoroughly cover the entire field of human-computer interaction, addressing major advances in knowledge and effective use of computers in a variety of application areas. The volumes constituting the full 27-volume set of the conference proceedings are listed on pages IX and X.

I would like to thank the program board chairs and the members of the program boards of all thematic areas and affiliated conferences for their contribution to the highest scientific quality and the overall success of the HCI International 2016 conference.

This conference would not have been possible without the continuous and unwavering support and advice of the founder, Conference General Chair Emeritus and Conference Scientific Advisor Prof. Gavriel Salvendy. For his outstanding efforts, I would like to express my appreciation to the communications chair and editor of *HCI International News*, Dr. Abbas Moallem.

April 2016   Constantine Stephanidis

HCI International 2016 Thematic Areas
and Affiliated Conferences

Thematic areas:

- Human-Computer Interaction (HCI 2016)
- Human Interface and the Management of Information (HIMI 2016)

Affiliated conferences:

- 13th International Conference on Engineering Psychology and Cognitive Ergonomics (EPCE 2016)
- 10th International Conference on Universal Access in Human-Computer Interaction (UAHCI 2016)
- 8th International Conference on Virtual, Augmented and Mixed Reality (VAMR 2016)
- 8th International Conference on Cross-Cultural Design (CCD 2016)
- 8th International Conference on Social Computing and Social Media (SCSM 2016)
- 10th International Conference on Augmented Cognition (AC 2016)
- 7th International Conference on Digital Human Modeling and Applications in Health, Safety, Ergonomics and Risk Management (DHM 2016)
- 5th International Conference on Design, User Experience and Usability (DUXU 2016)
- 4th International Conference on Distributed, Ambient and Pervasive Interactions (DAPI 2016)
- 4th International Conference on Human Aspects of Information Security, Privacy and Trust (HAS 2016)
- Third International Conference on HCI in Business, Government, and Organizations (HCIBGO 2016)
- Third International Conference on Learning and Collaboration Technologies (LCT 2016)
- Second International Conference on Human Aspects of IT for the Aged Population (ITAP 2016)

Conference Proceedings Volumes Full List

Engineering Psychology and Cognitive Ergonomics

Program Board Chair: **Don Harris, UK**

- Guy Andre Boy, USA
- Nicklas Dahlstrom, UAE
- Matt Ebbatson, Australia
- Shan Fu, P.R. China
- John Huddlestone, UK
- Hung-Sying Jing, Taiwan
- Wen-Chin Li, UK
- Peng Liu, P.R. China

- Andreas Luedtke, Germany
- Jan Noyes, UK
- Paul Salmon, Australia
- Axel Schulte, Germany
- Siraj Shaikh, UK
- Neville Stanton, UK
- Patrick Waterson, UK

The full list with the program board chairs and the members of the program boards of all thematic areas and affiliated conferences is available online at:

http://www.hci.international/2016/

HCI International 2017

The 19th International Conference on Human-Computer Interaction, HCI International 2017, will be held jointly with the affiliated conferences in Vancouver, Canada, at the Vancouver Convention Centre, July 9–14, 2017. It will cover a broad spectrum of themes related to human-computer interaction, including theoretical issues, methods, tools, processes, and case studies in HCI design, as well as novel interaction techniques, interfaces, and applications. The proceedings will be published by Springer. More information will be available on the conference website: http://2017. hci.international/.

General Chair
Prof. Constantine Stephanidis
University of Crete and ICS-FORTH
Heraklion, Crete, Greece
E-mail: general_chair@hcii2017.org

http://2017.hci.international/

Contents

Team Cognition

Cognition in Complex and High Risk Environments

Cognition in Aviation

Mental Workload and Performance

Toward Quantitative Modeling of User Performance in Multitasking Environments

Shijing Liu[✉], Amy Wadeson, and Chang S. Nam

North Carolina State University, Raleigh, NC, USA
{sliu14, aewadeso, csnam}@ncsu.edu

Abstract. Multitasking performance requires the ability to perform multiple tasks in the same time period by switching between individual tasks. To quantify the performance, a quantitative model for user performance in a multitasking environment was proposed in this study. This model was based on Shannon's information theory and quantified the information produced from each subtask in the multitasking environment. The Multi-Attribute Task Battery-II (MATB-II) was employed as a platform of multitasking. There were two phases of the experiment and ten participants completed the experiment. Results showed an overall improvement in user performance after reassigned task weights according to the proposed approach. Findings also indicated there was an effect of task difficulty on multitasking performance. The proposed model provided an approach to estimate and improve user performance in a multitasking environment.

Keywords: Multitasking · Quantitative modeling · Task difficulty · User performance

1 Introduction

Multitasking is required in many jobs and the goal of multitasking is to perform multiple tasks simultaneously by switching between individual tasks [1, 2]. Previous research demonstrated different approaches for assessing user performance in a multitasking environment [3–5], but only few studies quantitatively analyzed multitasking performance. This study proposed a quantitative model to estimate user performance in a multitasking environment.

The modeling of human information processing has been contributing to human-computer interaction since the early 1950s [6–8]. The Hick-Hyman Law [6, 7] was built upon a systematic relationship between the number of alternate stimuli and choice-reaction times. The law predicts a linear relationship between reaction time and transmitted information. Fitts' Law [8, 9] states a linear relationship between task difficulty and movement time. These human information processing models were widely applied in this area and originally applied to single-task scenarios. In 1948, Shannon [10] published a mathematical theory of communication, which laid the foundation of information theory and was employed in many areas including human-computer interaction. In this study, a quantitative model was proposed based on these human information processing models to estimate user performance quantitatively and improve their

© Springer International Publishing Switzerland 2016
D. Harris (Ed.): EPCE 2016, LNAI 9736, pp. 3–9, 2016.
DOI: 10.1007/978-3-319-40030-3_1

multitasking performance. The Multi-Attribute Task Battery II (MATB-II) was applied as a multitasking environment in this study.

The remainder of this paper is organized as follows: Sect. 2 introduces the proposed quantitative model and discusses a two-phase study demonstrating the application of the proposed model. Section 3 presents the results from the experiments while Sect. 4 explains and discusses the details of the findings. The last section discusses the implications of the proposed model and future research.

2   Methods

2.1   Quantitative Model and MATB-II Tasks

In this study, Multi-Attribute Task Battery II (MATB-II) was employed as a platform for multitasking [11]. Four subtasks were applied during the experiment: Light, Scale, Tracking, and Communication. Figure 1 shows the interface of MATB-II tasks.

The Light task requires the user to respond to the absence of the green light and the presence of the red light (top left of Fig. 1). The Scale task requires the user to observe and detect a deviation of the moving scale from the midpoint (left, middle of Fig. 1). The Communication task plays audio messages with particular "callsigns" and requires the user to choose the announced channel and frequency (bottom left of Fig. 1). The Tracking task has two modes: manual and Automatic. When the task is under manual

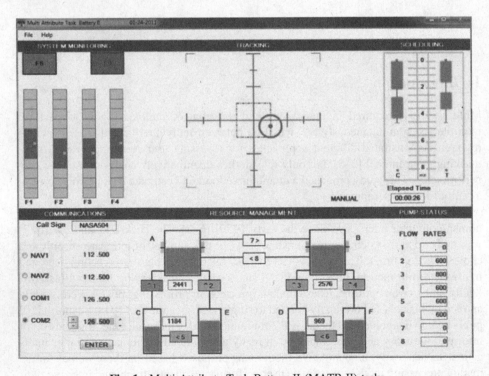

Fig. 1. Multi-Attribute Task Battery II (MATB-II) tasks

mode, the user needs to control a joystick with their left hand and keep the cursor in the center area (top, middle of Fig. 1). A Workload Rating Scale (WRS) is built into the MATB-II program and is based on the NASA Task Load Index [12]. The subjective workload assessed by WRS include six subscales: mental demand, physical demand, temporal demand, performance, effort, and frustration. The rating score ranges from 0 to 100 for each subscale. The questionnaire is presented after each trail.

To estimate the information produced by each subtask in MATB-II, baud rate (bit per second or bps) of each subtask is employed and defined based on Shannon's information theory.

$$B(i) = \frac{H(i)}{\Delta T(i)} \tag{1}$$

where $H(i)$ is the total information produced by subtask i and $\Delta T(i)$ is the time interval of two events of subtask i. When the subtask i is Light, Scale, or Communication,

$$H(i) = \log_2[p(i)] \tag{2}$$

where $p(i)$ is all possible events of subtask i. For MATB-II tasks of Light, Scale, and Communication, the events contained in each task have equal probability. For example, there are two events contained in the Light task (green and red lights) and each of them have a probability of occurrence of 0.5. Hence, all possible events of Light is $p(Light) = 2$ and the information produced in this task is $H(Light) = \log_2[p(i)] = 1$ bit.

When the subtask i is Tracking, which involves a circular cursor with diameter D and a target with width W, based on Fitts' Law [8, 9] and Shannon's information theory [10], the information produced from this subtask is

$$H(i) = \log_2\left(\frac{2D}{W}\right) \tag{3}$$

To investigate user performance among different levels of task difficulty, different overall baud rate (B_{TOT}) was assigned by manipulating the time interval for each subtask to represent different difficulty levels during the experiment. To assess user performance among individual subtasks, a response ratio of each subtask [13] was applied to the model to determine the weight of each subtask. The response ratio ($RR(i)$) is defined as correct response per trial for subtask i. The weight of subtask i is denoted as $w(i)$ and

$$\sum w(i)RR(i) = 1 \tag{4}$$

Overall baud rate of MATB-II tasks is defined as B_{TOT}.

$$B_{TOT} = \sum w(i)B(i) \tag{5}$$

To estimate the weight of each subtask, this approach includes two phases. During the first phase, all subtasks are assigned with equal weight and all response ratios are assumed to equal to 1. After a user completes a set of tasks in first phase, the response ratio of each subtask is calculated and the weight of each subtask is estimated according to Eq. (4). To maintain the same level of task difficulty and to balance among each individual tasks, a new set of tasks with different weights is assigned according to Eq. (5).

2.2 Participants

Ten users were recruited to participate in this study. Participants consisted of 6 males and 4 females, with an average age of 25 years old. All participants reported normal or corrected-to-normal vision and were right handed. All participants were native English speakers. All participants completed two phases of this study.

2.3 Experiment Design

Three levels of task difficulty were manipulated by setting up different overall baud rate (B_{TOT} = 0.5, 1.0, and 1.6 bps, respectively). There were two phases in this study with the three levels of overall baud rate kept the same for both phases. All participants were required to complete both phases.

Before the first phase, a training session of MATB-II tasks was provided to each participant. During the first phase, each participant was required to complete 6 trials (3 levels × 2 replicates) of MATB-II tasks. All participants were required to complete the tasks as quickly and accurately as possible. Each trial was 5 min. At the end of each trial, the NASA-TLX questionnaire was presented. After the participant completed the questionnaire, s/he was allowed a 3 min rest before the next trial. Phase I took 60 min for each participant.

After Phase I, user performance was analyzed and a new set of MATB-II tasks was assigned to each participant. All participant needed to complete the second phase of the experiment at least one day after first phase. Phase II included 6 5-minute trials (3 levels × 2 replicates) of MATB-II tasks. There was no training session during Phase II. It took approximately 50 min for each participant.

3 Results

All participants completed two phases of MATB-II tasks. For each phase, four subtasks were performed by each participant. The response time and response ratio of the Light (RT_Light and RR_Light), Scale (RT_Scale and RR_Scale), and Communication (RT_COMM and RR_COMM) tasks were recorded during experiments. Mean root mean square (MRMS) of the distance between the target and the center point for the Tracking task was also recorded. At the end of each trial, a Workload Rating Scale (WRS) was presented and completed by the participant. The mean rating scores were recorded for all trials in order to estimate the workload of each trial. Table 1 shows mean values of user performance parameters.

Table 1. Means of user performance parameters

Level	Easy		Medium		Difficult	
Phase	I	II	I	II	I	II
RT_Light	1.512	1.332	1.730	1.332	1.752	1.466
RT_Scale	2.534	2.243	2.877	2.131	3.301	2.979
RT_COMM	1.705	1.391	1.756	1.520	1.989	1.950
RR_Light	0.996	1.000	0.995	1.000	0.971	0.986
RR_Scale	0.963	0.968	0.977	0.986	0.966	0.972
RR_COMM	0.921	0.954	0.910	0.977	0.935	0.953
MRMS	19.89	17.27	31.97	28.09	50.51	41.89
WRS	30.09	19.33	39.41	32.28	58.55	55.87
RT_COMM	1.705	1.391	1.756	1.520	1.989	1.950

Most parameters of user performance showed the appearance of non-normal data in normality test, except for response time in the Scale task (RT_Scale) and WRS. A nonparametric method, Kruskal-Wallis one-way ANOVA, was applied to investigate the differences in user performance among different difficulty levels. Table 2 shows the p-value from ANOVA for each parameter.

Table 2. ANOVA of difficulty level for user performance

	Phase I	Phase II
RT_Light	0.215	0.129
RT_Scale	0.003*	0.0004**
RT_COMM	0.703	0.035*
RR_Light	0.186	<0.0001**
RR_Scale	0.080	0.652
RR_COMM	0.666	0.353
MRMS	<0.0001**	<0.0001**
WRS	0.004**	0.0003**

Note. * significance level: $p < 0.05$. ** significance level: $p < 0.01$.

All parameters of the changes between two phases showed the appearance of non-normal data in normality test. To compare user performance between two phases, a Wilcoxon Signed Rank test was applied for each parameter and each difficulty level between two phases. Table 3 shows the mean changes in each parameter and implies all significant results from the Wilcoxon Signed Rank test.

Table 3. Parameter comparion between two phases

Difficulty level	Easy	Medium	Difficult
RT_Light	−0.180*	−0.398**	−0.286**
RT_Scale	−0.291	−0.746**	−0.322*
RT_COMM	−0.314*	−0.236	−0.039
RR_Light	0.003	0.005	0.015*
RR_Scale	0.005	0.009	0.006
RR_COMM	0.033	0.067**	0.018
MRMS	−2.622**	−3.874*	−8.623**
WRS	−10.768**	−7.133	−2.684

Note. * significance level: $p < 0.05$. ** significance level: $p < 0.01$.

4 Discussion

The results of all user performance parameters showed an overall improvement during Phase II compared to Phase I. After reassigning task weights for each individuals, users spent less time to complete Light, Scale, and Communication tasks at all difficulty levels, meanwhile, they correctly responded more to signals from Light, Scale, and Communication tasks than during Phase I. Users also had less MRMS for Tracking task at all difficulty levels during Phase II. The subjective rating scores of workload (WRS) implied a decrease at all levels during second phase.

Findings indicated the effect of task difficulty level on user performance in multitasking environment. During both phases, user response time in the Scale task, MRMS of the Tracking task, and the overall workload (WRS) showed significant differences among task difficulty level. In addition, during Phase II, response ratio implied significant results among task difficulty levels.

Comparison of parameters between two phases demonstrated significant improvement in user performance after reassigned subtasks to users based on their performance during Phase I. The findings of response time of the Light, Scale, and Communication tasks indicated decreases at all three difficulty levels and more than half of them showed significant changes in Phase II. The findings of response ratio implied an overall increase in Phase II. Only two treatments of this parameter showed significant increases after reassigning the subtasks in MATB-II. A potential reason is that users already had high response ratios among these subtasks (RR(Light) > 0.97, RR(Scale) > 0.96, and RR(COMM) > 0.91) during Phase I. After reassigning the subtasks, users were still able to maintain a higher level of correct responses among different difficulty levels and showed an overall increase in their performance. The findings of the Tracking task revealed significant decreases of MRMS among all difficulty levels. Results of workload ratings (WRS) showed an overall decrease among all levels.

5 Conclusion

This study proposed a quantitative model to assess user performance in multitasking environment and demonstrated the approach of task weight assignment based on individual's performance to improve overall multitasking performance. Results implied an overall improvement in user performance after reassigning subtasks to each participant. Findings in this study also indicated there was an effect of task difficulty levels on user performance and several parameters showed significant difference among different levels of task difficulty. This approach is able to provide a guideline for multitasking users to train themselves and improve their performance based on different multitasking system and individual performance. Principles of multitasking operation can be established on the proposed model to achieve different task goals (e.g., satisfaction, response ratio, task efficiency, etc.).

There should be other potential factors than task difficulty influence on user performance in multitasking. Future research could investigate the effect of other factors on multitasking performance (e.g., training effect, individual differences).

References

1. Delbridge, K.A.: Individual differences in multi-tasking ability: exploring a nomological network (2000)
2. Konig, C.J., Buhner, M., Murling, G.: Working memory, fluid intelligence, and attention are predictors of multitasking performance, but polychronicity and extraversion are not. Hum. Perform. **18**(3), 243–266 (2005)
3. Spink, A., Park, M., Jansen, B.J., Pedersen, J.: Multitasking during Web search sessions. Inf. Process. Manage. **42**(1), 264–275 (2006)
4. David, P., Xu, L., Srivastava, J., Kim, J.H.: Media multitasking between two conversational tasks. Comput. Hum. Behav. **29**(4), 1657–1663 (2013)
5. Alexopoulou, P., Morris, A., Hepworth, M.: A new integrated model for multitasking during web searching. Procedia-Soc. Behav. Sci. **147**, 16–25 (2014)
6. Hick, W.E.: On the rate of gain of information. Quart. J. Exp. Psychol. **4**(1), 11–26 (1952)
7. Hyman, R.: Stimulus information as a determinant of reaction time. J. Exp. Psychol. **45**(3), 188 (1953)
8. Fitts, P.M.: The information capacity of the human motor system in controlling the amplitude of movement. J. Exp. Psychol. **47**(6), 381 (1954)
9. Fitts, P.M., Peterson, J.R.: Information capacity of discrete motor responses. J. Exp. Psychol. **67**(2), 103 (1964)
10. Shannon. C.E.: A mathematical theory of communication. Bell Syst. Tech. J. **27**, 379–423, 623–656 (1948)
11. Santiago-Espada, Y., Myer, R.R., Latorella, K.A., Comstock Jr., J.R.: The Multi-Attribute Task Battery II (MATB-II) software for human performance and workload research: a user's guide. NASA Tech Memorandum, 217164 (2011)
12. Hart, S.G., Staveland, L.E.: Development of NASA-TLX (Task Load Index): results of empirical and theoretical research. Adv. Psychol. **52**, 139–183 (1988)
13. Phillips, C.A., Repperger, D.W., Kinsler, R., Bharwani, G., Kender, D.: A quantitative model of the human–machine interaction and multi-task performance: a strategy function and the unity model paradigm. Comput. Biol. Med. **37**(9), 1259–1271 (2007)

Sensitivity, Bias, and Mental Workload in a Multitasking Environment

Monika Putri, Xiaonan Yang, and Jung Hyup Kim[(⊠)]

Department of Industrial and Manufacturing Systems Engineering,
University of Missouri, Columbia, MO, USA
{mapmtf,xyr29}@mail.missouri.edu, kijung@missouri.edu

Abstract. In this paper, we used signal detection theory (SDT) as a tool to evaluate human performance in a multitasking environment. The primary objective of using SDT is to assess an operator's sensitivity (d') and bias (β). In addition, NASA-TLX was used to measure participants' workload under different complexity scenarios. During the experiment, participants were asked to detect abnormal and alarm signals on a gauge monitoring display. They also needed to perform multi-attribute task battery (MATB) tasks at the same time. The gauge-monitoring screen contains total 52 gauges (flow, level, temperature, and pressure). The MATB consists of system monitoring, target tracking, and dynamic resource management. The results of this study demonstrate that participants showed various levels of sensitivity (d') in the gauge-monitoring task based on the degree of task complexity.

Keywords: Signal detection theory · Human-in-the-loop simulation · Mental workload

1 Introduction

Operators who perform tasks under supervisory control continuously keep track of new and high priority events (Ratwani et al. 2010). The control room environment in oil and gas refineries is one example of this. The room consists of multiple, complex human-machine systems. The operator must observe numerous different control loops while concurrently performing other attention-demanding tasks (Kim et al. 2015; Noah et al. 2014). Although the systems generate lots of data, the amount of information transmitted to the operator is always smaller than the stimulus information. Hence, it is necessary to understand how the operators reform their detectability, under a multitasking environment, to improve control conditions and avoid mistakes caused by missing the critical information. According to the previous research done by Pashler (1994), multitasking is one of the main causes of increasing human errors and reaction time. The multitasking environment results in degradation of information to the operator. Swets and Biedsall's (1955) found that humans who are working with multiple displays are making their choices among a number of signal alternatives. In addition, a cooperative multitasking involves task switching activities, which causes a higher error rate and slower reaction time during the tasks (Spector and Biederman 1976).

© Springer International Publishing Switzerland 2016
D. Harris (Ed.): EPCE 2016, LNAI 9736, pp. 10–18, 2016.
DOI: 10.1007/978-3-319-40030-3_2

In this study, we examined an impact of the complexity level in a multitasking environment (primary task: gauge monitoring task, secondary task: MATB). The signal rate of the gauge monitoring task was used to design the different levels of complexity. Each task requires a different cognitive resource, such as visual searching, target tracking, and diagnostic control. To conduct the experiment, a human-in-the-loop (HITL) simulation was used. A set of gauges shapes of flow, level, pressure, and temperature were used and underlay the design of the overview display (OD) that represents an actual refinery's operations (Bullemer et al. 2009). The HITL experiment allowed us to observe participants' direct responses and activities generated by characteristic functions of the given task. The activities comprised detecting abnormal events in a continuous gauge monitoring task. We applied SDT to measure human performance in a multitasking environment. SDT evaluates the psychometric function that describes how performance increases with stimulation degrees (García-Pérez and Alcalá-Quintana 2011). It measures an individual's ability to detect signals in a dual-task environment. The outcomes of SDT consist of Hit, Miss, False Alarm, and Correct Rejection. Using the outcome data, we will be able to calculate operator perceptual sensitivity (d') and operator bias, (β) (Walker and Brewster 2000). Operator bias is defined as the likelihood that a participant will favor one direction as opposed to the other, whereas sensitivity measures operator accuracy in differentiating the signal from the noise (Lerman et al. 2010). In addition, NASA-TLX was used to measure participants' workload during the experiment. NASA-TLX is a multi-dimensional rating task that measures an overall workload score in a dynamic environment.

The goal of this study is to investigate operator sensitivity, bias, and workload in a multitasking environment. The findings are not only beneficial for understanding operator behavior but also developing an operator decision-making model in a multitasking environment.

2 Methods

2.1 Participants

A total of 18 university students participated in this study. Participants included undergraduate and graduate students. The average age was 22 for male students and 23 for female students (M = 22.61, SD = 4.36). 45 % of participants were male and 55 % were female. Every participant had normal vision and no upper-body impairments that may have limited the use of a mouse as an interface.

2.2 Apparatus

To create a more realistic assessment in a multitasking environment, the gauge monitoring human-in-the-loop (HITL) simulation was used as a primary task (Kim et al. 2014). It contained five functional areas to represent all the major gauges (see Fig. 1). Each gauge showed different colored-outlines to indicate a normal, abnormal, or alarm state (see Table 1). We also used the multi-attribute task battery (MATB) as a second task. It consists of system monitoring, tracking, resource management, communication,

Table 1. Examples of different gauge states

Gauge Contour Color	Alarm Type
HVGO Reflux	Abnormal (dark blue colored-line)
VRFO Product	Low Alarm (yellow colored-line)
Heater Outlet	High Alarm (blue colored-line)
Total Pass Flow	Hi-Hi Alarm & Lo-Lo Alarm (red colored-line)

and scheduling task, but the communication task was deactivated during the experiment (see Fig. 2). Every experimental scenario was developed based on the actual refinery's operation. Participants experienced two levels of complexity scenarios (low and high) during the experiment. The total number of events in the high complexity scenario category was twice as large as the low complexity scenario category.

There were 12 alarm events of low complexity and 24 alarm events of high complexity. Moreover, the MATB was used to keep the balance of complexity in each scenario. For example, when the number of alarm events decreased, the number of events in the MATB increased.

3 Procedure

The experiment was conducted as a two-factor experiment with repeated measures (within-subject factors: scenario complexity and day), and a multi-session study, which would be continued for five days. Day 1 was a training session, and Day 2 and 3 were

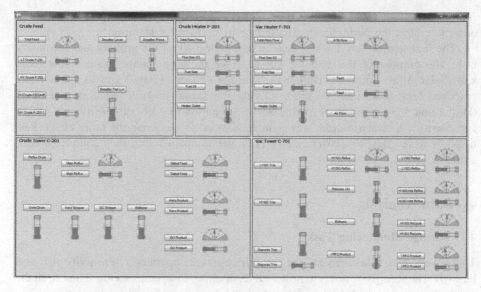

Fig. 1. The gauge monitoring HITL simulation

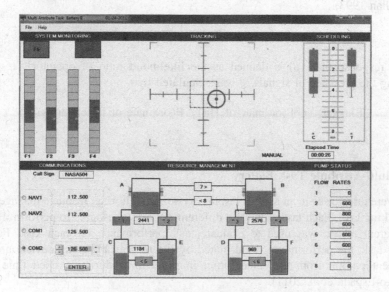

Fig. 2. MATB display

practice sessions. The data from Day 4 and 5 was used to analyze operator's sensitivity and bias. A statistical model was developed to analyze the performance under different complexity scenarios. Day 1 required 60 min for an introduction of initial training trials. Day 2 and 3 involved additional practice tests to ensure that participants were fully aware of all tasks. Day 4 and 5 were considered the actual experiment days in order to collect the performance data for the assessment of learning.

The first step of Day 1 was a general orientation about the primary and secondary task. The purpose of this training was to make the participants aware of the basic knowledge of all functions. During the practice sessions (Day 2 and 3), participants practiced both tasks multiple times. During the actual process monitoring sessions (Day 4 and 5), participants experienced six scenarios (3 low complexity and 3 high complexity). A scenario order was counterbalanced to eliminate the order effect. Participants were asked to answer NASA-TLX questionnaires after they completed each scenario.

4 Data Analysis

4.1 Gauge Monitoring Task

There were two measurements for the primary task: operator's sensitivity (d') and bias (β). The sensitivity refers to how well an operator discriminates the signal from the noise (Lerman et al. 2010). d' was calculated by subtracting the z-score that corresponds to the false alarm rate from the z-score that corresponds to the hit rate (Macmillan 1993).

$$\text{Sensitivity (d') = } |Z(\text{Hit}) - Z(\text{False Alarm})| \tag{1}$$

The response bias (β) is defined as the likelihood ratio of operator's response regarding the presence of signals. β was calculated by

$$\text{Bias } (\beta) = P(\text{ordinate of Hit}) / P(\text{ordinate of false alarms}) \tag{2}$$

4.2 Multi-Attribute Task Battery

There were three tasks in an MATB display: system monitoring, resource management, and tracking task. Each task requires a different cognitive resource to perform. Hence, the different metric was used to evaluate task performance on each task. For the tracking task, the performance is calculated by the root mean square deviation of the target center point from the center point in pixel units during a fixed time lapse (Santiago-Espada et al. 2011).

$$RMSD\_C = Square\,Root\,(SS/NUM) \tag{3}$$

The value range is from 0 for the center position to 300 for continuous maximum X and Y offset. *NUM* is the number of samples (15-s intervals), and SS is the sum of the squares of the X-offset plus the Y-offset. By using this, the tracking performance (A_T) was calculated by

$$A_T = \frac{(the\ highest\ RMSD\_C - current\ tRMSD\_C)}{the\ highest\ RMSD\_C} \tag{4}$$

For the system-monitoring task, the performance (A_S) was calculated by

$$A_S = \frac{H_s}{TA_s} \times 100 \tag{5}$$

H_s = Total number of correct actions in system-monitoring task.
TA_s = Total number of signal events.
For the resource management task, the performance (A_R) was calculated by

$$A_R = \frac{Total\ Normal - state\ Tanks}{Total\ Sampling\ Interval\ x\ 2\ (for\ two\ tanks)} \times 100 \tag{6}$$

A_R is identified as the total normal-state tanks divided by the total sampling interval multiplied by two tanks. There are 18 sampling interval in total that is derived from each 9 min-length scenario.

4.3 NASA TLX

The NASA-TLX (NASA Task Load Index) is a multidimensional subjective workload rating technique. NASA TLX is commonly used to measure operators' workload (Cao et al. 2009; Hancock et al. 1995; Hart and Staveland 1988). It considers the magnitude of six possible load types: mental demand, physical demand, and temporal demand, own performance, effort, and frustration. It weighs the six types of load through a series of 15 combinations (close to 100 – high workload; close to 0 - low workload). In this study, the workload is defined as the expense caused by operators to achieve a certain performance level (Singh et al. 2008).

5 Results

We analyzed the participant's responses by using a two-way ANOVA. The dependent variables were sensitivity (d'), operator's bias (β), performance on tracking, system-monitoring, resource management, and NASA-TLX score. The independent variables were scenario complexity and day.

5.1 Gauge Monitoring Task

The ANOVA results showed the effect of scenario complexity and day for d' and β. For the sensitivity (d'), it was significantly influenced by the scenario complexity, $F_{1,17} = 4.25$, p < 0.05. However, for the operator bias (β), there was a no significant effect on the scenario complexity and day (Table 2).

Table 2. Descriptive statistics for sensitivity and operator bias

Metrics	Complexity	Day 4		Day 5	
		M	SD	M	SD
d'	Low	4.1636	0.4121	4.254	0.3594
	High	3.912	0.846	4.007	0.715
β	Low	23.22	15.77	19.51	8.37
	High	19.89	12.47	22.61	14.08

5.2 MATB

For the tracking task, there was a significant effect on scenario complexity, $F_{1,17} = 22.56$, $p < 0.001$. However, there was no significant effect for the system-monitoring and resource management task (Table 3).

Table 3. Descriptive statistics for system monitoring, resource management, and track

Metrics	Complexity	Day 4		Day 5	
		M	SD	M	SD
A_S	Low	80.45	20.51	84.17	23.88
	High	79.08	18.93	78.58	23.24
A_R	Low	93.83	9.85	92.28	14.67
	High	89.81	12.28	93.00	10.03
A_T	Low	49.41	12.04	49.08	11.61
	High	38.98	14.42	44.88	13.04

5.3 Mental Workload

The NASA-TLX results showed that participant's mental workload was significantly influenced by the scenario complexity ($F_{1,17} = 11.43$; $p < 0.001$) (Table 4).

Table 4. Descriptive statistics for NASA-Task Load Index

Metrics	Complexity	Day 4		Day 5	
		Mean	St. Dev	Mean	St. Dev
NASA-TLX	Low	50.37	15.93	48.15	18.21
	High	56.96	13.24	54.74	16.11

6 Discussion and Conclusion

In this research, we studied sensitivity (d') and operator's bias (β), and mental workload of human operators in a multitasking environment by using the signal detection theory (SDT) and NASA-TLX.

The results showed that the operator's detectability regarding an alarm signal was significantly influenced by the number of visual stimuli from the primary task (the gauge monitoring task). When the scenario complexity was low, sensitivity (d') was better than during the high complexity condition. However, operator bias was not influenced by this, which means that the allocation of visual attention exists between the primary and secondary tasks. In this experiment, the participants had to pay attention to find abnormal situations in both displays. This divided the attention of participants. If they spent an equal amount of time detecting signals from both tasks, the number of missed signals on the gauge monitoring task during the high complexity condition would be larger than in the low complexity condition. Hence, the sensitivity was low when the participants executed high complexity scenarios, but this did not influence the performance on the system-monitoring task.

For the secondary task, the scenario complexity had a significant influence on the tracking task. The tracking task performance was better under the low complexity scenarios. However, the results of the system monitoring and resource management were not significantly influenced by the complexity. It means the complexity level of the gauge monitoring task could affect performance on the tracking task, although the tracking had more physical demands than mental demands. The performance on the tracking task was based on the deviation of the target point from the center point. A joystick controlled the target point. So, participants could control a joystick better in the low complexity condition. Tracking data showed that the switching time to the tracking task was longer than other tasks because of physical motions related to the joystick control. Therefore, we can conclude that the visual stimulus level in a multitasking environment could influence task performance related to physical activities.

For mental workload, we found a negative correlation between the sensitivity and NASA-TLX rating. With the increasing of the complexity level, the sensitivity worsened, and the NASA-TLX score increased.

Although we did not include any physiological measures to assess human performance in a multitasking environment, all findings suggest that multitasking performance is influenced by the visual stimulus level. In other words, the effect of the visual stimulus is significant on performing a visual searching task and physical control task in a multitasking environment. For future research, we will collect eye and head tracking data to investigate a relationship between the visual stimulus level and the multitasking performance. The results of this research will contribute to advance our understanding of behavior modification caused by visual stimuli and the operators' decision-making process in a multitasking environment.

References

Bullemer, P., Reising, D.V., Jones, M.: ASM® Consortium White Paper (2009)

Cao, A., Chintamani, K.K., Pandya, A.K., Ellis, R.D.: NASA TLX: software for assessing subjective mental workload. Behav. Res. Methods 41(1), 113–117 (2009)

García-Pérez, M.A., Alcalá-Quintana, R.: Interval bias in 2AFC detection tasks: sorting out the artifacts. Atten. Percept. Psychophys. 73(7), 2332–2352 (2011)

Hancock, P., Williams, G., Manning, C.: Influence of task demand characteristics on workload and performance. Int. J. Aviat. Psychol. **5**(1), 63–86 (1995)

Hart, S.G., Staveland, L.E.: Development of NASA-TLX (Task Load Index): results of empirical and theoretical research. Adv. Psychol. **52**, 139–183 (1988)

Kim, J.H., Rothrock, L., Laberge, J.: Using Signal Detection Theory and Time Window-based Human-In-The-Loop simulation as a tool for assessing the effectiveness of different qualitative shapes in continuous monitoring tasks. Applied ergonomics **45**(3), 693–705 (2014)

Kim, J.H., Rothrock, L., Laberge, J.: Arousal and performance in a process monitoring task using signal detection theory. In: Paper presented at the Proceedings of the Human Factors and Ergonomics Society Annual Meeting (2015)

Lerman, D.C., Tetreault, A., Hovanetz, A., Bellaci, E., Miller, J., Karp, H., Keyl, A.: Applying signal-detection theory to the study of observer accuracy and bias in behavioral assessment. J. Appl. Behav. Anal. **43**(2), 195–213 (2010)

Noah, B., Kim, J.-H., Rothrock, L., Tharanathan, A.: Evaluating alternate visualization techniques for overview displays in process control. IIE Trans. Occup. Ergonomics Hum. Factors **2**(3–4), 152–168 (2014)

Pashler, H.: Dual-task interference in simple tasks: data and theory. Psychol. Bull. **116**(2), 220 (1994)

Ratwani, R.M., McCurry, J.M., Trafton, J.G.: Single operator, multiple robots: an eye movement based theoretic model of operator situation awareness. In: Paper presented at the Proceedings of the 5th ACM/IEEE International Conference on Human-Robot Interaction (2010)

Santiago-Espada, Y., Myer, R.R., Latorella, K. A., Comstock Jr., J.R.: The Multi-Attribute Task Battery II (MATB-II) software for human performance and workload research: a user's guide. NASA Tech Memorandum, 217164 (2011)

Singh, I.L., Singh, A.L., Tiwari, T., Saha, P.K.: Multi-task performance in computer-aided systems: an appraisal. J. Indian Acad. Appl. Psychol. **34**(1), 115–125 (2008)

Spector, A., Biederman, I.: Mental set and ental shift revisited. Am. J. Psychol. 669–679 (1976)

Walker, A., Brewster, S.: Spatial audio in small screen device displays. Pers. Technol. **4**(2–3), 144–154 (2000)

Integrated Model for Workload Assessment Based on Multiple Physiological Parameters Measurement

Jufang Qiu and Ting Han[✉]

School of Media and Design, Shanghai Jiao Tong University,
Shanghai 200240, China
hanting@sjtu.edu.cn

Abstract. Aviation safety has been the focus of attention since the birth of the first plane. As the safety of aircrafts itself has been greatly improved, aviation human factors have now become the main cause of aviation accidents. This paper mainly aims at building a workload comprehensive evaluation model with effective features deriving from the physiological parameters of the pilots. In order to extract the specific features related to the pilot's workload, each physiological parameter collected in our experiment was tested for its validity and reliability separately. Finally, four main variables related to pilot's workload were derived from the features screened as the pilot workload assessment comprehensive variables with the principal component analysis (PCA) and the absolute value of the four main variables all decrease when the workload of pilots increases.

Keywords: Aviation safety · Human factor · Workload assessment · Physiological parameter · Principal component analysis

1 Introduction

Air transport industry faced all kinds of difficulties in the early days. At that time, the safety of the mechanical system in aircrafts is the main cause of various aviation accidents due to the underdevelopment of science and technology. However, aviation safety has been greatly improved with the development of avionics and mechanical manufacturing technology in recent decades. Nowadays, air transportation has become one of the safest type of transportation. How to continue to enhance the security of this area has been the greatest challenge for the aviation safety organizations. Though human factors accounts for different proportions in aviation accidents in different researches, most of them showed a percentage between 70 % and 90 % [1]. As a result, aviation human factors gradually attracted people's attention. Previous studies have shown that cockpit ergonomic is the most direct cause of flight crew's misoperation [2]. Therefore, researches on human factors in aircraft cockpit are especially important in order to improve aviation safety. For sake of the adaptation between the design of cockpit and the task requests as well as execution capacity of the pilots, the human (pilots) centered design concept was gradually formed during the process of aircraft design, especially in the design of the cockpit.

© Springer International Publishing Switzerland 2016
D. Harris (Ed.): EPCE 2016, LNAI 9736, pp. 19–28, 2016.
DOI: 10.1007/978-3-319-40030-3_3

Due to the appearance of new technologies like vertical takeoff and landing, low visibility landing as well as new noise reduction methods, the workload level of modern pilots shows a significant rise than before, and this change has a great impact on aviation safety. There has been studies indicated that pilot's mental workload plays a crucial role in solving problems during flight [3], and in recent years a greater interest in assessing workload during flight testing was aroused. There are two different ways to measure pilot's workload, subjective assessment and objective assessment. The former was used quiet a lot in the early days. Later, people found that the physiological parameters of pilots like heart rate, respiration and blood pressure would change when pilots are under different level of workload since they always try to maintain their performance at an acceptable level which would lead to a decline in parasympathetic nervous activity and an increase in sympathetic nervous activity [4]. For now, the physiological parameters used in subjective workload assessment includes electroencephalogram (EEG), electromyography (EMG), galvanic skin reflex (GSR), electrocardiogram (ECG), blood volume pressure (BVP), skin temperature and respiration.

Basing on the background described above, this paper mainly aims at building a workload comprehensive evaluation model with effective features deriving from the physiological parameters of the pilots.

2　Workload

2.1　The Definition of Workload

Though the concept of "workload" often appears in studies about human factors, there is no complete agreement reached over the definition of it so far. Some researchers have different opinions on the origin of workload, while others disagree over the mechanisms, consequences and measuring method of it [5]. However, the main aspects of workload seems to be concentrated in three categories: the quantity of work or events that need to be finished; time or one specific aspect of time that people focus on; the subjective mental feelings of pilots [6]. Here are some common definitions of workload:

- The information processing capability and resources that operators have in order to meet the system requirements;
- The difference between the information processing capacity that operators need to have in order to meet the performance expectations and the ability that operators really have;
- The efforts that operators make in order to realize control and monitor. When operators perform different tasks at the same time, it achieves the maximum;
- The decrease of capacity in performing other tasks which need to use the same processing resources when operators are performing one task;
- The relative reaction ability, the key point is to predict what operators would be able to achieve in the future.

There may be new operational definitions and verifications of workload in the future, and people in different areas will continue to define it in different ways.

2.2   Measuring Criteria and Measuring Technology of Workload

The main reason of measuring workload is to quantify the physiological cost of pilots when they are carrying out tasks so that we can predict the performance of the operation staff and the whole system. One problem in measuring workload is that the workload measured in laboratory environments is usually different from that in true operating environment. In order to minimize the difference, O'Donnell and Eggemeier proposed several criteria in measuring workload [7]:

- The measuring technology must be sensitive to the change of task difficulty and it should be reliable.
- The measuring technology should be diagnostic enough to point out the origins of workload change and quantify their contribution.
- The measuring technology should not be intrusive. It can not influence the performance of subjects.
- The measuring technology should be acceptable for subjects.
- The number of devices which will affect performance should be as less as possible.
- The measuring technology should be able to capture instantaneous changes of workload timely and quickly.
- The measuring technology should be reliable enough to ensure repetitive measurement.
- The measuring technology should not be sensitive to the requirement of other tasks.

These criteria can help researchers to select and develop the measuring technology better. However, the difference between different subjects can also have an effect on the experimental results. For sake of obtaining more accurate results, some researchers set weight for the subjective rating scale of subjects before calculating, others set baselines, especially in case of physical measurement.

Since there is still no unified definition about the concept of "workload", researchers in different fields use different technologies to measure it. Mainly, the measuring technologies can be classified into three categories: subjective rating scales, performance evaluation, and physical measurement. Different technologies are sensitive to different aspects of workload.

Subjective Rating Scales. Subjective measurement of workload mainly focuses on quantifying the explanation and judgement of subjects about what they experienced. Some have pointed out that subjective rating scales are lack of reliability and validity.

Performance Evaluation. Performance evaluation of workload can be divided into primary task assessment and secondary task assessment. The former is dedicated to evaluating operator's performance directly when they are carrying out the designed tasks, which is quite effective when the work request exceeds the ability of the operator. The latter can provide a good indicator of operator's remaining operating capacity when they are carrying out the main tasks. It will be more diagnostic when they are used together.

Physical Measurement. The physiological parameters commonly used in researches about physical measurement of workload are electroencephalogram (EEG), electromyography (EMG), galvanic skin reflex (GSR), electrocardiogram (ECG), blood volume pressure (BVP), skin temperature and respiration. Almost all researchers agree that different physiological parameters significantly correlate to different aspects of workload.

The future direction of workload measurement is to develop measuring methods that are more formal and can couple multiple physiological parameters.

3   Multi-channel Physiological Parameter Measurement System

The experiment in our study was carried out in the Man-Machine-Environment System Engineering laboratory in Shanghai Jiao Tong University. The BioHarness Wireless Data Logger was the crucial equipment used in our experiment. Besides, the integrated flight monitor system was important as well.

3.1   Physiological Parameter Detecting Device

We used the BioHarness Wireless Data Logger produced by Zepher to collect the physiological parameters we need (Fig. 1). The Data Logger contains an infrared temperature sensor and a tri-axial acceleration transducer. It has 16 data recording channels totally, including ECG, respiration and ROM (range of motion).

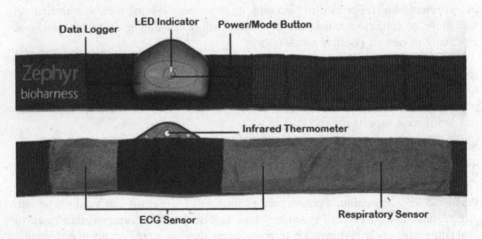

Fig. 1. BioHarness wireless data logger

The physiological parameters used in our study are heart rate [8], respiration [9], ROM and IBI (inter beat interval) [10]. ROM is composed of the total range of motion, the peak acceleration as well as the minimum acceleration and peak acceleration in three different axes. The IBI data was used for heart rate variability analysis.

3.2   Flight Monitor Integrated System

The integrated flight monitor system includes the simulated cockpit, visual system, video monitoring system and equipment condition monitoring system.

The Simulated Cockpit. The simulated cockpit contains the flight control workstation, the display area, control area and peripherals. The flight control system can provide flight control models for the whole system and the simulated flight mission was designed basing on the flight dynamic parameters generated by it. The display area includes primary flight display and navigation display and the control area contains the common control unit such as the throttle, the steering wheel and the handle (Fig. 2).

Fig. 2. The simulated cockpit

The Visual System. The visual system contains a three-channel projector and a circular projection screen, which can make our pilots feel more depth and more real during the simulated flight experiment so that the physiological parameters we collect would be more realistic.

The Video Monitoring System. The primary role of the video monitoring system is to record the hand action, facial expression of the subjects and the scene condition during our experiment. It can help the subjects to recall their actual experience during operations when they are asked to finish a self-assessment of workload after the simulated flight experiment.

The Equipment Condition Monitoring System. The equipment condition monitoring system is designed for monitoring the working condition of the whole integrated flight monitor system. It is able to adjust the test flow and ensure the test is conducted strictly in accordance with the requirements.

4 Flight Simulation Experiment

In order to get the physiological parameters we need, we designed a full process simulated flight mission, basing on the existing Boeing 777-200ER simulated cockpit in our laboratory. It includes a total of six different stages: takeoff, climb, cruise, falling, approach and landing, which is designed to be similar to the true flight condition as much as possible. The participants can control the aileron and elevator of the simulated airplane with the joystick in the cockpit during the experiment. They can also get control of the rudder and brake using the pedal. Besides, the throttle lever, the flaps and landing gear can all be controlled.

Six subjects (age 20.83 ± 2.04) from School of Aeronautics and Astronautics in Shanghai Jiao Tong University participated in our experiment. Since the BioHarness Wireless Data Logger used in our experiment needs to be worn on the breast, which is quite inconvenient for women, all of the six subjects were men. For avoiding disturbance caused by special factors, all the subjects were in good condition of health and had normal or rectified vision. None of them had musculoskeletal injury or mental disease related to angiocarpy, respiration or the central nervous system within a year. Besides, they all had ample sleep before taking part in the experiment. Hoping that our research result would be more reliable, all the subjects were asked to repeat the same experiment twice and the interval between them was 7 to 30 days.

After being told about the goal and content of our experiment, the participants began to carry out the simulated flight mission, and their multiple physiological parameters, including heart rate, respiration, range of motion and IBI, were measured with the BioHarness Wireless Data Logger at the same time. Since different physiological parameters contain different information of the sympathetic nervous system and the parasympathetic nervous system [11], a single physiological parameter can hardly express all the information related to the workload of the pilots, so we recorded these four aspects of physiological parameters in our experiment, hoping that the final workload assessment model we get would be more reliable. At last, all the subjects were asked to recall the workload they actually felt at different stages during the simulated flight experiment and finish the NASA-Task Load Index [12] separately.

5 Feature Extraction and Principal Component Analysis

According to the study of Karavidas M.K., Lehrer P.M., et al., the workload of the pilots was relatively lower during take off and cruise, and it turned higher in landing [13]. So the collected physiological parameters were divided into three sections according to the three different stages in the simulated flight mission (takeoff, cruise and landing), basing on the premise that synchronization was achieved between all the physiological parameters recorded and all the points of time during the completion of the simulated flight mission. All the physiological parameters were preprocessed and standardized before processing so that the interference arising by contamination of artifacts and the difference between all participants can be minimized [14].

5.1   Feature Extraction

In order to extract the specific features related to pilot's workload, each feature derived from the raw physiological parameter was tested for its validity and reliability separately.

Heart Rate. Heart rate is controlled by both the sympathetic nervous system and the parasympathetic nervous system. Usually, the increase of workload will lead to the increase of heart rate [15]. In our research, we tested the mean value, the standard deviation and the mean absolute value of the first order difference of heart rate.

Respiration. Previous research has shown that pilot's breathing is significantly related to the change of workload. Pilots may be hyperventilating in case of extreme workload, which would have serious effects on flight safety. The mean value, the standard deviation and the mean absolute value of the first order difference of respiration rate was tested in our research.

Range of Motion. The movement, posture and gesture of a man can be measured in three ways: using acceleration sensors or inertial measurement systems, using pressure sensors and using tracking systems basing on videos [16]. In our research, we used the data collected by the eight ROM channels of the BioHarness Wireless Data Logger. They are range of motion, peak acceleration and the minimum acceleration and peak acceleration in three different axes.

Heart Rate Variability. Both the parasympathetic nervous system and the sympathetic nervous system are origins of heart rate variability. The increase of workload will lead to the decrease of parasympathetic activity. Researchers have found that heart rate variability will also be weaker when task complexity increase. We preprocessed the original IBI data through interphase correction [17], detrending [18] and resampling. The four features derived in time domain are mean value of IBI, standard deviation of NN intervals (SDNN), root mean square of successive differences (RMSSD) and the percentages of NN intervals which exceed 50 ms (pNN50). Basing on Fast Fourier Transform (FFT), we get other 9 features in frequency domain, they are LF peak, HF peak, LF power, HF power, the percentage of LF power, the percentage of HF power, normalized LF power (nLF), normalized HF power (nHF) and LF/HF.

According to the criterion that there should be significant difference ($p < 0.05$) between the features during take off, cruise and landing, we totally extracted 12 features from the 27 features derived from the raw physiological parameters by using independent T-test, they are the mean value of heart rate, mean |H1-H2| (the mean absolute value of the first order difference of heart rate), the mean value of respiration rate, mean |R1-R2| (the mean absolute value of the first order difference of respiration rate), range of motion, peak acceleration, the mean value of IBI, LF power, HF power, nLF, nHF and LF/HF. All of them showed good reliability.

5.2   Principal Component Analysis

Principal component analysis (PCA) [19] was used to reduce the dimensions of the feature space. After applying PCA to the 12 features extracted in the previous step, we got four main factors related to pilot's workload and the cumulative contribution of them is 82.322 %. A workload comprehensive evaluation model was generated at the same time with the coefficients we got in PCA (Table 1).

Table 1. Component matrix without small coefficients

	Factor 1	Factor 2	Factor 3	Factor 4
LF/HF	0.846			
LF power	0.817			
nLF	0.814			
nHF	−0.805			
HF power	0.792			
Mean IBI		−0.759		
Mean heart rate		0.745		
Mean $|R_1-R_2|$		0.732		
Mean respiration rate		0.718		
Mean $|H_1-H_2|$		0.598		
Peak acceleration			0.86	
Range of motion				0.908

Since all the features in factor 1 were in the time domain and all the features in factor 2 were in the frequency domain, we call factor 1 "time domain factor" and factor 2 "frequency domain factor". The other two factors are named "activity factor" and "acceleration factor". The absolute value of all these four main factors will decrease when the level of workload increases.

Our study showed that heart rate, respiration, range of motion and heart rate variability of the pilots would all change under different level of workload, which demonstrated the feasibility of using the special features extracted from these physiological parameters to assess the workload of pilots during flight. According to the result of PCA, time domain features may contain quite different information about workload in comparison with frequency domain features. Besides, the activity data of pilots is also important in research about workload.

6   Conclusion

This paper is a step toward automatic assessment of pilot's workload, which will be quite useful in the airworthiness approval of new aircrafts. Previous research has shown that the workload of pilots can not be evaluated precisely by using one single physiological parameter. Though we synthetically studied heart rate, respiration, range of motion and heart rate variability in our research, but our division of flight phase is relatively simple. In the future, the assessment of pilot's workload could be more precise through collecting more types of physiological parameters and classifying different flight phase more precisely. Besides, none of the subjects in our research was professional even though they all received a short-term training before participating our experiment. Their piloting skill was relatively poor in comparison with professional pilots, which may have led to a relatively low level of simulation. Collecting the physiological parameters of professional pilots may help to get better results. Finally, simply evaluating the overall workload may have its limits since workload is a variable with multiple dimensions. Finding the specific features that can be used for the assessment of different aspects of workload may be the future research direction.

Acknowledgement. This research is supported by National Basic Research Program of China (973 Program No. 2010CB734103), Shanghai Pujiang Program (13PJC072), Shanghai Jiao Tong University Interdisciplinary among Humanity, Social Science and Natural Science Fund (13JCY02). Moreover, we thank to the students of Shanghai Jiao Tong University who contributed to this research.

References

1. Shappell, S., Detwiler, C., Holcomb, K., et al.: Human error and commercial aviation accidents: an analysis using the human factors analysis and classification system. Hum. Factors: J. Hum. Factors Ergon. Soc. **49**(2), 227–242 (2007)
2. Tangwen, Y., Shan, F.: Ergonomic evaluation of aircraft cockpit based on model-predictive control. In: 5th International Conference on IEEE Computational Intelligence and Communication Networks (CICN) 2013, pp. 607–612 (2013)
3. Borghini, G., Astolfi, L., Vecchiato, G., et al.: Measuring neurophysiological signals in aircraft pilots and car drivers for the assessment of mental workload, fatigue and drowsiness. J. Neurosci. Biobehav. Rev. **44**, 58–75 (2014)
4. Gawron, V.J., Schiflett, S.G., Miller, J.C.: Measures of in-flight workload (1989)
5. Wickens, C.D., Huey, B.M. (eds.): Workload Transition: Implications for Individual and Team Performance. National Academies Press, Washington (1993)
6. Lysaght, R.J., Hill, S.G., Dick, A.O., et al.: Operator workload: Comprehensive review and evaluation of operator workload methodologies. Analytics Inc Willow Grove Pa (1989)
7. O'Donnell, R.D., Eggemeier, F.T.: Workload assessment methodology (1986)
8. Regula, M., Socha, V., Kutilek, P., et al.: Study of heart rate as the main stress indicator in aircraft pilots, pp. 639–643. IEEE (2014)
9. Harriott, C.E., Zhang, T., Adams, J.A.: Evaluating the applicability of current models of workload to peer-based human-robot teams, pp. 45–52. ACM (2011)
10. Hoover, A., Singh, A., Fishel-Brown, S., et al.: Real-time detection of workload changes using heart rate variability. Biomed. Signal Process. Control J. **7**, 333–341 (2012)
11. Koelstra, S., Mühl, C., Soleymani, M., et al.: Deap: a database for emotion analysis; using physiological signals. IEEE Trans. Affect. Comput. **3**, 18–31 (2012)
12. Hart, S.G., Staveland, L.E.: Development of NASA-TLX (Task Load Index): Results of empirical and theoretical research. J. Adv. Psychol. **52**, 139–183 (1988)
13. Karavidas, M.K., Lehrer, P.M., Lu, S.E., et al.: The effects of workload on respiratory variables in simulated flight: a preliminary study. J. Biol. Psychol. **84**(1), 157–160 (2010)

14. Heger, D., Putze, F., Schultz, T.: Online workload recognition from EEG data during cognitive tests and human-machine interaction. In: Dillmann, R., Beyerer, J., Hanebeck, U. D., Schultz, T. (eds.) KI 2010. LNCS, vol. 6359, pp. 410–417. Springer, Heidelberg (2010)
15. Mulder, L.J.M.: Assessment of cardiovascular reactivity by means of spectral analysis. Thesis, RijksUniversiteit Groningen, The Netherlands (1988)
16. Kappeler-Setz, C.: Multimodal emotion and stress recognition. Diss., Eidgenössische Technische Hochschule ETH Zürich, Nr. 20086 (2012)
17. Thuraisingham, R.A.: Preprocessing RR interval time series for heart rate variability analysis and estimates of standard deviation of RR intervals. J. Comput. Methods Programs Biomed. **83**(1), 78–82 (2006)
18. Colak, O.H.: Preprocessing effects in time-frequency distributions and spectral analysis of heart rate variability. J. Digital Signal Process. **19**(4), 731–739 (2009)
19. Anuradha, P., Rallapalli, H., Narasimha, G., et al.: Efficient workload characterization technique for heterogeneous processors, pp. 812–817. IEEE (2015)

A New Method
for Mental Workload Registration

Thea Radüntz[✉]

Unit. 3.4 'Mental Health and Cognitive Capacity',
Federal Institute for Occupational Safety and Health,
Nöldnerstr. 40/42, 10000 Berlin, Germany
raduentz.thea@baua.bund.de

Abstract. Complex and highly automated systems impose high demands on employees with respect to cognitive capacity and the ability to cope with workload. Objectively registering mental workload at workplaces with high cognitive demands would enable prevention of over- and underload. Although urgently needed, such technical measurement is currently unfeasible. Hence, the goal of this work is the establishment of precisely such an objective method.

In this article we briefly present a new method for registering mental workload by means of the electroencephalogram (EEG). Based on so called Dual Frequency Head Maps (DFHM) every 5 s we obtain an index of mental state ranging between the classes low, moderate, and high workload.

Finally, we present results from a sample set of 54 people during the execution of the cognitive tasks 0-back, stroop test and AOSPAN in a laboratory setting. We compare them with our expectations based on the knowledge of task requirements on the executive functions as well as with further workload relevant biosignal data, performance data, and the NASA-TLX as a subjective questionnaire method. By this we gain proof of the integrity of the new method.

Keywords: Mental workload · Electroencephalogram (EEG) · Signal processing · Pattern recognition

1 Introduction

The computerization of the modern working world is evolving ever more rapidly and aims to facilitate our life. However there is a growing consensus surrounding the negative consequences of inappropriate workload on employee health and on the safety of persons. The consequences may arise from the inability to cope with increasing demands imposed on an individuals cognitive capacity and hence due to high mental workload [4,5,8]. On the other hand the proliferation of automation can also be linked to monotonous tasks that reduce employees arousal and induce underload [1,2,6,9,10].

© Springer International Publishing Switzerland 2016
D. Harris (Ed.): EPCE 2016, LNAI 9736, pp. 29–37, 2016.
DOI: 10.1007/978-3-319-40030-3_4

Although the relation between workload and performance is well studied and there has been years of research targeting the registering of mental workload, there is no generally accepted, reliable, objective, and continuous method for this. Such a method would allow for defining the individual optimal workload range in which task solving is most efficient. Our aim is to develop a method that relies on features from brain activity, the center of human information processing. Neuronal brain state monitoring can then be used for ergonomic evaluation and improvement of human-machine systems and hence contribute to the optimization of workload.

This article describes the development of a continuous method for neuronal mental workload registration. Cognitive tasks were conducted in a laboratory setting aiming to identify EEG features indicative for mental workload. For our task battery we selected tasks reflecting executive functions [7]. Such functions are responsible for everyday actions demanding non-schema-based processing and requiring attentional control. Hence, the EEG features obtained should allow for the development of a generalized method that can measure mental workload independently from tasks.

2 Methods

2.1 Procedure and Subjects

The investigation took place in the shielded lab of the Federal Institute of Occupational Safety and Health. Materials, procedures and the sample set have already been described in [13]. To recapitulate, the sample consists of 54 people between 34 and 62 years of age and shows high variability in respect to the cognitive capacity and hence to the expected mental workload. The experiment was fully carried out with each subject in a single day and consisted of a training phase where the subjects were familiarized with the tasks and the main experiment.

We used several workload measuring methods. Each of these has its own pros and cons. Hence, the collection of additional workload indexing data was aimed to consolidate the development of our method by giving us the opportunity to control possible subject-dependent confounders but also further information in case of doubts at the end.

2.2 Tasks

Different cognitive task requirements were realized through the implementation of a task battery with the E-Prime application suite. Nine tasks of diverse complexity and difficulty inducing different levels of mental workload are included in our test battery [11,13].

In this paper we concentrate on the analysis and evaluation of three tasks: 0-back as the easiest one, stroop test as an inhibition task, and AOSPAN as a demanding dual task (see Figs. 1, 2, 3). The latter is a translated version of the AOSPAN task developed by [14]. The analysis of rest measurements serves as a reference point measurement.

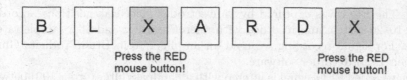

Fig. 1. 0-back task: Press the mouse button if the presented letter is 'X'.

Fig. 2. Stroop task as an inhibition task: Differently colored words appear on the screen one at a time. Press the mouse button (yellow, green, red, blue) that matches the font color, ignoring the meaning of the word. Try to work quickly and accurately. (Color figure online)

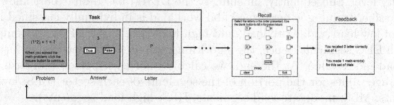

Fig. 3. AOSPAN as dual task (image adapted from [14]): memorize a set of letters in the order presented while simultaneously solving math problems. Trials consist of 3 sets of each set size, with the set sizes ranging from 3–7.

2.3 Subjective Ratings

Paired comparisons of the workload sources were conducted after each task during the training phase as the first part of the computerized version of the NASA-TLX questionnaire method [3]. Subjects were asked to rate the workload sources in 15 pairwise comparisons of NASA-TLX's six workload dimensions: mental demand, physical demand, temporal demand, performance, effort, frustration.

As part of the main experiment, following each task we then conducted the second part of the NASA-TLX, the ratings of its subscales. Subjects were asked to rate the task for each of the six workload dimensions within a 100-point range with 5-point steps. They indicated their rating by clicking on a 5-point step box with an optical mouse.

2.4 Physiological Measures

In the main experiment during the execution of the tasks we registered the electroencephalogram (EEG), as well as further biosignal data (i.e. heart rate, blood pressure).

EEG. The EEG was captured by 25 electrodes placed at positions according to the 10–20-system and recorded with reference to Cz and at a sample rate of 500 Hz. For signal recording we used an amplifier from BrainProducts GmbH and their BrainRecorder software.

The recorded EEG signal is filtered with a bandpass filter (order 100) between 0.5 and 40 Hz. Subsequently, independent component analysis (ICA) is applied to the signal and the calculated independent components are visually inspected and classified as either an artifact or signal component. The signal components are projected back onto the scalp channels. The artifact-corrected EEG signal is transformed to average reference and cut into segments of 10 s length, overlapping by 5 s. Subsequently, the workload relevant frequency bands (θ: 4–8 Hz, α: 8–12 Hz) are computed over the segments using the Fast Fourier Transformation (FFT).

The newly developed method of dual frequency head maps (DFHM) is based on our analysis of the EEG spectra demonstrating an increase of the frontal theta band power and a decrease of the parietal alpha band power with increasing task difficulty level. Subsequently, labelling of the DFHM based on expert knowledge and classifier training is performed and workload is individually classified in the range of low load, moderate load, and high load [12]. The DFHM are computed for each EEG segment. Hence, the algorithm computes in an interval of 5 s a new workload index value. At the end, we calculate for each person and task three percentage values for the portion of the segments of each sector (LLS: low load segments, MLS: moderate load segments, HLS: high load segments).

Cardiovascular parameters. Blood pressure was recorded continuously by the FMS Finometer Pro device. A finger cuff was placed around the subject's finger and systolic and diastolic blood pressure as well as the heart rate were detected automatically. The recorded data was processed in the time domain.

2.5   Performance

We concentrated on the analysis of the individual accuracy rates for all three tasks. For AOSPAN, correct responses include the number of sets in which the letters are recalled in correct serial order and correct math problem solving.

2.6   Statistical Analysis

Six ANOVAs were carried out utilizing repeated measures design, one within-subject factor (portion of LLS, portion of HLS, systolic BP, HR, accuracy rate or NASA-TLX). For the factors portion of LLS and HLS, systolic BP, and HR we had five levels (the three tasks and the two rest measurements) while for the factors accuracy rates and NASA-TLX we had only three levels (the three tasks). Differences between the levels were examined and tested with a post-hoc test (Bonferroni).

3 Results

3.1 Subjective Ratings and Performance

Subjective ratings. Figure 4(a) shows the average workload index for the selected tasks 0-back, stroop test, and AOSPAN as representatives of a low, a moderate and a high workload tasks. Workload means changed significantly during the experiment (Greenhouse-Geisser $F(1.94; 102.61) = 92.00$, p<0.001). Post-hoc analysis revealed significant changes of the subjectively rated mean workload index between all tasks.

Performance. Figure 4(b) shows the average accuracy rates for the selected tasks 0-back, stroop test, and AOSPAN. Accuracy rate means changed significantly during the experiment (Greenhouse-Geisser $F(1.12; 59.21) = 377.15$, p<0.001). Post-hoc analysis revealed significant changes of the mean accuracy rates between all tasks.

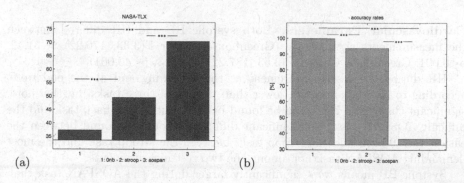

Fig. 4. (a) NASA-TLX computed for 0-back, stroop test, and AOSPAN over 54 subjects. (b) Accuracy rates computed for 0-back, stroop test, and AOSPAN over 54 subjects.

3.2 Physiological Measures

EEG. Analysis of the classified EEG segments demonstrates a proportion increase of the high load segments and a proportion decrease of the low load segments with increasing task difficulty level. Means of LLS and HLS changed significantly during the experiment (Greenhouse-Geisser $F(2.99; 158.02) = 98.51$, p<0.001; Greenhouse-Geisser $F(2.53; 134.07) = 64.26$, p<0.001). Results obtained from the assessment of the EEG segments are presented in Fig. 5.

Post-hoc analysis of the proportion of HLS showed that the means were significantly larger as more difficult the tasks were. Significant differences were identified between all tasks as well as between the tasks and the rest measurements. No significant differences could be found between the rest measurement at the begin and at the end of the experiment.

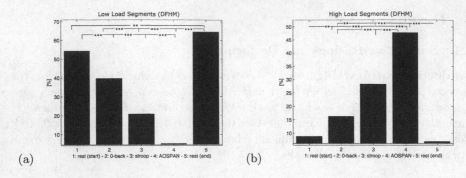

Fig. 5. EEG - proportion of LLS (a) and HLS (b) computed for 0-back, stroop task, and AOSPAN over 54 subjects.

The proportion of LLS revealed significant changes between all measurements.

Cardiovascular Parameters. Both systolic BP and HR differed between the measurements significantly (Greenhouse-Geisser $F(3.33; 176.22) = 31.42$, $p<0.001$; Greenhouse-Geisser $F(3.53; 187.22) = 25.13$, $p<40.001$).

HR during the rest measurement at the beginning and at the end were, according to post-hoc analysis, lower than during all three tasks. Furthermore, significant changes in HR could be found between the easy 0-back task and the difficult AOSPAN task. No significant differences could be found between the easiest task 0-back and the stroop task, between the stroop task and the most demanding AOSPAN task nor among the two rest measurements.

Systolic BP means were significantly larger during the AOSPAN task than in 0-back and stroop tasks. Additionally, they were significantly larger during the three task measurements and the rest measurements. No significant changes

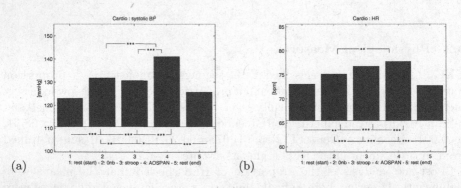

Fig. 6. Systolic BP (a) and HR (b) computed for 0-back, stroop task, and AOSPAN over 54 subjects.

could be found between the two rest measurements nor between the 0-back and the stroop task.

Results of systolic BP and HR are presented in Fig. 6(a) and (b).

4   Discussion

The registration of mental workload by means of the EEG is the central issue addressed by this paper. We induced different levels of mental workload on the basis of a task battery but for the sake of convenience, we concentrated here on the 0-back, stroop and AOSPAN tasks. Cognitive requirements of the first task are quite low and the task can be assumed to be an easy task. The stroop task is more demanding due to higher requirements on the ability for inhibition. It can be classified as a moderate to difficult task but not as challenging as the AOSPAN task. The AOSPAN task demands memory control while dealing with distraction due to the math problem solving. It is a dual-task with high workload requirements.

Subjective ratings derived from the NASA-TLX questionnaire as well as performance data demonstrate significant workload differences between all three tasks. These results emphasize our assumption of gradual workload differences between the tasks. Cardiovascular parameter indicate significant differences between the rest measurements at the begin and the end of the experiment and the three tasks. They also show significant differences between the demanding AOSPAN task and the easy task. However, no significant differences could be observed among the rest measurements nor between 0-back and stroop task. Although there exists a positive tendency, it does not reach the significance level.

The EEG and the frequently observed variability of the θ- and α-band according to attention, fatigue and mental workload, constitute the theoretical background for the new method of the DFHM. The obtained index can be used for neuronal mental state monitoring and ranges between low, moderate, and high workload. Results analyzing the proportions of the HLS and LLS are in concordance with the results expected based on difficulty levels resulting from the requirements of the tasks. The most demanding AOSPAN task contains significantly less segments of low load than the other tasks and the rest measurements. The stroop task includes less LLS than the 0-back task and the rest measurements, while the 0-back task includes less than the rest measurements. Furthermore, the rest measurement at the beginning has less LLS than the rest measurement at the end indicating that the workload at the beginning is a bit higher than at the end of the experiment. All these differences were found to be significant.

In respect of the HLS, the AOSPAN task again shows substantially higher values than all other measurements. Considering also its small proportion of LLS, AOSPAN is a high mental workload task. Stroop task includes significantly higher proportions of HLS than 0-back and the rest measurements. Finally, 0-back task comprises less segments of high load than the rest measurements. Interestingly, there is no significant difference of HLS's proportion among the rest measurements although there is tendency indicating that the activation of the subjects at the beginning is a bit higher than at the end, similar to the findings from the analysis of the LLS's proportion. Hence, we can assume that the index is able to distinguish between very small gradual differences, in particular when both HLS and LLS are considered simultaneously.

To sum up, our results from the new DFHM method for measuring mental workload are solidly in line both with the accuracy rates and the subjective ratings. Furthermore, they are in concordance with our expectations that result from the known task requirements.

Acknowledgments. We would like to thank Dr Sergei Schapkin, Dr Patrick Gajewski, and Prof Michael Falkenstein for selection of the battery's tasks. We would like to thank Mr Ludger Blanke for technical support during the timing tests for the tasks. In addition, we would like to thank Ms Xenija Weißbecker-Klaus, Mr Robert Sonnenberg, Dr Sergei Schapkin, and Ms Marion Freyer for general task testing and for conducting the laboratory experiments. Furthermore, we would like to thank Ms Marion Exner for daily operational support and our student assistant Jon Scouten for proofreading.

More information about the project where our EEG data were acquired can be found under the following link: http://www.baua.de/de/Forschung/Forschungsprojekte/f2312.html?nn=2799254.

References

1. Debitz, U., Gruber, H., Richter, G.: Psychische Gesundheit am Arbeitsplatz. Teil 2: Erkennen, Beurteilen und Verhüten von Fehlbeanspruchungen, vol. 2, 3rd edn. InfoMediaVerlag (2003)
2. Hacker, W., Richter, P.: Psychische Fehlbeanspruchung. Psychische Ermdung, Monotonie, Stttigung und Stress. (Spezielle Arbeits- und Ingenieurpsychologie in Einzeldarstellungen), vol. 2, 2nd edn. Springer, Heidelberg (1984)
3. Hart, S.G., Staveland, L.E.: Development of the NASA TLX: results of empirical and theoretical research. In: Hancock, P., Meshkati, N. (eds.) Human Mental Workload, pp. 139–183. North Holland, Amsterdam (1988)
4. Kompier, M.A.J., Kristensen, T.S.: Organisational work stress interventions in a theoretical, methodological and practical context. In: Dunham, J. (ed.) Stress in the Workplace: Past, Present and Future, pp. 164–190. Whurr Publishers, London (2001)
5. Landsbergis, P.A., Cahill, J., Schnall, P.: The changing organisation of work and the safety and health of working people: a commentary. J. Occup. Environ. Med. **45**(1), 61–72 (2003)
6. May, J.F., Baldwin, C.L.: Driver fatigue: the importance of identifying causal factors of fatigue when considering detection and countermeasure technologies. Transportation Research Part F 12, pp. 218–224 (2008). Accessed 03 Nov 2011
7. Miyake, A., Friedman, N.P., Emerson, M.J., Witzki, A.H., Howerter, A., Wager, T.D.: The unity and diversity of executive functions and their contributions to complex "frontal lobe" tasks: a latent variable analysis. Cogn. Psychol. **41**(1), 49–100 (2000). http://psych.colorado.edu/tor/Papers/Unity_Diversity_Exec_Functions.pdf. Accessed 17 Mar 2014

8. Niosh, N.: The changing organization of work and the safety and health of working people. Technical report 2002-116, National Institute for Occupational Safety and Health (NIOSH) (2002)
9. Parasuraman, R., Molloy, R., Singh, I.L.: Performance consequences of automation induced complacency. Int. J. Aviat. Psychol. **3**, 1–23 (1993)
10. Parasuraman, R., Mouloua, M., Molloy, R.: Monitoring automation failures in human machine systems. In: Mouloua, M., Parasuraman, R. (eds.) Human Performance in Automated Systems: Curent Research and Trends, pp. 45–49. Earlbaum, Hillsdale (1994)
11. Radüntz, T.: Neuronal mental workload registration during execution of cognitive tasks. In: Harris, D. (ed.) EPCE 2014. LNCS, vol. 8532, pp. 59–69. Springer, Heidelberg (2014)
12. Radüntz, T.: Kontinuierliche Bewertung psychischer Beanspruchung an informationsintensiven Arbeitsplätzen auf Basis des Elektroenzephalogramms. Ph.D. thesis, Department of Computer Science, Humboldt-Universität zu Berlin, Berlin (2016). http://edoc.hu-berlin.de/docviews/abstract.php?id=42402
13. Radüntz, T., Freude, G.: Towards a continuous method for mental workload registration. In: Harris, D. (ed.) EPCE 2015. LNCS, vol. 9174, pp. 176–187. Springer, Heidelberg (2015). http://dx.doi.org/10.1007/978-3-319-20373-7_17
14. Unsworth, N., Heitz, R.P., Schrock, J.C., Engle, R.W.: An automated version of the operation span task. Behav. Res. Methods **37**(3), 498–505 (2005). http://webs.wofford.edu/boppkl/coursefiles/Thesis/articles/UnsworthHeitz_2005_autoospan.pdf. Accessed 02 Apr 2014

An Analysis of Fatigue and Its Characteristics: A Survey on Chinese Air Traffic Controller

Le-ping Yuan, Guang-fu Ma, and Rui-shan Sun[✉]

Research Institute of Civil Aviation Safety,
Civil Aviation University of China, Tianjin, China
lpyuan@hotmail.com, sunrsh@hotmail.com,
875414062@qq.com

Abstract. Previous research has shown that fatigue may reduce alertness and negatively impact job performance [1]. An over fatigued worker may increase the probability of an accident or incident. The purpose of this research study was to examine fatigue conditions and identify fatigue characteristics among air traffic controllers in China. Researchers utilized a survey to gain a clearer understanding of participant perceptions pertaining to fatigue. Survey items consisted of the following constructs: subjective fatigue, sleep quality, working factors, daily life factors, and personality. The results indicated that sleep quality and workload were major issues that caused the feeling of fatigue in the air traffic controllers surveyed. It is noticeable that daily life impact also contributed to the controller's fatigue.

Keywords: Air traffic controllers · Fatigue · Aviation safety

1 Introduction

The civil aviation industry in China has been rapidly developed in recent years and has become the second largest aviation market in the world after the United States. With the rapid development of the aviation industry, the phenomenon of fatigue is increasingly becoming prominent throughout the civil aviation industry, particularly for air traffic controllers in China. Fatigue may lead to a decreased alertness and raise safety hazards [1]. According to the United Kingdom CHIRP (the Confidential Human Factors Incident Reporting Programme), 13 % of operation errors were directly caused by the controllers' fatigue in the U.K. [2]. Reported by the Xiamen ATC Safety Reporting System in China, 18 % of the errors made by air traffic controllers were associated with fatigue [2]; The National Transportation Safety Board (NTSB) in the U.S. has considered fatigue as one of the most important aviation safety issues that need to be solved [3].

Air traffic controllers in China are facing not only increasing work pressure, but also growing fatigue risks, due to a significant increase in the national air traffic. According to the Xinhua News Agency, Eastern Airlines flight MU2528 failed to contact with the ATC when approaching to Wuhan airport in the year of 2014, because two tower controllers fell asleep on duties. Fortunately this incident did not turn into a fatal tragedy, however, it posed a serious threat to aviation safety [4]. Previous

© Springer International Publishing Switzerland 2016
D. Harris (Ed.): EPCE 2016, LNAI 9736, pp. 38–47, 2016.
DOI: 10.1007/978-3-319-40030-3_5

researchers have conducted a number of research studies in order to address fatigue and various fatigue assessment methods have been generated.

Fatigue assessment methods mainly involve two categories: one is subjective measurement using questionnaires, such as the NASA-TLX scale, multidimensional fatigue self-assessment scales, Japan fatigue scale, fatigue scale FS-14, and Karolinska sleepiness scale (KSS) [5]; The other category is an objective measurement method by means of instruments, equipment and other auxiliary tools. These methods can record and measure human physiological and behavioral changes of certain indexes to reflect the degree of fatigue. These instruments and tools contain electrical equipment, eye tracking, flicker fusion frequency detectors, head position sensors, etc. [6]. Saroj and other researchers reviewed electroencephalogram (EEG) signals, eye-movement data, and other ways to analyze subjects' performance in driving simulation. Researchers found EEG was one of the most effective indicators for fatigue detection [7, 8].

Although EEG, eye-movement data and other similar methods can accurately reflect one's fatigue, the experimental data is subject to human and environmental impacts. Investigation of fatigue of air traffic controllers is mainly conducted by using fatigue survey questionnaires. Wang Tian-fang conducted a local fatigue self-assessment scale research study [9], whose purpose was to understand fatigue and depression of patients with chronic disease. The researchers of this study developed a survey that consisted of the following parts: Personal information, subjective fatigue assessment, workload factors, sleep status, life event impacts, and personality features. To gain a clearer understanding of air traffic controllers fatigue, the following research questions were addressed:

1. How bad it is? And what are the fatigue characteristics (general, physical, mental, and level of motivation) of participants?
2. How do fatigue and its contributing factors connected?

2 Methods

2.1 Survey Questionnaires

In order to identify risk factors that may lead to controllers' fatigue and understand fatigue characteristics, the researchers designed an air traffic controller fatigue survey questionnaire. The 6 components of the survey are listed in Table 1.

2.2 Reliability and Validity Analysis

Because Pittsburgh sleep quality index has been strictly tested in terms of reliability and validity, and personal information questionnaire, work-related factors questionnaire and life events impact questionnaire are objective investigation to controllers' life and of work-related information, it is not necessary to make an analysis of reliability and validity pertaining to the parts discussed above.

In this study, the researchers conducted reliability and validity analysis for the Subjective Assessment of Fatigue by using SPSS.22.0. Analysis results showed that

Table 1. Survey components.

Items	Purpose and Content
Personal information	Basic personal information included: family, personal living habits, preferences and health information, awareness to fatigue. In addition, basic information such as age, sex, job, growing environment, and education.
Subjective assessment of fatigue	The fatigue scale was designed to investigate controllers' fatigue. This part was based on the multidimensional fatigue inventory MFI-20 and included general fatigue, physical fatigue, mental fatigue and reduced motivation, 16 entries in total. There were 5 points from "not true" to "entirely true". There were 16–80 points in total, each dimension had a score of 4–20 points, and higher scores represent more serious fatigue.
Work-related factors questionnaire	This questionnaire incorporated schedule, workload and work environment factors, altogether 19 items. In terms of scheduling, it mainly investigate controllers' working time, duty time, numbers of overtime, rest after two consecutive hours, and shifts impact on controllers' sleeping habits. In the work survey section, numbers of flights, unusual events handling, operation limitations were mainly contributing to controllers' high workload. As for work environment, mainly investigate controllers rest environment, equipment performance, staffing and training, team characteristics and humanitarian environment.
Sleep quality index	The scale mainly referred to the Pittsburgh sleep quality index (PSQI) [10] which was prepared by the psychiatrist doctor Buysse from the University of Pittsburgh. The questionnaire contained seven dimensions: subjective sleep quality, sleep latency, sleep time, sleep efficiency, sleep disorders, using of medicine and daytime dysfunction. The scale was revised to four dimensions considering the reality of air traffic controller work.
Life events impact questionnaire	Some events in one's daily life whether good or bad, will definitely bring influence to metal state. Therefore, life events are involved as part of the controllers' fatigue investigation. This scale covers seven groups: work related, career, relationships, marriage and family, economic, physiological conditions and system pressure. Seventeen events were taken into account.
Personality traits questionnaire	People with different personalities handles problem differently. In this part, the Big Five Inventory for person traits investigation was used [11]. There were five dimensions involved: extraversion, agreeableness, conscientiousness, neuroticism, and openness. We try to use personality investigation to find out the relationship between personal traits and fatigue.

Cronbach's Alpha coefficient was 0.803, which indicated a high reliability. Additionally, the factor analysis method and the orthogonal variance maximum rotating method were applied. Four factors whose characteristic roots were bigger than 1, and their cumulative variance contribution rated for 84 %. Sixteen factor loadings were bigger than 0.5, which means it had good discriminability.

3 Results

The researchers distributed survey questionnaires to an ATC facility in China, including tower control, approach control, area control, and flight services. Eighty-five survey questionnaires were distributed, and eighty participants completed the survey. Table 2 shows the demographic information.

Table 2. Demographic numerical values

		n = 80
Gender	Male	70 (87.5 %)
	Female	10 (12.5 %)
Age	20~30 years	40 (50.0 %)
	31~40 years	23 (28.8 %)
	41~50 years	17 (21.2 %)
Position	Tower Controllers	20 (25.0 %)
	Approach Controllers	30 (37.5 %)
	Area Controllers	19 (23.8 %)
	Flight Service Controllers	11 (13.7 %)

3.1 Fatigue of Controllers in General

According to the fatigue scoring rules, the scores between 16 and 28 stand for no fatigue. The score span 29–41, 42–54, 55–67, and 68–80 represent mild, moderate, severe and extremely severe fatigue respectively. The results showed the general fatigue condition of controllers: 1 % no fatigue, 18 % mild fatigue, 58 % moderate fatigue, 19 % severe fatigue, and 4 % extremely severe fatigue.

The survey consisted of four different dimensions: general fatigue, physical fatigue and mental fatigue, and reduced motivation. The statistical results are shown in Table 3: 55 % controllers reported they had severe fatigue and above; 30 % of the controllers considered themselves serious physical fatigue and above; 46 % of the controllers considered themselves serious mental fatigue and above; 38 % of the controllers indicated they had reduced motivation.

Results showed that 58 % of the controllers at a moderate level of fatigue. Additionally, 23 % of the controllers had reached the extent of severe fatigue and above, especially in two aspects: mental fatigue and reduced motivation. Therefore, the mental workload and reduced motivation were identified as the two most serious fatigue dimensions.

Table 3. Distribution of different dimensions of fatigue

Fatigue / Four dimensions	No fatigue	Light fatigue	Moderate fatigue	Severe fatigue	Extreme fatigue
General fatigue	3%	10%	32%	32%	23%
Physical fatigue	4%	16%	34%	20%	10%
Mental fatigue	4%	16%	42%	32%	14%
Reduced motivation	14%	22%	34%	25%	13%

3.2   Controllers' Fatigue by Different Operational Positions

The results of controllers' fatigue conditions with different positions are shown in Table 4. In general, fatigue of the controllers working at four different positions was rated as moderate. Physical fatigue scores were lower than mental fatigue scores, which indicated that controllers have higher mental pressure. This may because most of the time the controllers were doing their brain works. As for approach controllers, their mental fatigue scores were higher than tower controllers, area controller, and flight service controllers. This indicated that approach controllers had a higher level of mental fatigue, which may be caused by complex airspace operations and busy air traffic. Flight service controllers had less working motivation than others. This may be because flight service controllers 24 h work shifts led to a lack of job interests.

Table 4. The fatigue status of controllers from different positions

Positions	Total points	General fatigue	Physical fatigue	Mental fatigue	Reduced motivation
Tower controllers	49.0 ± 5.3	13.1 ± 2.0	11.6 ± 1.4	13.9 ± 2.1	13.1 ± 2.6
Approach controllers	50.1 ± 4.7	13.3 ± 1.8	11.2 ± 1.7	15.6 ± 1.7	13.9 ± 2.2
Area controllers	50.5 ± 4.9	12.9 ± 2.3	11.6 ± 2.3	12.9 ± 2.3	13.9 ± 2.4
Flight service controllers	50.7 ± 4.3	12.5 ± 1.9	11.4 ± 1.5	11.1 ± 1.4	14.5 ± 2.9

3.3   Analysis of Controllers Sleeping

Analysis of Controllers Sleep Quality. Survey results showed that the general condition of controllers' sleep quality was good. Only 10 % of the controllers was assessed their sleep quality as very poor. Nearly half of the controllers slept 6–7 h each day. 67 % of the controllers' sleep efficiency was greater than 85 %, and 9 % of the controllers' sleep efficiency was below 74 %. 56 % of the controllers had long sleep latency factors, which may indicate that controllers needed a long time to fall asleep.

Table 5. Correlation analysis between sleep quality and fatigue

Four dimensions	Sleep quality correlation index	Sig
General fatigue	0.51	<0.01
Physical fatigue	0.27	<0.05
Mental fatigue	0.60	<0.01
Reduced motivation	0.05	>0.05

Correlation analyses of sleep quality and four dimensions of fatigue were conducted (results shown in Table 5). With a 99 % confidence level, controllers' general fatigue was related to sleep quality. In addition, sleep quality had a strong relationship with mental fatigue. In 95 % confidence level, sleep quality had weaker correlation with physical fatigue, but it had no relation with reduced motivation.

Sleep Factor Analysis of Different Fatigue Level. The researchers analyzed seven sleep factors for the controllers with high level of fatigue and low level of fatigue (results are shown in Table 5). According to factor analysis, the most prominent problem affecting sleep quality was sleep latency. Controllers cannot easily fall asleep in a short time, which may be related to controllers' long time night shifts. Controllers with high level of fatigue generally were accompanied with short sleeping time, usually between 5 and 7 h. Controllers with high level of fatigue were less efficient in sleeping, while controllers with light fatigue had higher efficient sleep quality. This indicated that sleep efficiency impacted on controller fatigue. The influence of sleep disorders among the controllers groups was not obvious. High-fatigued controllers' daytime dysfunction received higher scores (Table 6).

Table 6. A comparison of sleeping quality factors of different fatigue levels

Sleep quality factors	Subjective sleep quality	Sleep latency	Sleep time (h)	Sleep efficiency	Sleep disorders	Using sleep medicine	Daytime dysfunction	Total scores
All controllers	1.9 ± 0.8	1.7 ± 0.9	6.4 ± 1.0	0.6 ± 0.9	1.4 ± 0.6	0.3 ± 0.6	1.8 ± 0.7	8.3 ± 3.2
Light fatigue controllers	1.7 ± 0.8	1.6 ± 0.9	6.5 ± 0.9	0.5 ± 0.9	1.4 ± 0.6	0.2 ± 0.5	1.7 ± 0.7	7.7 ± 3.1
High fatigue controller	2.6 ± 0.7	2.2 ± 0.8	6.0 ± 1.1	1.2 ± 1.0	1.5 ± 0.5	0.5 ± 1.0	2.2 ± 0.7	11.2 ± 2.6

Sleep and Fatigue Analysis of Different Positions. Considering fatigue differences between different positions, the researchers analyzed sleeping factors of controllers with different positions. As shown in Table 7, generally the controllers with different positions showed a similar sleep condition.

3.4 Analysis of Controllers' Work-Related Factors

The self-assessment of workload results are showed as Table 8. The majority of the controllers reported they had a moderate level of workload. 60 % of approach

Table 7. Sleep condition contrast for different position controllers

Position	Total points	Subjective sleep quality	Sleep disorders	Daytime dysfunction	Sleep time
Tower controllers	8.7 ± 3.7	1.9 ± 0.8	1.6 ± 0.5	1.6 ± 0.7	6.4 ± 1.1
Approach controllers	8.1 ± 3.0	2.0 ± 0.7	1.3 ± 0.6	1.7 ± 0.9	6.5 ± 0.8
Area controllers	8.4 ± 4.0	1.8 ± 0.8	1.4 ± 0.6	1.6 ± 0.8	6.5 ± 1.1
Flight service controllers	8.1 ± 2.5	1.6 ± 0.8	1.2 ± 0.4	1.6 ± 0.9	6.5 ± 0.9

controllers suffered from high workload. Through on-site investigation, the researchers found that the ATC facility had a serious approach controller shortage. Executive controller continuously working for two hours would not have a break time, and just moved to coordinating positions to work. In most cases a coordinated controller was working with two executive controllers at the same time.

Table 8. Workload of controllers

	Low workload	Moderate workload	High workload
Tower controllers	0 %	67 %	33 %
Approach controllers	0 %	40 %	60 %
Area controllers	0 %	71 %	29 %
Flight service controllers	0 %	82 %	18 %

The researchers analyzed the on-duty rest of controllers with different positions. The results (Table 9) indicated that 75 % of the tower controllers after 2 h work did not have enough rest, while 25 % of them had enough rest. Similarly, 71 % of the approach controllers surveyed reported that they had no enough rest; By contrast 29 % had enough rest. Additionally, 56 % of the area controllers felt they had enough rest, while 44 % provided a negative answer.

Table 9. Rest of controllers

	Enough rest	Fatigue	Not enough rest	Fatigue
Tower controllers	25 %	49.2 ± 5.4	75 %	58.2 ± 4.7
Approach controllers	29 %	50.7 ± 3.7	71 %	67.7 ± 3.9
Area controllers	44 %	50.1 ± 4.2	56 %	54.1 ± 5.3

Survey of factors pertaining high workload demonstrated that weather and military restrictions were two main factors contributing to high workload (as shown in

Table 10). Other major factors were spatial complexity, and internal and external communication.

The results also showed that the majority of controllers mentioned ATC equipment performance had a significant impact on controllers' workload (as shown in Table 11), especially in terms of equipment stability and accuracy.

Table 10. Factors leading to high workload

	Military restrictions	Spatial complexity	Weather	Internal and external communication	Exception handing	Taking new controllers	Others
Ratio	21 %	16 %	23 %	16 %	15 %	7 %	2 %

3.5   Analysis of Life Event Impacts

Table 11. Equipment performance impact on controller

Influence level	1	2	3	4	5
Proportion	15.8 %	28.9 %	28.9 %	15.8 %	10.5 %

In order to understand how life events impacted controllers' fatigue, the Life Change Units (LCU) was included in the survey. Correlation and regression analyses among variables were analyzed by using SPSS 22.0. Pearson correlation coefficient between life events and fatigue was 0.64 ($P < 0.01$).

Regression analysis between fatigue and life events is showed in Table 12.

Table 12. Regression analysis between fatigue and life events

	Beta	R^2	F
Life events	0.64^{**}	0.42^{*}	55.36^{*}

Goodness of fit R^2 was high (0.42), which showed a linear relationship between fatigue and life events. Fitting equation can be concluded as:

$$Y = 1.020X + 9.794 \tag{1}$$

Regression analysis between high fatigue and life events is as shown in Table 13. R^2 was 0.54, which indicated a close relationship between life events and high fatigue in high-fatigued controllers. Controllers with high life events scores usually suffered from a high level of fatigue.

Table 13. Regression analysis between high fatigue and life events

	Beta	R^2	F
Life events	0.73**	0.54	17.76**

3.6 Analysis of Controllers Personality and Fatigue

In this section, controllers with high fatigue scores and low fatigue scores were selected for data analysis (results are as shown in Table 14). Personality scores of controllers with mild fatigue were higher than those controllers with high level of fatigue, especially in terms of extraversion, agreeableness and openness. This indicated controllers who tend to be extroverted, be good at interacting with people and learning new things may suffered less from fatigue.

Table 14. Personality scores for controllers of different fatigue levels

	Extraversion	Agreeableness	Conscientiousness	Neuroticism	Openness
All controllers	24.2 ± 1.8	18.9 ± 1.9	22.1 ± 1.9	19.0 ± 1.9	20.3 ± 2.8
Light fatigue controllers	26.3 ± 2.1	20.7 ± 2.4	21.3 ± 2.3	20.2 ± 2.4	22.6 ± 2.6
High fatigue controllers	16.3 ± 1.7	15.4 ± 1.8	18.2 ± 1.8	16.7 ± 2.0	14.9 ± 2.5

Table 15. T test about extraversion scores between mild fatigue and high fatigue controllers

		Levene's Test for Equality of Variances		T-test for Equality of Means						
		F	Sig.	t	Sig. (2-tailed)	Mean Difference	Std. Error Difference	95 % Confidence Interval of the Difference		
								Lower	Upper
Personality scores	Equal variances assumed	4.114	0.009	2.080	0.015	2.723	1.310	0.000	5.447
	Equal variances not assumed			2.731	0.013	2.723	0.997	0.649	4.798

In order to verify the relationship between personality and fatigue, a T test was applied in data analysis. The results showed extraversion scores of mild fatigue controllers had a significant difference with high fatigue controllers. The F value (4.114) for extraversion scores was calculated in a 95 % confidence level (as shown in Table 15). The variance of extraversion scores between mild fatigue and high fatigue existed significant differences. The results of T tests shown that the probability of the t-value was 0.013. The hypothesis was rejected indicating that there was a significant difference between light fatigue and high fatigue.

The same method was applied for agreeableness, conscientiousness, neuroticism and openness scores. Results showed that agreeableness and openness between mild fatigue controllers and high fatigue controllers exist significant differences. However, there are no significant differences in conscientiousness and neuroticism.

4 Conclusion

The researchers of this study utilized a survey to understand air traffic controllers' fatigue in China. Six components were included in the survey, they are: personal information, subjective assessment of fatigue, workload-related factors investigation, sleep quality, life event impacts, and personality. The survey was carried out in an air traffic control facility in China. The researchers also analyzed the reliability and validity of the survey. The researchers found that sleep quality, working factors and daily life factors were contributed for fatigue of air traffic controllers surveyed.

On-site survey seems obtain a cheerful ending. However, our work mainly analyzed the feelings of fatigue with other factors. Hopefully further in-depth analysis and more surveys in China are expected to make this study perfect.

References

1. Bultmann, U., Kant, U., Schroer, C.A., et al.: The relationship between psychosocial work characteristics and fatigue and psychological distress. Int. Arch. Occup. Environ. Health **75** (4), 259–266 (2000)
2. Sun, T., Chen, Y.: Fatigue of air traffic control management and prevention. Air Traffic Management, pp. 4–10 (2005)
3. Mitchell, L.S., Megan, A.K., Gaea, M.P.: Human Performance and Fatigue Research for Controllers. Technical report, The MITRE Corporation (2010)
4. Xinhua News Agency: http://news.xinhuanet.com/2014-08/19/c_1112128634.htm
5. Smats, E.M.A., Garssen, B., Bonke, B.: The Multidimensional Fatigue Inventory (MFI) psychometric qualities of an instrument to assess fatigue. J. Psychosom. Res. **39** (3), 315–325 (1995)
6. Sagberg, F.: Road accidents caused by drivers falling asleep. Accid. Anal. Prev. **31**(6), 639–649 (1999)
7. Lal, S.K.L., Craig, A.: A critical review of the psychophysiology of driver fatigue. Biol. Psychol. **55**(3), 173–194 (2001)
8. Peopie, P.S., Dinges, D.F., Maislin, G., et al.: Evaluation of Techniques for Ocular Measurement as an Index of Fatigue and the Basis for Alertness Management. Drivers (1998)
9. Wang, T., Xiaolin, X.: Fatigue check list. The Journal of Traditional Chinese Medicine, pp. 348–349 (2009)
10. Buysse, D.J., Reynolds, C., Monk, T.H., et al.: The pittsburgh sleep quality index: a new instrument for psychiatric practice and research. Psychiatry Res. **28**(2), 193–213 (1993)
11. John, O.P., Donahue, E.M., Kentle, R.L.: The Big Five Inventory-Versions 4a and 54. University of California, Berkeley, Institute of Personality and Social Research, Berkeley, CA (1991)

Workload Functions Distribution Method: A Workload Measurement Based on Pilot's Behaviors

Yiyuan Zheng[1(✉)], Yuwen Jie[1], Tong Zhang[1], and Shan Fu[2]

[1] Shanghai Aircraft Airworthiness Certification Center of CAAC, Shanghai, People's Republic of China
leodeisler@sjtu.edu.cn
[2] Shanghai Jiao Tong University, Shanghai, China

Abstract. According to the airworthiness regulation, FAR25.1523 published by Federal Aviation Administration, the minimum flight crew must be established so that it is sufficient for safe operation considering the workload on individual crew members. Considering workload evaluation, typically, the measurements classified into three types: performance measures, subjective rating scale measures and psychophysiological measures. However, although these measurements are widely used in various fields, they could not reflect the behavior of flight crew during flight tasks comprehensively, especially their workload functions. Normally, the basic workload functions based on the flight crew behaviors consist of six aspects: flight path control, collision avoidance, navigation, communication, operation and monitoring of aircraft engines and systems and command decisions. In this study, upon the above six aspects, a measurement named Workload Function Distribution Method was developed, considering flight crew behaviors including fixations, actions and communications in flight tasks. In order to verify the Workload Function Distribution Method, three flight tasks with different complexity were carried out among 6 flight crews in a CRJ200 flight simulator. The three flight tasks were standard instrument approach, non-precision approach with normal weather condition and non-precision approach with turbulence. Furthermore, one of the subjective rating scale measures, NASA-TLX, was used as a verification method which collected after each task. The experiment results indicated that Workload Function Distribution Method could distinguish the different complexity of flight tasks, and related to the NASA-TLX Scale.

In conclude, Workload Function Distribution Method was built up in this study. This measurement could effectively represent the flight crew workload based on their behaviors in flight tasks.

Keywords: Fixation · Operation · Workload · Workload function

1 Introduction

As described in the airworthiness regulation [1] and the related Mean of Compliances [2], the minimum flight crew was established by considering the workload on individual crew members. However, how to define workload is still controversial. Several

D. Harris (Ed.): EPCE 2016, LNAI 9736, pp. 48–55, 2016.
DOI: 10.1007/978-3-319-40030-3_6

researchers have given out some acceptable definitions. Stassen et al. regarded the workload as the mental effort that human operator devotes to control or supervision relative to his capacity [3]. Eggemeier et al. assumed that the mental workload refers to the portion of operator information processing capacity or resources that is actually required to meet system demands [4]. Kramer and Sirevaag held that the workload was the cost of performing a task in terms of a reduction in the capacity to perform additional tasks that use the same processing resource [5]. According to these definitions, the workload should be considered as a capacity proportion rather than an exact value. Typically, workload measurement could be divided into three types in aviation: performance measures, subjective rating scale measures and psychophysiological measures [6]. In aviation, performance measures include examining the deviation between actual flight and expected path [7], and response time and accuracy of flight crew [8]. The most widely used subjective rating scale measures are Modified Cooper-Harper scale, NASA-TLX, and Bedford Scale [9]. Psychophysiological measures usually considered eye movement, heart rate and respiration [10]. However, all these measures have their own limitations. Wickens noted that performance measures may not be sufficient or adequate in some conditions [11]. Subjective rating scale measures are sometimes uncertain on the repeatability and validity, and data manipulations are often questioned as being inappropriate [12]. Psychophysiological measures are influenced by other factors, such as heart rate is quite different in day and night [13].

In order to reflect flight crew's workload more specifically and comprehensively, Workload Function Distribution Method, which combined basic workload functions in flight, was built up in this paper. According to CS 25.1523, the basic workload functions depending on the flight crew behaviors consist of six aspects: flight path control, collision avoidance, navigation, communication, operation and monitoring of aircraft engines and systems and command decisions. Workload Function Distribution Method was implemented in three approach scenarios: Standard Instrument Approach, Non-Precision Approach, and Non-Precision Approach with turbulence. Meanwhile, NASA-TLX was used as a comparative and verification indication.

2 Method

2.1 Subjects

Twelve commercial airline male pilots were invited to participate in this experiment. All of them are Chinese. The age range of these pilots was from 30 to 50 years old (Mean = 38.3 ± 7.55yr). Mean total flight hours of them were 6543.6 ± 4680.9 h (range from 1000 to 18000 h), and mean flight hours in the last two weeks before the experiment were 10.55 ± 9.32 h (range from 0 to 80 h). Each pilot has been either captain or co-captain of CRJ-200 for more than 1 year (Mean = 4.32 ± 3.78 yr). Simultaneously, they have all been recruited as captains or co-captains for other types of aircrafts (6 for B737, 4 for A320, and 2 for B747). Before the experiment, all the subjects signed an informed consent form prior to participation.

2.2 Equipment

The experiment was carried out in a CRJ-200 full - flight simulator. It is a qualified flight simulator (level C) conforming to the guidance presented in Federal Aviation Administration Advisory Circular (AC 120-40B) - Airplane Simulator Qualification [14].

Besides the flight simulator, an eye tracker (Tobbi Glass, Sweden), which sample rate was 50 Hz, was used to determine the fixation areas and corresponding durations of the subjects during the experiment. The minimum fixation period was 200 ms.

The performance of each pilot was recorded by a wide angle video camera (pixel: 640*480, sampling frequency: 10 Hz) which was installed behind the emergency exit door on the flight deck. The recording accurately described the actions of pilots over time and space during the experiment.

2.3 Procedure

In order to distribute the subject's behaviors into the six workload functions aspects, several rules were established as following first:

(a) Flight path control

If the operations were carried out on Mode Control Panel (MCP) and Control Wheel, including moving time (i.e., hand moving from one device to another).
    If the fixations were focused on Primary Flight Display (PFD).

(b) Collision avoidance

If Traffic Collision Avoidance System (TCAS) alert appeared.

(c) Navigation

If the fixations were focused on Out of Window (OTW) or Multi-Function Display (MFD).

(d) Communication

If the communications existed between flight crews or between crew and Air Traffic Controller (ATC).

(e) Operation and Monitoring of aircraft engines and systems

If the fixations were focused on Engine Indication and Crew Alerting System (EICAS).
    If the operations were not carried out on Control Wheel.

(f) Command decisions

If the operations were not dependent on checklist.

The twelve pilots constituted six flight crews, and participated in the experiment including three approach scenarios, which were Standard Instrument Approach, Non-Precision Approach, and Non-Precision Approach with turbulence. Before the experiment, each subject were required to be trained in the simulator for one hour to be familiar with the configurations and the procedures of the scenarios. In the experiment, the subjects conducted the three tasks sequentially. Simultaneously, one flight instructor stayed with the flight crew in the simulator, who was responsible for the configurations of each scenario, and acted as the role of ATC. After each scenario, every subject was asked to fulfill the NASA-TLX scale. The whole duration of the experiment had been last for two weeks.

3   Results

The results of the experiment were divided into five aspects. Firstly, the NASA-TLX scales results were given out to represent the workload differences among the three types of approach. Then, the one function conditions, the two functions conditions and the three functions conditions were analyzed sequentially. Last but not least, the four to six functions were combined together for analyzing. Only the behaviors of Pilots Flying (PF) were provided here.

(a)   NASA-TLX scales

From the results of the NASA-TLX scales, the subjective workloads were significantly different among the three types of approach ($F(2, 15) = 3.865$, $p = 0.044$). However, the differences between each two of the three were insignificant. Among them, Standard Instrument Approach had the maximum mean workload (Mean = 48.64, SD = 14.33), Non-Precision Approach had the minimum mean workload (Mean = 31.81, SD = 4.80), and the mean workload of Non-Precision Approach with turbulence was in the middle (Mean = 42.75, SD = 10.54).

(b)   One Workload Function

The mean proportions of one workload function comparing with overall task time among the three types of approach was shown as Fig. 1. The difference of one

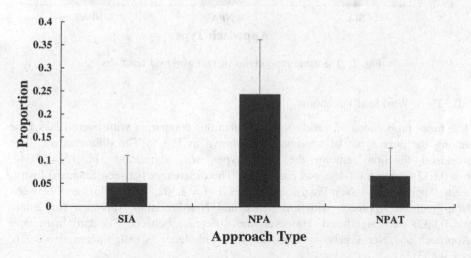

Fig. 1. The mean proportions of one workload function

workload function among the three types was significant ($F(2,15) = 9.903$, $p = 0.002$). An extra T-test was conducted. The differences between Standard Instrument Approach and Non-Precision Approach ($t = 3.614$, $p = 0.005$), and between Non-Precision Approach with turbulence and Non-Precision Approach ($t = 3.280$, $p = 0.008$) were significant. However, the difference between Standard Instrument Approach and Non-Precision Approach with turbulence was insignificant ($t = 0.483$, $p = 0.640$).

(c) Two Workload Functions

The mean proportions of two workload functions comparing with overall task time among the three types of approach was shown as Fig. 2. The difference of two workload functions among the three types was significant ($F(2,15) = 28.798$, $p = 0.000$). An extra T-test was conducted. All the differences between Standard Instrument Approach and Non-Precision Approach ($t = 7.145$, $p = 0.000$), between Standard Instrument Approach and Non-Precision Approach with turbulence ($t = 4.256$, $p = 0.002$), and between Non-Precision Approach with turbulence and Non-Precision Approach ($t = 3.743$, $p = 0.004$) were significant.

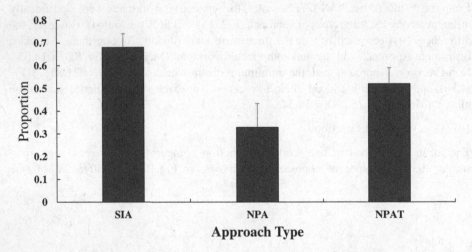

Fig. 2. The mean proportions of two workload functions

(d) Three Workload Functions

The mean proportions of three workload functions comparing with overall task time among the three types of approach was shown as Fig. 3. The difference of three workload functions among the three types was significant ($F(2,15) = 4.344$, $p = 0.032$). An extra T-test was conducted. The differences between Standard Instrument Approach and Non-Precision Approach ($t = 3.502$, $p = 0.006$), and between Non-Precision Approach with turbulence and Non-Precision Approach ($t = 2.486$, $p = 0.032$) were significant. However, the difference between Standard Instrument Approach and Non-Precision Approach with turbulence is insignificant ($t = 0.216$, $p = 0.833$).

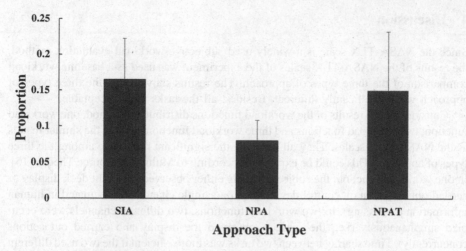

Fig. 3. The mean proportions of three workload functions

(e) Four to Six Workload Functions

The mean proportions of four to six workload functions comparing with overall task time among the three types of approach was shown as Fig. 4. The four to six workload functions difference among the three types was insignificant ($F(2,15) = 1.075$, $p = 0.366$). An extra T-test was conducted. None of differences between Standard Instrument Approach and Non-Precision Approach ($t = 1.046$, $p = 0.320$), between Standard Instrument Approach and Non-Precision Approach with turbulence ($t = 0.157$, $p = 0.878$), and between Non-Precision Approach with turbulence and Non-Precision Approach ($t = 1.763$, $p = 0.108$) were significant.

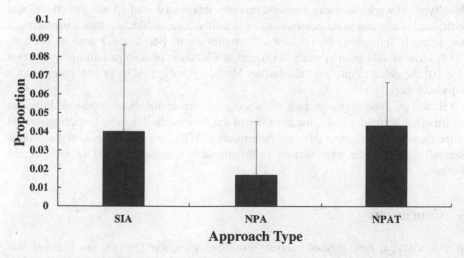

Fig. 4. The mean proportions of four to six workload functions

4   Discussion

Since the NASA-TLX scale is a widely used subjective workload evaluation method, the results of the NASA-TLX scales of the experiment was used as a baseline workload comparison of the three types of approach. The results showed that the three types of approach were significantly different. Besides, all the tasks were acceptable.

Considering the results of the workload functions distribution method, one workload function, two workload functions and three workload functions all had the similar results as the NASA-TLX scales. They all reflected the significant difference among the three types of approach. This could be explained according to Multiple Resource Theory [15]. In one workload function, the subjects usually either observed the flight deck display or carried out an action on control device (i.e., one single channel was actuated in human information processing). In two workload functions, two different channels were occupied simultaneously (i.e., the subjects observed the display and carried out actions concurrently). Time sharing between two tasks was more efficient if the two used different structures than if they used common structures [16]. Buhusi and Mack suggested that in time sharing tasks, brain circuits could reallocate the attentional and memory resources [17]. Similar results were found in three workload functions, in which auditory, visual and manual channels worked at the same time. All these workload functions conditions were tolerable by the pilots, and the different proportions of the workload functions could represent the workload differences on the pilots of the three types of approach. In four to six workload functions, the proportions were less than 0.05, and the difference was insignificant. This was reasonable, because in designing operating procedures of the tasks, to perform over four workload functions simultaneously was unacceptable. Information resource channel conflicts would lead to potential human error [18].

According to the experiment results, Workload Function Distribution Method could efficiently indicate different workload of the tasks, especially in one workload function, two workload functions and three workload functions. Comparing with the tradition three types of workload measurements, this new developed method was directly related to the flight task, and more comprehensive. Furthermore, unlike other measurements, it was scarcely influenced by the ambient environment. Besides, the area of interests (AOIs) was usually used to study the attention allocation or scan pattern of flight crews [19, 20]. Workload Function Distribution Method involved AOIs in evaluating pilot's workload directly.

However, some improvements still should be carried out about Workload Function Distribution Method. Firstly, the usability of the new method is more complicated than other measurements, especially on determining AOIs and the actions of the pilots. Secondly, more tasks with various distinguishable complexity need to validate the method.

5   Conclusion

In this study, a new method named Workload Function Distribution Method was developed based on the pilot's behaviors. Three types of approach were selected as experiment scenarios. According to the results, one workload function, two workload functions and three workload functions all had the similar results as the NASA-TLX scales, and could efficiently indicate pilot's workload. Further work would be carried out to make the method more convenient.

References

1. EASA, Certification Specifications for Large Aeroplanes CS-25 (2009)
2. EASA, CS-25 BOOK2 Acceptable Means of Compliance (2009)
3. Stassen, H., et al.: Final Report of Control Engineering Group on Mental Load, in Mental Workload: Its Theory and Measurement, pp. 235–252. Plenum Press, New York (1979)
4. Eggemeier, F.T., et al.: Workload Assessment in Multi-Task Environments Multiple-Task Performance, pp. 207–216. Taylor and Francis, London (1991)
5. Kramer, A.F., Sirevaag, E.J., Braune, R.: A psychophysiological assessment of operator workload during simulated flight missions. Hum. Factors J. Hum. Factors Ergonomics Soc. 29(2), 145–160 (1987)
6. Corwin, W.H., et al.: Assessment of Crew Workload Measurement Methods, Techniques and Procedures, vol. 1. Process, Methods and Results (1989). DTIC Document
7. Gawron, V.J.: Human Performance, Workload, and Situational Awareness Measures Handbook. CRC Press, Boca Raton (2008)
8. Di Nocera, F., Camilli, M., Terenzi, M.: A random glance at the flight deck: pilots' scanning strategies and the real-time assessment of mental workload. J. Cogn. Eng. Decis. Mak. 1(3), 271–285 (2007)
9. Farmer, E., Brownson, A.: Review of workload measurement, analysis and interpretation methods. Eur. Organ. Safety Air Navig. 33 (2003)
10. Cain, B.: A Review of the Mental Workload Literature (2007). DTIC Document
11. Wickens, C.D., Huey, B.M.: Workload Transition: Implications for Individual and Team Performance. National Academies Press, Washington DC (1993)
12. Annett, J.: Subjective rating scales: science or art? Ergonomics 45(14), 966–987 (2002)
13. Ramaekers, D., et al.: Heart rate variability and heart rate in healthy volunteers. Eur. Heart J. 19, 1334–1341 (1998)
14. FAA, A.C., Airplane Simulator Qualification (AC 120–40B), F.A. Adminstration, (ed.), Washington, DC (1991)
15. Wickens, C.D.: Multiple resources and mental workload. Hum. Factors J. Hum. Factors Ergonomics Soc. 50(3), 449–455 (2008)
16. Wickens, C.D., McCarley, J.S.: Applied Attention Theory. Taylor & Francis, Boca Raton (2007)
17. Buhusi, C.V., Meck, W.H.: Relative time sharing: new findings and an extension of the resource allocation model of temporal processing. Philos. Trans. R. Soc. B Biol. Sci. 364 (1525), 1875–1885 (2009)
18. Zheng, Y., et al.: Developing a measurement for task complexity in flight. Aerosp. Med. Hum. Perform. 86(8), 698–704 (2015)
19. Kasarskis, P., et al.: Comparison of expert and novice scan behaviors during VFR flight. In: Proceedings of the 11th International Symposium on Aviation Psychology (2001)
20. Mumaw, R., Sarter, N., Wickens, C.: Analysis of pilot's monitoring and perfomance on an automated flight deck. In: International Symposium on Aviation Psychology (2001)

Interaction and Cognition

Influence of User Characteristics
on Coping with Stress

Matthias Haase[1]([⊠]), Martin Krippl[2], Swantje Ferchow[1],
Mirko Otto[3], and Jörg Frommer[1]

[1] Department of Psychosomatic Medicine and Psychotherapy, Medical Faculty,
Otto-von-Guericke University Magdeburg, Magdeburg, Germany
matthias.haase@med.ovgu.de
[2] Institute for Psychology, Department Methodology,
Psychodiagnostics and Evaluation Research,
Otto-von-Guericke University Magdeburg, Magdeburg, Germany
[3] Computing Center, Otto-von-Guericke University Magdeburg,
Magdeburg, Germany

Abstract. There is still a lack of empirical evidence on the effects of user-characteristics on behavior towards computer systems. With regard to this, usage behavior has been surveyed intensively during the last few years by means of partial huge samples. However, most studies use secondary sources (e.g. questionnaires) rather than investigating actual behavior as the dependent measure. The present study therefore aims to examine the impact of individual user characteristics on dealing with situations experienced as challenging when interacting with a computer system. This process revealed that findings in personality research can be transferred to human-computer interaction.

Keywords: Companion system · User characteristics · Personality traits · Problem solving · Wizard of Oz experiment

1 Introduction

Weizenbaum's computer program ELIZA [1], which represented a homage to person-centered psychotherapy according to Carl Rogers [2], was assumed to have background knowledge, logical reasoning and the ability to felt understood after a short time. Users' reactions revealed the human tendency to experience even simple computer systems as empathic and trustworthy after even marginal interaction. Nass and colleagues [3, 4] came to similar conclusions and referred to the fact that humans adopt behavior patterns from face-to-face contact in human-computer interaction. Many users interact with their computer systems as if they had human motives and intentions. With respect to individuality, it can be suggested that every single user experiences the same system in different ways. Therefore, people will show diversity in their interaction behavior. Those differences might be especially observable during challenging situations, at the moment of change from unobstructed interaction to interaction experienced as challenging or requiring the person to solve a task.

© Springer International Publishing Switzerland 2016
D. Harris (Ed.): EPCE 2016, LNAI 9736, pp. 59–68, 2016.
DOI: 10.1007/978-3-319-40030-3_7

On this account, the present paper surveys changes during an interaction with a simulated, natural-linguistically controlled computer system. The focus is on the impact of user characteristics on interaction behavior when faced with a challenging situation.

2 Problem Solving and User Characteristics

Before classifying users in their contact and behavior with technical devices, it is first necessary to detect suitable user characteristics. However, there is hardly any research in this field meeting empirical standards [5], as most surveys center on usage behavior. Studies conducted this way allow for only limited conclusions to be drawn as they do not directly evaluate the interaction process with computer systems. They usually use questionnaires where the participants have to rate factors such as interaction behavior, attitude towards technology or frequency of technology usage.

2.1 User Characteristics in Human-Computer Interaction

The aforementioned statements are not meant to imply a complete lack of consideration of this topic in the literature. The most frequently surveyed user characteristics regarding actual behavior are personality, age, gender, technological experience and technological affinity.

The impact of personality theories has been considered since the early days of the field, mainly with regard to the dimensions of the Big Five personality traits [6]. Currently they are used in the technology acceptance model (TAM) with focus on the dimension of extraversion [7, 8].

For various reasons, it is not possible to make a clear statement on the impact of age and gender as user characteristics. There are numerous studies examining the effect of age, but these are difficult to compare. Most of them focus only on one age cohort, and comparisons between cohorts are rare. For older users, it is not only age that has an effect on the use of computer systems, but also factors like socio-economic status, educational level, extent of computer anxiety and interest in computer usage [9].

Findings concerning gender are indeterminate and seem to change over time. For example, Howard [10] found that females showed a higher level of computer anxiety compared to males, whereas King and colleagues [11] identified the reverse effect. Likely on the basis on such results, some authors argue that gender has no effect on human-computer interaction [12]. However, it seems undisputable that females tend to have significantly less self-confidence regarding the usage of computer systems compared to males [13]. This can be explained by gender differences in attributional styles [14]. Females tend to see failures or problems in computer usage or interaction as their own fault, which is known as internal attribution, whereas males tend to place blame for their failures and problems with someone or something else (external attribution) [13].

Technological experience is closely associated with technological affinity. According to Hassenzahl [15], the motivational aspect is fundamental when examining the extent of computer experience, which should be considered when looking at user patterns and usage models [16]. Furthermore, correlations exist between computer experience and attitudes towards technology in general [17] as well as self-efficacy [18].

2.2   Findings Regarding User Characteristics and Problem Solving

According to Dörner [19], a problem arises when a barrier prevents a subject from (1) experiencing its present state as satisfying and (2) attaining a desired goal state. Here, a distinction needs to be made between simple and complex problems. A complex problem is characterized by the need for reduction to the essential interdependence of involved variables, situational change over time and a lack of transparency [20].

The ways in which humans cope with those complications are determined primarily by their personality characteristics. There are clear connections between the Big Five personality traits, coping with stress and handling situations experienced as challenging. People with high levels of openness and extraversion are less stress sensitive [21, 22]. Optimal performance is achieved at lower stress levels for introverts and higher stress levels for extraverts [22]. Higher levels of neuroticism increase perceived stress, which may lead to depressive withdrawal, melancholy and a reduction of self-esteem [21, 23]. With regard to conscientiousness, there is no explicit evidence for a stress-reducing effect.

Furthermore, the influence of age on performance should be considered. There is evidence that older people with higher domain knowledge tend to reach their limits of effectiveness faster than younger people with lower domain knowledge [24].

For gender, the aforementioned attributional styles still apply. It can be supposed that females use internal attribution with regard to problems or failures during an interaction with a computer system. According to Abramson and colleagues [25], this attributional style is the basis for the theory of learned helplessness. This means that people who tend to attribute their failures as internal, global and stable are more likely to feel helpless in challenging situations.

3   Methods

The current study attends to the effect of user variables on interaction behavior with a simulated, speech-controlled and automated computer system. More concretely, we investigated the impact of situations experienced as challenging on interaction behavior.

After examining the aforementioned findings from previous research, we generated and examined the following research questions: What impact do stressful situations, hereafter referred to as challenge situations, have on participants' task performance while interacting with a computer system? Do correlations exist between user characteristics and performance?

3.1   Sample

We recruited participants aged between 18 and 29 as well as over 60 years old. Obtaining an equal distribution of age, gender and educational level was taken into account. Distinctions were made between participants with a "higher educational level" (general matriculation standard, studies at a university or a university of applied sciences) and "lower educational level" (secondary school or secondary modern school certificate, apprenticeship as highest educational/occupational qualification). Altogether we

Table 1. Sample distribution regarding age groups and gender

	Male	Female	Total
Age (18–29 years)			
Higher/lower educational level	22/13	23/12	70
Age (over 60 years)			
Higher/lower educational level	14/14	13/18	59
Total	63	66	129

gathered 130 participants, of which one could not be properly assigned to a level of education (Table 1).

3.2   Wizard of Oz Experiment

We developed a Wizard of Oz (WoZ) experiment which suggested to participants that they were interacting with an autonomous and automated computer system. The simulation was controlled by operators who worked in a separate room. A brief explanation of the experimental setting follows [27, 28].

An experimental supervisor briefed participants that they would be interacting with a computer system via speech input and output. At the beginning, the system asked for personal information to allow participants to get familiar with speech control and the operating mode. Subsequently, story tasks and maintaining restrictions were given by the system. Participants had to arrange their luggage for a trip with the help of the system under certain time restrictions. In doing so, they were able to choose items out of 12 categories (jackets, tops, trousers, shoes, etc.). The instructions given by the system encourage participants to imagine that they need luggage for a summer vacation. At this point, all restrictions are transparent and the task proceeds without limitations. This stage is called baseline (BSL). After selecting items from the eighth category, participants receive a limitation without prior notice requiring them to not only insert but also remove items. Participants receive assistance from the system on how to unpack items. This stage is called the weight limit barrier (WLB). Two categories later, participants have to handle another challenge situation, called the weather information barrier (WIB); they are informed that this would be a winter vacation rather than a summer one as previously assumed. They needed to adapt their strategy to the current conditions under not clearly defined time restrictions. At this point, a randomly selected portion of our sample got an affect-oriented intervention. This empathic intervention was based on general factors of psychotherapy (resource activation, problem actualization, accomplishment and clarification) [29]. Former studies have already shown that interventions given by computer systems can influence the interaction process [30, 31]. The other randomly selected participants proceeded without any further interventions. At the end, all participants got the opportunity to change some items in their luggage (revision stage (RES)). With reference to Funke [20], we can differentiate between a simple set of problems at WLB and a complex set of problems at challenges WIB and RES.

Dialog success: Besides satisfaction, performance can be seen as the most important part of user experience [32] and is defined as follows: Performance "includes measuring the degree to which users can accomplish a task or set of tasks successfully. Many measures related to the performance of these tasks are also important, including the time it takes to perform each task, the amount of effort to perform each (such as number of mouse clicks or amount of cognitive effort), the number of error committed…" [32, p. 44]. Thus, performance can be evaluated without having to rely on the subjective appraisal of users or test supervisors, allowing it to be termed an "objective goal variable". Because we used a speech-based control system, we were able to measure changes in interaction behavior at different experimental stages, which provides information about users' performance. The performance dimension "dialog success" describes participants' efforts to adapt to the altered conditions (challenge situations).

In terms of the technical implementation, participants' interaction behavior had to be operationalised initially, which was conducted using so called "logs" [33]. During the experiment, all contributions of speech output from the computer system, including their exact times, were logged. Afterwards, outputs were identified which represented a reaction to participants' interaction contributions (e.g. phrases, single words or longer silence). This allowed for a categorization of participants' interaction contributions without regard to the contents of transcripts, with the two categories of system is able to process contribution (positive logs) and system is not able to process contribution (negative logs). Negative logs are characterized by synonym failure (e.g. participant said stockings instead of socks) and all utterances outside of a clearly defined domain [27]. The positive logs represent all participant contributions that could be processed by the system.

Using the experimental values, it is possible to generate a "log quotient" ($Quotient_{logs} = \frac{N_{positivlogs}}{N_{alllogs}}$) for each participant. The log quotient permits an intra- and inter-individual comparison of different time stages during the experiment. A high value indicates that a participant was more successful in adapting to the conditions.

3.3 Psychometric Questionnaires

Before the last-minute experiment, we collected data regarding socio-biographic variables and aspects of experience with and usage of technical devices. We also conducted a system evaluation upon experiment completion. We made a separate appointment where participants completed various psychological questionnaires concerning coping with stress, interpersonal problems, attributional styles as well as technological affinity. In addition, they filled in a questionnaire regarding the Big Five personality traits, the NEO Five-Factor Inventory (NEO-FFI) [26], which measures the factors of neuroticism, extraversion, openness for experience, agreeableness and conscientiousness.

4   Results

We used repeated-measures ANOVAs for data analysis to analyze the effects of different independent variables on dialog success. We conducted one within-subject ANOVA to test only the effect of the different conditions (time). Here, we found a statistically significant interaction effect of time (F(2.74, 20.54) = 138,19, p < 0.001)[1]. One ANOVA was conducted with time as the within-subject factor and age (young vs. olds) as the between-subject factor. This revealed a significant main effect of age (F(1, 126) = 8.75, p < 0.004), showing young participants to have more dialog success, while the significant interaction of time and age (F(3.74, 345.65) = 3.651, p = 0.016) showed that these differences occurred only in the phases WIB and RES, but not during the first two (BSL and WLB) (Fig. 1).

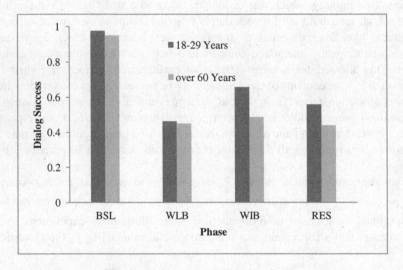

Fig. 1. Dialog success over time by age

We also looked for a main effect of psychotherapeutic-based intervention. Averaged over all test intervals, no statistically significant difference could be found (F(1, 124) = 1.03, p < 0.311) between the control and experimental groups regarding the dialog success. Neither was there a significant interaction effect of time and intervention (F(2.74, 339.44) = 0.027, p = 0.991). Therefore, it was not necessary to consider these groups separately in further measurements.

Several other ANOVAs were conducted with time as the within-subject and one of the Big Five factors or computer experience as the between-subject factor. To run the ANOVAs we had to split the sample for each independent variable (NEO-FFI scales, computer experience). We used a median split to subdivide these independent variables

---

[1] We used the Greenhouse-Geisser correction of degrees of freedom where a significant Mauchly test indicated lack of sphericity.

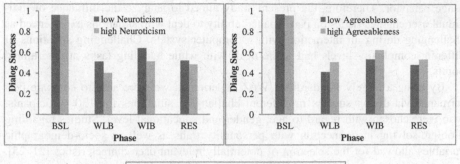

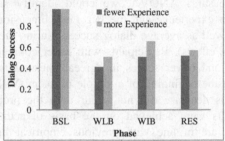

Fig. 2. Dialog success over time divided by NEO-FFI neuroticism (top left), NEO-FFI agreeableness (top right) and computer experience (bottom).

into two groups (lower vs. higher value). The following ANOVAs revealed statistically significant main effects for neuroticism ($F(1, 124) = 5.94$, $p < 0.016$), agreeableness ($F(1, 124) = 5.274$, $p < 0.023$) and computer experience ($F(1, 124) = 4.58$, $p < 0.034$). On closer examination of descriptive statistics, it became obvious that participants with a lower value of neuroticism, higher value of agreeableness and more computer experience (Fig. 2) showed better performance at WLB and WIB in particular. There were few differences between groups (lower vs. higher value) during BSL. The last challenge (RES) revealed the re-harmonization of the dialog success in the examined groups. In conclusion, participants who showed lower dialog success were older and had higher scores in neuroticism, lower scores in agreeableness and less computer-experience. The measurements showed no significant main effects for gender or the NEO-FFI scales for extraversion, openness and conscientiousness.

The three-way-interaction between time, age and extraversion revealed a statistically significant effect ($F(2,74/340,09) = 2.75$, $p < 0.047$). Another significant effect could be revealed for the interaction of computer experience with age and time ($F(2,78/344,18) = 3.89$, $p < 0.011$). All other interaction effects were not significant.

5   Conclusion

The implementation of a computer system perceived to be trustworthy, available and able to adapt presupposes an individualization process. Relevant user characteristics need to be identified from the beginning for improved classification and prediction of usage behavior. Therefore, the present study aimed to analyze the influence of individual user characteristics on participants' ability to deal with situations experienced as challenging during an interaction with a computer system. Challenging situations of different complexity levels had to be dealt with while handling tasks at determined points.

By using a largely standardized WoZ experiment, we were able to compare performance via dialog success in different challenging situations for 130 participants, who were chosen with regard to age, gender and educational level. Studies regarding problem-solving in connection with personality traits as well as socio-demographic variables allowed for the selection of potentially relevant user characteristics [21–25]. By using repeated-measures ANOVA, we could identify significant correlations between age, computer experience and the Big Five dimensions of neuroticism and agreeableness [26] as well as average dialog success during the course of interaction (tests of within-subject effects). Participants with lesser computer experience, higher scores in neuroticism and lower scores in agreeableness showed considerably less dialog success even at the beginning of a simple problem (WIB). Among older participants, however, this decrease did not occur until the problem complexity was increased. These results were achieved on the basis of actual interactions with a computer system and are in line with previous empirical findings in personality research. It was only for extraversion that no significant differences could be detected, whereas a difference (tests for within-subject effects) existed between measurement points and extraversion when considering age. This may originate from the fact that the time intervals had different lengths, with the duration of BSL equal to the total duration of all three challenges (WIB, WLB, RES) combined. Furthermore, the comparatively small sample size may underlie certain variability.

Nevertheless, the detected results substantiate the need for an individualization process as a fundamental basis for the acceptance of advancing automated computer systems to the point of companion systems.

Acknowledgements. The presented study is performed in the framework of the Transregional Collaborative Research Centre SFB/TRR 62. A Companion-Technology for Cognitive Technical Systems funded by the German Research Foundation (DFG). The responsibility for the content of this paper remains with the authors.

References

1. Weizenbaum, J.: ELIZA: a computer programm for the study of natural language communication between man and machine. Commun. ACM **9**(1), 36–45 (1966)
2. Rogers, C.R.: Client-centered psychotherapy. Sci. Am. **187**, 1–7 (1952)
3. Nass, C., Moon, Y., Carney, P.: Are people polite to computers? Responses to computer-based interviewing systems. J. Appl. Soc. Psychol. **5**(29), 1093–1110 (1999)
4. Reeves, B., Nass, C.: The Media Equation: How People Treat Computers, Television, and New Media Like Real People and Places. CSLI Publications, Cambridge University Press, Stanford, New York (1996)

5. Brandtzaeg, P.B.: Towards a unified Media-User Typology (MUT): a meta-analysis and review of the research literature on media-user typologies. Comput. Hum. Behav. **26**, 940–956 (2010)
6. Weinberg, G.M.: The Psychology of Computer Programming. Van Nostrand Reinhold, New York (1971)
7. Svendsen, G.B., Johnsen, J.-A.K., Almås-Sørensen, L., Vittersø, J.: Personality and technology acceptance: the influence of personality factors on the core constructs of the Technology Acceptance Model. Behav. Inf. Technol. **32**(4), 323–334 (2013)
8. Behrenbruch, K., Söllner, M., Leimeister, J.M., Schmidt, L.: Understanding diversity – the impact of personality on technology acceptance. In: Kotzé, P., Marsden, G., Lindgaard, G., Wesson, J., Winckler, M. (eds.) INTERACT 2013, Part IV. LNCS, vol. 8120, pp. 306–313. Springer, Heidelberg (2013)
9. Wagner, N., Hassanein, K., Head, M.: Computer use by older adults: a multi-disciplinary review. Comput. Hum. Behav. **26**(5), 870–882 (2010)
10. Howard, G.S.: Computer Anxiety and Management Use of Microcomputers. UMI Research Press, Ann Arbor (1986)
11. King, J., Bond, T., Blandford, S.: An investigation of computer anxiety by gender and grade. Comput. Hum. Behav. **18**(1), 69–84 (2002)
12. Naumann, A., Hermann, F., Niedermann, I., Peissner, M., Henke, K.: Interindividuelle Unterschiede in der Interaktion mit Informations- und Kommunikationstechnologie. In: Gross, T. (ed.) Mensch und Computer 2007: Interaktion im Plural. Oldenbourg, München (2007)
13. Dickhäuser, O., Stiensmeier-Pelster, J.: Erlernte Hilflosigkeit am Computer? Geschlechtsunterschiede in computerspezifischen Attributionen. Psychologie in Erziehung und Unterricht **27**, 486–496 (2002)
14. D'Amico, M., Baron, L.J., Sissons, M.E.: Gender differences in attributions about microcomputer learning in elementary school. Sex Roles **33**(5–6), 353–385 (1995)
15. Hassenzahl, M.: The thing and I: understanding the relationship between user and product. In: Blythe, M., Overbeeke, C., Monk, A.F., Wright, P.C. (eds.) Funology: From Usability to Enjoyment, pp. 31–42. Kluwer Academic Publishers, Dordrecht (2003)
16. Deng, L., Turner, D.E., Gehling, R., Prince, B.: User experience, satisfaction, and continual usage intention of IT. Eur. J. Inf. Syst. **19**(1), 60–75 (2010)
17. Loyd, B.H., Gressard, C.: The effects of sex, age, and computer experience on computer attitudes. AEDS J. **18**(2), 67–77 (1984)
18. Igbaria, M., Iivari, J.: The effects of self-efficacy on computer usage. Omega **23**(6), 587–605 (1995)
19. Dörner, D.: Problemlösen als Informationsverarbeitung. Kohlhammer, Stuttgart (1976)
20. Funke, J.: Complex problem solving: a case for complex cognition? Cogn. Process. **11**(2), 133–142 (2010)
21. Schneider, T.R., Rench, T.A., Lyons, J.B., Riffle, R.R.: The influence of neuroticism, extraversion and openness on stress responses. Stress Health: J. Intl. Soc. Invest. Stress **28**(2), 102–110 (2012)
22. Williams, P.G., Smith, T.W., Gunn, H.E., Uchino, B.N.: Personality and stress: individual differences in exposure, reactivity, recovery, and restoration. In: Contrada, R.J., Baum, A. (eds.) Handbook of Stress Science: Biology, Psychology, and Health, pp. 231–246. Springer, New York (2011)
23. Ebstrup, J.F., Eplov, L.F., Pisinger, C., Jørgensen, T.: Association between the Five Factor personality traits and perceived stress: is the effect mediated by general self-efficacy? Anxiety Stress Coping **24**(4), 407–419 (2011)

24. Lindenberger, U., Kliegl, R., Baltes, P.B.: Professional expertise does not eliminate age differences in imagery-based memory performance during adulthood. Psychol. Aging **7**(4), 585–593 (1992)
25. Abramson, L.Y., Seligman, M.E., Teasdale, J.D.: Learned helplessness in humans: critique and reformulation. J. Abnorm. Psychol. **87**(1), 49–74 (1978)
26. McCrae, R.R., Costa, P.T.: A contemplated revision of the NEO Five-Factor Inventory. Pers. Individ. Differ. **36**(3), 587–596 (2004)
27. Frommer, J., Rösner, D., Haase, M., Lange, J., Friesen, R., Otto, M.: Project A3 - Detection and Avoidance of Failures in Dialogues. Pabst Science Publisher, Lengerich (2012)
28. Haase, M., Lange, J., Rösner, D., Frommer, J.: Eigenschaften von Nutzern in der Mensch-Computer-Interaktion. In: Peters, S. (ed.) Die Technisierung des Menschlichen und die Humanisierung der Maschine: Interdisziplinäre Beiträge zur Interdependenz von Mensch und Technik, pp. 54–74. Mitteldeutscher Verlag, Halle (2015)
29. Grawe, K.: Grundriß einer Allgemeinen Psychotherapie. Psychotherapeut **40**, 130–145 (1995)
30. Bickmore, T., Gruber, A., Picard, R.: Establishing the computer–patient working alliance in automated health behavior change interventions. Patient Educ. Couns. **59**(1), 21–30 (2005)
31. Hone, K.: Empathic agents to reduce user frustration: the effects of varying agent characteristics. Interact. Comput. **18**(2), 227–245 (2006)
32. Tullis, T., Albert, B.: Measuring the User Experience: Collecting, Analyzing, and Presenting Usability Metrics. Elsevier, Amsterdam (2013)
33. Rösner, D., Frommer, J., Friesen, R., Haase, M., Lange, J., Otto, M.: LAST MINUTE: a multimodal corpus of speech-based user-companion interactions. In: Workshop abstracts, LREC 2012, Istanbul, Turkey, pp. 2559–2566. ELRA, Istanbul (2012)

The Effect of Multiple Perspectives Information on the Characteristics of Human's Spatial Cognition in the Human-Human Interaction of Spatial Cognition Tasks

Xianliang Mu, Lifen Tan, Yu Tian, and Chunhui Wang[✉]

National Key Laboratory of Human Factors Engineering,
China Astronaut Research and Training Center, Beijing 100094, China
1078042576@qq.com, {wluyao9802, chunhui_89}@163.com,
cctian@126.com

Abstract. Spatial cognition is an important branch of cognition science. The behavior in the spatial cognition interactions between people was studied in our research. And the results will contribute to the design of robot's cognitive system that similar to those of human which will make the robot much more intelligent to aids in human-robot cooperative work. We have designed several experimental scenes with different degree of ambiguity. In different scenes, the assistants will communicate with a commander through language and gesture on a single perspective or double perspectives. Based on these experiment, we can master the feature of human's spatial language expression and the rule of choosing spatial reference frame in the human-human interaction of spatial cognition tasks. The following three results are summed up. (1) The assistants are inclined to use the "egocentric" and "exocentric" frames of reference. (2) The frequency of choosing reference frames increases with the improvement of scene ambiguity. (3) Compared with single perspective, the assistants need much less number of reference frames on the double perspectives.

Keywords: Spatial cognition · Cooperative work · Spatial reference frame · Perspective-taking

1 Introduction

Spatial cognition refers to the processing of spatial information that perceived by people, such as the three-dimensional objects' size, shape, location, distance and the relationship between them in the psychological space or physical space. The spatial cognition tasks and human-human interaction are very common in our daily life. When people working together in spatial cognition tasks, the commander may communicate with the assistant or the assistant can observe the world on the commander's perspective to finish the work well. Actually, the assistant may be human or robot.

In the traditional human-robot interaction, human makes decisions through the analysis of information from his own perspective and the robot's perspective, and then he will interact with the robot through mouse, keyboard, handles, pedals, etc. The robot

© Springer International Publishing Switzerland 2016
D. Harris (Ed.): EPCE 2016, LNAI 9736, pp. 69–78, 2016.
DOI: 10.1007/978-3-319-40030-3_8

will fulfill specific task after it has received the commands. Under this interactive mode, the robot with a low intelligence level cannot understand the human's intention well. And the human's capacity of perceiving, attending the scene information has not been fully employed. People have a really high workload when they interact with robots with low intelligence level.

In the future, we hope that robots can communicate with people and have the capability of perspective-taking to help people fetch tools or assemble machines.

2   Method

In the human-human interaction, the key issue is how to eliminate ambiguity and it's the same with human-robot interaction. So the assistant should get the commander's intention as soon as possible to fulfill a task efficiently. In our study, we focus on the feature of human's spatial language expression and the rule of choosing spatial reference frame in the human-human interaction of spatial cognition tasks. According to literature [1–6], there are five frames of reference: exocentric (world-based, such as "Go north"), egocentric (self-based, "Turn to my left"), addressee-centered (other-based, "Turn to your left"), deictic ("Go here [points]"), and object-centric (object-based, "The fork is to the left of the plate").

We have designed several experimental scenes with different degree of ambiguity. The assistants will observe the scene on two different perspectives. One is the perspective of themselves and the other is combing the perspectives of the commander and the assistant. In different scenes, the assistants will communicate with a commander through language and gesture on a single perspective or double perspectives. The participants' utterances were collected. Then we extracted the categories of reference frames that participants used and recorded how many times they had used.

Based on the experiment, we can master the feature of human's spatial language expression and the rule of choosing spatial reference frame in the human-human interaction of spatial cognition tasks.

3   Experiment

3.1   Subjects

We recruit 12 participants who are between 20 and 40 years old serving as assistants, and they are not suffering from disease or color blindness. Besides, they should have a normal ability of expression.

3.2   Experiment Scene

As shown in Fig. 1, we design 6 scenes which have different levels of ambiguity. "P" stands for assistant, "M" stands for commander, "A", "B", "C" stand for goals, and the "arrow" points at the goal that the commander wants to get. The black rectangle stands for an obstacle. In the first three scenes, the assistant can identify the target "A" through

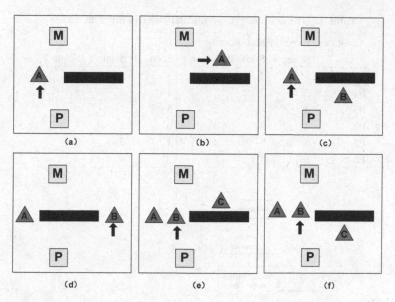

Fig. 1. Experimental scene: (a) target "A" can be seen by M and P, (b) M can see the target "A" but P can't see the it, (c) M can see the target but P can see "A" and "B", so P should exclude "B" to choose "A" automatically, (d) identify target "B" through communication, (e) M can see "A", "B" and "C", while P can see "A" and "B", so the target "B" should be identified through communication, (f) M can see "A" and "B", while P can see "A", "B" and "C", so the target "B" should be identified through communication.

perspective-taking easily. In the other three scenes, each one has a different degree of ambiguity. Once the commander sent out a verbal order, the assistant should find the goal as soon as possible through communicating with commander and perspective-taking. In different scenes, the participants' utterances were collected. And we extracted the categories of reference frames that participants used and recorded how many times they had used, as shown in Fig. 3.

3.3 Experiment Progress

The 12 assistants will accomplish the experiment in turn, and all the 6 experiment scenes should be done as shown in Fig. 1. What's more, in order to avoid the influence of order, we arrange the assistants' order through a method called "balanced Latin square design", as shown in Table 1.

The assistants named P7 ~ P12 will follow the same order designed above. In addition, the former 6 assistants will do the spatial cognition experiment on a single perspective. Then, it will take some time for the assistants to do a questionnaire test. We will make use of the data to analyze the subjective factors that affect experimental results. Later, these 6 assistants will do the spatial cognition experiment on two per-spectives, namely, the assistant's own perspective and the commander's perspective. Also, the other questionnaire test should be accomplished by the assistants. The later 6

Table 1. The assistants' experimental order in different scenes

Assistants	Experimental order					
	Scene a	Scene b	Scene c	Scene d	Scene e	Scene f
P1	1	2	6	3	5	4
P2	2	3	1	4	6	5
P3	3	4	2	5	1	6
P4	4	5	3	6	2	1
P5	5	6	4	1	3	2
P6	6	1	5	2	4	3

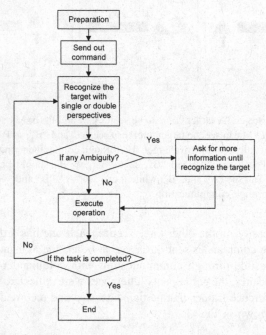

Fig. 2. A flow chart of the experiment

assistants will do the double perspectives test first and then accomplish the single perspective test.

The detailed procedure of single or double perspectives is shown below.

a. Prepare to conduct experiment.
b. The commander send out the order, "Please fetch the red screw driver to me."
c. The assistant starts to search the red screw driver.
d. The assistant can see the experimental scene through his own perspective or double perspectives. (The assistant can get the commander's perspective by a PC displayer.)
e. If there are any ambiguities, the assistant will ask for more information.
f. The assistant will identify and deliver a target.

g. The commander will tell the assistant if he has got a correct target. And if the choice is wrong, the assistant have to repeat step c ~ g. If the choice is correct, the assistant will follow the next step.
h. The experiment end.
i. The assistant will accomplish the questionnaire text.
j. The man who is responsible for data collection should record the data as soon as possible.

The Fig. 2 gives a description in a flow chart form.

4   Results

4.1   Analysis Between Assistants

We processed the data and got the correlation matrix of different reference frames. As shown in Table 2, a significant negative correlation was found between egocentric and exocentric. So people who chose the egocentric would seldom choose the exocentric and vice versa. The reason is that P3 and P4 are northerners who prefer exocentric and the others are southerners who prefer egocentric. What's more, the data showed that assistants preferred to use these two frames of reference. So we added the egocentric to exocentric and got a new figure, Fig. 3. It is much more significant to see this preference. Besides, all of the assistants chose the object-centric quite often, whether northerners or southerners.

Table 2. Correlation matrix

	exocentric	egocentric	addressee-centered	object-centric	deictic
exocentric	1	**−0.946**	−0.138	−0.198	−0.157
egocentric	–	1	−0.058	0.011	−0.053
addressee-centered	–	–	1	0.34	**0.98**
object-centric	–	–	–	1	0.375
deictic	–	–	–	–	1

As we know, different people may have different capability of spatial cognition. So we calculated the total amount of each assistant's choice of spatial reference frames, as shown in Fig. 5. The statistic of the result is shown in Table 3, in which the low variance indicates that the assistants have similar capabilities of spatial cognition (Fig. 4).

4.2   Analysis of Different Scenes

In Fig. 6, the frequency of choosing reference frames increases with the improvement of scene ambiguity. However, the ambiguity of the scene is hard to be explained quantitatively. We just focus on the trend in the figure. What's more, assistants preferred to use egocentric and exocentric in each scene.

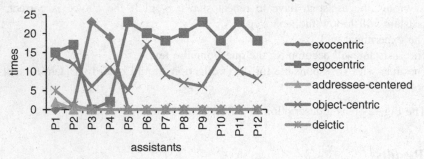

Fig. 3. The choice of spatial reference frames for 12 assistants throughout the experiment

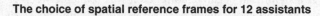

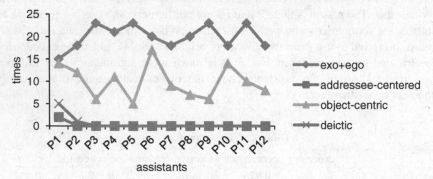

Fig. 4. Add exocentric to egocentric

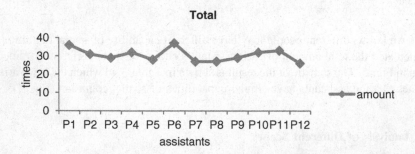

Fig. 5. The total amount of each assistant's choice of spatial reference frames

Table 3. The statistic of the total amount of each assistant's choice of spatial reference frames

Mean	Standard Error of Mean	Standard deviation	Variance	Skewness	Standard Error of skewness
30.58	1.026	3.554	12.629	0.558	0.637

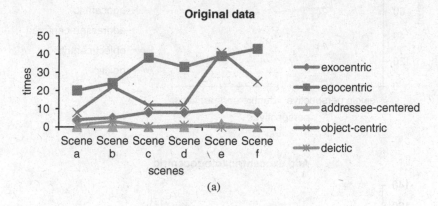

(a)

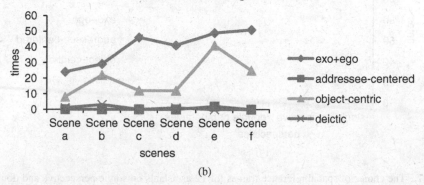

(b)

Fig. 6. The choice of spatial reference frames for 12 assistants in different scenes: (a) original data, (b) add exocentric to egocentric

4.3 Analysis of Single and Double Perspectives

In Fig. 7, compared with single perspective, the assistants need much less number of reference frames on the double perspectives. It means that abundant visual image information will improve the performance of human-human interaction. What's more, assistants preferred to use egocentric and exocentric in each case.

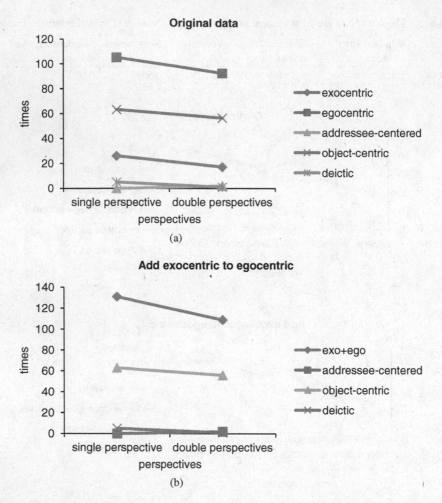

Fig. 7. The choice of spatial reference frames for 12 assistants on single perspective and double perspectives: (a) original data, (b) add exocentric to egocentric

5 Discussion

There are various characteristics of human's spatial cognition. In our study, we just focus on human's spatial language expression and the rule of choosing spatial reference frame. Besides, the effect of single and double perspectives on human's choice of spatial reference frame was studied here, and the effect of the third perspective needs further research.

6 Conclusion

We can get some conclusions from this human-human interaction experiment in the spatial cognition task.

a. When we design the robot's cognitive system that similar to those of human, we need to take the difference between southerners and northerners into consideration. The northerners prefer exocentric while the southerners prefer egocentric. In addition, these two kinds of spatial reference frames and the object-centric reference frames are frequently-used in the human-human interaction of spatial cognition tasks. So these three reference frames should be the key point of cognitive modeling task. Besides, the deictic reference frame has a strong relevance with gesture, such as "Go here [points]". Assistant can easily understand the commander's command through combining the gesture and language information. If you want to improve the naturalness of the human-robot interaction system, the deictic reference frame should be considered.

b. In the scene c, d, e, f, the ambiguities of scenes are much higher. There will be much more interactive behavior between people. So we should figure out the human's spatial language expression pattern and the rule of choosing spatial reference frame in these scenes. And these results will contribute to cognitive modeling work.

c. Multiple perspectives information will improve the performance of human-human interaction. Particularly, the commander will take much less time to communicate with the assistant. A second perspective can improve the efficiency of human-human cooperative work.

Acknowledgments. This study was supported by the Experimental Technique Youth Fund Project (No. SYFD1400618) and the Foundation of National Key Laboratory of Human Factors Engineering (No. SYFD140051802). Author Xianliang Mu, Lifen Tan, Yu Tian, Chunhui Wang were supported by the foundation of National Key Laboratory of Human Factors Engineering (No. HF2013-Z-B-02, NO.HF2011Z-Z-B-02). In addition, the authors would like to thank anonymous reviewers for their comments about the research and suggestions for improving this paper.

References

1. Levelt, W.J.M.: Some perceptual limitations on talking about space. Limits in perception: essays in honour of Maarten A. Bounman, pp. 323–358 (1984)
2. Carson-Radvansky, L.A., Radvansky, G.A.: The influence of functional relations on spatial term selection. Psychol. Sci. **7**, 56–60 (1996)
3. Carson-Radvansky, L.A., Logan, G.D.: The influence of functional relations on spatial template construction. J. Mem. Lang. **37**, 411–437 (1997)

4. Goldin-Meadow, S.: When gestures and words speak differently. Curr. Dir. Psychol. Sci. **6**, 138–143 (1997)
5. McNeill, D.: Hand and Mind: What Gestures Reveal About Thought. University of Chicago Press, Chicago (1992)
6. Mintz, F.E., Trafton, J.G., Marsh, E., Perzanowski, D.: Choosing frames of reference: perspective-taking in a 2-D and 3-D navigational task. Hum. Factors Ergon. Soc. Meet. **48**, 1933–1937 (2004)

Event-Related Potential Study on Visual Selective Attention to Icon Navigation Bar of Digital Interface

Yafeng Niu[1(✉)], Chengqi Xue[1], Haiyan Wang[1], Lei Zhou[1],
Jing Zhang[1], Ningyue Peng[1], and Tao Jin[2]

[1] School of Mechanical Engineering,
Southeast University, Nanjing 211189, China
nyf@seu.edu.cn
[2] Mechanical and Electrical Engineering Institute,
China University of Petroleum, Qingdao 266580, China

Abstract. In order to investigate the user cognitive processing of visual selective attention to icon navigation bar in the digital interface, 20 subjects were required to notice and remember the activated icons in the navigation bar selectively and judge whether or not target icon had presented in the navigation bar and if so press the button quickly. Their behavior and event-related potential (ERP) data were collected. Experimental results demonstrate that P200 and N400 components of navigation bar selective attention exist obvious differences in amplitude and latency under different activated icon quantities. In the recognition process of target stimulus icon, accuracy rate and reaction time both exist regular changes with the activated icon quantities, and target stimulus recognition N200 component distributing in different brain areas exists obvious differences.

Keywords: Icon navigation bar · Selective attention · Event-related potentials · P200 · N400 · N200

1 Introduction

As one of the important part of interactive digital interface, navigation bar takes on the roles of orientation, linking, transition and searching, helping users find their target area more accurately. In general, rationality of the navigation bar design is one significant index for measuring the usability of digital interface and the satisfaction of user experience. Navigation bar is the most popular interface navigation method, which makes the interface more recognizable for users, eliminating the communication gap and realizing natural, friendly and convenient communication between users and computers. In this paper, by investigating the user cognitive processing of visual selective attention to icon navigation bar, some general navigation bar design methods are proposed, which provide guidance for design of navigation bar and interface information architecture, enhancing the ability to convey information, reducing cognitive load of users, furthering improving the design quality of digital interface.

© Springer International Publishing Switzerland 2016
D. Harris (Ed.): EPCE 2016, LNAI 9736, pp. 79–89, 2016.
DOI: 10.1007/978-3-319-40030-3_9

Since Sutton created event-related potential (ERP) technique in 1965, ERP has been widely used in many fields, such as psychology, physiology and cognitive neuroscience. Simply, ERP refers to potential differences of brains when granting or revoking a particular stimulus applied on the sensing system or brain regions [1]. With the characteristics of high time resolution, ERP can realize synchronization lock of brain signals and experimental operations, and its amplitude, latency and spatial frequency of potential and current can provide detailed response information of brains, which directly reflect nerve electric activity and establishing the corresponding relations between operations and brain areas or brain signals [2].

P200, one early component of ERP, is associated with the early recognition of visual information, which has been widely used in the cognitive process of visual search experiment [3], task related processing [4] and early stage semantic processing of visual information [5]. N200, one early component of attention, has different manifestation and significance in different tasks and channels [6], especially in experimental tasks, such as visual searching [7], facial memory [8], feature matching [9] and Stemberg working memory. N400 is proposed by Kutas [10] through studying end ambiguity words, mainly reflecting semantic cognitive process, which is induced by stimuli, such as syntax [11], picture [12] and voice [13].

At present, researchers at home and abroad have studied icon understanding [14] and icon memory [15], however ERP research for visual selective attention to icon navigation bar has not been barely studied. Selective attention refers to only noticing some stimuli or certain aspects of stimulus among outside stimuli. For the icon navigation bar of digital interface, icons are divided into activated and inactivated states, and only activated icons are available. Therefore, inactivated icons are all distractions when users want to realize corresponding functions or commands by clicking on activated icons. Visual selective attention to icon navigation bar is extremely important in practical applications. For instance, Fig. 1 displays a real time status of Word for Mac, and only "cut", "copy" and "undo" typing are inactivated, hence users can only select and click the rest activated icons. In this paper, by adopting ERP technique and serial mismatch experimental paradigm, user cognitive processing of visual selective attention to icon navigation bar is investigated.

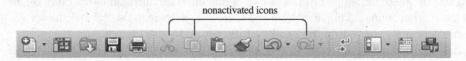

Fig. 1. Real-time status of Word for Mac icon navigation bar

2 Experimental Method

2.1 Subjects

Twenty undergraduates, with ten males and ten females, whose ages are all between $20 \sim 30$ years old, are chosen as subjects. They all satisfy the following conditions: physical and mental health, no mental illness history, right-handed, normal or rectified vision, and with many years' experience in using graphics device. Subjects are trained to be familiar with task flow and operation requirements before the formal experiment. During the experiment, subject with electrode cap sits comfortably in front of the screen in ERP laboratory, with their eyes 550 ∼ 600 mm away from the screen and both horizontal and vertical perspective controlled in 2.3 degrees.

2.2 Tasks and Procedures

To avoid the influence of personal preference and industry familiarity, military, communication and information related icons which subjects are all not familiar are chosen as stimulus materials, and all icons have been desaturated and undertaken the visual effect unified image processing. In addition, to avoid the influence of icon peripheral contour, rounded borders are added to icons and icon sizes are in 48 × 48 pixels. Navigation bar totally contains 5 icons, and these icons are divided into activated ones and inactivated ones, among which icons in high brightness are activated and darker icons are inactivated.

Firstly, a white cross appeared in the center of the screen with the background to be black, and continuously lasted for 500 ms then disappeared. Next, icon navigation bar appeared and presented for 2000 ms then disappeared. At this stage, subjects were required to remember the activated icons in the navigation bar. Afterwards, the screen turned to be black and continuously lasted for 500 ms. Subjects could relax and blink eyes to eliminate visual persistence. At last, target stimulus icon appeared and lasted indefinitely until subjects had identified weather this icon had appeared in the second stage. What they should do was to press key A if the target stimulus icon repeatedly appeared, otherwise press key L. In this experiment, activated icons in the navigation bar were set in random and time interval was 500 ms every two trials. Total experiment was divided into 4 blocks according to the quantity of activated icon in the navigation bar (1, 2, 3, 4). Each block consists of 60 trails and there was a short break between each block. The experimental process was demonstrated in Fig. 2.

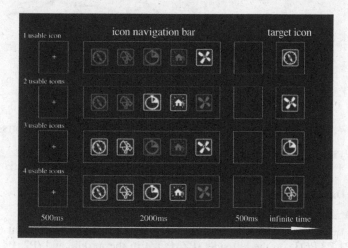

Fig. 2. Flow diagram of experiment

2.3   EEG Recording

ERP experimental equipment is placed in a closed ERP/behavior laboratory which is soundproof, with magnetic insulation and brightness adjustable. 19 inches CRT monitor works in visual presentation and the keyboard is used for reaction. Synamp2−64 channel signal amplifier, Scan 4.3.1 EEG recorder analysis system and Ag/AgCl electrode cap provided by American Neuroscan Company are used. Especially, electrode caps are placed according to the international 10−20 system. Reference electrode is placed in the bilateral mastoid connection. Grounding electrode is placed in the center point connection of FPZ and FZ, which records the horizontal and vertical EOG synchronously. Filter pass-band is 0.05−100 Hz, and sample frequency is 500 Hz/channel. Contact resistance between electrode and scalp is required to be less than 5 kΩ.

3   Data Analysis

3.1   Behavioral Data Analysis

Behavioral data includes the accuracy rate and reaction time of target stimulus icon recognition. As shown in Fig. 3, with the quantity of activated icon varying from one to four, average accuracy rate of target stimulus icon recognition is as follows: 2 (0.976) > 1 (0.968) > 3 (0.928) > 4 (0.856). This illustrates that accuracy rate generally shows a trend of decline with the increase of target stimulus icon number. The difference of accuracy rate between one or two icon number is not significant. As shown in Fig. 4, with the quantity of activated icon varying from one to four, average reaction time of target stimulus icon recognition is as follows: 4 (1174.233 ms) > 3 (1112.774 ms) > 2 (919.758 ms) > 1 (856.304 ms). This illustrates that reaction time presents increasing trend with the increase of target stimulus icon number.

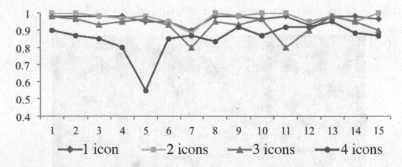

Fig. 3.   Line chart of target stimulus icon recognition accuracy rate

3.2   EEG Data Analysis

3.2.1   ERP Analysis of Icon Navigation Bar

EEG epoch time is from icon navigation bar appearance to 700 ms. Eight electrodes including (P1,P3,PO3) on the left side, (PZ, POZ) in the middle and (P2, P4, PO4) on the right side are selected as the analysis electrodes for P200, and seven electrodes including (C6, CP6) on the right central region, (FC4, FC6) on the right frontal lobe and (FT8, TP8, T8) on the temporal lobe are set as the N400 analysis electrodes.

(1) P200

For P200 component analysis, EEG average amplitude during 100 ms ~ 200 ms period after the appearance of icon navigation bar is selected for statistical analysis. 4 (quantity of stimulus icon variation: 1, 2, 3 and 4) × 3 (different region: left, middle and right) repetitive measure analysis of variance (ANOVA) is performed. The results show that, regions have a significant main effect (F = 23.298, p = 0<0.05), while there is no significant interaction effect between regions and icon quantities (F = 1.929, p = 0.079 > 0.05), and no significant difference exists between different icon quantities (F = 0.603, p = 0.615 > 0.05).

Paired-sample T tests of different icon number (1, 2, 3 and 4) respectively on the left, right and in the middle are performed. Result displays that absolute value of the average on the left side is larger than that on the right side and in the middle when icon number changes (one icon: 1.57uv > 1.01uv > 0.94uv, p < 0.05; two icons: 1.82uv > 1.30uv > 0.57uv, p < 0.05; three icons: 2.25uv > 1.69uv > 1.38uv, p < 0.05; four icons: 2.26uv > 1.50uv > 1.40uv, p < 0.05).

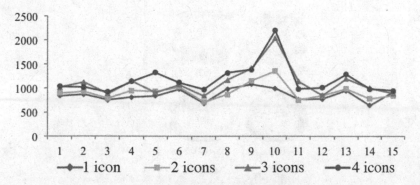

Fig. 4. Line chart of target stimulus icon recognition reaction time

Paired-sample T tests of P1, P3 and PO3 electrodes on the left are performed under different icon numbers (1, 2, 3 and 4). When the icon number is one or two, there is no significant difference of these three electrodes (p > 0.05), while the icon number is three or four, absolute value of the average for PO3 is significantly larger that of P1 and P3 (three icons: 2.92uv > 1.95uv > 1.87uv, p < 0.05; four icons: 2.83uv > 1.98uv > 1.96uv, p < 0.05). As shown in Figs. 5 and 6, when the icon number is three or four, P200 has a significant effect on the left region and the maximal amplitude is around PO3.

(2) N400

For N400 component analysis, EEG average amplitude during 300 ms ~ 500 ms period after the appearance of icon navigation bar is selected for statistical analysis. 4 (number of stimulus icon variation: 1, 2, 3 and 4) × 3 (different region: left, middle

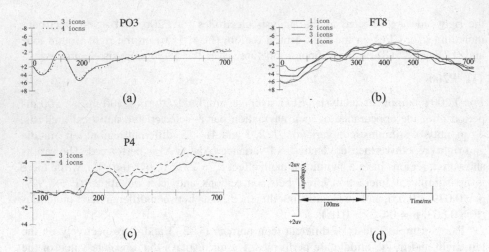

Fig. 5. All EEG components oscillogram of navigation bar and target stimulus icon under different conditions (a) navigation bar PO3 electrode P200 component; (b) navigation bar FT8 electrode N400 component; (c) target stimulus icon P4 electrode N200 component; (d) unit of measure

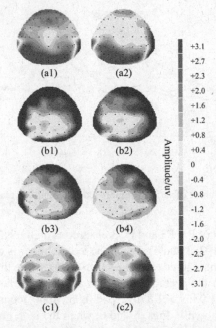

Fig. 6. All EEG components oscillogram brain topographic mapping in maximal potential period under different conditions (a1) P200: 3 icons (165 ms, 5.719uv); (a2) P200: 4 icons (165 ms, 5.180uv); (b1) N400: 1 icon (368 ms, -3.287uV); (b2) N400: 2 icons (361 ms, -3.964uv); (b3) N400: 3 icons (342 ms, -3.927uv); (b4) N400: 4 icons (330 ms, -3.000uv); (c1) N200: 3 icons (161 ms, -2.809uv); (c2) N200: 4 icons (177 ms, -3.462uv)

and right) ANOVA is performed. The results show that, regions have a significant main effect (F = 104.332, p = 0<0.05), while there is no significant interaction effect between regions and icon quantities (F = 0.997, p = 0.429 > 0.05), and significant difference exists between different icon quantities (F = 2.855, p = 0.042 < 0.05).

Paired-sample T tests of different icon number (1, 2, 3, and 4) respectively on the right central region, right frontal lobe and temporal lobe are performed. Results displayed that absolute value of the average on the temporal lobe is larger than that on the right central region and right frontal lobe when icon number changes (one icon: 1.75uv > 1.45uv > 1.02uv, p < 0.05; two icons: 2.83uv > 2.19uv > 1.87uv, p < 0.05; three icons: 2.56uv > 2.04uv > 1.74uv, p < 0.05; four icons: 1.96uv > 1.44uv > 1.22uv, p < 0.05).

Paired-sample T tests of FT8, TP8 and T8 electrodes on the temporal lobe are performed under different icon numbers (1, 2, 3, and 4). Result shows that, absolute value of the average for FT8 is larger than that of TP8 and T8 (one icon: 2.02uv > 1.83uv > 1.40uv, p < 0.05; two icons: 3.51uv > 2.86uv > 2.12uv, p < 0.05; three icons: 3.12uv > 2.54uv > 2.03uv, p < 0.05; four icons: 2.39uv > 2.01uv > 1.49uv, p < 0.05). As shown in Figs. 5 and 6, when the icon number changes, N400 has a significant effect on the temporal lobe and the maximal amplitude is around FT8.

3.2.2 ERP Analysis of Target Stimulus Icon

EEG epoch time is −100 ms before target stimulus icon appearance to 700 ms. Eight electrodes including (P1, P3, PO3) on the left side, (PZ, POZ) in the middle and (P2, P4, PO4) on the right side are selected as the analysis electrodes for N200, and seven electrodes including (C6, CP6) on the right central region, (FC4, FC6) on the right frontal lobe and (FT8, TP8, T8) on the temporal lobe are set as the N400 analysis electrodes.

(1) When target stimulus icon exists in the activated icons of navigation bar.
For N200 component analysis, EEG average amplitude during 100 ms ∼ 200 ms period after the appearance of target stimulus icon is selected for statistical analysis. 4 (icon number variation: 1, 2, 3 and 4) × 3 (different region: left, middle and right) ANOVA is performed. The results show that, regions have a significant main effect (F = 11.065, p = 0<0.05), while there is no significant interaction effect between regions and icon quantities (F = 0.333, p = 0.919 > 0.05), and no significant difference exists between different icon quantities (F = 0.843, p = 0.474 > 0.05). Paired-sample T tests of different icon number (1, 2, 3 and 4) respectively on the left, right and in the middle are performed. When the icon number is one or two, there is no significant difference of these three positions (p > 0.05), while the icon number is three or four, absolute value of the average on the right side is significantly larger than that in the middle (three icons: 1.33uv > 0.67uv, p = 0.023 < 0.05; four icons: 2.07uv > 1.43uv, p = 0.023 < 0.05). Paired-sample T tests of P2, P4 and PO4 electrodes on the right side are performed. When the icon number is three or four, absolute value of the average for P4 is significantly larger than that for P2 (three icons: 1.81uv > 0.96uv, p = 0.002 < 0.05; four icons: 2.49uv > 1.74uv, p = 0.029 < 0.05). As shown in Figs. 5 and 6, electrodes on the right side have a significant effect and the maximal amplitude is around P4.

For N400 component analysis, EEG average amplitude during 300 ms $\sim$ 500 ms period after the appearance of target stimulus bar is selected for statistical analysis. 4 (icon number variation: 1, 2, 3 and 4) $\times$ 3 (different region: right central region, right frontal lobe and temporal lobe) ANOVA is performed. The results show that, regions have a significant main effect ($F = 50.103$, $p = 0<0.05$), while there is no significant interaction effect between regions and icon quantities ($F = 1.766$, $p = 0.109 > 0.05$), and no significant difference exists between different icon quantities ($F = 1.799$, $p = 0.154 > 0.05$). Paired-sample T tests of regions and electrodes for these three positions under different icon quantities are performed. The results show that there are no significant difference between different regions and electrodes under different icon quantities ($p > 0.05$).

(2) When target stimulus icon do not appear in the activated icons of navigation bar.
Both analysis method of N200 and N400 are the same as above. The results demonstrate that, both N200 and N400 show no significant difference between different regions and electrodes under different icon quantities ($p > 0.05$).

4 Discussions

4.1 Behavioral Data Discussion

The research results indicated that target stimulus icon recognition accuracy rate displayed a trend of decline with the increase of activated icon number, which was as the following rule, 2 > 1>3 > 4. When there was only one stimulus icon appears in the navigation bar, recognition accuracy was not in the first place, which could be explained according to the vulnerability of short-term memory storage. That was to say, any outside distraction could lead to oblivion. The quantity of distractors reached four when one stimulus icon turned up, therefore subjects were more easily distracted and to forget. Reaction time increased as the stimulus icon number varying from one to four, which was as follows, 4 > 3>2 > 1. Resource limited theory proposes that cognitive resources of people were limited, mainly manifested in the limited capacity of working memory [16]. Task difficulty increase would lead to attention resources shortage, resulting in a higher cognitive load, which reflected in this experiment was the prolonged reaction time. Miller [17] found that for numbers, letters or words, short-memory span of subjects are all 7 ± 2. In this study, graphic symbols with more information were adopted, leading to narrowed memory span. Meanwhile, combining with the specifications and standards of interface design, five navigation icons were set for study, with activated icon number varying from one to four. Murch [18] proposed that choosing six distinguishable icon colors was scientific and rational. Black, white, and gray were used in the navigation bar, which met the standard for color selection, while it was more complicated in practical applications, which needed to be further studied.

4.2 P200 Data Analysis

The maximal wave peak for selective attention component P200 of icon navigation bar located on the left side of parietal-occipital lobe and the maximal amplitude was around PO3 electrode. Driver's study [19] on visual attention indicated that attention disorders would present when there was damage on the rear end of left and right parietal lobe or the connection point of left and right parietal-occipital lobe. In this paper, nerve function area of navigation bar selected attention was around PO3, which was consistent with Drive's study. Selective attention of activated icons in the navigation bar was the process of activated icons selection and short-time storage. Yiwen Wang's study [20] demonstrated that parietal-occipital lobe had distinct effect for short-time storage and P230 had the maximal amplitude, which provided strong evidence for the appearance and distribution of P200 component. Working memory brain model showed that semantic storage could activate the rear of left-parietal lobe, which verified the brain region distribution of P200 component. Moreover, it could be speculated that memory of the activated icon might be a series of process through the semantic element translation, management and storage.

4.3 N400 Data Analysis

The results indicated that the maximal wave peak for selective attention component N400 of icon navigation bar located on the right frontal-temporal lobe and the maximal amplitude was around FT8 electrode. Sakai's research on fMRI [21] showed activation of prefrontal lobe was attributed to selecting task related information would not be distracted by irrelevant distractors, while activation of temporal lobe inboard was because the repeated response to information which had been stored but already offline. Activation of frontal-temporal lobe in this paper was consistent with Sakai's study. N400 component was the semantic ambiguity wave, while there was no direct relationship between N400 and semantic ambiguity wave in this study, which indicated that emergency of N400 was due to the semantic association or interference of inactivated icons to activated icons during navigation bar selected attention and memory process. As displayed in Figs. 5 and 6, N400 existed with no relation to activated icon quantities, which further verified that N400 would be evoked if distraction existed in visual stimulation. Latency of N400 under different activated icon number was as follows, 4 (330 ms), 3 (342 ms), 2 (361 ms) and 1 (368 ms), which indicated that N400 appeared later with fewer activated icon quantity, and N400 was evoked later when more semantic distractors generated by inactivated icons existed. This study was consistent with Nobre's research on the latency timing and semantic difference [22].

4.4 N200 Data Analysis

The results indicated that the maximal wave peak for target stimulus icon recognition component N200 located on the right parietal region and the maximal amplitude was around P4 electrode. N200 appeared in the visual working memory task conducted by Vogel [23], and the distraction was more concentrated on the right parietal region, which reflected that the information maintenance of working memory, in accordance with the result reached in this paper that concentrated distribution located on the right parietal region when target stimulation appeared. N200 component included N2a and N2b, and N2a referred to visual mismatch negative wave, while N2b was relative to target stimulation recognition [1]. In this study, N200 mainly referred to N2b component. When target stimulus icons had appeared in the activated icons of navigation bar, N200 (N2b) had a significant difference on the parietal region, whereas there was no significant difference. Simson proposed that task related visual stimulation would evoke N2b component and the most obvious response located on the back of brains [24], which was consistent with the appearance and distribution of N200 studied in this paper. The average amplitude of N200 for right hemisphere was significantly larger than that of the left hemisphere, reflecting the asymmetry of visual information processing and hemisphere functional difference on the right and left hemisphere.

5　Conclusions

ERP technique was adopted in this paper, and cognitive process of icon navigation bar was investigated from the perspective of visual selective attention. The results showed that that P200 and N400 components of navigation bar selective attention existed obvious differences in amplitude and latency under different activated icon quantities. In the recognition process of target stimulus icon, accuracy rate and reaction time both existed regular changes with the activated icon quantities, and target stimulus recognition N200 component distributing in different brain areas exists significant differences. This study exhibited important reference and application value in revealing cognitive rules for icon navigation bar, enhancing the ability to convey information for navigation bar and exploring more effective navigation bar and digital interface design method. In the next work, novel EEG techniques and experimental paradigms will be explored, further focusing on the user cognitive research about properties of navigation bar, such as icon distribution, visual effect, color, contrast ratio and border.

Acknowledgement. The paper is supported by National Natural Science Foundation of China (71471037, 71271053, 51405514) and Natural Science Foundation of Jiangsu Province (BK20150636).

References

1. Zhao, L.: Experimental Instruction of ERPs. Southeast University Press, Nanjing (2010)
2. Niu, Y.F., Xue, C.Q., Wang, H.Y., Li, J.: The preliminary exploration and study on brain mechanism of cognitive load in the DHCI of complex system. Ind. Eng. Manag. **17**(6), 72–75 (2012)
3. Luck, S.J., Hillyard, S.A.: Electrophysiological correlates of feature analysis during visual search. Psychophysiology **31**, 291–308 (1994)
4. Potts, G.F., Tucker, D.M.: Frontal evaluation and posterior representation in target detection. Cogn. Brain. Res. **11**, 147–156 (2001)

5. Zhao, L., Li, J.: Visual mismatch negativity elicited by facial expressions under non-attentional conditions. Neurosci. Lett. **410**, 126–131 (2006)
6. Folstein, J., Petten, C.: Influence of cognitive control and mismatch on the N2 component of the ERP: a review. Psychophysiology **45**, 152–170 (2008)
7. Kiss, M., Van Velzen, J., Eimer, M.: The N2pc component and is links to attention shifts and spatially selective visual processing. Psychophysiology **45**(2), 240–249 (2008)
8. Bindemann, M., Burton, A.M., Leuthold, H., Schweinberger, S.R.: Brain potential correlates of face recognition: geometric distortions and the N250r brain response to stimulus repetitions. Psychophysiology **45**(4), 535–544 (2008)
9. Wang, Y., Cui, L., Wang, H., Tian, S., Zhang, X.: The sequential processing of visual feature conjunction mismatches in the human brain. Psychophysiology **41**, 21–29 (2004)
10. Kutas, M., Hillyard, S.A.: Reading senseless sentences: brain potentials reflect semantic incongruity. Science **207**, 203–205 (1980)
11. Pulvermüller, F., Shtyrov, Y.: Automatic processing of grammar in the human brain as revealed by the mismatch negativity. Neuroimage. **20**, 1020–1025 (2003)
12. Kuperberg, G.R.: Neural mechanisms of language comprehension: challenges to syntax. Brain Res. (Spec. Issue). **1146**, 23–49 (2007)
13. Connolly, J.F., Phillips, N.A.: Event-related potential components reflect phonological and semantic processing of the terminal word of spoken sentences. J. Cogn. Neurosci. **6**, 256–266 (1994)
14. Gong, Y., Yang, Y., Zhang, S.Y., Qian, X.F.: Event-related potential study on concretness effects to icon comprehension. J. Zhejiang Univ. (Eng. Sci.). **47**(6), 1000–1005 (2013)
15. Niu, Y.F., Xue, C.Q., Li, X.S., Li, J., Wang, H.Y., Jin, T.: Icon memory research under different time pressures and icon quantities based on event-related potential. J. Southeast Univ. (Engl. Ed.) **30**(1), 45–50 (2014)
16. Wang, H.B., Xue, Q.C., Huang, J.W., Song, G.L.: Design and evaluation of human-computer digital interface based on cognitive load. Electro-Mech. Eng. **29**(5), 57–60 (2013)
17. Miller, G.A.: The magic number seven, plus or minus two: some limits on our capacity for processing information. Psychol. Rev. **63**, 81–93 (1956)
18. Murch, G.M.: Color graphics-blessing or ballyhoo? excerpt. In: Baecker, R.M., Grudin, J., Buxton, W.A.S., Greenberg, S. (eds.) Readings in Human-Computer Interaction: Toward the Year 2000. Morgan Kaufmann, San Francisco (1987)
19. Driver, J.: The neuropsychology of spatial attention. In: Pashler, H. (ed.) Attention. Psychology Press, Hove (1998)
20. Wang, Y.W., Lin, C.D., Wei, J.H., Luo, Y.J.: ERP evidences of dynamic dissociation of short-term storage and rehearsal. Acta Psychologica Sinica **36**(6), 697–703 (2004)
21. Sakai, K., Passininhan, R.E.: Prefrontal selection and medial temporal lobe reactivation in retrieval of short-term verbal information. Cerebr Cortex. **14**, 914–921 (2004)
22. Nobre, A.C., McCarthy, G.: Language-related field potentials in the anterior-medial temporal lobe. J. Neurosci. **15**(2), 1090–1098 (1995)
23. Vogel, E.K., Machizawa, M.G.: Neural activity predicts individual differences in visual working memory capacity. Nature **428**, 748–751 (2004)
24. Simson, R., Vaughan, H.G., Ritter, W.: The scalp topography of potentials in auditory and visual discrimination tasks. Electroencephalogr. Clin. Neurophysiol. **42**, 528–535 (1977)

Differences of Affective Learning with Own-Race and Other-Race Faces: An Eye-Tracking Study

Junchen Shang[1] and Xiaolan Fu[2($\boxtimes$)]

[1] College of Psychology, Liaoning Normal University, Dalian 116029, China
junchen_20081@163.com
[2] State Key Laboratory of Brain and Cognitive Science, Institute of Psychology,
Chinese Academy of Sciences, Beijing 100101, China
fuxl@psych.ac.cn

Abstract. Minimal affective learning is a phenomenon wherein people can learn about the affective meaning of other people with brief behavioral descriptions. Prior research mainly focused on affective learning with own-race faces. Own-race bias is a robust phenomenon describing that people can recognize own-race faces more efficiently than other-race faces. In the current study, we investigated whether own-race bias would influence minimal affective learning. Chinese participants learned Chinese and Caucasian faces paired with behaviors of different valence. After learning, they were asked to evaluate the learned faces and novel faces. Their eye movements and pupil diameters were continuously monitored during the experiment. We analyzed the change in pupil dilation to assess how much cognitive effort was required for affective learning. The results showed that participants only learned positive information with faces. Learning performance for other-race faces was similar with own-race faces. In addition, change of pupil dilation was larger when learning other-race than own-race faces, suggesting a greater cognitive effort for affective learning with other-race faces. Taken together, the results demonstrated that affective learning for other-race faces was more difficult than own-race faces. This research provided more support for the notion that different cognitive strategies were employed by faces of different race.

Keywords: Affective learning · Own-race bias · Eye movements · Pupil dilation

1 Introduction

When we make an impression of a person, we compare the person to previous memory. Psychological research revealed that our impressions of a person are easily changed by previous affective information [1, 2]. This phenomenon is called minimal affective learning. In a typical affective learning research, participants see neutral faces presented with sentences describing positive, neutral or negative behavior, later made judgments about the faces. Faces paired with negative behaviors were evaluated more negatively than those paired with neutral, positive behaviors. In turn, faces paired with neutral

© Springer International Publishing Switzerland 2016
D. Harris (Ed.): EPCE 2016, LNAI 9736, pp. 90–96, 2016.
DOI: 10.1007/978-3-319-40030-3_10

behaviors were evaluated more negatively than those with positive behaviors [1, 3]. Affective learning effect is robust and reliable within Western culture [1–4]. One recent study with Chinese participants found similar results [5]. However, since these studies have only examined minimal affective learning with faces of participants' own race, it remains unclear whether race will affect the learning effect with faces.

We argue that learning affective associations with faces may be impacted by race. The "own-race bias" (ORB; also called the cross-race effect or other-race effect, and outgroup homogeneity effect) is a robust phenomenon in face learning and recognition, wherein people are better able to recognize own-race faces compared to other-race faces [6]. This effect is reliable across cultural and racial groups [7]. According to [8], the context in which faces appear may strongly impact face perception. There are four types of context: within-face features, within sender features, external features from the environment surrounding the face, and within-perceiver features. Affective learning processes and own-race bias are within-perceiver features, both can impact face perception.

Prior research has rarely examined whether affective learning can be modulated by own-race bias, except for [9]. Reference [9] demonstrated an overlap between own-race bias and fear conditioning. In this research, two black and two white neutral faces were shown to both white and black Americans. During the learning phase, one face from each race was paired with an electric shock. Then, in the extinction phase, there were no shocks. Skin conductance responses were measured to assess the conditioned fear response. The results indicated that participants showed a conditioned response to both black and white faces during acquisition, while they only showed a significant conditioned response to other race faces in extinction. Thus, other-race faces are more likely associated with negative information. However, this research [9] did not experimentally investigate why people associated other-race faces more easily with aversive stimulus. They speculated that human might have evolved to take persons who were from another race or outgroup as a threat. In addition, stimuli in fear conditioning were always strongly aversive, such as an electric shock, whereas stimuli in minimal affective learning are mildly affective in nature [1]. It is unknown whether the own-race bias would influence this type of learning.

Our goal in the present study was to test whether minimal affective learning with own-race faces is different with other-race faces. In the main experiment, Chinese participants learned to associate own-race and other-race faces with negative, neutral or positive behavior. Then, they rated these faces plus novel faces. We compared learning effect of own-race faces with other-race faces. If other-race faces were threat stimuli, participants should only learn negative information with them. In addition, a recent study found that healthy participants recalled the behavior paired with faces and recognized the faces after affective learning [10]. It is possible that affective learning is partially impacted by memory of the face-behavior pairings. Since other-race faces are more difficult to remember, affective learning for other-race faces may be more difficult than own-race faces.

Furthermore, recent studies used eye-tracking to investigate the face-processing strategies of different race [11–15]. For example, participants' pupils were more dilated when encoding other-race faces [12, 13]. The pupil dilation indicated that other-race face encoding required more cognitive load or mental effort, leading to lower efficiency in processing other-race than own-race faces. In the present study, we also used eye-tracking and pupillometry to measure the cognitive effort invested when encoding the face and behavioral sentences, in order to explain the differences in affective learning. We predicted that our participants would show larger changes in pupil dilation when learning Caucasian faces than Chinese faces.

To sum up, we aimed to answer two questions: (1) Is affective learning effect of other-race faces different with own-race faces? (2) Does affective learning of other-race faces require more mental effort than own-race faces?

2   Method

2.1   Participants

Thirty-four Chinese undergraduate students (15 male, 19 female, M age = 22.65, SD age = 2.42) voluntarily took part in the experiment for payments. Participants all had normal or corrected-to-normal vision.

2.2   Materials

Digitized grayscale pictures of 40 faces displaying neutral expressions (20 Caucasian, 20 Chinese) were used in the study. The Chinese faces were taken from a Chinese facial expression database [16], and the Caucasian faces were taken from the faceset used by [17]. The original images were cropped around the face to exclude hair and ears using Adobe Photoshop CS, and were adjusted to equal mean luminance. The faces were randomly divided into four sets, with 5 Caucasian faces and 5 Chinese faces in each set. One set of faces were paired with negative behaviors, one set of faces with neutral behaviors, one set of faces with positive behaviors, and one set of faces were presented without behaviors. Thirty behavioral sentences were selected from [1], and were translated into Chinese. The pairing of faces and behaviors was counterbalanced across participants.

The stimuli were displayed on a 17-in LCD monitor at approximately 70 cm away from participants' eyes. The images covered 12 of visual angle horizontally and 17 of visual angle vertically. The face images and sentences were incorporated on a 1280×1024 pixel white background. The stimuli were presented and responses were recorded using E-Prime Version 2.

Eye movements were recorded at a sampling rate of 250 Hz with an infrared camera on an iView X RED 500 system (SensoMotoric Instruments, Germany). Chin and forehead rests were used to minimize the participant's head movements. Only the left eye of each participant was tracked continuously throughout the experiment. Prior to the experiment, calibration of eye fixations was conducted using a nine-point fixation procedure.

2.3   Procedure

Participants were seated in a room with dim light. We adopted the minimal affective learning task [1]. The main experiment was comprised of two phases: learning phase and test phase. During the learning phase, the participants were presented with 30 face-sentence pairs, and were instructed to remember each pair by imaging each person performing the behavior described in the corresponding sentence. In the beginning of each trial, a fixation cross was presented in the center of the screen for 500 ms. Then, one face-sentence pair was shown for 5 s. The intertrial interval was 1 s, after which the next trial started. Each face-sentence pair was presented four times in random order.

During the test phase, participants evaluated the 30 learned faces, plus 10 novel faces, as negative, neutral, or positive. Each trial started with a 500-ms fixation cross. Then, a face was presented in the center of the screen. Participants were instructed to make "quick snap" judgments about each face. The face was displayed until the participant pressed labeled keys. The intertrial interval was 1 s, after which the next trial started. The faces were shown in random order. The response options were coded as negative = 1, neutral = 2, and positive = 3 [17]. The participants' pupil diameters were continuously monitored during the experiment. The change in pupil dilation was analyzed to assess how much cognitive effort was required for affective learning.

3 Results

Analyses were performed in two parts: rating data in the test phase, pupil dilation during the learning phase. The eye-tracking data was analyzed with BeGaze software (Senso-Motoric Instruments, Germany). For analysis, we rejected trials in which there were no fixations within the borders of the face area. 3.4 % of all trials were rejected as invalid.

3.1 Behavioral Data

The rating scores were submitted to 4 (Behavior: negative vs. neutral vs. positive vs. no behavior) × 2 (race: Caucasian vs. Chinese) repeated-measures ANOVA. Descriptive statistics are presented in Table 1. The main effect of behavior was significant, $F(3, 99) = 14.71$, $p < .001$, $\eta2 = .31$. Pairwised comparisons (Bonferroni) showed that people evaluated faces presented with negative behaviors more negatively than those presented with neutral ($p = .012$) or positive behaviors ($p < .001$), and those with neural behaviors more negatively than those with positive behaviors, p = .021. Novel faces were rated as more negatively than those with positive behaviors ($p < .001$), suggesting that positive learning occurred. However, ratings of novel faces were not different with faces presented with negative behaviors ($p > .84$), or those presented with neutral behaviors ($p > .14$), suggesting that negative learning did not occur. We did not found significant effect of race, $F(1, 33) = .007$, $p > .93$, $\eta2 < .001$, or

Table 1. Mean (and standard deviation) affective ratings of faces as a function of valence of behavior and race of stimulus.

	Positive behavior	Neutral behavior	Negative behavior	No behavior
Chinese faces	2.19 (0.47)	1.95 (0.33)	1.79 (0.37)	1.88 (0.36)
Caucasian faces	2.14 (0.34)	1.99 (0.33)	1.76 (0.32)	1.83 (0.36)

interaction between behavior and race, $F(3, 99) = .38$, $p > .77$, $\eta2 = .01$. The results indicated that race of face did not influence affective learning.

3.2 Pupil Dilation

We used horizontal pupil diameter to extract changes in pupil dilation toward Caucasian faces and Chinese faces in the learning phase. We used a transformation procedure to calculate a ratio percentage in pupil dilation for each trial [18]. According to [18], the ratio percentage score represents the range of change in pupil dilation, which indicated cognitive effort when viewing a face. Ratio percentage score is calculated as follows: ([minimum overall pupil diameter–current pupil diameter]/[maximum overall pupil diameter–minimum overall pupil diameter]).

A 2 (race: Caucasian, Chinese) × 3(valence of paired behavior: positive, negative, neutral) repeated-measures ANOVA was conducted on pupil ratio percentages. A main effect of race emerged, $F(1,33) = 6.14$, $p = 0.019$, $\eta2 = .16$, suggesting that the range of change in pupil dilation was larger when participants fixed on Caucasian faces, comparing to Chinese faces (see Fig. 1.). The main effect of valence was not significant, $F(2,66) = 2.46$, $p > 0.09$, $\eta2 = .07$. Finally, we did not observe a significant race × valence interaction, $F(2,66) = .75$, $p > 0.47$, $\eta2 = .02$. Thus, these results support the prediction that learning other race faces required more cognitive effort as compared with own race faces.

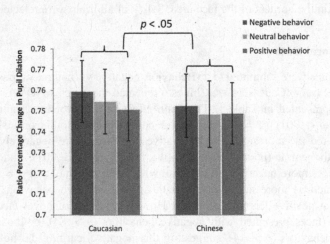

Fig. 1. Change in pupil dilation as a function of face race while encoding face-sentence pairs. Error bars reflect standard error.

4   Discussion and Conclusion

In the present study, Chinese participants learned positive information with faces in minimal condition of affective learning. However, there is no negative learning. This is not consistent with previous research in which both positive learning and negative learning occurred [1, 5]. It should be noted that reference [17] used the same paradigm with reference [1], but they only observed negative learning. The reason for the mixed findings of these studies may be individual differences in affective learning. Verosky and Todorov [3] observed that some participants did not rate faces associated with positive behaviors more positively than faces associated with negative behaviors. In their study, only 35 of the 57 participants' judgments showed strict ranking of the associations: positive > neutral > negative. In our study, the pattern should be positive > neutral > novel > negative. It was hard to use this strict criterion to exclude participants because there were only 34 participants. If we excluded half of participants, the data would be lack of statistic power. Nonetheless, it reminds us that minimal affective learning is hard to form since the affective stimulus is mild, which may result in mixed results. Future studies should test our findings by recruiting a larger sample of participants.

Affective learning effect of other race faces is similar with own race faces. This is not consistent with research of fear conditioning in which other-race faces were more easily associated with aversive information [9]. The reason may be that the present study involved different learning processes with fear conditioning. Fear conditioning is based on associative learning, while minimal affective learning in the present study is based on rule-based learning [1].

Moreover, participants demonstrated a greater change in pupil dilation when associating other-race faces with behaviors as compared to own-race faces. These results are completely consistent with [12, 13]. This may reflected enhanced cognitive exertion while learning other-race faces. This also provide support for the in-group/out-group theory of own-race bias [19]: processing of in-group faces is efficient and automatic, while processing of out-group faces is less efficient and non-automatic. In order to get equal performance of learning with the own race faces, participants had to make greater cognitive effort with other race faces.

In conclusion, the results of current study demonstrated that own-race bias influenced affective learning. In line with the idea that different cognitive strategies were employed by faces of different race, we found evidence that affective learning is also modulated by race. The findings expended our understanding of both affective learning and own-race bias. This point is helpful in the research areas of human computer interaction, such as affective computing and design of emotional machine. Furthermore, since culture influences multiple cognitive and affective processes [20], it would be interesting to compare affective learning effect across cultures. Furthermore, in the present study, we only tested Chinese faces and Caucasian faces, it is not clear whether affective learning effect for other race face, such as black faces, would be differenct with own race faces. Future studies should also test affective learning effect for faces from different out groups.

Acknowledgments. This study was supported by grants from the National Natural Science Foundation of China (31400869). We thank Huizhong Wu and Yuqiong Jiang for data collection.

References

1. Bliss-Moreau, E., Barrett, L.F., Wright, C.I.: Individual differences in learning the affective value of others under minimal conditions. Emotion **8**, 479–493 (2008)
2. Todorov, A., Olson, I.R.: Robust learning of affective trait associations with faces when the hippocampus is damaged, but not when the amygdala and temporal pole are damaged. Soc. Cogn. Affect. Neurosci. **3**, 195–203 (2008)
3. Verosky, S.C., Todorov, A.: Generalization of affective learning about faces to perceptually similar faces. Psychol. Sci. **21**, 779–785 (2010)
4. Verosky, S.C., Todorov, A.: When physical similarity matters: mechanisms underlying affective learning generalization to the evaluation of novel faces. J. Exp. Soc. Psychol. **49**, 661–669 (2013)
5. Shang, J., Fu, X.: Differences in allocations of attention to faces during affective learning of Chinese people. In: Liu, D., Alippi, C., Zhao, D., Hussain, A. (eds.) BICS 2013. LNCS, vol. 7888, pp. 192–200. Springer, Heidelberg (2013)
6. Meissner, C.A., Brigham, J.C.: Thirty years of investigating the own-race bias in memory for faces a meta-analytic review. Psychol. Public Law **7**, 3–35 (2001)
7. Ng, W., Lindsay, R.C.L.: Cross-race facial recognition: failure of the contact hypothesis. J. Cross Cult. Psychol. **25**, 217–232 (1994)
8. Wieser, M.J., Brosch, T.: Faces in context: a review and systematization of contextual influences on affective face processing. Front. Psychol. **3**, 1–13 (2012)
9. Olsson, A., Ebert, J.P., Banaji, M.R., Phelps, E.A.: The role of social groups in the persistence of learned fear. Science **309**, 785–787 (2005)
10. Blessing, A., Keil, A., Gruss, L.F., Zöllig, J., Dammann, G., Martin, M.: Affective learning and psychophysiological reactivity in dementia patients. Int. J. Alzheimer's Dis. **2012**, 1–9 (2012)
11. Blais, C., Jack, R.E., Scheepers, C., Fiset, D., Caldara, R.: Culture shapes how we look at faces. PLoS ONE **3**, e3022 (2008)
12. Goldinger, S.D., He, Y., Papesh, M.H.: Deficits in cross-race face learning: insights from eye movements and pupillometry. J. Exp. Psychol. Learn. Mem. Cogn. **35**, 1105–1122 (2009)
13. Wu, E.X.W., Laeng, B., Magnussen, S.: Through the eyes of the own-race bias: eye-tracking and pupillometry during face recogniton. Soc. Neurosci. doi:10.1080/17470919.2011. 596946
14. Hills, P.J., Pake, J.M.: Eye-tracking and the own-race bias in face recognition: revealing the perceptual and socio-cognitive mechanisms. Cognition **129**, 586–597 (2013)
15. Brielmann, A.A., Bülthoff, I., Armann, R.: Looking at faces from different angles: Europeans fixate different features in Asian and Caucasian faces. Vis. Res. **100**, 105–112 (2014)
16. Wang, Y., Luo, Y.: Standardization and assessment of college students' facial expression of emotion. Chin. J. Clin. Psychol. **13**, 396–398 (2005)
17. Anderson, E., Siegel, E.H., Bliss-Moreau, E., Barrett, L.F.: The visual impact of gossip. Science **332**, 1446–1448 (2011)
18. Allard, E.S., Wadlinger, H.A., Isaacowitz, D.M.: Positive gaze preferences in older adults: assessing the role of cognitive effort with pupil dilation. Aging Neuropsychol. Cogn. **17**, 296–311 (2010)
19. Sporer, S.L.: Recognizing faces of other ethnic groups: an integration of theories. Psychol. Public Policy Law **7**, 36–97 (2001)
20. Han, S., Ma, Y.: A culture-behavior-brain loop model of human development. Trends Cogn. Sci. **19**, 666–676 (2015)

A Complex Perspective of System Situation Awareness

Lei Wang$^{(\boxtimes)}$ and Yong Ren

Research Institute of Civil Aviation Safety, Civil Aviation University of China,
Tianjin 300300, China
wanglei0564@hotmail.com, renrxy@outlook.com

Abstract. Though the concept of Situation Awareness (SA) was put forward over two decades, it is still a popular issue in the field of human factors. However, the current 'situation' has been changed a lot from the times when SA theory was born. More and more system parts have been designed to meet the requirement of context-aware, which means they have been distributed some cognitive function in a system. We propose out the concept of System Situation Awareness (SSA) and try to extend the range of awareness from human to system. SSA is influenced by the system's ability of context-aware and human's ability of situation awareness. The complex mechanism exists between human and system when maintaining SSA. This concept implies that the system would probably lose its SA when its context-aware ability gets weaken or lost. We should focus more on system design to enhance SSA with the approach of human system integration.

Keywords: Situation awareness · System situation awareness · Complexity

1 Introduction

Situation awareness (SA) has been developed as an important construct in field of human factors in the past two decades. The most prestigious definition on SA was put forward by Endsley who defined situation awareness as 'the perception of the elements in the environment within a volume of time and space, the comprehension of their meaning and the projection of their status in the near future [1] '. There is no doubt that Endsley's SA model and theory is still very dominant and influential in human factors and ergonomics community.

However, the discussions and even arguments on this concept and its inner mechanism never stopped since when it was born [2–13]. One of researcher's focus points is that whether SA is a pure psychological phenomenon. Endsley's definition [1, 14, 15] emphasizes mainly on perception and understanding of the environment with some aspects of future projection. Lots of researchers with psychological background are favourable to this definition and they have been drawn to study largely on the awareness, the cognitive side of SA. By contrast, less researchers like Smith and Hancock emphasized more on the interaction between the human and the environment [16]. Smith and Hancock pointed out that situational awareness is the invariant in the agent-environment

© Springer International Publishing Switzerland 2016
D. Harris (Ed.): EPCE 2016, LNAI 9736, pp. 97–103, 2016.
DOI: 10.1007/978-3-319-40030-3_11

system that generates the momentary knowledge and behaviour required to attain the goals specified by an arbiter of performance in the environment [16].

Generally to say, current researchers focused more on awareness and less on situation. As a matter of fact, nowadays the 'situation' has been changed a lot from the times when the SA theory was put forward, e.g. more and more tangible interaction objects are being introduced in our working environment. We started to neglect the physical aspect of things [17]. In this study, in order to adequately understand the new features between situation and awareness, we try to put forward the concept of System Situation Awareness (SSA) and extend the range of situation awareness from human to system.

2   System Situation Awareness

With the development of information and interaction technology, more and more products or system parts have been designed to meet the requirement of context-aware. This means some parts have been distributed cognitive function in a system. We take the evolution of flight deck as an example and find that there is huge change from B727 to B787 (see Fig. 1), especially the difference on displays, more new information systems such as Head-Up Display (HUD) were introduced into B787. The flight deck system of B787 provides crew with more support on information collecting and analyzing.

Flight Deck of B727   Flight Deck of B787

Fig. 1. The evolution of flight deck from B727 to B787

The systems are designed with more new functions which will help human operators to finish some tasks more easily. However, sometimes they will lose the ability of situation awareness when their functions get failed. Stanton pointed that sometimes it is the system that 'loses' situation awareness, not individual operators [19]. Salmon and his colleagues claimed that systems can be responsible for losing situation awareness [20, 21]. If the system awareness is considered in, previous situation awareness models focusing on the side of human cognition are probably not suitable for use. Therefore, the right approach for situation awareness today is to investigate interactivity of multi-agent (humans and systems) consciousness [11]. We propose out the concept of System Situation Awareness (SSA) and try to extend the range of awareness from human to system. System Situation Awareness can be defined as the situation awareness of human and environment agent in system. SSA would be influenced by the system's ability of context-aware and human's ability of situation awareness.

3 Complexity of System Situation Awareness

Firstly we should see situation awareness from a systemic perspective. The 'situation' means environment around operators who possessing the 'awareness'. Apparently there are two ways to improve SA. It is as showing as Fig. 2, one way is from situation side to improve 'situation' by human centered design and another one is from awareness side to improve human ability and performance by training. But in fact now we have a black box here, we do not know the complex mechanism between them exactly. We just know that they are two elements keeping dynamic and interactive in complex systems such as flight deck, nuclear power control room and so on. So the key question is to know the complex mechanism between situation and awareness.

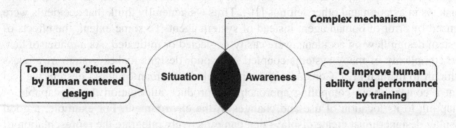

Fig. 2. The complex mechanism between situation and awareness

We think System Situation Awareness is an interactive and adaptive process between human agent and environment agent. For human operator, the situation is not a static picture in mind but keep changing all the way. The awareness process is complex and lots of conscious and subconscious mental mechanisms are involved in it. Due to the intermediary role of a long term working memory, several human cognitive stages are connected in the process of human-computer interaction. In this process, new information and stored information are integrated together and system situation awareness is enriched step by step, eventually forming a complete understanding of the system states and environment, this kind of interaction between human consciousness and system environment could be seen as an adaptive process. According to the complexity theory, the initiative and positive interaction between agents and environment is the basic driving force of system development and evolution. For example in modern cockpits, SA has to be thought as a human-systems multi-agent activity [11]. The study of Radvansky and Copeland shows that spatial shifts requires the participants to update their situation model of the environment, which demands cognitive effort, which then makes information about associated objects less available [22]. Boy pointed out that situations are related to the complexity of human operator's extrinsic environment and intrinsic capabilities [11]. Flach proposed that SA defines the problem of human performance in terms of understanding the adaptive coupling between human and environment [18]. Seeing it from methodology level, it is a reflection of reduction method if we just take the human agent's awareness into consideration. It is a holistic view if we take human agent and environment into account but neglect the interaction between them. The view of complexity has surpassed the view of reductionism and holism, which takes the dynamic, non-linear and emergence issue of system into thinking. To some extent, we think that SSA has the characteristic of complexity.

4   Implications of System Situation Awareness

Firstly, this concept implies that we should pay more attention on system design to improve the situation awareness of whole system. Decker pointed out that it leads the term of situation awareness is overused in accident investigation while we always just regard SA as human agent's business [10]. Eighty-five percent of reports produced by the Australian Transportation Safety Bureau in 1996 contained references to a 'loss of situation awareness' [23]. Loss of situation awareness has become the favored cause for mishaps in aviation and other settings [10]. Thus we generally think that accidents were caused by error of human agent instead of system agent. To some extent, the effects of system design flaw on accidents were easily neglected or mitigated. As a matter of fact, the complexity of many systems coupled with poor designs makes system awareness difficult to maintain [2]. Considering the principles of human centered design, we feel that a context-aware computing approach can produce automation that is capable of adapting to its location of use and changes in the environment. For example, a good display designer must create displays that can effectively integrate the representation of two classes of information for routine performance and the broader environment (in anticipation of unexpected events) [24]. Then enhancing System Situation Awareness will become the main goal of system design. Dey define context as 'any information that can be used to characterize the situation of an entity' [25]. Context-aware devices may also try to make assumptions about the user's current situation. Moreover, social context could be taken into consideration in flight deck design for improving SSA. We know that there is a huge difference between eastern culture and western culture. Western technology and eastern culture would clash within the flight cockpit [27]. For the western make aircraft, the culture context should be better considered in for users (eastern pilots) in the design stage.

Secondly, this concept implies us to reconsider the measurement of situation awareness. Current method of measuring situation awareness generally is to estimate the perception, comprehension and projection level of perceived situation in a subject way. If we expand the definition of Situation Awareness to System Situation Awareness, previous SA measurement method which focusing on cognition side of human agent will be not be suitable. Previous SA measurement methods focused more on human instead of the whole system. A new method or criterion of measuring SSA should be developed. Boy [11] constructed a model of the various kinds of situations ranging from the real, available, perceived, expected, to desired situations. Probably we can assess the level of available situation in a system. That means the availability of situation for human operator would be an important index of measure SSA.

In addition, from the perspective of complexity and adaption, the arguments on product or process concerning situation awareness could be unified. Because the SA is a dynamic process, it is a product at any time point.

5   A Case Study

In this section we give a case study on an aviation accident to illustrate the importance of improving SSA. On February 12, 2009, Colgan Air Flight 3407 crashed when instrument approaching to Buffalo International Airport of United States. The aircraft crashed into a residence around 8 km from the Buffalo airport. The aircraft type is Bombardier Dash 8. All passengers on board and one person on the ground lost their lives. The final investigation indicated that this crash was a Loss-of-Control (LOC) accident [26]. LOC is the flight accident type with the largest occurrence rate.

The report pointed that at first Air Traffic Controller cleared the aircraft to descend to 2300 feet and intercept the instrument approach course. The auto flight system was set to hold at 2300 feet. Once this auto flight was set, the pilot in flying kept the engine power near idle and slowed to flap-extension speed. As the landing gear lowered and flaps extended, the auto flight system continually pitched the aircraft nose-up to increase Angle of Attack (AOA) and maintain lift and altitude, causing the airspeed to decay. The cue of indicated airspeed and low-speed converged, and the stick shaker started to alert of an impending stall. At the same time, the auto pilot system disconnected – as it was designed. In a condition of great surprise, the captain finished a wrong operation and applied inappropriate nose-up inputs and failed to increase engine power. This Dash 8 aircraft experienced a full aerodynamic stall, the pilot counteracted the stick pusher but it's too late to recover it.

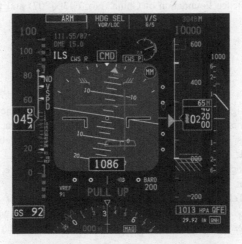

Fig. 3. The primary display in flight deck

In this case, in fact the automation had access to the data needed to make it 'aware' of its low-energy state, but the display in flight deck did not convey the implications of this important information to pilot in the right time. The flight crew members seemed to have been frozen by surprise, likely because they had not noticed the decay of airspeed from display. This was an automation surprise [2, 25]. Crew members have not noticed that the speed was dangerously slow. The National Transportation Safety Board (NTSB) concluded that the airspeed indicator in this cockpit lacked low-speed awareness features [26]. The primary display in this flight deck is as showing in Fig. 3. In this case, it is hard to say pilot lost the situation awareness or the system lost situation awareness. This accident may have been avoided if the primary display system had incorporated a context-aware design solution.

6   Conclusions

The traditional concept of situation awareness was put forward nearly thirty years ago. However, most SA models focused more on the awareness, the cognitive side of SA. Meanwhile nowadays the 'situation' updated quickly, many new technologies have been introduced into working environment. Many system parts have been distributed some cognitive function in a system. Therefore we proposed out the concept of System Situation Awareness (SSA) and extended the range of awareness from human to system. SSA is influenced by the system's ability of context-aware and human's ability of situation awareness. Meanwhile, the complex mechanism exists between human and system when maintaining SSA.

This concept implies that the system would probably lose its SA when its context-aware ability gets weaken or lost. It concluded that we need to focus more on system design to enhance SSA with the approach of human system integration.

Acknowledgments. We appreciate the valuable suggestions from Dr. Guy A. Boy of Florida Institute of technology in improving this paper. We also appreciate the support of this work from the National Natural Science Foundation of China (No. 61304207) and the China Scholarship Council.

References

1. Endsley, M.R.: Design and evaluation for situation awareness enhancement. In: Proceeding of the Human Factors Society 32nd Annual Meeting, Santa Monica, CA (1988)
2. Sarter, N.B., Woods, D.D.: Situation awareness – a critical but ill-defines phenomenon. Int. J. Aviat. Psychol. 1, 45–57 (1991)
3. Smith, K., Hancock, P.A.: Situation awareness is adaptive, externally directed consciousness. Hum. Factors 37(1), 137–148 (1995)
4. Vidulich, M.A.: Testing the sensitivity of situation awareness metrics in interface evaluations. In: Endsley, M.R., Garland, D.J. (eds.) Situation Awareness Analysis and Measurement, pp. 227–246. Lawrence Erlbaum Associates, Mahwah (2000)

5. Stanton, N.A., Chambers, P.R.G., Piggott, J.: Situational awareness and safety. Saf. Sci. **39**, 189–204 (2001)
6. Hollnagel, E.: Extended cognition and the future of ergonomics. Theor. Issues Ergonomics Sci. **2**(3), 309–315 (2001)
7. Wickens, C.D.: Situation awareness: review of Mica Endsley's 1995 articles on situation awareness theory and measurement. Hum. Factors **50**(3), 397–403 (2008)
8. Dekker, S.W.A., Hummerdal, D.H., Smith, K.: Situation awareness: some remaining questions. Theor. Issues Ergonomics Sci. **11**, 131–135 (2010)
9. Kasdaglis, N., Newton, O., Lakhmani, S.: System state awareness a human centered design approach to awareness in a complex world. In: Proceedings of the Human Factors and Ergonomics Society Annual Meeting. SAGE Publications (2014)
10. Dekker, S.W.A.: The danger of losing situation awareness. Cogn. Technol. Work **17**, 1–3 (2015)
11. Boy, G.A.: On the complexity of situation awareness. In: Proceedings 19th Triennial Congress of the IEA, Melbourne, Australia, pp. 9–14 (2015)
12. Stanton, N.A., Salmon, P.M., Walker, G.H.: Let the reader decide: a paradigm shift for situation awareness in socio-technical systems. J. Cogn. Eng. Decis. Making **9**(1), 44–50 (2015)
13. Endsley, M.R.: Situation awareness misconceptions and misunderstandings. J. Cogn. Eng. Decis. Making **9**(1), 4–32 (2015)
14. Endsley, M.R.: Measurement of situation awareness in dynamic systems. Hum. Factors **37** (1), 65–84 (1995)
15. Endsley, M.R.: Toward a theory of situation awareness in dynamic systems. Hum. Factors: J. Hum. Factors Ergonomics Soc. **37**(1), 32–64 (1995)
16. Smith, K., Hancock, P.A.: Situation awareness is adaptive, externally directed consciousness. Hum. Factors **37**(1), 137–148 (1995)
17. Boy, G.A.: From automation to tangible interactive objects. Ann. Rev. Control J. **38**(1), 1–11 (2014)
18. Flach, J.M.: Situation awareness: proceed with caution. Hum. Factors **37**, 149–157 (1995)
19. Stanton, N.A., Salmon, P.M., Walker, G.H., Jenkins, D.P.: Is situation awareness all in the mind? Theor. Issues Ergonomics Sci. **11**, 29–40 (2010)
20. Salmon, P.M., Stanton, N.A., Walker, G.H., Jenkins, D.P., Ladva, D., Rafferty, L., Young, M.S.: Measuring situation awareness in complex systems: Comparison of measures study. Int. J. Ind. Ergonomics **39**, 490–500 (2009)
21. Salmon, P.M., Lenne, M.G., Walker, G.H., Stanton, N.A., Filtness, A.: Exploring schema-driven differences in situation awareness across road users: an on-road study of driver, cyclist and motorcyclist situation awareness. Ergonomics **57**, 191–209 (2014)
22. Radvansky, G.A., Copeland, D.E.: Walking through doorways causes forgetting: situation models and experienced space. Mem. Cogn. **34**, 1150–1156 (2006)
23. ATSB: Human factors in fatal aircraft accidents. Australian Transportation Safety Bureau. ACT, Canberra (1996)
24. NTSB: Accident report - Loss of control on approach Colgan Air, Inc. operating as Continental Connection Flight 3407 Bombardier DHC-8-400. National Transportation Safety Board, Washington, D.C (2010)
25. Wickens, C.D.: Situation awareness and workload in aviation. Curr. Dir. Psychol. Sci. **11**, 128–133 (2002)
26. Dey, A.K.: Understanding and using context. Pers. Ubiquitous Comput. **5**(1), 4–7 (2001)
27. Jing, H.S., Batteau, A.: The Dragon in the Cockpit: How Western Aviation Concepts Conflict with Chinese Value Systems. Ashgate, Farnham (2015)

Development of an Experimental Setup to Investigate Multimodal Information Representation and Superposition for Elderly Users in Healthcare Context

Matthias Wille[(✉)], Tobias Seinsch, Rebecca Kummer, Peter Rasche,
Sabine Theis, Christina Bröhl, Alexander Mertens,
and Christopher Schlick

Institute of Industrial Engineering and Ergonomics, RWTH-Aachen University,
Bergdriesch 27, 52062 Aachen, Germany
{m.wille, t.seinsch, r.kummer, p.rasche, s.theis,
c.broehl, a.mertens, c.schlick}@iaw.rwth-aachen.de

Abstract. This paper describes the development of an experimental setup to test the multimodal information representation and superposition for elderly users in a categorical decision task. Due to the demographic change more and more elderly people will have to be supported monitoring their health on their own with new digital devices. Therefore it should be investigated how multimodal information presentation can help to compensate restrictions in perception that often come along with age. After reflecting the theoretical background an experimental setup is described. This setup will be realized as a native Android App to ensure ecological validity. The construction of the App and different tests measuring timing irregularities in the technical setup are also described.

Keywords: Multimodal perception · Elderly · Dual task · Categorical decision task

1 Introduction

Current electronic devices and consequently human-computer interaction have found their way into everyday life and now take part in many interactions which were formerly based on direct human interaction. Additionally, our society is aging rapidly which is why a growing user group of elderly, who are neither "digital natives" nor "digital emigrants", will have to interact with the growing number of digital devices. Especially, if thinking about electronic healthcare devices, the question appears how these users interpret the signals a device sends and if there are differences compared to younger users, who have grown up with computer technology.

The use of mobile ICT systems for patients to independently monitor their own health has great potential to compensate for the expected results of demographic change by delinking medical care from local availability of medical staff. Here, telemedicine systems and services refer to the use of information technology and communication technologies within the provision of healthcare processes.

© Springer International Publishing Switzerland 2016
D. Harris (Ed.): EPCE 2016, LNAI 9736, pp. 104–115, 2016.
DOI: 10.1007/978-3-319-40030-3_12

The interdisciplinary research project "Tech4age", founded by the German Federal Ministry of Education and Research (BMBF), investigates how elderly users can be supported in using modern ICT for healthcare applications. One work package focuses on multimodal information representation and superposition and how (or if) this can compensate some of the restrictions in perception that can come along with age. The present paper describes the theoretical background and the development of an experimental setup including the development of an Android App for testing.

2   Theoretical Background

2.1   Common Restrictions in Perception for the Elderly (Unimodal)

For the ergonomic design of human-computer interaction, the consideration of the physiological changes in performance of sensory, cognitive and motor system associated with the aging process is essential. Here, the relevant explanation and prediction models for age differentiated performance have changed in recent years from deficit-oriented models to individual compensation strategies [1, 2]. This so-called "compensation" models take into account that the acquired knowledge and adapted practices and success strategies offer an individual range of possibilities [3, 4], which for example can be used for human-computer interaction [5]. Therefore the idea of "differential aging" was developed, emanating from the heterogeneous development of human skills (both in terms of capabilities and skills) [6]. The average power loss during aging can be explained by the accumulation of represent individual courses that remain for a long time constant and fall significantly only after reaching an individual limit in old age.

If someone takes a look on the specific changes that accompany aging it is obvious that they occur in every sense: Starting with the visual sense aging brings along a deficit in almost every visual function and therefore in the perception of the environment [7]. Reasons for the decline are the reduced elasticity as well as the yellowing of the lense [8]. As one consequence it is difficult for elderly to work with objects near to their eyes [9] as it can be the case with handheld devices. Taking a look at the faculty of hearing presbyacusis is a common consequence of the aging process. It leads to a generally impaired hearing ability but especially to worsened performance in high frequency areas between 1000 and 8000 Hz and in most cases speech comprehension is impaired as well [10, 11]. Furthermore older adults show reduced sensitivity in differentiating different frequencies especially those produced by the consonants "s", "sch", "f" and "z" [8]. Aging also leads to a reduction of tactile capabilities and skin sensibility [12] leading to difficulties in perceiving vibrations greater than 60 Hz [13].

Between 20 and 60 years, the reaction time is enlarged by approximately 13 % – 20 %. This process takes place very steadily. Between the 20th and 96th year of life, the response time for simple auditory requirements increases about 0.6 ms per year, with disjunctive requirements by about 1.5 ms per year at higher requirements these values continue to rise (as in a four-ways test by approximately 3 ms per year) [14, 15]. The properties of each object thus have a decisive influence on the reaction time, the age-related differences increase in proportion with the number of choices [16]. Substituting the use of a technical system with a task, which consists of three four-ways elements, resulting in an increase in reaction time of 9 ms per year. A 70-year-old would accordingly react 450 ms slower in the operation of a corresponding technical system as at the age of 20 years.

2.2 Multimodal Interaction and Reaction Time Experiments

In nearly all areas of our everyday life we react to feedback or stimuli that engage multiple senses. Thereby it is of special significance that we connect the input of the different senses in order to integrate the amount of information on an object or event [17].

One of the first and most basic scientific works regarding multimodality is repre-sented by the multiple resource model by Wickens [18]. It is based on the assumption that specific resources exist for certain functions such as processing level (perceptual-cognitive vs. motoric) or modality (visual vs. acoustic). Consequently there is more interference between tasks that require the same resources than resources that address different resources [19]. Talsma [20] showed that the multisensory integration takes place in a range up to 40 ms after stimulus presentation, meaning that stimuli that are presented with a distance of 40 ms are perceived as one unit.

In the context of modern technology multimodality plays an important role espe-cially when it comes to the design of effective interfaces for touchscreen-devices [21]. Notifications of modern smartphones are often presented in a multimodal way and appear in form of blinking, sounds and vibrations. Many studies already showed dif-ferent advantages of multimodal feedback:

According to Lee et al. [21] audio-visual feedback either alone or in combination with tactile feedback produces shorter reaction times. Furthermore they showed that audio-visual response is rated as more comfortable. In the context of this study par-ticipants had to dial a phone number on a touchscreen either in a single or a dual task combined with a recognition task. The tactile vibration feedback was presented by an 8.4 inch (21.34 cm) touch screen and for the auditory feedback a loudspeaker behind the screen has been used. The visual stimuli that had to be recognized were shown on a 19 inch (48.26 cm) monitor.

However, recently there are also contradictory findings in the literature. According to them especially haptic feedback either alone or in combination with visual response reduces reaction time [22]. Thus "the average of the conditions without haptic feedback had a mean of 0.77 s, while the average of the conditions with haptic feedback had a significantly shorter mean of 0.69 s" [22, p. 84]. However they used a search selection drag-and-drop task which leads to the assumption that for different contexts there are different feedback modalities that are advantageous. In this case visual and auditory stimuli were presented through a computer and haptic feedback from a vibrating mouse.

In the context of the application of multimodal feedback also technical experience has to be taken into account. By using almost the same experimental setup Jacko et al. [23] showed that experienced users benefit from ever kind of multimodal feedback whereas for less experienced users especially audio-haptic response is beneficial. These findings may be important for the use of modern technology by older people because according to Ellis and Allaire [24] age and computer knowledge show a negative correlation.

Multimodal interaction and elderly. Taking a look on older users of modern technological devices someone needs to consider further particularities: When taking into account the processing of multimodal stimuli older people do have a greater vulnerability for visual bias if bimodal stimuli are presented [25]. Examples are the greater distractibility by items on screens and slowed processing of visual signals [23]. DeLoss, Pierce, and Anderson [26] showed that compared to younger people elderly show a prolonged multisensory integration. Therefore they used the sound-induced flash illusion paradigm [27]. Within this paradigm participants have to report the number of flashes that are presented at the same time as beeps occur. Sounds and visual signals where presented by a computer. An interesting theory states, that this longer and less exact multisensory integration could be a reason for the more frequent occurrence of falls by elderly [28].

Multimodal interaction in categorization tasks. In addition to these findings about age-related changes Rozencwajg and Bertoux [29] stated that performance of older adults in categorization task declines by using an adjusted Wechsler's similarity test. Regarding to Lenoble, Bordaberry, Rougier, Boucart and Delord [30] elderly show prolonged reaction times and more errors in classification of objects. However it must be noted that these findings are depending on centeredness and contrast of presented objects.

Previous research did already show that in general multimodal stimuli have a positive influence on categorization tasks. According to Molholm, Ritter, Javitt and Foxe [31] the presentation of congruent animal sounds combined with pictures of animals lead to an improvement of the decision whether the picture portrayed an animal or not. If someone compares the application of multisensory material in simple reaction tasks and choice tasks it is becoming clear that it enhances performances in both types of tasks but that its effect on choice tasks is even greater than on less complex tasks [32].

2.3   Knowledge Gaps and Motivation

The above mentioned studies show that, although multimodal information representation in general leads to better and faster performance, the detailed effects of multimodal information representation are highly task specific. Furthermore in a lot of experiments every feedback modality is presented by a different device which does not seem to be ecologically valid. That is why we decided to developed an experimental setup where multimodal feedback and interaction are given on one handheld device – a smartphone. That way a high ecological validity is given, as these devices are common in our days and are also often the devices where healthcare applications for the elderly take place (e.g. medication reminder to ensure adherence).

3   Experimental Plan

3.1   Main Idea

To investigate age effects in multimodal information representation and superposition we are planning to test a minimum of 30 subjects with ages ranging from 18 to 80 years in a categorical decision task. The stimuli will consist of haptic, auditory and visual cues presented alone or in each possible combination (haptic + auditory; haptic + visual; visual + auditory; haptic + auditory + visual) and will be presented in random order. To minimize other influences like learning strategies we will use only two categories and keep the stimuli as well as their unimodal characteristics very simple, clear to distinguish and easy to assign to one of the categories.

Each unimodal stimuli has only two forms of appearance: constant (category A) or rhythmic (category B). While "constant" means a continuous tone/vibration/image presentation of 500 ms "rhythmic" means an on/off pattern of the same tone/vibration/ image presentation where three phases of presenting the stimuli for 100 ms are divided by two pauses with 100 ms each. This way both categorical stimuli types have the same length. While interpreting reaction times one has to keep in mind that the first 100 ms of the stimuli are the same and deliver no hint for the categorical decision task. As tone we will use a standard sinus wave with 750 Hz, so it is clear hearable in all age groups. The vibration signal will be the standard vibration of the Google Nexus 5. The visual signal will be a clear white square in the middle of the screen.

The experimental setup is programmed as native Android App and presented on a smartphone. As mentioned earlier we see it as important regarding ecological validity to present the whole setup on one devices in contrast to many laboratory studies, where signals are often presented on different devices (e.g. on a classic monitor for visual and acoustic stimuli and an extra vibration box plus external reaction buttons). However, using a native Android App can lead to more timing irregularities as discussed in the next chapter.

The experimental setup will be run as single task, where the whole focus of attention of the participants is on the reaction to the stimuli and under dual task condition, where participants will have to watch a movie in parallel while some questions about the content were asked later to ensure people divide their attention also towards the video. This dual task condition was chosen again because of its ecological validity, representing a typical everyday life situation where people might watch TV, while some signal might be incoming from an electronic device.

3.2 Procedure

After welcome the participant some demographic values like age and sight restrictions are collected followed by a visual test and audiometry. Then the participants are introduced to the setting by explaining their task and having a test run for about ten minutes, so the participants get familiar with the stimuli and the task. After that the single or dual task condition will start (order permuted). Each of those conditions will run for 30 min. The interstimulus interval will be 30 s plus a random time of up to 15 s which will ensure that about 40 stimuli can be proved so each of the 7 multimodal combinations will be presented about 5 times.

3.3   Statistical Analysis

Statistical analysis will be done by an ANOVA with repeated measurements using SPSS. Independent variable will be single or dual task as well as all multimodal stimuli combinations. Dependent variables will be reaction time (reactions longer as 3 s will be count as miss), misses and wrong categorizations. Age will be used as covariate in the analysis variances to determinate its influence (the traditional testing of age groups is not in line with the above described individual aging). A post hoc multiple regression analysis will furthermore investigate how much variance is determinated by sight and hearing restrictions based on the tests before the experiment.

4   Technical Development of an Android App as Multimodal Reaction Time and Categorical Choice Experiment

4.1   App Structure

The App is used in landscape mode. It has 2 buttons on the right side for reacting to category A or B. For lefthanders there is the possibility to switch the side of the buttons in a hidden preferences menu. Sound and vibration are initiated by the hardware and the visual stimulus is presented in the middle. Figure 1 shows an early prototype of the App.

Fig. 1. A prototype version of the Android App showing the reaction buttons on the right side. The image of the tiger at the top as well as the data window on the bottom will not be included in the final version and are for testing only. The slider on the left side is thought for online rating of subjective strain but still has to prove its validity in pretests.

Within the preferences of the actual developer version the experimenter can also set the stimuli dimensions included in the test (haptic, acoustic, visual), the interval between the stimuli (10–30 s), the random time which is added to the interval to make stimuli appearance less predictable (0–15 s) and the duration of the whole experiment, thought for easy pretest variation. Furthermore the subject number, age of participant, sex, diopter of both eyes, used fingers for reaction and a free field for comments can be added before the data is send via email.

The data structure is event based and has time since app start in milliseconds as first column followed by other columns describing the discrete event. The parameter calculation (e.g. reaction time) is done in SPSS later using successive differences.

4.2 Timing Tests

One potential problem while using an App for reaction time experiments are timing irregularities. Especially as computers are never (really) tight and mean reaction time differences between two experimental conditions are sometimes less than 50 ms. To determine these irregularities we programmed an app in the first place which sends a ping every 100 ms which was compared to the system time to show up timing irregularities. To simulate some interaction the whole screen changed color every 100 ms and a button was included that triggered an acoustic and vibration signal by pressing. Table 1 shows the timing irregularities of that test App on two devices based on 5 min testing (n of ping = 3000).

Table 1. Mean variation and deviation of time stamps in milliseconds during test series with Nexus 5 (Android 6.0) and LG G3 (Android 5.0)

	Without button pressing		With button pressing	
	Nexus 5	LG G3	Nexus 5	LG G3
Mean variation	0,292	0,724	5,8175	11,1375
Mean amount of variation	0,63	0,95	6,32	11,275
Standard Deviation	0,896	1,574	12,1125	23,3025

As it could be seen in Table 1 the timing irregularities are for ping are less than 1 ms if no button is pressed. However, with some kind of interaction the amount of variation rises to 6–11 ms. Hereby the new Android 6.0 performs nearly twice as well as Android 5.0. Furthermore it could be seen by comparing the mean variation with the mean amount of variation that most timing irregularities are in form of a lag.

However, the interpretation of those timing irregularities might lead wrong, as they just describe the time when some action is recalled, not necessarily the time when some action is also completely displayed or played. Therefore we ran another test using a camera with 120 Hz filming. This test focused on the difference between the time a button was pressed (or released) and the time the system reacts to that interaction (by changing the color of the button) – the touch response time. Table 2 illustrates that there is a lag of about 55 ms for releasing the button and a lag of 72 ms for pressing the button which is align with findings on other hardware[1]. Both accompanied by timing irregularities as seen in the standard deviation. So while a linear lag can be subtracted for interpretation of reaction times the irregularities lead to blurred results, which are

---

[1] http://www.phonearena.com/news/Funky-metrics-HTC-One-M8-has-the-fastest-46ms-phone-display-touch-response-time-so-far_id54887.

Table 2. Time lag in milliseconds between system time and video observed time of reaction (touch response time) using Nexus 5 with Android 6.0

Pressing button			Release button		
Time by video	System time	lag	Time by video	System time	lag
2034	2101	67	2168	2235	67
2478	2553	75	2620	2687	67
2829	2896	67	2963	3013	50
3147	3214	67	3265	3315	50
3474	3549	75	3608	3666	58
3851	3918	67	3976	4026	50
4236	4311	75	4370	4428	58
4646	4713	67	4839	4880	41
5131	5224	93	5257	5307	50
5466	5542	76	5567	5625	58
5692	5759	67	5784	5843	59
5952	6011	59	6044	6103	59
6270	6354	84	6379	6437	58
Mean lag		72,23	Mean lag		55,77
Standard deviation		8,88	Standard deviation		7,33

hard to interpret if the mean difference between two experimental conditions is only small in amount.

In conclusion of these timing tests, we decided that the ecological validity of an experimental setup as native App is more important than some minor timing irregularities, especially for our use case of healthcare applications for the elderly: The lag, estimated as 72 ms for pressing reaction button plus 6 ms on internal time stamps, will be the same on all experimental conditions and therefore not influence the comparison. The irregularities, estimated as 12 ms for internal time stamps (if interaction is given) plus 8 ms for pressing button, is in its sum of 20 ms far below most effects found in literature.

4.3   Lesson Learned Coding the App

In the first stage of implementation, the stimulus was invoked by a CountDownTimer[2]. The CountDownTimer is to schedule a countdown until a time in the future, with regular notifications on intervals along the way. Since the stimulus should not be invoked in a regular interval, but in a specific time range (regular interval + random time) the timer needed to be extended. Therefore the first operation within the onTick()-method was generating a random number to determine the time, the stimulus has to be delayed. This led to an influence on the UI and a bad user experience.

---

[2] http://developer.android.com/reference/android/os/CountDownTimer.html.

However, after some researches in scheduling of time-based actions in Java-Code the Handler[3] and its method "postDelayed()" seemed to fit perfectly, since it is optimized to schedule runnables to be executed at some point in the future. Furthermore the UI does not get affected because the runnable within the Handler has its own Thread. After the code was processed, the Handler was called recursively until the time the experiment is finished. The use of the Handler in this specific case is shown in the code-example below.

```java
public void timeBasedStimulus()
{
  // avoid another start of this method
  isRunning = true;

  // minutes * seconds * milliseconds , seconds *
milliseconds
  final long experimentDuration = duration * 60 * 1000;
  final long staticIntervall = intervall * 1000;
  final long endTimeMillis = System.currentTimeMillis() +
experimentDuration;

  int r = 0;
  if(random > 0)
  {
    r = new Random().nextInt(random);
  }
  // milliseconds to seconds
  long randomIntervall = r * 1000;

  final Handler handler = new Handler();
  handler.postDelayed(new Runnable()
  {
    @Override

  public void run()
```

---

[3] http://developer.android.com/reference/android/os/Handler.html.

```
{
      try
      {
        // generate a stimulus
        final Stimulus stimulus = createNextStimulus();
        doStimulus(stimulus);
        // write the stimulus description into an array
(for evaluation)
        createStimulusRow(stimulus);
      }catch (Exception e)
          {
        e.printStackTrace();
          }

      if(System.currentTimeMillis() <= endTimeMillis)
      { // start next stimulus
        if(random > 0)
        {
          handler.postDelayed(this, staticIntervall + new
Random().nextInt(random) * 1000);
        } else {
          handler.postDelayed(this, staticIntervall);
        }
      }else { //end of experiment
        Context context = getApplicationContext();
        Toast.makeText(context, "Versuchsende",
Toast.LENGTH_LONG).show();
        isRunning = false;
      }
    }
  }, staticIntervall + randomIntervall);

}
```

5   Discussion

While investigating how multimodal information representation can compensate perception restrictions that can come along with age we presented an experimental setup as an Android App. Although we experienced and described a timing lag regarding touch response time and even more critical (although smaller) irregularities in timing we decided to use such an App because of its ecological validity, which we judge as more important in our use case of healthcare applications for the elderly.

Other researcher might also have a look at some frameworks for psychological experiments on Android as given in Open Sesame[4] or Expyriment[5].

Acknowledgement. The interdisciplinary research project Tech4Age is funded by the German Federal Ministry of Education and Research (BMBF) under Grant No. 16SV7111. It is part of the Institute of Industrial Engineering and Ergonomics of RWTH Aachen University. For more details and information, please see www.tech4age.de.

References

1. Schlick, C.M., Bruder, R., Luczak, R.: Arbeitswissenschaft. Springer, Heidelberg (2010)
2. Naegele, G.: Zwischen Arbeit und Rente: gesellschaftliche Chancen und Risiken älterer Arbeitsnehmer, 2nd edn. Maro Verlag, Augsburg (2004)
3. Astor, M., Koch, C., Klose, G., Reimann, F., Rochhold, S., Stemann, M.: Zu alt, um Neues zu lernen? Chancen und Grenzen des gemeinsamen Lernens von älteren und jüngeren Mitarbeitern. In: QUEM-Materialien der Arbeitsgemeinschaft Betriebliche Weiterbildungsforschung e.V. (AWBF), vol. 77, pp. 1–165 (2006)
4. Adenauer, S.: Die Potenziale älterer Mitarbeiter im Betrieb erkennen und nutzen. In: Angewandte Arbeitswissenschaft, vol. 172, pp. 19–34 (2002)
5. Jochems, N.: Altersdifferenzierte Gestaltung der Mensch-Rechner-Interaktion am Beispiel von Projektmanagementaufgaben. In: Schlick, C.M. (ed.) Schriftenreihe Industrial Engineering and Ergonomics, Dissertation RWTH Aachen. Shaker-Verlag, Aachen (2010)
6. Czaja, S.J.: Computer technology and the older adult. In: Helander, M.G., Landauer, T.K., Prabhu, P. (eds.) Handbook of Human-Computer Interaction, 2nd edn, pp. 797–812. Elsevier, Amsterdam (1997)
7. Sun, F.C., Stark, L., Nguyen, A., Wong, J., Lakshminarayanan, V., Mueller, E.: Changes in accommodation with age: static and dynamic. Am. J. Otometry Physiol. Opt. **65**(6), 492–498 (1988)
8. Amann, A.: Umwelt, Mobilität und Kompetenzen im Alter. In: Amann, A. (ed.) Kurswechsel für das Alter, pp. 105–119. Böhlau Verlag, Wien (2000)
9. Granjean, E.: Fitting the Task to the Man: An Ergonomic Approach. Taylor & Francis limited, London (1982)
10. Marsiske, M., Klumb, P., Baltes, M.M.: Everyday activity patterns and sensory functioning in old age. Psychol. Aging **12**(3), 444–457 (1997)
11. Schieber, F.: Aging and the senses. In: Birren, J.E., Sloane, R.B., Cohen, G.D. (eds.) Handbook of Mental Health and Aging, pp. 252–306. Elsevier Academic Press, San Diego (1992)
12. Wandke, H., Blessing, L.: Gestural Interfaces for elderly users: help or hindrance. In: Kopp, S., Wachsmuth, I. (eds.) Gesture in Embodied Communication and Human-Computer Interaction. Lecture Notes in Computer Science, vol. 5934, pp. 269–280. Springer, Heidelberg (2012)
13. Charnes, N., Demiris, G., Krupinski, E.: Designing Telehealth for an Aging Population – A Human Factors Perspective. CRC Press, Boca Raton (FL) (2012)

---

[4] http://osdoc.cogsci.nl/getting-opensesame/android/.
[5] http://www.expyriment.org/.

14. Vercruyssen, M.: Age and motor performance for the elderly. In: van Berlo, L.J., Rietseman, J. (eds.) Gerontechnology - Human factors for an Aging Population - Course Material First International Post-graduate Course on Gerontechnology. Center for Biomedical and Health Care Technology, Eindhoven (1993)

15. Small Sr., A.M.: Design for Older People. In: Salvendy, G. (ed.) Handbook of Human Factors, pp. 496–504. John Wiley & Sons, New York (1987)

16. Botwinick, J., Storandt, M.: Age-differences in reaction-time as a function of experience stimulus-intensity and preparatory interval. J. Genet. Psychol. 123(2), 209–217 (1973)

17. Spence, C.: Crossmodal correspondences: a tutorial review. Attention Percept. Psychophysics 73(4), 971–995 (2011)

18. Wickens, C.D.: The structure of attentional resources. In: Nickerson, R. (ed.) Attention and performance VIII, pp. 239–257. Lawrence Erlbaum, Hillsdale, New Jersey (1980)

19. Wickens, C.D.: Multiple resources and performance prediction. Theor. Issues Ergon. Sci. 3 (2), 159–177 (2002)

20. Talsma, D.: Predictive coding and multisensory integration: an attentional account of the multisensory mind. Frontiers Integr. Neurosci. 9(19), 13 (2015)

21. Lee, J.-H., Poliakoff, E., Spence, C.: The effect of multimodal feedback presented via a touch screen on the performance of older adults. In: Altinsoy, M., Jekosch, U., Brewster, S. (eds.) HAID 2009. LNCS, vol. 5763, pp. 128–135. Springer, Heidelberg (2009)

22. Vitense, H.S., Jacko, J.A., Emery, V.K.: Foundation for improved interaction by individuals with visual impairments through multimodal feedback. Univ. Access Inf. Soc. 2(1), 76–87 (2002)

23. Jacko, J., Emery, V.K., Edwards, P.J., Ashok, M., Barnard, L., Kongnakorn, T., Moloney, K.P., Sainfort, F.: The effects of multimodal feedback on older adults' task performance given varying levels of computer experience. Behav. Inf. Technol. 23(4), 247–264 (2004)

24. Ellis, R.D., Allaire, J.C.: Modeling computer interest in older adults: the role of age, education, computer knowledge, and computer anxiety. Hum. Factors: J. Hum. Factors Ergon. Soc. 41(3), 345–355 (1999)

25. Dobreva, M.S., O'Neill, W.E., Paige, G.D.: Influence of age, spatial memory, and ocular fixation on localization of auditory, visual, and bimodal targets by human subjects. Exp. Brain Res. 223(4), 441–455 (2012)

26. DeLoss, D.J., Pierce, R.S., Andersen, G.J.: Multisensory integration, aging, and the sound-induced flash illusion. Psychol. Aging 28(3), 802–812 (2013)

27. Shams, L., Kamitani, Y., Shimojo, S.: Illusions: what you see is what you hear. Nature 408 (6814), 788 (2000)

28. Setti, A., Burke, K.E., Kenny, R.A., Newell, F.N.: Is inefficient multisensory processing associated with falls in older people? Exp. Brain Res. 209(3), 375–384 (2011)

29. Rozencwajg, P., Bertoux, M.L.: Categorization and aging as measured by an adapted version of Wechsler's similarities test. Curr. Psychol. Lett. Behav. Brain Cogn. 24(2), 82–96 (2008)

30. Lenoble, Q., Bordaberry, P., Rougier, M.B., Boucart, M., Delord, S.: Influence of visual deficits on object categorization in normal aging. Exp. Aging Res. 39(2), 145–161 (2013)

31. Molholm, S., Ritter, W., Javitt, D.C., Foxe, J.J.: Multisensory visual–auditory object recognition in humans: a high-density electrical mapping study. Cereb. Cortex 14(4), 452–465 (2004)

32. Hecht, D., Reiner, M., Karni, A.: Multisensory enhancement: gains in choice and in simple response times. Exp. Brain Res. 189(2), 133–143 (2008)

An Interface Analysis Method
of Complex Information System
by Introducing Error Factors

Xiaoli Wu[1,2(✉)], Yan Chen[1], and Feng Zhou[1,2]

[1] College of Mechanical and Electrical Engineering,
Hohai University, Jinling Road. 200, Changzhou 213022, China
wuxlhhu@163.com
[2] Institute of Industrial Design, Hohai University,
Jinling Road. 200, Changzhou 213022, China

Abstract. With the rapid developments of computer technology and information technology, human-machine interfaces of aircrafts, ships, nuclear power plants, battlefield command system, and other complex information systems have evolved from the traditional control mode to digital control mode with visual information interface. This paper studies error factors of information interface in human-computer interaction based on visual cognition theory. A feasible error-cognition model is established to solve some design problems which result in serious failures in information recognition and analysis, and even in operation and execution processes. Based on Rasmussen, Norman, Reason and other error types as well as the HERA and CREAM failure identification models, we performed classification and cognitive characterization for error factors according to information search, information recognition, information identification, information selection and judgment as well as the decision-making process and obtained the comprehensive error-cognition model for complex information interface.

Keywords: Error factors · Design factors · Human-computer interface · Interaction · Visual cognition · Error-cognition model

1 Introduction

With the rapid developments of computer technology and information technology, human-machine interfaces of great intelligent manufacture equipment, nuclear power plants, even aircrafts, ships, battlefield command systems, and other complex information systems have evolved from the traditional control mode to digital control mode with information interaction interface. Compared with the conventional analog control which is generally monitoring and operating system, digital control shifts the role of operators from manual controlers to regulators and decision-makers, which increases the process of operator's visual cognition and needs a set of cognitive behaviors perform the task (as shown in Fig. 2). Because complex information interaction interfaces are characterized by the large quantity of information and complex information relationships, an operator may enter the complex cognition and lead to task

© Springer International Publishing Switzerland 2016
D. Harris (Ed.): EPCE 2016, LNAI 9736, pp. 116–124, 2016.
DOI: 10.1007/978-3-319-40030-3_13

Fig. 1. Analog control of an intelligent system (Left) and displays of digital control (Right)

failure, even serious system failures and major accidents due to operation errors, misreading, misjudgment, late feedback, and other cognitive difficulties (Fig. 1).

Complex information task interface is characterized by transforming systematic abstract information into user interfacial elements which are easy to identify and understand. Graphical user interface conveys several elements, including character, text, image, icon, colour, dimension, and so on. When the information displayed is complex, only the reasonable navigation design and structure design of information hierarchy can reach the rationality of information interaction. Thus, the design problem of information interaction interface has evolved into a hot spot and focus problem which was concerned mutually by researchers in human-factors engineering, automatic control, cognitive psychology, systematic science, design science and other disciplines. Then, whether the design factors of information interaction interface could begin with the source of task failures – error factors? The key point lies in how to understand correctly the interaction mechanism between 'error and cognitive', then, can we propose a reasonable design strategy for the optimization of visual information interface.

2 Objective

Many methods of classifying the human errors sprang up in the field of cognitive science and engineering application research. Based on the cognitive psychology, Norman (1981) divided operation errors into the three types: error, slip and mistake. To optimize the design of the system, Rasmussen (1986) proposed three types of cognitive control layers: skill layer, rule layer and knowledge layer and classified the errors systematically based on the three types. Reason (1987) thought the opinion proposed by Norman that operation errors include two types: negligence and error is not comprehensive, and he divided them into three types: mistake, slip and lapse. Later, Reason further consummate the error classification on the basis of the three types, and he believed that there were 8 basic error types: false sensation, attention failure, memory slip, inaccurate recall, mispercetion, error judgment, inferential error and unintended actions. Swain (1998) classified the errors into three modes: error of omission, error of commission, extraneous error. Li L.Sh (2004) proposed that inattention and overattention should be the main study objects of user error. Above classification methods have become major error types in the studies of human error, and combined with Human Reliability Analysis method are applied in engineering field.

Currently, few people in the field of visual information interface have started researches in the base of error factors, especially applied to aviation, military and other complex systems which are displayed by multilevel subsystems, whose error factors are concentrated in visual information display of executive monitoring, search and other tasks and its cognition mechanism of errors is an important hitting-point for improving interface design as well as the key for reducing cognition difficulties. Wu (2014, 2015) proposed a new interface design method by introducing error factors and established the error-cognition stratification model for complex information task interfaces. This paper studies error factors of information interface in human-computer interaction based on visual cognition theory. A feasible error-cognition model is established to solve some design problems which result in serious failures in information recognition and analysis, and even in operation and execution processes.

3   Methods

According to the CREAM and HEPA, we established operators' cognitive behavior model based on extended CREAM and the cognitive error recognition framework of operators' behavior based on HEPA, and obtained a possible human error mode for complex monitoring interfaces. We performed classification, extraction and cognitive characterization for cognitive behaviors of four monitoring tasks: monitoring/discovering, inquiring the state, planning the response and performing the response. Then, we established error-cognition set through the mapping relationship from error factors to cognition. According to the specific classification of every error types, we divided error factors into five types, including misperception set, perception confusion set, attention failures set, memory lapse set and inattention set.

The study analyzes different types of error factors from visual cognitive theories, further analyzes error factors at different levels through cognitive theories and sorts out relevant attention theories. Theeuwes et al. (1998, 2004) have held the opinion that, the occurrence of attention capture mainly depends on the significance level of the feature of one stimulus relative to that of other stimuli. The higher the feature significance level of a stimulus, the higher the possibility of its generating attention capture. Fleetwood and Byrne (2002, 2006) have found through experimental observation that, the first factor which influence the user's visual search is the quantity of icons, the second is the target boundary, and the last one is the quality and resolution of icons. In a conclusion, error-cognition model is established through the relevance between user error and cognition.

4   Model

4.1   Cognitive Behavior Model of Operators

According to error classification Norman (1981) and Reason (1987) proposed, misperception types are extracted from the visual cognitive perspective as the main object of study. In the visual information interface, they are mainly shown as: information misreading/misjudgment, omissions and other error factors caused by attention invalidation, attention transfer, visual interference and visual limitation in the visual search.

As shown in Fig. 2, based on the information central processing of monitoring task interface, forming the cognitive process from information input to information feedback. During the process, we need to analyze the operator's cognitive behaviors based on the execution of the task. Information search, information recognition, information identification, information selection and judgment as well as the decision-making process are just operator's cognitive behaviors of information observation, explanation, planning and execution during the process of executing the task. Thus, this paper will continue to explore the information process of complex monitoring task interface in depth.

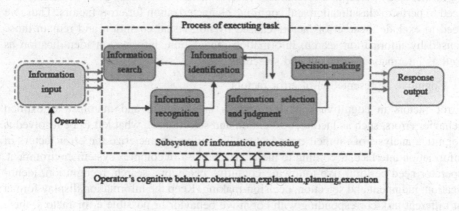

Fig. 2. Central processing of information of monitoring task interface

4.2 Analytical Model of Cognitive Error Recognition Based on HEPA

We can combine extended operator's cognitive behavior model with corresponding analytical model of error recognition, and further recognize the cognitive error of the interfacial task. The technology of HERA proposed by Kirwan (1997), which integrates several methods and enables the analysis results to be tested each other, is reliable relatively. Thus, this paper will apply error recognition framework to analyze the cognitive error recognition of information search, recognition, judgment and selection, as well as decision-making.

According to the process of operator's cognitive behavior, operator's task, task function as well as task steps and structure are unfolded, corresponding with the analytical opinion of human reliability, which includes task analysis, objection analysis, operation analysis, planning analysis, error analysis, psychological error mechanism analysis, performance shaping factor analysis as well as human error identification in systems tool analysis.

According to operator's cognitive behavior model based on extended CREAM (Hollnagel 1996, 1998), we extracted the main cognitive behavior in every period, and integrate into synthetic procedure of information search, recognition, judgment and selection as well as decision-making as its task function. Then, we analyzed the cognitive error recognition of different modules. Figure 3 shows the error recognition analysis of operator's cognitive behavior.

4.3 Cognitive Characterization of Error Factors

1. Classification of error factors

Through the extraction of error factors in the four cognitive behavior processes including monitoring/discovering, inquiring the state, response planning and response performing, we obtained error factor combination of cognitive behavior classification. To further study perception mechanism of error factors in visual cognitive interface, we need to perform classification and cognitive characterization for error factors. Thus, we need to exclude those error factors caused by non-visual cognition and remain those caused by information search, information recognition, information identification as well as information judgment and selection.

2. Cognitive representation of error factors

Error factors in cognitive behavior process are implicit, and manifest as explicit behavior errors, such as incorrect execution and selection, so what left to be resolved is cognitive analysis of implicit error factors. To further characterize the error factors of information interface, according to the interfacial task in complex system environment, operator need perform five following cognitive behaviors: search, recognition, identification, judgment and selection, decision-making. Keep the information display format of different task corresponding with cognitive behavior or possible error factors, then, we can characterize the errors.

   In complex monitoring task system, there are several possible task to be executed, such as monitoring status data, inquiring task information, monitoring threat and security state information, and so on. Display interface of complex information system displays navigation, situation pictures, status data and other information. The monitoring task likely to be performed: plan creating, monitoring state inquiring, burst scheduling, and so on. We can classify the monitoring interfacial task either by abrupt affairs and common tasks or by the order in which to perform tasks. Thus, as shown in Table 1, we listed the monitoring interface tasks and corresponding error factors to extract the error characterization of monitoring interface of complex system.

4.4 Analytical Model of Error-Cognition

We classified n possible error factors in process of cognitive behavior into m nonvoid subsets($1 \leq m \leq n$). There are s(n, m) methods of classification, and every method represents the process of cognitive behavior to information. For each integer $n \geq 1$ and $m \geq 1$, exists $S(n,k) = \frac{1}{k!} \sum_{i=0}^{k-1} (-1)^i C_k^i (k-i)^n$. Table 2 shows the error-cognition mapping.

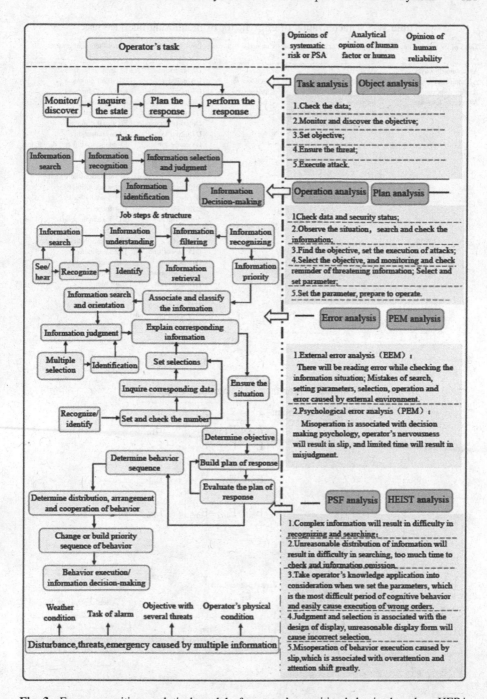

Fig. 3. Error recognition analytical model of operator's cognitive behavior based on HEPA

Table 1. Characterization of error factor of monitoring interface task

Tasks of monitoring interface A	Display format of information B	Cognitive behavior C	Error factor D	representation of error E
A1monitor/discover	B1 dynamic display	C1search	D1 ignorance	E1 ambiguity states
A2inquire state	B2 static display	C2recognize	D2 omission	E2 visual limitation
A3plan response	B3 navigation	C3identify	D3 miss	E3 visual bluntness
A4execute response	B4 status data	C4judge&select	D4 misreading	E4 visual illusion
	B5 information icon	C5decision-making	D5 misjudgment	E5 attentional load
	B6 alarm reminder		D6 misunderstanding	E6 visual disturbance
			D7 haven't seen	E7 overattention
			D8 confusion	E8 attention shift and distraction
			D9 cannot remember	E9 too nervous to do anything
			D10 input error	E10 cognitive bias
			D11 misregistration	E11 unreasonable match
			D12 cannot see clearly	E12 weak visibility
			D13 hard to distinguish	E13 thinking load
			D14 match incorrectly	E14 forget
			D15 cannot find	E15 inaccurate recall
			D16 delay	E16 lack of memory aids
			D17 inadequate	E17 intentionality decrease
			D18 irrelevant	E18 false memory
			D19 react too early	E19 unconsciousness
			D20 no reaction	E20 omission caused by inattention
			D21 select incorrectly	E21 time pressure
			D22 slip	

Table 2. Error factor to cognition mapping

Cognitive domain	1	2	3	⋯	n
C_1	E_{11}	E_{12}	E_{13}	⋯	E_{1n}
C_2	E_{21}	E_{22}	E_{23}	⋯	E_{2n}
⋮	⋮	⋮	⋮	⋯	⋮
C_i	E_{i1}	E_{i2}	E_{i3}	⋯	E_{in}
⋮	⋮	⋮	⋮	⋯	⋮
C_m	E_{m1}	E_{m2}	E_{m3}	⋯	E_{mn}

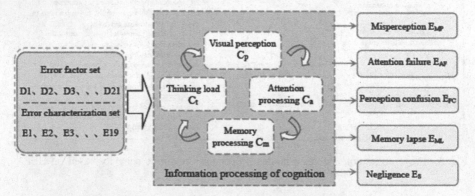

Fig. 4. Error-cognition model of visual information interface

Based on the error factor set, error characterization set as well as the process of cognition to information, we obtained five types of error-cognition: misperception, attention failure, perception confusion, memory lapse and negligence (as shown in Fig. 4).

5 Conclusion

1. The design problems, resulting in serious failures in information recognition and analysis, and even in operation and execution processes, could begin with error factors;
2. The relevance between error and cognition is existed, which could be established the error-cognition model to analysis design problems in information interface.

Acknowledgement. This work was supported by Fundamental Research Funds for the Central Universities (Grant No. 2015B22714), science and technology projects of Changzhou (CJ20140033), the Project of Philosophy and Social Science Research in Colleges and Universities in Jiangsu Province (2014SJD065).

References

Fleetwood, M.D., Byrne, M.D.: Modeling icon search in ACT-R/PM. Cogn. Syst. Res. **3**, 25–33 (2002)

Fleetwood, M.D., Byrne, M.D.: Modeling the visual search of displays: a revised ACT-R/PM model of icon search based on eye-tracking and experimental data. Hum.-Comput. Interact. **21**(2), 153–197 (2006)

Hollnagel, E.: Reliability analysis and operator modeling. Reliablity Eng. Syst. Safety **52**(3), 327–337 (1996)

Hollnagel, E.: Cognitive Reliability and Error Analysis Method. Elsevier science Ltd, Oxford (1998)

Kirwan, B.: Human error identification techniques for risk assessment of high risk systems-part 2: towards a frame work approach. Appl. Ergonomics **29**(5), 299–318 (1998)

Li, L.: Human Computer Interface Design. Science Press, Beijing (2004). (in Chinese)

Norman, D.A.: Categorisation of action slips. Psychol. Rev. **88**, 1–15 (1981)

Norman, D.A.: The psychology of everyday things. Basic books (1988)

Rasmussen, J.: Informaiton processing and human machine interaction: an approach to cognitive engineering. North-Holland, Amsterdam (1986)

Reason, J.: Human Error. Cambridge University Press, New York (1990)

Reason, J.: Human error: models and management. Br. Med. J. **320**, 768–770 (2000)

Swain, A.D., Guttmann, H.E.: Handbook of Human Reliability Analysis with Emphasis on Nuclear Power Plant Applications. NUREG/CR-1278, Nuclear regulatory commission, Washington, DC (1983)

Theeuwes, J., Burger, R.: Attentional control during visual search the effect of irrelevant singletons. J. Exp. Psychol. Hum. Percept. Perform. **24**, 1342–1353 (1998)

Theeuwes, J.: Top-down search strategies cannot override attentional capture. Psychon. Bull. Rev. **11**(1), 65–70 (2004)

Wu, X., Xue, C., Niu, Y., Tang, W.: Study on eye movements of information omission/misjudgment in radar situation-interface. In: Harris, D. (ed.) EPCE 2014. LNCS, vol. 8532, pp. 407–418. Springer, Heidelberg (2014a)

Wu, X., Xue, C., Feng, Z.: Misperception model-based analytic method of visual interface design factors. In: Harris, D. (ed.) EPCE 2014. LNCS, vol. 8532, pp. 284–292. Springer, Heidelberg (2014b)

Wu, X.: Study on error-cognition mechanism of task interface in complex in formation system. School of Mechanical Engineering, Southeast University, Nanjing (2015). (in Chinese)

The Analysis of Online News Information Credibility Assessment on Weibo Based on Analyzing Content

Quan Yuan[⊠] and Qin Gao

Department of Industrial Engineering,
Tsinghua University, Beijing 100084, China
yuan-q15@mails.tsinghua.edu.cn,
gaoqin@tsinghua.edu.cn

Abstract. As a representative of online news information carrier, social media contain much information that difficult to be differentiate between true and false. Sina Weibo is the most popular social media in China and need to be took into account. This paper first identify criterions and cues for assessing the credibility of online news through literature review. Second, we interviewed 5 experts in the news information judgment process. According to the interview, we reviseed the effective criteria and cues for helping users assess the online news information. Third, we design and develop an assistant webpage as a tool to help Weibo users assess the credibility a specific Weibo news by visualizing cues related to its source, content, dissemination, and topic. Future work are to test the effectiveness and efficiency of the tool and improve it.

Keywords: Information credibility · Online news · Sina Weibo · Assistant assessment · Content analyzing

1 Introduction

As technology rapidly develops, the Internet has already enter into worldwide families of millions. The convenient Internet not only brings people information without leaving home, but also makes people easier to send messages to other people: People can easily communicate with others immediately without the constraint of distance through online chart tools, can read current news all over the world at first time when the event occur through web news portals, and can speak their words out letting others see them through social network.

However, as everyone can be the publisher of the information, Internet also brings many rumors and bogus news to people, which look so real that most of us cannot tell the truth. As online information circulate quickly, once a rumor tend to spreads in many people, it is very likely to cause huge losses for people. Thus, we should pay attention to the information credibility problems in the Internet.

Like Facebook and Twitter, Sina Weibo is one of the representative new social media in China. Weibo has the significant influence on Chinese. In June 2015, there exists 212 million monthly active users in Weibo. So it is absolutely an important social platform

© Springer International Publishing Switzerland 2016
D. Harris (Ed.): EPCE 2016, LNAI 9736, pp. 125–135, 2016.
DOI: 10.1007/978-3-319-40030-3_14

which can be the source of Internet rumors. In March 3, 2011, Fukushima Nuclear Power Plant leaked because of the big earthquake. In March 16, a fake news claiming the leak had affected China, and iodate salts could prevent the damage spreads on the Internet, particularly in Weibo, in an explosive speed. Most of Internet users believed it, buying iodate salts crazily. The stock around China was insufficient, and it seriously impacted the lives of Chinese. Once a rumor is read by users, it can mislead the truth to another direct, causing damage in many aspects. It is necessary for us to search for a way to assist Internet users in judging online information credibility, particularly in Weibo.

The objective of our research is to propose a method which can guide Internet users to the scientific approach to judging the credibility of information in the Internet according to the content of information, and develop an assistant webpage with the method based on Weibo, and conduct an experiment to verify the effectiveness of the method and the usability of the website.

2   Judgment Process, Criterions and Cues in Judgment

Information credibility is what degree a person believe the information is true when receiving it. It is content-based, but different from different people and different environment, and easily affected by kinds of reasons.

2.1   Judgment Process

Before people judging the credibility of online information, they generally make sure the topic of the information is interesting for them [1]. They begin the judging process in judge whether the website providing the information is authoritative and credible [2]. People continue the credibility judging process only if they trust on the platform. Rather than accuracy, people usually expect more efficiency when judging credibility [3], and people have limited capacity in mind [4]. Thus people will not spend much time on it, but prefer to use a small part of information they have, such as words, pictures and other cues, [5] for judging in terms of some heuristic including reputation, endorsement, consistency, expectancy violation and persuasive heuristic [6] and one or two criterions [7] from usefulness, completeness, accuracy, currency, and importance. [8] Consequently, people sometimes cannot do a correct judgment to an information.

If the motivation for judging is not enough for getting conclusion, people will give up. Even if people have their own conclusion, because of the shortage of process, there may be the misjudgment about judging information credibility.

2.2   Judging Criterions

Metzger reviewed current recommendations helping people judge credibility of information, and evaluated the existing cognitive models for credibility assessment, and provided the future online credibility education and practice [7]. He suggested five criterions for judging process including accuracy, authority, objectivity, currency and coverage. However, Internet users always follow accuracy, authority, objectivity and coverage, but ignore currency. When the time and energy for assessment are limited, they will just use two in five criterions, e.g., accuracy and coverage, and even use only one criterion for the final decision. When user judge the credibility, they are always partial to beautiful interface. For assisting users, we can emphasize criterions that are easier to be ignored for them.

Table 1 is the criterions with its details and definitions.

Table 1. Judging criterions in the process of information credibility assessment [7, 9]

Judging criterions	Short definitions
Accuracy	Information provides a true description of reality
	Information is trustable, giving the same result on successive trials
	Information is able to accurately describe reality
Authority	Information is presented in authorized forums
	Information is based on the findings of scientific research
Objectivity	A piece of information is presented as an objective description of reality
	Information provides an impartial and unbiased description of reality
Currency	Information is timely, recent, or up-to-date
	Information provides multi-aspect description of current reality
	Information provides something really new
Coverage	Information covers a broad range of facts and opinions
	Information is focused enough to match the needs of a person or a group
	Information is considered as helpful to meet the need of a person or a group

2.3   Judging Cues

Schwarz and Morris suggested that providing for Internet users some cues that can supporting to evaluate the credibility of online text was useful and valuable [10]. Castillo, Mendoza and Problete classified cues that influence people's judgment of online information credibility into information contents, information sources, topics, and information dissemination [11]. In addition, Flanagin and Metzger considered that visual styles of information also intensively affected the assessing of credibility, [12] and Fogg even believed that the influence of visual styles was more important than information content and source [3].

Information Contents: Properties related only to the content of information, including misspelling, misuse of grammar and punctuation, reference of literature or data, professional and clear content, understandability, reasonability, advertisement, URL, tags, and so on [7, 10, 13].

Information Sources: Properties about the publishing sites and author of online information. For sites, there are many cues that can affect the credibility of information it publishing, including visitor volume, wining prizes, ranking, official, domain type, and simple navigation, structural websites, notification of review from editor, interaction function (search, information confirming, prompt response for user service), reputation [7]. The cues about author influencing the judgment are gender, geographic location, active degree, expert in topic area, officially proving, and contact details [13, 14]. Specially, in social platform, the head portrait, followers and followees are also important for users assessing the credibility [13, 15].

Topics: The topic about the information content and its properties. Currencyis the most obvious cues of topic [7].

Information Dissemination: Description of how the information dissemination. Popularity in experts, visitor volume classified by geographic location, in the front of the list of search results, sharing times are all the properties [10, 13].

Visual Styles: Properties of the ways the information visually present to users, independent with other properties of information itself. Personalizing homepage, [13] professional, attractive, consistent design of sites is included in visual styles.

Table 2 shows affecting cues about online information credibility.

3 Expert Interviewing

Considering the importance of motivation and people are usually interested in news, in order to make sure which criterions and cues have positive effects on judging outcome, and to add some criterions and cues that may not be mentioned in literatures, interviews with expert in judging credibility of news information were conducted.

3.1 Interview Process

Participants: Five experts in news information credibility assessment, including four Chinese editors of newspapers and one Journalism professor from Tongji University, three male and two female. One editor works for academic journal of Beijing Institute of Technology, and two works for daily news now, one has worked for daily news. They are occupied in jobs related to news, and are all experienced in the credibility about news information.

Interview Questions: Including some open end explorative questions about experts' experience in news credibility assessment, and a questionnaire inquiring the experts' ranking for the positive effect on five criterions and five cues mentioned above. Main aspects of questions were experts' opinions about online news information credibility, the judging process expert usually use in their work, the properties of fake news, and how to help general people assess online news credibility. And in the questionnaire, the 7-point Likert scales were used to measure different levels of agreement to the positive effect of items including criterions and cues from "1 = totally disagree" to "7 = totally agree". The definition of items were provided in the questionnaire.

Procedure: One interview was conducted face to face, and other four interviews was conducted by online video chatting. The interview time for each participant was

Table 2. Cues in the process of information credibility assessment

Type of cues	Cue	Definite items
Information contents	Language errors	Misuse of grammar and punctuation
		Misspelling
	Special contents	URL
		References
		Advertisement
	Quality of content	Professional and clear content
		Comprehensibility
		Reasonability
Information sources	Popularity of the website	Visitor volume
		Prizes
		Ranking
	Professionality of the website	Official platform
		Reputation
	Design and function of the website platform	Simple navigations and structural website
		Notification of review from editors
		Interaction function
	Personal information of authors	Gender
		Contact information
	Properties of authors	Active degree
		Expert in information topic area
		Officially proved
Topics	Currency	Lag between topic event occurring and information published
		Lag between topic event occurring and users seeing it
	Evaluations to the topic event	Opinions in the original website platform
		Opinions in other online platforms
Information dissemination	Event topic spread	Popularity in experts
		In the front of the list of search results, Sharing times
Visual styles	Visual design	Personalizing homepage
		Professional design
		Consistency of the website

$40 \sim 90$ min. We first asked open questions to experts about their works and specific cases for judging news credibility they had experienced, then let them fill in the questionnaire about useful criterions and cues.

3.2   Interview Results

Properties of Online News: Compared to news on traditional media, online news cares more about 'new', and is required to be faster by people. At the same time, the examine steps of online news is simpler and fewer than traditional news. Even so, official news is still more credible than we media on the Internet. Judging credibility of online news only in terms of content is extremely difficult for everyone.

Types of Fake News: There are three different fake news. The first one is completely fake news, representing the news whose content is absolutely fake, such as the medicine that guarantee to cure all diseases. The second fake news is partial fake news, representing the news that contain true part and fake part, which are common on the Internet. The third fake news is bias news. The bias news include no fake part, but hide some fact or enlarge some fact in content. It is the type of majority fake news, causing most damage to people.

Suggestions to Internet Users: Do not easily believe online news. Source, experts' opinion and integrity of news are all important for credible news. The news whose related news are from only one source is not credible.

Revise of Criterions: According to the questionnaire data, items that mean value of point are greater than 4 and variance of point are small are keep. Useful criterions includes accuracy, authority and objectivity.

Revise of Cues: According to the questionnaire data, items that mean value of point are greater than 4 and variance of point are small are keep. Useful type of cues were information contents, information sources, topics and information dissemination.

4   Assistant Webpage Tool Design

An assistant webpage is designed to help people assess online news in Weibo. The webpage is developed by Python, PHP, JavaScript, CSS and HTML, visualizing the useful cues to Weibo users. Figure 1 illustrates a part of webpage.

According to the different types of cues, the assistant webpage is divided into three parts, presenting information contents and sources, information spread, and topics. Every part is constituted by different functional pieces, and each functional piece visualizes different cues respectively.

Table 3 shows the structure of webpage with affecting cues.

4.1   First Part: Information Contents and Sources Part

First part contained the information contents and sources assistance. And this part is design as familiar with Weibo as possible considering the consistency for users.

There are two functional pieces in the first part. The left piece presents the content of Weibo news and information of its author, including author's head portrait, followers, followees, numbers of weibos, active degree and related field, showed by the

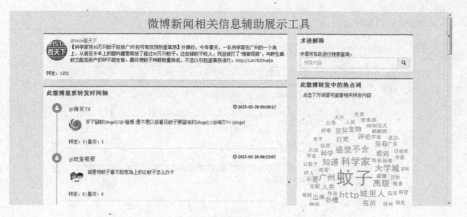

Fig. 1. The overall design of the assistant webpage

Table 3. The structure and content of the assistant webpage

Type of cues	Cues	Definite items	Webpage part	Functional piece
Information contents	Quality of the content	Professional and clear content	First part	Explanations of terms in the information
		Reliable data		
Information sourses	Properties of authors	Expert in news topic area	First part	Authors' Keywords
		Officially proved identity		Identification in Weibo
Topics	Currency	Following up the development of the information topic	Second part	Retransmission timeline
	Evaluations to the topic event	Opinions in the website	Third part	Relevant news in Weibo
		Opinions in other platforms		Relevant news in other websites
Information dissemination	Event topic spread	Opinions of experts	Second part	Retransmission timeline
				The clouds of hot words

rate of sending weibos and keyword of author's weibos. The right piece presents the means of terms in news content from Wiki, helping users understand the news.

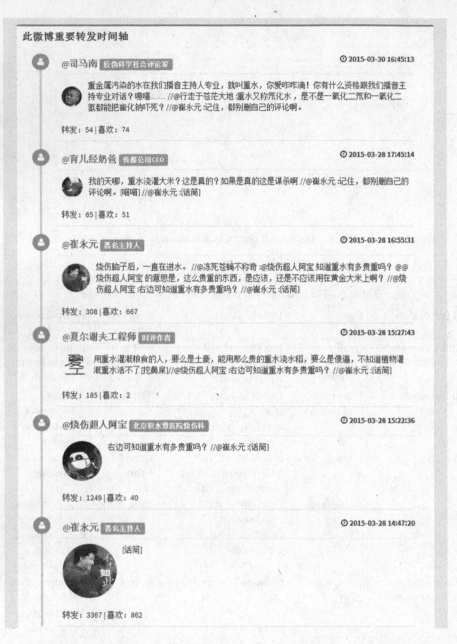

Fig. 2. The timeline functional piece in the second part of the assistant webpage

4.2 Second Part: Information Dissemination Part

Second part of assistant webpage contained the information dissemination of Weibo news. The spread is by 'retransmit weibos' function, like retweet in Twitter.

Fig. 3. The cloud of key words functional piece in the second part of the assistant webpage

The second part also contains two functional pieces. The left piece is the timeline of key retransmission of the Weibo news, called retransmission timeline. Hot retransmissions from officially proving users and their identity in Weibo are presented ordering by time, gathering the experts' opinion in it. Figure 2 shows the details of retransmission timeline piece.

The right functional piece is the cloud of hot words of all the retransmission by Weibo users. It contains the words that are mostly mentioned in retransmission, and displays the content of related retransmission when clicking a word. The cloud of hot words represent the opinion of general users in spreading process. Figure 3 is the details of the piece.

4.3   Third Part: Topics Part

Third part of assistant webpage shows the cross-platform relevant news about the same topics. It has two functional pieces presenting relevant news in Weibo and at other news websites respectively.

5   Conclusion

In this study, a method of helping the Internet users judge the credibility of online news information was proposed through literature reviewing and interviews with experts in news credibility assessment. The method contained a judgment process, three judging criterions and four affecting cues. The judgment process described how people thought in the process of credibility assessment: People firstly judged the credibility of sources, then selected several elements in the information; according to the elements people conducted the assessment and finally got the results; moreover, judging process observed the interest-driving rules, considering efficiency but not accuracy. The judging criterions which had positive effects on assessment included accuracy, authority and objectivity. And the four types of positive affecting cues are information contents, information sources, relevant news of the topic and information spread, every type contained several small cues.

An assistant webpage based on Weibo, helping online users judge the credibility of the news information by visualizing the positive affecting cues in the method, was designed. The first part of the webpage showed the content and source information in Weibo, adding the explanation of terms in the content. And the second part visualizing the news spread information, containing the timeline of the experts' opinion and the cloud of the general users' hot word in the retransmission of the Weibo news. The third part gathered the relevant news in Weibo and added the news in official online news media.

There were three main limitations in the study. Firstly, we had just verified the effectiveness of the method in Weibo news. The initial object of the research was to get a method that could help Internet users for the process of all the online information credibility assessment, and the method was conducted to help people judging online news in all the Internet website, and the webpage was applied only for Weibo. In other words, the assisting range was narrow. Secondly, the webpage only visualized the affecting cues of the method, but without the judging criterions, which were just used to test the assistant effects. At last, the effects of the assistant webpage had not been measured. The future study can concentrate on expanding the applying range of the method, visualizing the judging criterions in the method, and improving the design of the assistant webpage.

References

1. Chaiken, S., Trope, Y.: Dual-Process Theories in Social Psychology. Guilford Press, New York (1999)
2. Rieh, S.Y.: Judgment of information quality and cognitive authority in the web. J. Am. Soc. Inform. Sci. Technol. **53**(2), 145–161 (2002)
3. Fogg, B.J.: Prominence-interpretation theory: explaining how people assess credibility online. In: CHI 2003 Extended Abstracts on Human Factors in Computing Systems, pp. 722–723 (2003)
4. Simon, H.A.: A behavioral model of rational choice. Quart. J. Econ. **69**(1), 99–118 (1955)
5. Hilligoss, B., Rieh, S.Y.: Developing a unifying framework of credibility assessment: construct, heuristics, and interaction in context. Inf. Process. Manage. **44**(4), 1467–1484 (2008)
6. Metzger, M.J., Flanagin, A.J., Medders, R.B.: Social and heuristic approaches to credibility evaluation online. Journal of Communication **60**(3), 413–439 (2010)
7. Metzger, M.J.: Making sense of credibility on the web: models for evaluating online information and recommendations for future research. J. Am. Soc. Inform. Sci. Technol. **58**(13), 2078–2091 (2007)

8. Petty, R.E., Cacioppo, J.T.: The elaboration likelihood model of persuasion. Communication and Persuasion. Central and Peripheral Routes to Attitude Change. Springer Series in Social Psychology, pp. 1–24. Springer, New York (1986)
9. Savolainen, P.T., Mannering, F.L., Lord, D., Quddus, M.A.: The statistical analysis of highway crash-injury severities: a review and assessment of methodological alternatives. Accid. Anal. Prev. **43**(5), 1666–1676 (2011)
10. Schwarz, J., Morris, M.: Augmenting web pages and search results to support credibility assessment. In: Proceedings of the SIGCHI Conference on Human Factors in Computing Systems, pp. 1245–1254 (2011)
11. Castillo, C., Mendoza, M., Poblete, B.: Information credibility on twitter. In: Proceedings of the 20th International Conference on World Wide Web, pp. 675–684 (2011)
12. Flanagin, A.J., Metzger, M.J.: The role of site features, user attributes, and information verification behaviors on the perceived credibility of web-based information. New Media Soc. **9**(2), 319–342 (2007)
13. Morris, M. R., Counts, S., Roseway, A., Hoff, A., Schwarz, J.: Tweeting is believing?: Understanding microblog credibility perceptions. In: Proceedings of the ACM 2012 Conference on Computer Supported Cooperative Work, pp. 441–450 (2012)
14. Armstrong, C.L., McAdams, M.J.: Blogs of information: how gender cues and individual motivations influence perceptions of credibility. J. Comput.-Mediated Commun. **14**(3), 435–456 (2009)
15. Westerman, D., Spence, P.R., Van Der Heide, B.: A social network as information: the effect of system generated reports of connectedness on credibility on twitter. Comput. Hum. Behav. **28**(1), 199–206 (2012)

How the Alignment Pattern and Route Direction Affect the Design of the Bus Stop Board: An Eye Movement Experimental Research

Na Lin[1], Chuanyu Zou[1,2], Yunhong Zhang[1(✉)], and Yijun Chen[3]

[1] Human Factor and Ergonomics Laboratory,
China National Institute of Standardization, Beijing, China
{zouchy, zhangyh}@cnis.gov.cn
[2] Research Group of Graphical Symbols and Way Guidance,
China National Institute of Standardization, Beijing, China
[3] School of Design, Central Academy of Fine Arts, Beijing, China

Abstract. An eye movement study was conducted to study the visual factors which influencing the searching efficiency of bus stop board. 31 ordinary adults were measured to investigate the effects of the alignment patterns, the positions of the arrow indicating bus route direction on the searching efficiency of the different sexual passengers at different age stage by Eye-tracking. The eye movement experiment took the bus stop names as material, set simulated bus route, and made series of bus stop boards with different color combinations and graphic designs. The result shows that the difference in search time and fixation times between the positions of the direction arrow and the alignment patterns of the bus name list is significant. When the arrow was below of the bus stop name list, it cost much less time for distribute alignment bus stop boards than for top alignment ones in searching destination bus stop; and when the bus stop name list was in distribute alignment, those bus stop boards which the direction arrow was below the bus stop name list had a significant advantage over those that the arrow was above in searching time and fixation times. As a conclusion, the obtained results could be a reference for design the bus stop board.

Keywords: Bus stop board · Alignment patterns · Arrow position · Searching efficiency · Fixation time · Eye-tracking

1 Introduction

The bus stop boards are a kind of public information signs set at bus stops, which generally are formed by graphical symbols, text and colors, to provide passengers with travel information [1]. Bus stop boards are important guidance tools for passengers travelling by bus. Bus stop boards with low visual search efficiency are easily lead to stranded passengers and congestion at the bus stop. Many ergonomics researchers focus on the visual cognition characteristics of the bus stop boards to make the design conformed to passengers' visual cognitive processing habits. Bus stop boards with good design will help passengers travel fast and convenient.

© Springer International Publishing Switzerland 2016
D. Harris (Ed.): EPCE 2016, LNAI 9736, pp. 136–146, 2016.
DOI: 10.1007/978-3-319-40030-3_15

In previous studies, data showed that there were many problems on the bus stop boards' visual design. For example, it was difficult for passengers to read the information on the bus stop boards which installed in various cities, the fonts' size were too small, the colors were dull and dreadfully alike, the information were incomplete [1]. As there were no indications about the travel directions and the approaching stops, those also caused inconvenience for passengers to confirm the current stops [2].

Xie et al. [2] found that "using response time and accuracy in searching bus stop boards as indicators, the visual search performance on recognizing the current stop will be improved a lot with adding highlighted display", and "the performance of highlighted arrow and color is much better than that of using bigger font size". Chen [3] found some existing problems on bus stop signs "can't identify one/two way of bus route", "lack the position information of the stop at opposite side, forward or backward", "lack the route diagrams on relative transferring bus routes", and "the approximate orientation of bus running route in the city". Zheng Zhe Chen also put forward several suggestions on designing the bus stop signs. Zheng [4] gave several advices and new concepts on fonts, diagrams and graphical designing methods which based on the psychology and visual cognitive process theories. Ding et al. [5] conducted a case investigation on SHANGHAI bus stop boards from the following aspects: color scheme, information completeness, beautiful appearance, convenience, English translation, night illumination and the need of disabled groups. Ding et al. [5] also suggested several improvement aspects on the design.

The above researches collected some existing questions on bus stop boards' design via various methods including questionnaire method, behavior experiment method and theoretical analysis method. But they haven't studied into the visual cognitive process in bus stop boards design.

With the rapid technical development, eye movement theory and tracer technique are widely used in the road traffic research on various design and setting fields, including the design of the cab console panel, the design of vehicle vision, the design of vehicle color (e.g. vehicle body color, cab color, and signal lamp color), the design of road line, the design of road crossing, the design of tunnel entrance and exit, the design and setting of road traffic facilities, signs and markings, the design of street trees and isolation belt plants. The design of bus stop board is the focal point of this paper, which is similar with the design of road traffic facilities, signs and markings. In order to improve the design and setting of road traffic facilities, signs and markings, some researchers study the eye movement features, visual characteristic, and their relationships [6, 7]. As eye movement can reflect the visual information searching mode effectively, it has more important value in explaining the mental mechanism of visual cognitive process. Relative research findings have been widely used in cognitive studies on website, advertisement and graphics.

Visual search is a complicated cognitive process, normally, it focuses on find out the specific stimulation in a stimulus context, which is performance oriented. From the explicit behavior, the visual search gained the outside stimulus information and fulfilled the information processing by a series of saccades and fixations [8]. Lots of factors influence the efficiency of visual search, in which the physical properties of stimulus is one of the most important factors. As early as in 2006, some researchers studied the saccade mechanism of visual search using eye tracer technique. Ding (2007) eye movement study found that there were obvious asymmetry features of left eye and right eye movements when participants did graphic visual search. The main asymmetry features are: the average fixation time of the left side view was significantly longer than that of the right side view; the search saccade distance of the left side view was shorter than that of the right side view; the searching saccade speed of the left side view was slower than the right side view; the beat frequency of the left side view was significantly more than that of the right side view. For search strategy, the average fixation duration of vertical search was significantly longer than that of horizontal search [9].

Many studies were conducted on the information display methods to improve the speed and quality of the visual interfaces information communication by designers and researchers. Hu et al. found that using highlighted display methods (e.g. color, flashing, title) can significantly enhance the users' visual search efficiency. An appropriate color code may effectively reduce the visual search time. Their study indicated the highlighted display might influence user' searching strategy: when using highlighted display interface, participants can collect limited resources together and reduce useless search to enhance the search efficiency. On the contrary, when using non-highlighted display interface, participants mainly use sequential search strategy, they are unable to collect limited resources together, so the invalid searches are increasing and the search efficiency is poor [10]. Ge (2009) indicated there were some differences in the cognitive processing and checking methods on road information structure. The main difference was that the eye movements vary by participants. A symmetric road information structure could improve the users' efficiency on reading road traffic signs. Eye movement data indicated that the fixation points and retrace time were reduce a lot, and the gazing time was significantly shorter when using symmetric structures. So the symmetric structure for road traffic signs can improve the visual search efficiency obviously. A symmetrical structure information effect does exist [11].

On the point of search strategy, some researchers found that when participants employed directive search strategy, the number of fixation was significantly lower, the saccade trajectory length was shorter, and the fixation time was much less, in result, the search efficiency was better. While when participants employed sequential search strategy, the number of fixation was much more, the saccade trajectory length was longer, and the fixation time was much more, in result, the search efficiency was worse. The research indicated visual interface structure, label and the project semantic features might influence the participants search strategy and reduce the number of fixation to improve search efficiency [12]. In this paper, we try to use the eye movement tracer method to study the influence of various highlighted visual interfaces on the bus stop boards' visual search efficiency to collect experimental data for improving the bus stop boards' design.

2   Method

2.1   Experiment Design

Within-subject and between-subject crossed four factors design was conducted to investigate the effects of the alignment patterns, the positions of the arrow indicating bus route direction on the searching efficiency of the different sexual passengers at different age stage. A 2 (the positions of the arrow indicating bus route direction: above vs. below the bus stop name list) × 2 (the alignment patterns of the bus stop name list: top alignment or distribute alignment) within-subject factorial design with two additional control condition were used in this experiment. The additional independent variables were: age (young vs. older) and gender (male and female). In this experiment, the search time and fixation times were measured by eye-tracking to assess and compare which type of bus stop board design is better.

2.2 Participants

Thirty-one ordinary adults from 20 to 66 years old (14 male and 17 female, mean age = 40.42, standard deviation of age = 15.83) were recruited and paid to participate in the experiment. All subjects were divided into two groups, one group was young from 20 to 44 (9 male and 8 female, mean age = 27.18, standard deviation of age = 5.34); the other group was senior from 45 to 66(8 males and 6 female, mean age = 56.50, standard deviation of age = 5.96). All had normal or corrected-to-normal visual acuities and healthy physical conditions, without ophthalmic diseases. They did not have any history of neurological and mental diseases. And the participants were divided into two groups, one group were younger group which included nine male and eight female, and the other group were senior group which included eight male and six female.

2.3 Stimulus

The eye movement experiment took the bus stop names as material, set simulated bus route, and made series of bus stop boards with different color combinations and graphic designs. From Beijing city bus station name library selects the bus station name and form 11 virtual circuit made of green bottom mispronounced character matching bus stop pictures, of which each bus stop containing 46 bus station. One of them was as the practice trial. Each route has 4 target station to search which represent four experimental level and the position effect of the target stations were balanced. 40 search trials were randomly divided into 7 groups, each group included of 4–8 trials. The 4 target search trials of the same line were evenly distributed in each group. The 4 bus stops of the same line were not adjacent for each other. Each experimental level has designed 10 standard trials to emphatically analyze which there were 20 stations between the target station and the current station, and the rest are filled trial. The standard trial of each experiment level was evenly distributed in each experimental group, and their locations were not in the first or in the last of each experimental group. The positions of the standard trials in each experimental group were pseudo randomly arranged.

As generating the virtual circuit bus stop, the station name is selected to avoid the special place (such as Zhongnanhai, Badaling station) and the very familiar place (such as Sanyuan Bridge). And the station names was arranged by pseudo random and the station names with different words (including 2 words, 3 words, 4 words, 5, 6 words, 7 words) was evenly distributed throughout the virtual circuit. The station order was arranged by considering the geographical location to avoid a clear violation of the common sense (Fig. 1).

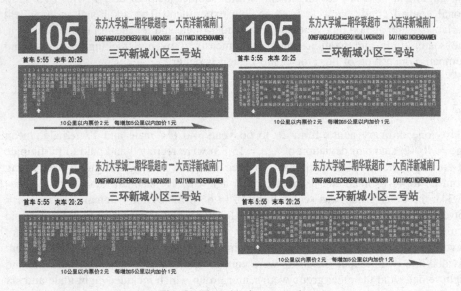

Fig. 1. The stimulus example

The locations of the initial stations were distributed random. The station name with 2 words was not as the initial station and terminal station. Target stations were selected by taking into account the word number, the location and other factors. The terminal station are not the target station. The image resolution was 1284×812 and the image example was as follow:

2.4   Apparatus

Experiments were conducted in a quiet and bright environment which simulated outdoors condition. It was installed in the laboratory in the Institute of Human Factors and Ergonomics in China National Institute of Standardization. The eye-tracker was SMI iView X RED made by SMI Corporation and its sampling rate is 60 Hz. And DELL Latitude D620 was as the experimental host with 2116 Hz core frequency, 2G memory card, independent graphics card. The host was connected to two monitors, one monitor was 19 inch display which was presented stimuli for subjects and subjects responded through the mouse and keyboard, while the eye tracker below the display recorded the subjects' eye movement data; the other display device showed the subjects' eye movement for the objects during the experimental process. And the resolutions of all the display terminals were 1280×1024 and their refresh rates were 60 Hz. The experimental programs was automatically generated by SMI Center Experiment.

2.5 Procedures

The eye movement experiment on the design of bus stop board was conducted in the Institute of Human Factors and Ergonomics lab in China National Institute of Standardization. After arriving at the laboratory, participants signed the informed consent and completed a general survey about their demographic information. The participants were asked to sit into the simulator to get ready for the test. After that, the participants were required to complete the visual search task by simulating reading the bus stop boards. The experiment are vertically arranged in the height adjustable special experimental table. Before the experiment, the height of the table and display position were adjusted to make the participants' eyes and display center on a line. The viewing distance is about 60–70 cm, and the head tracking range is 40*40 cm. Before viewing the bus stop board, an eye movement calibration was done to ensure data precisely. Then, participants read experimental instruction and did some exercises to ensure participants understand the instruction and conduct the visual search task correctly. If participants don't know the experimental process, then let him/her do practice again. After practice, the experimenter would validate simply the search strategy which the subject used, but do not make any judgments and tips. Then, they entered the formal experiment. During viewing the bus stop boards, the participants' eye movement data were recorded. There was three to five minutes resting between each group. After viewing all the pictures, the participants were required to tell which search strategy he/she used. Each participant spent about one hour finishing the experiment. The searching time and fixation times were recorded by SMI eye-tracker as efficiency indexes when the participants reading different designed bus stop boards. The experimental instruction was as follows:

> "You will see a series of bus stop pictures. Before each picture presenting, it will show you a few words in the center of the screen, and that is the station where you are going to. When you memory the target station, please press the spacebar. Then, please find out the target station and count the number of the interval of stations between the target station and the current station on the next bus stop. The number does not contain the current station, also does not include the target station, and it only include the stations in the middle. After determining the number of stations, please input the number through the keyboard, then press the space bar to enter the next trial. When you input the number of stations, the screen will not have any presentation, you should input it as usual. The whole process is not reversible, it means that you can't look back a picture or text, so please ensure that each your operation is accurate. If you are ready to begin the experiment, please switch off the mobile phone or set it at the quiet mode."

2.6 Data Analysis

According to the experimental design, the data of standard trials were analyzed through the BeGaze software. The standard trial was divided three regions of interest which were current station, target station and the middle region between the two stations. The time that first enter the target station was as the search time, and the fixation times in the middle regions were as the fixation times. They were as indexes for further data analysis. According to the behavior data and the search strategy that subjects used, the first fixation time data were corrected, and the trials with incorrect behavior data were excluded. The eye movement data of all standard trials were exported from the SMI BeGaze software and analyzed by IBM SPSS 20 Statistics software (IBM-SPSS Inc. Chicago, IL). The repeated-measure ANOVA was applied to analysis the data of searching time and fixation times.

3 Results

3.1 The Means of Search Time and Fixation Times for Each Condition

Tracking test was conducted to compare the effect of the Bus Stop Board's Design with different alignment patterns and route direction. The search time and fixation times data were analyzed. A $2 \times 2 \times 2 \times 2$ mixed-measure ANOVA was conducted to evaluate age group(above 40 years old and below 40 years old), gender group(male and female), alignment patterns (top alignment or distribute alignment) and route direction(above the bus stop names and below the bus stop names). Search time and fixation times for each condition are summarized in Table 1.

Table 1. The mean search time and mean fixation times of the four conditions[a]

	Conditions	Mean search time	Mean fixation times
Alignment patterns	top alignment	9.25E3 (1044.57)	21.42 (2.36)
	distribute alignment	8.27E3 (867.46)	23.25 (2.78)
Route direction	above the bus stop names	1.06E4 (856.81)	26.32 (2.86)
	below the bus stop names	6.93E3 (756.53)	18.34 (2.12)
Gender group	male	8.22E3 (937.38)	19.05 (3.18)
	female	9.30E3 (1041.84)	25.62 (3.54)
Age group	above 40 years old	1.067E4 (1041.84)	27.09 (3.54)
	below 40 years old	6.85E3 (937.38)	17.57 (3.18)

[a]Standard errors are given in parentheses.

3.2 Repeated-Measure ANOVA of Search Time Which First Entered the Target Station Region

With regard to the search time, a repeated-measure ANOVA was applied to the search time data of the different conditions, a significant main effect of route direction was found $(F(1,30) = 20.79, p < 0.001)$, a significant main effect of age group was found $(F(1,30) = 7.74, p < 0.05)$, and a significant interaction was found, $F(1,15) = 9.29$,

$p < 0.01$. The planned comparisons revealed that the search time of male condition was remarkably shorter than that of female condition ($p < 0.05$), and the search time of the condition that the route direction was below the bus stop names was remarkably shorter than that of the condition that the route direction was above the bus stop names ($p < 0.05$). The results indicated that the main effect of gender group and alignment patterns of was not significant ($p > 0.05$) (see Table 2). It means that the search time was not affected by gender and alignment patterns.

Table 2. Repeated-measure ANOVA results of search time which first entered the target station region.

	SS	df	MS	F value	Sig. (Two-tailed)
Age Group	3.55E7	1	3.55E7	7.44	0.011
Gender Group	4.43E8	1	4.43E8	0.60	0.447
Alignment patterns	2.90E7	1	2.90E7	0.55	0.463
The positions of route direction	4.09E8	1	4.09E8	20.79	0.000
The positions of route direction × Alignment patterns	3.15E8	1	3.15E8	9.29	0.005

3.3 Repeated-Measure ANOVA of Fixation Times in the Middle Station Region

With regard to the fixation times, a repeated-measure ANOVA was applied to the fixation times data of the different conditions, a significant main effect of route direction was found ($F(1,30) = 23.51$, $p < 0.001$). The planned comparisons revealed that the fixation times of the condition that the route direction was below the bus stop names was remarkably less than that of the condition that the route direction was above the bus stop names ($p < 0.001$).The results indicated that the main effect of age group and the interaction of the positions of route direction and alignment patterns was critical significant ($p = 0.056$, $p = 0.058$) (see Table 2). And the main effect of gender group and alignment patterns of was not significant ($p > 0.05$) (see Table 2), which means that the fixation times was not affected by gender and alignment patterns (Table 3).

Table 3. Repeated-measure ANOVA results of fixation times in the middle station region

	SS	df	MS	F value	Sig. (Two-tailed)
Age Group	2746.51	1	2746.51	4.00	0.056
Gender Group	1306.63	1	1306.63	1.90	0.179
Alignment patterns	101.03	1	101.03	0.85	0.364
The positions of route direction	1930.54	1	1930.54	23.51	0.000
The positions of route direction × Alignment patterns	1540.13	1	1540.13	3.93	0.058

4 Discussion

In recent years, eye movement research has been applied to multiple design fields, such as design of webpages, books, city landscape, etc. Researchers answered that design elements of books different formats whether could influence reading velocity or efficiency [13]. In the eye movement observation indicators and under the study of searching performance tasks, one of the main observation indicators was fixation times that users stared at a location, it reflects people information dealing abilities and processing hardness [6]. The more fixation times be used, the less efficiency for searching, it might cause by bad layout display [14]. Early in 1989, Hendrickso regarded fixation times as one of indicators and assessed efficiency of different type menus [14].

Another indicator was the first time to enter target area, which was assessed searching efficiency. More first enter-time indicated more visual searching processing time to get target and lower efficiency of searching activity [14]. The study result revealed that when direction arrows were below station lists, users spent less searching time. It was not the final purpose that direction arrows as sign of judging the bus driving route direction. Therefore, arrows were below bus station lists as reminders whenever needed, it also attracted passengers less attention when they were finding the target station. Further analysis displayed that arrows were below bus station lists which was justify align use less searching time than align top. It provided extra clue for users, saved cognitive recourses and improved searching efficiency.

The same result was found in the test of fixation times that staring at the middle district. When arrows were below the station lists, users spent less fixation times, it means that arrows below influenced users with little interference, and they had greater attention, it was good for target process searching [11]. In addition, similar to the first time to enter target area, further analysis of fixation times of middle district showed that when direction arrows were below the bus station lists,the alignment patterns of justify align spent less fixation times than align top. That is to say, bus stations lists justify align used less time for information processing.

Preceding research proved that less fixation times showed faster processing speed and users could get more processing information. Time length of stare showed difficulty degree of information processed and extracted. Symmetry structure information contains little cognition that was easy to understanding, recognizing and processing. In the research, justify align approaches the style of symmetry structure, which was better for users process information. Therefore, when route direction located below and bus station list justify align, it is a better format design to improving searching efficiency.

Age was remarkably different at the user searching time. The study revealed that, the older users spent more searching time. It was related to many mental functions deterioration with age growing, especially for the cognitive capacity. Based on preceding research, Schaie chose five representative capacities, the ability of inductive reasoning, space orientation, statistics, vocabulary comprehension and vocabulary fluent, which as the basic mental abilities for testing cognitive function. The results showed it was necessary recession with age growing whether horizontal comparison or vertical comparison [15]. It was related to sensory function degeneration in varying degrees, meanwhile, processing rate was reducing and working memory was trending toward degeneration. Some studies indicated that visual function was the mediating variable for the older users' memory width and fluid intelligence, degeneration of visual function was the key in the mental ability ageing [16]. So the study result showed the older users need more time to finish searching tasks, it related to the declining reaction capacity.

5   Conclusion

Bus station board as the necessary public facility for people's travelling, and its humanized degree reflects the developing level of a state or a city. The research indicated that alignment patterns of station names configuration was non-significant difference between justify align and align top, but the positions of route direction was significant difference between above and below, the location below name lists was more efficient. It also revealed that ageing effect was found in the bus station searching test. The study results offered data support for bus stop design. In follow-up work, researchers will continue researching bus station board and relevant facilities from cognitive processing angle, and offer date support for bus station board improvement. Also, they will research for special group such as ageing people, and finally keep the design of bus station board better suit people's needs.

Acknowledgement. The authors would like to gratefully acknowledge the support from the National Key Technology R&D Program of the Ministry of Science and Technology (2012BAK28B03, 2014BAK01B03), China National Institute of Standardization through the "special funds for the basic R&D undertakings by welfare research institutions"(522014Y-3344).

References

1. Li, Z.N.: Research on the visual design of urban bus stop board. Packaging World **01**, 77–78 (2014)
2. Xie, H., Fang, W.N., Ding, L.: Experimental research on cognitive ergonomics of highlighted display used in bus stop board. In: The 2007 International Conference on Industrial Design, p. 12 (2007)
3. Chen, Z.Z.: Improved design for indicating information on bus-stop boards. Sci. Technol. Inform. **03**, 190–207 (2014)
4. Zheng, Y.: Aspects should be paid attention to concerning with the design of static public transport stop boards. Art Design **05**, 010–011 (2005)
5. Ding, H.Y., Zhu, W.Q., Guo, J.L.: Investigation and analysis of bus stop sign in Shanghai. Urban Public Transp. **12**, 37–39 (2009)
6. Li, Y.F.: The application of eye movement technique in road traffic system. Shanghai Auto **5**, 56–59 (2010)
7. Wang, H.R.: The application and prospect of research on eye movement technology in road traffic. Med. J. Commun. **2**, 119–123 (2014)
8. Ren, Y.T., Han, Y.C., Sui, X.: The saccades and its mechanism in the process of visual search. Adv. Psychol. Sci. **14**(3), 340–345 (2006)

9. Ding, J.H., Li, Y., Hu, R.R., Yan, Y.M.: Spatial asymmetry of visual search between different locations: an eye movements study. Psychol. Sci. **30**(1), 116–119 (2007)
10. Hu, F.P., Ge, L.Z., Xu, W.D.: Item highlighting influence on visual searching strategies studies. Acta Psychologica Sinica **37**(3), 314–319 (2005)
11. Ge, X.L., Hu, X.K., Ge, L.Z.: Eye movement study on symmetry effect in structure of road traffic signs. Chinese J. Appl. Psychol. **15**(3), 284–288 (2009)
12. Hu, F.P., Chen, Y.C., Ge, L.Z.: Page label and page structure influence on visual searching strategies in page layout. Chinese J. Ergonomics **13**(4), 4–7 (2007)
13. Xu, J.: Domestic design for eye movement study in the field of psychology. Beijing Union Univ. J. **7**, 72–75 (2013)
14. Yan, B.: Application of Eye Movement in Web Usability Test, Beijing Post and Communication University (2011)
15. Peng, H., Wang, D.: Cognitive mechanism of basic mental ability ageing. Develop. Psychol. Sci. **8**, 1251–1258 (2012)
16. Mao, X., Peng, H.: Function of visual and perception pressure in the basic mental ability ageing. Psychol. J. **1**, 29–38 (2016)

Study on the Effects of Semantic Memory on Icon Complexity in Cognitive Domain

Jing Zhang, Chengqi Xue[⊠], Zhangfan Shen, Xiaojiao Chen,
Jiang Shao, Lei Zhou, and Xiaozhou Zhou

School of Mechanical Engineering,
Southeast University, Nanjing 211189, China
ipd_xcq@seu.edu.cn

Abstract. It is a studying worthy problem whether highly visual complexity must bring low cognitive efficiency in icon design of visual interface. Although the visual noise of unreasonable and improper complexity seriously impacts the efficiency of users' access and visual search tasks, few are able to determine the effects of memory on icon complexity in cognitive domain. The goal of the present study was to investigate the interaction between semantic memory and icon in a complexity perceptual layering method. The CP (Complexity of Presentation) and CM (Complexity of Memory) are presented in this article by a complex perceptual layering. Three laboratory experiments are conducted to assess the cognitive performances of three different complexities (low, medium and high) in three CP dimensions (shape feature, color feature, texture feature). Results revealed that, (1) One influence of semantic memory on icon complexity is the familiarity, the cognitive efficiency is enhanced when stimulus are processed in a high complex semantically meaningful way. (2) The cognitive performance of low complexity coding and high complexity coding is greater than the medium coding in the familiar test and the correlation test. (3) When searching for a similar target with stimulus in different complex levels, the gaze opacity and heat map data demonstrate the efficiency of medium-low and high-low are the highest. Based on the experimental results, it is validated that the interaction between semantic memory and icon complexity is a visual dimensionality reduction in a complexity perceptual layering.

Keywords: Icon complexity · Semantic memory · Cognitive domain · Complexity perceptual layering · Icon design factors

1 Introduction

In various digital interfaces of computers and other devices, icons are often thought to be more useful at communicating tools than words because of their ability to transcend language barriers and present meaning in a condensed form [1]. The complexity selection of icons directly influences the cognitive efficiency users received from the graphical information. People are susceptible to irregular icons when identifying targets from a wide variety of icon-based interfaces, which may lead to clutter, confusion, and even human error. Correct icon complexity can help users to distinct appropriate icons and respond more quickly. It is well known that semantic memory has an impact on

© Springer International Publishing Switzerland 2016
D. Harris (Ed.): EPCE 2016, LNAI 9736, pp. 147–157, 2016.
DOI: 10.1007/978-3-319-40030-3_16

performance [2]. The icon design depends on two kinds: the fixed semantic factors and the visual factors (such as icon style, shape, color and texture). Previous psychological studies only focused on icon's visual factors and then concluded that the icon's cognitive efficiency would decrease with the increasing of the complexity. Although the visual noise of unreasonable and improper complexity seriously impacts the efficiency of users' access and visual search tasks, few are able to determine the effects of memory on icon complexity in cognitive domain. Therefore, the interaction between semantic memory and icon in a complexity perceptual layering method can help to provide a novel and valuable guidance to icon complexity.

In cognitive load of visual information processing, the early icon complexity research have conducted the following studies: Measures of the icon complexity study developed by Garcia as early as 1994 included six icon properties: icon foreground, the number of objects in an icon, the number of holes in those objects, and two calculations of icon edges and homogeneity in icon structure which uses image-processing techniques to measure icon properties [3]. McDougall et al. (1999) determined three characteristics of icons: concreteness, distinctiveness, and complexity, which reflected the primary importance in the measurement [4]. Maurizio (2009) used a fuzzy approach to reveal the evaluation of image complexity and classified as high, medium and low [5].

In terms of working memory, there were few approaches to study the icon complexity. A study of the memory capacity for the value of an icon or symbol by Harber and Hershenson (1973) found that the memory depends largely on the effort required for an accurate interpretation of its meaning [6]. Forsythe et al. (2008) investigated the role of complexity and familiarity in basic-level picture processing and their findings were in good agreement with a previous study of experiment method on the familiar test by Snodgrass [7]. However, event-related potentials (ERPs) provide lots of ideal methods to investigate behavioral findings about semantic memory influence users' cognition largely by modulating recollection [8].

In general, the previous studies on icon complexity focused on the styles and the constituent factors of icon belong to the visual presentation. But, these studies ignored the fact that acquiring information from icons was a cognitive behavior related with semantic memory. Previous studies have, in fact, separately provided evidences supporting the idea that both semantic memory and visual complexity influence the cognitive performance. This research is the first endeavor to investigate the interaction of the two factors on icon complexity.

2 Cognitive Icon Complexity

People retrieve information stored in long-term memory in two ways: episodic memory and semantic memory [9]. Semantic memory is retrieval of knowledge about the world without reference to any specific event, whereas episodic memory refers to retrieval of personally experienced events. The cognitive processing of visual information involves five important components: stimulate, percept, recognize, memory and comprehend. Semantic memory in the memory component directly affects comprehension as recognition is enhanced when stimuli are processed in a semantically meaningful way. Familiarity refers to a fast acting process that reflects a quantitative assessment of memory strength, while similarity plays an associative role and recollection is the retrieval of qualitative contextual information about a previous event [10].

As is shown in Fig. 1, to study the functional interaction of semantic memory and its perceived complexity on cognitive performance, the present study define the icon complexity into two kinds: CP (Complexity of Presentation) and CM (Complexity of Memory). CP represents the basic visual features of icon (shape feature, color feature, texture feature, etc.) in the shallow level of cognitive processing, whereas CM represents the internal relationship (familiarity feature, similarity feature and correlation feature) between memory and image complexity.

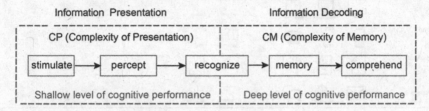

Fig. 1. The Cognitive Process of Icon Design Information

3 Materials and Methods

3.1 Participants

Twenty-eight subjects (15 males and 13 females) were present undergraduates (n = 7), postgraduate (n = 13) and doctoral candidates (n = 8) from Southeast University. They ranged in age from 20 to 35 years, with a mean age of 24 years. They had no color blindness or hypochromatopsia, with the corrected visual acuity over 1.0. They were required to practice and train to know the experimental procedure and operation requirements. Each participant sat in a comfortable chair in a soft light and sound-proofed room, and eyes gazed at the center of the screen. A 21.5-in. CRT monitor with a 1920 × 1080 pixel resolution was used in the experiment. The distance between participant eyes and the screen was approximately 60 cm, while the horizontal and vertical picture viewing angle was within 2.3° [11].

3.2 Materials

The experimental materials were semantic icons selected from real digital interface and the size of icon image is 128 * 128px. As is shown in Fig. 2, eighty-one icons were selected and redesigned based on expert score and Likert scale. Each row represents three same sematic icons in CP under nine semantic category names: Time, Transport, Music, Weather, PC, Message, Document and Movie.

The CP represent three different complexities form low to high: shape feature coding with easy lines, color feature coding with three colors and texture feature coding with design details and background graphics. The three columns represent three

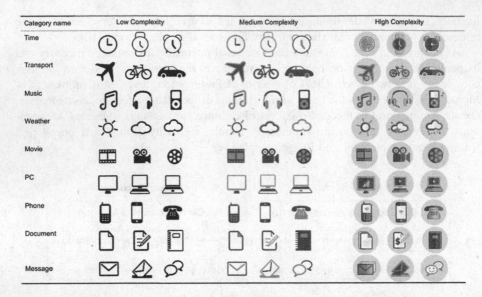

Fig. 2. Semantic icons with CP coding under nine category names

different relationships in CM: familiarity, similarity and correlation, as shown in Fig. 3. Four color combinations were used in color feature from simple to complex: white/black, blue/green, white/green/blue and white/green/blue/beige. These color combinations were proved to improve a subject's visual search performance on an LCD monitor with high vision saliency in highly saturation and brightness [23]. The color value (L, a, b) of the colors used in the present study are shown in Table 1 followed the opponent-color theory.

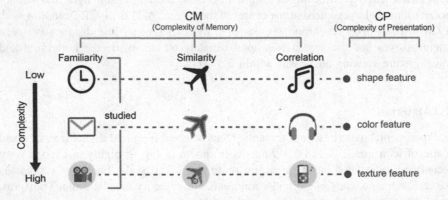

Fig. 3. The experimental materials in CP and CM

Table 1. The Lab value of the colors used in the present study

	Color				
	Green	Blue	Beige	White	Black
L	69	34	90	100	0
a	−54	32	2	0	0
b	51	−68	11	0	0

3.3 Procedures

This experiment was divided into three phases: study phase, distraction phase and test phase. In the study-test blocks, category names were displayed in central vision and then the associated icons were shown to the participants to remember as semantic memory (see Fig. 4A). Then the participants were instructed to do some distract mental arithmetic for 1 min. Test phase involves three test trials: familiarity test (see Fig. 4B), similarity test (see Fig. 4C) and correlation test (see Fig. 4D). Each test trial starts with a fixation cross (+) displayed for 1000 ms in the center of the screen, followed by a blank screen for 200 ms. The semantic icon/word was then presented for 1500 ms, followed by a blank screen for 500 ms and then replaced by nine icons for 2000 ms. Participants were instructed to find which one of the icons was same/similar/correlated to the sematic icon and click the left mouse bottom.

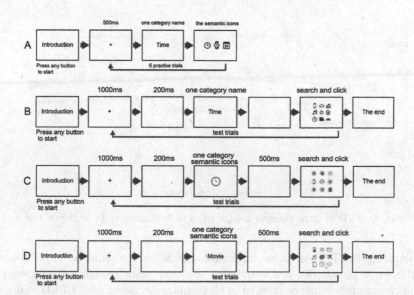

Fig. 4. The schematic of the experimental flow (A) Practice trials. (B) Familiarity test trials. (C) Similarity test trials. (D) Correlation test trials

The eye movement data includes the mouse trajectory, click location, reaction time, TVD (total visit duration), TFD (total fixation count), Gaze Opacity and heat map and which were acquired by Tobii X2-30 Eye-tracking Device in the experiment are recorded for data analysis.

4   Results

4.1   TVD and MFD Data Analysis

In terms of behavioral data in the present experiment, there were 28 subjects, but the data were available in only 24. Behavioral data included the accuracy of target stimulus identification and the reaction time. In normal circumstances, the reaction time includes the visual visit time, the decision making time and the behavioral reaction time. After repeated testing, the decision making time and the behavioral reaction time is constant and the TVD (total visit duration) can be regard as the reaction time. It was found by analyzing the experimental accuracy that the accuracy was over 99 % in all test trials, thus such data were not statistically significant. During the visual processing, when the total time of a certain point over 100 ms can be defined as fixation and then the information processing occurs. The information coding efficiency can be calculated as MFD (mean fixation duration) = TFD (total fixation duration)/TFC (total fixation count) [12]. Therefore, the reaction time analyzed as TVD is described in Fig. 5 and the MFD is described in Fig. 6.

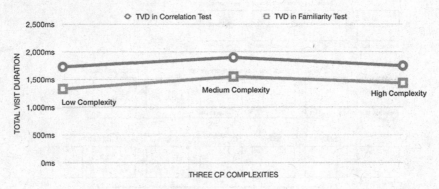

Fig. 5. TVD to three different complexities in familiarity and correlation test

Comparing the TVD of three different complexities for semantic target stimulus identification in familiarity and correlation test, the mean recognition efficiency of familiarity was higher than correlation in all complexity coding as the TVD in the two tests were: 1333.33 ms < 1728.75 ms in Low complexity, 1553.33 ms < 1898.75 ms in medium complexity, 1436.67 ms < 1746.25 ms in high complexity. The information coding efficiency of correlation was higher than familiarity in medium and high complexity as the MFD in the two tests were: 218.89 ms > 213.28 ms in medium complexity, 222.64 ms > 219.10 ms in high complexity, while the MFD in low

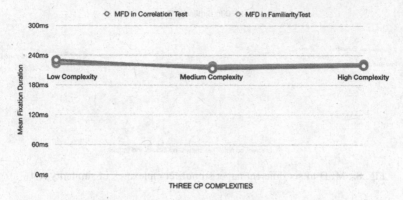

Fig. 6. MFD to three different complexities in familiarity and correlation test

familiarity was 222.96 ms < 230.28 ms which suggested the different excellent coding advantages in familiarity. Moreover, according to the result in MFD two tests, medium complexity in correlation test (MFD = 213.28 ms) was the most efficient, which broke the traditional view that RT is growing by the increased complexity.

In the second similarity test, the search tasks included six kinds of target-stimuli in different complex levels: low-medium, low-high, medium-low, medium-high, high-low and high- medium. The TVD and TFD are shown in Figs. 7 and 8. The result demonstrates the medium-low (1013.33 ms in TVD and 225.93 ms in MFD) is the highest efficiency and low-high (1226.67 ms in TVD and245.9 ms in MFD) and medium-high (1663.33 ms in TVD and 225.93 ms in MFD) are most difficult to be perceived.

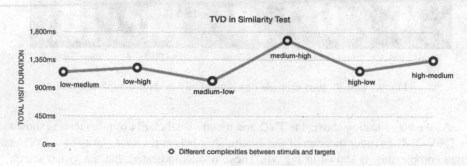

Fig. 7. TVD to six different target-stimuli complexities in similarity test

4.2   Gaze Opacity and Heat Map Data Analysis

The GO (Gaze Opacity) in eye movement data reveals the clear visual scopes and the amount of information processing of an image. The GO assigns different opacities in black and white to represent the gaze degree and the visual search efficiency increased as the GO narrowed and the TVD decreased. With a portfolio analysis of the TVD and

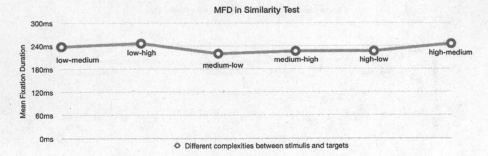

Fig. 8. MFD to six different target-stimuli complexities in similarity test

GO, the search efficiency of the different complexity encodings in three tests can be estimated. As is shown in Fig. 9, the number of icons in the clear visual scopes of GO were counted in ascending order classified from "1" to "5" as the visual clarity. Here, visual clarity is 5 when the number of clear icons > 7 and visual clarity is 1 when the number of clear icons $\leq$ 2.

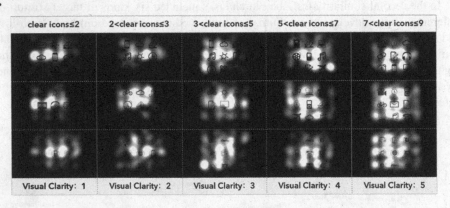

Fig. 9. Classification example of visual clarity in three complexities

As the classification above, the TVD and mean visual clarity of three tests is shown in Table 2. The scatter diagram of the relationship between visual clarity and TVD in three complexities is shown in Fig. 10. These results indicated that the visual search efficiency of medium-low and high-low in similarity test were highest, whereas the visual search efficiency of the medium complexity coding in three tests were lowest. According to these two kinds of target-stimuli in different complex levels, the visual cognitive performance for lower complexity level from higher level was significantly better.

To investigate this problem between the target-stimuli and interested distractors, the heat map of nine high complexity coding materials in the correlation test were used to analysis the interested areas. As shown in Fig. 11, the red dots in the heat map

Table 2. TVD and MVC in three tests

Familiarity test	Low Complexity	Medium Complexity	High Complexity			
TVD (ms)	1333.33	1553.33	1436.67			
Mean Visual Clarity	3	4	4			
Correlation test	Low Complexity	Medium Complexity	High Complexity			
TVD (ms)	1728.75	1898.75	1746.25			
Mean Visual Clarity	5	4	4			
Similarity test (stimuli-target)	Low-Medium	Low-High	Medium-Low	Medium-High	High-Low	High-Medium
TVD (ms)	1153.33	1226.67	1013.33	1663.33	1173.33	1343.33
Mean Visual Clarity	3	2	5	4	5	2

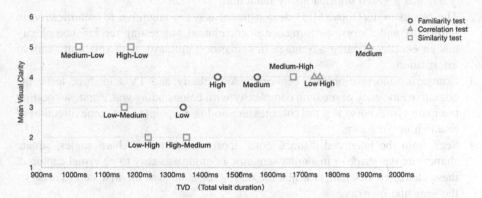

Fig. 10. Scatter diagram of the relationship between visual clarity and TVD in three complexities

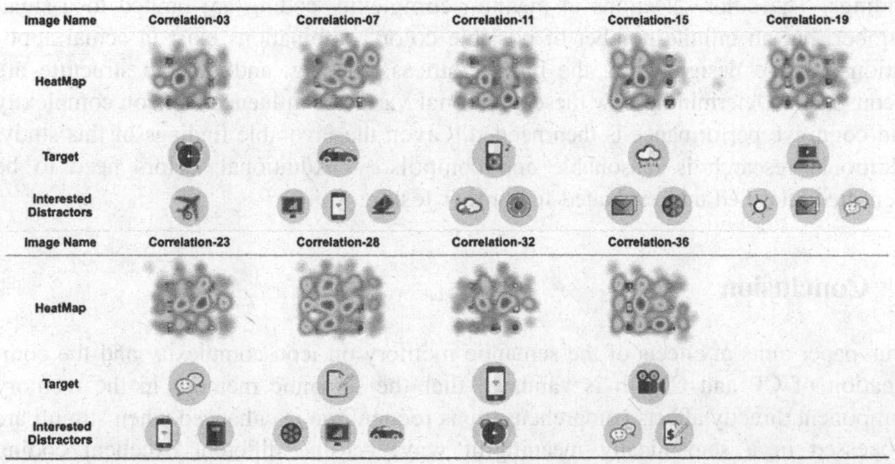

Fig. 11. The heat map, targets and interested distractors in similarity test

represent the most concentrated icons and the results suggested that the most interested distract icons were composed of sharp angles, square shape, circular shape or in similar semantic contour.

5   Discussion

1. The experiment validated the icon complexity of CP and CM in matches the icon complexity, as visual cognitive performance for lower complexity level from higher level was significantly better than from higher level, which prove the perceptual layering decoding processes from easy complexity (CP) to high complexity (CM) was a visual dimensionality reduction.
2. The results in TVD and MFD demonstrated a better cognitive re-identification in familiarity and a worse performance in correlation, suggesting the low complexity has an excellent coding advantage in semantic familiarity with small amounts of information.
3. Comparing the relationships between visual clarity and TVD in three tests, the cognitive efficiency of medium complexity with color-coding was worst, suggesting the main visual noise was the color texture and these pointed out some direction of research in the future.
4. Seen from the interested distract icons, icons composed of sharp angles, square shape, circular shape or in similar semantic contour was easy to be visual captured, these characteristics indicated that the outline of icons was the first step to analysis the semantic memory.

The scope of this paper is limited to the different uses of semantic memory for icon complexity for a meaningful information transmission. The scope of semantic memory can be expanded as there may be some other relevant factors can enhance the cognitive performance. Based on the experimental conclusion, questions are raised about the findings. The color selections in medium complexity coding are limited to a small number, but an infinite number of possible color combinations exist in actual applications. In the design work, the hue, lightness, spacing, and graphic structure are inconsistent. Determining how these additional variables influence the icon complexity and cognitive performance is then needed. Given the favorable findings of this study, additional research is reasonable and compulsory. Additional factors need to be identified, clarified and evaluated for further testing.

6   Conclusion

This paper aims at effects of the semantic memory on icon complexity and the combination of CP and CM. It is validated that the semantic memory in the memory component directly affects comprehension as recognition is enhanced when stimuli are processed in a semantically meaningful way. As the different excellent coding advantages of CP and MP were established in familiarity test, similarity test and correlation test, some icon design points about semantic memory could be clarified by the current study. The two kinds of icon complexity can guide the icon design separately, as users' cognitive efficiency of high complexity coding can be increased in a familiar way, which broke the traditional view that RT is growing by the increased complexity. The data analysis and conclusion of this thesis can provide a novel and valuable efficiency guidance for icon design factors, so as to effectively improve the use efficiency of information icon complexity design in reality.

Acknowledgments. This paper is supported by the National Nature Science Foundation of China Grant No.71471037, 71271053 and the Fundamental Research Funds for the Central Universities and Scientific Innovation Research of College Graduates in Jiangsu Province (No. KYLX15_0062).

References

1. Gittens, D.: Icon-based-human–computer interaction. Int. J. Man-Mach. Stud. **24**, 519–543 (1986)
2. Gobet, F.: Expert memory: a comparison of four theories. Cognition **66**(2), 115–152 (1998)
3. Garcia, M., Badre, A.N., Stasko, J.T.: Development and validation of icons varying in their abstractness. Interact. Comput. **6**, 191–211 (1994)
4. McDougall, S.J.P., Curry, M.B., de Bruijn, O.: Measuring symbol and icon characteristics: norms for concreteness, complexity, meaningfulness, familiarity, and semantic distance for 239 symbols. Behav. Res. Methods Instrum. Comput. **31**, 487–519 (1999)
5. Cardaci, M., Di Gesù, V., Petrou, M., et al.: Fuzzy Sets Syst. A fuzzy approach to the evaluation of image complexity **160**, 1474–1484 (2009)
6. Harber, R.N., Hershenson, M.: The Psychology of Visual Perception. Holt, Rinehart & Winston, New York (1973)
7. Forsythe, A., Mulhern, G., Sawey, M.: Confounds in pictorial sets: the role of complexity and familiarity in basic-level picture processing. Behav. Res. Methods **40**, 116–129 (2008)
8. Johansson, M., Mecklinger, A., Treese, A.C.: Recognition memory for emotional and neutral faces: and event-related potential study. Cogn. Neurosci. **16**, 1840–1853 (2004)
9. Tulving, E., Donaldson, W.: Organisation of Memory, pp. 381–403. Academic Press, New York (1972)
10. Greve, A., Van Rossum, M.C., Donaldson, D.I.: Investigating the functional interaction between semantic and episodic memory: convergent behavioral and electrophysiological evidence for the role of familiarity. NeuroImage **34**, 801–814 (2007)
11. Wang, H.L., Feng, T.Y., Suo, T., Liang, J., Meng, X.X., Li, H.: The process of counterfactual thinking after decision-making: Evidence from an ERP study. Chin. Sci. Bull. **55**, 1113–1121 (2010)
12. Kammerer, Y., Gerjets, P.: Effects of search interface and internet-specific epistemic beliefs on source evaluations during web search for medical information: an eye-tracking study. Behav. Inform. Technol. **31**, 83–97 (2012)

Cognitive Relevance Mechanism Analysis of DHCI Structure and Composition

Lei Zhou[1(✉)], Chengqi Xue[1], Haiyan Wang[1], Jing Zhang[1],
Xiaojiao Chen[1], Xiaozhou Zhou[1], Yafeng Niu[1], and Tao Jin[2]

[1] School of Mechanical Engineering, Southeast University, Nanjing, China
zhoulei@seu.edu.cn
[2] School of Mechanical and Electrical Engineering,
China University of Petroleum, Qingdao, China
52592736@qq.com

Abstract. Organizational conflict and phenotypical conflict are fundamental reasons that reduce human-computer interactive efficiency through digital interface. In order to solve these problems, doing research on cognitive relevance mechanism of DHCI structure and composition is necessary. This paper first constructed theoretical model between DHCI information design and user cognition. Second, introduced current research status of related field both domestic and foreign. Finally, proposed an experiment plan on 3 different smart phone App designs, elaborated the experiment objective and procedure. This research provided a new thinking way for DHCI information design.

Keywords: DHCI · Interface structure · Interface composition · User cognition · Cognitive relevance

1 Contradiction Mechanism of DHCI Information Design and User Cognition

In recent years, digital human-computer interface (DHCI) has been widely used in many fields, which has greatly alleviated the crisis in information presentation space, which exists because of information expanse. Information presentation mode has been changed from tile-type entity presentation forms into blocks, hierarchical integration forms. Users no longer need to frequently go back and forth between multiple panels, but interactive problems between human and machine/computer have not been fundamentally resolved. On the contrary, new issues such as information loss, focus chaos has intensified. Well, how these phenomena happened?

Superficially, the users' low searching efficiency is caused by unreasonable interface visual presentation; the users can't find their objectives. But this kind of thinking way neglects the effect of information structure, which has obvious guiding effect on the users. For example, by the influence of the mental schema of the Gestalt psychology, information blocks usually cause uniting process of the information-in-block and selective shield of the information in other blocks. As the result, closely related information should apply the nearest, grouped presentation mode. Another example, super link can improve information connectivity, on the other side, the possibility of

D. Harris (Ed.): EPCE 2016, LNAI 9736, pp. 158–166, 2016.
DOI: 10.1007/978-3-319-40030-3_17

information loss grows greatly. The users may leave their objectives farther and farther because of easy link, even completely change their target.

1.1 Organizational Conflict Between Interface Information and User Cognition

In the environment of digital information, organizational conflict between interface information and user cognition is caused by flexible information requirement and rigid interface structure. Human's information requirement has 3 dimensions— information, relation and time dimension, information and relation could group together easily because of time axis. But DHCI just has 2 dimensions—information and relation, it's flat type. Against dynamic information requirement in our brain, the information structure on the interface is fixed and static. Users need to frequently jump from one level to the other to remedy the loss of time axis. So, dimension difference is the root of organizational conflict that influences our memory schema to extract and match information.

1.2 Phenotypical Conflict Between Interface Information and User Cognition

Phenotypical conflict reflects in the discrepancy between theoretical route and the realistic route. In principle, users get their goals according to the prepared information structure. But actually, the information to people is concrete and graphical, users need to read the figures first to decode the meaning. It's prone to be disturbed by image influence, people's attention schema may not in line with their searching objective.

As shown in Fig. 1, the balance between user and DHCI contains two parts— structure balance and composition balance. Structure balance arises from time dimension loss on the interface, and composition balance arises from figuration of design and conceptualization of cognition and structure. As an analogy, information structure and composition are like the bone and the flesh, the figure we could see relies on the support of bone, but this kind of support effect can be easily omitted because of its concealment.

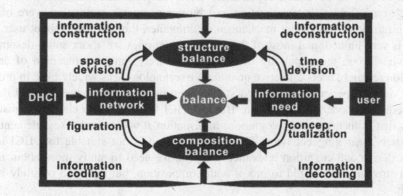

Fig. 1. DHCI structure and composition relevance mechanism

In the end of the analysis, information structure has leading impact on the composition, and the composition is the performance of structure. Then, the problem appears, how the information structure and composition of interface affect people's cognition? This article intends to start a research in order to solve this problem.

2 Research Situation in China and Abroad

In related field, scholars in China and abroad have done much detailed research and got some achievement, which can be listed as follows:

In the field of information process, researches were conducted on information filter, information compression technologies. Some described a large-scale implementation of a video recommendation system in use by the largest media group in Latin America [1]. Some designed methods to solve the afore-mentioned problems for patent retrieval [2–4]. Some presented and illustrated a procedure for similarity analysis of the large data compression [5]. Some proposed methods through reducing the principal component vector to cut the amount of information [6, 7].

In the field of information visualization field, some analyze the visualizing large, heterogeneous data in hybrid-reality environments [8]. Some elaborated data flow under different time scales through concrete examples [9, 10]. The use of graph ordering algorithms for visual analysis of data sets using visual similarity matrices was proposed [11].

In the field of human-computer interactive field, some researched visual analysis instruments that influence cognition and decision-making [12, 13]. Some studied interactive learning materials in mathematics or other fields [14, 15]. Some studied a number of foundational concepts related to interaction and complex cognitive activities syncretized into a coherent theoretical framework [16, 17].

In the field of image thinking and cognitive science, many researches were about the image thinking and cognitive organs [18–21]. Affective design were also interested in the origins and models that arose consumer lure [22–32].

In summary, current studies paid more attention to data transferring, information filter, information compression fields, and the technologies are relatively mature enough to provide an effective guarantee for DHCI fundamental construction. And research on information visualization and human-computer interaction were mainly about information processing mechanism of computer, the real study about user cognition is very limited, and most of the small amount ones are about entity design and functional layout, the popularity of the results is very finite. In the field of design cognition research, users' affective quantitative technology was widely used in product design, users experience and related studies, and established some emotional design and prediction models for cognition. But in DHCI field, affective element is just one factors that influences users' cognition, information structure is the key element that leads users' searching behavior. The existed method is not suitable to DHCI information design and cognition relevance analysis, we need to study more about information structure, and forbid to mix it with composition, but this kind of study is not enough.

3 Cognitive Relevance Experiment Design of Information Structure and Information Composition

3.1 Experiment Design

The experiment is planned to test under the premise of the same composition variables, how the structure discrepancy influence cognitive effect. Smart phone interface is chosen for cognitive relevance study of information structure and information composition. The reason of this choice is because smart phone interface has become into one of the most familiar DHCI in our daily life with the flourish of mobile service. Choosing the App layout of smart phone as the typical example of DHCI information structure also shows great similar characteristics with webpage interface and system interface, which presents great public awareness and universal conclusion.

Experiment task is designed as finding pointed App in different information structures, and main cognitive index are searching time and correct rate. Experiment applies the same App icons as the composition to control the discrepancy of information composition to cognitive effect.

This experiment applies single probe change examine paradigm, single task experiment. It requires subjects remember App icon first, then find the target App icon on the interface. This experiment contains 3 different kinds of information structures. Among them, structure 1 is constitute of 75 App icons, 5 parallel pages and 4 shortcut keys (Fig. 2), 75 App icons are exhibited on 5 pages respectively, shortcut keys are posited at the bottom of the interface. Each searching risk is started with an initial page not locating the objective (except the shortcut keys), subjects can shift from pages through clicking the © mark on the interface. Its information structure can be abstractly represented in Fig. 3. The white circle represents form element, which means group or node in structures, while the black circle represents goal element, which here means App icons.

Fig. 2. Structure 1 interface

Structure 2 consists 1 main page, 4 shortcut keys and 7 files, each file contains 9 App icons (Fig. 4). Different from structure 1, subjects can get into sub-pages through clicking files, and get back to the main page through clicking blank space. Choose the

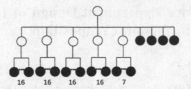

Fig. 3. Abstract structure 1

Fig. 4. Structure 2 interface

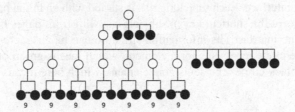

Fig. 5. Abstract structure 2

non-objective page as the initial page except the shortcut key to ensure the integrity of the route. The App layout in structure 2 are very different from structure 1. Its information structure can be abstractly represented in Fig. 5.

Structure 3 contains 2 parallel pages, each page have 6 files, which accommodate 4 to 6 App icons, no shortcut key design (Fig. 6). Subjects can use the ◎ icon to shift from main pages at the middle lower part of the interface; Meanwhile, they can also get into the sub-page through clicking the file, and get out of it through clicking the blank space just like the operation in structure 2. Attention is paid to set the initial page for searching to ensure the route integrity. Interface layout is set different from structure 1 and 2 to forbid memory effect. Its information structure can be abstractly represented in Fig. 7.

The experiment is planned to apply 3*75 within-subjects design. Factor 1 is structures, with 3 levels—structure 1, 2 and 3; Factor 2 is 75 App searching task.

Fig. 6. Structure 3 interface

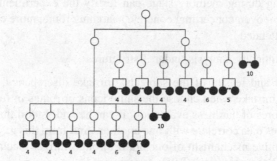

Fig. 7. Abstract structure 3

This experiment will last 3 days, in each day 1 structure 75 searching is tested, App presentation turn is pseudorandom, and the experiment procedure is shown in Fig. 8.

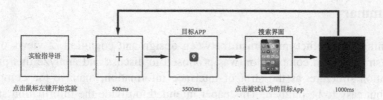

Fig. 8. Experiment procedure

This experiment is planned to use E-prime software for programming. The subjects are to be told the test content and train before formal experiment. First present the target App icon, and start to timing. Subjects remember the objective and press the preset key to enter the test smart phone interface. Then the timing of memory part is over and the timing of searching part is on. Subjects are asked to press the preset key when find the goal, then finish the time keeping of searching part, record the App icon clicked. And then defer 1 s to get into the next task. Make 15 tasks a group, and take a break of 1 min after each group. When 3days' experiment is over, ask the subjects immediately how is their feeling about the difficulties of the 3 layouts, set 3 levels of hard, medium and easy, with the mark of 3, 2, 1. The subjects are required to score their hardness evaluation.

3.2   Experiment Destination

(1) Variance analysis of memory and searching time under 3 structures

Under 3 different structures, subjects' reaction can be divided into memory and searching stages individually. The time consuming during searching stage can reflect the relationship between DHCI information structure and cognitive performance, while the time consuming during memory stage can testify the experiment reliability from another aspect. Moreover, concerning concrete searching route, more complex compare analysis can be extended.

(2) Mistake and difficulty analysis under 3 structures

Analyze the trend and reason of the subjects' mistake discrepancy, and explain the potential cause of mistake when choose the same icons or routes in further. According to the subjects' scores of hardness evaluation, it can be understood that how introspect and instant activities data correlate with one another. And from this result, we can study more hidden cognitive mechanism of our brain through further electroencephalogram (EEG) or event related potentials (ERP) experiments.

(3) The influence from information composition to structure

In these 3 kinds of structures, No. 1 has 2 levels, while No. 2 and 3 have 3 levels. Through this experiment design, we can compare the sophisticated cognitive differences of compositions in the same structure or level.

4   Summary

Concerning the conflict mechanism between design and cognition, 2 views of information structure and composition was proposed to discuss and analyze this problem. Information structure, as the strut of interface information, manage the composition format but easy to be omitted. This paper intended to divide the information structure and composition effects in cognitive process by controlling the experiment variables, so as to study the related mechanism. This study could provide theoretical reference and intelligent supply for human-computer interaction research in many fields such as design science, information science, cognitive science, system science and ergonomics.

Acknowledgement. This paper is supported by Natural fund of Jiangsu Province (No. BK20150636), National Natural Science Foundation of China (No. 71471037, 71271053, 51405514).

References

1. Pereira, R., Lopes, H., Breitman, K., et al.: Cloud based real-time collaborative filtering for item–item recommendations. Comput. Ind. **65**, 279–290 (2014)
2. Chen, Y.-L., Chiu, Y.-T.: An IPC-based vector space model for patent retrieval. Inf. Process. Manage. **47**, 309–322 (2011)
3. 吴洪波. 大规模信息过滤技术研究及其在 Web 问答系统中的应用. 中国科学院计算技术研究所 (2003)
4. 谷文成,柴宝仁,韩俊松. 基于支持向量机的垃圾信息过滤方法. 北京理工大学学报, vol. 10, pp. 1062–1071 (2013)
5. Vachkov, G., Ishihara, H.: On-line unsupervised learning for information compression and similarity analysis of large data sets. In: Proceedings of Mechatronics and Automation 2007 (ICMA 2007), Harbin, pp. 105–110 (2007)
6. Notsu, A., Honda, K., Ichihashi, H., et al.: Information compression effect based on PCA for reinforcement learning agents' communication. In: Proceedings of the 13th International Symposium on Advanced Intelligent Systems (ISIS), Kobe, pp. 1318–1321 (2012)
7. 王清波. 基于信息压缩的无线植入式脑机接口中算法及系统研究. 浙江大学 (2011)
8. Khairi, R., Alessandro, F., Aaron, K.: Visualizing large, heterogeneous data in hybrid-reality environments. IEEE Comput. Graph. Appl. **33**(4), 38–48 (2013)
9. James, C., Michael, B.: Visualisation tools for understanding big data. Environ. Planning B Planning Des. **39**(3), 413–415 (2012)
10. Basole, R.C., Clear, T., Hu, M.: Understanding interfirm relationships in business ecosystems with interactive visualization. IEEE Trans. Visual. Comput. Graph. **19**(12), 2526–2535 (2013)
11. Mueller, C., Martin, B., Lumsdaine, A.: A comparison of vertex ordering algorithms for large graph visualization. In: Sydney, AUSTRALIA: Asia/Pacific Symposium on Visualisation 2007, 141–148 (2007)
12. Sedig, K., Ola, O.: The challenge of big data in public health: an opportunity for visual analytics. Online J. Publ. Health Inf. **5**(3), 1–21 (2014)
13. Kelton, A.S., Pennington, R.R.: Internet financial reporting: the effects of information presentation format and content differences on investor decision making. Comput. Hum. Behav. **28**(4), 1178–1185 (2012)
14. Noroozi, O., Busstra, M.C., Mulder, M., et al.: Online discussion compensates for suboptimal timing of supportive information presentation in a digitally supported learning environment. Educ. Technol. Res. Dev. **60**(2), 193–221 (2012)
15. Parsons, P., Sedig, K.: Adjustable properties of visual representations: improving the quality of human-information interaction. J. Assoc. Inf. Sci. Technol. **65**(3), 455–482 (2014)
16. Sedig, K., Parsons, P.: Interaction design for complex cognitive activities with visual representations: a pattern-based approach. AIS Trans. Hum. Comput. Interact. **5**(2), 84–133 (2013)
17. Du, H.M., Yu, W.D.: The study of graphic design encoding based on knowledge coupling. Procedia Soc. Behav. Sci. **51**, 480–488 (2012)
18. 董军.形象思维模拟的可能途径. 世界科技研究与发展, 28(3) (2006)
19. Hai-shan, Y., Chao-yi, L.: Clustered organization of neurons with similar extra-receptive field properties in the primary visual cortex. Neuron **35**, 547–553 (2002)
20. Anderson, M.L.: Evolution of cognitive function via redeployment of brain areas. Neuroscientist **13**(2), 13–21 (2007)
21. Schnitzler, A., Gross, J.: Normal and pathological oscillatory communication in the brain. Nat. Rev. Neurosci. **6**(4), 285–296 (2005)

22. 潘云鹤.形象思维中的形象信息模型的研究. 模式识别与人工智能, 4(4), 7–14 (1991)

23. 罗仕鉴,朱上上,应放天等.产品设计中的用户隐性知识研究现状与进展. 计算机集成制造系统, 16(4) (2010)

24. Dorst, K., Cross, N.: Creativity in the design process: co-evolution of problem-solution. Des. Stud. **22**, 425–437 (2001)

25. 秦忠宝.基于混合知识表示的设计创新及知识获取研究. 西北工业大学 (2006)

26. Xu, S., Lau, F.C.M., Tang, F., Pan, Y.: Advanced design for a realistic virtual brush. Comput. Graph. Forum **22**(3), 533–542 (2003)

27. 张艳河,杨颖,罗仕鉴等.产品设计中用户感知意象的思维结构. 机械工程学报, 46(2) (2010)

28. Desmet, P.M.A., Monk, A.F., Overbeeke, K., Wright, P.C.: Measuring emotion: development and application of an instrument to measure emotional responses to products, pp. 111–123 (2003)

29. Khalid, H.M., Helander, M.G.: Customer emotional needs in product design. Concurrent Eng. **14**(3), 197–206 (2006)

30. Desmet, P.M.A., Hekkert, P.: Framework of product experience. Int. J. Des. **1**(1), 57–66 (2007)

31. Hsee, C.K., Tsai, C.I.: Hedonomics in consumer behavior. In: Handbook of Consumer Psychology, pp. 639–658 (2008)

32. Yua, N., Kong, J.: User experience with web browsing on small screens: experimental investigations of mobile-page interface design and homepage design for news websites. Inf. Sci. **330**(10), 427–443 (2016)

Team Cognition

Human-Agent Teaming for Effective Multirobot Management: Effects of Agent Transparency

Michael J. Barnes[1], Jessie Y.C. Chen[1(✉)], Julia L. Wright[1], and Kimberly Stowers[2]

[1] U.S. Army Research Laboratory,
Aberdeen Proving Ground, Aberdeen, MD, USA
{michael.j.barnes.civ,yun-sheng.c.chen.civ,
julia.l.wright8.civ}@mail.mil
[2] University of Central Florida, Orlando, FL, USA
kstowers@ist.ucf.edu

Abstract. The U.S. Army Research Laboratory is engaged in a multi-year program focusing on the human role in supervising autonomous vehicles. We discuss this research with regard to patterns of human/intelligent agent (IA) interrelationships, and explore the dynamics of these patterns in terms of supervising multiple autonomous vehicles. The first design pattern focuses on a human operator controlling multiple autonomous vehicles via a single IA. The second design pattern involves multiple intelligent systems including (a) human operator, (b) IA-asset manager, (c) IA-planning manager, (d) IA-mission monitor, and (e) multiple autonomous vehicles. Both scenarios require a single operator to control multiple heterogeneous autonomous vehicles, and yet the complexity of both the mission variables and the relations among the autonomous vehicles makes efficient operations by a single operator difficult at best. Key findings of two recent research programs are summarized with an emphasis on their implications for developing future systems with similar design patterns. Our conclusions stress the importance of operator situation awareness, not only of the immediate environment, but also of the IA's intent, reasoning and predicted outcomes.

Keywords: Intelligent agents · Transparency · Patterns of human–agent interaction · Human factors · Supervisory control

1 Introduction

Autonomous systems are becoming part of the framework of American life. They are also changing the dynamics of future combat in ways that are not altogether predictable. Although the advantages are obvious (e.g., reduction in casualties, force multiplication and increased capabilities) [1, 2] their disadvantages (e.g., possible fratricides, civilian casualties, and mission disruptions) can only be estimated [3, 4]. It is important not only to minimize the potential dangers of autonomy but also to increase tactical flexibility by developing user interfaces that ensure that humans have ultimate decision authority [5].

© Springer International Publishing Switzerland 2016
D. Harris (Ed.): EPCE 2016, LNAI 9736, pp. 169–178, 2016.
DOI: 10.1007/978-3-319-40030-3_18

When human operators must supervise or control many systems, the problems are multiplicative [6]. The operator, who is bounded by short-term memory limitations, must maintain situation awareness (SA) of a dynamic and potentially volatile environment while supervising multiple heterogeneous autonomous vehicles (AVs) [5]. To address these challenges, we discuss the implications of patterns of interaction between software-based intelligent agents (IA) and humans, and give examples of experiments that verify their usefulness (see [7] for an overview of design patterns for human-cognitive agent teaming). The definition of an IA varies [8]. In this context, an IA acts autonomously in the sense that it processes environmental information, has clear-cut objectives, and develops courses of actions (COAs) to achieve its objectives. Patterns of interaction refer to reusable human–agent architectures which are adapted to multiple problem spaces that share generic features. Below, we discuss two patterns which manage the type (or level) of information necessary for the human to supervise the IA while simultaneously maintaining SA of both the unfolding environment and the IA's intent, reasoning, and perceived outcomes. The first pattern is relatively simple and involves the human interacting with a single supervisory agent that serves as an intermediary and supervisor for multiple AVs. The second pattern requires the operator to interact with multiple intermediate agents. These agents can interact with each other but each is dedicated to a specific task: choosing the heterogeneous AVs, developing a route plan, and monitoring the AVs' progress. The purpose of identifying effective patterns is to pinpoint essential elements of human–agent systems for possible generic solutions in complex environments. Specifically, our emphasis in this effort is on determining the effectiveness of IA transparency in promoting operator awareness of both the physical environment and the IA's assumptions about the environment [8]. The construct of transparency and its application to patterns of human-IA interaction is discussed below.

2   The Situation Awareness-Based Agent Transparency (SAT) Model

Operator trust is an important research topic for both automated and autonomous systems, as it is a key determinant in the calibration of reliance on such systems. Trust can be measured either as an attitude (subjective measure) or as a behavior [9]. Subjective scales have been shown to correlate with automation reliability, the perception of the IA's capabilities, and task difficulties as well as individual differences [10]. Lee and See [11] defined appropriate trust as human reliance on automation that minimizes disuse (failure to rely on reliable automation) and misuse (over-relying on unreliable automation) [12]. Lee [13] suggested that to make the underpinnings of the automation algorithm transparent, it is necessary to display the purpose, process and performance (3-Ps) of the automation, with the caveat that too much information is counterproductive. Based on these and related concepts, U.S. Army Research Laboratory researchers developed a Situation awareness-based Agent Transparency (SAT) model (Fig. 1) to elucidate aspects of SA affecting trust [8]. SAT posits three transparency levels (L) of information to support the operator's SA of the IA's decision process: (a.) L1 – IA's actions and intent (b.) L2 – IA's reasoning process, (c.) L3 – IA's predicted outcomes and uncertainty [14, 15]. The purpose of the SAT model is to define the type of information necessary to give the operator insight into the IA's basic plan, its intent, reasoning process and its objective end-state. Our hypothesis is that each level of transparency contributes to improving operators' appropriate trust calibration. However, an obvious problem of managing n-systems is that the SAT information for multiple systems could easily overwhelm the operator.

- To support operator's **Level 1 SA** *(What's going on and what is the agent trying to achieve?)*
  - *Purpose*
    - *Desire* (Goal selection)
  - *Process*
    - *Intentions* (Planning/Execution)
    - Progress
  - *Performance*
- To support operator's **Level 2 SA** *(Why does the agent do it?)*
  - Reasoning process *(Belief)(Purpose)*
    - Environmental & other constraints
- To support operator's **Level 3 SA** *(What should the operator expect to happen?)*
  - Projection to Future/End State
  - Potential limitations
    - Uncertainty; Likelihood of error
    - History of performance

Fig. 1. The SAT model [8]

3 Pattern 1: Supervisory Agent

Autonomy and the necessity of human supervision appear to be contradictory. Especially when the operator is managing multiple systems, supervising many autonomous systems would seem to defeat the purpose of making them autonomous in the first place. The first pattern (Fig. 2) uses the power of an IA to reduce operator workload while maintaining the human's decision prerogatives. The IA (RoboLeader) acts as an intermediate supervisor monitoring the lower level systems and reporting back to the human supervisor through a chat window. Furthermore, the IA suggests an algorithmic solution to the operator who can either implement the IA's solution or use the operator's own solution [16].

The advantage of this pattern is that the human operator can multitask, monitor the AVs when alerted by the IA, and also determine the utility of the agent's solution to the

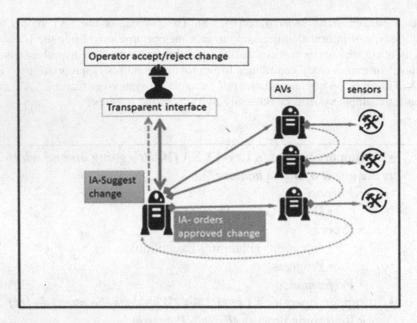

Fig. 2. Pattern 1, the IA (RoboLeader) supervises AVs and suggests re-planning when the AVs original plan is no longer feasible, requiring the human operator to either accept the IA's re-plan or over-ride the IA.

alerted problem. Multiple research projects have used the RoboLeader paradigm to explore a number of pertinent human-agent teaming issues, including manipulating the number of AVs supervised, IA reliability, the degree of autonomy, the type of autonomy, and IA transparency [8, 16–19]. The paradigm proved to be effective in numerous simulated combat-related scenarios, resulting in a variety of useful human-agent design guidelines [1, 8]. In general, results showed that the RoboLeader agent benefitted the operators' concurrent task performance and reduced their workload while allowing operators to maintain their SA. Importantly, individual differences in gaming experience, spatial abilities, and perceived attentional control proved to be crucial factors in human-agent interactions—implying that training and decision support should be geared to individual aptitudes and experience—not "one size fits all" solutions [8].

Pertaining to our current emphasis on the role of transparency in trust calibration, our lab recently examined the efficacy of SAT level-2 information (reasoning explanation) during convoy operations [19]. In this effort, operators monitored an unmanned aerial vehicle (UAV), a manned ground vehicle (MGV), and an unmanned ground vehicle (UGV). We focused on IA reasoning transparency by manipulating the amount of explanatory information conveyed to the operator during high workload mission segments: the operator was monitoring three assets while also detecting threats to their own vehicle using the 360° SA displays (Fig. 3). The IA advisories (which made suggestions concerning when to re-route the convoy) were only accurate 66 % of the time, requiring the operator to monitor the situation continually.

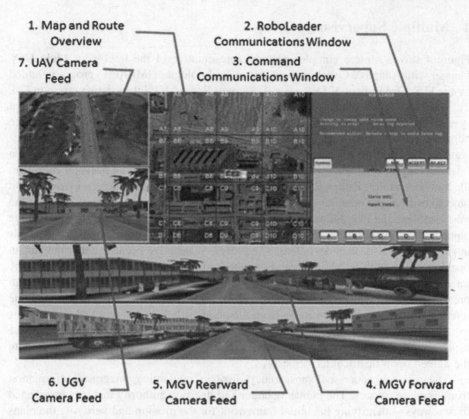

1. Map and Route Overview

7. UAV Camera Feed

2. RoboLeader Communications Window

3. Command Communications Window

6. UGV Camera Feed

5. MGV Rearward Camera Feed

4. MGV Forward Camera Feed

Fig. 3. Operator control unit for convoy operations requiring monitoring multiple elements, identifying threats and making convoy route changes based on command updates.

The results supported our hypothesis that explanatory information (e.g., "Change to convoy path recommended: Activity in area: Dense Fog") would reduce misuse of automation. Operators rejected incorrect advisories significantly more often when given the rationale for the advisory. However, adding non-essential information to the explanation (a time stamp which was potentially useful to determine if the explanation is current) contributed to misuse of IA by decreasing correct rejections. This finding supports Lee's [13] argument that when adding information to increase the transparency of a display, the information must adhere to the environment (or the task) for which it was intended. In Wright et al.'s case, a parsimonious explanation improved the ability of the operator to override incorrect advisories. In summary, having an IA interface between the AVs and the operator decision-maker proved to be a useful pattern of AV control under a variety of experimental conditions [8]. The caveat is that successful interaction between the IA and the operator depended on concise display formats that provided insight into the IA's reasoning.

4 Multiple Supervisory Agents

Figure 4 shows a more complex pattern representative of the Intelligent Multi-UxV Planner with Adaptive Collaborative/Control Technologies (IMPACT) program funded by the U.S. Department of Defense's Autonomy Research Pilot Initiative program [20, 21]. IMPACT researchers are investigating issues associated with multiple intelligent systems interacting both with one another and with the human operator to execute numerous combat missions. They are independent in the sense that each IA can generate a COA, and they are interdependent in the sense that to successfully complete a mission, they must interact with one another while taking their final decision cues from the human operator. Pattern 2 involves an Asset Manager agent which receives mission objectives from the operator and decides which AVs and sensors are best suited to the mission. Next, the Plan Manager compiles plans for routing the vehicles to arrive at the objective at a particular time whereas the Mission Monitor agent monitors the AVs in-route progress for plan deviations. The process is adaptive because either the human operator or the Mission Monitor can interrupt the mission and start the process over by interacting with the Asset Manager and Plan Manager to develop a revised plan to present to the operator. Each system tries to optimize mission objectives and the integrated plan requires permission from the operator before the Asset Manager gives execution instructions to the AVs. In Fig. 4, the integrator is the Asset Manager whose tasks include generating the information for the transparency display as well as sending the agreed upon instructions to the AVs.

The research addressed transparency displays containing integrated information from multiple sources. The human operator had decision authority that was manifested in two ways—identifying the initial framework for the mission and verifying the plans supplied by the Asset Manager. In our experiments, information integrated into the Asset Manager was used to generate three levels of SAT including: L1 – plan elements, L2 – rationale, and L3 – IA's predicted outcomes and uncertainty. We conducted two studies to investigate the effects of agent transparency on operators' task performance and trust. Because of the inherent complexity of the experimental conditions, the displays (Fig. 5) used in the experiments contained SAT information on the map, in text, as well as on graphics developed by U.S. Air Force researchers [22]. In addition, the user interface had tactical alerts from the command module showing the commander's intent, environmental, and situational changes. We explored interface options over two experiments in an attempt to isolate the effects of SAT levels and interface features. In particular, in the second experiment, we changed the L3 interface to better display the projected outcomes. L3 information was conveyed using the Air Force's revised graphics showing the relative weights of the predicted outcomes (e.g., time to target, fuel consumption, sensor coverage) on an integrated line graph [22].

In the first simulation experiment, we investigated the SAT model by incrementally varying the type of SAT level (L1 vs. L1 + 2 vs. L1 + 2 + 3) with scenarios counterbalanced over conditions. Each scenario developed a base defense vignette such as an unknown craft spotted near the shoreline adjacent to the naval base. The participants were given two options (A and B) that resulted in different asset compositions (naval, ground or aerial AVs), planned routes, and type of sensors. Updates from the command

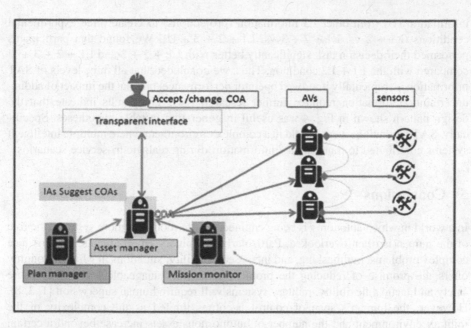

Fig. 4. N- intelligent systems coordinating planning, executing, and monitoring a dynamic mission by sending mission instructions to N autonomous vehicles after receiving guidance from the operator.

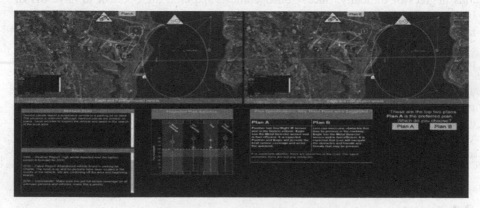

Fig. 5. The improved transparency display used in the second experiment showing the relative outcomes predicted for options A and B.

modules supporting either plan A (IAs' favored COA) or B (IAs' less favored option) are shown in Fig. 5. The results indicated that trust calibration (correct rejections and correct positive responses-hits) improved for the latter two conditions compared with the L1 (baseline information) condition. Additionally, subjective trust scores also increased for the third condition (L1 < L1 + 2 + 3) [23]. In the second experiment, aside from improving the user interface as discussed above, we separated the uncertainty information (U) from other L3 information (projections) to create three experimental conditions (L1 + 2 vs. L1 + 2 + 3 vs. L1 + 2 + 3 + U). We found that participants performed their decision task significantly better with L1 + 2 + 3 and L1 + 2 + 3 + U compared with the L1 + L2 condition. Thus, we concluded that all three levels of SAT information incrementally improved operator performance, but that the impact of adding uncertainty information required further research [24]. The results indicate that the design pattern shown in Fig. 4 was useful in generating testable hypotheses. Specifically, SAT predictions were upheld in a complex environment where multiple intelligent systems contributed to transparency information during realistic tri-service scenarios.

5   Conclusions

In a world in which autonomy is being engineered into more and more systems, the role of the human is often overlooked. Particularly in military environments, humans face complex problems, multitasking, and increased volatility; situations in which autonomy offers the promise of reducing the problem space to manageable levels. To ensure safety and tactical flexibility, military systems will require human supervision [1–3, 8]. However, the human's span of control becomes limited as the complexity of the military environment and the number of autonomous assets increase beyond a certain limit [6]. Two patterns of autonomous control were discussed that reduced supervisory loading while ensuring human control of multiple heterogeneous autonomous assets. In both paradigms, humans interacted with IAs to control autonomous assets under various degrees of difficulty. Successful operations required the operator to have SA of both the changing military situation and the IAs' decision-making processes. The SAT model of transparency was tested for both patterns indicating the feasibility of effective supervisory control by enhancing the operator understanding of the IA's intent, reasoning, and projected outcomes [8, 14, 19, 23, 24].

Acknowledgements. This research was supported by the U.S. Department of Defense Autonomy Research Pilot Initiative, under the Intelligent Multi-UxV Planner with Adaptive Collaborative/ Control Technologies (IMPACT) project. The authors wish to thank Olivia Newton, Ryan Wohleber, Nicholas Kasdaglis, Michael Rupp, Daniel Barber, Jonathan Harris, Gloria Calhoun, and Mark Draper for their contribution to this project.

References

1. Barnes, M.J., Chen, J.Y., Jentsch, F., Redden, E.S.: Designing effective soldier-robot teams in complex environments: training, interfaces, and individual differences. In: Harris, D. (ed.) HCII 2011. LNCS, vol. 6781, pp. 484–493. Springer, Heidelberg (2011)
2. U.S. Department of Defense, Briefing on Autonomy Initiatives (2012)
3. U.S. Defense Science Board: Role of Autonomy in DoD Systems. Office of the Undersecretary of Defense, Washington, D.C. (2012)

4. Endsley, M.: Autonomous Horizons: System Autonomy in the Air Force – A Path to the Future (Volume I: Human Autonomy Teaming). U.S. Department of the Air Force, Washington (2015)
5. Chen, J.Y.C., Barnes, M.J.: Human-agent teaming for multirobot control: a review of human factors issues. IEEE Trans. Hum. Mach. Syst. **44**, 13–29 (2014)
6. Lewis, M.: Human interaction with multiple remote robots. Rev. Hum. Factors Ergon. **9**, 131–174 (2013)
7. Schulte, A., Donath, D., Lange, D.: Design patterns for human-cognitive agent teaming. In: Conference on Engineering Psychology & Cognitive Ergonomics. Lecture Notes on Computer Science, Springer (2016)
8. Chen, J.Y.C., Procci, K., Boyce, M., Wright, J., Garcia, A., Barnes, M.J.: Situation awareness–based agent transparency. Technical report ARL–TR–6905, U.S. Army Research Laboratory, Aberdeen Proving Ground, Maryland (2014)
9. Meyer, J., Lee, J.: Trust, Reliance, Compliance. In: Lee, J., Kirlik, A. (eds.) The Oxford Handbook of Cognitive Engineering. Oxford University Press, Oxford (2013)
10. Schaefer, K.E., Billings, D.R., Szalma, J.L., Adams, J., Sanders, T.L., Chen, J.Y.C., Hancock, P.A.: A meta-analysis of factors influencing the development of trust in automation: implications for human-robot interaction. Technical report ARL-TR-6984, U.S. Army Research Laboratory, Aberdeen Proving Ground, Maryland (2014)
11. Lee, J.D., See, K.A.: Trust in automation: designing for appropriate reliance. Hum. Factors **46**, 50–80 (2004)
12. Parasuraman, R., Sheridan, T.B., Wickens, C.D.: A model for types and levels of human interaction with automation. IEEE Trans. Syst. Man Cybern. Part A Syst. Hum. **30**, 286–297 (2000)
13. Lee, J.D.: Trust, trustworthiness, and trustability. In: The Workshop on Human-Machine Trust Robust Autonomous Systems, 31 Jan. 2012, Ocala, FL, USA (2012)
14. Endsley, M.R.: Toward a theory of situation awareness in dynamic systems. Hum. Factors **37**, 32–64 (1995)
15. Endsley, M.R.: Situation awareness misconceptions and misunderstandings. J. Cognit. Eng. Decis. Making **9**, 4–32 (2015)
16. Chen, J.Y.C., Barnes, M.J.: Supervisory control of multiple robots: effects of imperfect automation and individual differences. Hum. Factors **54**, 157–174 (2012)
17. Chen, J.Y.C., Barnes, M.J.: Supervisory control of multiple robots in dynamic tasking environments. Ergonomics **55**, 1043–1058 (2012)
18. Wright, J.L., Chen, J.Y.C., Quinn, S.A., Barnes, M.J.: The effects of level of autonomy on human–agent teaming for multi–robot control and local security maintenance. Technical report, ARL–TR–6724, U.S. Army Research Laboratory, Aberdeen Proving Ground, Maryland (2013)
19. Wright, J.L., Chen, J.Y.C., Barnes, M.J., Hancock, P.A.: The effect of agent reasoning transparency on automation bias: an analysis of performance and decision time. Technical report, U.S. Army Research Laboratory, Aberdeen Proving Ground, Maryland (in press)
20. U.S. Department of Defense – Research & Engineering Enterprise.: Autonomy Research Pilot Initiative. http://www.acq.osd.mil/chieftechnologist/arpi.html
21. Draper, M.: Realizing Autonomy via Intelligent Adaptive Hybrid Control: Adaptable Autonomy for Achieving UxV RSTA Team Decision Superiority, Yearly report. U.S. Air Force Research Laboratory, Dayton, OH (2013)
22. Behymer, K.J., Mersch, E.M., Ruff, H.A., Calhoun, G.L., Spriggs, S.E.: Unmanned vehicle plan comparison visualization for effective human-autonomy teaming. In: Proceedings of the 6th Applied Human Factors and Ergonomics International Conference Las Vegas, NV (2015)

23. Mercado, J.E., Rupp, M., Chen, J.Y.C., Barber, D., Procci, K., Barnes, M.J.: Intelligent agent transparency in human-agent teaming for Multi-UxV management. Hum. Factors **58**(3), 401–415 (2016)
24. Stowers K., Chen J.Y.C., Kasdaglis N., Newton O., Rupp, M., Barnes M.: Effects of situation awareness-based agent transparency information on human agent teaming for multi-UxV management. Technical report, U.S. Army Research Laboratory, Aberdeen Proving Ground, Maryland (2016)

Human-Autonomy Teaming Patterns
in the Command and Control of Teams
of Autonomous Systems

Douglas S. Lange[(⊠)] and Robert S. Gutzwiller

Space and Naval Warfare Systems Center Pacific (SPAWAR),
San Diego, CA, USA
{doug.lange,robert.s.gutzwiller1}@navy.mil

Abstract. Design patterns have been found useful in several domains. This paper helps motivate their use in the field of human-autonomy teaming and provides three example patterns that could be contributed to the language of patterns available to system developers. In our examples we focus on the motivations and consequences in terms of human and team performance when describing the features of the individual patterns. These replace forces more commonly used in software engineering or other fields. Practitioners and researchers alike will benefit from a vetted vocabulary of established patterns of the form presented.

Keywords: Autonomous system · Cognitive agent · Cognitive assistant · Command and control · Design patterns · Teaming · Supervisory control · Systems engineering

1 Introduction

Command and control (C^2) has long been an example of human-autonomy teaming. In particular, commanders have been directing teams of autonomous systems since the concept of C^2 began. These autonomous systems were collections of infantry or artillery or perhaps squadrons of aircraft or ships. The decisions behind the autonomy being displayed came from biological brains rather than biologically inspired artificial intelligence.

1.1 Command and Control

Commanders guide the operation of a team. There is a goal or mission to be accomplished, an environment to operate in that may include an opposing force, and there are the team members themselves. In some cases the commander is separate from the team

© Springer International Publishing Switzerland 2016
D. Harris (Ed.): EPCE 2016, LNAI 9736, pp. 179–188, 2016.
DOI: 10.1007/978-3-319-40030-3_19

and in essence supervises the operation. In others, the commander is an integral part of the team (e.g., an infantry squad) and teams with the other autonomous units (i.e., the other members of the squad).

According to Willard [1], C^2 is accomplished through the following tasks:

- Ensure that all decisions remain aligned with the mission and the commander's intent.
- Assess the status of plan execution utilizing a common operational picture that is also provided to the team members.
- Monitor the status of the plan against the plan's timeline.
- Oversee compliance with procedures to avoid mistakes and achieve efficiencies.
- Respond to emerging information that differs significantly from expectations.
- Reapportion assets due to changes in availability or changes to requirements and priorities.

Beyond the control of autonomous teams or units, human-autonomy teaming has found its way into the command environment itself. Projects have shown that intelligent agents can assist a human commander in exercising C^2 [2]. Thus, human-autonomy teams can become responsible for controlling teams of autonomous systems employed to execute the mission.

SKIPAL [2] is an example where the role of autonomy is strictly within the task of maintaining situational awareness. The human's role is both as a consumer of the information and as an instructor to the autonomy. Other research [3–5] includes the possibility of utilizing autonomy to plan, monitor, and reapportion assets for missions. Autonomy can even respond on the human's behalf with permission of the human to handle rapidly occurring events [5].

1.2 Design Patterns

The use of a semi-formal language to describe design patterns began with the fields of architecture and land use [6, 7]. Christopher Alexander proposed that buildings and towns are created as collections of patterns that are the result of forces and processes. Communicating these patterns among practitioners in the field provides a powerful design tool.

Design patterns and pattern languages became a popular tool for software engineering in the 1990s and later for multi-agent systems [8–13]. It is proposed in [14] that the study of human-autonomy teaming adopt this approach for describing and communicating critical design patterns, enabling reuse of these patterns across systems and mission domains. To accomplish this goal, the same critical elements employed by previous pattern users must be described:

- Pattern Name
- The forces driving the problem to be solved
- The solution
- The positive and negative consequences of using the pattern
- Implementation advice

References [7–13] provide catalogs of some discovered patterns in their particular domains.

To begin the process, we must first provide a good if informal definition of the problem to be solved and the forces in play. A systems engineering view indicates that the work objective is the place to start [14]. This sets the goal for a work process that will be employed by a human-autonomy team. An environment must also be defined along with a system boundary. The objective and environment together form the forces for the problem. The process indicates the solution. In any process there will consequences, and in particular for a human-autonomy teaming process, there will be consequences on the performance of the human, the autonomy, and the joint human-autonomy team in how the process is defined. Different methods of implementation will affect how the consequences play out and the development of the capabilities desired.

In this paper, we attempt to describe patterns of human-autonomy teaming utilized in our development of task management aids for a human-autonomy team exercising the C^2 of teams of autonomous systems. These are not patterns that we ourselves first discovered. They have been experimented with by many others, and we know of them through research literature. To engage in dialog on human-autonomy teaming, we will attempt to employ the pattern methods suggested in [14].

1.3 Forces in Human-Autonomy Teaming

The forces leading to the motivation to utilize a particular software engineering pattern might include the effects of computational complexity or difficulty in extending the software for future requirements [8]. We propose to look at forces from human performance and teaming research [17, 18]. In particular, we will use the Input, Process, Output (IPO) model to derive forces. Examples of forces derived from this model are: motivation, expertise, composition, team mental models, communication, cooperation, coordination of execution, and shared awareness. Patterns may be selected to counter or enhance particular forces, while the consequences may affect other components of the IPO model.

2 Task Management for Supervisory Control

We will be discussing the C2 of teams of Unmanned {air, surface, subsurface, ground} Vehicles (UxV). It is important to distinguish between different instances of human-autonomy teaming that will be involved in describing the Intelligent Multi-UxV Planner with Adaptive Collaborative Control Technologies (IMPACT) project. Per our approach for pattern descriptions [14] we will do this is by focusing on the different Work Objectives (WObjs) and Work Processes (WProcs).

Through the IMPACT project we are experimenting with concepts necessary to develop a C^2 capability to allow a small number of people to control multiple teams of autonomous vehicles. The WObj of the overall system is therefore to achieve success for the various missions that are taken on by the commander responsible for the UxV teams. There is a supervisory relationship that is formed between the controllers and UxV that are conducting the missions. This relationship is mediated through IMPACT.

In this paper, we will focus on the subordinate human-autonomy relationships that we believe enable the human controllers to handle the workload of a complex environment that could include many teams of many vehicles. We are not focused on the tasks and conduct of the vehicles or vehicle teams themselves, but rather the tasks of the controllers in maintaining C^2 over the vehicle teams. The use of autonomous assistants has been suggested for this class of problem before [15].

2.1   Task Generation

The IMPACT Task Manager (TM) is currently being developed, but exists as a functioning prototype with partial functionality. Some of the capabilities discussed will be those that are still in development, but the patterns exist in previous work as well, for instance in the Cognitive Assistant that Learns and Organizes [15] and other experiments in the use of task learning [16]. This is an important feature of patterns. They show up frequently.

TM monitors its environment, learns to recognize the need for and generate tasks, manages active tasks and assists the user in completing tasks. The TM is instrumented in order to improve performance. The WObj for the human-autonomy team is to execute the necessary C^2 tasks that will allow the command to succeed at its mission.

TM is programmed to recognize the need for some tasks. For instance, TM monitors a chat stream and recognizes text patterns that indicate the need to generate a new instance of a particular task type. Other tasks can be generated through machine learning that occurs through observing the human user and relating the user's actions to the current state of the C^2 environment. The human's actions serve to label the situation to enable lifelong learning by the cognitive assistant. Other user actions, such as correcting a mistakenly generated task, serve to teach the TM.

2.2   Task Assignment

Tasks that are created by the TM on its own, or through the human's initiative are then assigned for execution. The TM can choose either an autonomous assistant or a human, or a team of humans and autonomy to execute the task. The key to this flexibility is the task structure [5] that breaks tasks into methods and subtasks. Instrumentation can collect data on performance allowing TM to predict how each agent (human or machine) will perform.

Working agreements established by the users dictate how much authority the TM has in assigning tasks. The human users also have the ability to manually change the assignments that are created by the TM.

2.3   Task Execution

For some tasks, the TM will have aids that can help a user through the task. These can be programmed for tasks that are anticipated. For those that are not, we envision using capabilities similar to those in [15] for automated assistants to learn to help or perform tasks. When capable of performing tasks the methods are entered into the task structure and the assistant will be available to be assigned a task or subtask.

3   Patterns

We will discuss three patterns that we would propose are being used to allow human-autonomy teaming within IMPACT between a human user and the TM. Two of these patterns illustrate a heterarchical rather than a hierarchical relationship, suggesting that we do not have a supervisory control situation. Instead, humans and autonomous agents are teaming roughly as partners, though the roles do give added authority to the human. The final pattern discussed also creates a temporarily strict supervisory control authority. Using a template inspired by software design patterns (e.g., [8]), and the top-level patterns discussed in [14], we describe these patterns.

3.1   Instructor and Student

Figure 1 indicates the top-level pattern from [14] that is relevant for this aspect of TM. Both the TM and the human user are identifying tasks from the environment. The TM is accomplishing this by reading data from the C2 system and performing either programmed or learned pattern recognition. The human user is presumably doing pattern recognition as well, but we will not address this aspect of human cognition here. Either is able to initiate tasks in the system, which are subsequently assigned to an agent (either human or machine).

Fig. 1. Agent works in cooperation with the human operator being an element of the worker per [14].

Intent: Provide a means for expanding the pattern recognition and task catalog of the TM.

Motivation: We do not know a priori all of the tasks that will need to be accomplished. C^2 has been largely a human endeavor in part because it is difficult to discretize the tasks and events in the C^2 environment. Our programs do not know as well as human experts do, when tasks should be initiated. We can perform task analyses to expand our knowledge and influence our design, but the nature of the domain requires the ability to adapt.

Applicability: Instructor-Student is applicable whenever there is a means to represent a discretization of the environment and an opportunity for the human to indicate the nature of an element of the environment. There must be instrumentation in place to facilitate representation of the environment. The representation then allows us to form a useful model of the patterns required for identifying the discrete element (e.g., a task).

Structure and Participants: See Fig. 1 for the basic structure. The human is in the role of *instructor* while the cognitive agent is in the role of *student*. Both use the tools available in the system to gain situational awareness and to instantiate discretized elements (tasks).

Human Requirements and Consequences: This pattern requires effort and motivation by the human participant. If because of stresses the human does not take the opportunity to teach the agent, then the agent will not be able to assist through recognizing instances for task creation. One likely cause of this decision will be an inadequate learning environment for the agent. If either the instrumentation is insufficient, or the algorithms used produce poor models, then the user is likely to lose trust (rightly) in the ability of the agent to learn. This pattern when successfully implemented helps form a consistent team mental model. The student (autonomy) learns to classify events by creating a model that estimates the model held by the human instructor. Output performance measures of quality and quantity of tasks completed form the ultimate measure of the instructor-student team. The performance consequences are discussed in [16] and depend on the human's teaching strategy and the machine learning capabilities of the agent.

3.2   Working Agreements

This aspect of TM also follows the top level pattern depicted in Fig. 1. The TM is serving as a scheduler for human and automated agents.

Intent: Provide a means for a human user to indicate preferences concerning how task allocation and execution should be accomplished.

Motivation: We want to establish the rules by which the allocation of tasks will be conducted. This allows the human user to successfully predict the pattern of operations increasing trust in the autonomy. It also puts the human on at least equal footing with the autonomy. The autonomy has algorithms, models, and sensors to use to make a decision as to how to assign tasks. This provides a means for the human to contribute to the decisions.

Applicability: Working agreements are applicable whenever two agents must cooperate and have differing kinds of models for making decisions. The working agreement bridges the mismatch in knowledge and understanding with agreed upon guidelines [19].

Structure and Participants: See Fig. 1 for the basic structure and Fig. 2 for a possible user interface. Both the human and the autonomy access the working agreement in

	Preference	Assigned (Constrained) to	Unconstrained Task
Point Inspection	USER ☑	☑	☒
Identify Target(s)	USER ☑	ASSISTANT ☑	◯
Monitor Video Feed/Images	USER ☑	☑	☒
Does Vehicle Reach Location	USER ☑	☑	☒
Situation Assessment	USER ☑	USER ☑	☒
Within sensor range?	USER ☑	USER ☑	☒
Overwatch	USER ☑	USER ☑	☒
LPOP	USER ☑	☑	☒
Fuel Status	USER ☑	USER ☑	☒
Last Eyes On	USER ☑	☑	☒

Fig. 2. A possible user interface for accessing a working agreement

order to guide decisions. In all efforts that we are aware of, the agreement is between a human and an autonomous agent, although it is clearly modeled after human-human agreements.

Human Requirements and Consequences: This pattern brings about a team mental model concerning how work will be accomplished [17]. It also affects how team composition is adjusted for individual tasks. An agent's (particular human's) motivation is a source of information for the input of an agent to the working agreement. Working agreements can directly affect the quality and quantity of work performed and therefore measuring these factors can be useful. We also believe that working agreements increase trust in the automation by the humans involved as it gives the autonomy more predictable behavior based on a model accessible to the humans.

3.3 Ultimate Override

This aspect of TM takes a heterarchical relationship and imposes a hierarchy onto it. Figure 3 shows the base pattern graphically.

Fig. 3. The human user assumes all of the initiative for the WProc

Intent: Provide a means for a human user to take full control over a WProc. When the operator performs certain operations, there is no negotiation with the agent and any working agreement is overlooked.

Motivation: There are times when we want to ensure that the human has the final say. In many situations the human have the legal responsibility over WProc and WObj, while the automated system does not. Knowing that this option exists may give the human teammate more trust in employing the automation. However, it is also possible that in providing such manual overrides, users may under trust the autonomy [20].

Applicability: This pattern is applicable wherever there are legal or ethical guidelines that insist upon human responsibility. It is also applicable any time when the models available for the autonomy are known to be insufficient and human decision-making may become essential.

Structure and Participants: See Fig. 3 for the basic structure. Capabilities that employ this pattern are fundamentally taking the team away from Fig. 1 to a structure where the human exerts all of the initiative and the autonomy performs tasks assigned using the tools available.

Human Requirements and Consequences: This pattern removes all semblance of a team mental model. The initiative is completely contained within the human participant. This also changes the team composition and view of participant expertise. The autonomy essentially becomes a narrow technical expert, while the human moves to a supervisory role. The motivation of the human participant is all important in this pattern, while the autonomy essentially does not exhibit motivation (Fig. 4).

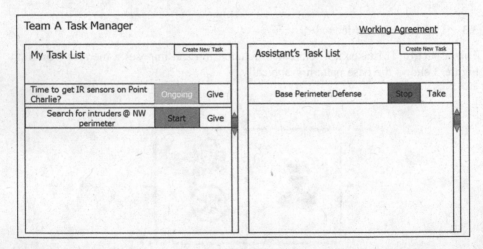

Fig. 4. When the user decides to "Give" or "Take" tasks while using the TM, ultimate override is being exerted. For that period and relating to those tasks, the TM makes no decisions, but reflects the motivated will of the supervisor.

4 Conclusions

We have described three patterns that we are employing in the development of a TM to support the C2 of teams of autonomous vehicles. We utilize the systems engineering approach from [14] along with the descriptive templates of sources such as those used in the domain of software engineering [8]. Alexander [6] would have us utilize an extensive catalog of such patterns and weave a specifying description of our projects developing a pattern language.

Further work must be done to fully develop such a catalog, and we plan on employing experiments to measure the human and team performance consequences of our use of these patterns. We must also be conscious of the possibility that consequences will differ across domains, and believe that research can enlighten us in this area. Ultimately, the core patterns of human-autonomy teaming will be those that can be reliably used across many application domains.

References

1. Willard, R.F.: Rediscovering the art of command & control. In: Proceedings of the US Naval Institute, vol. 128, no. 10 (2002)
2. Lange, D.S., Lai, E.C., Carlin, M., Ling, A.S., Keifer, K., Deans, B., Nitz, K., Tam, L., Bolton, J., Graves, B., Reestman, B.: SKIPAL: the incorporation of machine learning technology into the strategic knowledge integration web. In: The 15th International Command and Control Research and Technology Symposium (2010)
3. Apker, T.B., Johnson, B., Humphrey, L.: LTL templates for play-calling supervisory control. In: American Institute of Aeronautics and Astronautics SciTech Forum (2016)
4. Behymer, K.J., Mersch, E.M., Ruff, H.A., Calhoun, G.L., Spriggs, S.E.: Unmanned vehicle plan comparison visualizations for effective human-autonomy teaming. In: The 6th International Conference on Applied Human Factors and Ergonomics (2015)
5. Lange, D.S., Gutzwiller, R.S., Verbancsics, P., Sin, T.: Task models for human-computer collaboration in supervisory control of teams of autonomous systems. In: The IEEE International Inter-Disciplinary Conference on Cognitive Methods in Situation Awareness and Decision Support (2014)
6. Alexander, C.: The Timeless Way of Building. Oxford U.P., New York (1979)
7. Alexander, C., Ishikawa, S., Silverstein, M.: A Pattern Language: Towns, Buildings, Construction. Oxford U. P., New York (1977)
8. Gamma, E., Helm, R., Johnson, R., Vlissides, J.: Design Patterns Elements of Reusable Object-Oriented Software. Addison-Wesley, Reading (1977)
9. Fowler, M.: Analysis Patterns: Reusable Object Models. Addison-Wesley Professional, Reading (1996)
10. Pree, W.: Design Patterns for Object-Oriented Software Development. Addison-Wesley Professional, Reading (1994)
11. Brown, W., Malveau, R., McCormick, H., Mowbray, T.: Anti Patterns: Refactoring Software, Architectures, and Projects in Crisis. Wiley, Chichester (1995)
12. Coplien, J.O.: Pattern Languages of Program Design. Addison-Wesley Professional, Boston (1995)
13. Juziuk, J.: Design Patterns for Multi-Agent Systems. Linnaeus University, Sweden (2012)

14. Schulte, A., Donath, D., Lange, D.S.: Design patterns for human-cognitive agent teaming. In: Harris, D. (ed.) EPCE 2016. LNAI, vol. 9736, pp. 231–243. Springer, Heidelberg (2016)
15. Myers, K., Berry, P., Blythe, J., Conley, K., Gervasio, M., McGuinness, D., Morley, D., Pfeffer, A., Pollack, M., Tambe, M.: An intelligent personal assistant for task and time management. AI Mag. **28**(2), 47–61 (2007)
16. Lange, D., Carlin, M., Ivanchenko, V., Luqi, B.V.: Human and software factors for successful system adaptation. In: The Twelfth International Command and Control Research and Technology Symposium (2007)
17. Gutzwiller, R.S., Lange, D.S.: Task teams: supervisory control and task management of autonomous unmanned systems. In: Lackey, S., Shumaker, R. (eds.) VAMR 2016. LNCS, vol. 9740, pp. 1–9. Springer, Heidelberg (2016)
18. Gutzwiller, R.S., Lange, D.S., Reeder, J., Morris, R.L., Rodas, O.: Human-computer collaboration in adaptive supervisory control and function allocation of autonomous system teams. In: Shumaker, R., Lackey, S. (eds.) VAMR 2015. LNCS, vol. 9179, pp. 447–456. Springer, Heidelberg (2015)
19. de Greef, T., Arciszewski, H., Neerincx, M.: Adaptive automation based on an object-oriented task model: implementation and evaluation in a realistic C2 environment. J. Cogn. Eng. Decis. Mak. **4**(2), 152–182 (2010)
20. Parasuraman, R., Riley, V.: Humans and automation: use, misuse, disuse, abuse. Hum. Factors **39**(2), 230–253 (1997)

Influence of Time Delay on Team Performance in Space Robotic Teleoperation

Mengdi Liu[1(✉)], Yijing Zhang[2,3], Cheng Zhu[4], and Zhizhong Li[1]

[1] Department of Industrial Engineering,
Tsinghua University, Beijing, People's Republic of China
lmd15@mails.tsinghua.edu.cn, zzli@tsinghua.edu.cn
[2] National Key Laboratory of Human Factors Engineering,
Beijing, People's Republic of China
[3] China Astronaut Research and Training Center,
Beijing, People's Republic of China
ldlzyj@163.com
[4] Science and Technology on Information Systems Engineering Laboratory,
National University of Defense Technology,
Changsha, Hunan, People's Republic of China
zhucheng@nudt.edu.cn

Abstract. Team teleoperation, which is commonly seen in dangerous and inaccessible environments, is challenging by the complexity and dynamics of the environment, especially when there is time delay. This study was focused on Two-Operator-Two-Robot teleoperation and discussed the influence of time delay on team performance. In this study, we collected operational performance data, eye movement data and subjective rating to compare the performance of an object moving task with 0 s and 3.73 s time delay. Preliminary results of the experiment indicate that the increase of time delay significantly increase completion time and decrease fraction of time moving (MRATIO). In addition, time delay significantly increase the variance of the number of collisions and joint limit reach, which suggest that the inter-individual difference become greater under time delay.

Keywords: Team performance · Time delay · Teleoperation

1 Introduction

Teleoperation, i.e. the manipulation of remotely located machines, is commonly seen in disaster relief, space exploration, and other dangerous or inaccessible environments. As an example, space robots often have to be tele-operated in the process of shuttle docking at space station and various maintenance and repair tasks in the space.

Resulted from the nature of space, there are several challenges in space robotic teleoperation. Time delay caused by long distance is one of the major problems, which may directly affect operators' perception and interpretation of the current situation. It is critical for operators to maintain awareness of robotic arms' position and configuration under time delay condition.

D. Harris (Ed.): EPCE 2016, LNAI 9736, pp. 189–197, 2016.
DOI: 10.1007/978-3-319-40030-3_20

Time delay from action input to visual feedback display is an acknowledged shortcoming of current virtual environment and teleoperation technology [1]. There have been some studies focused on Single-Operator-Single-Robot teleoperation with time delay, most of which showed that time delay significantly reduces operator's performance in error rate, completion time, efficiency and other measures of performance. Thompson showed that the linear relationship of time delay and completion time occurred when the constraint difficulty increased [2]. Hill found, in his comparison of seven performance measures in a time-delayed manipulation task, that time delay decreased the performance in terms of error rate and efficiency [3]. In his study, the efficiency was measured by fraction of time moving (MRATIO) and mean time per move (MBAR). In addition, it's commonly accepted that operators tend to adopt a move-and-wait strategy in case of time delay [3, 4].

Compared with single operator teleoperation, teamwork in teleoperation makes it possible to undertake complex tasks. However, at the same time, teamwork makes teleoperation more challenging because operators have to work together harmoniously to overcome difficulties. Time delay may significantly influence team performance and safety by increasing collisions between robotic arms, leading to great damage [5]. There are few literatures on Multi-Operator-Multi-Robot teleoperation with time delay yet.

The control loop of Two-Operator-Tow-Robot teleoperation system can be shown as Fig. 1. Time delay occurs in every stage of information transition process, especially during the transition process between masters and slaves. Moreover, we can find that the result of a single operation commanded by a operator affects not only on the environment but also his teammate. Higher attention demand for the situation of teammate and his robotic arm is an important feature of teamwork. Chong worked on Multi-Operator-Multi-Robot teleoperation problem, tried to conduct visual and audition aids to decrease the influence of time delay, and found that unavoidable time delay is the most severe problem affecting team performance and safety in terms of error rate and completion time [5–8].

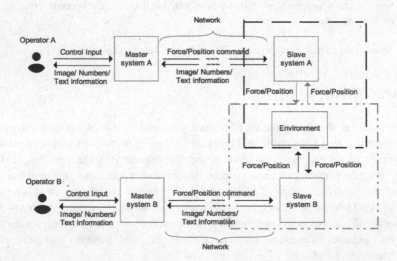

Fig. 1. The control loop of Two-Operator-Two-Robot teleoperation system

In most of previous studies on teleoperation with time delay, team performance was mostly measured in terms of error rate and completion time. However, there is few discussion about other aspects of team performance, sauch as operators' situation awareness and workload. According to NASA Generic Robotics Training (GRT) performance assessment metric [9], scan pattern and reach/joint limits and singularities are also important measures to evaluate operators' skill and performance.

In this study on Two-Operator-Two-Robot teleoperation, team performance was measured with operational performance metrics, eye movement metrics and subjective rating. The goal is to compare teleoperation team performance with and without time delay.

2   Method

2.1   Participants

Sixteen pairs of right-handed male engineering undergraduate students in Tsinghua University participated in the experiment (mean age = 19.8, SD = 1.2) and were randomly assigned to teams. None of them had previous experience in operating a robotic arm, using joysticks or teleoperation.

2.2   The Virtual Robot Experimentation Platform

In this study, the experiment was conducted on the virtual robot experiment platform (V-REP) developed by COPPELIA ROBOTICS. The arm was simulated based on SIASUN SR6C industrial robotic arm, which had six degrees of freedom: shoulder pitch, shoulder yaw, elbow pitch, elbow yaw, wrist pitch and wrist roll.

As is shown in Fig. 2, the participants controlled the robotic arm with a posture joystick (right side) and a translation joystick (left side). Their eye movements were tracked by SMI iView RED.

Fig. 2. A participant in experiment

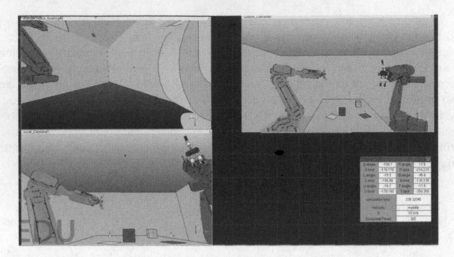

Fig. 3. Visual display of orange arm operator

Cameras were located on the wall of the room, above the table and on the end effector of the arms. The positions and angles of the cameras besides the wall and above the table were fixed while the cameras on the end effectors of the arms moved with the arms. While operating the arms, the operators could display simultaneously as many as three camera views and a digital panel window. The visual display is illustrated in Fig. 3 (take the view of the operator using the orange arm as an example). The view of the camera on the end of a robotic arm is located on upper left and the direction of the coordinate system changed with the movement of the arm. The upper right view and the lower left view are shot by the cameras on the wall and above the table respectively.

2.3 Tasks

Each participant was responsible for operating a robotic arm and cooperating with his teammate to complete the object moving task. As shown in Fig. 4, each participant was required to move an object to the target area correspondingly. Only when both objects were located in their target area, the task was completed. The task fail if it was not completed in 15 min. In addition, collisions and joint limit reach should be avoid as possible. Since the moving paths were designed to be crossed each other and verbal communication was mot allowed, each participant had to pay attention to the position and configuration of the robotic arm operated by his teammate while making decision on movement direction and velocity.

For each participant, this task involves four steps: (1) adjusting the posture of arm to aline the gripper to the object, (2) grasping the object, (3) moving the object and aligning it to the target area, (4) releasing the object. If the object was not put into the target area, it can be picked up and re-moved until the task success or the time was out.

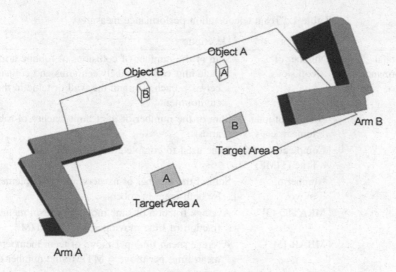

Fig. 4. Illustration of the task

2.4 Experiment Design

The independent variable in this study was time delay (two different levels, 0 s vs. 3.73 s). Specifically, although time delay occured in every stage of information transition process (as shown in Fig. 1), here we only studied the transition delay from masters to slaves.

Three types of measures were recorded to evaluate team teleoperation performance, including operational performance metrics, eye movement metrics and operators' subjective evaluation, as listed in Table 1. Only data in successful trials was used to measure operational performance.

Each team was required to perform two replicates with each time delay level. To counteract learning and fatigue effects, the order was counterbalanced.

2.5 Procedure

Before the experiment session, the participants attended a 2-hour training session to learn about the operation of a robotic arm and the experiment task. The training consisted of 15 min Power Point introduction about the configure of the arm, the way to operate joysticks and the task, 65 min individual operation practice, 10 min rest and 30 min team operation practice. The task of team operation practice was similar to the formal experiment task and verbal discussions were allowed during the practice. All participants were able to complete the training session.

In the experiment session, the participants filled out the SART-10D and TWA questionnaires after each trial. Before each trial, the eye tracker was calibrated.

Table 1. Team teleoperation performance measures

	Measures	Description
Operational performance metrics	Number of collisions	Sum of the number of collisions of robotic arms, including collisions between arms and collisions between each arm and the wall or table in the environment
	Number of joint limit reaches	Sum of the number of joint limit reaches of robotic arms
	Completion time (TIME)	Time used to complete the task
	Number of moves	Sum of the number of masters' moves implemented by both team members
	MRATIO [3]	Average fraction of time moving of team members; fraction of time moving = MTIME[a]/TIME;
	MBAR [3]	Average mean time per move of team members; mean time per move = MTIME/the number of master moves
Eye movement metrics	Average saccade amplitude	Recorded in 60 Hz
	Blinking frequency	Recorded in 60 Hz
Subjective evaluation	SART score	Average SART-10D score of team members
	Workload (WL) [10]	Average team workload assessment score (WL) of team member

[a]MTIME: total time that the master was moving

3 Results

3.1 Operational Performance

During the experiment, the position and status of slaves (robotic arms) and masters (the joysticks) were recorded with 2.5 Hz. According to these data, the operational performance were compared between different time delay levels from three aspects, i.e. accident rate (including collisions and joint limit reaches), completion time and controlling efficiency (including number of moves, MRATIO and MBAR). Note that when discussing accident rate and completion time, only data in successful trials were used. The data were analyzed with paired t-test and Wilcoxon signed rank signed test.

- Accident rate
  The average collision number with 0 s delay (M = 3.46, SD = 2.99) was greater than average collision number with 3.73 s delay (M = 5.75, SD = 7.4). Similarly,

when time delay increased from 0 s to 3.73 s, average number of joint limit reaches increased from 0.38 to 1.58, with standard deviation 0.51 and 3.41, respectively. However, statistical analysis show no significant difference on the number of collisions and joint limit reaches between different levels of time delay due to the large variance.

With time delay, the standard deviation of the number of collisions (F = 0.16, p = 0.01) and joint limit reaches (F = 0.02, p < 0.001) increases significantly, which implies that instability of the participants' performance increases, meaning individual ability may play an important role.

- Completion time
  Similar to the conclusion in Single-Operator-Single-Robot studies, completion time increased significantly when time delay presented (F = 6.471, p = 0.0217; see Fig. 5). Average completion time was lifted from 484.48 s to 610.70 s, meaning a 126.1 % increase.
- Control efficiency
  In this study, we evaluated the control efficiency through the number of master moves, MRATIO and mean time per move (MBAR).

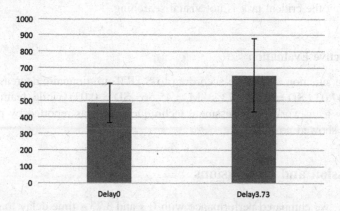

Fig. 5. Completion times (error bar represent standard deviation)

There was no significant effect of time delay on the number of master moves and MBAR. The results showed that even in the scenario without time delay, the number of master moves was high, which suggested that in team teleoperation, the participants may tend to use move-and-wait strategy whenever there was time delay or not.

Hill found MRATIO, or the fraction of time moving, is the most sensitive variable to time delay [3]. The result of this study showed a similar result, MRATIO decreased significantly when the time delay increase from 0 s to 3.73 s (t = 2.49, p = 0.02; see Fig. 6), implying significant decrease of control efficiency.

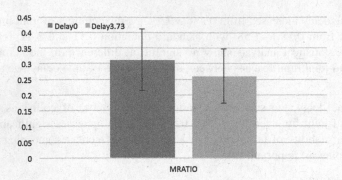

Fig. 6. MRATIO (error bar represent standard deviation)

3.2 Eye Movement

Eye tracking data was recorded from one of the participants in each team. As for saccade amplitude, it had a 6.8 % increase from 10.62° to 11.34°, though without significance. Similarly, the blinking frequency also showed no significant difference. These results might suggest that, in the task of this experiment, information acquisition is difficult, but the critical task is not visual searching.

3.3 Subjective Evaluation

Self-reported situation awareness according to SART questionnaire decreased slightly (0 s: M = 47.03, SD = 0.3; 3.73 s: M = 45.56, SD = 0.03) while team workload evaluated by team workload assessment technique (also was reported by participants themselves) showed no difference.

4 Discussion and Conclusions

In this study, we compared performance with 0 s and 3.73 s time delay to discuss the influence of time delay on team teleoperation performance.

According to the experiment results, time delay significantly influenced completion time and MRATIO. These results indicated that time delay significant decreased team performance because of less control efficiency and slower operating speed. Additionally, the significant increase of the variance of the number of collisions and joint limit reaches also suggested that inter-individual difference may play an important role and the operation performance became less stable. However, in this case, time delay did not significantly influence the eye movement or subjective evaluation. However, it would be difficult to say that the influence of time delay to Multi-Operator-Multi-Robot operation is less than its influence to Single-Operator-Single-Robot operation. Differently from the results in Single-Operator-Single-Robot studies, in team teleoperation, there is no significant transition from continuous to the interrupted move-and-wait strategy, according to the analysis of the number of master moves. In team teleoperation, the task is more challenging and operators have to pay attention to the situation of not only their own robot but also the robots of team members. Thus, operators may tend to use move-and-wait strategy whenever there is time delay or not.

Acknowledgement. This study was supported by National Natural Science Foundation of China (No. 71371174, 61273322).

References

1. Adelstein, B.D., Lee, T.G., Ellis, S.R.: Head tracking latency in virtual environments: psychophysics and a model. In: The Human Factors and Ergonomics Society 47th Annual Meeting (2003)
2. Thompson, D.A.: The development of a six degree-of-constraint robot performance evaluation test. In: 13th Annual Conference on Manual Control (MIT Proc), pp. 289–292 (1977)
3. Hill, J.W.: Comparison of seven performance measures in a time delayed manipulation task. IEEE Trans. Syst. Man Cybern. **smc-6**(4), 286–295 (1976)
4. Sheridan, T.B., Ferrellt, W.R.: Remote manipulative control with transmission delay (1963)
5. Chong, N.Y., Kawabata, S.I., Ohba, K., Kotoku, T., Komoriya, K., Takase, K., Tanie, K.: Multioperator teleoperation of multirobot systems with time delay: part I—aids for collision-free control. Presence Teleoperators Virtual Environ. **11**(3), 277–291 (2002)
6. Chong, N.Y., et al.: Remote coordinated controls in multiple telerobot cooperation (2000)
7. Chongl, N.Y., et al.: Development of a multi-telerobot system for remote collaboration (2000)
8. Chong, N.Y., et al.: Multioperator teleoperation of multirobot systems with time delay: part II—testbed description. Teleoperators Virtual Environ. **11**(3), 292 (2002)
9. Forman, R.E.: Objective performance metrics for improved space telerobotics training. (Master of Science in Aeronautics and Astronautics), Massachusetts Institute of Technology, Massachusetts Institute of Technology. Retrieved from Available from database (2011)
10. Lin, C.J., et al.: Development of a team workload assessment technique for the main control room of advanced nuclear power plants. Hum. Factors Ergon. Manuf. Serv. Ind. **21**(4), 397–411 (2011). doi:10.1002/hfm.20247

Sub-patterns for Human-Autonomy Teaming: Variations on a Delegation Theme

Christopher A. Miller[✉]

Smart Information Flow Technologies (SIFT),
319 First Ave. N., Minneapolis, MN 55401, USA
cmiller@sift.net

Abstract. Building on Shulte et al. [1], we deepen the concept of design patterns for human-autonomy teaming by introducing two distinctions. First, Patterns are composed of a Problem Pattern and a Solution Pattern, both of which should be described and linked so they can be recognized in design. Second, Patterns are hierarchically related in that SubPatterns capture more specific instances of their SuperPattern parents and, thus, can provide more specific design guidance. Both additions are explored within the general concept of supervisory control and specific instances from the Rotorcraft Pilot's Associate program are analyzed using the formalism developed in the paper.

Keywords: Supervisory control · Delegation · Design patterns · Human-autonomy teaming · Workload · Unpredictability · Competency

1 Introduction

The concept of a *design pattern* was introduced by Christopher Alexander—an architect—in his 1977 book *A Pattern Language* [2]. Alexander's concept, and its later adoption by software engineers [3], was meant to link recurrent problems and their similar solutions. Thus, the "pattern" is not just a description of a designed solution, but rather of a recurring process of similar problems with similar solutions. Alexander says "Each pattern describes a problem that occurs over and over again … and then describes the core of the solution to that problem, in such a way that you can use this solution a million times over, without ever doing it the same way twice" [2]. One example in architecture is the recurring problem having rooms be sunny and yet also not overheat. A variety of architectural solutions have been derived—ranging from placing windows on sides of the room that don't get the sun during the hottest hours, to extended eaves, to sky lights, to window tints, to blinds, screens, drapes, etc.

The goal is to create a "pattern language" which not only characterizes the various elements and relationships of the solutions, but also the "conflicting forces" [2] and values in variations of the problem that give rise to preferences for specific solutions. In architecture this might mean characterizing:

- First, the *Solution Patterns* as described (e.g., windows not on room sides with the hot sun, etc.) along with a vocabulary of entities and relationships (e.g., windows, room sides, sun positions, 'hot hours', etc.),

© Springer International Publishing Switzerland 2016
D. Harris (Ed.): EPCE 2016, LNAI 9736, pp. 198–210, 2016.
DOI: 10.1007/978-3-319-40030-3_21

- As well as the attributes and relationships of the problem, the *Problem Patterns*, which the solutions are meant to resolve, along with their entities and relationships (e.g., rooms with sufficient light that are also do not overheat),
- And finally describing the values and priorities by which a solution pattern may be adopted in one instance or by one designer over others.

In the remainder of this paper, I will attempt to apply this "pattern" of patterns to some sub-patterns for the "super-pattern" of human-machine supervisory control [4].

2 Supervisory Control as a Design Pattern

Supervisory control [4] is a dominant paradigm for human-automation interaction (HAI) today, yet it is not the only approach. Is supervisory control a design pattern–"a link between recurrent problems and their similar or identical solutions"? It seems very reasonable to make this claim. In its initial formulation [5], Sheridan and Verplank were generalizing from a "pattern" in human supervisor-subordinate relationships and extending it to HAI. There are clear alternatives. This is important since a design pattern should not be all-encompassing, but rather appropriate in a subset of frequently encountered contexts. Sheridan [4] identified at least three other HAI approaches: direct control, indirect control through an interface (i.e., teleoperation), and computer aided control. There are also HAI relationships which are not supervisory. One characterization comes from Wiig [6] and involves 7 "Cs": Combat, Competition, Control, Cloistering, Coordination, Collaboration and Cooperation. Of these, Supervisory Control fits neatly into only the third category.

The entities and relationships that characterize supervisory control as a design pattern have already been specified in multiple sources, most recently in the paper by Schulte, Donath and Lange in this volume [1]. These consist, in their formalism, of:

- A *Work Process* consisting of a *Work Object* (i.e., a goal or mission) which takes place in an *Environment*, using *Material and Energy Supplies* and *Information*. The Work Process generates *Output* which alters the Environment in some way.
- The Work Process itself is performed by a *Work System* which is composed of *Worker(s)* and *Tool(s)*. Workers understand and pursue the Work Object using some degree of initiative and thus can be either *human* or some forms of *advanced automated agents* capable of these higher cognitive functions. Workers alone are able to break down the Work Object into tasks and to assign those tasks to Tools. By contrast, Tools only perform tasks when used or told to do so by the Worker. Though they may be adaptive to the environment, and may also perform higher cognitive functions, they do so only within the roles and duties assigned to the by the Worker(s).
- Note that *Automation*, or *Autonomous Agents*, are a special case that be either Worker or Tool can, depending on their roles and capabilities.
- Two relationships are defined between Worker and Tool elements: a *Hierarchical Relationship* in which tasks are decomposed by one element (Worker only) and

delegated for performance by the Tools, and a *Heterarchical Relationship* in which multiple entities may cooperate to perform the Work Object, presumably in either Worker or Tool roles. Both imply bi-directional information flow but control differs between the two.

Supervisory Control is, then, characterized by a Worker (who may be Human or an Advanced Agent) in a hierarchical relationship with Tools to perform a Work Object. There may be more than one entity in both the Worker and Tool groups and relationships within those subgroups may be hierarchical or heterarchical. Tools themselves may range from "dumb" to highly advanced automation and intelligent agents but do not take initiative in assigning themselves tasks with an understanding of the Work Objective. This relationship may be depicted, using Shulte et al.'s notation, as shown in Fig. 1. Note that the multiple entities in shades of gray are meant to indicate options (i.e., one or more of each may be used) and the dashed-line circles are meant to convey groups of, in this case, possible entities. Thus, this figure connotes the "superpattern" of supervisory control[1]

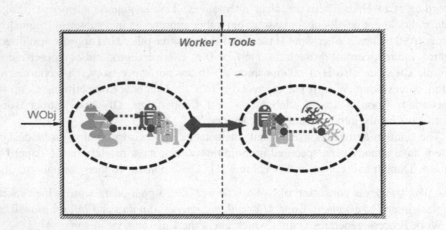

Fig. 1. A proposed "superpattern" for Supervisory Control.

If supervisory control is a design pattern, in the sense of [2], then it must be useful for resolving a set of conflicting forces. But this implies that, insofar as those force sets repeat in patterns of their own, it must admit sub-patterns which permit tradeoffs and differential valuation for different problem sets.

---

[1] I have avoided placing humans in the tool portion of the figure. While it is clear that there are supervisory relationships between humans and other humans, we might call this "supervision" rather than supervisory control. Schulte would, I think, argue that the human ability to understand the work objective and form intentions about how (and maybe whether) to pursue it, keeps them from fitting the "Tool" in his description.

3 Conflicting Forces: Problem Patterns and Their Solution Patterns

Are there conflicting forces that drive tradeoffs in the use of Supervisory Control and give rise to specific "subpatterns" as instances of it? If so, what is their nature and what aspects of context are pertinent to the application of the parent pattern?

At the highest level of abstraction, the conflicting forces characterizing the problem addressed by supervisory control can be stated as *one or more humans want to accomplish goals in specific ways without incurring the full workload and skills required to achieve the goals themselves*. This may be because they *cannot* incur that work due to physical, mental, locational, etc. reasons, or because they simply don't wish to, or because they are less competent. Thus, this forms the core set of conflicting forces and can be depicted as in Fig. 2. This figure introduces a "superpattern" depicted as a *Problem Pattern* which is solved by an abstract *Solution Pattern*. The Solution

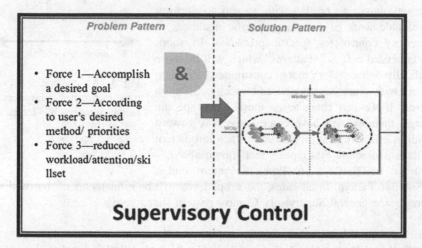

Fig. 2. Proposed Problem Pattern and Solution Pattern that link design decisions to use Supervisory Control.

Pattern is what perhaps more commonly comes to mind as a "design pattern" (cf. [3]), but design power comes from knowing the circumstances in which a solution is appropriate—that is, what problem it is a solution for. Problem Patterns are characterized by conflicting forces [2] and these should be captured in problem description.

I will use the convention of stating problem forces on the left side and the solution pattern on the right to imply that problems with these conflicting forces (i.e., problems of this type) are solved by solutions of this type. The forces themselves will be simply stated for now, with their relationships (notionally, Boolean AND, OR, XOR, NOT) illustrated. In examples below, I will introduce an added notation for prioritization or values which discriminate between those forces.

There is much more to be said about variations in the problem(s) which supervisory control may or may not solve but, as will be seen below, these are appropriately the focus of "sub-patterns"—that is, alternative patterns which are themselves types of supervisory control but which impose additional constraints on the solution pattern and which are intended and "good for" solving different types of problem patterns.

4   SubPatterns of Supervisory Control

Supervisory Control can be seen as a design or Solution Pattern which is good at resolving the conflicting forces that characterize its Problem Pattern. But this gives us little traction by itself, since one always has to apply and interpret Supervisory Control in a more specific setting. If all we know is the high level, comparatively abstract Problem-Solution pattern expressed above, we are left with no way to perform the valuable work of designing specific instances of supervisory control for specific problems. In short, what is needed are "Sub-Patterns" which will be more specifically-defined for more constrained Problem Patterns with more constrained and specific Solution Patterns. If we can characterize these more specific pairings, then we will have come some way toward providing effective design guidance. Each subpattern will have a structure that repeats that shown above— that is, it will have a sub-Problem Pattern and a sub-Solution Pattern. In all cases, the subpatterns will be refinements of, but will still adhere to, the general Supervisory Control pattern stated above.

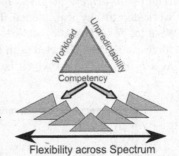

Fig. 3. A tradeoff between three interrelated parameters for human-automation interaction (after [7]).

4.1   Problem Pattern Variations—Finer Grained Conflicting Forces

What finer-grained sets of conflicting forces can we identify within the broad set identified for Supervisory Control? We characterized one set (each embodying or aggregating many subforces) in Miller and Parasuraman (2007) [7]: the *workload* (particularly cognitive workload) the human experiences in attempting to control a system, the *unpredictability* of the system to the human and the *competence* of the overall Workers + Tools system under the expected configuration and environmental conditions. We have drawn this relationship as an adjustable triangle to indicate that there is a fundamental tradeoff between these three dimensions (see Fig. 3).

Performance to a given level of competency can only be achieved through some mix of workload and unpredictability. A user's workload can be reduced by allocating some functions to subordinates (human or automated), but only with increased unpredictability to the user (at least for those functions); conversely, reducing unpredictability by having the user perform functions increases workload. It is sometimes possible to reduce both workload and unpredictability through better design—corresponding to shortening the height of the triangle.

Another implication is that these approaches are endpoints of a spectrum with many alternatives between, each representing a different tradeoff between workload, unpredictability and competency and each a different mix of human and automation roles. The range of alternatives and exactly how they are implemented may be constrained, but an alternative must be selected. This selection is the process of *designing*, and it is exactly where selecting among solution patterns would be appropriate.

Other dimensions are certainly relevant to supervisory control, but many can be compressed into those three (workload, competency, unpredictability). A list of potential other factors and their relationship is presented in Fig. 4. This list is undoubtedly incomplete and its elements are not orthogonal. Indeed, much work in human factors has addressed their complex relationships for the past several years without complete success. I am attempting a preliminary list of elements which contribute to conflicting forces pertinent to designing supervisory control implementations to enlarge the vocabulary of entities in the Problem Pattern description. From these finer-grained forces we can define more specific sub problems classes. For example: how is supervisory control accomplished with agents/tools of varying competencies? With supervisors of varying competencies? When missions are of high vs. low risk? When the supervisor is not co-located and can't communicate with the subordinate? Etc.

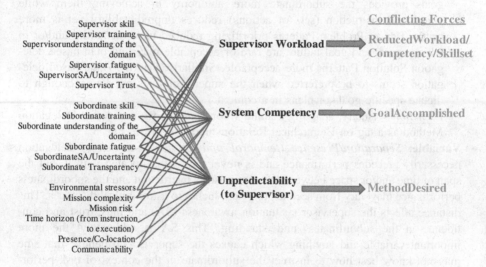

Fig. 4. Some finer-grained dimensions that affect the conflicting forces for the Supervisory Control SuperPattern and its SubPatterns.

4.2 Solution Pattern Variations—Finer Grained Entities and Relationships

Since Sheridan and Verplank defined the "supervisory control" relationship in 1978 [5], Google Scholar says there have been almost 50,000 published articles using that phrase in their title. In principle, each of these represents or discusses a separate instance of the SuperPattern "Supervisory Control"... but surely there are useful Solution subpatterns within that set—ideas that restrict the broad class of supervisory control to subclasses designed to solve more specific problems. The ability of a pattern representation scheme to account for these variations will be key to its descriptive power. Just as a map may be designed to afford broad international navigation, but not to get a driver from one street address to another, so too a pattern description may need to be augmented or limited to function at different levels of description.

A full categorization of this space is well beyond the scope of this paper, but some dimensions along which supervisory control systems differ can be suggested. Below, I will emphasize the delegation or instruction (cf. [7]) act which is crucial to the Hierarchical Relationship and which transfers control authority from supervisor to subordinate. Important variations in the attributes, number and capabilities of both supervisors and subordinates also exist and should be examined, but have not been yet.

- **Variable**: *Delegation Method* — We have previously proposed [8] that delegation can be performed through various mixtures of stated Goals, Plans, Constraints/Stipulations, and Values or Policies. The common or appropriate mixture of these elements for differing conditions may, itself, constitute a sub-pattern within the general delegation pattern.
  - *Relation to Problem Forces*–We know [9] that instruction which emphasizes goals provides the subordinate more autonomy in achieving them while plan-based instruction (sets of actions) reduces unpredictability yet is more brittle. Hence, Problem Patterns prioritizing reduced unpredictability and/or in which upsets and goal failure are rare or acceptable may find plan-based delegation Solution Patterns more acceptable. Similarly, Priority/Value-based delegation seems to be preferred when the supervisor does not know enough to dictate specific goals or plans in a context.
  - *Depiction*–Visually, adapting Schulte's conventions, we can depict Delegation Method as a tag on Hierarchical Relationship as shown in Fig. 5.
- **Variable:** *Separation/Presence* *(temporal and physical)*—an act of delegation necessarily precedes performance and is never entirely co-located with it, but the span of time and/or space between the supervisor's instruction and the subordinate's performance may vary from seconds to years, inches to astronomical distances. This distance affects the supervisor's situation awareness (SA) and thus, trust and confidence in the subordinates' understanding. This SA is, ultimately, the more important variable and anything which causes the supervisor to believe that s/he may not know best how to instruct the subordinate in the context of task performance will likely have the effects described below.
  - *Relation to Problem Forces*–Separation affects information flows and frequently mandates more a priori negotiation producing, I hypothesize, a rough bell curve for instruction detail. At very low separation, supervisor intervention ability may drive down the perceived need for substantial instruction. As separation increases, confidence in instructional ability declines, yielding higher levels of delegated autonomy and on delegation at higher task and authority levels or using value-based delegation methods.

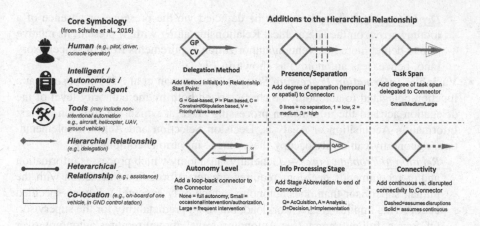

Fig. 5. Proposed depiction additions to enable presentation of additional, finer-grained aspects of the Hierarchical Relationship and, therefore, to permit sub-Patterns to be represented and discussed.

- *Depiction*— We will depict a relative degree of separation by means of inserted lines on the Hierarchical Relationship connector as in Fig. 5.
- **Variable:** *Task Span*—an act of delegation conveys the responsibility to perform a task or function, but that function may be "larger" or "smaller" in terms of the number and variety of subfunctions it includes. The size of this span is related to information flows and the need for a priori negotiation.
  - *Relation to Problem Forces*— Obviously, delegating "larger" tasks to subordinates does a better job (insofar as they are performed adequately) of reducing the supervisor's workload and skill requirements. It can also, though, make performance more unpredictable and recovery from error worse still because it effectively hides errors from the operator [10].
  - *Depiction*— We depict relative degree of task span via the size of the end arrow in the Hierarchical Relationship as shown in Fig. 5.
- **Variable:** *Autonomy Level*—a delegation act conveys some responsibility and authority to select and perform alternatives from among the sub-functions which could accomplish the delegated task, but this authority need not be absolute; the agent may need to ask further permission for certain functions or resources. Further, autonomy might not be complete if plans or actions need to be reviewed and approved by the supervisor before they are enacted. Yet another reason is if the Supervisor can intervene and seize control of the tools directly rather than managing them through the subordinate.
  - *Relation to Problem Forces*—As with Task Span, to which it is related, delegating more autonomy to the subordinate reduces workload and skill requirements from the supervisor to the degree that the subordinate is competent (and trusted). But increased autonomy for the subordinate means increased risks that tasks may not be performed exactly as the supervisor wishes—and hence can drive the need for intervention and/or "check-ins" and subsequent authorization.

- *Depiction*—Autonomy level can be depicted via the presence or absence of a looping arrow on the Hierarchical Relationship along with, if present, its relative size to depict more intervention/authorization requirements from the supervisory (and, hence, less autonomy) as shown in Fig. 5.
- **Variable:** *Information Processing Stage*—Parasuraman et al. [11] proposed that a function delegated to autonomy be characterized both by the authority level of the delegation act and the information processing stage at which the function occurs: Information Acquisition or Analysis, Decision Selection and Action Implementation. Autonomy can easily occupy these stages in various combinations.
  - *Relation to Problem Forces*—Generally, autonomy which processes information and/or recommends decisions requires greater information interaction with the human supervisor than does autonomy which only executes a human-specified action. This implies greater workload, but more predictability for the supervisor. Of course, full autonomy (see Autonomy Level above) requires autonomy over these stages for performance of the task assigned. As Galster et al. have shown [12], autonomy at the later sequential stages (decision selection and implementation) either requires greater attention to earlier stages from the supervisor or risks "out of the loop" errors and associated time loss as the operator retrieves SA.
  - *Depiction*—We can depict the primary information processing stage(s) in which the subordinate is tasked to act via an abbreviation added to the end arrow of the Hierarchical Relationship—see Fig. 5.
- **Variable:** *Connectivity*—some subordinate relationships are designed assuming active monitoring and continuous control inputs by the supervisor. These subordinates either fail, or enter a "fail-safe" state when those conditions are violated. Others are designed to operate with occasional sustained communications loss— usually by relying on a more "covering" delegation act that occurred in an earlier time span. The use of additional "layers" of delegation in the form of back up plans or general policies is also common.
  - *Relation to Problem Forces*—Connectivity is clearly related to Autonomy level in that lower levels of autonomy require connectivity. Thus, its impact on the problem's conflicting forces is similar: design for subordinate action during lost connectivity implies reduced workload on the part of the supervisor during non-communicative periods, but this increases unpredictability. The net result is frequently either design for increased autonomy or greater effort to pre-mission planning and authorization stages.
  - *Depiction*— We depict presumption of connectivity via the use of solid vs. dashed lines on the Hierarchical Relationship Connector in Fig. 5.

These are a few "sub-pattern descriptor elements" which, I believe, can be profitably used to depict specific variations under the general heading of the Supervisory Control superpattern. There are clearly many other elements which could be added, and I have admittedly focused only on the hierarchical relationship. Below, I will explore whether these elements can help us discriminate between Solution and Problem Patterns for different types of Supervisory Control implementations.

5 Some Instances of Supervisory Control Sub-patterns

As a simple example using the concepts developed above, consider the Rotorcraft Pilots' Associate (RPA)—a system created to aid the pilots of an advanced attack/scout rotorcraft [13, 14]. RPA was an intelligent cognitive aiding system which was aware of the intent of the two pilots and of the overall mission, thus it is a Worker in Schulte's sense. The pilots and the Associate worked with a suite of advanced Tools—sensors, communications, weapons and defensive systems, as well as decision aids which processed and integrated results. While the overall relationship between the pilots and the Associate was largely hierarchical and an instance of supervisory control, there were cooperative relationship elements as well. But over the many functions the humans and systems in RPA performed, there were many different interaction styles and relationships. Thus, it is a reasonable source of alternate supervisory control examples. We will examine two such subsystems/functions to illustrate the above representational scheme and the similarities and differences it highlights.

One RPA function was recommending cover locations during an enemy contact. When this event was detected, the Associate determined whether pilots needed and wanted to react. If so, it tasked less intent-aware Tools to analyze terrain and known threats to prepare a set of "cover locations"—locations the aircraft could get to rapidly where it would be safe from fire and visibility. The Associate then determined whether these locations had adequate priority to be presented on the pilot's displays.

Figure 6 presents this relationship pattern, which I have tentatively labelled "Prepare High Criticality Input," as a sub-instance of the general Supervisory Control Pattern (as shown by the expansion from the small image in the upper left). Otherwise, this subPattern uses the same structure as its parent: a Problem Pattern characterized by conflicting forces and a Solution Pattern showing participating elements and their relationships. I have introduced a rough priority to the Problem Pattern forces. Up and down arrows indicate higher or lower priority, and no arrow indicates neutral priority. Chief importance goes to the time critical and high criticality aspects here—failure to get useful cover information quickly enough can result in the loss of the ship and crew.

To the right of this figure is the Solution Pattern. Two humans interact with an intent-aware agent (the Associate) to interpret the WObj for this task. They permit/instruct the Associate to prepare cover location recommendations via pre-mission authorizations. The Associate tasks intelligent, but not intent-aware Tools (decision aids, sensor processors) to develop recommendations when a threat is detected. The relationship from Workers to Tools is Hierarchical, but more detail is provided about it via the enlarged green arrow. The Delegation Method is primarily goal-based (to have cover recommendations) but there are also constraints and values on what would constitute a good location. There is essentially no Separation since all Workers are co-located with the Tools and there is no significant time lag between the request and the task execution period. The Task Span is very narrow– just computing recommendations and presenting them, not executing them, much less additional

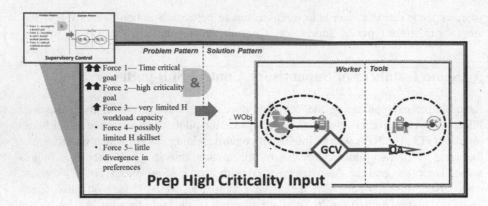

Fig. 6. A Problem and Solution Pattern for a particular subclass of Supervisory Control relationships characterized as Preparing High Criticality Inputs.

deployment or evasion tasks– and falls into the acquisition and analysis Information Processing stages (not decision or implementation). The Autonomy Level, for this task is very high, however, since there is no ability for the Workers to override or interrupt the recommendation of locations. There is a presumption of continuous Connectivity.

Contrast this with preparing a SPOT report upon enemy contact. Such reports are supposed to be sent back to aid in higher echelon and theater SA and coordination. They are important, but their criticality is not nearly as high as deploying to cover upon enemy contact. The conflicting forces on the left side of Fig. 7 reflect this.

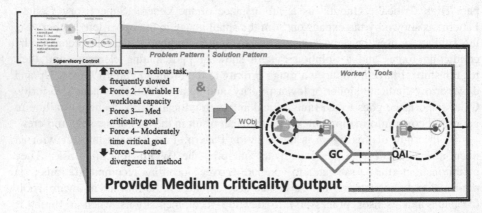

Fig. 7. A Problem and Solution Pattern for another subclass of Supervisory Control relationships characterized as Provide Medium Criticality Output.

The right side of Fig. 7 shows the Solution Pattern. It is similar to Fig. 6 above, as expected for alternate implementations of a superpattern, but there are differences. The delegation method from Workers to Tools is primarily goal-based (to have the report prepared and sent) but there are also some constraints on when it can be sent without explicit authorization (e.g., user workload levels). There is some temporal separation since although all Workers are co-located with the Tools, authorization for when the report can be sent autonomously is done pre-mission. The Task Span is fairly narrow—just processing information for input to the report, presenting it and sending it if the user agrees (or evaluating workload levels and permission and sending it autonomously if previously authorized), though this is somewhat larger than for coverage locations above. Tasks fall into the Information Acquisition, Analysis stages and Implementation stages. The Autonomy Level, for this task, however, is intermediate since the system is usually supposed to submit its prepared report to the Human for review and editing before sending. There is a presumption of continuous connectivity.

6   Conclusions

I have argued for broadening of the perspective on a design pattern from a strict focus on the solution to, as I believe was Alexander's [2] intent, linking Problem Patterns to Solution Patterns into SuperPatterns and then decomposing them into SubPatterns for more design power. I have explored these relationships in the context of a proposed Supervisory Control "SuperPattern" with both a Problem Pattern (defined by conflicting forces) and a Solution Pattern. I showed how such a pattern can be decomposed into subpatterns with more specific problem and solution patterns. I suggested initial approaches to characterizing conflicting forces for supervisory control subpatterns, as well as specific dimensions (with methods for depicting them) along which supervisory control implementations (especially the Hierarchical relationship) are achieved.

This approach was illustrated via two different functions from the RPA system. I showed that the formalism was capable of identifying differences in both the Problem Pattern and the Solution Pattern for these different functions. I was even able to suggest SubPatterns associated with high criticality inputs vs. medium criticality outputs. This hierarchical approach to linking Problem and Solution patterns and then decomposing them seems both viable and to provide more design power because it identifies more specific characteristics which help to discriminate when (in what circumstances) one instance or implementation approach to supervisory control works vs. others.

Acknowledgments. I am indebted to Axel Schulte, Diana Donath & Doug Lange for the study on which this paper is based, as well as the NATO RTO-HFM-247 Technical Team, particularly Jay Shively, for encouraging discussion on the topic.

References

1. Schulte, A., Donath, D., Lange, D.S.: Design patterns for human-cognitive agent teaming. In: Harris, D. (ed.) EPCE 2016. LNAI, vol. 9736, pp. 231–243. Springer, Heidelberg (2016)
2. Alexander, C.: A Pattern Language: Towns, Buildings, Construction. Oxford University Press, Oxford (1977)

3. Gamma, E., Helm, R., Johnson, R., Vlissides, J.: Design Patterns. Design Patterns. Addison-Wesley, Boston (1995)
4. Sheridan, T.: Supervisory Control. In: Salvendy, G. (ed.) Handbook of Human Factors, pp. 1244–1268. Wiley, New York (1987)
5. Sheridan, T., Verplank, W.: Human and computer control of undersea teleoperators. MIT Man-Machine Systems Laboratory, Cambridge. Technical report (1978)
6. Wiig, K.: Knowledge Management Methods: Practical Approaches to Managing Knowledge. Schema Press, Arlington (1995)
7. Miller, C., Parasuraman, R.: Designing for flexible interaction between humans and automation. Hum. Factors 49(1), 57–75 (2007)
8. Miller, C.: Delegation for single pilot operation. In: 2014 HCI-Aero ACM, New York (2014)
9. Vicente, K.: Cognitive Work Analysis. Erlbaum, Mahwah (1999)
10. Miller, C., Shaw, T., Emfield, A., Hamell, J., Parasuraman, R., Parasuraman, R., Musliner, D.: Delegating to automation: performance, complacency and bias effects under non-optimal conditions. 2011 HFES 55(1), 95–99 (2011). SAGE, Los Angeles
11. Parasuraman, R., Sheridan, T., Wickens, C.: A model for types and levels of human interaction with automation. IEEE SMC A Syst. Hum. 30, 286–297 (2000)
12. Galster S.: An examination of complex human-machine system performance under multiple levels and stages of automation. Dissertation for Catholic University of America (2003)
13. Dornheim, M.: Apache tests power of new cockpit tool. Aviat. Week Space Technol. 151, 46–49 (1999)
14. Miller, C., Hannen, M.: The rotorcraft pilot's associate: design and evaluation of an intelligent user interface for cockpit information management. Knowl. Based Syst. 12, 443–456 (1999)

Interaction Design Patterns for Adaptive Human-Agent-Robot Teamwork in High-Risk Domains

Mark A. Neerincx[✉], Jurriaan van Diggelen, and Leo van Breda

TNO, Kampweg 5, 3769 DE Soesterberg, Netherlands
{mark.neerincx, jurriaan.vandiggelen,
leo.vanbreda}@tno.nl

Abstract. Integrating cognitive agents and robots into teams that operate in high-demand situations involves mutual and context-dependent behaviors of the human and agent/robot team-members. We propose a cognitive engineering method that includes the development of Interaction Design patterns for such systems as re-usable, theoretically and empirically founded, design solutions. This paper presents an overview of the background, the method and three example patterns.

Keywords: Design patterns · Human-Agent teamwork · Cognitive robots · Cognitive engineering · High-Risk domain

1 Introduction

A clear need exists for the deployment of robots to establish effective and safe operations in high risk domains, e.g. for firefighting, search and rescue, and defense. To meet this need, research in the field of supervisory control provided advanced multi-modal user interfaces for the robot operators, focusing on dedicated, small human-robot settings (e.g., two operators that control an Unmanned Aerial Vehicle, UAV, or a single operator that (tele-)operates an Unmanned Ground Vehicle, UGV). To enhance the robot's functions and usability, its level of automation has been increased, so that the operator's role became more supervisory in nature, overseeing the automated activation of pro-grammed events (e.g., making sure the appropriate event is activated at the appropriate time) and managing unexpected changes to the automated mission plan. Associated operator interfaces for the robots have been developed that take into account issues associated with automation management, including vigilance, attention management, clumsy automation, etc. Subsequently, next-generation multiple-robot systems have been developed that can be supervised and controlled by a single supervisor at a higher abstraction level, due to system's increased capability to make 'lower level decisions'. For the supervisory control of single and multiple robots, inventories of critical human factors issues were made, e.g. on situation awareness, workload, performance and safety. Standard operator interface design guidelines associated with supervisory control were developed to facilitate interoperability across (semi) autonomous platforms, and

© Springer International Publishing Switzerland 2016
D. Harris (Ed.): EPCE 2016, LNAI 9736, pp. 211–220, 2016.
DOI: 10.1007/978-3-319-40030-3_22

for identifying, prioritizing, and addressing human factors challenges associated with robot supervisory control [4, 11, 19, 20, 22, 26].

However, the content and scope of these guidelines fail to address current operational demands and to steer the required developments and applications of robotics and artificial intelligence. The supervisory control paradigm still regards robots as "obedient servants" that only do work after they have been explicitly told to do so by a human operator, which could cause an unacceptably high workload. Furthermore, the human is not necessarily the best decision maker, as the robot may possess information which is unknown to the operator. As the amount of robots (or UxV's) is increasing and these robots are being employed in a wider variety of tasks, they should become more proactive in their behavior than in the supervisory control paradigm. To realize this, we should aim at robots as team-members [6]. A major challenge for such an approach is to integrate the (intelligent) robots into the dynamic teamwork in such a way that the robots complement human capabilities, relieve them from demanding tasks (e.g., observation, reconnaissance, search, securing and sampling) and do not pose additional demands on them (cf., [18]). That is, we aim at the development of robots that become more and more able to act as adaptive team-members (e.g., by sharing knowledge, pursuing team goals, and coordinating "own" actions with actions of others). In our approach, such a system encompasses networked Humans, Agents and Robots, which show Teamwork (HART) in a "smart environment" (i.e., networked interactive things and knowledge bases; see Fig. 1). The agents support goal-oriented behaviors, driven by task, context, team and user models [3, 12], and the ontology provides the knowledge representations to establish joint knowledge-based behaviors (based on shared mental models, transactive memory systems, and shared situation awareness; [10]).

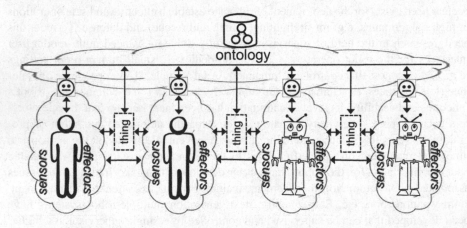

Fig. 1. Human-Agent-Robot Teamwork (HART) in a smart environment

As the behaviors of the humans, agents and robots are adaptive (i.e., towards one another and towards the dynamic outside), design and implementation of the optimal set of behaviors is intrinsically complex. Whereas several methodologies for agent-based software engineering exist (e.g. [13]), these methodologies focus on systems that consist completely of software agents and robots, and do not consider the human interactions that is required in HART. To fill this gap, we propose to use Interaction Design (ID) patterns as an integral part of cognitive engineering, addressing the mutual dependent human, agent and robot behaviors in an explicit Interaction Design Rationale. These ID-patterns (1) justify the design choices with theoretical and empirical foundations, (2) show the similarities between different instantiated interaction designs and (3) may be put into a library of reusable (justified) HART ID-patterns.

2 Design Patterns

Alexander [1] was the originator of the pattern concept, defining it as a description of "[…] a problem which occurs over and over again in our environment, and […] the core of the solution to that problem, in such a way that you can use this solution a million times over, without ever doing it the same way twice". His philosophy of constructive, coherent and meaningful design in architecture, inspired the development of pattern languages in many other domains and application fields. Examples are Workflow Patterns [27]), User Interface Design Patterns [25, 28], Interaction Design [5], Design Patterns for sociality in human-robot interaction [14], human-computer interaction [7], patterns to manage software complexity [9], and patterns for collaborative technology [24].

For our purpose of explicating the HART Design Rationale during research and development, the following characteristics are important. A pattern is a structured description of an invariant solution to a recurrent problem within a context. It abstracts true interactions, is generative and includes notion of temporality. The HART ID-patterns should capture good practice and provide theoretical account, i.e., they (1) represent "big ideas" with their design rationale, (2) reflect design values, (3) contain common concepts to communicate the design rationale (as a "lingua franca"), (4) are grounded in the domain and include examples, and (5) have different levels of abstraction and scales.

3 Pattern Engineering

We propose to integrate the ID-pattern development process into a general situated Cognitive Engineering methodology that derives a coherent base-line of use cases, requirements and claims from work, domain, human factors and technology analyses [21]. This baseline describes the *what* (requirements), *when* (use cases) and *why* (claims) of the design, whereas the patterns describe *how* the human-agent interaction will take place [17]. These interaction patterns are generalization of specific user interface and dialogue instantiations (the interdependent multi-actor "look-feel-and-hear").

For HART patterns, we distinguish the following key concepts [23]:

- *Actor*: In a HART system the actor can be *Human*, *Agent* or *Robot*. Note that we use the term "Actor", where Schulte et al. [23] use the term "Worker". Actor refers to "activity" instead of work and is as such a more general term. In this way, we can describe generic patterns on joint human-agent/robot activities that take place within and outside work organizations (e.g. informal caregiving).

- *Relationship*: The relationship between actors can be *Supervisory* and/or *Collaborative*. These two parameters are similar to the distinction of Schulte et al. [23] between hierarchical and heterarchical relationships. However, we distinguish the main concept "Relationship" to enable the creation of patterns that adjust such relationships during the work processes.
- *Location*: Actors can perform their work at the *Same* (co-location) or a *Distant* (distributed) location. Also here, we are focusing on the dynamics, e.g., patterns that describe agent support for " roaming operators" (see Sect. 4.2).
- *Pattern status*: the status of the pattern can be *Proto* (i.e., in construction) or *Grounded* (e.g., empirically validated in an experiment).

Pattern engineering aims at the generation, sharing, use and evolution of design knowledge [16]. To make progress in the field of HART, the research and design can make use of available patterns and anticipate for the refinement or construction of relevant patterns, taking the following steps:

1. Identify key design problems
2. Search for available design patterns
3. If no pattern can be found, and if it is a general, recurrent design problem:

   - Start with a *Proto Pattern*[1], a pattern "in construction", i.e., a design problem and solution documented in a pattern form (yet lacking empirical grounding)

4. Provide different instantiations (examples)
5. Test, refine and validate these examples
6. If successful:

   - Make the Design Pattern accessible in library (of best practices)

4   Example ID-Patterns

This section presents briefly three example ID-patterns to share HART research progress: for making working agreements, for establishing adequate human supervision of the delegated tasks and for anticipating required colocation actions.

4.1   Adjustable Human-Agent Working Agreements

Our first example focuses on the enabling of making adjustable working agreements between humans and agents to establish the required adaptability of the teamwork. This pattern aims to overcome a common problem present in most modern SCADA systems (Supervisory Control And Data Acquisition), where either the system behaves fully autonomously, or where the full control is allocated to the human. Using an agent and this design pattern, a third option is introduced which supports dynamic and adaptive human-agent (sub)task allocation (i.e., the SCADA system is evolving into a HART system). For specific work contexts, the human can set agreements with the agent on how the tasks will be allocated.

---

[1] cf. http://c2.com/cgi/wiki?ProtoPattern.

Title	Obtain adjustable human-agent working agreements on object handling

Design Problem

- The information that the team has to process for object handling is highly dynamic, causing high peaks and deep hollows in workload
- The agent can perform "only" well-delineated information processing tasks adequately
- The human operator should remain in the loop (1) to maintain the Situation Awareness for adequate performance of the complex or unsteady tasks, (2) to assess the work strategy, and (3) to maintain overall responsibility

Design solution

The *human* operator can choose the conditions and rules for delegating tasks to the agent with the objectives to harmonize operator workload and maintain situation awareness (SA) under the dynamic conditions for optimal team performance. The human-agent relationship is *supervisory* and *collaborative*. The human operator, who is in charge of the work process (as "Creditor"), sets (1) the delegation criteria (e.g., the area of operation and characteristics of possible objects in this area that the agent is obliged to handle) and (2) the corresponding handling tasks (e.g., identify and monitor). As an electronic partner, the agent will meet this social commitment and act according to the defined settings with the corresponding obligations, i.e., as "Debtor", show the task outcomes with the conditions that led to these outcomes (e.g., sensed attributes of an object). In this way, agents can be committed to provide an advice on the handling of specific (critical) objects, while handling (standard) objects themselves. A formal language has been developed to implement such commitments in a human-agent system [15].

Use when

When a clear-cut part of the work can be automated and humans are needed (a) to deal with the uncertain or ill-defined information, and (b) to take the overall responsibility for the information-processing strategy and outcome.

Design rationale

HART-system behaviors are prompted and constrained by norms (e.g., flight regulations). To address situational dynamics, the responsibilities for specific task objects (e.g., tracks) are actively divided by the human operator by specifying the range of distinctive object attributes (e.g., flight height, region, ...) that the agent has to process (i.e., is obliged to identify). The human operator can maintain the overall responsibility of the work well, because (1) she initiates and may always adjust the agreement, and (2) the agent's behavior is transparent (i.e., showing the current object attributes and rules that led to the identification outcome). In other words, the agent will act according to the agreement settings with the corresponding obligations and, as "Debtor", show the conditions that led to the task outcomes (e.g., speed, direction, height and distance of an object, which led to agent's identification "neutral"). In general, the human takes the more difficult objects and the agent is left with the easy ones (e.g., neutral objects that take an air or sea way and identify themselves).

Example

A prototype of a "track handling agent" for a naval operator was developed [2] and tested [8]. The general task is to assess tracks in the environment of the ship and decide whether it is "unknown", "friendly", "assumed friendly", "neutral", "suspect" or "hostile". These tracks are the domain-related instantiations of objects for which a number of tasks can be executed (e.g., classification, identification, guidance and/or engagement).

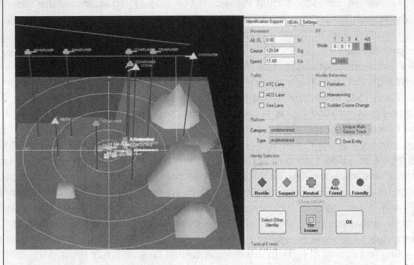

Via color- and form-coded icons, the source (human or agent) and outcome of the identification is shown in the display. Object attributes are shown when clicking on the corresponding icon. A timeline shows the tasks that have been and are being performed for the operator and the agent. In a separate tab, the work agreement settings can be specified and edited. For example, for the identification task, the operator can set a speed threshold of 400 mph. If higher than 400, the agent has to give an advice on the identity of the track, whereas below 400 the agents sets the identity itself. This granular work distribution with object attributes matches closely humans way of dynamic work distribution (e.g., when the number of signals, the response times to these signals, and/or the workload are high).

Status

Grounded [8]: The effects of the "track handling agent" was evaluated in a high-fidelity command & control setting with eight naval officers. The overall efficiency increased with 60%, particularly for the complex scenarios (65%). Downsides of the agent did not appear.

4.2   Transfer from Distant to Co-location

The second design pattern aims at providing a solution for the problem that human control has some context requirements which must be fulfilled before control can be passed to the human. One of these context requirements is spatial location. For example, when the system operates in fully autonomous mode, and a problem occurs, the human operator should be able to make it back to the workstation within a certain time limit.

Title	Demand operator to stay in vicinity of workstation.
Design Problem	
The agent predicts that human intervention might be necessary soon, which cannot be done from a mobile device. It asks the operator to stay in the vicinity of the workstation.	
Design solution	
Popup window with short explanation of the type of expected problems and time frame. The operator can ask the agent for more explanation, and decide to agree or disagree to stay in the vicinity.	
Use when	
Agent expects to switch from autonomous mode to a semi-autonomous mode which requires a stationary operator.	
Design rationale	
Operator is more likely to follow the system's advice to stay in the vicinity if (s)he understand why this is necessary.	
Example	
In the control room of a ship with Dynamic Positioning, an agent that provides proximity notification allows operators to roam about the vessel. This notification provides a summary of the proximity need. The operator can resolve, reject, annotate or ask for more information. 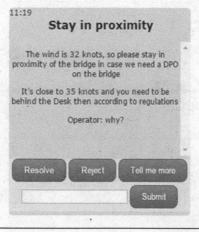	
Status	*Proto*

4.3 Management of Interaction Processes

The interaction design patterns such as the ones described above have been designed to realize sensible human-agent interaction by themselves. This does not guarantee that the human can cope with multiple interactions running simultaneously. The third design pattern that we will discuss aims to solve that problem.

Title	Manage multiple interactions between user and system

Design Problem

When many interactions with the agent are required simultaneously, the user gets overloaded with information.

Design solution

A container window which contains all separate interactions as separate tiles. The important interactions are shown intrusively (i.e. in color and large), and the less important interactions are shown non-intrusive (smaller and greyed out). The container shows the most important 7 windows in an intrusive way. The user can choose to dismiss any interaction as non-important using the "resolve" button.

Use when

Multiple different types of interactions are required simultaneously.

Design rationale

By limiting the amount of intrusive interactions to seven, human operators are capable of processing them simultaneously.

Example

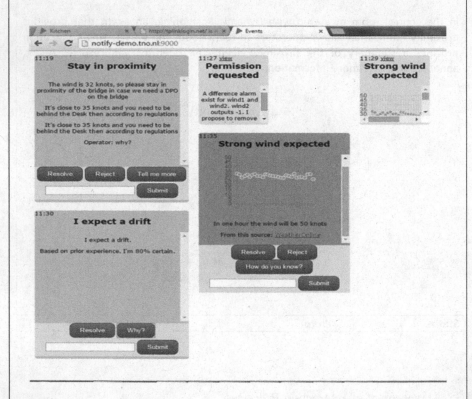

Status	*Proto*

5   Conclusions

Integrating cognitive agents and robots into teams that operate in high-demand situations involves mutual and context-dependent behaviors of the human and agent/robot team-members. Figure 1 shows the concept of Human-Agent-Robot Teamwork (HART), encompassing agent- and ontology-mediated human-robot collaboration in order to establish adaptive teamwork. We propose a cognitive engineering method that includes the development of Interaction Design patterns for such systems as re-usable, theoretically and empirically founded, design solutions. These patterns are used to explicate and share HART research and development results. In this way, a pattern for making working agreements has been constructed and tested. For establishing adequate human supervision of the delegated tasks, an approval-request pattern was constructed, and for anticipating required colocation actions, a vicinity-advice patterns was constructed. These patterns can be instantiated for different use cases and into specific interaction designs, in order to realize the required adaptive human-robot teamwork.

Acknowledgements. This research is supported by the EU FP7 project 609763 (TRADR), and the TNO Defense research program V1340 on Unmanned Systems.

References

1. Alexander, C., Ishikawa, S., Silverstein, M.A.: Pattern Language: Towns, Buildings, Construction. Center for Environmental Structure series. Oxford University Press, Berkeley (1977)
2. Arciszewski, H.F., De Greef, T.E., Van Delft, J.H.: Adaptive automation in a naval combat management system. IEEE Trans. Syst. Cybern. A Syst. Hum. **39**(6), 1188–1199 (2009)
3. Bagosi, T., de Greeff, J., Hindriks, K.V., Neerincx, M.A.: Designing a Knowledge Representation Interface for Cognitive Agents. In: Baldoni, M., Baresi, L., Dastani, M. (eds.) EMAS 2015. LNCS, vol. 9318, pp. 33–50. Springer, Heidelberg (2015). doi:10.1007/978-3-319-26184-3_3
4. Banbury, S., Gauthier, M., Scipione, A., Hou, M.: Intelligent adaptive systems: literature research of design guidance for intelligent adaptive automation and interfaces. Defence Research and Development Canada - Toronto, CR 2007-075 (2007)
5. Borchers, J.O.: A pattern approach to interaction design. AI SOC. **15**(4), 359–376 (2001)
6. Bradshaw, J.M., Feltovich, P., Johnson, M., Breedy, M., Bunch, L., Eskridge, T., Jung, H., Lott, J., Uszok, A., van Diggelen, J.: From Tools to Teammates: Joint Activity in Human-Agent-Robot Teams. In: Kurosu, M. (ed.) HCD 2009. LNCS, vol. 5619, pp. 935–944. Springer, Heidelberg (2009)
7. Dearden, A., Finlay, J.: Pattern languages in HCI: a critical review. Hum. Comput. Inter. **21**(1), 49–102 (2006)
8. De Greef, T.E., Arciszewski, H.F.R., Neerincx, M.A.: Adaptive automation based on an object-oriented task model: implementation and evaluation in a realistic C2 environment. J. Cognitive Eng. Decis. Mak. **4**, 152–173 (2010)
9. Gamma, E., Helm, R., Johnson, R., Vlissides, J.: Design Patterns: Elements of Reusable Object-Oriented Software. Addinson-Wesley, Reading (1995)

10. Gevers, J.M.P., Uitdewilligen, S., Margarida Passos, A.: Dynamics of team cognition and team adaptation: introduction to the special issue. Eu. J. Work Organ. Psychol. **24**(5), 645–651 (2015)
11. Harrison, J.A., Forster, M.J.: Human systems integration requirements in systems acquisition. In: Booher, H.R. (ed.) Handbook of Human Systems Integration (2003). Wiley, Hoboken (2003)
12. Hindriks, K.V.: Programming rational agents in goal. In: El Fallah Seghrouchni, A., Dix, J., Dastani, M., Bordini, H.R. (eds.) Multi-agent Programming, pp. 119–157. Springer, New York (2009)
13. Jennings, N.R.: An agent-based approach for building complex software systems. Commun. ACM **44**(4), 35–41 (2001)
14. Kahn, P.H., Freier, N.G., Kanda, T., Ishiguro, H., Ruckert, J.H., Severson, R.L., Kane, S.K.: Design patterns for sociality in human-robot interaction. In: Proceedings of the 3rd ACM/IEEE International Conference on Human-Robot Interaction, pp. 97–104. ACM (2008)
15. Kayal, A., Brinkman, W.P., Neerincx, M.A. van Riemsdijk, M.B.: A social commitment model for location sharing applications in the family domain. Int. J. Hum. Comput. Stud. (to appear)
16. Kohls, C.: The theories of design patterns and their practical implications exemplified for e-learning patterns. Dissertation, Katolischen Universität Eichstätt-Ingolstadt. Eichstätt (2013)
17. Mioch, T., Ledegang, W., Paulissen, R., Neerincx, M.A., Van Diggelen, J.: Interaction design patterns for coherent and re-usable shape specifications of human-robot collaboration. In: EICS 2014 (Rome, Italy, June 17–20), pp. 75–83. ACM (2014)
18. Murphy, R.R.: Disaster Robotics. MIT Press, Cambridge (2014)
19. NATO. The NATO Unmanned Aircraft Systems Human Systems Integration Guidebook (2012)
20. NATO. The NATO Human View Handbook (2007)
21. Neerincx, M.A.: Situated cognitive engineering for crew support in space. Pers. Ubiquitous Comput. **15**(5), 445–456 (2011)
22. Reising, J. (ed.): Uninhabited Military Vehicles (UMVs): Human factors Issues in Augmenting the Force. NATO RTO technical report RTO-TR-HFM-078. NATO, Brussel (2009)
23. Schulte, A., Donath, D., Lange, D.S.: Design patterns for human-cognitive agent teaming. In: 13th Conference on Engineering Psychology & Cognitive Ergonomics. LNCS. Springer
24. Schümmer, T., Lukosch, S.: Patterns for Computer-Mediated Interaction. Wiley, Chichester (2007)
25. Tidwell, J.: Designing Interfaces. O'Reilly Media, Inc., Sebastopol (2010)
26. Van Breda, L. (ed.): Supervisory Control of Multiple Uninhabited Systems – Methodologies and Enabling Human-Robot Interface Technologies. NATO RTO technical report AC/323 (HFM-170)TP/451. NATO, Neuilly-sur-Seine Cedex, France (2012). ISBN:978-92-837-0167-5
27. Van der Aalst, W., Hofstede, A.H.M., Kiepuszewski, B., Barros, A.P.: Workflow patterns. Distributed Parallel Databases **14**(1), 5–51 (2003)
28. Van Welie, M., Van der Veer, G.C.: Pattern languages in interaction design: structure and organization. In: Proceedings of Interact 2003, Zürich, Switzerland, pp. 527–534. IOS Press, Amsterdam, 1–5 September 2003

A Teamwork Model for Fighter Pilots

Ulrika Ohlander[1,2(✉)], Jens Alfredson[1], Maria Riveiro[2],
and Göran Falkman[2]

[1] Saab Aeronautics, Saab AB, Linköping, Sweden
{ulrika.ohlander,jens.alfredson}@saabgroup.com
[2] University of Skövde, Skövde, Sweden
{maria.riveiro,goran.falkman}@his.se

Abstract. Fighter pilots depend on collaboration and teamwork to perform successful air missions. However, such collaboration is challenging due to limitations in communication and the amount of data that can be shared between aircraft. In order to design future support systems for fighter pilots, this paper aims at characterizing how pilots collaborate while performing real-world missions. Our starting point is the "Big Five" model for effective teamwork, put forth by Salas et al. [1]. Fighter pilots were interviewed about their teamwork, and how they prepare and perform missions in teams. The results from the interviews were used to describe how pilots collaborate in teams, and to suggest relationships between the teamwork elements of the "Big Five" model for fighter pilots performing missions. The results presented in this paper are intended to inform designers and developers of cockpit displays, data links and decision support systems for fighter aircraft.

Keywords: Team effectiveness · Teamwork · Fighter aircraft · Fighter pilots

1 Introduction

A majority of air missions are conducted by teams of aircraft, and effective teamwork among fighter pilots is a pre-requisite for a successful outcome of missions [2].

Team performance is the result of the teamwork, what the team accomplishes, and team effectiveness is about how the team members acts and interacts when performing the task. A team can perform well and even accomplish its goals, despite ineffective functioning. Hence, focusing only on the outcome and results of the teamwork will not give enough information about how the team reached its goals. In order to understand team effectiveness, it is necessary to investigate the internal processes of the team [1]. Teamwork is practiced in almost all kinds of settings, for example sports, management, product development, health care, as well as in the military. Research on teams is vast, and much of the previous literature focuses on human aspects related to teams, such as team building and leadership. The need for communication is often emphasized in the literature as a success factor, but in most other studied cases, the ability to communicate does not depend on technology as much as in the case between aircraft. The extreme conditions and circumstances, for example time pressure, high stakes, combined with this limited ability to communicate, make the teamwork for pilots challenging. In order

© Springer International Publishing Switzerland 2016
D. Harris (Ed.): EPCE 2016, LNAI 9736, pp. 221–230, 2016.
DOI: 10.1007/978-3-319-40030-3_23

to overcome the limitations associated to current support systems and design more effective systems for the future, this paper aims at investigating which factors make teamwork successful in this domain. To the best of our knowledge there is currently no such description in the literature.

The main contribution of this paper is the description of the teamwork in teams of fighter pilots. The aim is to describe how to these types of teams achieve effectiveness and successful outcomes of their missions. It has been shown that well-designed technology can improve team performance [3]. The teamwork elements that must be supported by technology in the studied environment are therefore of special interest. Since the teamwork between fighter pilots relies heavily on technological support, and there are certain limitations to which data can be distributed and displayed, the presented results are intended to guide in selecting the information that should be processed and presented to the pilots.

2 Teamwork Model

This section describes important theories and findings in team research and relates them to teams of fighter pilots.

A team of military fighter pilots typically consists of two or four aircraft, sometimes more. Since teamwork is present in many different settings, teams can be grouped depending on their characteristics such as team membership, work cycles and output. There are for example project teams, management teams and service teams. A team of fighter pilots can be classified as an *action team*. Other examples of action teams are response teams (medical, fire fighters), sports teams and aircrews. The classification is used to describe teams which are highly skilled specialist teams, cooperating in unpredictable circumstances [4]. Naturally, the task the team is formed to solve affects how the team works. There are mainly two categories of team tasks: collaborative and coordination tasks [1]. In a coordination task, team members depend on each other to perform subtasks in a certain priority, and perhaps there are specialized members for certain actions, for example in a medical team performing surgery. In a collaborative task, the team members are equally able to solve all the subtasks. The team task for a team of fighter pilots is in most cases collaborative. But there might be exceptions from this, for example when one of the team members is flying an aircraft with special equipment.

Many models for teamwork have been proposed in different areas. Salas et al. [1] made a review and found more than 138 relevant models of teamwork. They synthesized the factors that had been found to have an impact on team effectiveness and they named the model The "Big Five" of teamwork. The "Big Five" model contains five central factors and three coordinating mechanisms, thus in total eight elements, necessary for successful teamwork. The approach used when the model was created, and the general applicability, makes it a good starting point for team research. The Big Five model has been analyzed both in military team settings [5], as well as in general, office/school types of teams [6]. Moreover, it has been found to be relevant for teams of fighter pilots [7].

In this work, when we are exploring the meaning of the elements in this specific context, we choose not to differ between the five factors and the three coordinating mechanisms. Instead, we label all eight components teamwork *elements*. The "Big Five" elements and their definitions as given by Salas et al. are listed in Table 1. An adapted illustration of the model with relationships between the elements as suggested by Salas et al. is shown in Fig. 1.

Table 1. The "Big Five"of effective teamwork and their definitions, after Salas et al. (2005)

Big Five Element	Definition
Team leadership	Ability to direct and coordinate the activities of other team members, assess team performance, assign tasks, develop team knowledge, skills, and abilities, motivate team members, plan and organize, and establish a positive atmosphere
Mutual performance monitoring	The ability to develop common understandings of the team environment and apply appropriate task strategies to accurately monitor teammate performance
Backup behavior	Ability to anticipate other team members' needs through accurate knowledge about their responsibilities. This includes the ability to shift workload among members to achieve balance during high periods of workload or pressure
Adaptability	Ability to adjust strategies based on information gathered from the environment through the use of backup behavior and reallocation of intrateam resources. Altering a course of action or team repertoire in response to changing conditions (internal or external)
Team orientation	Propensity to take other's behavior into account during group interaction and the belief in the importance of team goals over individual members' goals
Shared mental models	An organizing knowledge structure of the relationships among the task the team is engaged in and how the team members will interact
Mutual trust	The shared belief that team members will perform their roles and protect the interests of their teammates
Closed-loop communication	The exchange of information between a sender and a receiver irrespective of the medium

Teamwork is a dynamic activity. The team is formed, the task assigned, planned, performed, finished and evaluated. The cycle of task performance is vital to investigate in order to understand the teamwork as also pointed out by Salas et al. [1]. Teams perform in episodes, and these processes have been investigated and described in [8]. A suggested task performance cycle with the "Big Five" elements for a team of fighter pilots is shown in Fig. 2 [9].

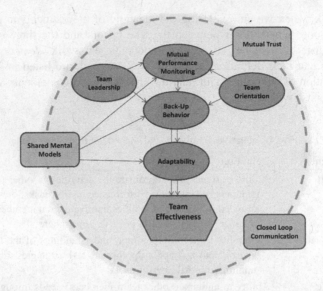

Fig. 1. The "Big Five" for team effectiveness, after Salas et al. [1]. The "Big Five" factors are represented by ovals while supporting mechanisms are shown as squares. The arrows represent propositions by Salas et al. for how the elements relate to each other.

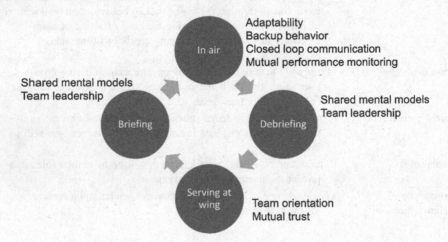

Fig. 2. Task performance cycle for fighter pilots with the "Big Five" elements [9]

3   Method

A qualitative research approach was applied and interviewing was selected as the most suitable method, since the aim of this work was to characterize how pilots collaborate while performing real-world missions. The interviews were conducted as described below following general guidelines for qualitative research [10].

3.1 Conducted Interviews

Open-ended interviews were conducted with ten experienced active fighter pilots. The participants were all male and their average age was 38 years (29–45). Their average flying time on fighter jets was 1500 h (500–3000). The interviews lasted between 40 min up to 2 h depending on the subject's availability. During the interviews, the subjects were first asked in general about their experiences and views on teamwork as fighter pilots. Then, they were presented with the teamwork elements printed on loose paper slips, a total of eight pieces. They were informed about the definitions of the elements as proposed by Salas et al. [1], and they were asked to rank the eight paper slips and to put the most important element during the performing of a mission on top. In addition, the pilots were asked to discuss and reflect on the teamwork elements and to explain what they thought the elements could mean for a group of fighter pilots during a mission. The interviews were recorded and transcribed afterwards for analysis.

4 Results

4.1 Ranking of Teamwork Elements

The average ranking of the most important teamwork elements during mission execution between all interviewees was calculated. The resulting list, with the mean value of the ranking in parenthesis, is presented below:

1. Mutual performance monitoring (3.4)
2. Closed loop communication (4.0)
3. Shared mental models (4.1)
4. Adaptability (4.3)
5. Mutual trust (4.4)
6. Team orientation (4.8)
7. Team leadership (5.0)
8. Back-up behavior (6.1)

4.2 Description of the Teamwork Elements

In this section, each element in the teamwork model is described in the context of a team of fighter pilots. The descriptions are the results of the interviews.

Mutual Performance Monitoring. Mutual performance monitoring was ranked among the pilots as the most important teamwork element in the air. Without knowing where the others are, their status and what they are doing, it is almost impossible to perform a mission. However, the importance of not checking on each other for mistakes was stressed. The monitoring depends on technical solutions, such as data links and cockpit displays. Since the aircraft are moving very fast, it is sometimes difficult to rely on the information on the displays; it might be updated too slowly to be useful in some cases. If, for example, someone is making a sharp turn it takes too long before this is visible on the others' screens. But, not only is the current status of interest, information about what the teammates are planning to do is also highly desirable. Also, in many cases it is not suitable to communicate status and intentions on the radio. If a pilot feels he cannot ask about this information he is left guessing from the teammate's behavior in the air. And as one pilot said: "If I don´t know, I might have to shoot myself, and then perhaps we will waste a missile."

Closed Loop Communication. Closed loop communication was also considered important during the mission; it was ranked as number two by the pilots. In general, the discipline concerning the closed loop was not regarded as a problem, since there are clear procedures that determine how communication via radio is carried out, with call signs and acknowledgements. And in the cases where people might skip the routines, the pilots concluded that they know each other so well that they know how each person usually manages the radio. As long as the original plan is followed, the need for a closed loop was considered less important, "I can see that he is doing what we planned". This element should probably in this context be regarded as not only referring to the necessity of a closed loop, but the capability and occurrence of communication between the team members at all. However, the information transferred via data link can help in keeping the closed loop. The utility of clear acknowledgements via data link was expressed. If the information is on the displays, there is no need to ask. Also, the absence of a closed loop would sometimes be taken as a sign of cognitive overload. If someone remains silent on the radio, perhaps he/she is too busy with something else and was not able to hear to the message. The absence of acknowledgements generally adds workload also to the team leader since he/she cannot move on with the planned actions until he/she knows that the message has been received. The safety aspect of closed loop communication was also articulated, especially when the plan is changed, "It is crucial to know whether everybody understand, or the situation may become dangerous."

Shared Mental Models. The element shared mental models was interpreted by the pilots as originating from the tactics and standard procedures that the team complies to. Before the mission, the team members plan and discuss the mission and the goals during the briefing session. The pilots considered it to be very important that everybody share the same understanding about the mission. The standardized procedures ensure common grounds and predictability. "If we all have the same mental models, I can count on that most people will take the same decisions." It was also recognized that the better the shared mental models are, the less talk is needed.

Adaptability. Adaptability was interpreted as the ability to change plans and adapt to new situations. It was considered as an important factor since it is impossible to plan a mission in every detail. Some contingency will always remain, and unexpected events may occur. However, there are difficulties with being adaptive in this environment with the limited communication. The possible gains must always be judged against the risk of a failure due to communication difficulties and misunderstandings. In many cases it is best to "stick to the plan".

Mutual Trust. The team members trust that their colleagues will do what is expected of them during the mission. Mutual trust was argued to be the result of good team leadership. The leader was considered to be responsible for the trust among the team members. The team members on their hand trust the team leader to act during the mission. During missions, pilots with different ranks can be mixed in one team. It is not uncommon that a pilot with a lower rank is trusted to act as the team leader over a higher ranked colleague.

Team Orientation. Pilots are trained and disciplined to work in teams; not many types of missions are performed by single pilots. Team orientation was considered to be fairly unproblematic and a natural trait among the interviewed pilots, something they assume always to be present among their teammates. The pilots expressed it as "the team above self." However, this does not mean that it can be taken for granted. The importance of team orientation is fostered and emphasized by the organization. One aspect of team orientation that was mentioned was that during stressful situations it is easy to lose awareness about the whole situation and what the others are doing. The pilot can get so focused on his own situation that he "forgets" about the rest of the team and does not realize that perhaps some other team member is better positioned and can step in and take over.

Team Leadership. During the actual execution of the mission, team leadership was ranked as less important. The interviewed pilots argued that a good team leader does the main part of the job at the briefing before the mission. A good team leader listens to the team, and lets everybody take part in the discussions when the tactics are decided. With good leadership, team members agree and understand the tactics, and they know what is expected of them without the need of detailed orders during mission execution. It was considered important for the pilots to be an active part of the preparations and to have the opportunity to discuss alternatives. However, when the discussion is finished and the tactics are decided, team members must respect the decision of the team leader. "No problem solving regarding tactics in the air, it must be clear who decides." Further, when unforeseen events occur in the air, the leader is expected to take control and give clear instructions on how to proceed.

Backup Behavior. The respondents agreed that the need for backup behavior is something they are aware of and try to build into the system. If, for example, the team leader is forced to leave the group for some reason, there is always a deputy appointed to step in. Since the team task to a large extent is collaborative, and in most cases all participants are equally able to perform the subtasks of the mission, backup behavior might be difficult to distinguish from adaptability. Both these elements are essentially equal to flexibility. The priority for the team is to get the job done, who actually does what seems to be of less importance. This could explain why the ranking is low; the pilots did not really regard is at a back-up behavior if someone else got in the position to use the radar or fire a shot. Only when someone was out of weapons, low in fuel or had to leave the group, it was considered as a backup behavior.

Relationship Between the Teamwork Elements. For establishing the relations between the teamwork elements we use the performance cycle presented in Sect. 2. This cycle suggests where each teamwork element comes into play.

The elements team orientation, team leadership and mutual trust were previously identified as prerequisites for a mission, and are mainly established and manifested on ground [9]. Team leadership was considered to be central for the mutual trust and in the establishing of shared mental models during briefings before the mission. The element shared mental models was found to be a prerequisite for mutual performance monitoring. The elements the pilots ranked as most important for a successful mission were mutual performance monitoring and closed loop communication. These are also the two elements where the pilots need technology, such as radio, data links and displays to perform. Backup behavior and adaptability are the elements that are central during mission performance, which are dependent on mutual performance monitoring and closed loop communication to be present before they can be accomplished.

Based on these findings, a suggested relationship between the eight teamwork elements, and how team effectiveness is built up during a mission, is shown in Fig. 3.

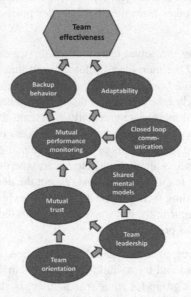

Fig. 3. The found relationships between the "Big Five" elements for effective teamwork for teams of fighter pilots.

5   Discussion

The "Big Five" model for effective teamwork was found to be relevant and well suited as a starting point for research of teams in the military fighter domain. The model has previously been used for research on peace keeping army teams where it was also found to be applicable [5]. Team orientation is described by Salas et al. as an attitude in contrast to the other elements that are behavioral. This makes team orientation a natural starting point for the chain of relationships. According to the propositions by Salas et al. team leadership would influence the team's ability to engage in mutual performance monitoring and backup behavior. However, in this context it was found that the team leadership was considered to be central for the mutual trust and in the establishing of shared mental models during briefings before the mission. Shared mental models was in accordance to the propositions by Salas et al. found to be a fundamental prerequisite for mutual performance monitoring, adaptability, and back-up behavior. In the original model by Salas et al. the element closed loop communication is a coordinating mechanism without connections to the other elements. However, there are propositions given, but not incorporated in the model, regarding how closed loop communication may connect to mutual performance monitoring, back-up behavior and adaptability. During the performing of an air mission closed loop communication was found to be a prerequisite to mutual performance monitoring, and is therefore put in the model in this place. The need for the pilots to communicate does not only occur during the actual mission, but also during briefing and debriefing, but then there are no technical limitations.

6 Conclusions

The aim of this paper was to describe how fighter pilots work in teams and what factors they think are central for achieving effective and successful missions. To this end ten fighter pilots were interviewed about their experiences from team work. The findings regarding each teamwork element inform how teamwork is viewed by the interviewed subjects in this specific domain. The findings resulted in a suggested relationship between the elements of the "Big Five" model by Salas et al. (2005), adapted to the domain.

Team leadership was considered to be central for the mutual trust and in the establishing of shared mental models during briefings before the mission. Shared mental models was in accordance to the propositions by Salas et al. found to be a fundamental prerequisite for mutual performance monitoring, adaptability, and back-up behavior. The elements the pilots ranked as most important for a successful mission were mutual performance monitoring and closed loop communication.

7 Future Work

Each pilot builds his awareness of the situation through mutual performance monitoring and closed loop communication. Since the pilots are separated, and many times they do not even see each other's aircraft, the teamwork is depending on technology during missions. There are several identified issues that could be further explored in order to better support the team with technology:

- The task to maintain both one's own situation and keep track of the whole team at the same time is difficult. There is a risk that a pilot gets so engaged in his own situation that he forgets to check whether someone else can help out or even perform the whole task instead.

- As of today, the potential benefits of changing plans needs to be balanced with the risk that the new plan is not received and understood by the whole team. The limited acting space, i.e. the team's adaptability, should be expected to improve with better communication and mutual performance monitoring.
- The ability to communicate and understand each other's intentions, especially with very short notice could be further explored and developed in order to support the teamwork.

Other domains might also benefit from our findings in the area of teamwork and effective team collaboration. The proposed elaborated model, adapted for teamwork of fighter pilots, together with a deeper understanding of how these high-performing and mature teams collaborate can hopefully inform and inspire how teams with similar characteristics can accomplish effective teamwork.

Acknowledgements. This research was funded by NFFP (National Aviation Research Programme, NFFP6-2013-01201), which is founded by VINNOVA (Swedish Governmental Agency for Innovation Systems), the Swedish Armed Forces and the Swedish Defence Material Administration. The authors also like to thank Saab AB and the University of Skövde for supporting the project.

References

1. Salas, E., Sims, D., Burke, S.: Is there a "Big Five" in teamwork? Small Group Res. **36**(5), 555–599 (2005)
2. Castor, M.: The use of structural equation modelling to describe the effect of operator functional state on air-to-air engagement outcomes. Doctoral thesis, Linköping University (2009)
3. Salas, E., Cooke, N.J., Rosen, M.A.: On teams, teamwork, and team performance: discoveries and developments. Hum. Factors **50**(3), 540–547 (2008)
4. Sundstrom, E., De Meuse, K.P., Futrell, D.: Work teams: application and effectiveness. Am. Psychol. **45**(2), 120–133 (1990)
5. Duel, J.: Teamwork in action: military teams preparing for, and conducting peace support operations, Tilburg University (2010)
6. Moen van Rosmalen, T.: The development of a questionnaire on the subjective experience of teamwork, based on Salas, Sims and Burke's "the big five of teamwork" and Hackman's understanding of team effectiveness'. Master thesis, The Norwegian University of Science and Technology (2012)
7. Ohlander, U., Alfredson, J., Riveiro, M., Falkman, G.: Understanding team effectiveness in a tactical air unit, In: Harris, D. (ed.) Engineering Psychology and Cognitive Ergonomics. LNCS, vol. 9174, pp. 472–479. Springer, Switzerland (2015)
8. Marks, M.A., Mathieu, J.E., Zaccaro, S.J.: A temporally based framework and taxonomy of team processes. Acad. Manage. Rev. **26**(3), 356–376 (2001)
9. Ohlander, U., Alfredson, J., Riveiro, M., Falkman, G.: Elements of team effectiveness: a qualitative study with pilots. In: Proceedings of CogSIMA, San Diego, CA (2016)
10. Patton, M.Q.: Qualitative Research & Evaluation Methods: Integrating Theory and Practice, 4th edn. SAGE Publications Inc, Thousand Oaks (2015)

Design Patterns for Human-Cognitive Agent Teaming

Axel Schulte[1(✉)], Diana Donath[1], and Douglas S. Lange[2]

[1] Universität der Bundeswehr München, Neubiberg, Germany
{axel.schulte, diana.donath}@unibw.de
[2] Space and Naval Warfare Systems Center Pacific, San Diego, CA, USA
doug.lange@navy.mil

Abstract. The aim of this article is to provide a common, easy to use nomenclature to describe highly automated human-machine systems in the realm of vehicle guidance and foster the identification of established design patterns for human-autonomy teaming. With this effort, we intend to facilitate the discussion and exchange of approaches to the integration of humans with cognitive agents amongst researchers and system designers. By use of this nomenclature, we identify most important top-level design patterns, such as delegation and associate systems, as well as hybrid structures of humans working with cognitive agents.

Keywords: Assistant system · Autonomous system · Cognitive agent · Cooperative control · Delegation · Design patterns · Teaming · Supervisory control · Systems engineering · Unmanned vehicles · Vehicle guidance · Work system

1   Introduction

Today, higher cognitive functions (e.g., perception, planning, and decision-making) that are traditionally exclusively owned by the human, are becoming an integral part of automated functions. In the last one or two decades the term "autonomous system" has widely been used to describe complex automated systems working largely independent from a human operator. However, the more capable the automation has become, the more essential the challenging issue of human-system functional allocation and integration has turned out to be [1]. We share the concern of Bradshaw et al. [2] that an undifferentiated use of the term of "autonomy" and the proliferation of automation can lead to unfruitful discussions and oddly defined development programs. We see the need for a conceptual framework unifying the nomenclature and description of systems in which human beings interact with complex automation. Therefore, in this article, we attempt to identify and formally describe common grounds among researchers in this field. Despite our concerns, we want to adhere to the term of "Human-Autonomy Teaming (HAT)" to describe systems in which humans work with highly automated agents. Where those agents carry attributes like "autonomous" or "intelligent", we will assign the unified term *cognitive agent* in this nomenclature. We establish a procedure and a common language to describe concepts of HAT. Our goal is to contribute to a

© Springer International Publishing Switzerland 2016
D. Harris (Ed.): EPCE 2016, LNAI 9736, pp. 231–243, 2016.
DOI: 10.1007/978-3-319-40030-3_24

more objective debate, to facilitate the effective communication between researchers, and to provide guidance to practitioners. Our approach, in general, is twofold. Firstly, we suggest a common symbolic language, as well as a procedure to follow to describe systems, system requirements, and top-level system designs. Both have a stronger focus on human-automation work share and integration aspects than traditional systems engineering practices and tools (e.g., Unified Modelling Language, UML). We borrow the notion of design patterns from the domain of systems and software engineering and adapt it for use in human factors engineering of highly automated dynamic systems. Secondly, we encourage the analysis of current HAT research and development approaches in order to identify solutions and best practices from empirical studies. This article shall also provide advice for designers of HAT systems how to approach the design process in a strictly top-down manner.

1.1 Design Patterns in Engineering

Christopher Alexander proposed that every building and town is composed of patterns [3]. The patterns are a result of forces and processes that combine such that towns or buildings develop in particular ways. By developing a language of these patterns, Alexander et al. were able to describe the forces that produced patterns as well as the consequences of those patterns [4]. Pattern descriptions also specified their relationships to other patterns so that one could create a network of patterns to describe a project. Finally, Alexander et al. set out processes by which the patterns could be used. They envisioned the descriptions of forces and consequences as useful in making arguments to decision making bodies. They also described how one could specify a project from top-down using patterns to make decisions about the ultimate design.

Design patterns and pattern languages became a popular tool for software engineering in the 1990s. This is usually traced to Gamma et al. in 1995 [5]. That patterns describe a repeated problem and the core of a solution to that problem class is their fundamental value. Gamma et al. tried to be more explicit than Alexander concerning the components of a pattern. Four critical elements were listed: the pattern name, the description of the problem, the description of the solution, and the consequences. A more detailed template was created, and their book [5], like the second volume of Alexander's work [4] provided a catalog of some discovered patterns, each entry describing a suitable problem space, the solution template, positive and negative consequences, and providing implementation advice. The popularity of software patterns led to further efforts to catalog patterns for software analysis [6] and design [7], and data models [7]. Discussions of negative patterns often found in systems or organizations were described as anti-patterns [8] with discussions of how to correct the problems. Conferences were held to capture the experience of practitioners in program design as a counterweight to scientific activities that focused on new approaches [9].

Ultimately, a pattern literature for HAT will accomplish the same goals that Alexander initially set out in the domain of architecture and land-use. Patterns serve to communicate generalized solutions to problems faced by engineers. Alexander believed that one could look through a catalog of patterns, identify the key features and forces of a project, and select the appropriate starting points. Then using the linkages provided among the patterns in his catalog one could bring in other appropriate patterns until one had a description of the solution in the form of a language of patterns. Our forces will include human performance issues, limitations of autonomy, communication issues, and many other critical factors. If our patterns can describe forces, features, consequences, and linkages to other patterns, pattern languages as solution descriptions may be possible within this domain.

1.2   Design Patterns in Human Factors, Ergonomics, and HAT

In the field of human factors and ergonomics, the description of design patterns also became fashionable recently. Borchers [10] is one of the first who described the linkage between human-computer interaction and design patterns. Kruschitz and Hitz [11] also provide a good overview. Kahn et al. [12] looked at design patterns for sociality in human-robot interaction.

Sheridan's well-known Levels-of-Automation (LoA) scale (e.g. [13]) is one of the early design patterns in human-automation interaction. System designers very successfully use this scale or one of its derivatives (e.g. [14, 15]) in many different application fields, sometimes even without knowing. In that sense, we see these kinds of Management-by-Consent/Management-by-Exception-based LoA-scales as a collection of often-found design patterns. They apply for supervisory control relationships [13] between human and machine. In this use case, LoA-scales provide an excellent source for deciding how to design the interaction for certain specific functions. Scales of levels-of-autonomy (e.g. [16, 17]) refer more to design options for the scope of a full system. Their focus is predominantly on the description of the independence of the system from human intervention.

Juziuk [18] provides a comprehensive listing and overview of efforts to document design patterns in multi-agent systems. This gets us closer to what we need for HAT, in that cognitive agents and their relationships to each other are considered.

In the following chapters, we want to create a generalized framework and methodology for describing a wider variety of configurations in different scopes. We will present an approach to derive system requirements and to describe top-level system designs for systems involving HAT based on design patterns.

2   Basic Concepts

The traditional systems engineering view is solely on the formulation of requirements and the design of the technical functions of a system. The human operator only appears as an actor, usually located outside the system boundary. This approach is reasonable when automation is relatively simple, in the sense that it can perform specific clear-cut part-tasks. There, one can well describe the relationship between the (technical) system and the human user through use cases calling for a certain user-system interaction.

In this article, in contrast, we want to take account for the following trends: (1) the automation in HAT will become much more capable, (2) the work share and interaction between the user and the system will be much less stable (e.g. adaptive automation [19]), and (3) the task performance of human and automation will be highly dependent on a cognitive level. Hollnagel and Woods [20] speak of joint cognitive systems in this context. Consequently, our approach focuses on two aspects, (a) the description of the purpose we want to design a HAT system for before the actual design, and (b) the incorporation of the human user within the process and system boundary.

2.1 The Work Process

The process of meaningful, goal-oriented co-action of humans (e.g., operators) and machines (e.g., unmanned vehicles (UVs) with automation), including artificial cognitive agents, shall be called a Work Process (WProc) (see Fig. 1a). A Work Objective (WObj), i.e., the mission or the purpose of work, defines and initiates the WProc. The WObj usually comes as an instruction, order, or command (e.g., a UV mission assignment). The proper definition of the WObj is of high priority and most critical for the definition of the system boundaries and the design. The WProc is embedded into a Work Environment (WEnv). WEnv inputs to the WProc are the physical Environment (Env) (e.g., atmosphere, threats), material and energy Supplies (Sup) (e.g., fuel, weapons), and Information (Inf) (e.g., ATC clearances, airspace regulations). Finally, the WProc generates certain physical or conceptual effects to the environment, i.e. the Work Process Output (WPOut) (e.g., target photo/video, destruction of target, provision of information to other WProc).

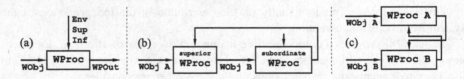

Fig. 1. (a) Work process; (b) hierarchical work processes; (c) networked work processes

The WProc itself imposes meaningful actions upon a particular Work Object (WO) (e.g., target to be destroyed, materials to be transported, premises to be secured) being part of the WEnv. The WEnv may also host other WProcs. In case one WProc interacts with other WProcs, this can be organized as a hierarchical structure, i.e. a superior WProc generates the WObj for one or many sub-ordinate WProcs and monitors their results, thereby forming supervisory loops (see Fig. 1b). Alternatively, the WProcs might be organized as a networked structure, i.e., parallel WProcs depend on each other in a way that their WPOuts cause environmental changes relevant to other WProcs, or provide supplies or information to other WProcs, thereby forming a more or less tight mesh of interdependent WProcs, each following individual WObjs (see Fig. 1c).

A proper work process design should be the starting point for each development of a system involving HAT. At this stage, *"it is more important to understand what the [... system] does [...], than to explain how it does it"* [20]. However, defining the

WObj, the system boundary, and the interfaces of the WProc you want to design for is a hard task to do. The result will heavily influence the system design. From our experience in engineering HAT systems, we suggest a list of guidelines as in Table 1.

Table 1. Guidelines for Work Process design

1. Identify the ***Work Objective*** (**WObj**) you want to design a system for.
   - Therefore, describe the ***purpose*** your customer wants to achieve.
   - Since we want to design a ***human-machine system***, it is always a good idea to start with describing the ***job of that human*** (team).
   - If the human team members are working with very different or locally distributed workstations, ***consider*** defining ***multiple*** separate **WObj**s for hierarchical or networked **WProc**s.
2. Identify other relevant ***Work Processes*** (**WProcs**) your **WProc** is networked with.
   - Therefore, consider ***agencies actively providing orders*** or commands to your **WProc**.
   - Consider ***agencies actively providing*** relevant ***information*** or supplies to your **WProc**.
   - Furthermore, consider agencies that ***receive*** the **WPOut** you are providing.
3. Draw a network of all relevant ***Work Processes*** (**WProcs**) including your **WProc**.
   - Clearly denote the ***individual*** **WProcs**.
   - Clearly mark the most important ***information flow*** through the network. Properly distinguish between **WObj**s, **WEnv** inputs, and **WPOuts**.
   - This exercise will provide a good starting point for defining the inputs and outputs of *your* **WProc** (i.e., the **WProc** you want to design a system for) *as a black box*. In this context, it might be helpful also to consider the introduction of a Work Object (**WO**).

Figure 2 shows an example of a common WProc design taken from civil aviation. The example consists of three individual WProcs, including WProc: Airline Flight, which is the process we want to design a system for. This process changes the WEnv by transporting passengers (WO: PAX). It is in a hierarchical subordinate relationship to WProc: Airline Dispatching that provides WObj: Flight and supplementary information, and to which flight and aircraft status information is fed back. With WProc: Air Traffic Control, a network is established, in which radar surveillance takes place, and requests and clearances are exchanged.

Each WProc has a certain life cycle and can be broken down into a potentially large number of subsequent and/or concurrent sub-processes. During the life cycle of a WProc, it may be exposed to many use cases. For system design, it is important to collect and describe these use cases and sub-processes that finally result in tasks to be performed either by a human, a cognitive agent, or by conventional automation. Without going deeply into well-established methods of systems engineering and cognitive task analysis (e.g. [21]) in this article, Table 2 provides some guidelines from our experience in the consequential top-down design of HAT systems.

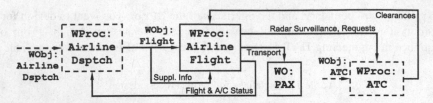

Fig. 2. Example for a common Work Process design with hierarchical and networked structures

Table 2. Guidelines for Work Process Use Case Analysis

1. Identify the relevant *Use Cases* you want to design a system for.
   - Therefore, analyze all *relevant loops* and *meshes*, in which your **WProc** is involved and interacts with other **WProcs**, the **WEnv**, and the **WO**.
   - Identify all *possible specifications* of the **WObj**, the **Env**, the **Sup**, the **Inf**, and the **WPout**.
   - Make sure not to drift into *design discussions* on how your **WProc** shall be implemented now.
2. *Collect all inputs and outputs* of your **WProc** from the various use cases.
   - This will be rather straightforward, given the use cases have been well described.
   - However, this process may cause you to *rethink* some of the use cases.
   - As a result, you will get a good *user requirements specification* for the system you want to design.
3. Describe the *life cycle phases* your **WProc** is supposed to go through.
   - Describe the *dynamics* of your **WProc** by the most important or frequent use cases as *subsequent, parallel, and/or nested sub-processes* (e.g., "take off", "transit", "operation").
   - *Determine* necessary subsequent and/or parallel *tasks* to be performed (e.g., "hold flight altitude", "shoot photo", "get clearance") for each of the found sub-processes. Caution, do not pre-determine any human-automation functional allocation or any design yet!
   - Again, this can provide lengthy debates. *Postpone* those *discussions* for when you have more time and money to spend.

2.2 The Work System

Now we are ready to open the black box. From now on, we look at the physical system that runs the WProc described so far (i.e., the system we want to design). We will name this a Work System (WSys), which is our first *design pattern*. It is important to note that the WSys inherits the complete definition of the corresponding WProc we described before. Within the box, in principle, there are two essential roles to be taken to run the WProc: the Worker and the Tools. Consequently, the WSys is composed of two components, each taking one of the roles (see Fig. 3).

The main characteristic of a Worker is to *know, understand, and pursue* the WObj *by own initiative*. Without this initiative, the WProc would not be carried out. Therefore, a WSys cannot exist without a *human* Worker, by definition. Otherwise, we would not speak of a WSys, but rather of a mere technical artifact, i.e. a Tool. Only Tools would not make a WSys, nor perform a WProc, due to the lack of purpose. The Worker is the only instance and responsible for breaking down the

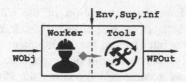

Fig. 3. Design pattern WSys as physical instance of the corresponding WProc comprising the roles of the Worker and the Tools being in a Hierarchical Relationship (HiR, green arrow) (Color figure online)

WObj into relevant tasks. The Tools, on the other hand, will receive tasks from the Worker and will only perform them when told to do so. Hence, the Worker and the Tools are always in a Hierarchical Relationship (HiR, green arrow in Fig. 3) that may be characterized by more detailed design patterns.

We would like to mention that in an earlier article [22], we defined "autonomy" by use of the WSys as the authorization of the Worker to self-define the WObj. Only the *human* Worker shall exercise this authority, for ethical and other reasons.

Table 3. Guidelines for initial Work System Design

1. Transition from **WProc** view to **WSys** view.
   - The starting point is the **WProc** or network of **WProcs** you designed according to Table 1. *Each WProc will become a WSys* keeping exactly the same specifications and periphery.
   - *Open* only the *black box of your* **WSys**, i.e. the **WSys** you want to design.
   - Keep all other **WProcs** (and also **WOs**, if needed) as black boxes. If you feel the urge to also open one of them, consider a *re-design* of the network of **WProcs**.
2. Initial **WSys** design.
   - Populate the **WSys** with the necessary physical entities (e.g., humans, vehicles, control stations).
   - Start with the *human* **Worker** and the *conventional* **Tools** (i.e., machines and automation not necessarily carrying attributes like "intelligent" or "autonomous") to develop a first product vision.
   - Take advantage of any available *market solutions*.
3. Human-Agent/Automation Task Allocation.
   - Now *allocate the tasks* you found in your task analysis to the human **Worker** and/or automated functions. Some, unfortunately only very few, allocations are quite obvious due to their physical (e.g., aircraft flies) or legal/ethical (e.g., human decides on weapon deployment) requirements. However, many others are not!
   - If a task is undoable (by humans or system/automation), consider further breakdown of that task into sub-tasks.
   - The cognitive tasks, which turn out to be allocated to humans and automation (by sharing or trading) are the most interesting ones. They might require a *cognitive agent* (cf. chapter 3).

Traditionally, only a human or a human team represents the Worker. Machinery and automation would constitute the Tools. Thereby, a conventional human-machine system is created, involving manual control, and in presence of automation, also human supervisory control [13]. However, the notion of the WSys provides, additional information concerning the WObj, i.e., the purpose of work, and the system boundary, including the definition of the interfaces to the environment. Finally, the Tools shall never contain a full WSys, or humans. From our experience, nested WSys are not an option. As an alternative, we recommend modeling the structure as a hierarchy of individual WProcs. Table 3 provides some guidelines from our experience for an initial WSys design.

3   Introduction of the Cognitive Agent into the Work System

With the advent of more advanced methods to provide higher cognitive capabilities on behalf of automated functions, the introduction of Cognitive Agents (CogA, little 'R2D2' in Fig. 4) into the WSys becomes an option. In the past, the focus in this field was predominantly on the provision of suitable information processing methods and algorithms (e.g., artificial intelligence, computer vision, soft computing; cf. e.g. [23]). Two trends have been followed in the past two decades concerning the role such an agent could potentially take in system design. Firstly, so-called autonomous systems, i.e. systems that aimed at performing user-given tasks, as much as possible independent from human intervention; and secondly, decision support, assistant, or associate systems, acknowledging that a human predominantly performs the work, while supported by a machine agent [24].

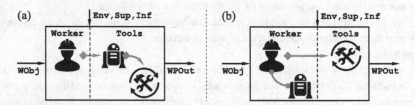

Fig. 4. (a) Design pattern WSys with CogA as Tool in HiR; (b) Design pattern WSys with CogA as Worker in HeR (Color figure online)

We want to acknowledge these trends by introducing two new elementary design patterns. Figure 4(a) shows a design pattern, where there exists a HiR (green arrow) between the Worker and the CogA being part of the Tools. Within the Tools, a HiR (green arrow) between the CogA and other automated Tools exist. Figure 4(b) shows a design pattern, where in addition to the HiR between the human Worker and the Tools (cf. Fig. 3), there exists a Heterarchical Relationship (HeR, blue connector) between the human Worker and the CogA being part of the Worker in this case. Concerning this HeR, we would like to introduce one restriction, i.e. the CogA shall not be given the authority to define or even question the WObj. The human Worker shall always have the final authority do decide.

Figure 5 shows some examples of existing setups we constructed using the elements human Worker, Tools, CogA, HiR, and HeR. Figure 5(a) depicts a regular non-HAT system, in which two human operators cooperate while using technical equipment (e.g., a two-pilot flight-deck crew operating an aircraft). Figure 5(b) might be useful to either reduce the crew size (e.g., single pilot operations [25]), or to increase the span of control (e.g., larger "autonomy" of UVs [16]; single agent operation of multiple UVs [26]). In this case, the CogA is delegated certain tasks which otherwise a human crewmember would execute. In both examples, the effect could be mostly attributed to a reduction of the taskload of the human Worker. Elements of adaptive functional allocation might also be involved [27]. Figure 5(c) is an extension to (b) where there is more than one agent tasked by a human operator, each controlling its individual system (e.g., task-based guidance of multiple UVs [28]). Again, the challenge here is the increase of the span of control by means of spreading the taskload. Figure 5(d) goes even further down that road. Here, the human user controls a cooperating team of multiple agents, each of which operating its own equipment (e.g., pilot controlling a cooperating team of multiple UVs [29]; multi-agent system controlling multiple UVs [30]).

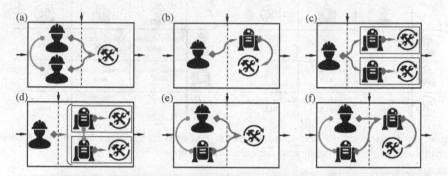

Fig. 5. Examples for WSys setups constructed from the elements human Worker, Tools, CogA, HiR, and HeR

However, an increase of automation complexity and span of control, as exercised in (b)–(d), may also result in automation-induced shortcomings. These effects have been reported by many researchers (e.g., [31] for a classical source). To counteract suchlike problems, a number of scientists suggested approaches as in Fig. 5(e). Here, the agent works in cooperation with the human operator being an element of the Worker (e.g., pilot assistance or associate systems [32]). Core elements here are the agent's initiative in achieving the WObj, and the ability of the agent to decode the human's mental states as a basis for cooperation. Means of assistance can be attention allocation, mixed-initiative operation, and adaptive automation techniques [19]. Finally, Fig. 5(f) shows a setup, in which a human is controlling a system via agent delegation, while at the same time being assisted by an agent being part of the Worker (e.g., assisted guidance of a single UV operator [33]; assisted multi-UV mission management [34]). In the two latter cases (e) and (f), where a CogA is part of the Worker, the CogA inherits the required attributes of the role of a Worker as claimed in Sect. 2.2, i.e., to know, understand and pursue the WObj by its own initiative [22, 24].

At this stage, it is obvious that there can be constructed many more configurations, especially when we look at distributed multi-user, multi-agent systems with complex HiR/HeR structures.

4 Actor-Relationship-Actor Tuples

As became clear during the discussion of Fig. 5 in the previous chapter, there are possible very many WSys configurations only by combining one or few of the symbols provided (i.e., human Worker, CogA, Tools, HiR, and HeR). Thereby, researchers and practitioners can depict their individual solutions described in literature, and hence, make them comparable. In this chapter, we now want to look at the possible {Actor-Relationship-Actor}-tuples, which can occur in all possible WSys. Figure 6 gives an annotated overview of all possible tuples.

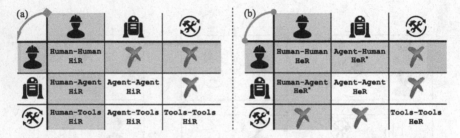

Fig. 6. (a) Hierarchical, (b) heterarchical{Actor-Relationship-Actor}-tuples; (shaded: human involved; *: equal configurations; cross: invalid option)

A hierarchy of an agent or a tool over a human, or a tool over an agent we do not want further to consider. The same applies to a heterarchy of a tool with either a human or an agent, for obvious reasons. Tuples, which do not involve humans, may not directly be interesting for HAT systems. However, they certainly can influence the behavior of the automation "under the hood", and therefore, be worthwhile to look at, at least from a pure engineering stance. Also, the pure human-human relationships, either hierarchical or heterarchical, may not directly be relevant for HAT systems, except of course for WSys with more than one human. Apart from that, they may serve as valuable source for design metaphors. Finally, we do not want to allow a Human-Agent HeR, where the agent is part of the Tools, since per definition there is always a HiR between Worker and Tools.

Within the scope of the modeled WSys, the {Actor-Relationship-Actor}-tuples describe the binary relationships between two entities. The possible combinations include tuples with well-established design patterns.

The tuple {Human-HiR-Tools} describes the basic setting of human supervisory control [13]. By the time when Sheridan established his LoA-scale, automation used to be mostly rather clear-cut control automation following relatively simple rules or algorithms. In most of these systems, the human exclusively owned higher cognitive capabilities. It was acknowledged in later works [14] that automation could also take over higher cognitive tasks. New scales for LoA have been developed (e.g. [14, 15]), which, to a certain degree, reflect the situation that automation became capable of assuming functions of information acquisition and analysis. These scales are applicable to the tuple {Human-HiR-Agent}. Since then, many works have been conducted, supporting the relevance of this tuple and provide valuable design patterns 7(e.g., [26, 28, 35]). Van Breda and coauthors also provide a good overview [36].

Finally, the {Human-HeR-Agent}-tuple has become particularly interesting in situations where automation-induced human erroneous action should be prevented. We already mentioned a few citations in this context [22, 24, 32–34]. Also further international approaches to adaptive associate systems should be mentioned that are representative to many others [37, 38].

5 Conclusions

In this article, we describe a method for documenting human-autonomy teaming (HAT) design patterns. Therefore, we followed a strict top-down procedure, inspired by systems engineering and cognitive ergonomics. Coming from a general human-systems view, we ended up at the level of frequently recurring actor-relationship-actor-tuples, which may serve as containers for similar or competing design patterns to be found, described, and discussed. However, the benefit of this approach heavily depends on the researchers' and practitioners' efforts to describe their solutions to HAT problems using the offered method. In doing so, we could avail of a great opportunity for rational discussions on future highly automated systems.

References

1. Klein, G., Woods, D.D., Bradshaw, J.M., Hoffman, R.R., Feltovich, P.J.: Ten challenges for making automation a "team player" in joint human-agent activity. IEEE Intell. Syst. **6**, 91–95 (2004)
2. Bradshaw, J.M., Hoffman, R.R., Woods, D.D., Johnson, M.: The seven deadly myths of "Autonomous Systems". IEEE Intell. Syst. **3**, 54–61 (2013)
3. Alexander, C.: The Timeless Way of Building. Oxford University Press, New York (1979)
4. Alexander, C., Ishikawa, S., Silverstein, M.: A Pattern Language: Towns, Buildings, Construction, Oxford University Press, New York (1977)
5. Gamma, E., Helm, R., Johnson, R., Vlissides, J.: Design Patterns: Elements of Reusable Object-Oriented Software. Addison-Wesley, Reading (1995)
6. Fowler, M.: Analysis Patterns: Reusable Object Models. Addison-Wesley, Menlo Park (1996)
7. Pree, W.: Design Patterns for Object-Oriented Software Development. Addison-Wesley, Reading (1994)
8. Brown, W., Malveau, R., McCormick, H., Mowbray, T.: Anti Patterns: Refactoring Software, Architectures, and Projects in Crisis. Wiley, New York (1998)

9. Coplien, J.O.: Pattern Languages of Program Design. Addison-Wesley Professional, Reading (1995)
10. Borchers, J.O.: A pattern approach to interaction design. AI Soc. **15**(4), 359–376 (2001)
11. Kruschitz, C., Hitz, M.: Human-computer interaction design patterns: structure, methods, and tools. Int. J. Adv. Softw. 3(1&2) (2010)
12. Kahn, P.H., et al.: Design patterns for sociality in human-robot interaction. In: 3rd ACM/IEEE International Conference on Human Robot Interaction (2008)
13. Sheridan, T.B.: Telerobotics, Automation, and Human Supervisory Control. MIT, Cambridge (1992)
14. Parasuraman, R., Sheridan, T.B., Wickens, C.D.: A model for types and levels of human interaction with automation. IEEE SMC Trans. **30**(3), 286–297 (2000)
15. Miller, C.A., Parasuraman, R.: Beyond levels of automation: an architecture for more flexible human-automation collaboration. HFES **47**(1), 182–186 (2003)
16. Clough, B.T.: Unmanned aerial vehicles: autonomous control challenges, a researcher's perspective. In: Murphey, R., Pardalos, P.M. (eds.) Cooperative Control and Optimization, pp. 35–52. Springer, New York (2002)
17. Huang, H.M.: Autonomy levels for unmanned systems (ALFUS) framework. Volume I: Terminology, version 2.0. NIST special publication, pp. 1–47 (2008)
18. Juziuk, J.: Design Patterns for Multi-agent Systems. Linnaeus University, Sweden (2012)
19. Scerbo, M.: Adaptive automation. Neuroergonomics, pp. 239–252. Oxford University Press, New York (2006)
20. Hollnagel, E., Woods, D.D.: Joint Cognitive Systems: Foundations of Cognitive Systems Engineering. CRC Press (2005)
21. Roth, E.M., Woods, D.D.: Cognitive task analysis: an approach to knowledge acquisition for intelligent system design. In: Topics in Expert System Design, pp. 233–264 (1989)
22. Schulte, A., Meitinger, C., Onken, R.: Human factors in the guidance of uninhabited vehicles: oxymoron or tautology? Cogn. Technol. Work **11**(1), 71–86 (2009)
23. Russell, S., Norvig, P.: Artificial Intelligence: A Modern Approach. Prentice Hall, Englewood Cliffs (1995)
24. Onken, R., Schulte, A.: System-Ergonomic Design of Cognitive Automation. Studies in Computational Intelligence, vol. 235. Springer, Heidelberg (2010)
25. Shively, R.J., Brandt, S.L., Lachter, J.: Application of Human Automation Teaming (HAT) patterns to Reduced Crew Operations (RCO). In: HCII Conference (2016)
26. Miller, C.A., Funk, H.B., Dorneich, M., Whitlow, S.D.: A playbook interface for mixed initiative control of multiple unmanned vehicle teams. In: IEEE DASC (2002)
27. Miller, C.A., Parasuraman, R.: Designing for flexible interaction between humans and automation: delegation interfaces for supervisory control. Hum. Factors **49**(1), 57–75 (2007)
28. Uhrmann, J., Schulte, A.: Concept, design and evaluation of cognitive task-based UAV guidance. Int. J. Adv. Intell. Syst. (2012)
29. Schulte, A., Meitinger, C.: Introducing cognitive and co-operative automation into UAV guidance work systems. In: Human-Robot Interaction in Future Military Operations. Ashgate. Series Human Factors in Defence, pp. 145–170 (2010)
30. Baxter, J.W., Horn, G.S., Leivers, D.P.: Fly-by-agent: controlling a pool of UAVs via a multi-agent system. Knowl. Based Syst. **21**(3), 232–237 (2008)
31. Bainbridge, L.: Ironies of automation. Automatica **19**(6), 775–779 (1983)
32. Onken, R., Walsdorf, A.: Assistant systems for aircraft guidance: cognitive man-machine cooperation. Aerosp. Sci. Technol. **5**(8), 511–520 (2001)
33. Theißing, N., Schulte, A.: Designing a support system to mitigate pilot error while minimizing out-of-the-loop-effects. In: HCII Conference (2016)

34. Strenzke, R., Uhrmann, J., Benzler, A., Maiwald, F., Rauschert, A., Schulte, A.: Managing cockpit crew excess task load in military manned-unmanned teaming missions by dual-mode cognitive automation approaches. In: AIAA GNC Conference (2011)
35. Lange, D.S., Gutzwiller, R.S.: Human-autonomy teaming patterns in the command and control of teams of autonomous systems. In: HCII Conference (2016)
36. Van Breda, L., et al.: Supervisory control of multiple uninhabited systems: methodologies and enabling human-robot interface technologies. NATO RTO HFM-170 Report (2012)
37. Taylor, R.M., Howells, H., Watson, D.: The cognitive cockpit: operational requirement and technical challenge. contemporary ergonomics, pp. 55–59 (2000)
38. Miller, C.A., Hannen, M.D.: The Rotorcraft Pilot's Associate: design and evaluation of an intelligent user interface for cockpit information management. Knowl. Based Syst. **12**(8), 443–456 (1999)

Application of Human-Autonomy Teaming (HAT) Patterns to Reduced Crew Operations (RCO)

Shively R. Jay[1]([⊠]), Summer L. Brandt[2], Joel Lachter[2],
Mike Matessa[3], Garrett Sadler[4], and Henri Battiste[4]

[1] NASA Ames Research Center, Moffett Field, Sunnyvale, USA
robert.j.shively@nasa.gov
[2] San Jose State University, Moffett Field, Sunnyvale, USA
{summer.l.brandt,joel.lachter}@nasa.gov
[3] Rockwell Collins, Moffett Field, Sunnyvale, USA
mike.matessa@rockwellcollins.com
[4] NVH Human Systems Integration, Moffett Field, Sunnyvale, USA
garrett.g.sadler@nasa.gov, henri.battiste@gmail.com

Abstract. Unmanned aerial systems, advanced cockpits, and air traffic management are all seeing dramatic increases in automation. However, while automation may take on some tasks previously performed by humans, humans will still be required to remain in the system for the foreseeable future. The collaboration between humans and these increasingly autonomous systems will begin to resemble cooperation between teammates, rather than simple task allocation. It is critical to understand this human-autonomy teaming (HAT) to optimize these systems in the future. One methodology to understand HAT is by identifying recurring patterns of HAT that have similar characteristics and solutions. This paper applies a methodology for identifying HAT patterns to an advanced cockpit project.

Keywords: Design Patterns · Human-autonomy teaming (HAT) · Reduced crew operations (RCO)

1 Introduction

In this paper we propose the use of design patterns to aid in characterizing commonly occurring human-autonomy teaming (HAT) situations. The concept of design patterns, originally introduced by Christopher Alexander [1] in the context of architectural design, and extended to the domain of software engineering by Beck and Cunningham [2], provides abstractions that capture a general repeatable solution to commonly occurring problems. That is, they provide descriptions or templates for how to solve a problem that can be used in many different situations. While not finished designs that

---

© Springer International Publishing Switzerland 2016
D. Harris (Ed.): EPCE 2016, LNAI 9736, pp. 244–255, 2016.
DOI: 10.1007/978-3-319-40030-3_25

can be transformed directly into code, these design patterns have served as aids to more efficient development.

More specifically, design patterns can speed up the development process by providing tested, proven development paradigms. Effective software design requires considering issues that may not become visible until later in the implementation. Reusing design patterns helps to prevent subtle issues that can cause major problems and improves code readability for coders and architects familiar with the patterns. In addition, patterns allow developers to communicate using well-known, well-understood names for software interactions.

We believe that the design of HAT solutions might also benefit from the use of patterns. In this paper, we will discuss the methodology for developing such patterns and examine example applications to a project investigating reduced crew size on commercial airlines. Because this project involves replacing one member of a tightly coupled team with automation, it provides a very ripe environment in which to apply this methodology.

2 Design Patterns for Reduced Crew Operations

NASA is currently investigating the feasibility of reduced crew operations (RCO) for transport category aircraft. RCO envisions having one pilot on board domestic flights, and two pilots on board long-haul operations, where one of the two pilots is often off of the flight deck resting in the bunk. An important element of NASA's RCO research seeks to develop a concept of operation (ConOp) that covers the roles and responsibilities of the principal human operators, the automation tools used by them, and the operating procedures for human-human and human-automation interaction. The human-automation function allocation, in particular, is an ongoing NASA focus, drawing upon insights gathered from subject matter experts in industry, academia and government during technical interchange meetings and from empirical human-in-the-loop research [3–5].

The proposed NASA RCO ConOp [6] includes three basic human roles: the pilot on board (POB), the dispatcher, and when necessary, a ground pilot. The POB (unless incapacitated) would serve as the captain and pilot-in-command. As such, s/he would determine when to call on automation and ground support. The POB's main tasks would be to manage risk and resources (both human and automation).

Onboard automation would assist the POB with many tasks currently performed by the pilot monitoring, such as flight management system (FMS) input, assisting with checklists and validating inputs.

Ground-based automation would assist the dispatcher in a variety of tasks. Dispatch tasks would be similar to current operations (e.g., preflight planning, monitoring aircraft positions, and enroute reroutes), but for those tasks currently performed jointly with the pilot, the dispatchers (aided by automation) would absorb some of the POB's workload (e.g., creating new flight plans, vetting them with air traffic control (ATC) and uplinking them to the aircraft). In this ConOp, automation would assist the dispatcher with creation of pre-flight briefings, flight path monitoring, selection of divert airports, and optimizing reroutes. Automation would also be responsible for monitoring many flights and alerting the dispatcher to aircraft needing assistance. In addition, the POB could call the dispatcher for consultation on important decisions where s/he might previously have consulted the first officer (e.g., diagnosing an aircraft system caution light or determining the fuel consequences of a holding instruction).

Under high-workload or challenging off-nominal operating conditions, such as an engine fire or cabin depressurization, where the flight's needs exceed the capacity of a dispatcher responsible for many other aircraft, a ground pilot would be assigned to the flight for dedicated piloting support. The ground pilot would have remote access to fly the aircraft as needed. Similarly, if the POB was found to be incapacitated (by automation or the dispatcher), a ground pilot would be assigned to that aircraft and assume the role of pilot-in-command.

The remainder of this paper will discuss the methodology for developing design patterns for RCO.

3 Steps to Build a Pattern

Schulte [7, 8], in conjunction with Neerincx and Lange [9], proposed using a set of primitives to build HAT patterns. They proposed three types of agents: (1) human operators, (2) intelligent/cognitive agents, and (3) automated tools. The agents, which can either be co-located or distributed, can be connected by cooperative, supervisory, or communications links.

As described by Schulte [7, 8], a critically important preliminary task in the construction of HAT patterns is the identification of the *Work Objective*. The *Work Objective* identifies the aspects that initiate and characterize the mission or purpose of the work. The *Work Objective* provides a black box description of the *Work Process*, which includes informational inputs (e.g., ATC clearance), environmental inputs (e.g., airspace) and supply inputs (e.g., fuel). The *Work Process*, utilizing all of these inputs and the *Work Objective*, produces a *Work Process Output* (e.g., reducing target speed) on the *Work Object* (e.g., speed of aircraft) that distributes meaningful physical and conceptual actions to human-automation team members within the overall *Work Environment*.

Using these primitives, we have been working to build patterns that describe HAT in the RCO context. An initial use case was developed, and by walking through each step, the agents and links required to depict one such pattern were identified.

Agents		Links
👤	Human Operator	Communication Only
🤖	Intelligent/Cognitive Agent	Supervisory
🛠	Automated Tools	Cooperative

Fig. 1. Legend for RCO design pattern steps; Cooperative and supervisory links imply communication.

3.1   Initial Use Case 1: Fuel Leak

FLYSKY12 is en route from SFO to BOS. There is one POB and a dispatcher flight following.

In this initial use case, there is an onboard fuel leak. The *Work Objective* is to manage the fuel leak. The *Work Process* consists of the steps necessary to resolve the situation. Here, the output is a divert to an alternate airport. Figure 1 provides a legend for the steps and links detailed in Fig. 2. The culmination of steps produced our initial RCO design pattern.

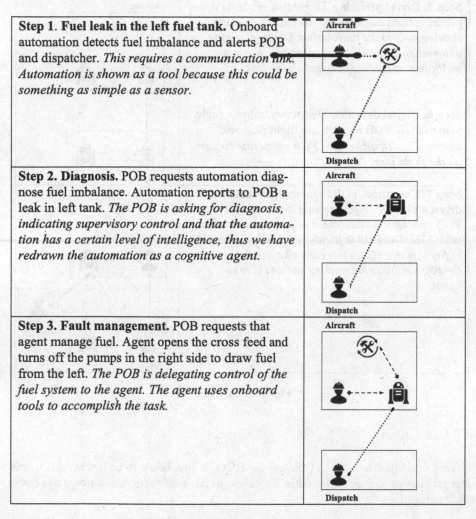

Step 1. Fuel leak in the left fuel tank. Onboard automation detects fuel imbalance and alerts POB and dispatcher. *This requires a communication link. Automation is shown as a tool because this could be something as simple as a sensor.*	Aircraft Dispatch
Step 2. Diagnosis. POB requests automation diagnose fuel imbalance. Automation reports to POB a leak in left tank. *The POB is asking for diagnosis, indicating supervisory control and that the automation has a certain level of intelligence, thus we have redrawn the automation as a cognitive agent.*	Aircraft Dispatch
Step 3. Fault management. POB requests that agent manage fuel. Agent opens the cross feed and turns off the pumps in the right side to draw fuel from the left. *The POB is delegating control of the fuel system to the agent. The agent uses onboard tools to accomplish the task.*	Aircraft Dispatch

Fig. 2. RCO initial use case design pattern steps

Step 4. Decision to divert. POB contacts dispatch about need to divert. *There is coordination between POB and dispatcher.*	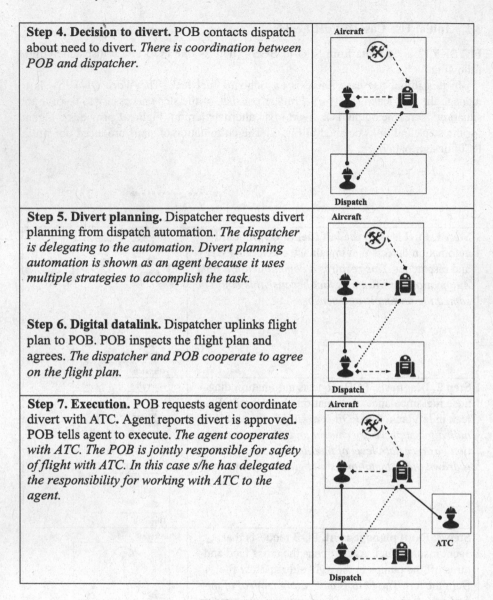
Step 5. Divert planning. Dispatcher requests divert planning from dispatch automation. *The dispatcher is delegating to the automation. Divert planning automation is shown as an agent because it uses multiple strategies to accomplish the task.* **Step 6. Digital datalink.** Dispatcher uplinks flight plan to POB. POB inspects the flight plan and agrees. *The dispatcher and POB cooperate to agree on the flight plan.*	
Step 7. Execution. POB requests agent coordinate divert with ATC. Agent reports divert is approved. POB tells agent to execute. *The agent cooperates with ATC. The POB is jointly responsible for safety of flight with ATC. In this case s/he has delegated the responsibility for working with ATC to the agent.*	

Fig. 2. (continued)

4   Use Cases

Having developed a base HAT pattern for RCO, it now needs to be determined if it is general enough to account for other use cases. In this next section, additional use cases are examined.

4.1   Use Case 2: Thunderstorm

Initial Conditions. FLYSKY12 is en route from SFO to ORD. There is one POB and a dispatcher flight following. The *Work Objective* is to avoid a thunderstorm. Again, the *Work Process* consists of the steps necessary to resolve the situation with the output to divert to an alternate airport. Figure 3 represents the final design pattern.

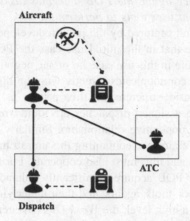

Fig. 3. Use case 2 design pattern

Step 1. Detection and alerting of thunderstorm. Dispatch automation informs dispatcher of convective cell growing on flight path of FLYSKY12. *This requires a communication link between dispatch automation and the dispatcher (covered by supervisory link in the pattern).*

Step 2. Dispatcher informs POB of cell. *This requires a link between the dispatcher and the POB. This link is as a cooperative link (as in the pattern) because, by regulation, the dispatcher and POB share responsibility for safe operation of the flight (including detecting and responding to thunderstorms).*

Step 3. Modification of flight plan. Dispatcher requests modified flight plan from dispatch automation. Dispatch automation returns modified flight plan. *The delegation of flight path planning to the automation requires a supervisory link. As with the previous use case, this planning requires consideration of multiple strategies making this automation an agent.*

Step 4. Dispatch uplinks modified flight plan. *Uses the link between dispatch and POB from Step 2.*

Step 5. POB requests clearance for flight plan from ATC. *POB and ATC are both responsible for safety of flight and thus this is a cooperative link. This differs from the pattern above where the link from ATC to the aircraft went to the agent.*

Step 6. ATC rejects clearance. ATC tells POB that aircraft must take additional six-minute delay for new arrival slot coming into ORD. *Cooperative link from Step 5.*

Step 7. Planning for delay. POB asks automation for alternatives to take six-minute delay. Automation provides two alternatives: (a) Slow down, saves fuel but risks further movement/growth of cell (b) Hold past cell, more fuel burn but lower risk of further deviations. *Like Steps 2 and 3 in the previous use case, POB is delegating this task to the automation, requiring a supervisory link. The automation is developing multiple strategies for taking the delay, making it an agent.*

Step 9. POB requests clearance from ATC, modified with holding after passing cell; ATC approves request. *Same cooperative link from Steps 2 and 5.*

Step 10. POB tells agent to implement the new clearance. Agent sets autopilot in accord with clearance. *Once again, the POB delegates tasks to the agent. As in the previous use case, the agent uses tools to perform the task.*

This use case is also well captured by the pattern developed in our initial use case. The only modifications are that in the initial use case the POB delegates negotiation with ATC to the agent, while in this use case he or she negotiates directly and that the onboard automation never communicates directly with the dispatcher. This is perhaps unsurprising since the basic structure of this pattern is specified in our RCO ConOp. The POB and the assigned dispatcher are jointly responsible for the flight, assisting each other in a cooperative relationship. Similarly, the POB and the ATC responsible for the sector of airspace containing the aircraft have complementary roles in assuring safety of flight, and thus must also cooperate. Further, our ConOp specifies that both dispatch and the POB acquire significantly enhanced automation. Thus, in most situations the operators, tools, agents, and their underlying relationships are fixed by our ConOp. Further, at a high level, the *Work Objective* remains constant for RCO: getting the aircraft to the best airport possible for the airline (usually its destination and ideally on time) while maintaining safety of flight. The relevant informational, environmental, and supply inputs also remain constant (although possibly with different weightings) across operations. Of course, a number of specifics could change depending on the situation. For example, while the POB and dispatch are jointly responsible for a flight, it is not necessary that dispatch be contacted in every situation (e.g., if ATC issued a two-mile deviation for traffic).

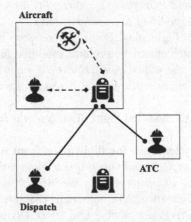

Fig. 4. Use case 3 design pattern

4.2   Use Case 3: Non-cooperative Pilot

There are, however, use cases for which we believe more significant changes to this pattern would be necessary. In particular, pilots may become incapacitated, or, in rare but well publicized instances, become threats to the aircraft themselves (e.g., Jet Blue 191, Germanwings 9525, EgyptAir 990). If we hope to guarantee safety and security in these cases, the dispatcher and possibly the cognitive agent will need significant authority to effectively supervise the POB. Here we outline a possible use case involving such a situation.

Initial Conditions. FLYSKY12 DEN-DCA on final into DCA. There is one POB and a dispatcher flight following. The *Work Objective* is to complete a safe flight with a potentially incapacitated pilot. Again, the *Work Process* is the steps necessary to resolve the situation with the output being the onboard agent assuming the pilot-in-command role. Figure 4 represents the final design pattern.

Step 1. Pilot takes aircraft off course. At WIRSO (424 feet) POB decouples autopilot and turns north (toward the White House) instead of south. Onboard automation detects deviation from flight plan and alerts POB and dispatcher. *Same communication links from Step 1 of the initial use case.*

Step 2. ATC intervenes. ATC directs POB to correct course. *As with previous use cases, ATC is also responsible for safety of flight, indicating a cooperative link.*

Step 3. Automation calculates point of no return, informs pilot that s/he will be locked out if no corrective action is taken by that time (in this case the time would be minimal; the White House is less than 30 s from WIRSO). *As the aircraft approaches restricted airspace, the automation takes on additional authority, marking a change in the relationship between the agent and the POB: the agent is now supervising the POB rather than being supervised by the POB.*

Step 4. POB locked out. No corrective action is taken. The agent locks out POB and alerts the dispatcher. (Dispatch assumed to have the power to return control to POB, but does not here.) *The agent continues its supervisory role relative to the POB.*

Step 5. Agent squawks 777 and corrects course. *The agent has supervisory control over the FMS and other flight deck controls as in the previous use cases.*

Step 6. Establishing link with dispatcher. Agent informs dispatcher of corrective action. *This requires only a communication link between the agent and the dispatcher as in the previous use cases. However, it is presumed that, at this point the agent would either form a cooperative link with the dispatcher or the dispatcher would take over supervision of the agent.*

In this use case, major changes were needed to accommodate the events. Yet this change is only reflected in the subtle change from the POB and the cognitive agent cooperating with the agent supervising the POB, requiring that the agent have a great deal of autonomy and authority. Intuitively, this change in authority is a major change in the pattern; however, the level of authority (although implied through delegation) has not been an explicit component of these design patterns. Perhaps to fully explore some of this design space, it will need to be added.

Step 1. Fuel leak in the left fuel tank. Onboard automation detects fuel imbalance and alerts POB and dispatcher.	No CRM skill indicated
Step 2. Diagnosis. POB requests automation diagnose fuel imbalance. Automation reports to POB a leak in left tank.	Management skill in a supervisory relationship between POB and agent (labeled M), with the agent having a capability to identify problems (Decision Making level one, labeled D1)
Step 3. Fault Management. POB requests that agent manage fuel. Agent opens the cross feed and turns off the pumps in the right side to draw fuel from the left.	Management in a supervisory relationship between agent and aircraft (labeled M), with the agent informing the POB only if necessary (Sheridan management level nine, labeled M9)
Step 4. Decision to divert. POB contacts dispatch about need to divert.	A relationship between POB and dispatcher with Cooperation (awareness of needs of other), Decision Making (eliciting divert options), and Management (delegating divert location task to the dispatcher), labeled C/D/M
Step 5. Divert planning. Dispatcher requests divert planning from dispatch automation.	Management in a supervisory relationship between dispatcher and agent (labeled M), with the agent having a Decision Making ability to select an option (NOTECHS level three, labeled D3)
Step 6. Digital datalink. Dispatcher uplinks flight plan to POB.	Continued relationship between POB and dispatcher with Cooperation (awareness of needs of other), Decision Making (eliciting divert options), and Management (delegating divert location task to the dispatcher), labeled C/D/M
Step 7. Execution. POB requests agent coordinate divert with ATC. Agent reports divert is approved. POB tells agent to execute.	Management in a supervisory relationship between POB and agent (labeled M). Cooperative Decision Making between the agent and ATC (labeled D), with the agent having a Decision Making ability to select an option (NOTECHS level three, labeled D3)

Fig. 5. Re-examination of RCO design pattern using additional measures

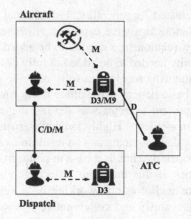

Fig. 6. RCO design pattern using additional measures

5 HAT Measures

Our HAT design patterns effectively captured the similarities between our first two use cases, as well as the structural differences between those and the final use case with the non-cooperative pilot. However, the reader may be concerned that in developing these patterns we have made a number of arbitrary distinctions. In fact, we spent considerable time debating which piece of automation was a cognitive agent versus a tool and the type of connections between the various agents. To aid in making these decisions, we turned to a number of metrics that have been used by researchers in related fields. Specifically, we looked at the degree to which agents exhibited situation awareness indexed by the levels of situation awareness described by Endsley [10], the management capabilities of agents as indexed by Sheridan's levels of automation [11], and decision-making ability assessed using the Non-Technical Skills framework (NOTECHS) categories [12]. In addition to categorizing the decision-making authority of the agent, NOTECHS have several other scales that allow us to assess whether communications links involve Management, Joint Decision making, and/or Cooperation.

We used these measures to give a more quantitative assessment of the automation in our initial use case. In Fig. 5, we re-examined each step, giving the reasoning behind these assessments. A new design pattern was drawn in Fig. 6 to reflect the additional measures.

6 Discussion

In this relatively new field of human-autonomy teaming, this analysis suggests that defining design patterns may help describe and prescribe human-autonomy relationships. This paper attempts to build a pattern to describe the human-autonomy teaming resident in a reduced crew operations design. Building on a use case, researchers were able to identify a basic pattern (see Fig. 1). This pattern describes the agents (human and otherwise) and the logical connections between them. Once this base pattern was defined, new use cases evaluated its generality. For nominal and routine off-nominal operations, most of the relationships were captured. However, for extreme use cases (non-cooperating pilot), new relationships needed to be added. Further, it became clear that the dimension of authority needed to be added to fully describe the environment. It may be that a family of patterns is required to fully describe complex situations in all contexts, but that a single basic pattern may suffice for normal operations.

A challenge with the present exercise was getting the correct level of detail in defining HAT design pattern elements. Highly general elements can gloss over critical distinctions, while narrowly defined elements can result in overly complex and hard to generalize patterns. The cooperative link is a case in point. In this exercise we realized that there were two varieties of this link, one reflecting relatively unstructured *collaboration* between humans and/or agents working on a single task (e.g., a ground operator and a pilot simultaneously and collaboratively searching for the best divert airport); and one reflecting a more structured *coordination* while working on separate subtasks (e.g., an automated agent developing a list of divert options and an operator culling this list while generating new criteria/constraints for the automated agent). Answering whether or not to include distinctions such as these will probably require multiple efforts to generate and apply HAT design patterns.

We have seen that a design pattern (or family of design patterns) can be used to describe this environment and its relationships, but how can it be of use? One way is to re-use patterns when developing system designs in other (new) environments. We can use patterns to prescribe the relationships and level of automation required to achieve design goals. Design patterns can also be used in a diagnostic manner. The non-cooperating pilot example showed that the cognitive agent needed a higher degree of authority than had previously been assigned. Exercising the use cases can determine if a pattern (or existing system) is able to execute that case and can diagnose where additional autonomy and/or authority might be required.

Members of NATO HFM-247 working group are applying this methodology to their individual projects to determine the overall generalizability and utility. If successful, this may be a significant step forward in understanding human-autonomy teaming.

Acknowledgements. This study was supported by the NASA Safe and Autonomous System Operations project and Reduced Crew Operations subproject. We would like to thank Dr. Walter Johnson for his support and insightful edits.

References

1. Alexander, C., Ishikawa, S., Silverstein, M.: A Pattern Language: Towns, Buildings, Construction. Oxford University Press, New York (1977)
2. Beck, K., Cunningham, W.: Using pattern languages for object-oriented programs. In: Proceedings of OOPSLA 1987 Specification and Design for Object-Oriented Programming (1987)

3. Comerford, D., Brandt, S.L., Wu, S.-C., Mogford, R., Battiste, V., Johnson, W.W.: NASA's single pilot operations technical interchange meeting: proceedings and findings, Report No. NASA-CP-2013-216513, NASA Ames Research Center, CA (2012)
4. Lachter, J., Brandt, S.L., Battiste, V., Ligda, S.V., Matessa, M., Johnson, W.W.: Toward single pilot operations: developing a ground station. In: Proceedings of the International Conference on Human-Computer Interaction in Aerospace, Santa Clara (2014)
5. Brandt, S.L., Lachter, J., Battiste, V., Johnson, W.W.: Pilot situation awareness and its implications for single pilot operations: analysis of a human-in-the-loop study. In: Proceedings of the 6th International Conference on Applied Human Factors and Ergonomics, Las Vegas (2015)
6. Bilimoria, K.D., Johnson, W.W., Shutte, P.C.: Conceptual framework for single pilot operations. In: Proceedings of the International Conference on Human-Computer Interaction in Aerospace, Santa Clara (2014)
7. Schulte, A.: Human Systems Engineering (HSE) Approach to Human-Autonomy Teaming, NATO STO HFM-247 Task Group Presentation (2015)
8. Schulte, A., Donath, D., Lange, D.S.: Design patterns for human-cognitive agent teaming. In: Harris, D. (ed.) EPCE 2016. LNCS(LNAI), vol. 9736, pp. 231–243. Springer, Heidelberg (2016)
9. Neerincx, M., Lange, D.: HAT Patterns, NATO STO HFM-247 Task Group Presentation (2015)
10. Endsley, M.R.: Toward a theory of situation awareness in dynamic systems. Hum. Factors 37, 32–64 (1995)
11. Parasuraman, R., Sheridan, T.B., Wickens, C.D.: A model for types and levels of human interaction with automation. IEEE Trans. Syst. Man Cybern. Part A: Syst. Hum. 30(3), 286–297 (2000)
12. Flin, R., Martin, L., Goeters, K.-M., Hörmann, H.-J., Amalberti, R., Valot, C., Nijhuis, H.: Development of the NOTECHS (Non-Technical Skills) system for assessing pilots' CRM skills. Hum. Factors Aero. Saf. 3, 95–117 (2003)

Effect of Speech Display on Team Mutual Awareness and Diagnosis Performance

Yingzhi Zhang[✉] and Zhizhong Li

Department of Industrial Engineering,
Tsinghua University, Beijing, People's Republic of China
zhangyz_0208@163.com, zzli@tsinghua.edu.cn

Abstract. In many complex industrial systems, a team works together on digital systems. Team members need to gather information efficiently to maintain mutual awareness and do well in dealing with what may happen in the system. This research studies the effect of speech display in mutual awareness tools on team mutual awareness, individual performance, mental workload and team performance in simulated emergent diagnosis tasks of nuclear power plants at different task complexity levels. An experiment was conducted with 48 subjects (24 teams). Every team completed two scenarios. The results showed that speech display improved team mutual awareness in the low-complexity scenario. However, the teams without speech display did better in analyzing the accident than the teams with speech display in the low-complexity scenario. Furthermore, the teams with speech display were under higher workload.

Keywords: Speech display · Mutual awareness · Team performance · Complex industrial system

1 Introduction

In many complex industrial systems, team members work together to ensure the effective operation of the system. They have to respond quickly to any emergencies that may occur in the system. So besides having a real-time understanding of how their own part operates, they also need to keep an up-to-the-minute understanding of how other team members interact with the system, which is related to mutual awareness.

Situation awareness is defined as "the knowledge of a dynamic organization structure maintained through perceptual information gathered from the environment" [1]. When a team works together, one sort of situation awareness, called mutual awareness, is "A's awareness of activities of B, including the aim, state, possible effects and ramifications etc." [2]. For diagnosis tasks, including mutual awareness tools can improve mutual awareness and thus improve team performance to some degree [11].

To maintain mutual awareness and do well in dealing with what may happen in the system, team members need to gather information efficiently. The selection of information display is an important factor that influences the efficiency of information gathering.

Our research studied the effect of speech display in mutual awareness tools on team mutual awareness, individual performance, mental workload, and team diagnosis

© Springer International Publishing Switzerland 2016
D. Harris (Ed.): EPCE 2016, LNAI 9736, pp. 256–265, 2016.
DOI: 10.1007/978-3-319-40030-3_26

performance at two levels of task complexity. The speech display was used only in mutual awareness tools and there is no voice prompt for one's own states.

Five questions are to be answered:

Question 1: How will speech display influence team mutual awareness?
Question 2: How will speech display influence individual performance?
Question 3: How will speech display influence mental workload?
Question 4: How will speech display influence team performance?
Question 5: Will the conclusion differ at different task complexity?

2 Literature Review

2.1 Visual, Auditory and Multimodal Display

In most complex systems, visual displays are most often used. However, there are some limitations in visual display modality and thus auditory display modality can serve as a complementary choice in addition to visual display modality to enhance performance in complex tasks and reduce cognitive load [3].

Also, researches have stressed the use of multimodal display that combines visual display and auditory display.

The advantages of multimodal display include: synergy (presenting various dimensions of information of the same event), redundancy (presenting information in various ways), and the increase of bandwidth of information transfer [4].

Dowell et al. (2008) described three situations where multimodal display can be applied: multitask situations, usually with visual demand for primary tasks and auditory demand for side tasks, multimedia presentations, which present the information through multiple channels, and situations when the screen is too small to present all information visually [5].

2.2 Selection of Information Display Modality

Various experiments analyzed the influence of information display modality selection on individual performance, situation awareness and mental workload based on different scenarios.

One example is an experiment conducted by Kalyuga et al. (2009). Visual-only display, auditory-only display, and redundant (both visual and auditory) display were used to present information. Redundant display resulted in the best learning performance, followed by auditory display and visual display [6].

As Moreno and Mayer (2002) suggested, the reason why redundant display results in better performance may lie in the "sharing of load across visual and auditory processing in working memory" [7].

Dowell et al. (2008) conducted an experiment to examine the effect of information display on comprehension performance, taking information complexity into consideration. The results showed that redundant display and visual display did an equally good job and speech display results in worse performance in high information complexity [5].

Examples above are all single-task situations. In some occasions, a side task is performed while the primary task (usually an ongoing visual task) is processed, which is called the dual-task situation. There are two views on selection between "visual-visual" display (visual primary task and visual side task) and "visual-auditory" display (visual primary task and auditory side task) in dual-task situations.

Some argue that "visual-auditory" display can result in better performance. Wickens explained this using models of multiple resources. The resource management of different channels is relatively independent and thus an auditory side task interfere with the visual primary task less than a visual side task [8].

However, there exists an opposite view. As the primary visual task is ongoing and the auditory task is discrete, some assert that the auditory side task will take attention away from the visual primary task easily and adversely affect the performance of the primary task, which is called a "preemption" effect [9]. So they think "visual-visual" display is a better choice.

Horrey & Wickens (2004) took both views into consideration and posited that this is a trade-off which needs to be balanced when designing information display in dual-task situations [10].

3   Method

In our research, speech display was included in a simulated simplified nuclear power plant. An experiment was conducted with 48 participants (24 teams). Every pair of participants acted as two operators working together in the nuclear power plant. They were in charge of the nuclear island (Fig. 1) and the conventional island (Fig. 2), respectively. They were asked to complete some daily work alone and some diagnosis tasks together.

3.1   Participants

The participants were 48 male undergraduate students major in science or engineering, with an average age of 21.2. Most of them knew little about nuclear power plants before participation. To avoid the influence of unfamiliarity, every pair of participants who know each other well were grouped into a team. Participants in one team all have known each other for more than 0.5 years and 62.50 % have known each other for 3−4 years.

The participants were randomly divided into two groups. One used system with speech display that would "speak out" the other team member's actions and alarms. The other used system without speech display.

3.2   System

Every pair of the participants conducted the experiment on two computers in a quiet room. The system was a simulated simplified nuclear power plant with a mutual

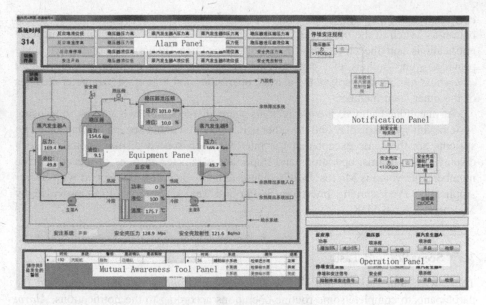

Fig. 1. Interface for nuclear island

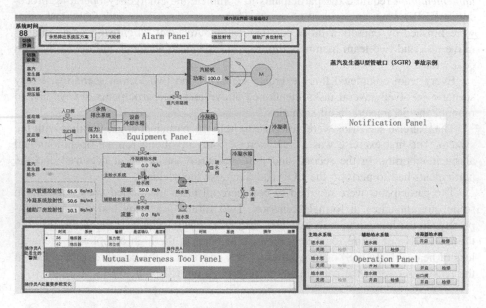

Fig. 2. Interface for conventional island

awareness toolkit, which was first developed by Yuan (2013) [11]. In our study, we did some modification and added a speech display.

The interface of each operator consists of five parts: the *alarm panel* displays an alarm with red alarm tile as any system parameter exceeds its normal range; the *equipment panel* displays all the equipment and parameters, with an interface-switching button to switch to the other team member's interface; the *notification panel* displays notifications and the emergency operation procedures (EOPs); the *operation panel* provides some buttons that can be clicked to control the equipment; the *mutual awareness tool panel* displays the alarms, operations and important parameter changes of the other team member.

As mentioned above, the participants were divided into two groups, one using system with speech display and the other using system without speech display. The two systems are the same except that the interface with speech display include speech display of the alarms, operations and important parameter changes of the other team member. The voice is Microsoft lili Chinese female voice. It is developed with Server Application Programming Interface (SAPI) and Text to Speech (TTS) provided by Microsoft Speech SDK.

3.3   Scenarios and Tasks

There were four type of tasks in the experiment. *Routine operations* required the participants to complete some routine operations according to the notifications. *Alarm monitoring* required the participants to click the alarm tiles when it turned red. *EOP implementation* required the participants to complete the emergency operating procedures (EOPs) when an accident occurred. These three tasks were individual tasks that were finished by oneself without communication. *Accident diagnosis* was a collaborative task and two team members discussed to diagnose accident and decide how to deal with it.

Every team completed three exercise scenarios and two formal scenarios. Every scenario involved several tasks mentioned above and the participants always had to monitor the parameters in all scenarios.

The exercise scenarios were designed to help the participants get familiar with the system. The first exercise was a free exercise, only involving routine operations and alarm monitoring. In the second and third scenarios, an accident occurred and the participants had to perform the EOP and diagnose the accident.

The participants were required to complete all tasks mentioned above and finish some questionnaires in formal scenarios. Two formal scenarios had different complexity. In the low-complexity scenario, loss of coolant accident (LOCA) occurred in the inlet valve of the residual heat removal system. In the high-complexity scenario, loss of heat sink (LOHS) occurred and LOCA occurred in the pressure relief valve of the pressurizer while the participants were performing EOPs of LOHS.

3.4   Independent Variables

This was a 2×2 mix design with two independent variables.

Speech display (with speech display vs. without speech display) is a between-subjects variable. Half of the participants (24 participants, 12 teams) used system with speech display.

Task complexity (low-complexity vs. high-complexity) is a within-subjects variable. Every team completed two scenarios with different task complexity. In the low-complexity scenario, only one accident occurred. The team needed to diagnose the accident after the EOPs. In the high-complexity scenario, another accident occurred while they were performing the EOPs of the first accident. The team needed to diagnose the accident and decide whether to take a certain action.

3.5   Dependent Variables

There were seven dependent variables.

Mutual Awareness Score. In each formal scenario, the participants finished a questionnaire designed with SAGAT method to evaluate the participant's knowledge and understanding of the other team member's status. From the questionnaire we obtained the individual mutual awareness scores. The team's mutual awareness score is the average of the individual scores of the two team members.

Individual Situation Awareness Score. We were interested in whether speech display would cause a loss in individual situation awareness. Like mutual awareness score, individual situation awareness score was measured with a questionnaire and we took the average as the final score.

Alarm missing Rate. It is the percentage of alarms that were missed by the participants. This was recorded by the system to evaluate individual performance.

Average Reaction Time. It is the average time from the appearance of an alarm to the confirmation of the alarm. This was recorded by the system to evaluate individual performance.

Mental Workload. In each formal scenario, the participants finished a NASA Task Load Index (NASA-TLX) questionnaire. The participants were required to use 1−10 to measure their mental demand, physical demand, temporal demand, performance, effort, and frustration level. The overall mental workload was the sum of the scores in the six dimensions.

Diagnosis Score. It measures the accuracy of the participants' diagnosis. The score has four levels(0, 5, 10, 15), higher if the diagnosis conclusion was closer to the correct answer.

Analysis Score. This measure reflects how well the diagnosis was performed by counting how many key issues were addressed in the discussion during the diagnosis process. The percentage of key issues mentioned by the participants was transformed to a 0−10 score.

3.6   Procedure

The experiment lasted about 2.5 h. First, the experimenter introduced the experiment to the participants. Then the participants were given a one-hour training on the principle and operation of the simulated nuclear power plant as well as a quiz to ensure that they mastered what they were taught. After the quiz, they completed the three exercise scenarios in about 40 min. Then they completed the two formal scenarios in about 50 min. The order of the formal scenarios were randomized. During each scenario, the system froze at some time and a questionnaire was given to the participants to measure mutual awareness and individual situation awareness. Then the scenario continued and they perform the EOPs and diagnose the accident. After the diagnosis, mental load was assessed.

4 Results

4.1 Mutual Awareness

The effects of speech display, task complexity, and their interaction on mutual awareness score were assessed using the repeated measure ANOVA at the significance level of 0.05. There was no significant effect of speech display on mutual awareness score. Mutual awareness score in the low-complexity task was significantly higher than that in the high-complexity task ($F = 41.050$, $p < 0.001$). There was a significant interaction effect between speech display and task complexity ($F = 4.826$, $p = 0.039$).

To further analyze the effect of speech display on mutual awareness score, a t-test was conducted at both task complexity levels respectively. Mutual awareness score of teams with speech display was marginally significantly higher than that of teams without speech display in the low-complexity task ($t = 1.841$, $p = 0.080$). There was no significant effect in the high-complexity task.

4.2 Individual Situation Awareness

Homogeneity of variance was rejected using Box test and Levene test at significance level 0.05. The effect of speech display on individual situation awareness score was assessed at both task complexity levels respectively using Mann-Whitney U test at the significance level of 0.05. There was no significant effect of speech display on individual situation awareness score at both task complexity levels. The effect of task complexity on individual situation awareness score was assessed when team used a system with and without speech display respectively using Wilcoxon signed-rank test. Individual situation awareness score in the low-complexity task was significantly higher than that in the high-complexity task whether a team used a system with ($p = 0.03$) or without ($p = 0.03$) speech display.

4.3 Alarm Missing Rate

There was no alarms at the conventional island in the high-complexity scenario and thus we only analyzed alarm missing rate in the low-complexity task. Normality was rejected using Anderson-Darling test at the significance level of 0.05. The effect of speech display on alarm missing rate in the low-complexity task was assessed using Mann-Whitney U test at the significance level of 0.05. No significant effect was found.

4.4 Average Reaction Time

Similarly, average reaction time was analyzed only for the low-complexity task. Normality was rejected using Anderson-Darling test at the significance level of 0.05. The effect of speech display on average reaction time in the low-complexity task was assessed using Mann-Whitney U test and no significant effect of speech display was found on average reaction time.

4.5 Mental Workload

The effects of speech display, task complexity, and their interaction on the overall mental workload were assessed using the repeated measure ANOVA at the significance level of 0.05. There were no significant main effects and interaction effects.

However, when we analyzed each dimension of mental workload separately, we found that the performance dimension of the teams with speech display was significantly higher than the teams without speech display ($F = 5.576$, $p = 0.022$). The performance dimension of mental workload measures the extent that the participants thought they had performed the tasks in the experiment well. The teams with speech display inclined to think that they had not performed the tasks well.

4.6 Diagnosis Score

Diagnosis score was a four-level ordered categorical variable. The effects of speech display and task complexity on diagnosis score were assessed using a Logistic model. Diagnosis score in the low-complexity task was found to be significantly higher than that in the high-complexity task ($Chi\text{-}square = 24.799$, $p < 0.001$). There was no significance effect of speech display on diagnosis score.

4.7 Analysis Score

The effects of speech display, task complexity, and their interaction on analysis score were assessed using the repeated measure ANOVA at the significance level of 0.05. There were no significant effect of speech display on analysis score. Analysis score in the low-complexity task was significantly higher than that in the high-complexity task ($F = 19.181$, $p < 0.001$). There was a marginally significant interaction effect between speech display and task complexity ($F = 2.952$, $p = 0.100$).

To further assess the interaction effect, a t-test was conducted on the effect of speech display on analysis score at both task complexity levels, respectively. We found that analysis score of the teams with speech display was significantly lower than that of the teams without speech display in the low-complexity task ($t = -2.894$, $p = 0.008$). There was no significant effect in the high-complexity task.

5 Discussion and Further Plan

According to the results, speech display improved mutual awareness only in the low-complexity task. One possible reason is that information load in the high-complexity task was so high that no more attention could be paid to the other team member even with speech display. Moreover, we found that the performance dimension of mental workload of teams with speech display was higher. One possible reason is that the participants realized that they missed some important information as they could not remember all the information displayed by speech. Thus, they thought they had not performed well in the experiment. We also found that analysis score of the teams with speech display was lower in the low-complexity task. This indicates that speech display had an adverse effect on performance to some degree.

In this study, we analyzed the effect of speech display in mutual awareness tools on team mutual awareness, individual performance, mental workload and team performance on two levels of task complexity. For the next stage, tone without speech could be used and the effect of this kind of auditory display could be examined.

Acknowledgements. This work was supported by the National Natural Science Foundation of China (Grant No. 71371104) and the Open Funding Project of National Key Laboratory of Human Factors Engineering (Grant No. HF2012-K-02).

References

1. Gutwin, C., Greenberg, S.: Effects of awareness support on groupware usability. In: Proceedings of International Conference on Human Factors in Computing System, pp. 511–518 (1998)
2. Schmidt, K.: Some notes on mutual awareness, COTCOS-Report, Universidade Técnica da Dinamarca, disponível em http://citeseerist.psu.edu/330273.html, último acesso em Jan 1998
3. Oviatt, S., Coulston, R., Lunsford, R.: When do we interact multimodally? cognitive load and multimodal communication pattern. In: Proceedings of the 6th International Conference on Multimodal Interfaces, pp. 129–136 (2004)
4. Sarter, N.: B,: Multimodal information presentation in support of human-automation communication and coordination. Adv. Hum. Perform. Cogn. Eng. Res. **2**, 13–35 (2002)
5. Dowell, J., Shmueli, Y., Kingdom, U.: Blending speech output and visual text in the multimodal. Interface **50**(5), 782–788 (2008)
6. Kalyuga, U., Chandler, P., Sweller, J.: cc in Multimedia Instruction, vol. 371, April 1998, pp. 351–372 (1999)
7. Moreno, R., Mayer, R.E.: Learning science in virtual reality multimedia environments: role of methods and media. J. Educ. Psychol. **94**(3), 598 (2002)
8. Wickens, C.D.: Multiple resources and performance prediction. Ergon. Psychol. Mech. Model. Ergon. **83** (2005)

9. Wickens, C.D., Liu, Y.: Codes and modalities in multiple resources: a success and a qualification. Hum. Factors J. Hum. Factors Ergon. Soc. **30**(5), 599–616 (1988)
10. Horrey, W.J., Wickens, C.D.: Driving and side task performance: the effects of display. Hum. Factors. **46**(4), 611–624 (2004)
11. Xihui, Y., Zhizhong, L.: Effects of mutual awareness on team performance in accident diagnosis under computerized working environment. Dept. of Industrial engineering, Tsinghua University (2015)

Cognition in Complex and High Risk Environments

A-PiMod: A New Approach to Solving Human Factors Problems with Automation

Joan Cahill[1(✉)], Tiziana C. Callari[1], Florian Fortmann[2],
Denis Javaux[3], and Andreas Hasselberg[4]

[1] School of Psychology, Centre for Innovative Human Systems (CIHS),
Trinity College Dublin, Dublin, Ireland
cahilljo@tcd.ie
[2] R&D Division Transportation, OFFIS – Institute for Information Technology,
Escherweg 2, 26121 Oldenburg, Germany
[3] Symbio Concepts & Products S.P.R.L,
Sur les Coteaux, 264690 Bassenge, Belgium
[4] Deutsches Zentrum für Luft- und Raumfahrt e.V. (DLR),
Institut für Flugführung, Lilienthalplatz 7, 38108 Brunswick, Germany

Abstract. The objective of this paper is to present a new adaptive automation concept which (1) addresses the still open human factors problems with automation from a team centred perspective and (2), as part of this, offers a new 'team' centred approach to solving these problems. In so doing, this paper poses questions about what it means to work in a team, what kind of expertise a third crew member (i.e. automation) offers, and how team members might share information about their state, intentions and actions. In elucidating this new automation concept, this paper introduces new role/work practice concepts for pilots, and a potential roadmap for adaptive automation and single crew operations.

Keywords: Adaptive automation · Stakeholder evaluation · Crew state monitoring · Pilot decision making

1 Introduction

1.1 Introduction to Research Problem

Crew information needs (and the requirement for workload and decision support) vary according to the crew composition, the specific experiences of the two crew members (i.e. familiarity with type, familiarity with route and time elapsed since last flown that route), and the specific flight circumstances on the day (traffic and weather).

Given automation advances over the last decade, Pilots share responsibility for different flight tasks with cockpit systems. Adaptable systems are systems which require human delegation of task and 'function authority' to automation during real-time operational performance (i.e. the task distribution is controlled by the user) [1]. Adaptive automation (AA) is defined as a 'form of automation that allows for dynamic changes in control function allocations between a machine and human operator based on states of

© Springer International Publishing Switzerland 2016
D. Harris (Ed.): EPCE 2016, LNAI 9736, pp. 269–279, 2016.
DOI: 10.1007/978-3-319-40030-3_27

the collective human–machine system' [2, 3]. As such, task distribution changes can be controlled autonomously by the system.

The air accident and flight safety literature reports on the many still-open issues in relation to automation design. For example: Flight Air France 447 (2009) [4], Flight Spanair 5022 (2008) [5], Flight Helios Airways HCY 522 (2005) [6], Flight China Airlines 140 (1994) [7], and Flight Air Inter 148 (1992) [8]. Critically, several human factors problems have been documented. This includes: automation surprises, degraded situation awareness, unintentional blindness, workload concerns and issues pertaining to over-reliance on automation.

With increasing flight hours, fatigue and increased traffic growth, all crews can benefit from an "experience aid". Ideally, the user and the "experience aid" (or assistance system) constitute a cooperative system - they share tasks and perform them as a team.

1.2   Introduction to A-PiMod Project

The Applying Pilots' Model for Safer Aircraft (A-PiMod) project aims to address problems relating to crew/automation teamwork and workload management. The high level goal of the project is to design a new adaptive automation concept based on a hybrid of three elements – (1) Multi-Modal Pilot Interaction, (2) Operator Modelling, and (3) Real-Time Risk Assessment. This research is funded by the European Commission and has been undertaken since September 2013.

2   Research Design and Status

The high level Human Machine Interaction (HMI) design/evaluation methodology combines formal HMI design/evaluation activities (i.e. interviews and simulator evaluation), informal HMI design/evaluation approaches (i.e. participatory design activities), along with an integrated stakeholder approach to evaluation [9]. The concept of a Community of Practice (COP) proposed by Wenger underpins the stakeholder evaluation approach [10]. The current COP panel comprises fifteen participants (see Fig. 1 below). Stakeholder participation involves consultative interaction along with engagement in technical research tasks [11]. Overall, nineteen COP sessions and two phases of simulator evaluation have been undertaken. The first phase of simulator evaluation involved eight participants, while the second phase involved twelve participants.

The Radar Diagram below (see Fig. 1) shows the two overlaying levels of expertise both from the internal and external stakeholders. The composition of the internal stakeholders is represented in blue, while the composition of the external stakeholder is represented in amaranth. The red dotted line corresponds to the 2-level expertise.

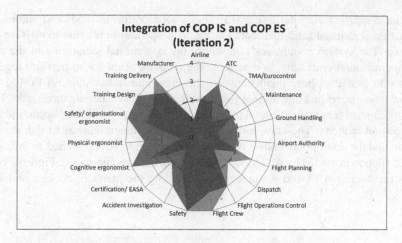

Fig. 1. Current state of stakeholder competency knowledge in A-PiMod

3 Key Results and Emerging Concept

3.1 Human Factors Problems and Proposed Approach

Field research with the pilots resulted in the identification of several categories of human factors problems. This includes (1) human factors specific to automation, (2) more general HF/operational problems - that might be addressed by improved automation design and (3) existing technology/information gaps in terms of cockpit design – that might be addressed by an improved automation design. For more information, please see Appendix 1.

The theoretical starting point for addressing human factors issues with automation is the assessment of crew/automation/aircraft state in relation to the achievement of the mission level goal (i.e. mission level risk assessment), and the identification of a suitable task distribution at cockpit/agent level, to achieve this (see Appendix 2). Automation has a role in relation to (1) real-time risk assessment, (2) the identification of a course of action, (3) the selection/implementation of a course of action (i.e. the delegation of work to automation is part of the course of action selection), and (4) the identification of a suitable task distribution based on crew state .

3.2 Automation Concept

The emerging concept can be conceptualised on several levels - (1) a task/experience aid, (2) a proactive risk/safety tool, (3) a crew state monitor and (4) a decision support system. The goal is to support crew in situations when they may need help irrespective of experience, and/or in situations when the crew has less experience, and/or in situations where the crew is experiencing high workload, under pressure and potentially fatigued.

The team comprises the pilot flying (PF), the pilot monitoring (PM) and automation. Automation is a virtual team-member. The team co-operates in relation to mission level decisions. The system continuously monitors the operational situation and the allied crew/automation/aircraft state, to determine the tasks the team has to perform together, and how to best distribute them between the crew and automation. A-PiMod flags potential risks - providing operational guidance in relation to managing those risks. Pilots have final control (i.e. make the final decisions), but are responsible and accountable for their decisions/actions. The crew forms their own judgement/ideas as to risk status of situation and the appropriate course of action. The crew are not mandated to follow the decision support provided by A-PiMod (this is an aid, not a requirement). Figure 2 below depicts the overall A-PiMod architecture – including the mission, cockpit and agent levels.

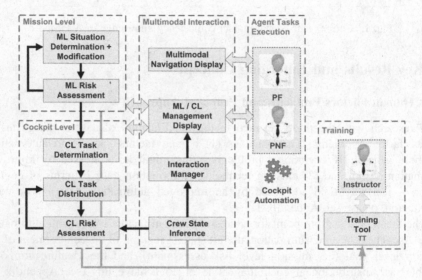

Fig. 2. Architecture Concept and Technology Components/Modules

3.3 Pilot Interaction in the Cockpit

Pilot interaction in the cockpit can be characterized in relation to the following points:

- User friendly and flexible information/decision support
- The crew interact using voice/touch and traditional controls
- This interaction is tracked by the system (i.e. what tasks performing, level of fatigue, involvement in activity): this is referred to as 'crew state monitoring'

- The crew obtain feedback via a new cockpit user interface (Mission and Cockpit Level Management Display - MCMD) as to:
  - The risk status of the operational situation (this includes an assessment of the status of joint crew/automation system)
  - What to do – including the provision of best options/alternatives based on different 'technical' contributing factors (i.e. fuel remaining, status of alternates etc.)
- The proposed MCMD features two related sub-displays – the mission and cockpit level displays
- The crew can over-ride system proposals/decisions – except in certain critical situations (i.e. incapacitation)

4   Discussion

4.1   Cockpit Centred .V. Task Centred Approach

A-PiMod adopts a team centred approach as opposed to a crew centred approach. We are focussing on the outcome; considering what is best for the safe and efficient completion of the mission/flight, and not particularly trying to adapt to human needs. As indicated in the architecture concept [12], if the pilot flying/pilot monitoring is overloaded and this threatens the completion of the mission, the task distribution is adapted at the agent level.

4.2   Crew State Monitoring

The real gain in A-PiMod relates to crew state monitoring – that is focussing the pilot's attention on their state (i.e. crew state) along with that of their crew member - and on the current and future state of the aircraft. If overloaded and/or under pressure, pilots may forget or not consider all the safe options. However the 3rd crew member (automation) will not, so a quick check will refresh the possible options, to allow a safe decision to be made. In this context, a key challenge is how to get the two human crew members to share their 'current state' with the 3rd crew member such that it is meaningful, informative but not self-incriminating in any post hoc analysis. Normal human interactions can easily accommodate this in simple pre-flight social interactions. Formalising it such that the 3rd crew member can make useful sense of it may be more problematic.

The assessment of crew state is not just about workload, it's about the crew experience, flight hours, familiarity with route, when last flown there, training background etc. If the Pilots are not familiar with the route, then the crew state might be assessed as less optimal. From a Pilots perspective, the starting point for crew state monitoring is the crew briefing/flight planning. This might occur a week before the flight. Or at least, at the time of the pre-flight, flight planning and briefing task. For crew state monitoring to work, we need to establish a picture/sense of the crew state from the very beginning of the flight. The A-PiMod system needs to know what the join crew status is and any threats associated with this. Potentially, we will need the crew to provide feedback about their state in advance of the flight. Further, it takes into account real-time crew behaviour. This involves monitoring the crew state via the assessment of (1) crew activity (gesture), and (2) crew interaction with cockpit systems including new multi-modal input (i.e. touch, voice and gesture) and traditional controls.

4.3   Interpreting Crew State Information

Careful attention needs to be given to the means/basis by which crew state information (i.e. eye tracking data, gesture data, voice, and touch data) is used to form an assessment of crew state. The evaluation of this feedback depends on what we know about the crew. For example, if crew are not looking at the right area of the screen and/or blinking a lot, it may not be a problem. In this case, the crew might be very familiar with the route and also, on the first day of their roster. However the system might interpret this behaviour differently if the crew are unfamiliar with the route, and on the last day of their roster (i.e. if expect more or less fatigue).

4.4   Teamwork Concept and Nature of Automation

The question of how the system interprets quietness in the cockpit is controversial. One of the crew members might be taking a controlled rest (i.e. flight over the Atlantic). In this case, one would not expect any briefing/verbalizations between the crew members. Maybe A-PiMod has a role at this time, to ensure the other crew member (PF) is kept in a safe state. Accordingly, A-PiMod might issue soft alerts so that they remain active and engaged. If A-PiMod is to become a 'trusted 3rd crew member', it needs to behave as one does in 'normal' situations. Potentially, it needs to engage in some form of 'social' interaction as much as technical interactions in order to be fully integrated in the 'team'. This latter issue has not been explored in A-PiMod and warrants more attention.

How assertive a team member is automation? When and how can it voice its concerns – and potentially, over-ride? In most (but not all situations), the cockpit crew have the final authority and can veto automation. As such, this reflects an 'adaptive systems' logic. However, A-PiMod's crew state monitoring technology will detect certain situations, when it is necessary from a safety perspective for automation to 'take charge' (for example, situations of crew incapacity). Specifically, there may be different levels of crew state monitoring. For example, (1) passive support, (2) active support and (3) intervention/over-ride. In this sense, A-PiMod represents an adaptive automation approach.

4.5   Adaptive Automation and Roadmap to Single Crew Operations

The proposed third Pilot/adaptive automation concept has the potential to support single crew operations and remote crew operations (i.e. provision of ground support). In principle, the implementation of single crew operations necessitates a fully adaptive automation approach. As indicated in this research, a fully adaptive automation approach requires detailed and reliable/robust modelling and assessment of both crew and aircraft states. The former (i.e. crew states) links to the new cockpit display (MCMD) and specifically the integration between crew modelling and crew monitoring (and specifically real time monitoring of crew use of the proposed HMMI - touch, voice, gesture and eye-tracking). The latter (i.e. aircraft state) may require complete integration between A-PiMod and other aircraft systems, and potentially wider ATM and ground systems (i.e. ATM system picture/multiple missions). Not all of this may be fully achievable in terms of what is demonstrated at the end of the A-PiMod project, and may require additional research/development.

5   Conclusions

Overall, the stakeholder evaluation/validation approach adopted has facilitated the preliminary specification and evaluation of a new adaptive automation concept and associated technology requirements. Specifically, the integration of a range of formal and informal HMI methods, with a stakeholder evaluation approach has proved effective in terms of enabling both operational and safety validation. Critically, the emerging adaptive automation concept is predicated on feedback in relation to flight crew experience with automation (and associated problems). Automation is conceptualized as a third crew member – providing support to crew in both high and low workload situations – to optimise flight safety and ensure the mission level goal is achieved. A-PiMod cannot supplant experience. However, it is ready to provide extra information in relation to risks/hazards and potential courses of action – if required by crew. In this way, as noted by a COP pilot, the proposed A-PiMod system features different "levels" of response, similar to the way a Captain would have with different co-pilots of varying experience.

Acknowledgements. The research leading to these results/preliminary outcomes has received funding from the European Commission's Seventh Framework Programme (FP7/2007-2013) under grant agreement N. 605141 - Applying Pilot Models for Safety Aircraft (A-PiMod) Project. We would like to thank member of the A-PiMod Project Team and our COP members – particularly, Paul Cullen, William Butler, Martin Duffy and Stephen Duffy.

Appendix 1: Human Factors Problems

See Table 1

Table 1. Human Factors Problems

Type	Example
HF problems specific to automation	Poor teamwork between crew and automation (crew have poor understanding of automation status)
	Poor teamwork between crew and automation (automation not understanding crew intentions)
	Sometimes Pilot knows more than automation – experience to know can continue with flight plan and not impacted by thunderstorm
	As such, issue not just whether crew understand automation, but whether automation acting in way that understand intentions of Pilot
	Overconfidence and getting lazy – danger/problem if not keeping track of status of automation
	Over-reliance on automation and loss of situation awareness
	Performance drops when not enough workload – need to be involved
	Pilot deskilling/degrading flying skills due to over-reliance on automation
	Automation not provide context information (except for Windshear and Terrain awareness)
	Lack of standardization across different aircraft types
More general HF/operational problems – that might be addressed by improved automation design	High workload – need task support
	Crew composition – gaps in experiences levels
	High workload and loss of situation awareness
	Fatigue – need task support
	Emergency situations – need task support
	Poor crew CRM
	Low workload – not involved, easily fall out of loop

(*Continued*)

Table 1. (*Continued*)

Type	Example
Existing technology/information gaps in terms of cockpit design – that might be addressed by improved automation design	Currently no risk assessment information provided – useful to obtain this information and associated decision options
	Currently, no crew state monitoring
	Currently, no detection of degraded crew performance – only post hoc analysis (i.e. Flight Data Monitoring)
	Currently, no monitoring of quality of teamwork between crew i.e. detecting degraded CRM
	Lack of information integration with company – Flight Operations Control
	Poor weather information – predictive information re weather and associated risk assessment

Appendix 2: Automation Perspectives and Theoretical Starting Points

See Table 2

Table 2. Perspective/Starting Points

#	Perspective/Starting point	Description	Example Questions
1	Aircraft control	Key questions in relation to aircraft/flight plan (aviate, navigate etc.)	What is the current status of the aircraft in relation to the flight plan and current situation (location, heading, speed, fuel, aircraft tech status, weather, traffic and terrain)
			Where am I
			Where should I beChanges to the above – navigation, guidance and control

(*Continued*)

Table 2. (*Continued*)

#	Perspective/Starting point	Description	Example Questions
2	Automation status	Key questions in relation to automation status and work-share between crew and automation	Is the auto-flight system engaged? What is automation doing now (what tasks is it responsible for now, automation mode)? What tasks should it be doing now?
3	Human Factors/Crew	Key questions in relation to crew status	Are both crew members doing their work in line with SOP? What tasks currently doing, or yet to do, or should of done but not done? Level of situation awareness (i.e. flight plan, flight plan course, aircraft status, automation status etc.). Understanding of risk status of situation? Understanding of course of action? Implementing right course of action?
4	Mission Risk	Key questions in relation to flight plan/mission level risk assessment	What is the risk status of my flight/flight plan? What do I need to do now and/or in the future?

References

1. Kaber, D.B., Prinzel, L.J.: Adaptive and Adaptable Automation Design: A Critical Review of the Literature and Recommendations for Future Research. NASA/TM-2006-214504 (2006)
2. Hilburn, Byrne, Parasuraman: Horwood Limited (publishers), John Wiley & Sons (Halsted Press) (1997)
3. Kaber, D.B., Riley, J.M.: Adaptive automation of a dynamic control task based on secondary task workload measurement. Int. J. Cogn. Ergonomics **3**, 169–187 (1999)
4. Flight AF 447 Final Report on the accident on 1st June 2009 to the Airbus A330-203 registered F-GZCP operated by Air France flight AF 447 Rio de Janeiro (Published July 2012). Retrieved from Bureau d'Enquêtes et d'Analyses pour la sécurité de l'aviation civile (BEA). 1 June 2009. http://www.bea.aero/docspa/2009/f-cp090601.en/pdf/f-cp090601.en.pdf

5. Flight Spainair 5022 Final Report on the accident on 20th August 2008 involving a McDonnell Douglas DC-9-82 (MD-82) registration EC-HFP operated by Spainair at Madrid-Barajas Airport (Published 8 October 2008). Retrieved from Comisión Investigatión de Accidentes e Incidentes de Aviación Civil (CIAIAC). 20 August 2008. http://www.fomento.es/NR/rdonlyres/EC47A855-B098-409E-B4C8-9A6DD0D0969F/107087/2008_032_A_ENG.pdf

6. Flight Helios Airways HCY522 Final Report on the accident on 14th August 2005 involving a Boeing 737-31S registration 5B-DBY operated by Helios Airways at Grammatiko, Hellas (Published November 2006). Retrieved from Air Accident Investigation & Aviation Safety Board (AAIASB), 14 August 2005. http://www.moi.gov.cy/moi/pio/pio.nsf/All/F15FBD7320037284C2257204002B6243/$file/FINAL%20REPORT%205B-DBY.pdf

7. Flight China Airlines 140 Final Report on the accident on 26th April 1994 involving an Airbus Industrie A300B4-662R registration B1816 operated by China Airlines at Nagoya Airport (Published 19 July 1996). Retrieved from Aircraft Accident Investigation Commission. 26 April 1994. http://www.skybrary.aero/bookshelf/books/808.pdf

8. Flight Air Inter 148 Final Report on the accident on 20th January 1992 involving an Airbus A320 registration F-GGED operated by Air Inter Airlines in Vosges Mountains (near Mont Sainte-Odile). Retrieved from Bureau d'Enquêtes et d'Analyses pour la sécurité de l'aviation civile (BEA), 20 January 1992. http://www.bea.aero/docspa/1992/f-ed920120/htm/f-ed920120.html

9. Cahill, J., Callari, T.C.: A Novel Human Machine Interaction (HMI) Design/Evaluation Approach Supporting the Advancement of Improved Automation Concepts to Enhance Flight Safety. In: de Waard, D., Sauer, J., Röttger, S., Kluge, A., Manzey, D., Weikert, C., Toffetti, A., Wiczorek, R., Brookhuis, K., H., Hoonhout (eds.). Proceeding of the Ergonomics Society Europe Chapter 2014 Annual Conference Human Factors in high reliability industries Lisbon, Portugal. http://www.hfes-europe.org/human-factors-high-reliability-industries-2/

10. Wenger, E., McDermott, R.A., Snyder, W.: Cultivating Communities of Practice: A Guide to Managing Knowledge. Harvard Business Press, Boston (2002)

11. Cousins, J.B., Whitmore, E., Shulha, L.: Arguments for a common set of principles for collaborative inquiry in evaluation. Am. J. Eval. **34**(1), 7–22 (2013)

12. Javaux, D., Fortmann, F., Möhlenbrink, C.: Adaptive human-automation cooperation: a general architecture for the cockpit and its application in the A-PiMod project. In: Proceedings of the 7th International Conference on Advanced Cognitive Technologies and Applications (COGNITIVE 2015). International Academy, Research, and Industry Association (IARIA). ISBN: 978-1-61208-390-2 (2015)

Study on the Perceptual Intention Space Construction Model of Industrial Robots Based on 'User + Expert'

Jianxin Cheng[1(✉)], Wangqun Xiao[1,2], Xuejie Wang[2], Junnan Ye[1], and Le Xi[1]

[1] School of Art, Design and Media,
East China University of Science and Technology,
M.BOX 286 No. 130, Meilong road, Xuhui District, Shanghai 200237, China
cjx.master@gmail.com, xiaoyao-1916@163.com,
yejunnan971108@qq.com, xilutar@sina.com
[2] Academy of Art and Design, Anhui University of Technology,
No. 59, East Lake Road, Ma'anshan 243002, China
402860858@qq.com

Abstract. Nowadays, a new technological and industrial revolution is under gestation and the labor division as well as competition division is re-shaping. Meanwhile, the industrial robot has become the one contested by all high-end equipment field throughout the world. How to introduce emotion design into the robot will inevitably become a power weapon for robots shinning out in competition. Human beings have emotional appeals, and the emotional effect ignited based on product functional structure, material form, user aesthetic sense as well as experience, and the cross-over study among user emotional appeals, psychology, physiology and design will become front topics in the industrial design research field. No matter perceptual engineering or emotional design, they are mainly responsible for the scientific recognition and adoption of ambiguous perceptual or emotional factors appeared in the course of creation, which aim to try the utmost to solve the emotional problems via scientific approaches, and change the situation that people cannot scientifically as well as accurately deal with emotional problems based on the experience and feeling of designers. So, the primary problem to solve emotional recognition is how to scientifically and effectively construct the perceptual intention space of products. This paper carries out scientific research on the special filed industrial robot based on the research of constructing perceptual intention space, trying unremitt8ing efforts to know the most scientific and effective perceptual intention space. The model construction includes vocabulary acquisition, selection and establishment to determine the key elements of users and experts. The main task of perceptual vocabulary acquisition is to widely collect the perceptual intention of industrial robot purchasers and users and personal interview as well as questionnaire is adopted; the selection stage is to carry out hierarchical clustering and simplification of the vulgar, similar and opposite words and the KJ is adopted; the establishment stage is to refine and determine perceptual words based on experts counseling and refinement experiment (the experiment approach is to integrate the online questionnaire and field investigation), which cannot only help to have a good knowledge of the emotional appeals, perceptual intention vocabularies

© Springer International Publishing Switzerland 2016
D. Harris (Ed.): EPCE 2016, LNAI 9736, pp. 280–289, 2016.
DOI: 10.1007/978-3-319-40030-3_28

recognized by users but also make up for the inner voice of users. To conclude, this paper innovatively comes up with the idea of perceptual intention space construction model of industrial robots based on 'users and experts' appealing.

Keywords: Users · Experts · Industrial robot · Perceptual intention space

1 Introduction

Nowadays, a new round of scientific, technological and industrial revolution is brewing. A new trend appears to make manufacturing service-oriented and lead the upgrading of manufacturing. In developed countries like Europe and America, "reindustrialization" strategies are promoted, in an attempt to maintain leading advantages in technologies and industries, in order to take the lead in manufacturing. American President Obama has specially made four speeches over the past few years, highlighting that manufacturing should be revitalized. New plans have been declared in Germany, England, France and Japan to vigorously promote the vitalization of manufacturing (Zhou 2015). As mechanical products, industrial robots are generally considered as structural products, which have somewhat different requirements for "emotional quality" compared with ordinary consumer products. Design ideas have been persistently dominated by the "function first" concept. Research has primarily focused on "technologies" and "performances" of "items", but attached inadequate attention to emotional experience of products and humanistic care. To solve the problem about single development of technologies based on functions, material functions will be inevitably separated from spiritual functions. As a consequence, modern society's "reverse technological control", "material and spiritual separation" have been caused, which isn't in line with original intents of human beings (Xiao et al. 2014). As human beings appeal for emotions, it has become a cutting-edge topic of current studies on industrial design to carry out research on users' emotional appeals in combination with psychology, physiology and design in light of interactions of functional structures of products and their material forms with users' requirements for aesthetics and experiences, etc. However, emotions belong to psychological processes integrating multiple components, dimensions and levels. Covering knowledge about psychology, industrial design, engineering technologies, semiology, linguistics, aesthetics, sociology, computer technologies and ergonomics, emotional design of products have complicated, vague and variable characteristics that can be hardly controlled and grasped. As a result, it is highly difficult to perform emotional design of products and pertinent research (Lin 2012).

2 Research Background

Emotions have been usually neglected and suppressed for a long period in the field of science where rationality is the foremost. By the late 19th century, William James introduced emotional research into the field of psychology. Thereafter, emotional research had presented a relatively complete theoretical system for more than 100 years with the development of disciplines like physiology, cognitive science, behavioral science and sociology (Strongman 2006), gradually expanding form psychology to other fields, such as ergonomics (Vink 2005), engineering (Tractinsky et al. 2000) and computer science (Picard 2003). Although the research is still prosperous in this field home and abroad, neither specific definitions nor uniform names have formed up till now. For Asia, concept of "Kansei engineering" has been put forward in Japan, while "society of Kansei engineering" has been set up in both Japan and Korea. Currently, this wording is generally accepted by the academic circle of Europe (Yamamoto 1986). In spite of attaching great importance to Kansei science, "emotion" is a generally accepted wording (Luo and Pan 2007). Nevertheless, with an overview of much Chinese and foreign literature about emotional design, it may be discovered that Japanese theory of Kansei engineering and three-level theory put forward by an American professor known as Donald A Norman are the sole publicly acknowledged ones that can form a theoretical system at present (Ding et al. 2010).

The 1st International Conference on Design & Emotion convened in the Technische Universiteit Delft of Holland in 1999 and the founding of the "Society of International Design and Emotions" in the conference are hallmark events for research on emotional design as well. Dr. Desmet, from the Department of Industrial Design in the Technische Universiteit Delft, concentrates on research about emotional design and experience (Desmet et al. 2004). Proposing the concept of "product emotion", he has developed tools for measuring product emotions, including Emocards and PrEmo (Desmet 2003). Dr. Desmet has constructed a framework of product experiences with his colleagues, to explain users' all emotional responses in their interactions with products (Desmet and Hekkert 2007) and roles of products in emotional experiences (Demir and Desmet 2008). Considering that emotions are centers for human beings' quality of life (Desmet 2008), he has qualitatively and quantitatively conveyed relationships between evaluation and design projects. These research findings have provided theoretical foundations and technical support for research on emotional designs and measurements.

Regardless of "Kansei engineering" or "emotional design", research has been mainly conducted to examine those uncertain perceptual or emotional factors during human creations from the perspective of scientific cognition and applications, so as to solve material emotional problems of human beings by scientific means, thereby solving problems concerning emotional factors that can't be scientifically and accurately solved just based on designers' experiences and feelings. To deal with problems regarding emotional cognition, the foremost issue is how to scientifically and effectively construct perceptual image space for products.

3 Research Methods

By studying a great deal of literature, it may be discovered that research methods and key technologies for perceptual images of product design have been discussed in previous research on perceptual image space. Nevertheless, there is still space for further exploring the modes and routes for creating perceptual image space for products, including research about if it is proper and scientific to acquire perceptual vocabularies as well as multidimensional characteristics of perceptual image space. Perceptual vocabularies are critical premises for constructing perceptual image space of products. Accurate and scientific construction of perceptual image space of products is dependent upon if perceptual vocabularies are scientifically and rationally defined. In light of this problem, industrial robots are scientifically explored as a relatively special field, in an attempt to construct the most scientific and efficient perceptual image space for industrial robots. Such space may be constructed by gathering/selecting perceptual vocabularies, defining three stages, and two elements, including "users" and "experts".

3.1   Gathering Perceptual Vocabularies of Industrial Robots

In the process of gathering perceptual vocabularies, it is mainly necessary to extensively collect perceptual intentions of purchasers and users of industrial robots. In this study, information is collected by communication with users of industrial robots, personal interview and questionnaire survey as well as magazines, books and websites about industrial robots. In this way, 873 perceptual vocabularies are obtained at first, as shown in Fig. 1 as follows. In this stage, it is unnecessary to evaluate and deal with perceptual vocabularies in any ways. There is only a need to extensively collect adjectives related to feelings or cognitions presented by industrial products. The larger the scope, the wider the lexical coverage is. At last, perceptual vocabularies can be summarized and determined more scientifically.

Fig. 1. Gathering perceptual vocabularies of industrial robots (independently drawn)

3.2   Selecting Perceptual Vocabularies of Industrial Robots

In the process of selecting perceptual vocabularies, the main tasks are manual hierarchical clustering and simplification of vague, similar vocabularies and antonyms by classification, KJ method, summary and combination of several methods. In this paper, a

7-person group is founded to simplify perceptual vocabularies, including a boss of a industrial robot manufacturers, a boss of an enterprise purchasing industrial robots, an operator of the enterprise purchasing industrial robots, two experienced industrial designers, a salesperson and an undergraduate majoring in statistics. The research process is shown in Fig. 2 as follows. The group for simplifying perceptual vocabularies eventually simplifies 874 perceptual vocabularies collected in the last stage into 72 vocabularies to make 36 pairs of adjectives by classification, KJ method, summary and combination of several methods, including modern-traditional, hospitable-indifferent, expensive-cheap, scientific-backward, popular-personalized, graceful-vulgar, bright-dark, concrete-abstract, generous-cautious, hard-soft, thin-thick, rhythmic-serene, streamlined-geometric, unique-ordinary, lively-rigid, coordinated-lofty, light-heavy, interesting-dull, complete-separated, concise-complex, leisure-work, durable-flimsy, young-old, emotional-rational, free-constrained, practical-ornamental, creative-imitative, opportunistic-pessimistic, handsome-manly, coordinated-lofty, kind-alienated.

Fig. 2. Selecting perceptual vocabularies of industrial robots (Self-portrait)

3.3   Defining Perceptual Vocabularies of Industrial Robots

Above 36 pairs of perceptual vocabularies are prepared into a questionnaire survey, to carry out an experiment with the participation of users in combination with expert consultation for the purpose of optimally extracting perceptual vocabularies. Concerning the experimental method, online survey questionnaire is integrated with the field survey questionnaire. Then, expert opinions are solicited. The online questionnaire survey is shown in Fig. 3 as follows.

This questionnaire survey is performed online and offline. In the online survey, the questionnaires are distributed by E-mail, QQ and WeChat. The offline field survey is conducted on users of industrial robots in areas like Shenzhen, Hefei, Wuhu and Ma On Shan, including Foxconn Technology Group, Anhui Jianghuai Automobile Co., Ltd, Chery Automobile Co., Ltd and Hualing Xingma Automobile (Group) Co., Ltd by anonymous answering. In completing the questionnaires, respondents shall fill up their age range and answer their familiarity with industrial robots. In the final online survey questionnaires, 1,382 people who are over 18 years old have known about industrial robots, so these questionnaires are valid. 300 questionnaires are distributed for the field survey, among which 249 valid questionnaires are recovered. The questionnaire surveys are summed up in Figs. 4 and 5 as follows.

Fig. 3. Questionnaire survey of vocabularies on characteristics of industrial robots (Self-portrait)

An expert consultation meeting is convened in light of results of the questionnaire surveys and relevant problems. 3 experts of industrial design, 2 experts of industrial robot users (enterprises) and 2 experts of industrial robot manufacturers are invited to discuss and add perceptual vocabularies put forward by experts. At last, 6 pairs of perceptual vocabularies are defined, including friendly-hostile, safe-dangerous, modern-traditional, beautiful-ugly, exquisite-rough, durable-flimsy.

3.4   Constructing Perceptual Image Space of Industrial Robots

Created by American psychologists in the 20th century, semantic differential method is an empirical method used for investigating mentality of respondents. In fields of sociology and psychology, it is widely used for comparative research concerning differences of individuals and groups, people's attitudes toward things and their views. The experiments on semantic differential method are mainly carried out in the form of questionnaire survey.

1st Stage of Experiment: Collecting and Selecting Samples of Industrial Robots.
At first, samples of industrial robots are collected. In this study, overall forms of industrial robots are explored, so pictures of the forms are collected from advertisements, magazines and exhibitions, etc. of industrial robots in market, so as to widely collect samples in different forms. In this way, research findings may be more significant and complete. After preliminarily selecting collected samples of industrial robots, 73 sampled products are left altogether. Once these 73 samples are confirmed by several people with pertinent design background, 37 samples in forms of cell phones are finally picked up. Next, 39 samples are grouped for treatment, in order to ease the burden of respondents. 30 majors of industrial design are invited from the East China University of Science and Technology and the Anhui University of Technology, including 10 postgraduates, 20 undergraduates, 15 males and females respectively. Respondents are asked to group 39 samples of industrial robots according to personal subjective feelings. After the number of the same grouping times is statistically

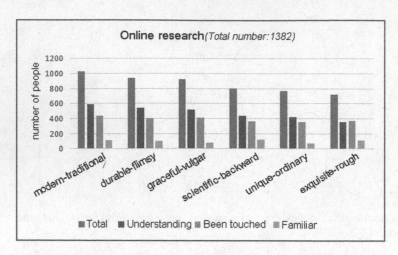

Fig. 4. Histogram statistics of online survey questionnaire (Self-portrait)

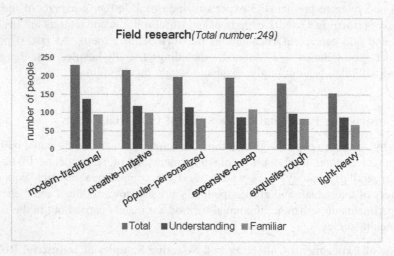

Fig. 5. Histogram statistics of field survey questionnaire (Self-portrait)

analyzed, 39×39 similarity matrix is listed to compare the frequency at which a sample appears in a group, namely degree of similarities. Subsequently, matrix data are input into the statistical software system, in order to perform analyses by multidimensional (2 to 6 dimensions) software system. Finally, the most representative 8 samples are obtained, as shown in Fig. 6.

2nd Stage of Experiment: Evaluation of Perceptual Intentions. In this stage, respondents are invited to take part in an experiment for evaluating images and semantics of 8 representative samples based on personal subjective feelings. A 7-scale attitude scale is set according to the scaling standard for semantic differential survey questionnaire. From the left to the right, 3 to −3 scores are granted for the scale.

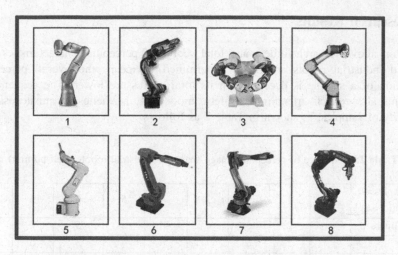

Fig. 6. Final samples of 8 most representative industrial robots (Self-portrait)

−3 means that the sample greatly deviates from the semantics, and 0 represents ordinary, while 3 indicates that the sample has pretty strong feelings represented by the image semantics. In this experiment, 40 respondents are randomly selected from users, including 23 skilled operators of industrial robots and 17 unskilled ones. Then, a questionnaire survey is carried out, and the mean of semantics is determined for the perceptual images as follows, as shown in Table 1.

Table 1. Evaluated mean of semantics for all images of representative samples (Self-portrait)

semantic samples	friendly- hostile	safe- dangerous	modern- traditional	beautiful- ugly	exquisite- rough	durable- flimsy
samples 1	0.956	0.861	0.648	0.982	1.014	0.246
samples 2	-0.154	-0.537	0.366	0.54	0.219	0.137
samples 3	1.5	0.915	0.874	1.694	0.89	0.313
samples 4	0.426	0.114	0.3	0.373	0.389	-0.314
samples 5	0.561	0.12	0.564	0.494	0.675	0.518
samples 6	0.13	0.264	0	0.252	0.421	0.451
samples 7	-0.239	-0.158	0.4	0.377	0.3	0.199
samples 8	-0.853	-0.316	0.117	0.1	0.198	0.466

4 Research Results

Based on above research, orders and total scores of perceptual characteristics of 8 sampled industrial robots are finally determined. It means the overall perceptual evaluation of a sample is decent when its total scores are lower. The sequence of sub-items also reflects friendliness, safety, modernity, aesthetics, exquisiteness and durability of samples, as shown in Table 2 as follows.

Table 2. Sequence of perceptual image space of industrial robots (Self-portrait)

samples semantic		1	2	3	4	5	6	7	8
friendliness		2	6	1	4	3	5	7	8
safety		2	8	1	5	4	3	6	7
modernity		2	4	1	6	3	8	5	7
aesthetics		2	3	1	6	4	7	5	8
exquisiteness		1	7	2	5	3	4	6	8
durability		5	7	4	8	1	3	6	2
total score		14	35	10	34	18	30	35	40

At last, perceptual image vocabularies that actually represent users' emotional needs and acknowledged by users are obtained. With the participation of experts, some perceptual vocabularies are beyond users' psychological expectations, but represent their potential emotional needs. This makes up previous failure to completely reflect users' thoughts by perceptual vocabularies in experiments on perceptual image cognitions and innovatively create a mode of "users + experts" for perceptual image space of industrial robots.

5 Conclusions and Prospect

In all stages where "users" and "experts" deeply get involved in the research from collection from selection and definition of perceptual vocabularies to the experiments for collecting/selecting sampled products of industrial robots and evaluation of emotional images, sequence of perceptual image space is eventually determined to construct a mode of "users + experts" for perceptual image space of industrial robots. This mode is somewhat creative, scientific and reasonable. Nonetheless, the perceptual image space constructed by this mode may be further optimized and deeply explored. Provided that current pictures of sampled industrial robots for experiments are replaced by physical objects, the research findings will be more reliable and scientific. In the mean time, numerous difficulties will be brought to experiments. Furthermore, industrial robots sampled for experiments may be developed into three-dimensional digital models with the same dimensions and experiments may be performed on virtual reality platforms. This will make the research findings more reliable and scientific while avoiding the difficulties for collecting physical samples of industrial robots.

References

Zhou, J.: Intelligent manufacturing – "Made in China 2025" in the main direction. China Mech. Eng. **26**(17), 2273–2284 (2015)

Xiao, W., Cheng, J., Ye, J., Xi, L.: Study on "Intuitive Semantics" of orient traditional creation wisdom contained in the design of modern mechanical products. Commun. Comput. Inf. Sci. **1**, 129–133 (2014)

Lin, L.: Expression model KE emotional imagery products multidimensional variables Construction and Evaluation. Southeast University, Nanjing (2012)

Strongman, K.T.: Emotional Psychology: From Theory to Everyday Life. China Light Industry Press, Beijing (2006)

Vink, P.: Comfort and Design. CRC Press, London (2005)

Tractinsky, N., Katz, A., Ikar, D.: What is beautiful is usable. Interact. Comput. **13**(2), 127–145 (2000)

Picard, R.W.: Affective computing: challenges. Int. J. Hum. Comput. Stud. **59**(1–2), 55–64 (2003)

Yamamoto, K.: Kansei engineering — the art of automotive development at Mazda, pp. 1–24. University of Michigan, Ann Arbor (1986)

Luo, S., Pan, Y.: Product design sensibility imagery theory, research and application technology. Mech. Eng. **43**(3), 8–12 (2007)

Ding, J., Yang, D., Cao, Y., Wang, L.: The main emotional design theory, methods and research trends. J. Eng. Des. **17**(1), 12–18 (2010)

Desmet, P.M.A., Hekkert, P., Hillen, M.G.: Values and Emotions:an empirical investigation in the relationship between emotional responses to products and human values. In: The fifth European Academy of Design Conference, Barcelona, Spain, pp. 1–13 (2004)

Desmet, P.M.A.: Multilayered model of product emotions. Des. J. **6**(2), 4–11 (2003)

Desmet, P.M.A., Hekkert, P.: Framework of product experience. Int. J. Des. **1**(1), 57–66 (2007)

Demir, E., Desmet, P.M.A.: The roles of products in product emotions—an explorative study. In: Design Research Society Biennial Conference, Sheffield, UK, pp. 324/1–324/15 (2008)

Desmet, P.M.A.: Product Emotion. Elsevier, Amsterdam (2008)

The Influence of Visual Cues and Human Spatial Ability on Intra-vehicular Orientation Performance

Junpeng Guo, Guohua Jiang[(⊠)], Yuqing Liu, Yu Tian,
and Bohe Zhou

National Key Laboratory of Human Factors Engineering,
China Astronaut Research and Training Center, Beijing, China
dragonguo@126.com, jgh_isme@sina.com

Abstract. Astronauts often experience disorientation when floating inside their spacecraft due to the lack of gravity. Previous research showed that the intra-vehicular orientation performance correlated with human spatial ability, but paid less attention to the visual cues in the environment. In this study, an experiment was conducted to explore the role of visual cues on spatial orientation performance inside a virtual space station module. Results implicated that visual cues might help in three-dimensional space orientation, but its effect varied between different spatial ability groups. People with low spatial ability might depend more on visual cues for orientation whereas people with high spatial ability could be independent of visual cues in spatial orientation. This finding reveals the effect of visual cues for orientation inside the spacecraft and provides useful guide for preflight orientation training.

Keywords: Spatial orientation · Virtual reality · Visual cues · Spatial ability · Weightlessness

1 Introduction

Humans have the ability to locomote through their immediate environment and keep track of their orientation and location without much cognitive effort [1–3]. This mainly relies on the effortless and reliable sensory integration process, such as the integration of visual, vestibular and proprioceptive cues [4–6]. Among these senses, visual cues play an important role. Firstly, visual information is the most direct information humans can perceive in daily life and it tells people the spatial relationship of different objects in an intuitional way [3, 7]. Secondly, in many cases, landmarks presented in vision are crucial for choosing turning direction at decision points and updating the egocentric or allocentric spatial relationship during locomotion [8, 9]. Furthermore, in the gravitational environment on earth, visual polarity cues usually appear in a congruent way with the gravity vector, so people can always easily retrieve spatial information about objects located gravitationally above or below [10].

But in the weightless world, such as astronauts in the space station, spatial orientation becomes a troublesome problem and humans need special efforts to fulfill the

© Springer International Publishing Switzerland 2016
D. Harris (Ed.): EPCE 2016, LNAI 9736, pp. 290–300, 2016.
DOI: 10.1007/978-3-319-40030-3_29

orientation tasks in many situations [10, 11]. These troubles are mainly caused by the lack of gravity. On earth, people are restricted to move on a two dimensional plane and most large body rotations occur about the body's head/foot axis, which is usually in alignment with gravity. But when gravity is absent, these restrictions are removed, and astronauts can rotate their bodies around arbitrary axes, which makes both locomotion and visual experience appear in an very unfamiliar way. In the spacecraft, visual verticals are usually established to help astronauts build a reference for orientation inside the module and reduce the adaptation time needed in the spatial orientation by making interior surfaces of space module look different [12], e.g. putting the lights overhead, the racks on bilateral walls and little equipment beneath the feet. But only the visual verticals are still insufficient for spatial orientation in weightless space as astronauts cannot always have the opportunity to view the module interiors from upright perspectives inside the space station. In weightlessness, they can float freely in various body orientations which having not experienced before entering into space and view the interior of the module from arbitrary or unexpected perspectives. Previous study showed that spatial orientation ability in a simulated weightless environment correlated significantly with human spatial ability factors such as mental rotation ability and visual field dependence as these spatial ability factors can indicate the ability to transform the imagery of spatial relationship between different perspectives [13–15], however, the role of visual cues was not discussed in detail. In practice, sometimes it is possible that the visual cues inside the module are obscured by smoke or fog in emergency [16], so it is also necessary to make it clear what the visual cues affect in the intra-vehicular spatial orientation tasks.

On the earth, it is impractical to provide all the possible body orientations using physical simulators that astronauts may float into in space for preflight training due to gravity. But with the help of computer science, virtual reality simulation has provided an alternative method for spatial orientation training and research under conditions similar to the weightlessness on the earth. In this study, we developed a training system for the intra-vehicular spatial orientation based on virtual reality technology, and set up an interior visual environment with/without abundant visual cues. Participants in the experiment were first tested for their spatial ability in 2&3D mental rotation and perspective-taking ability tests, and then participated in the task for intra-vehicular spatial orientation which was similar to the paradigm used in previous studies [13, 17], but with some adjustments. We anticipated that visual cues could help in the intra-vehicular spatial orientation task as it could help participants establish a reference for orientation in the module and identify targets' location. As demonstrated by previous studies, mental imagery could be used to perform the task, so we also expected that this result could be repeated in our experiment.

2 Materials and Methods

2.1 Participants

Forty adults (20 men and 20 women, mean age = 23.53, SD = 3.45, ranging from 20 to 27) with college-level education participated the experiment. None of these participants had conducted the intra-vehicular spatial orientation task or the same spatial ability tests before the experiment. The study was approved by the IRB and all participants signed the informed consent prior to the experiment.

2.2   Measurement of Spatial Ability

Two spatial ability factors, mental rotation and perspective-taking, were measured both in their 2D and 3D versions. The 3D Mental Rotation Ability (MRA) was measured by Cube Comparison Test (CCT) using paper-and-pencils, and the 2D MRA was also measured by Card Rotation Test (CRT) through paper-and-pencils. The 3D Perspective-taking Ability (PTA) was measured by the paradigm developed by Guay [18] on computer, and the 2D PTA was also measured by the paradigm developed by Kozhevnikov and Hegarty [19] using specially developed software. The specific parameters used in the spatial ability tests were shown in Table 1.

Table 1.   Parameters setting in the four spatial ability tests

Parameters	Trial Numbers	Time Limitation	Test Platform	Performance Indicator
2D Perspective-Taking	24	25 s	Computer Software	Percent Correct
3D Perspective-Taking	24	40 s	Computer Software	Percent Correct
2D Mental Rotation	Maximum is 20	6 min in total	Paper-and-pencil	Right answers minus wrong ones
3D Mental Rotation	Maximum is 42	6 min in total	Paper-and-pencil	Right answers minus wrong ones

2.3   Intra-vehicular Spatial Orientation Task Appartus

The intra-vehicular spatial orientation task was conducted in the virtual environment developed by 3ds MAX and OGRE (Open Graphic Rendering Engine). Two kinds of the virtual environment were provided, as shown in Fig. 1. In Fig. 1 (a) there were distinct visual vertical cues visible, e.g. the ceiling and lights overhead, the floor beneath the feet and the different textures on bilateral walls. Whereas in Fig. 1 (b), there were only similar brown interior surfaces could be seen in the module. To provide an immersive environment for participants, the virtual interiors of the module were presented by Sony HMZ-T3 W HMD. Participants fulfilled the task sitting on a chair with a computer.

(a)   (b)

Fig. 1. Two kinds of the virtual interior environment used in the intra-vehicular spatial orientation task. (a) The interior environment with visual cues, e.g. the ceiling and lights overhead, the floor beneath the feet and the different textures on bilateral walls. (b) The interior enviroment without visual cues, only similar brown interior surfaces were presented.

2.4 Experiment Procedure

The whole experiment was conducted in two periods. In the first period, we measured the spatial ability of all the participants and calculated the participants' scores in the spatial ability tests; and then in the second period, according to the spatial ability scores in the first period the participants were divided into two groups for fulfilling the intra-vehicular spatial orientation tasks.

To be specific, during the first period, participants' spatial ability in 2D & 3D MRA and PTA were tested. Their scores in each test were obtained using the performance indicators as shown in Table 1. Then to give a comprehensive description of spatial ability for each participant, the scores in the four spatial ability tests were normalized at first and summed up afterwards to form a final number representing each participant's overall spatial ability score. Then in the second period, with the overall spatial ability test scores balanced, all the participants were assigned to two groups (visual cue group and no-visual-cue group) for the intra-vehicular spatial orientation task with an equal number of males and females in each group. In the visual cue group, the participants were presented virtual environments with visual vertical cues as shown in Fig. 1 (a). And in the no-visual-cue group, the participants were presented virtual environments with the similar brown interior surfaces as shown in Fig. 1 (b). Except for the visual cues, the two groups completed the orientation task through the same procedure. Averaged response time (RT) and percent correct (%C) in the intra-vehicular spatial orientation task were recorded for evaluating participants' performance.

To fulfill the intra-vehicular spatial orientation task, participants needed to image themselves floating in various places inside a simulated cubic space module, and view the intra-vehicular environment from the corresponding specific viewpoint, just as the floating astronauts might view the interior of the module from arbitrary or unexpected viewpoint. There was one recognizable object at the center of each interior surface, which made up an object array containing six items. The location of each object remained unchanged during the experiment. Participants could learn the spatial relationship of the six objects from a prototypical viewpoint in the first five trials as a practice. This could help them form a basic understanding of the spatial relationship among the six objects. In this prototypical orientation, the objects and their locations were: a camera (above), a spacesuit (right), a treadmill (below), a Chinese knot (left), and a hatch (behind). After the initial learning trials, their ability to image the spatial arrangement of the six objects from a rotated viewpoint was tested in successive formal trials.

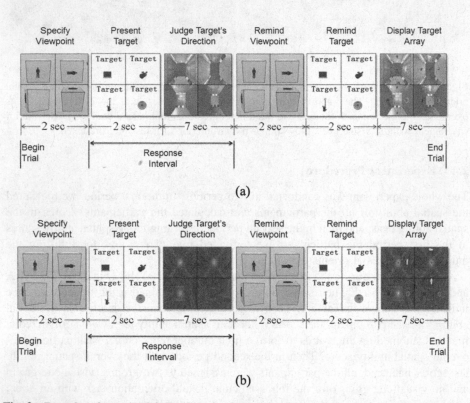

Fig. 2. Procedure for each trial. To illustrate four successive trials concurrently, the picture in each step was divided into four parts. The parts locating at the same position of the quads in every step composed an integral trial. (a) The procedure in visual cue group. (b) The procedure in no-visual-cue group

There were 12 different viewpoints in the entire task, distributing on three square surfaces that were perpendicular to each other. On each surface, there were four different orientations that in alignment with the two symmetrical axes of the surface, and each orientation represented a specific viewpoint. The task consisted of 72 trials. During each trial, the participants were first shown a picture that indicated the desired imaginary viewpoint. Next the target object whose direction needed to be indicated by the participants later was shown, and then the interior surface with/without visual cues was shown to the participants, but no object array appeared. The participants needed to indicate the relative direction to the target in body coordinates on this step. To make this indication, participants pushed one of five buttons on a numeric keyboard. After this, the imaginary viewpoint and target object was presented again, and the complete object array was displayed, rotated into the viewpoint called for in the trial. This allowed the participants to verify the correctness of their judgments based on the direct visual observation of the array in its rotated viewpoint. Participants could review the spatial arrangement of the object array in preparation for the next trial. The imaginary viewpoints distributed randomly during the entire task but same to all the participants. The procedure for each trial was shown schematically in Fig. 2. At the end of the intra-vehicular spatial orientation task, participants completed a strategy questionnaire, which included both multiple choice and open ended questions about the strategies they employed in fulfilling the task. The entire experiment of the two periods took approximately 2 h to complete.

3 Result

Since no significant difference was found in terms of gender, data from male and female participants were not distinguished in later analysis. Statistical analysis was conducted using SPSS. We first compared the participants' performance under different visual cue conditions. The percent correct performance in the intra-vehicular spatial orientation task for all the participants in both visual cues conditions was shown in Fig. 3. Generally, the participants in visual cue group performed better than no-visual-cue group, although the advantage was not significant. But further analysis showed that spatial ability moderated the relation between visual cues and intra-vehicular spatial orientation performance. Both in visual cue group and no-visual-cue group, parting the spatial orientation task results into two subgroups according to the participants' spatial ability: one subgroup contained the results of the better half participants in spatial ability and the other subgroup contained the remaining. Then the t test was conducted to compare the spatial orientation performance under different visual cue conditions both in higher spatial ability subgroups and lower spatial ability subgroups. And the moderate effects manifested as follows: on one hand, participants with higher spatial ability showed no significant differences in percent correct under visual cue/no-visual-cue conditions ($t(18) = 1.225$, $p = 0.128$); on the other hand, participants with lower spatial ability in the visual cue group performed better significantly in percent correct than those in the no-visual-cue group ($t(18) = 2.674$, $p = 0.008$). In terms of the response time, participants with higher spatial ability in the no-visual-cue group had significantly longer response time than the participants with higher spatial ability in the visual cue group ($t(18) = 3.002$, $p = 0.006$). No significant difference was found in the response time of participants with lower spatial ability under different visual cue conditions($t(18) = 1.292$, $p = 0.105$).

The correlation between participants' spatial ability and intra-vehicular spatial orientation performance under different visual cue conditions was also analyzed. For the participants in the no-visual-cue group, their scores in all the four spatial ability tests correlated significantly with their performance in the intra-vehicular spatial

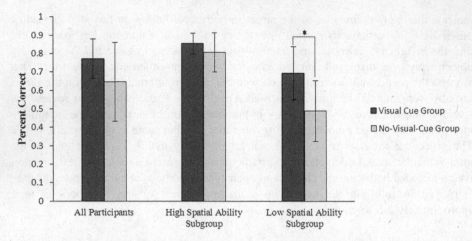

Fig. 3. Percent correct performance for both visual cue group and no-visual-cue group. In each group, parting the results into two subgroups according to the participants' spatial ability. The results of all participants (*left*), high spatial ability subgroup (*middle*), and low spatial ability subgroup (*right*) were shown with ± 1 standard error bars. The asterisk indicated significance at *p* level 0.01.

Table 2. Pearson correlation coefficients for spatial ability test scores and intra-vehicular orientation task performance (%C and RT) both in visual cue and no visual cue group

Test Type	2D Perspective-Taking	2D Mental Rotation	3D Perspective-Taking	3D Mental Rotation
%C in Visual Cue Group	0.128	0.286	0.273	0.378
RT in Visual Cue Group	−0.186	−0.152	−0.190	−0.291
%C in No-Visual-Cue Group	0.356*	0.423**	0.467**	0.684**
RT in No-Visual-Cue Group	−0.382*	−0.680**	−0.400*	−0.577**

**p < 0.01; *p < 0.05.

orientation task (both in response time and percent correct). But for the participants in the visual cue group, there was no significant correlation between the performance in the spatial orientation task and the scores in the spatial ability tests. The correlation coefficients were shown in Table 2.

Tabulation of the post-experiment strategy questionnaire results (Table 3) showed that for the participants in the no-visual-cue group, most of them learned the configuration of the object array by remembering paired opposite objects, whereas most of the participants in the visual cue group did this by relating the location of the objects with the visual cues on the interior surfaces of the modules. And when determining the target location, participants in the no-visual-cue group usually needed to image rotating their perspective to the viewpoint indicated in the trial, but majority of the participants in the visual cue group made their decisions by observing the location of the corresponding visual cues on the judgment step. And when asked in which imaged body orientation they found the spatial orientation task most difficult, most of the participants in both groups thought that the orientation deviated more from the prototypical orientation in initial learning trials, the more difficult they felt.

Table 3. Tabulation of post experiment strategy questionaire responses

Questions	Answer Category					
	Visual Cue Group (n = 20)			No-Visual-Cue Group (n = 20)		
How did you build up the knowledge of the object array configuration?	Relate objects with visual cues	Paired opposite objects	Other	Paired opposite objects	Attached meaning to objects	Other
	17	3		18	1	1
How did you make decisions about target location?	Observe the interiors location	Imaged self rotating	Imaged the module rotating	Imaged self rotating	Imaged the module rotating	Other
	18	2		16	4	
Which body orientation made the task most difficult?	90° deviated from the prototypical	180° deviated from the prototypical	270° deviated from the prototypical	90° deviated from the prototypical	180° deviated from the prototypical	270° deviated from the prototypical
	2	3	15	1	3	16

4 Discussion

We interviewed each participant informally at the conclusion of the entire experiment. Most participants said that although the initial learning trials had gave them some basic knowledge about the configurations of the object array, they still felt confused to make orientation decisions in the first several formal trials. But with the help of the opportunity to learn the spatial arrangement of objects on the last step in each trial, they could build up the complete and stable spatial knowledge soon. And the data of percent correct also showed that participants under both visual cue conditions usually could achieve rather high (above 80 %) percent correct after about 25 trials. This testified that the paradigm used in our study was effective in building up three-dimensional spatial knowledge for novices. As shown in the strategy questionnaire results, most of the participants in the visual cue group said that they remembered the objects on the interior surfaces simply by the relating the objects with the visual cues, e.g. they remembered clearly that the camera was hung on the ceiling, and the spacesuit was put on the wall with more apparatuses. And on the judgment step, they would first observe the location of the interior surfaces and then made the decision according to the interior surface's location. It could be seen that in this process, the participants did not need to utilize the imagery of the spatial relationship or even image rotating their perspectives. They just needed to observe the visual environment all the time and then they could get their judgments. This strategy that mainly adopted by these participants could also explain the no findings in significant correlation between the individual spatial ability and the intra-vehicular spatial orientation task in the visual cue group.

For the participants in the no-visual-cue group, they had no visual cues in helping them remember the location of the objects, so they had to think out other methods to build up the spatial configuration of the object array. Most of the participants did that by remembering paired opposite objects and imaging the rotation of themselves when needed to indicate target's location in the specific body orientation. This strategy they claimed was verified by the significant correlation between their scores in the spatial ability test and the intra-vehicular spatial orientation task.

It was reasonable to conclude that visual cues could be helpful in the intra-vehicular spatial orientation, especially for those with lower spatial ability. As mentioned above, visual cues could help participants in identifying the location of objects and made them clearer about their body orientation relative to the prototypical orientation during the task. Although for those participants with higher spatial ability there was no significant difference in percent correct of the intra-vehicular spatial orientation task, the significant differences in response time indicated that participants in the no-visual-cue group needed more cognitive efforts to fulfill the orientation task. This meant that the visual cues could make the intra-vehicular orientation task easier. For the participants with lower spatial ability, it might be more difficult for them to transform the imagery of various spatial relationships, which was not an easy job indeed, but the visual cues could help them avoid the strategy related with spatial ability and gave them the alternative way to complete the task by observing and remembering those visual cues, so the participants with lower spatial ability in the visual cue group could outperform those participants with lower spatial ability in the no-visual-cue group significantly.

5 Conclusions

Spatial orientation under terrestrial conditions needs not much effort in most situations, but it is a troublesome problem for astronauts living in the space station as there is no gravity providing some helpful restrictions. This study explored the role of visual cues inside the space module in spatial orientation tasks by means of establishing a virtual reality environment. Through the experiment, we found that, like the terrestrial situations, visual cues can also provide a lot of help in fulfilling the orientation tasks in weightlessness. The direct visual impression of the spatial relationship between the targets and visual cues can reduce the cognitive efforts needed in location judgments. Especially for population with lower spatial ability, it could be more difficult for them to undertake mental rotation or perspective-taking tasks to identify target location, but the visual cues could simplify the complex process to remembering the combination of targets and the corresponding visual cues. This could be thought as the good side of the visual cues. But in another aspect, astronauts should not rely too much on the visual cues for intra-vehicular spatial orientation. Because in some emergencies, it is possible that these visual cues might be partly or mostly obscured by fog and smoke caused by loss of pressure or even fire. But spatial orientation is vital in these emergencies because astronauts need to react as quickly as possible to reach the destination module for some further actions. So astronauts still need to acquire the essential skills for orientation in three-dimensional space so that they can obtain a good sense of direction under any conditions in the space station. These essential skills are similar to the skills adopted in solving the problems in the spatial ability tests, because they both need to image the perspectives change or body rotation when the external environment keeps stationary. And it also indicates that the prefight training should not only be done in the environments with abundant visual cues, but also done specially in the environments without visual cues.

Except for the visual cues that indicate vertical vectors and make interior surfaces have different appearances, the effects of the visual directional landmarks that directly indicate the different modules or some specific orientations and its interactional effects with individual spatial abilities are still needed to be explored in further studies.

Acknowledgments. This study was supported by the National Defense Basic Research Program of China (No. B1720132001). Author Junpeng Guo, Yuqing Liu and Bohe Zhou were supported by the foundation of National Key Laboratory of Human Factors Engineering (No. SYFD140051807).

References

1. Pick Jr., H.L., Rieser, J.J.: Childlren's cognitive mapping. In: Potegal, M. (ed.) Spatial Orientation: Development and Physiological Bases, pp. 107–128. Academic Press, New York (1982)
2. Rieser, J.J.: Access to knowledge of spatial structure at novel points of observation. J. Exp. Psychol. Learn. Mem. Cogn. **15**(6), 1157–1165 (1989)
3. Loomis, J.M., Da Silva, J.A., Fujita, N., Fukusima, S.S.: Visual space perception and visually directed action. J. Exp. Psychol. Hum. Percept. Perform. **18**, 906–922 (1992)
4. Ivanenko, Y.P., Grasso, R., Israel, I., Berthoz, A.: The contribution of otoliths and semicircular canals to the perception of two-dimensional passive whole-body motion in humans. J. Physiol. London **502**, 223–233 (1997)
5. Loomis, J.M., Klatzky, R.L., Golledge, R.G., Cicinelli, J.G., Pellegrino, J.W., Fry, P.: Nonvisual navigation by blind and sighted: assessment of path integration ability. J. Exp. Psychol. Gen. **122**, 73–91 (1993)
6. Rieser, J.J., Guth, D.A., Hill, E.W.: Sensitivity to perspective structure while walking without vision. Perception **15**, 173–188 (1986)
7. Howard, I.P.: Human Visual Orientation. John Wiley & Sons, New York (1982)
8. Wang, L., Mou, W., Sun, X.: Development of landmark knowledge at decision points. Spat. Cogn. Comput. **14**(1), 1–17 (2014)
9. Li, X., Carlson, L.A., Mou, W., et al.: Describing spatial locations from perception and memory: the influence of intrinsic axes on reference object selection. J. Mem. Lang. **65**(2), 222–236 (2011)

10. Clément, G., Reschke, M.F.: Neuroscience in Space. Springer Science & Business Media, New York (2010)
11. Oman, C.: Spatial orientation and navigation in microgravity. Spatial Processing in Navigation. Imagery and Perception, pp. 209–247. Springer, New York (2007)
12. Zhu, L., Yao, Y., Xu, P., et al.: Study on space station design elements for intra-vehicular navigation: a survey. In: 2011 International Conference on Electronic and Mechanical Engineering and Information Technology (EMEIT), vol. 9, pp. 4493–4496. IEEE (2011)
13. Oman, C.M., et al.: Three dimensional spatial memory and learning in real and virtual environments. Spatial Cogn. Comput. **2**(4), 355–372 (2000)
14. Richards, J.T., et al.: Training, transfer, and retention of three-dimensional spatial memory in virtual environments. J. Vestib. Res. **12**(5/6), 223–238 (2003)
15. Shebilske, W.L., et al.: Three-dimensional spatial skill training in a simulated space station: random vs. blocked designs. Aviat. Space Environ. Med. **77**(4), 404–409 (2006)
16. Aoki, H., Oman, C.M., Natapoff, A.: Virtual-reality-based 3D navigation training for emergency egress from spacecraft. Aviat. Space Environ. Med. **78**(8), 774–783 (2007)
17. Cizaire, C.C.J.L.: Effect of two-module-docked spacecraft configurations on spatial orientation. Massachusetts Institute of Technology (2007)
18. Guay, R., Mc Daniels, E.: The visualization of viewpoints. The Purdue Research Foundation (as modified by Lippa, I., Hegarty, M., & Montello, D.R., 2002), West Lafayette, IN (1976)
19. Kozhevnikov, M., Hegarty, M.: A dissociation between object-manipulation spatial ability and spatial orientation ability. Mem. Cogn. **29**, 745–756 (2001)

Multitasking and Interruption Management in Control Room Operator Work During Simulated Accidents

Jari Laarni[1(✉)], Hannu Karvonen[1], Satu Pakarinen[2],
and Jari Torniainen[2]

[1] VTT Technical Research Centre of Finland, Espoo, Finland
{jari.laarni, hannu.karvonen}@vtt.fi
[2] Finnish Institute of Occupational Health, Helsinki, Finland
{satu.pakarinen, jari.torniainen}@ttl.fi

Abstract. Our everyday life is full of interruptions, which cause problems in different situations. Therefore, efficient management of interruptions is a natural part of our daily activity, and we humans are experts at managing task switching and interruptions. Efficient management of interruptions is required in many tasks and domains such as in health care, aviation, car driving and office work. This paper focusses on control room (CR) operator work in nuclear power plants. CR operators have to manage interruptions in various plant states, and sometimes interruptions cause problems in their work. This paper is divided into two major parts: the first part is a short literature review of effects of multi-tasking and interruptions in work settings; the second part presents some experimental results of multitasking and interruption management during simulated accidents. Some suggestions are given to improve interruption and multitasking management in safety-critical domains.

Keywords: Multitasking · Interruption management · Nuclear power plant · Control room operator

1 Introduction

Interruptions are an inherent aspect of many work environments, such as emergency services [1]. Recently, about one-third of respondents of the European Survey on Living and Working Conditions answered that they were interrupted several times a day [2]. The rate of interruptions has also drastically increased during the last decades. A survey conducted in Germany showed that the rate of interruptions has doubled in the past 20 years, and according to this study, interruptions at work are evaluated among the most important causes of stress at work [3].

At the same time, multitasking is growing steadily, and it has become a natural and normal condition in many work domains so that it is more and more difficult to recognize that you are multitasking at work. According to [4], employees are facing an increased demand for multitasking, and when they have to perform multiple tasks at the same time, it may be even difficult to determine what the primary and secondary tasks are and what interrupts and disturbs what.

© Springer International Publishing Switzerland 2016
D. Harris (Ed.): EPCE 2016, LNAI 9736, pp. 301–310, 2016.
DOI: 10.1007/978-3-319-40030-3_30

But multitasking and frequent interruptions at work are not necessarily considered as a problem or a nuisance: sometimes employees may even be proud of their skill of performing several tasks simultaneously, and multitasking may also be a breath of fresh air compared with normal work [5]. Also, interruptions and multitasking have in some contexts been described as something that makes the work more attractive [6].

1.1   Effects of Multitasking and Interruptions

One of the main goals in studying interruptions and multitasking is to acquire knowledge of their effects on employees and their performance. Apparently, interruptions have both positive and negative effects. They affect task completion time and quality of work, and they also exert influence on cognition, emotions, workload and well-being in general.

Interruptions are not basically either bad or good, and, as suggested above, sometimes interruptions may have positive effects on performance [6–8]. In fact, interruptions may provide valuable task-related information just at the moment it is needed [8]. For example, it is feasible to send an alert to a colleague, if he/she is about to carry out an error [7].

According to the systemic view, workers must constantly trade-off between potentially positive and negative effects of interruptions, rather than avoiding interruptions altogether. The cost of interruption can be defined as a subjective measure of the price people are ready to pay to remain undisturbed while working in a particular task [9]. Hollnagel's [10] functional resonance model (FRAM), according to which both accidents and successes are caused by unexpected combinations of normal behavioral variability, can quite well explain how interruptions may have both positive and negative effects.

Even though moderate levels of multitasking may even increase performance, most existing research suggests that interruptions and excessive multitasking have harmful effects on performance and well-being [4]. For example, according to [9], multitasking is less efficient and more complicated than single tasking.

Overall, interruptions increase the task completion time, hamper decision making, and easily lead to slips, lapses and mistakes [11]. The main factors of interruption effects on quantitative task performance are increased memory load and task similarity [12]. One of the main problems of interruptions is that their harmful effects can last long after the interruption has ceased [13].

Interruptions also cause loss of time [14]. The task completion time of the task with interruption increases by two transition time intervals: interruption lag and resumption lag [15]. The 'interruption lag' is the switching time from the primary task to the secondary interrupting task, and the 'resumption lag' is the return time from the secondary task back to the primary task [15]. Both the accomplishment of the primary interrupted and secondary interrupting task may be delayed. According to [16], ill-placed interruptions can increase task performance time, especially because of increases in resumption time. In a situation in which the interruptions are nested and accumulated, the duration of the delay will further increase because of the additional cognitive burden [4].

In safety-critical domains, an important question is to show whether there is a causal link between interruptions and errors. For example, evidence for a relation between interruptions and medical errors are still quite weak [7]. According to [7], this is apparently caused by deficit methodological approaches, not because there would be evidence of absence of evidence.

Interruptions have shown to cause all kinds of cognitive effects, such as memory loss and less accurate recall of information [17], detrimental effects on decision making [18] and breaks in concentration [15]. When interrupted, people quite easily forget what they were initially doing. Successful prospective memory performance requires that we are able to recall something at a specific point of time in the future which is more demanding that simple remembering a particular fact [5]. And if your attention is constantly wandering from one information source to another, you may not be able to build a complete and coherent view of the status of the matter, when recalling the interrupted task [19].

Weigl et al. found that interruptions were significantly correlated with employees' workload over and above the contribution of other variables [8]. Kalich and Aebersold have also shown that interruptions had a negative effect on workload [20]. Frequent interruptions were associated with increased frustration in Weigl et al.'s study, and interruptions by colleagues had a strongest association to workload [8]. Cumulative interruptions may have an even more detrimental effect on workload [4]. In addition, interruptions under periods of high workload may have a more detrimental effect on task performance, since people take longer to resume the suspended tasks during these periods [16].

In addition to cognitive costs, interruptions may also cause emotional costs [21]. Interruptions had a negative effect on emotion and well-being [20, 22], and interruptions can increase feelings of stress and frustration [23], as proposed above.

1.2   Effects of Sensory Distractions

An ongoing task has to stop in case of interruption, but an ongoing task can continue in a distraction condition [12]. Irrelevant speech and noise are one of the most important causes of distraction in many work domains. Irrelevant sound has shown to disturb concentration and impair task performance. According to several experimental studies, most of the participants suffer from irrelevant sounds, even though there are notable and consistent individual differences in susceptibility to noise effects [24]. The effect has been shown to result in an average increase of errors of up to 30 % [24].

Abrupt changes in successive auditory signals have shown to be the main cause of the distraction effect [25], but the intensity of the auditory signal does not seem to have a clear effect on the irrelevant sound effect [24, 26]. A work environment, in which there is continuous background chatter, is less distracting than an environment in which several distinct speech events are present at the same time [24]. Irrelevant sound effects do not seem to diminish with time and repeated exposure to the disturbing sounds [27].

Background sounds, such as auditory warnings and irrelevant radio messages that occur in a random and unpredictable fashion, have also shown to impair concentration and increase errors [28, 29]. This effect may be caused by attentional capture effect in which the irrelevant sound diverts attention away from the primary task [30]. As suggested by Boehm-Davis and Remington [31], the fact that even subtle alarms and warning signals can distract attention may explain why workers find it frustrating and stressful to process alarms, even though they know that the alarm signals can be ignored.

1.3   Interruptions, Distractions and Multitasking in Nuclear Domain

To our knowledge, there is very little research on multitasking and the impact of interruptions in the nuclear domain, even though, based on a French survey, Griffon-Fouco and Ghertman [32] proposed that interruptions of job performance have shown to explain over 15 % of all nuclear power plant shutdowns.

Alarms can easily distract operators in CR environments. Alarms accompanied by auditory signals easily attract the operator's attention, and thus, interrupt his/her primary task execution. Many of the presented alarms are useless, and the operators consider them as annoying [33]. Mumaw et al. [33] proposed that a majority of alarm messages in the nuclear power plant (NPP) control room (CR) do not require operator action at all.

Carvalho et al. have investigated in many studies operator work and team communication in the main CR of a NPP [34, 35]. They have found that the operators have to cope with many irrelevant alarms in different operational modes which they cannot ignore without violating against emergency operating procedures [34, 35]. For example, it was found several times in their study that the operators turned off the alarm buzzer in order to muffle the disturbing sounds, even though it is forbidden to do that [35]. It was also observed that phone calls can be very distracting, if the operators are busy and have too many tasks to do in an incident situation [35]. On the other hand, internal communication with the crew played an important role to solve technical problems, and individual comments and questions of the crew members are not considered distracting [34, 35].

Apparently, multitasking and task interruptions are common in 'normal' operational conditions, and operators have also told that the amount of multitasking has clearly increased during recent years (personal communication). In simulated accident situations operators focus on accident management, and therefore interruptions that halt the execution of the primary task are infrequent. However, all kinds of distractions that disturb operators' concentration on their duties are frequent, and it would be, therefore, justifiable to study their effect on operator performance.

2   Methods

We have observed NPP main CR operators' work in order to investigate the effects of interruptions and task switching in simulated accident management situations and the management of multiple parallel tasks. In the analysis, we have utilized video data from operators' head-mounted cameras and a general-view camera. Head-mounted camera videos show at a crude level to what information the operator is paying his/her attention, and therefore they provide a mean to identify the task he/she is performing. We have analysed video data from loss-of-coolant accident (LOCA) simulation runs. Each observed operating crew consisted of three operators (reactor operator, turbine operator and shift supervisor).

In a separate study, we were interested in CR operators' personal opinions regarding interruptions encountered and frustration caused by these interruptions. Twenty-two operators responded to a questionnaire in connection with a simulator test in a Finnish NPP.

3   Results

3.1   Interruptions in Simulated Accidents

We studied interruptions in an NPP CR in a demanding operational situation by analysing data from a simulated accident scenario. A loss of coolant accident was simulated together with a failure in a plant protection signal. Interruption/intrusion was defined as everything that interrupted the ongoing task for a while. Figure 1 shows the interruptions encountered by shift supervisors, and reactor and turbine operators in three crews within a period of 40 min from the beginning of the failure to the end of the session. As can be seen, the shift supervisors were interrupted a bit more often than the other operators. For the shift supervisors, there also seems to be somewhat more interruptions in the first part of the scenario than in the latter part.

On the other hand, the interruptions were longer for reactor operators than for the other operators (see Fig. 2). Tasks that were most often interrupted were procedure reading/handling, monitoring screens, and panel operations. It was also found that a response to an interruption was typically immediate – as if the operators thought that the interruptee is obliged to respond immediately to the interrupter so that the latter does not need to wait for a long time.

A preliminary categorization of interruptions and their causes was conducted. In general, external interruptions were caused by alarms, phone calls and verbal expressions of other personnel. The response to an interruption was typically immediate. The shift supervisors interrupted reactor or turbine operators by asking a question or informing them on issues of importance more frequently than the other way around. This finding can be understood in that the shift supervisors are responsible for the main operational decisions, and they also have the main responsibility of co-ordinating the operators' work and communicating with people outside the CR. As said above, at the first phases of the scenario the shift supervisors were frequently interrupted, and they also had problems at times to get their tasks accomplished due to these interruptions.

We also observed the operators' procedure use from the perspective of multi-tasking. It was found that self-initiated interruptions were a characteristic feature of NPP CR operator multitasking. For example, operators had to frequently move from one user interface to another to seek information or to conduct a particular control action, and sometimes they had to shift their attention from one procedure path to another and execute a number of procedure steps from the latter path before returning back to the first task. It was, however, found that the operators tried to minimize the

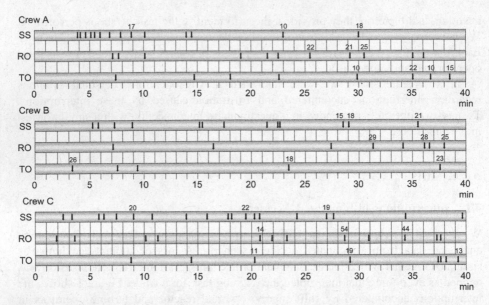

Fig. 1. Interruptions in a simulated accident scenario for three crews and three operator roles (SS = shift supervisor; RO = reactor operator; TO = turbine operator). Each arrow refers to one interruption. The duration of some of the longest interruptions is presented above the arrow (in seconds).

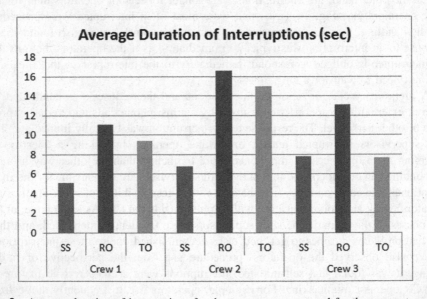

Fig. 2. Average duration of interruptions for three operator crews and for three operator roles

time spent for multitasking, and instead they tried to execute each path from the beginning to the end before they moved to another path. Even though the number of errors caused by task interruptions was apparently small, there was typically a small time delay when operators returned from one task to another.

3.2   Operator Perceptions of Interruptions

Regarding operators' perceptions of interruptions encountered and of frustration caused by these interruptions, it seemed to be that the distracting events that may occur in the CR did not frustrate them very much. The only exception to that were the alarm sounds that disturbed them to some extent. As an answer to the question whether the operator him-/herself interrupted another operator while the colleague was executing some task, the respondents thought that they did it at least a couple of times during the simulation run.

However, according to the survey, the operators still thought that the task at hand was sometimes interrupted due to background conversations, alarm sounds, and phone ring tones. As can be seen in Fig. 3, turbine operators were interrupted more frequently than the other operators by alarm sounds, other operators, and background conversations; shift supervisors were, in turn, more frequently interrupted by phone ring tones. This finding simply reflects the fact that a larger proportion of all phone calls are addressed to the shift supervisors.

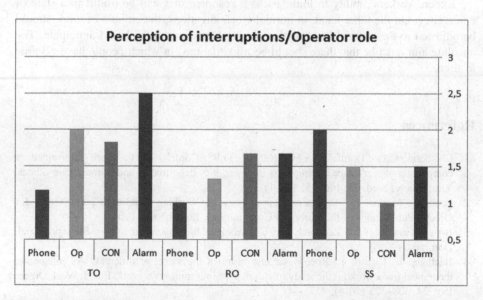

Fig. 3. Perception of some types of interruptions in the three operator positions. It was asked whether task accomplishment was interrupted during the session by the presented factors (Phone = phone ring tone; Op = another operator; CON = background conversation; Alarm = alarm sound) in a rating scale ranging from 1 to 4.

4 Conclusion

Our results have implications for theories of interruption management. According to the findings, existing views present a too simplistic view of the role of interruptions in multitasking, since they do not take into account the effect of task context on the specification of interruptions. For example, in the CR settings, it depends on the task performed whether, for example, an operator's utterance is defined as an interruption or a necessary element in a normal conversation.

We suggest that negative consequences of interruptions can be alleviated, for example, by better procedure and user interface design, alarm management, and team training. As an example of a procedure design issue, we state that strict adherence to procedures may even increase the adverse effect of interruptions: when using the procedure in a more adaptive and resilient way, the operator may better consider the total situation and therefore anticipate the interruptions. A more adaptive way of working requires that the operator is able to hierarchically decompose the main task into separate simple tasks, and he/she relies to a sufficient extent on knowledge in the world to guide him/her from one task to another.

If we look at multitasking and interruption handling especially from the perspective of resilience engineering, many conversational interruptions can support the enactment of resilient strategy and are thus useful (for examples of behaviors supporting resilience, see [36]). However, it is equally true that excessive multitasking and constant interruptions cause vulnerabilities that can result in errors and other problems.

Expert workers' ability to multitask is a resource that will be useful in a state of emergency. On the other hand, in normal work situations, the amount of work should be adjusted to the optimal level so that people have time to think and anticipate. The absolute aim must be that there should be no situations, in which people have no time to think.

References

1. Chisholm, C.D., Dornfeld, A.M., Nelson, D.R., Cordell, W.H.: Work interrupted: a comparison of workplace interruptions in emergency departments and primary care offices. Ann. Emerg. Med. **38**, 146–151 (2001)
2. Paoli, P., Merllié, D.: Third European Survey on Working Conditions 2000. Office for Official Publications of the European Communities, Luxembourg (2005)
3. BAuA: Factssheet 01. Zeitdruck und Co-Arbeitsbedingungen mit hohem Stresspotenzial, Dortmund (2013)
4. Baethge, A., Rigotti, T., Roe, R.A.: Just more of the same, or different? An integrative theoretical framework for the study of cumulative interruptions at work. Eur. J. Work Organ. Psy. **24**, 308–323 (2014)
5. Czerwinski, M., Horvitz, E., Wilhite, S.A: Diary study of task switching and interruptions. In: Proceedings of CHI 2004, Vienna, Austria, 24–29 April 2004
6. Forsberg, H.H., Muntlin, Å., von Thiele Schwarz, U.: Nurses' perceptions of multitasking in the emergency department: effective, fun and unproblematic (at least for me): - a qualitative study. Int. Emerg. Nurs. (in press)

7. Grundgeiger, T., Sanderson, P.: Interruptions in healthcare: theoretical views. Int. J. Med. Inform. **78**, 293–307 (2009)
8. Weigl, M., Müller, A., Vincent, C., Angerer, P., Sevdalis, N.: The association of workflow interruptions and hospital doctors' workload: a prospective observational study. BMJ Qual. Saf. **21**, 399–407 (2012)
9. Sykes, E.R.: Interruptions in the workplace: a case study to reduce their effects. Int. J. Inform. Manag. **31**, 385–394 (2011)
10. Hollnagel, E.: Barriers and Accident Prevention. Ashgate, Aldershot, UK (2004)
11. Carayon, P., Wetterneck, T.B., Hundt, A.S., Ozkaynak, M., DeSilvey, J., Ludwig, B., Ram, P., Steven, S.: Evaluation of nurse interaction with bar code medication administration technology in the work environment. J. Patient Saf. **3**, 34–42 (2007)
12. Lee, B.C., Duffy, V.G.: The effects of task interruption on human performance: a study of the systematic classification of human behaviour and interruption frequency. Hum. Factors Ergon. Manuf. Serv. Ind. **25**, 137–152 (2015)
13. Dismukes, K., Young, G., Battelle, R.S.: Cockpit Interruptions and Distractions: Effective Management Requires a Careful Balancing Act. ASRS Directline 10 (1998)
14. Monk, C.A., Boehm-Davis, D.A., Trafton, J.G.: Recovering from interruptions: implications for driver distraction research. Hum. Factors **46**, 650–663 (2004)
15. Altmann, E.M., Trafton, J.G.: Memory for goals: an activation-based model. Cogn. Sci. **26**, 39–83 (2002)
16. Iqbal, S.T., Bailey, B.P.: Leveraging Characteristics of Task Structure to Predict Costs of Interruption. In: Proceedings of the ACM CHI, Montreal, Canada (2006)
17. Oulasvirta, A., Saariluoma, P.: Surviving task interruptions: investigating the implications of long-term working memory theory. Int. J. Hum.-Comput. Stud. **64**, 941–961 (2004)
18. Speier, C., Valacich, J.S., Vessey, I.: Information overload through interruptions: an empirical examination of decision making. Decis. Sci. **30**, 337–360 (1999)
19. Chishom, C.D., Collison, E.K., Nelson, D.R., Cordell, W.H.: Emergency department workplace interruptions: are emergency phycisians "interrupt-drive" and "multitasking"? Acad. Emerg. Med. **7**, 1239–1243 (2000)
20. Kalisch, B.J., Aebersold, M.: Interruptions and multitasking in nursing care. Jt. Comm. J. Qual. Patient Saf. **36**, 126–132 (2010)
21. Janssen, C.P., Gould, S.J.J., Li, S.Y.W., Brumby, D.P., Cox, A.L.: Integrating knowledge of multitasking and interruptions across different perspectives and research methods. Int. J. Hum.-Comput. Stud. (in press)
22. Farrimond, S., Knight, R.G., Titov, N.: The effects of aging on remembering intentions: performance on a simulated shopping task. Appl. Cogn. Psychol. **20**, 533–555 (2006)
23. Mark, G., Gudith, D., Klocke, U.: The cost of interrupted work: more speed and stress. In: Proceedings of CHI 2008, Florence, Italy, 5–10 April 2008
24. Beaman, C.P.: Auditory distraction from low-intensity noise: a review of the consequences for learning and workplace environments. Appl. Cogn. Psychol. **19**, 1041–1064 (2005)
25. Jones, D.M., Macken, W.I.: Irrelevant tones produce an irrelevant speech effect: implications for phonological coding in working memory. J. Exp. Psychol. Learn. **19**, 369–381 (1993)
26. Colle, H.A.: Auditory encoding in visual short-term recall: effects of noise intensity and spatial location. J. Verb. Learn. Verb. Behav. **19**, 722–735 (1980)
27. Tremblay, S., Jones, D.M.: The role of habituation in the irrelevant sound effect: evidence from the effects of token set size and rate of transition. J. Exp. Psychol. Learn. **24**, 659–671 (1998)
28. Clark, W.W., Bohne, B.A.: Effects of noise on hearing. JAMA **281**, 1658–1659 (1999)

29. Spooner, A.J., Corley, A., Chaboyer, W., Hammond, N.E., Fraser, J.F.: Measurement of the frequency and source of interruptions occurring during bedside nursing handover in the intensive care unit: an observational study. Aust. Crit. Care **28**, 19–23 (2015)

30. Hodgetts, H.M., Vachon, F., Tremblay, S.: Background sound impairs interruption recovery in dynamic task situations: procedural conflict? Appl. Cogn. Psychol. **28**, 10–21 (2014)

31. Boehm-Davis, D.A., Remington, R.: Reducing the disruptive effects of interruption: a cognitive framework for analysing the costs and benefits if intervention strategies. Accid. Anal. Prev. **41**, 1124–1129 (2009)

32. Griffon-Fouco, M., Ghertman, F.: Recueil de Données sur les Facteurs Humains à Electricité de France [Collection of data on the human factors with Electricity of France]. In: Operational Safety of Nuclear Power Plants, pp. 157–172. Vienna International Atomic Energy Agency, Vienna, Austria (1984)

33. Mumaw, R.J., Roth, E.M., Vicente, K.J., Burns, C.M.: There is more to monitoring a nuclear power plant than meets the eye. Hum. Factors **42**, 36–55 (2000)

34. De Carvalho, P.V.R.: Ergonomic field studies in a nuclear power plant control room. Prog. Nucl. Energ. **48**, 51–69 (2006)

35. De Carvalho, P.V.R., Vidal, M.C.R., de Carvalho, E.F.: Nuclear power plant communications in normative and actual practice: a field study of control room operators' communications. Hum. Factors Ergon. Manuf. Serv. Ind. **17**, 43–78 (2007)

36. Furniss, D., Back, J., Blandford, A., Hildebrandt, M., Broberg, H.: A resilience markers framework for small teams. Rel. Eng. Sys. Saf. **96**, 2–10 (2011)

Enhancing Cognitive Control for Improvement of Inspection Performance: A Study of Construction Safety

Pin-Chao Liao[✉], Jiawei Ding, and Xiaoyun Wang

Department of Construction Management, Tsinghua University, Beijing, China
pinchao@tsinghua.edu.cn

Abstract. Since safety inspection safeguards robustness of the construction projects, the cognitive issues of safety inspectors requires more understanding, catering improvement of management processes and policies. Researchers on safety management suggested that even though with the help of comprehensive checklist, inspectors were still prone to missing observation of critical risks during inspection. However, few of them clarified the nature of missing observations, as well as providing effective solutions with empirical support. This study aims at summarizing the pattern of missing observations during inspection from the perspective of cognitive psychology. A causal model of missing observation was established, a practical measure was proposed and verified through an experiment using eye-tracking device. The results revealed that, excessive inspection contents and ambiguity in description of checklist will increase the cognitive-control load of inspectors and results in observation miss. And a procedure-oriented checklist might be an effective solution to such defects.

Keywords: Safety inspection · Checklist · Cognitive-control load · Eye-tracking

1 Introduction

1.1 Safety Inspection Can Be Unreliable Due to Inspector's Observation Miss

Construction has been considered as one of the most dangerous industries globally. In the U.S., there are 6-10 accidents occur on jobsite every day [1]. According to the statistic from U.S. Bureau of Labor Statistics in 2013, accidents in construction had led to 828 deaths, which ranked the first place among all industries. These accidents also resulted in great direct and indirect economic loss, which accounted for 8 % of total costs of construction projects [2]. In U.K., workers in construction only took up 5 % of the employment nationwide, but accounted for 31 % of the work-related casualties [3]. Given the severe situation of construction safety, a variety of risk-controlling methods have been taken to lower the rate of fatal accidents and minimize both casualties and economic loss.

Safety inspection, as one of them, has commonly been applied by construction companies worldwide to control risks by early detection and correction. However, since

© Springer International Publishing Switzerland 2016
D. Harris (Ed.): EPCE 2016, LNAI 9736, pp. 311–321, 2016.
DOI: 10.1007/978-3-319-40030-3_31

safety inspections in construction are mostly conducted by human inspectors through observation, their performance in practice may not be as reliable as generally assumed. Generally, their mistakes can be categorized into two types [4], (I) falsely judging the scenario in safety to be at risk, and (II) missing observation of potential risks during inspection. Type I, though results in a waste of resources of production and safety management, is economically manageable and harmless to workers, while type II may cause serious casualties, as well as immeasurable economic loss. Beside the severe consequence, Type II could be evitable regardless of inspector's working experience. In fact, inspectors usually make mistakes in visual inspection due to undesirable jobsite condition (noise, lighting, etc.), various distractors along with targets, unreasonable inspection plan (frequency, sampling mode etc.), and lack of training or working experience [5, 6]. As revealed in a simulation experiment on construction inspectors [7], subjects with higher working age tended to have higher detection rate of potential risks. Nevertheless, even those with over ten years' experience could hardly identified 80 % of all the inbuilt risks within the test, which means there were up to 20 % of risks missed by inspectors in the visual observation. Thus, mistakes of type II, missing observation of risks, are much more fatal to the reliability of safety inspection for risk controlling, and therefore require more attention from both researchers and construction companies.

1.2   Observation Miss Results from Excessive Inspection Contents

As an integration of potential risks summarized from previous accident reports and individual inspection experience, checklist is applied as a comprehensive reference for the inspectors to avoid missing observation of risks appear in construction site, and ensure an effective inspection through item-by-item examination. However, as the complexity of workspace keeps growing these days, the number of items on the checklist increase dramatically with potential risks, making it exhausting for the inspector to simultaneously map all the checklist items with potential risks in limited inspection time. For instance, in the safety inspection of amusement rides, inspectors have to go through more than fifty items on their standard checklist during their 1–2 h inspection [8]. It is the same case in construction industry. Since the construction site involves hundreds of elements, including materials, equipment and workers, it is almost out of questions for inspectors to simultaneously map all the checking items with accompanying risks [9]. To make it worse, there is ambiguity in the description of inspection contents. Sometimes it may include such expression as to ensure the working environment being 'considered' [10], or sometimes it may leave the inspectors to determine what is 'proper' based on personal knowledge [11]. The existence of such 'grey area' may bring extra cognitive burden to the inspector in making qualitative decisions when matching these ambiguous checking items to potential risks [12]. As a result, most inspectors tend to perform a holistic observation instead, taking the checklist as a reminder, and only have a quick review on it before or after the overall inspection. This may probably undermine the function of checklist as a reference of item-by-item inspection, leaving chance for inspectors to miss observation of potential risks.

1.3 Prioritizing Risks by Construction Stage Can Be Effective in Reducing Observation Miss

To relieve the inspectors of overload, making it possible for them to have an item-by-item examination, it is necessary to cut down the number of checking items by giving priority to some of them under certain criteria. Prioritizing the checking items (Risk-based inspection, RBI) by the level of overall impact is a common practice in this purpose. Inspection based on this criteria is called Risk-based Inspection (RBI). RBI was first applied in chemical engineering, when looking into the safety inspection on the container and piping system of oil and natural gas. It was found to be useful in locating the emergent risks, providing guidance on immediate actions for inspectors and safety managers to prevent leaking accidents [13]. Motahari [14] summarized the risks of construction process of oil drilling platform, and then used the RBI to improve the inspection procedure through the classification of risks by their priority of impact. Jagars-Cohen et al. [15] introduced RBI into the construction industry. By ranking the risks according to the level of impact, he figured out the most critical risks within a construction projects of highways in Texas, and provided practical solutions for Texas Department of Transportation (TxDOT) to tackle with the shortage of inspectors and the problem of overload by giving priority to those critical risks during inspection. However, since the risks most likely to arise at construction site may be time-varying, critical risks identified under this criteria, which remain unchanged throughout the construction process, will not always represent the risks most likely to arise at the moment of the inspection. Although Zhang and Chi [16] proposed a time-varying inspection model, how does the model influence the observation patterns and improve inspection performance (reducing observation miss) remain unclear.

This study asked how inspectors miss observations on potential risks despite the aid of comprehensive checklist and tried to come up with an effective solution. The study examined the current status of safety inspection in construction industry, including the workload of inspectors and how they use checklist under such circumstance. Then, a theoretical model from cognitive perspective was established to clarify the nature of observation miss. Finally, based on the original checklist, a dynamic checklist on elevator installation was created under the guidance of installation manual, and the effectiveness of this checklist was verified through a simulation experiment using eye tracking device. By comparing the inspection performance fixation figure of subjects in both control group (applying original checklist) and experimental group (applying the dynamic checklist), we made conclusions on whether the dynamic checklist help to reduce the inspector's observation miss by drawing more attention of them on potential risks that most likely to arise in certain installation procedure.

2 Methodology

2.1 Causal Model of Observation Miss

Observation miss of inspectors was studied on the foundation of the theory of selective attention under load, which addresses how people's visual attention on certain targets is affected by different levels of perceptual load and cognitive control load. Literatures on safety inspection and visual search were deep reviewed to identify direct and indirect factors leading to observation miss. The approach of information integration was then applied to form a rough picture of this model. Interviews with 6 inspectors from the company was also conducted to examine whether the theoretical connections in this model were consistent with the real situation according to their personal experience. Given the replies in these six interviews and the information summarized from the literature on load theory of selective attention, the causal model of observation miss was proposed as followed (Fig. 1).

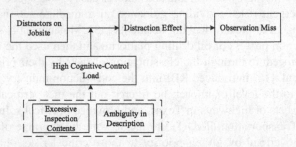

Fig. 1. The causal model of observation miss

In this model, excessive inspection contents leads to overload in working memory of the inspector to keep all of them in mind during the observation, while the ambiguous description of checking items adds to this burden, for the inspector may have a hard time judging whether an actual scenario meet the safety requirement described on the checklist. These two obstacles cause an increase in the difficulty of searching potential risks, and result in high cognitive-control load for the inspector. According to the load theory, this will then strengthens the distraction effect from common distractors existing in construction site, like scattered objects, construction noise, important phone calls and unnecessary talks. Finally, the distraction effect will be strong enough for the inspector, even an experienced one, to miss observation of underlying risks, which definitely impairs the reliability of inspection system.

2.2 Experimental Design

Before conducting the simulation experiment, a dynamic checklist oriented by the installation process of an elevator needs to be created ahead. In this study, a checklist for Fatal Prevention Audit (FPA) of an elevator company, containing 81 items of potential risks, was applied as the original version of this process-oriented checklist. 11 installation stages of elevators were also identified from an installation handbook of Generation II Comfort, which is the widest used type of elevator currently. Then, all the 81 items of risks were matched to these 11 installation stages to create a process-oriented checklist, basing on the judgment that whether a risk item was connected to the tasks of a particular stage. The connection here referred to the concurrence of elements (worker's movements, applied objects or tools used) appeared both in the description of a certain item on the checklist and tasks under a certain stage on the handbook. Finally, the mapping result was rectified and confirmed by two experienced safety auditors from the company through face-to-face interviews.

As for the simulation experiment, this study selected 40 photographs taken at 4 typical locations (Hoistway, Pit, Machine Room, and Storeroom) from different job-sites to create a virtual environment of elevator installation. These photographs were of the same installation stage ('Rail installation') in contents. Then, they were numbered and organized into 4 PPT slides, a single slide for photographs taken at an individual location, to simulate the real inspection context. 43 check points were included within these photographs, containing 30 risks of three types, worker' unsafe behavior, unsafe status of objects and unsafe working condition. These risks were determined through the selection of photographs to be as wide ranging in nature as possible, with the constraint of not being spatially conflicting to the others, to allow the inspectors to completely show their ability in detecting various types of them. However, as the storeroom was seldom the place where fatal accidents occurred, only 2 risks was set in this location. The final distribution of risks in 4 locations was presented in Table 1.

Table 1. The distribution of photographs and risks at different locations

Location	Hoistway	Pit	Machine room	Storeroom
No. of photographs	12	9	10	9
No. of risks	11	8	9	2

Five inspectors from the Beijing branch of the company were selected as subjects for this experiment, with working age ranging from 1.5 years to 25 years. Selecting subjects of wide-range working age from the same branch can avoid the interference of personal experience as well as inspection requirement of different branch on inspection performance in this experiment.

The experiment consisted of two sections, a pre-test and a pro-test. In the pre-test, subjects were provided with identical FPA checklists in original versions, and asked to examine this virtual environment through the observation of photographs in 4 slides to detect as many of hidden risks as possible. Once a risk was detected in a photograph, subjects were required to write down the number of photograph next to the relative item on the checklist. The time limit for this section was 13 min. In the pro-test, subjects were provided with a process-oriented FPA checklist specifically for the stage of 'Rail Installation'. The process-oriented FPA checklist remains in the style of the original one, except that items related to Rail Installation were highlighted by different color. Then they were asked to do the examination again based on the detection result of pre-test, and keep records of risks further detected as what they did in the first section. The time limit for this section was 7 min. The experiment was conducted in turns, and subjects were allowed to examine these 4 location in the random order during the test according to their preference in daily inspection, simply by switching the slides through hyperlinks. After the experiment, 2 indicators were calculated to evaluate the inspection performance of each subject, illustrated as followed,

$$\text{Detection Rate (DR)} = \frac{\text{No. of risks corrected identified}}{\text{Total no. of hidden risks}} \tag{1}$$

$$\text{Judgment Accuracy (JA)} = \frac{\text{No. of risks corrected identified}}{\text{No. of detected}} \tag{2}$$

In Eq. (1), risks corrected identified referred to those detected by subjects with the correct decisions on corresponding checking items. Total number of hidden risks here was 30, as introduced above. In Eq. (2), the risks detected referred to items with photographs numbers aside. These two indicators were both calculated and statistically compared in pre-test and pro-test to determine whether the application of process-oriented checklist causes any decrease in observation miss without sacrificing the accuracy of judgment.

To monitor the shifting focus of subjects on these photographs during the inspection process and collect data on attention distribution, an eye tracking device was applied for subjects to wear all the time in this experiment. The equipment used was SMI iView X, with sampling frequency 50 Hz of eye movement. After the experiment, the image data of simulation experiments were automatically recorded in the software of BeGaze for further analysis. To better understand the distribution of subject's attention on hidden risks, 'Areas of Interest' (AOI) were defined to locate the exact region of risks appeared in specific photographs, based on recorded images of inspection process. With the help of BeGaze, we could have the value of several indexes for eye movement in defined areas on the screen. Given these indexes, we could have the value of an indicator addressing search efficiency, calculated as followed,

$$\text{Search Efficiency (SE)} = \frac{\sum_{i=1}^{n} (AF)_i \times (FC)_i}{\textit{Total Time of inspection}} \tag{3}$$

In Eq. (3), AF_i referred to average fixation time on a certain AOI, while FC_i referred to fixation counts. As a result, the product of this two indicators would be the total time of fixation spent on a potential risks, which was taken as the valid time in one's searching task during the safety inspection. Besides, the total time of inspection was not 13 min in the pre-test, or 7 min in the pro-test. Instead, the time of reviewing checklist during the inspection should be deducted, for the subjects then were not actually conducting the observation of photographs. The deduction in total time could be clearly identified and calculated from the image data. This indicator was calculated in both pre-test and pro-test with a statistical comparison to determine whether the application of process-oriented checklist causes any decrease in the proportion of inspector's observation time spent on distractors rather than hidden risks.

3   Findings

3.1   Inspection Performance on Risks Detection

Table 2 below provides the average detection rate in both pre-test and pro-test. According to the results of t-test, there is a significant increase in detection rate (sig. = 0.01/0.03 < 0.05) after applying the process-oriented checklist in the pro-test, from 15 % to 24 % (23 %), whether the items unrelated to rail installation, yet being detected in pro-test, are included or not. Table 3 provides the average judgment accuracy in both pre-test and pro-test. The result of t-test reveals that there is no significant change in judgment accuracy (sig. = 0.93/0.92 > 0.05) after applying the proposed checklist in the pro-test. Figure 2 below takes into account the number of risks corrected identified versus the working age of inspectors. As is shown, R2 values are very low (R2 = 0.0103, 0.0727, 0.1314 ≪ 1), being far away from 1, in both the pre-test and pro-test, indicating no direct relationships between the detection rate of inspectors and their working experience. It's the same story of judgment rate (R2 = 0.0081, 0.0128, 0.0138 ≪ 1), indicating no direct relationships between the judgment rate of inspectors and working experience (Fig. 3).

Table 2. The t-test for detection rate

Checklist provided	Mean	Std. deviation	Std. error mean	Sig.
Original checklist	0.15	0.04	0.02	0.01
Process-oriented checklist (total)	0.24	0.04	0.02	
Original checklist	0.15	0.04	0.02	0.03
Process-oriented checklist (Related items only)	0.23	0.05	0.02	

Table 3. The t-test for judgment accuracy

Checklist provided	Mean	Std. deviation	Std. error mean	Sig.
Original checklist	0.62	0.17	0.07	0.93
Process-oriented checklist (Total)	0.63	0.09	0.04	
Original checklist	0.62	0.17	0.07	0.92
Process-oriented checklist (Related items only)	0.63	0.09	0.04	

3.2   Inspection Performance on Searching Efficiency

Table 4 below shows the percentage of valid search for 5 subjects in both the pre-test and the pro-test. To be mentioned, the data of subject No.1 is abandoned because of too

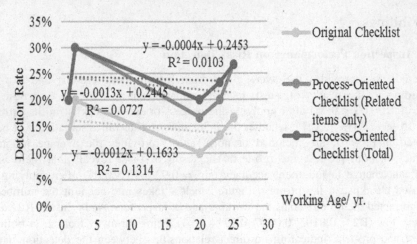

Fig. 2. The relationship between detection rate and working experience

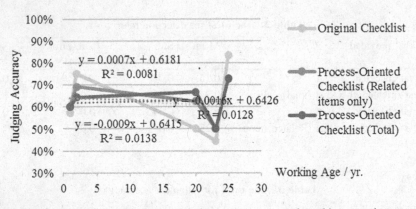

Fig. 3. The relationship between judgment accuracy and working experience

many head movement during the experiment, making the definition of AOI (Area of interest) to be inaccurate. The other missing data in this table are all from the pro-test. The reason is that since all the photographs are examined in the pre-test, subjects may not have a double check on each one of them in the pro-test, given the limited inspection time in this section. As for the data left, there is a significant increase in the proportion of valid search (Table 5, sig. = 0.03 < 0.05) after applying the process-oriented checklist in the pro-test, indicating that search efficiency of inspectors has been improved by the proposed checklist.

Table 4. Search efficiency in two sections

No. of Subject	Location	Hoistway	Pit	Machine Room	Storeroom
1	Pre-test	N/A	N/A	N/A	N/A
	Pro-test	N/A	N/A	N/A	N/A
2	Pre-test	13.33%	9.22%	2.99%	8.54%
	Pro-test	17.37%	12.72%	N/A	N/A
3	Pre-test	8.09%	4.88%	3.06%	5.26%
	Pro-test	8.68%	N/A	10.58%	N/A
4	Pre-test	2.79%	3.02%	2.53%	3.04%
	Pro-test	8.32%	4.73%	13.99%	6.20%
5	Pre-test	8.61%	N/A	N/A	N/A
	Pro-test	9.90%	N/A	N/A	N/A

*Search efficiency $= \frac{\sum_{i=1}^{k}(AF)_i \times (FC)_i}{Total\ Time\ of\ inspection}$, AF_i-Average Fixation time on a certain AOI, FC_i -Fixation Counts

Table 5. The t-test for search efficiency

Section of experiment	Mean	Std. deviation	Std. error mean	Sig.
Pre-test	0.06	0.04	0.01	0.03
Pro-test	0.10	0.04	0.01	

4   Discussions

As illustrated in the causal model, the reason why inspectors miss observation of potential risks despite the aid of checklist was that the usage of checklist usually deviates from its original purpose because of heavy cognitive-control load. In practice, the inspectors seldom used it simultaneously while examine the construction site, for the checklist are too complicated in contents without reasonable structure and indication of priority. Instead, checklist was commonly used as a reminder of the inspection contents before or after a holistic observation. These findings suggested that inspectors actually need a well-structured checklist corresponding to the nature of technical system being examined. In response to the defects, a dynamic checklist oriented by installation stage was proposed in this research. Then the experiment results provided a sustainable support to the effectiveness of proposed checklist in reducing observation miss by presenting an increase in both detection rate and search efficiency. To be mentioned, the detection rate may only serve as a reference for the improvement to avoid missing observations of risks. Because the risks detected in the pro-test may include those already been detected in the pre-test. Thus, the increase in searching efficiency is a more substantial support for the effectiveness of process-oriented checklist, as it revealed that more attention had been focused on potential risks after applying the proposed checklist. However, due to the difficulty of accessing qualified subjects, the sample size is not large enough to reach a conclusion of statistical significance. Besides, despite the effectiveness of structured checklist, it is better to be used as a complement after holistic observation in practice. Because there will always be defects in the design of a checklist, and a structured checklist with fewer inspection contents at a certain time may have risks in missing observation of targets outside the checklist.

5 Conclusions

The research illustrates the nature of observation miss in safety inspection through a causal model. The complexity of checklist, including having too much checking items as well as being ambiguous in descriptions, will increase the cognitive-control load for the inspectors. In that case, inspectors will then shift their inspection mode of inspectors from item-by-item examination to holistic inspection. As the high cognitive-control load strengthens the effect of interference from existing distractor on jobsite, inspectors will finally be prone to missing observations of potential risks during their holistic inspection. These findings provide a convincing answer to the question that why missing observation of potential risks still happens in safety inspection of construction industry given the comprehensive checklist applied by the inspectors. Besides, the role of working experience of the inspector was also clarified to have little influence on his inspection performance. Future research should aim to carry out a similar experiment on validating the dynamic checklist with larger sample. Although augmenting cognitive load of inspector is found to be effective in reducing observation miss, future research should focus on how to dynamically propose inspection items according to the location of inspectors and construction procedures.

References

1. Lucker, J.: Zero accidents on the job-you bet! J. Pavement Adv. World Pavements 16, 12–16 (1996)
2. Bureau of Labor Statistics: Census of Fatal Occupational Injuries (CFOI) - Current and Revised Data. http://www.blsgov/iif/oshwc/cfoi/cfch0012.pdf
3. Health and Safety Executive: Health and Safety in Construction in Great Britain (2014). http://www.hsegovuk/statistics/industry/construction/construction.pdf
4. Wang, C.H.: Economic off-line quality control strategy with two types of inspection errors. J. Eur. J. Oper. Res. 179, 132–147 (2007)

5. Duffuaa, S.O., El-Ga'aly, A.: Impact of inspection errors on the formulation of a multi-objective optimization process targeting model under inspection sampling plan. J. Comput. Ind. Eng. **80**, 254–260 (2015)
6. Hamzic, Z.: Development of an Optimization Model to Determine Sampling Levels. Missouri University of Science and Technology, Columbia City (2013)
7. Saha S.K, Greville C., Mullins T.: Simulation experiment: the effects of experience and interruption in predicting error rate for a construction inspection task. In: International Congress on Modelling and Simulation Proceedings, pp. 6–9, New Zealand (1999)
8. Fischer, S.L., Woodcock, K.: A cross-sectional survey of reported musculoskeletal pain, disorders, work volume and employment situation among sign language interpreters. J. Int. J. Ind. Ergon. **42**, 335–340 (2012)
9. Drury, C.G.: Human factors and automation in test and inspection. New York (2001)
10. Lind, S., Nenonen, S., Kivistö-Rahnasto, J.: Safety risk assessment in industrial maintenance. J. Qual. Maint. Eng. **14**, 205–217 (2008)
11. Murphy, K.S., DiPietro, R.B., et al.: Does mandatory food safety training and certification for restaurant employees improve inspection outcomes? Int. J. Hosp. Manag. **30**, 150–156 (2011)
12. Pham, M.T., Jones, A.Q., Sargeant, J.M., et al.: A qualitative exploration of the perceptions and information needs of public health inspectors responsible for food safety. BMC Publ. Health **10**, 345 (2010)
13. Conley M., Reynolds J.: Using risk based inspection to assess the effect of corrosive crudes on refining equipment. In: 15th World Petroleum Congress, Beijing, China (1997)
14. Jalali, M.M.S.: Risk Based Inspection: Developing Empirical Formula to Calculate Inspection Coverage. University of Stavanger, Stavanger (2011)
15. Jagars-Cohen, C., Chelsea, A., et al.: Priority-ranking workload reduction strategies to address challenges of transportation construction inspection. Transportation research record. J. Transp. Res. Board **2098**, 13–17 (2009)
16. Zhang, H., Chi, S.: Real-time information support for strategic safety inspection on construction sites. In: 30th International Symposium on Automation and Robotics in Construction and Mining, Montreal, Canada (2013). (J. Transp. Res. Board)

Conceptualizing Performance Shaping Factors in Main Control Rooms of Nuclear Power Plants: A Preliminary Study

Peng Liu[1(✉)], Xi Lv[2], Zhizhong Li[2], Yongping Qiu[3], Juntao Hu[3], and Jiandong He[3]

[1] Department of Industrial Engineering,
College of Management and Economics, Tianjin University, Tianjin, China
pengliu@tju.edu.cn
[2] Department of Industrial Engineering, Tsinghua University, Beijing, China
lvxl2@mails.tsinghua.edu.cn, zzli@tsinghua.edu.cn
[3] Shanghai Nuclear Engineering Research and Design Institute, Shanghai, China
{qiuyp,hujuntao,hejd}@snerdi.com.cn

Abstract. Human errors are widely-accepted to be a major contributor to incidents and accidents in complex, safety-critical systems. Human reliability is influenced by individual, organizational, and environmental factors, which are called as performance shaping factors (PSFs). Identifying and managing PSFs are important for quantifying human error probability in human reliability analysis (HRA) and preventing human errors in main control rooms (MCRs) of nuclear power plants (NPPs). This study proposes a conceptualization framework for PSFs to identify and organize PSFs in MCRs of NPPs. It describes PSFs at three levels, components, factors (i.e., dimensions), and indicators. The expected result is the full-set PSF model for MCRs of NPPs. The future study is to weight and rank the PSFs from this full-set PSF model and to identify the elite-set PSF model with key PSFs to inform the HRA quantitative analysis.

Keywords: Human reliability analysis · Performance shaping factors · Main control rooms · Nuclear power plants · Conceptualization

1 Introduction

Safety-critical systems (e.g., nuclear power plants and air traffic control) have extremely high requirements on safety and reliability. Technological, individual, organization, and social elements can influence the reliability of safety-critical systems. With the rapid developments of technologies, the contribution of human errors and organizational weakness to system failures is becoming significant. It is widely-accepted that human errors and organizational weakness are a major contributor to incidents and accidents in safety-critical systems. For nuclear power plants (NPPs), 80 % of significant events can be related to human and organization errors [1]. More than 50 % of operating events in NPPs in China were implicated with operator errors from 1991 to 2011 [2]. Highly reliable human performance is required to maintain the integrity of complex, safety-critical systems as NPPs.

© Springer International Publishing Switzerland 2016
D. Harris (Ed.): EPCE 2016, LNAI 9736, pp. 322–333, 2016.
DOI: 10.1007/978-3-319-40030-3_32

Human reliability is influenced by individual, organizational, and environmental factors, which are called as performance shaping factors (PSFs) [3]. A PSF can also be called as a performance influencing factor (PIF), error producing context (EPC), or common performance condition (CPC). Human error probability (HEP) can be quantified by the PSFs in the human reliability analysis (HRA). Three types of PSF-based quantitative methods were suggested. The HEP of a human failure event (HFE) can be obtained by modifying its nominal HEP with the multipliers of PSFs (see [4]), the HEP of a HFE can be a function of its PSFs (see [5]), or the HEP of a HFE in various combinations of PSF levels can be directly estimated by expert judgments or other techniques (see [17]). Therefore, in order to assess human reliability, first and most importantly, the PSFs in safety-critical systems should be identified.

Several sources can be used to identify PSFs in a complex system, including HRA methods, human performance database, accident investigation, and operator survey. Dozens of PSF classification systems were suggested. Three major problems of PSFs were found in the literature. First, the PSFs overlap with each other and their definitions are not clear within several HRA methods [6], and PSFs are defined at various levels between HRA methods. Second, the range of PSFs covered is not appropriate for several HRA methods [6]. That is, the content validity of several PSF systems is not satisfied [7]. For example, the PSFs related to organization and digital human-system interfaces are not well covered by the first-generation HRA methods. Third, several PSF models may cover too many PSFs, which may influence the quantitative predicting ability of HRA methods. The International HRA Empirical Study [6] suggested that addressing a wide range of PSFs may contribute to the HRA qualitative analysis, and however, it may influence the HRA quantitative analysis negatively. A PSF model with a few key factors can produce reasonable HEPs [6].

The current study will focus on the first two major PSF problems. It will conceptualize PSFs in digital MCRs following a systematic process and clarify the components, factors (i.e., dimensions), and indicators in PSF systems. The results of this study will be used to identify and weight the key PSFs for the HRA quantitative analysis, which is beyond the scope of the current study. The next is organized as follows. Section 2 will describe the conceptualization process, propose a model of PSF components, and introduce the sources of PSF factors and indicators that we referred to. Section 3 will present the suggested PSF model with the list of PSF factors and indicators. Section 4 will make a short discussion and conclude this study.

2   Conceptualization Process

This study proposes a conceptualization framework for PSFs in MCRs. It borrows the process to define task complexity in Liu and Li [8], which follows the general conceptualization process in social science [9]. Its basic idea is to describe PSFs at three levels, components, factors, and indicators. PSFs build the context of MCRs. Thus, the PSF components are the components in the MCR system. The components in a MCR, for example, include individual, crew, organization, etc. For each MCR component, it has one or more PSF factors (i.e., dimensions) that affect human performance. For example, the PSF factors for the individual component can be fatigue, experience/training, stress, etc. In social science, the term "dimension" is preferred. The term "factor" is used in place of "dimension" in the context of HRA. The PSF factors are abstract, and operationalized and represented by their indicators. Take the fatigue PSF for example, its indicators can be working continuously for considerable number of hours, frequent changes of shift, night work, etc.

Thus, the conceptualization process for PSFs has three steps:

- Step 1 is to identify and define components in the PSF system. Section 2.1 will propose a eight-component model for PSFs.
- Step 2 is to identify the PSF factors and indicators for each MCR component. Two researchers with the background of human factors and HRA identified approximately 500 indicators from the literature review. Section 2.2 will introduce the referred sources of PSF factors and indicators.
- Step 3 is to re-group and classify PSF indicators into PSF factors. These two researchers independently classified PSF indicators and reached the consensus finally. Section 3 will present the identified PSF factors and illustrate their indicators.

2.1   PSF Component

The MCR in NPPs is a complex sociotechnical system. Several models can be found to describe the components of sociotechnical systems and to classify contextual factors in several complex domains. In aviation, Edwards [10] and then Hawkins [11] developed the well-known SHELL model, in order to organize and classify contextual factors that influence pilot performance. The components in the SHELL model include Software, Hardware (i.e. physical elements), Environment, and Liveware (i.e. human elements). Several deviations of SHELL model [12, 13] were suggested to add the management and organization component. Bea [14] suggested a model of seven components for offshore structure systems, which are operators, organizations, procedure, equipment, structure, environments, and interfaces. Carayon et al. [15] suggested a model of five components in work systems for patient safety. They are person, organization, tasks, technology and tools, and environment. In the nuclear power industry, Kim and Jung [16] classified PSFs into four groups, human, system (including man-machine interface), task (including procedures), and environment (team and organization, physical working environment). Several common components are considered in the aforementioned models. They are human/liveware, organization/
management, environment, hardware/system structure/equipment, man-machine interface/human-system interface.

With regard to the digital MCRs in NPPs, we would like to decompose the PSF systems into eight components as follows:

- 1 Operator: Individuals that operating NPPs, including MCR operators and field operators. It covers individual characteristics, including the competency of problem solving (e.g., knowledge, skills, abilities) and other characteristics.

- 2 Crew: Operating crews in MCRs. It covers crew characteristics.
- 3 Organization: Support from higher-level organizations, including resource support, training support, safety culture, management support and policies.
- 4 Human-System Interface (HSI): Ways and means of interaction between the crew and the system. It mainly refers to the displays and controls in HSI.
- 5 System: Physical system *per se*.
- 6 Working Environment: Internal and external environments in MCRs.
- 7 Procedure: Computerized- and paper-procedures, guidelines, checklists, standards, etc.
- 8 Task: High-level cognitive activities in specific task environments.

Human elements in MCRs are classified into two components: operator and crew. The former refers to individual capacity, knowledge, trait, etc. The later refers to teamwork characteristics such as leadership, communication and coordination. Procedure and task are considered separately. Procedure will more refer to the usability and quality of procedure systems. Besides proceduralized tasks (i.e., following procedures step by step), crews have to perform other higher-level cognitive activities (e.g., continuous monitoring, situation assessment, diagnosis and analysis, response planning) [6], which are covered by the task component.

2.2 Sources of PSF Factors and Indicators

The PSF factors and indicators in the MCRs are extracted from four major sources: HRA methods, human performance database, human event reports, and other sources. Due to the limited space, we cannot name all of the sources that we referred to.

HRA methods provide dozens of PSF models. Each HRA method has its own PSF model. Here give several examples. The Technique for Human Error Rate Prediction (THERP) method [3] classifies PSFs into two types: external PSFs, including work environment (e.g., equipment design, written procedures or oral instructions), internal PSFs, including individual characteristics of operators (e.g., skills, motivations, and experience), and psychological and physiological stress. The Standardized Plant Analysis Risk-Human Reliability Analysis (SPAR-H) method [4] considers eight PSFs, available time, stress/stressors, complexity, experience/training, procedures, ergonomics/HMI, fitness for duty, and work process. Two new HRA methods, the Integrated Human Event Analysis System (IDHEAS) [17] and Phoenix [18] provide a complete set of PSFs.

Human performance database studies have PSF models to organize the contextual information. For example, the Scenario Authoring, Characterization, and Debriefing Application (SACADA) database [19] classifies PSFs into two groups: overarching factors (e.g., workload and time criticality) that affect all macrocognitive functions and factors that affect specific macrocognitive functions.

Human event reports provide the information of near-misses, incidents, and accidents related to humans. One well-known human event database in NPPs is the Human Event Repository and Analysis (HERA) system [20]. It identifies 11 types of PSFs including indicators.

Other sources include complexity surveys in MCRs, cognitive experiments, and human factors guidelines, etc. One latest study [21] by the authors, which identified and compared complexity factors in conventional and digital MCRs, is referred to. Cognitive experiments can provide the magnitude of the PSF effect on operators [22]. These sources are great complementary to the aforementioned sources.

3   Results

The expected result in the conceptualization process is to build a hierarchy model with three levels in the PSF system (see Fig. 1). The following text will detail the identified PSF factors including their indicators for each component.

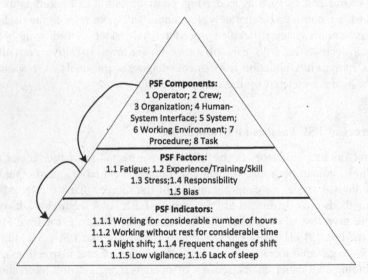

Fig. 1. Components, factors, and Indicators of the PSF system

3.1   Operator Component

Five PSF factors including their indicators belonging to the operator component are suggested as follows:

- 1.1 Fatigue
  - 1.1.1 Working continuously for considerable number of hours
  - 1.1.2 Working without rest for considerable time
  - 1.1.3 Night shifts
  - 1.1.4 Frequent changes of shift
  - 1.1.5 Low vigilance
  - 1.1.6 Lack of sleep
- 1.2 Experience/training/skill
  - 1.2.1 Amount of time passed since training

- 1.2.2 Periodic training not provided
- 1.2.3 Years of experience
- 1.2.4 Knowledge level on system/equipment
- 1.2.5 Similarity between the training and the actual situation
- 1.2.6 Problems in the training process
- 1.2.7 Insufficient training
- 1.2.8 Lack of experience
- 1.3 Stress
  - 1.3.1 Perceived urgency
  - 1.3.2 Apprehension or nervousness associated with the importance of an event
  - 1.3.3 Muscular tension
  - 1.3.4 Fear of failure
  - 1.3.5 Perceived severity
  - 1.3.6 Perceived threat to themselves and others
  - 1.3.7 Performing task under high-jeopardy risk
- 1.4 Responsibility
  - 1.4.1 Responsibility for society
  - 1.4.2 Responsibility for the person
  - 1.4.3 Responsibility for the plant
- 1.5 Bias
  - 1.5.1 Overconfidence
  - 1.5.2 Risk taking
  - 1.5.3 Cognitive bias

3.2 Crew Component

Six PSF factors including their indicators belonging to the crew component are suggested as follows:

- 2.1 Communication requirement
  - 2.1.1 A large amount of communication required
  - 2.1.2 Outside discussions with other staff or even offsite entities needed
- 2.2 Communication availability
  - 2.2.1 Unavailable communication systems
  - 2.2.2 Unreliable communication systems
  - 2.2.3 Standard communication structure/protocol not followed
  - 2.2.4 No communication/key information not communicated
  - 2.2.5 Communication not timely
- 2.3 Communication quality
  - 2.3.1 Received information is not consistent with the transmitted information
  - 2.3.2 Information misunderstood or misinterpreted
  - 2.3.3 Disturbing factors (e.g., noise and interruptions)
  - 2.3.4 Verbal communication with similar sounding words (e.g., "increase" and "decrease")

- 2.4 Leadership
  - 2.4.1 Progress not adequately monitored
  - 2.4.2 Supervisor too involved in tasks, inadequate oversight
  - 2.4.3 Lack of adequate, real-time command and control of activities
  - 2.4.4 Supervisor overconfident and tough
  - 2.4.5 No supervision, excessive trust, failed to question
  - 2.4.6 Team members' duties and tasks not specified
- 2.5 Team cohesion
  - 2.5.1 Lack of commitment and willingness to thoroughly complete the task
  - 2.5.2 Mistrust between team members
  - 2.5.3 Strained interpersonal relationships
- 2.6 Team collaboration
  - 2.6.1 Other members' performance and activities not monitored and checked
  - 2.6.2 Only focusing on their own tasks
  - 2.6.3 Unaware of her/his duties, goals, responsibilities, and role
  - 2.6.4 Lack of training to work together
  - 2.6.5 Limited experience in working together

3.3   Organization Component

Two PSF factors including their indicators belonging to the organization component are suggested as follows:

- 3.1 Safety culture
  - 3.1.1 Routine violation
  - 3.1.2 Safety-production trade-off. Making decisions with sacrificing safety. Focusing on production rather than safety
  - 3.1.3 Lack of openness in communication; limited communication channels; poor information flow
  - 3.1.4 Lack of willingness to fix problems
  - 3.1.5 Non-compliance with regulatory requirements
  - 3.1.6 Failure to correct known deficiencies and ignoring warning signs
  - 3.1.7 Deficiency in self-assessment and effectiveness review
  - 3.1.8 Overconfidence and complacency
  - 3.1.9 Oversight groups failed to question
- 3.2 Resource management
  - 3.2.1 Inappropriate organizational placement of personnel resources
  - 3.2.2 Inappropriate organizational assignment of tasks

3.4   Human-System Interface Component

Four PSF factors including their indicators belonging to the HSI component are suggested as follows:

- 4.1 Information availability
  - 4.1.1 Missing key indicators and cues information
  - 4.1.2 Key indicators and cues information masked
  - 4.1.3 Missing key alarms
  - 4.1.4 Little redundancy in key information
  - 4.1.5 No feedback
  - 4.1.6 Slow feedback
- 4.2 Information ambiguity
  - 4.2.1 Small indications/problems of visibility
  - 4.2.2 Slight change of information
  - 4.2.3 Cues/alarms not salient
  - 4.2.4 Symptom of one fault is masked by another fault
  - 4.2.5 Ambiguity of alarms
- 4.3 Information unreliability
  - 4.3.1 Misleading information that points to an incorrect diagnosis
  - 4.3.2 Conflicting information that points to more than multiple diagnosis or conflicts with other information sources
  - 4.3.3 False alarms
  - 4.3.4 Other events (e.g., fire) lead some indications to be missing, spurious, or failed
  - 4.3.5 Failed indicators
- 4.4 Information overload
  - 4.4.1 Many alarms
  - 4.4.2 Lots of information in displays or panels
  - 4.4.3 Much information changing simultaneously
  - 4.4.4 Many extraneous/unrelated alarms

3.5   System Component

Four PSF factors including their indicators belonging to the system component are suggested as follows:

- 5.1 System unreliability
  - 5.1.1 Multiple faults
  - 5.1.2 Low fault tolerance level
  - 5.1.3 Multiple equipments unavailable
- 5.2 System complexity
  - 5.2.1 Number of sub-systems and components
  - 5.2.2 Number of coupled components
  - 5.2.3 System interdependencies not well defined
  - 5.2.4 Low transparency of system structures or behaviors
  - 5.2.5 Non-transparent behaviors of the automatic system
  - 5.2.6 Difficult to find out what changes in the process are caused by fault(s) directly, and what changes are caused by the automatic system

- 5.3 System dynamics
  - – 5.3.1 Highly unstable plant situation, sensitive to operator operations
  - – 5.3.2 Number of dynamic changing variables
  - – 5.3.3 Quick change of critical parameters

3.6   Working Environment Component

Two PSF factors including their indicators belonging to the working environment component are suggested as follows:

- Habitability
  - – 6.1.1 Noise, which makes communication challenging
  - – 6.1.2 Too heat or too cold
  - – 6.1.3 Poor lighting/illumination
  - – 6.1.4 With radiation
  - – 6.1.5 With smoke
  - – 6.1.6 With toxic gas
- Workplace quality
  - – 6.2.1 Poor workplace layout and configuration
  - – 6.2.2 Narrow work space
  - – 6.2.3 Inappropriate postings/signs

3.7   Procedure Component

Two PSF factors including their indicators belonging to the procedure component are suggested as follows:

- 7.1 Procedure complexity
  - – 7.1.1 Number of steps
  - – 7.1.2 Transitioning between multiple procedures
  - – 7.1.3 Complicated logic between steps
- 7.2 Procedure quality
  - – 7.2.1 Ambiguity, unclear, non-detailed steps
  - – 7.2.2 Incorrect procedure content
  - – 7.2.3 Missing one or more steps. Procedure content not complete
  - – 7.2.4 Lack of necessary instructions
  - – 7.2.5 Mismatch between procedure and scenario
  - – 7.2.6 Conflicts between procedure and industry practice
  - – 7.2.7 Required to perform calculations to get the required information
  - – 7.2.8 Double negatives in procedure text
  - – 7.2.9 Confusing words (e.g., "increase" or "decrease") in procedure text

3.8 Task Component

Six PSF factors including their indicators belonging to the task component are suggested as follows:

- 8.1 Goal complexity
    - 8.1.1 Number of simultaneous goals
    - 8.1.2 Competing or conflicting goals
- 8.2 Information acquisition complexity
    - 8.2.1 Demands to memorize information
    - 8.2.2 Needs of mental calculations or translation
    - 8.2.3 Demands to track and monitor information continuously
    - 8.2.4 Needs to integrate and combine information from different parts of the process and information systems
    - 8.2.5 Problems in separating important from less important information
- 8.3 Information analysis complexity
    - 8.3.1 Ambiguity of the situation
    - 8.3.2 Difficult to identify the most important symptom of the fault
    - 8.3.3 Difficult to predict future plant states
    - 8.3.4 Difficult to find the chronological order of problems observed
    - 8.3.5 Difficult to prioritize the most important fault to focus on
- 8.4 Decision making complexity
    - 8.4.1 Several different alternative diagnosis to choose
    - 8.4.2 Several procedures to choose
- 8.5 Action implementation complexity
    - 8.5.1 A large number of manual actions required
    - 8.5.2 Special sequencing or coordination required
    - 8.5.3 Precision and careful operations required
    - 8.5.4 Control actions that require constant monitoring and manipulation
    - 8.5.5 Many procedures to perform simultaneously
- 8.6 Time pressure
    - 8.6.1 Limited time to focus on tasks
    - 8.6.2 Available time is lower than the required time
    - 8.6.3 Simultaneous tasks required or planned with demands of high attention
    - 8.6.4 Need to respond fast due to time pressure
    - 8.6.5 Urgently need to act on the process to stabilize it

4 Discussion and Conclusions

This study is to conceptualize the PSF model in digital MCRs of NPPs. It shows the preliminary result of this study. The obtained PSF hierarchy model can be expanded to deeper levels if necessary. It can add more PSF components, factors, and indicators. We must caution that the proposed PSF model is not the final one. We are still working on a sound, structured PSF model.

Three excellent PSF hierarchy models [16, 18, 23] have been provided. Kim and Jung [16] classified PSFs into four main groups: human, system, task, and environment. For each group, several subgroups were suggested. Groth and Mosleh [23] organized PSF into five major categories, organization-based, team-based, person-based, situation/stressors-based, and machine-based. Ekanem et al. [18] proposed the three-level of PSFs in which the top level includes HSI, procedures, resources, team effectiveness, knowledge/abilities, bias, stress, task load, and time constraint. One difference between the current study and the three studies may be that it clarifies the difference between components, factors, and indicators in a PSF system.

The final aim of this study is not just to provide a full-set PSF model. The full-set PSF model is required to inform the HRA qualitative analysis and to describe the contextual information from the operating events in NPPs. However, the full-set PSF model is not appropriate for the HRA quantitative analysis which requires a parsimonious PSF model. The future work is to rank and weight PSFs in NPP MCRs, in order to obtain the elite-set PSF model.

Acknowledgements. This work was supported by the National Natural Science Foundation of China under Grant 71371104.

References

1. IAEA: Managing Human Performance to Improve Nuclear Facility Operation. International Atomic Energy Agency, Vienna (2013)
2. Wang, Z., Li, Z.: Summary Reports of Operating Events in Chinese Nuclear Power Plants. China Environmental Science Press, Beijing (2012). (in Chinese)
3. Swain, A.D., Guttmann, H.E.: Handbook of Human Reliability Analysis with Emphasis on Nuclear Power Plant Applications. NUREG/CR-1278, U.S. Nuclear Regulatory Commission, Washington, D.C. (1983)
4. Gertman, D.I., Blackman, H., Marble, J., et al.: The SPAR-H Human Reliability Analysis Method. NUREG/CR-6883, U.S. Nuclear Regulatory Commission, Washington, D.C. (2005)
5. Embrey, D.E., Humphreys, P., Rosa, E.A., et al.: An Approach to Assessing Human Error Probabilities Using Structured Expert Judgment. NUREG/CR-3518, U.S. Nuclear Regulatory Commission, Washington, D.C. (1984)
6. Forester, J.A., Dang, V.N., Bye, A., et al.: The International HRA Empirical Study: Lessons Learned from Comparing HRA Methods Predictions to HAMMLAB Simulator Data. NUREG-2127, U.S. Nuclear Regulatory Commission, Washington, D.C. (2014)
7. OECD/NEA: Establishing the Appropriate Attributes in Current Human Reliability Assessment Techniques for Nuclear Safety. NEA/CSNI/R(2015)1, Organisation for Economic Co-Operation and Development (OECD), Paris, France (2015)
8. Liu, P., Li, Z.Z.: Task complexity: a review and conceptualization framework. Int. J. Ind. Ergon. **42**, 553–568 (2012)
9. Babbie, E.: The Practice of Social Research, 11th edn. Wadsworth, Belmont (2007)
10. Edwards, E.: Man and machine: systems for safety. In: Proceedings of British Airline Pilots Associations Technical Symposium, pp. 21–36. British Airline Pilots Associations, London (1972)

11. Hawkins, F.H.: Human Factors in Flight. Gower Technical Press, Aldershot (1987)
12. Kawano, R.: Steps toward the realization of "human-centered systems" - an overview of the human factors activities at TEPCO. In: Proceedings of 1997 IEEE 6th Conference on Human Factors and Power Plants, pp. 13/27–13/32. IEEE Press, Orlando, FL (1997)
13. Chang, Y.-H., Wang, Y.-C.: Significant human risk factors in aircraft maintenance technicians. Saf. Sci. **48**, 54–62 (2010)
14. Bea, R.G.: Human and organizational factors in reliability assessment and management of offshore structures. Risk Anal. **22**, 19–35 (2002)
15. Carayon, P., Hundt, A.S., Karsh, B.T., et al.: Work system design for patient safety: the SEIPS model. Qual. Saf. Health Care **15**(Suppl. 1), i50–i58 (2006)
16. Kim, J.W., Jung, W.: A taxonomy of performance influencing factors for human reliability analysis of emergency tasks. J. Loss Prevent. Proc. **16**, 479–495 (2003)
17. Whaley, A.M., Xing, J., Boring, R.L., et al.: Cognitive Basis for Human Reliability Analysis. NUREG-2114, U.S. Nuclear Regulatory Commission, Washington D.C. (2016)
18. Ekanem, N.J., Mosleh, A., Shen, S.-H.: Phoenix–a model-based human reliability analysis methodology: qualitative analysis procedure. Relib. Eng. Syst. Saf. **145**, 301–315 (2016)
19. Chang, Y.J., Bley, D., Criscione, L.: The SACADA database for human reliability and human performance. Relib. Eng. Syst. Saf. **125**, 117–133 (2014)
20. Hallbert, B., Boring, R., Gertman, D.: Human Event Repository and Analysis (HERA) System, Overview. NUREG/CR-6903, vol. 1. U.S. Nuclear Regulatory Commission, Washington, D.C. (2006)
21. Liu, P., Li, Z.: Comparison between conventional and digital nuclear power plant main control rooms: a task complexity perspective, Part I: overall results and analysis. Int. J. Ind. Ergon. **51**, 2–9 (2016)
22. Xing, J., Chang, J., Siu, N.: Insights on human error probability from cognitive experiment literature. In: 2015 International Topical Meeting on Probabilistic Safety Assessment and Analysis, Sun Valley, ID (2015)
23. Groth, K.M., Mosleh, A.: A data-informed PIF hierarchy for model-based human reliability analysis. Relib. Eng. Syst. Saf. **108**, 154–174 (2012)

An Approach to Define Design Requirements for a Hand Terminal of an Electronic Warfare System

Mehmet Turhan[(⊠)]

Radar and Electronic Warfare Systems Business Sector,
Aselsan Inc., Ankara, Turkey
mturhan@aselsan.com.tr

Abstract. Elicitation of requirements is critical for the conformance of a system. However, collecting user information and deriving it into unambiguous and verifiable design requirements present a challenge. Therefore non-functional design requirements are usually ended up with ambiguous statements like easy to use. Within the framework of this problem, this paper presents a user research conducted at the early stage of the development process of an electronic warfare system's hand terminal. As a result; the implicit user demands on system functions, the specifications of the hand terminal should provide to its users were collected from the stakeholders' perspective and the research data were clarified in a way guiding designers to define design requirements and realize the final design.

Keywords: Design requirements · Requirement elicitation · Perceived ease of use

1 Introduction

Requirements enable system developers to "design the right thing", beyond "designing the thing right [1] ". In order to "design the right thing", it is important to initiate system development process through well-defined requirements which are described as achievable, verifiable, unambiguous, complete, correct and consistent [2]. On the other hand, non-functional requirements related to the property and quality attribute that systems must have are usually described as ambiguous and difficult to measure contrary to definite and straight-forward functional requirements about what systems must do [3]. Even though non-functional requirements play crucial role in system development process [4], and neglecting them is counted as one of the top risks of requirements engineering [5], they are still poorly understood and difficult to elicit.

One type of non-functional requirements which derives from the needs, preferences and physical/cognitive capabilities of the users is design requirements. Even the importance of design requirements referring to the specifications that systems provide to its users is discussed through different sources [6, 7]; the elicitation of formal design requirements presents a challenge [8]. Therefore, practitioners often describe design specifications with ambiguous statements like "easy to use" or "user friendly" which have different meanings in different contexts [9]. Additionally, the early phases of

© Springer International Publishing Switzerland 2016
D. Harris (Ed.): EPCE 2016, LNAI 9736, pp. 334–342, 2016.
DOI: 10.1007/978-3-319-40030-3_33

system development process are already characterized by the greatest degree of uncertainty and crucial user information is usually lost or not gathered [10]. When critical user information is not realized in the early phases of the development process, modification costs increase drastically as the development process proceeds towards the end [11].

Within the framework of this problem, this research was conducted in order to determine design requirements that may contribute to the development of an electronic warfare system's hand terminal through which "...the user shall easily operate the functions of the system..." as stated in the technical specification document of the related project. By this means, the aim was to explain the implicit user demands on system functions and the specifications that the hand terminal should provide to its users in a way guiding the designers to define design requirements and to realize the final design.

2   Method

2.1   Participants

As a critical first step element to define requirements [12], the participants of the study were selected among stakeholders representing the actual actors of the system. However, when compared to the civilian, military population is too small. Especially regarding the end-users of a special military product, it is very difficult to find enough number of test participants because of time considerations and also bureaucratic reasons. Therefore, only six of 16 participants were potential end-users who had used the previous version of the related system (M = 31.3). Other 10 participants were recruited to represent a sample of development team personnel including systems, hardware and software engineers (M = 30.4).

2.2   Test Materials

Prototyping is assessed as one of the most effective ways for identification of stakeholder requirements at the early phases of development processes [13]. Low fidelity paper prototypes of two hand-held terminals were used in the study. These prototypes were designed to fulfill the functional specifications of the related system and to help user accomplish the same tasks through different user interfaces.

Even the outer dimensions of the prototypes (length: 125 mm, breadth: 80 mm, depth: 20 mm) and the graphical symbols used in the interfaces were the same; design specifications including menu structure, LCD screen, layout and positioning of interaction elements were differed in order to make design specifications comparable and gather more prosperous data (see Fig. 1).

The main difference between two designs was the type of LCD screens used. While a 16 characters by four lines LCD which could only display ASCII characters and some symbols was used at Prototype 1, Prototype 2 had a graphic LCD using a dot matrix pattern to display both text and image. This difference also provided a base to diversify other interface elements. By this means, half of the panel keys of Prototype 1 were

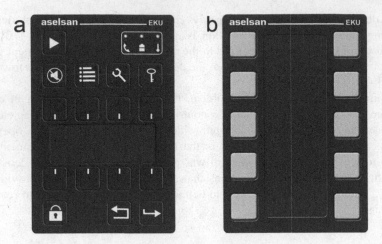

Fig. 1. (a) Prototype 1 and (b) Prototype 2

assigned to fixed functions separately; while functions of the all keys of Prototype 2 varied in accordance with the display interface. The summary of the differences between prototypes is given in Table 1.

Table 1. Main differences of the test materials related to interface elements.

	Prototype 1	Prototype 2
Display	Monochrome character LCD	Monochrome graphic LCD
	Horizontal alignment	Vertical alignment
Controls	16 keys	10 keys
	Fixed/variable function keys	Variable function keys

2.3   Data Collection Techniques

There are many methods and techniques to discover users' cognitive demands and needs such as questionnaire, survey, focus group, observation and etc. Two main approaches referring these methods and techniques are called formative and summative approaches. While summative approaches evaluate the final design at the end of the development process; formative approaches intent to form the required information in the early phases and describe what and how the design should do. Since the study aimed to investigate design requirements at the early stages of development process, formative approach was used.

The qualitative responses of the participants were gathered through semi-structured in-depth interviews and it was attempted to understand the implicit demands through probing. The participants were also asked to rate the perceived ease of use of the test materials. Therefore, in order to make the prototypes comparable quantitatively, subjective evaluation ratings were gathered as an experimental measure. Compromising four items of TAM3 [14], perceived ease of use was measured. The behavioral intention to use was also intended to be predicted through the evaluation questionnaire, and it was measured through one item. All items were examined through 5-point scales, labeled "strongly disagree" (1) and "strongly agree" (5) at the end points. Thus, formative data about the perceived ease of use and the intention to use were gathered.

2.4   Procedure

In their workspaces, the participants recruited were randomly assigned to one of the two prototypes first. Then, the participants were informed that they would evaluate two low fidelity prototypes having the same functional specifications with a view that their feedback would be used to define the requirements of the hand terminal design. Later; a demonstration of the prototypes including the functions of interface elements was given by the researcher. Afterwards, the same procedure was repeated for the other prototype.

The technical specifications of the related system demand both lower and higher user skills. Therefore, nine task scenarios were selected to represent a sample corresponding both basic and complex capabilities. The scenarios were demonstrated on cardboards as separate sequence diagrams. A sample task (the activations of predefined operational modes) represented in a sequence diagram was given in Fig. 2.

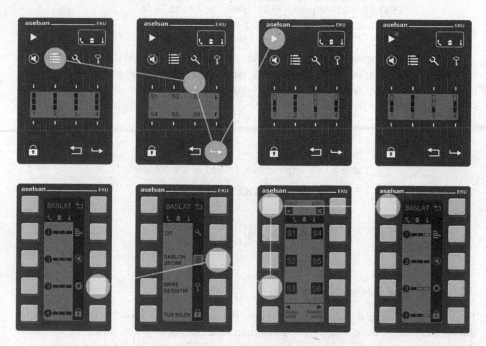

Fig. 2. Sample sequence diagrams of a task

After having completed the demonstrations, the participants were asked to fill in the questionnaire and the behavioral intension to use scale for each prototype respectively.

Later, any issues regarding the design specifications of the prototypes and problems referring to the task scenarios were probed through interviews.

3 Results

3.1 Results of Subjective Evaluation Ratings

Two paired-samples t-tests were conducted to evaluate the results of subjective ratings through main factors of the questionnaire; perceived ease of use (PEOU) and behavioral intention to use (BIU). As shown in Table 2, statistically significant differences were not found in the PEOU scores for Prototype 1 (M = 4.20, SD = 0.68) and Prototype 2 (M = 3.95, SD = 0.53), t (15) = 1.49, p > .05; and in the BIU scores for Prototype 1 (M = 4.06, SD = 0.93) and Prototype 2 (M = 4.19, SD = 0.75), t (15) = −.46, p > .05.

Table 2. Paired-samples t-test results.

	Paired differences				
	M	SD	t	df	Sig. (2-tailed)
PEOU (prototype pair)	0.25	0.67	1.49	15	0.16
BIU (prototype pair)	−0.13	1.09	−0.46	15	0.65

Even any significant differences between the level of prototype did not emerge, it is remarkable that (see Table 3), Prototype 1 was rated with higher scores in the PEOU factor (M_{P1} = 4.20, M_{P2} = 3.95); while getting lower scores in the BIU factor (M_{P1} = 4.06, M_{P2} = 4.19).

Table 3. Descriptive stats related to test materials.

	PEOU		BIU	
	M	SD	M	SD
Prototype 1	4.20	0.68	4.06	0.93
Prototype 2	3.95	0.53	4.19	0.75

3.2 Results of In-Depth Interviews

In order to achieve a holistic perspective; the issues mentioned by the participants during interviews were analyzed and assigned to a category system including two main themes, six sub-themes and seven design items. While one of the main themes was concerned with the extent to which the specifications of user interface designs and tasks performed were quickly and clearly interpreted (comprehensibility); the other was concerned with the extent to which the functions of the system were efficiently and effectively used (effectiveness). As well as seven design items regarding the design specifications of interfaces; the sub-themes were identified with regard to the variety of mentioned issues including intuitiveness (e.g. setting signal output violates common stereotypes), familiarity (e.g. interface layout is similar to ATM's), visibility of the system status (e.g. tracking warnings through distinctive indicators), task completion performance (e.g. accessing task window with one action), error prevention (e.g. display characters are big enough to read) and compatibility with hand use (e.g. controls are not easily accessible for one hand use).

Later, in order to elaborate the interrelation within category system; the main themes were associated with the related sub-themes and design items. As an example, when a participant said "I could lose time since my hand obscures the display while using keys", two interactions were set between effectiveness and task completion performance, and effectiveness and layout of interface elements. By this way, not only the interrelations between categories, but also the strength of these interrelations through the frequencies of mentioning were clarified, and the data were visualized into two maps (see Fig. 3).

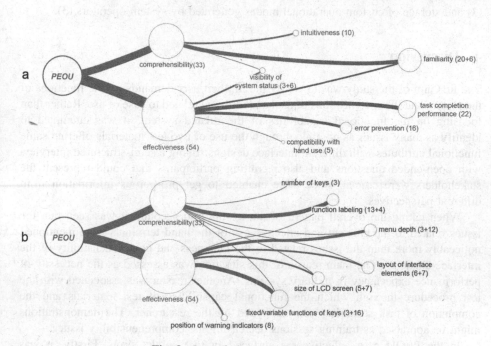

Fig. 3. Interrelations among categories

The results showed that, out of 87 mentioned issues about PEOU, 54 of them were about effectiveness of the system functions. On the other hand, the most frequently mentioned sub-theme was familiarity (26), followed by task performance (22) and error prevention (16). Other categories were referred less frequently. There were also a number of design items which were emphasized more. However, there was a homogeneous distribution when compared to sub-themes. Fixed/variable key functions (19), function labeling (17) and menu depth (15) were the most frequently mentioned design items related to PEOU. However, while function labeling (13) was associated with comprehensibility; fixed/variable key functions (16) and menu depth (12) were mostly associated with effectiveness.

A similar analysis was conducted to evaluate the issues mentioned within the topic of BIU. It was seen that, of out 25 issues, almost half of them were about PEOU of the hand terminals (12). There were two sub-themes which were not mentioned within PEOU issues. One of them is to ability to have a configurable architecture which can allow developers to integrate new functions to the hand terminals (4). The variable key functions and menu depth were associated with the issue. The other one was techno-logical appearances that hand terminals had (8). The bigger sized, graphic LCD screen of Prototype 2 was mostly referred when mentioning the perception of technological appearance.

Finally, apart from the interrelations among categories, there were a number of issues which were related to the functional aspects of the hand terminal. These included restoring to the default settings (5), blackout mode when operational security is required (3) and storage of custom operational modes generated by system operators (3).

4   Discussion

The first aim of the study was to clarify the implicit user demands on the functions of the system and the specifications of the hand terminal related to ease of use. Rather than focusing on the functional capabilities of the related system, it was attempted to identify as many issues as possible through the use of two test materials offering same functional attributes with different interface designs. Using a semi-structured interview with open-ended questions and also recruiting participants that could represent the stakeholders were crucial, since these enabled to get prosperous information from different perspectives.

When taking the overall pattern of the results into account, it was seen that the issues related to the efficient and effective use of the hand terminals were mentioned noticeably more than the issues related to the clearness and comprehensibility of the interface elements. The main reason of this situation was assessed as the necessity of performance expectancy in military systems. Another reason was associated with the test procedure through which the functional capabilities of test materials and the completion of task scenarios were explained by the researcher. The demonstrations might be appraised as training sessions decreasing the comprehensibility issues.

In the PEOU case, effectiveness surfaced in two subtle forms. Firstly, it was strongly associated with the issues of task completion performance and error preven-tion. It was not surprising, since military systems should aim to minimize factors degrading human performance and increasing errors. Additionally, it was observed that nearly all study participants focused on the worst cases by referring to the potential novice users and the task scenarios having more detailed levels. Secondly; the keys of interfaces, whether assigned to fixed or variable functions, were associated with effectiveness. When compared to variable function keys, fixed function keys serving direct access to the related menus were evaluated as determinants of task completion and error prevention. However, they were also criticized, since they could cause complexity and degrade human performance when there were an excessive number of functions. Apart from key functions; number of keys and menu depth were also mentioned and evaluated in a similar manner. Therefore, the trade-off among fixed/variable key functions, number of keys and menu depth presented an important parameter influencing perceived effectiveness. Another emphasized design item was the position of warning indicators. For the sake of the visibility of system status, warning indicators were noticeably demanded as hard, visual indicators positioned separately in the interface; instead of soft indicators placed on LCD displays. The theme comprehensibility, on the other hand, was mostly mentioned through familiarity. As well as referring to products which had similar interface layouts like previously used hand terminals and ATM's, the appropriateness of function labeling was associated with the perception of comprehensibility. While the use of descriptive wording, standard icons on keys and displays were appreciated, a notable amount of participants pointed out the ambiguity within control-display integration. The lack of key status presentation on the display face and the lack of direct marking between display and associated control, especially for variable function keys, caused the impenetrability of proper identification and utilization.

The other factor of the study, BIU, was also associated with PEOU through formerly mentioned performance expectancy requirements and also with two issues. One of them was to ability to have a configurable architecture perceived through variable key functions and menu depth; the other was technological appearance perceived through the size of LCD display. Prototype 2 was mostly referred when mentioning these issues, and also evaluated with higher scores than Prototype 1, even statistically significant differences were not found. It should be also noted that fixed function keys and menu depth of Prototype 1 serving direct access to the related menus were identified with efficient and effective use; thus Prototype 1 was rated with higher scores in the PEOU factor. Finally, there were a number of issues which are concerned with the functional aspects of the hand terminal should also have. These functional aspects were defined based on the experiences of the participants regarding the context of use. Therefore, the results of the study revealed that; even design requirements are considered non-functional requirements establishing constraints on the means to meet functional aspects of a system, in order to develop a system conforming users, design requirements should also shape functional requirements.

5 Conclusion

Even design requirements have an important role in conformance of a system, collecting user information and deriving them into unambiguous and verifiable requirements presents a challenge. This study supports the value of conducting user research at the early stages of development process with an approach using low fidelity prototypes, questionnaire and in-depth interviews to collect data, followed by a focused analysis to present user demands in a generalizable manner to derive research data into actionable design requirements. The information gathered has positive contribution to system development process; since not only the specifications that system should have are clarified and the design requirements are elicited, but also the user acceptance is aimed to be fostered in a mission critical military system.

References

1. Boehm, B.W.: Software Engineering Economics. Prentice-Hall, New York (1981)
2. IEEE, IEEE Std 830-1998: Recommended Practice for Software Requirements Specifications. IEEE Press (1998)
3. Hochmüller, E.: Requirements classification as a first step to grasp quality requirements. In: International Workshop on Requirements Engineering: Foundations for Software Quality, pp. 133–144. Presses Universitaires de Namur, Namur (1997)
4. Mylopoulos, J., Chung, L., Nixon, B.: Representing and using non-functional requirements: a process-oriented approach. IEEE Trans. Softw. Eng. 18(6), 483–497 (1982)
5. Lawrence, B., Wiegers, K., Ebert, C.: The top ten risks of requirements engineering. IEEE Softw. 18(6), 62–63 (2000)
6. Paech, B., Kerkow, D.: Non-functional requirements engineering - quality is essential. In: Regnell, B., Kamsties, E., Gervasi, V. (eds.) Proceedings of 10th International Workshop on Requirements Engineering: Foundation for Software Quality, pp. 237–250 (2004)
7. Taylor, A.: IT projects: sink or swim. Comput. Bull. 42(1), 24–26 (2000)
8. Allendoerfer, K.R.: An analysis of different methods for writing human factors requirements. In: Proceedings of 2005 Mini Conference on Human Factors in Complex Sociotechnical Systems (2005)
9. Abran, A., Khelifi, A., Suryn, W., Seffah, A.: Usability meanings and interpretations in ISO standards. Softw. Qual. J. 11, 325–338 (2003)
10. Ehrhart, L.S., Sage, A.P.: User-centered systems engineering framework. In: Booher, H.R. (ed.) Handbook of Human Systems Integration, pp. 295–373. Wiley, New York (2003)
11. Sutcliffe, A.: User-centered Requirements Engineering: Theory and Practice. Springer, New York (2002)
12. Bahill, A.T., Dean, F.F.: Discovering system requirements. In: Sage, A.P., Rouse, W.B. (eds.) Handbook of Systems Engineering and Management, pp. 205–266. Wiley, New York (2009)
13. Røkke, J.M., Muller, G., Pennotti, M.: Requirement elicitation and validation by prototyping and demonstrators: user interface development in the oil and gas industry. In: Systems Research Forum, pp. 89–108. World Scientific Publishing Company (2011)
14. Venkatesh, V., Bala, H.: Technology acceptance Model 3 and a research agenda on interventions. Decis. Sci. 39(2), 273–315 (2008)

Using a Serious Game to Illustrate Supervisory Control Technology

Robert E. Wray[✉], Benjamin Bachelor, Charles Newton, Kyle Aron,
and Randolph Jones

Soar Technology, Inc., 3600 Green Court Suite 600, Ann Arbor, MI 48105, USA
{wray, ben.bachelor, charles.newton,
aron, rjones}@soartech.com

Abstract. We describe the development of a serious game designed to illustrate the impact of a supervisory control technology. The technology is designed to help human operators deliver better training experiences in simulation. It automates low-level control tasks, thus reducing operator workload. The serious game embeds the technology and simulation in a different context. In the game, the player directs several aircraft in a simulation toward specific geographic points while avoiding "obstacles" and obeying "speed limits" in certain areas. The player's score is maximized when the player adjusts aircraft flight to the constraints, which change dynamically during gameplay. The supervisory control is employed as an "autopilot" to enable aircraft to automatically obey geographical restrictions. Users can play the game with and without the supervisory control technology. These modes allow the players to experience directly both overload and the workload reduction enabled by supervisory control. We contend that direct experience with a technology such as this can supplement design reviews and empirical piloting, helping stakeholders gain a more complete perspective of the desired operational role of the technology.

Keywords: Supervisory control · Simulation-based training · Serious games

1 Introduction

Many stakeholders in the development of user interface and interaction technologies are not the target audience for the deployed technology. We are developing a supervisory control technology that supports instructors adapting training scenarios more readily to the decisions and reactions of individual trainees in virtual simulations. The stakeholders in this effort, science and technology sponsors, requirements analysts, technology acquisition managers, must evaluate the technology somewhat indirectly. Early in technology development, they depend on the subjective reports of potential users and preliminary pilot studies rather than direct experience.

This paper describes a serious game developed to provide stakeholders a more direct experience of the underlying technology. Skipper (a simplification of "SCIPR", or Supervisory Control Illustrated via Pylon Racing) supplements design reviews, technology demonstrations, and verification studies. It allows anyone able to control a mouse to experience a complex control task with and without the presence of the

© Springer International Publishing Switzerland 2016
D. Harris (Ed.): EPCE 2016, LNAI 9736, pp. 343–353, 2016.
DOI: 10.1007/978-3-319-40030-3_34

supervisory control technology. Skipper directly employs both the supervisory control technology and the underlying simulation. Thus, it is not an illustration of the technology but a direct implementation of it targeted to a different use case and audience. We describe Skipper as a *serious game* because its purpose is to enable greater understanding in an interactive experience, in contrast with functional but passive demonstrations or an entertainment game.

The remainder of the paper describes the motivation for Skipper, its design and implementation, a discussion of its use for illustration and demonstration, and consideration of future game features.

2   Context and Motivation

Today, even for relatively simple simulation-based training, human operators are typically required to conduct, to control, and to direct its execution. For example, when a human pilot trainee is flying against simulated entities (semi-automated forces or SAFs) in an immersive simulation trainer, an operator is often employed to control and to adjust the actions of those SAFs as the scenario progresses [1]. As we have described elsewhere [2, 3], the need for human intervention results when what is needed for a highly effective training situation differs from presenting a good (realistic) tactical situation to the trainee. Thus, a realistic representation of the tactical behavior is not sufficient for also delivering a training situation that closely maps to training needs and capabilities of individual trainees.

For tactical aircraft pilot training, we have developed an instructional and exercise management support tool, the Training Executive Agent (TXA), designed to limit the need for dynamic intervention and thus reduce workload. The TXA facilitates and simplifies the management and control of SAFs as the exercise executes, reducing the need for additional staffing and easing the burden of operator control. The TXA builds on research principles from both supervisory control [4, 5] and adaptive training [6, 7]. It enables human operators to specify when and how a SAF entity should deviate from its native tactical behavior program. The TXA actively monitors execution and automatically directs behavioral adaptations based on exercise or training conditions. A verification study demonstrated the TXA can adapt execution to maintain scenario goals while requiring little human intervention [2].

The simulation in which the TXA is integrated is complex and powerful, offering the possibility of simulating simple exercises of a few entities and a single trainee but also large-scale live-virtual-constructive (LVC) exercises that integrate thousands of simulated (constructive) entities, many human trainees operating within virtual simulations, and live assets. For such a flexible and comprehensive simulation environment, there are many different stakeholders and potential stakeholders. How could we quickly communicate how the TXA could be used and what its potential impact might be? We employ traditional tools, such as design specifications, illustrative demonstrations, and empirical test results such as the one cited above. With Skipper, any potential stakeholder can gain a direct experience of supervisory control automation.

3   Game Design and Implementation

This section describes several key game design and implementation choice points in the development of the Skipper game. We describe high-level game design, the role of supervisory control in the game, and several detailed game-design decisions.

3.1   Serious-Game Requirements

Skipper's purpose is to provide players with a sense of what it is like to experience overload and to provide the feeling of that overload being sharply reduced via the TXA. We drew on common serious-game design and "gamification" concepts [8, 9]. The goal of this serious game was not to teach a new the player anything directly about the TXA itself, but rather to illustrate the concept of workload and supervisory control in fast-paced, reward-oriented, short session of gameplay. Thus, the goal of this serious game was a minor development in conceptual knowledge rather than the development of more advanced or broad-based skills, which are the focus of many serious games [10, 11].

The over-arching requirement is to provide players with a sense of what it is like to control SAFs in a simulation but without requiring detailed knowledge of the simulation and its user interfaces, or working knowledge of the tactics, techniques, and procedures that would be used in the real world system. Additionally, we required the experience be interactive, have a scoring/reward mechanism to provide immediate performance feedback, and to be able to be played in no more than 5–10 min.

We considered and adopted additional design requirements, focusing especially on the relationship between the game environment and player tasks and the actual operational environment and operator tasks. A careful mapping of this relationship is important because illustrating the role of technology via a game could be distracting or even misleading. The game design approach attempts to mitigate potential negative effects in three ways. First and most importantly, we designed Skipper and present it as a supplement to analytic and empirical methods for evaluating the technology [2, 12]. Thus, the game is one tool available to help stakeholders understand the technology but not the only one.

Second, after some internal evaluation and analysis, we decided that the serious game should employ the actual technologies used in the real application. In some sense, this approach was limiting. It constrained game-design choices in both game mechanic (what users could do within the game) and because it integrates with the simulation, also constrains the physical properties of entities within the game. For example, aircraft fly according to the flight dynamics defined by their physical design and propulsion systems, which means it takes time for aircraft to change speed and course. However, we decided that using the native technology offset these limits. Applying it ensures that the player-aiding version is a direct implementation of the application technology, which contributes to the validity of the experience.

Using the underlying technology also conveys the flexibility and generality of that technology. We are using it to adapt entity behavior in ways not anticipated or envisioned in the original simulation or with the TXA.

Third and finally, we chose to map player control tasks and game design choices to the real-world control task. Although there is some superficial similarity to the domain, controlling and directing aircraft, we went beyond this mapping to identify analogues between real-world tasks and the player control task that illuminate the why workload can become unmanageable. As we highlight further below, some of the flight rules in the environment change as the game progresses. Dynamic changes in flight requirements reflect a real-world requirement because some training-mission parameters and constraints may be changed on the fly as a scenario unfolds [3].

3.2   Game Design

The component-level design of Skipper is shown in Fig. 1. As illustrated by the shading, the underlying distributed simulation environment and the TXA supervisory control technology were incorporated directly into the game. To compute player scores, we used a previously-developed dynamic performance monitoring and scoring system, the Goal-Constraint System [13]. We developed a game-specific graphical user interface for the player to view the game state, interact with individual aircraft and enable/disable automated piloting functions. We also developed game-specific control behaviors for the TXA-based autopilot. These were necessary to customize autopilot adaptations to game states, as we discuss further below.

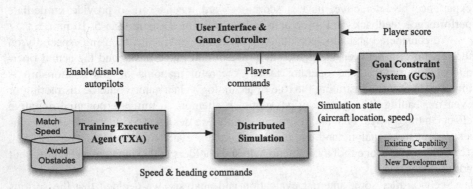

Fig. 1. Skipper system components

Figure 2 shows the primary player view presented in the game. The goal of game play is to direct one or more aircraft to specified location waypoints ("pylons") in an airspace. In the figure, `eagle` and `osprey` are the two aircraft the player is controlling. Pylons `Alpha`, `Bravo`, `Charlie`, and `Delta` are visible as well.

The player controls each aircraft via an aircraft controller, as shown in Fig. 3. These controllers (one for each aircraft) appear to the right of the game-state display illustrated in Fig. 2. The black leader line represents the player's desired heading for the aircraft. The player changes the heading by clicking to the desired heading. The length of the heading line indicates the player's desired speed for the aircraft. Speed control is segmented into four categorical values (concentric rings) to simplify speed control. The bar to the left shows altitude (in a future version of the game, we may add the ability to specify altitude and to require that pylon's be reached at different altitudes).

The current "target" pylon is also listed on this display. The player accrues points based on how quickly pylons are reached. Thus, the player's task is to adjust the speed and heading of each aircraft to fly as quickly as possible to its target pylon. When a target pylon is reached, a new pylon target is indicated, requiring the player to assign new headings for the aircraft to fly toward the new target. When the target pylon changes (either because the player reached it or because the timer

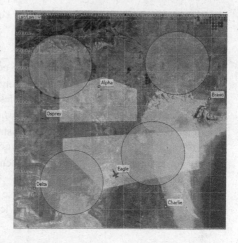

Fig. 2. Skipper's plan-view control display

associated with the pylon expired), the controller text briefly flashes red to help the player recognize that a new target pylon has been assigned.

As above, we desired the game to reflect the dynamic requirements imposed on operators during scenario execution. We undertook this goal in the game design by adding another element to the basic goal of "chasing pylons." Figure 2 illustrates two different kinds of areas where flight restrictions may apply. The circles represent "obstacles". When the obstacle flight restriction is in effect, aircraft flying within the obstacle accrue no points, even if closing on the pylon. The yellow polygons indicate "speed controlled" areas. In these areas, when the restriction is enforced, speed must not exceed the "slow-medium" speed indicated on the aircraft controller (the red circle in Fig. 3). Again, if it does, no points accrue. Thus, the player has several concurrent tasks that must be monitored and executed for each aircraft during play. These tasks are summarized in Table 1.

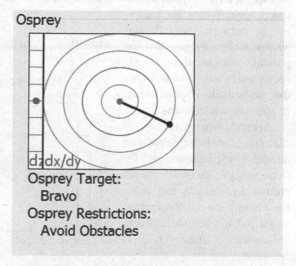

Fig. 3. Example of Skipper flight controller display (Color figure online)

Table 1. Summary of unaided player control tasks for each aircraft in the game

Control tasks (for each aircraft)	Description
Monitor target pylon	Determine the current target pylon and its location on the map
Determine course and speed to pylon	Compare current course/speed with respect to target pylon and compute a desired course and speed (if changes are needed)
Monitor flight restrictions	Determine if/when flight restrictions are in place
Determine course/speed given restriction	Compute adjustments to course and/or speed based on current flight restrictions
Monitor for termination of restrictions	Determine when a flight restriction no longer applies
Assign course and speed	Assign a course (heading) and speed to the aircraft by moving the heading leader

3.3　The Role of Supervisory Control

As we describe further below, in the absence of any aiding, most players find the two-aircraft version of the game very challenging. Thus, Skipper satisfies the goal of creating an experience that causes workload. Automation from the TXA can relieve some of this workload in the game. The supervisory control system is packaged as a "pilot assistant." Figure 4 shows how this "autopilot" is presented to the player when the autopilot is enabled.

The autopilot automates two aspects of control. First, when selected, the autopilot will adjust aircraft speed so that the aircraft flies at the maximum allowed speed for the speed zone. When this autopilot is engaged, aircraft will automatically fly as fast as possible outside of restricted-speed zones and slow down to the medium-slow speed when in speed-restricted areas.

Second, when `Obstacle Avoidance` is selected, the autopilot will compute and fly (reasonably) efficient routes around an obstacle and point the aircraft toward the current target pylon when the obstacle avoidance maneuver is complete.

Table 2 summarizes the player tasks for each aircraft when the autopilot function is enabled. In comparison to Table 1 the player's task is

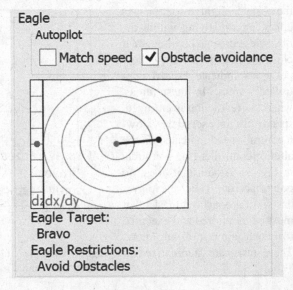

Fig. 4. Enabling autopilot allows the user to automate adjusting to speed restrictions and obstacle avoidance.

primarily different when deciding how to respond to restrictions. In the aided case, the player only needs to direct each aircraft's course toward pylons and activate/deactivate the pilot assistant settings as the restrictions change, rather than the more continuous monitoring and control of the aircraft that was needed for the unaided condition.

Table 2. Summary of aided player control tasks for each aircraft in the game

Control tasks (for each aircraft)	Description
Monitor target pylon	Determine the current target pylon and its location on the map
Determine course and speed to pylon	Compare current course/speed with respect to target pylon and compute a desired course and speed (if changes are needed)
Monitor flight restrictions	Determine if/when flight restrictions are in place
Activate/deactivate auto-pilot functions	*Choose what autopilot functions are active*
Monitor for termination of restrictions	Determine when a flight restriction no longer applies
Assign course and speed	Assign a course (heading) and speed to the aircraft by moving the heading leader

Finally, as a game-design choice, we left it the responsibility of the player to activate and deactivate the individual autopilot functions. It is within the TXA's technical capability to adjust the autopilot settings automatically as restrictions change (e.g., ignoring obstacles when there is no obstacle avoidance restriction in place and avoiding them when they are). This would have provided almost complete automation for the task. This level of automation is feasible for this simple game, but less realistic and feasible for large-scale, real-world training exercises. Thus, the choice to require the player to remain closely engaged with the task was designed to reflect the cognitive demands of the real-world task.

4 Player Reactions and Feedback

We have presented the game to stakeholders directly, showed it at several technology forums and tradeshows, and even allowed elementary-aged students to play the game at a school STEM event. We introduce the game and its goals and let players play the unaided and aided versions of the game. Scores are captured on a "leaderboard," allowing participants to compare their scores to others and compete for the high score of the day.

Via playtesting and tuning, we adjusted the base speed of aircraft and the timing of pylon target assignments so that the game flow is challenging but achievable. Most players find the two aircraft, unaided version of the game very challenging. The combination of multiple aircraft, changing flight restrictions, and changing pylons

Table 3. Examples of strategies and errors observed during unaided, 2-aircraft game play

Adaptation or error	Example
Immobilization	Player reports feeling overwhelmed and freezes and/or stops playing/trying to succeed
Task shedding [14]	Player does not try to avoid an obstacle if a significant deviation in course is required
Cognitive tunneling [15]	Player tends to focus on ensuring one aircraft is "compliant" and spends a much greater fraction of time focused on and manipulating that aircraft than the other
Error of omission	Player fails to adjust course or speed after a flight restriction is no longer relevant
Error of commission	Player applies an appropriate setting (such as a change in desired speed) for the incorrect aircraft

generates sufficient cognitive load that some common strategies for dealing with overload emerge. Some examples drawn from game-play observations are summarized in Table 3.

This table and the score analysis that follows are intended to illustrate the way users experience the game. We do not intend to present them as a formal assessment. For formal assessment, we would need to control more deliberately the way the game was presented to new players, the time players dedicated to the game, and the mechanisms for score collection.

Skipper players can compare their unaided and aided scores, which serves as a proxy for the impact of the supervisory control. The game has been tuned so that excellent control in the 2-aircraft version results in a score of about 500 points. Informal results from thirty-two adult game players are summarized in Fig. 5. The chart shows one estimated standard deviation above and below the average (boxes) and the total range of scores (error bars). Unaided players average about 350 points in the 2-aircraft scenario. The total range of scores and estimated standard distribution are comparatively large. However, some unaided players do as well as some players do when aided.

Aided players score about 450 points on average and the range and distribution of scores is much tighter. Further, there is a possible floor effect on low scores, with almost all of the

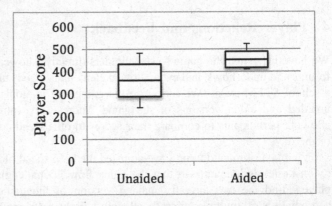

Fig. 5. Informal summary of player scores for unaided and aided gameplay in Skipper.

lower scores being within one standard deviation of the mean. These results suggest that the supervisory control is compensating for the overload that leads to lower scores in the unaided condition and helping players achieve a minimum level of accomplishment in the game. More meaningfully, stakeholders who have played the game report greater understanding of what role the technology is performing in training simulations and a clearer sense of the role it may play in future training systems.

5 Extensions to Support a More Complete Use Case

Overall, Skipper has met the goal of giving players the experience of being overloaded followed by the contrasting experience of being supported by automation for the pylon-racing task. Based on player feedback and suggestions, we are evaluating some minor adjustments to the game as listed below:

- **Altitude targets:** We originally planned to include altitude block requirements when reaching a pylon target. We did not include altitude changes in the first versions of Skipper because the game was sufficiently challenging with two aircraft to achieve significant player overload.
- **Automatic map generation:** One of the limits on replay in the current game is that the map, including pylon positions and flight-restricted areas, is fixed (the progression of pylon targets is variable). Other maps can be generated by-hand, but this is a time-consuming process. A more replayable game requires automatic generation of maps. Because target users were not expected to play the game more than a few times, the current approach has thus far proven acceptable.
- **Less realistic physical constraints:** As outlined earlier, Skipper uses an underlying simulation that is used for actual training. As a consequence, aircraft change speed and heading as aircraft do in the real world, which takes time. In order to optimize score, a player needs to take these physical limits into account. For example, to ensure that the speed has slowed to the maximum allowed speed prior to entering a speed-restricted area, the player must issue the change speed command well in advance of reaching the restricted area. For some players, this is confusing and distracting. It would likely be preferable to use instantaneous speed and heading changes to avoid these distractions during gameplay.
- **Enable autopilot in-game:** The current game is played in two distinct sessions in which the autopilot is disabled (unaided) or enabled (aided). An alternative design would be to enable the autopilot at some point during the game, either based on a fixed point in the scenario or after some amount of elapsed time. This would reduce a player's ability to compare aided and unaided scores for the same time period, but might reduce some player frustration (players dislike being overloaded) and the total time it takes to play the game. This choice is in tension with the goal of having players experience overload but may be apt for some settings, especially for demonstrations to school-aged players.

These changes might improve gameplay but likely would not significantly alter the player's perception of overloading or supervisory control. We are also considering a more substantial addition to the game, one that would provide a richer sense of the way the TXA supports operators in the operational environment.

To motivate this addition, consider the implementation of the autopilot functions in the game. The game allows the user to indicate that the autopilot function should be engaged, but it does not allow the user to specify *how* the autopilot should perform its function. Some players complained that the autopilot made different choices than they would have. For example, if an aircraft would only narrowly cut thru a restricted area when restrictions were in force, in many cases the score-maximizing choice is to not adapt behavior, especially for speed reductions (because of the time it takes to slow and speed back up). Some players expressed a preference that the autopilot make score-maximizing choices, rather than simply enforce restrictions.

In the next iteration of Skipper, we would like to allow players to define specific characteristics of their autopilots, either thru some choices about parameters of autopilots (like whether or not to engage within some range of the restricted area) or possibly to compose functional building blocks that define how their autopilots should operate. This change would reflect the way the TXA is used in real-world scenarios, where users define both when and how adaptive interventions should be made. It would also improve replayability and potentially player engagement, because the player might experiment with a number of different strategies for the autopilot functions. However, this change would also increase the complexity of the game and the amount of time players would need to spend with it. Further, it requires identifying a simple, understandable, but sufficiently powerful set of parameters or primitives that users could effectively use to specify their autopilots.

6 Conclusion

Skipper satisfies the goal of offering a representative experience of the tasks and workload demands that operators in a simulation-training domain experience without requiring any detailed technical knowledge of the application. It illustrates the potential advantages of automation support to game players, who, through game play, can directly compare the impact of automation, both in terms of subjective experience of workload and in different scores produced in aided and unaided conditions.

We suggest that this approach can be used to illustrate the role of automation in other domains. Because Skipper directly uses the underlying application technologies, the actual cost of developing a representative game task and implementing it was quite small (less than a person month of effort). Other applications and domains may present greater challenge in formulating a representative abstraction of the application requirements and the role of automation. However, the experience with Skipper suggests significant benefit in enabling stakeholders to engage with the technology directly to help deepen and expand their understanding of the technology.

Acknowledgments. This work is supported by the Office of Naval Research project N00014-1-C-0170 Tactical Semi-Automated Forces for Live, Virtual, and Constructive Training (TACSAF). The views and conclusions contained in this document are those of the authors and should not be interpreted as representing the official policies, either expressed or implied, of the

Department of Defense or Office of Naval Research. The U.S. Government is authorized to reproduce and distribute reprints for Government purposes notwithstanding any copyright notation hereon. We would like to thank collaborators and sponsors at NAWCTSD and ONR who have provided insights and operational perspectives in the development of TXA: CDR Brent Olde, Ami Bolton, Melissa Walwanis, and Heather Priest.

References

1. Tolk, A. (ed.): Engineering Principles of Combat Modeling and Distributed Simulation. Wiley, Hoboken (2012)
2. Wray, R.E., Bachelor, B., Jones, R.M., Newton, C.: Bracketing human performance to support automation for workload reduction: a case study. In: Schmorrow, D.D., Fidopiastis, C.M. (eds.) AC 2015. LNCS, vol. 9183, pp. 153–163. Springer, Heidelberg (2015)
3. Wray, R.E., Priest, H., Walwanis, M.A., Kaste, K.: Requirements for future SAFs: beyond tactical realism. In: 2015 I/ITSEC Conference. NTSA (2015)
4. Parasuraman, R., Sheridan, T.B., Wickens, C.D.: A model of types and levels of human interaction with automation. IEEE Trans. Syst. Man Cybernetics – Part A: Syst. Hum. **30**, 286–297 (2000)
5. Sheridan, T.B.: Humans and Automation: System Design and Research Issues. Wiley, New York (2002)
6. Durlach, P.J., Lesgold, A.M. (eds.): Adaptive Technologies for Training and Education. Cambridge, New York (2012)
7. Raybourn, E.M.: Applying simulation experience design methods to creating serious game-based adaptive training systems. Interact. Comput. **19**, 206–214 (2007)
8. Ruggiero, D., Watson, W.R.: Engagement through praxis in educational game design common threads. Simul. Gaming **45**, 471–490 (2014)
9. Deterding, S., Dixon, D., Khaled, R., Nacke, L.: From game design elements to gamefulness: defining "gamification". In: Proceedings of the 15th International Academic MindTrek Conference, pp. 9–15. ACM, Tampere (2011)
10. O'Neil, H.F., Wainess, R., Baker, E.: Classification of learning outcomes; evidence from the games literature. Curriculum J. **16**, 455–474 (2005)
11. Connolly, T.M., Boyle, E.A., MacArthur, E., Hainey, T., Boyle, J.M.: A systematic literature review of empirical evidence on computer games and serious games. Comput. Educ. **59**, 661–686 (2012)
12. Jones, R.M., Wray, R.E., Zaientz, J., Bachelor, B., Newton, C.: Using cognitive workload analysis to predict and mitigate workload for training simulation. In: Proceedings of the 6th International Conference on Applied Human Factors and Ergonomics (AHFE 2015), AHFE 2015. Springer, Las Vegas (2015)
13. Jones, R.M., Bachelor, B., Stacy, W., Colonna-Romano, J., Wray, R.E.: Automated monitoring and evaluation of expected behavior. In: International Conference on Artificial Intelligence, Las Vegas (2015)
14. Raby, M., Wickens, C.D.: Strategic workload management and decision biases in aviation. Int. J. Aviat. Psychol. **4**, 211–240 (1994)
15. Dirkin, G.R.: Cognitive tunneling: use of visual information under stress. Percept. Mot. Skills **56**, 191–198 (1983)

EID vs UCD: A Comparative Study on User Interface Design in Complex Electronics Manufacturing Systems

Lei Wu[1(✉)], Juan Li[2], Tian Lei[1], and Bin Li[3]

[1] Department of Industry Design, Huazhong University of Science and Technology, Wuhan 430074, People's Republic of China
{lei.wu,andrew.tianlei}@hust.edu.cn
[2] Department of Art and Design, Huaxia College, Wuhan University of Technology, Wuhan 430070, People's Republic of China
lijuan-xy@163.com
[3] School of Mechanical Science and Engineering, Huazhong University of Science and Technology, 430074 Wuhan, People's Republic of China
libin999@mail.hust.edu.cn

Abstract. This paper reports on an experimental study on user interface design in complex electronics manufacturing systems to measure the difference between ecological interface design (EID) and user-centered design (UCD). Based on cognitive psychology and human factors theory, we conducted a comparative research study. Prototypes of the interface were designed based on the EID and UCD which were undergoing NASA-TLX to evaluation the subjective workload of the users. The main findings of this study were as follows: (1) we found that the ecological interface design and user-centered design had significant differences in each levels; (2) the ecological interface design has a significant better effect on subjective workload compare to user-centered design in the complex electronics manufacturing systems ($P < 0.05$). The research results can help interface designers to deeply understand the difference between EID and UCD, which could guide the design of user interface in the complex industrial scenarios.

Keywords: Ecological interface design · User-centered design · User interface · Complex electronics manufacturing systems

1 Introduction

As we known, user-centered design (UCD) and ecological interface design (EID) are both of the two important design methods in the user interface design area. User-centered design is a research framework of design processes that the psychological limitations and physiological limitations of end users are given extensive attention at each stage of the interface design process [1]. Ecological interface design is an approach to user interface design that was introduced specifically for complex sociotechnical, real-time, and dynamic information systems. It has been applied in a

© Springer International Publishing Switzerland 2016
D. Harris (Ed.): EPCE 2016, LNAI 9736, pp. 354–362, 2016.
DOI: 10.1007/978-3-319-40030-3_35

variety of domains including process control such as nuclear power plants, aviation and complex electronics manufacturing systems, etc. [2].

Eason pointed out that sociotechnical system in manufacturing systems is an approach to complex organizational work design that researches the interaction between the user and user interface [3]. However, Vicente & Rasmussen described that complex manufacturing system designed based on traditional methods frequently loses the ability to support sudden failure in system design. System safety is often compromised by the operators' inability to adapt to new and unfamiliar situations [4]. Vicente argued that ecological interface design attempts to provide the operators with the necessary tools and information to become active problem solvers as opposed to passive monitors, particularly during the development of unforeseen failure events [5]. Upton pointed out that manufacturing systems were complex sociotechnical systems, the user interface is also beginning to show information complexity, real-time and dynamic features [6]. Situational awareness (SA) is the field of study concerned with understanding of the environment critical to end users in complex and dynamic work conditions. Designing for situation awareness helps designers understand how user acquire and deal with visual information in user interface of complex electronics manufacturing environment [7].

Currently, user interface in complex electronics manufacturing systems is increasing in information complexity. To take advantage of huge amounts of information in the user interface, we need information displays that transform production data into meaningful information organization. This means developing user interface that clearly connect performance goals to technical processes and physical electronics manufacturing equipment. Behind every user interface in complex electronics manufacturing systems, there lays different degree of information complexity. The solution isn't to reduce information, but to transform it into clear information architecture [8].

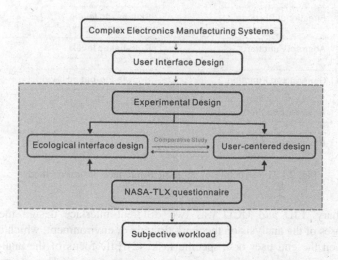

Fig. 1. The theoretical framework of this study

The user interface is the core to control of the electronics manufacturing equipment, user interface is the bridge of transmits the user command to the electronics manufacturing equipment. There were huge differences between the environments, design object, use pattern with the traditional consumer products (especially IT products). As a result, it is becoming more and more difficult for UI designers to anticipate events that occur within electronics manufacturing systems. However, little research has been focused on different subjective workload of the users between EID and UCD method with the user interface design in complex electronics manufacturing systems. Therefore, we started this design research. The theoretical framework of the study was shown in the Fig. 1.

2   Research Method

2.1   Interface Design Methodology: EID vs UCD

User-centered design used to identify user behavior and user's mental model and incorporating them into the user interfaces [9]. The UCD method used to focuses on single user interactions between the user and the user interface [10]. EID contains the abstraction hierarchy (functional purpose; abstract function; generalized function; physical function; physical form) and skills, rules, knowledge (skill-based level; rule-based level; knowledge-based level) framework [11, 12], as shown in Fig. 2.

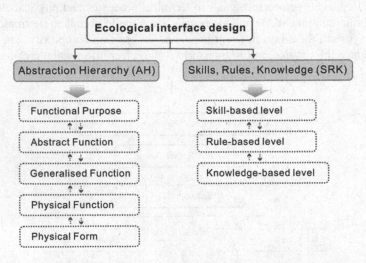

Fig. 2. The structure of ecological interface design method

In summary, EID and UCD was two different interface design methodology. (1) EID focuses of the analysis on the work domain or environment, which differs from UCD focus on the end user or a specific task. (2) EID focus of the analysis on the complex systems, real-time and dynamic systems, in contrast, UCD focus on the simple system, everyday use and static systems. (3) EID theory based on the abstraction hierarchy (AH), The skills, rules, knowledge (SRK) method, in contrast, UCD theory based on the interviews, focus groups, usability test and questionnaire method, as shown in Fig. 3.

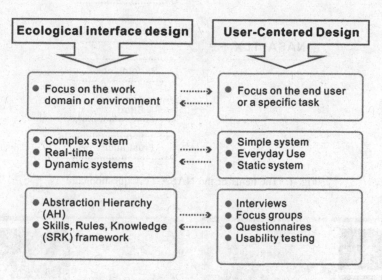

Fig. 3. The difference between EID and UCD

2.2 Experiment Design

The experiment was a within-group design, all participants were tested the two experimental materials. The independent variables in this research were user interface designed based on UCD and EID method in complex electronics manufacturing systems. The dependent variable was measured in NASA-TLX questionnaire. We used the NASA-TLX questionnaire for measuring user subjective workload. The questionnaire for NASA-TLX was designed to assess user's subjective workload assessments on operators working with the user interface. NASA-TLX is a multi-dimensional rating procedure that derives an overall workload score based on a weighted average of ratings on six subscales. These subscales include mental demands, physical demands, temporal demands, performance, effort and frustration, as shown in Fig. 4.

2.3 Material

As the experimental material in this research, we chose the user interface of the LED chip high-speed detection and sorting system, which could provide LED chip testing and sorting functions. Two prototypes of the user interface were designed based on the EID and UCD which is undergoing compare evaluation the subjective workload. Using the simulator technology, the materials were shown in a 19 inches LCD Monitor (16:10, 1440 * 900 pixels), as shown in Figs. 5 and 6.

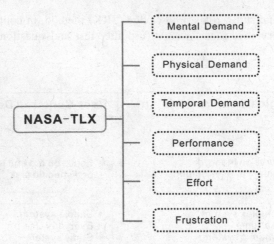

Fig. 4. The items of the NASA-TLX questionnaire

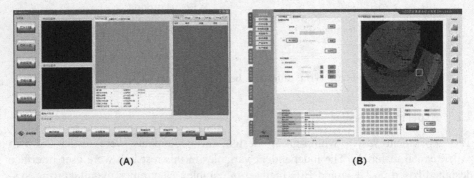

(A)   **(B)**

Fig. 5. The prototypes of the interface design based in UCD (A) and EID (B)

2.4   Participants

A total of 45 operators at Guangdong Zhicheng-Huake Optoelectronic Equipment Co. Ltd. were randomly selected to participate in this experiment, 22 male and 23 female, aged 20–25 (Mean age = 22.13, SD = 1.75) which female of subjects accounted for 51%, male subjects were 49%.

2.5   Procedure

Firstly, participants were asked to read the introduction of the experiment requirements, then signatures in the "Experimental Consent". Test environment was a quiet LED laboratory without interference and noise. Participants were instructed to switch off their mobile phones to reduce possible distractions during the experiment. Next, participants read a short guide manual about the experiment material to insure they were able to understand and solve the given task. When the participant was ready, we started

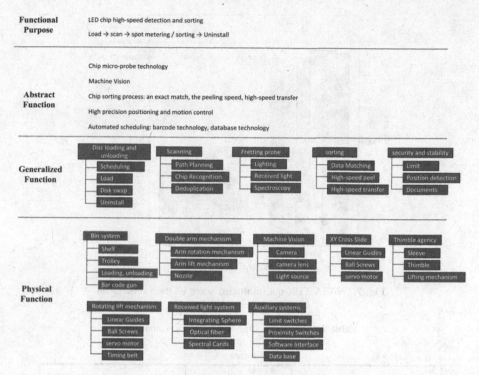

Functional Purpose	LED chip high-speed detection and sorting Load → scan → spot metering / sorting → Uninstall

Fig. 6. Work domain model in LED chip high-speed detection and sorting system

the experiment. Participants were asked to operate on the experimental material for the given task. The duration of each task was 2–3 min based on the task. After each of the experiment task, participants were asked to complete the NASA-TLX questionnaire immediately. The questionnaire answers were manually recorded by the operator. A total of 90 questionnaires were collected after the experiment (45 participants *2 tasks).

3 Results and Discussion

Using IBM SPSS Statistics 19 analysis, the results were as follows:

3.1 The Reliability Analysis

The cronbach's alpha = 0.941, displays the scale of the each project has high internal consistency. Furthermore, mean of mental demands in UCD is 5.58 (Std. Deviation = 1.20), mean of mental demands in EID is 2.62 (Std. Deviation = 1.59). Mean of physical demands in UCD is 5.64 (Std. Deviation = 0.98), mean of physical demands in EID is 2.84 (Std. Deviation = 1.41). Mean of temporal demands in UCD is 5.64 (Std. Deviation = 1.19), mean of temporal demands in EID is 2.93 (Std.

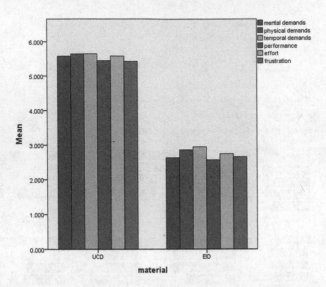

Fig. 7. NASA-TLX questionnaire score of each dimension

Table 1. Results of One-way ANOVA analysis

ANOVA

		Sum of Squares	df	Mean Square	F	Sig.
mental demands	Between Groups	196.544	1	196.544	99.656	.000
	Within Groups	173.556	88	1.972		
	Total	370.100	89			
physical demands	Between Groups	176.400	1	176.400	119.205	.000
	Within Groups	130.222	88	1.480		
	Total	306.622	89			
temporal demands	Between Groups	165.378	1	165.378	116.323	.000
	Within Groups	125.111	88	1.422		
	Total	290.489	89			
performance	Between Groups	187.778	1	187.778	144.669	.000
	Within Groups	114.222	88	1.298		
	Total	302.000	89			
effort	Between Groups	182.044	1	182.044	140.800	.000
	Within Groups	113.778	88	1.293		
	Total	295.822	89			
frustration	Between Groups	173.611	1	173.611	103.727	.000
	Within Groups	147.289	88	1.674		
	Total	320.900	89			

Deviation = 1.19). Mean of performance in UCD is 5.44 (Std. Deviation = 1.20), mean of performance in EID is 2.26 (Std. Deviation = 1.08). Mean of effort in UCD is 5.58 (Std. Deviation = 1.08), mean of effort in EID is 2.73 (Std. Deviation = 1.19). Mean of frustration in UCD is 5.42 (Std. Deviation = 1.23), mean of frustration in EID is 2.64 (Std. Deviation = 1.35), as shown in Fig. 7.

3.2 The ANOVA Analysis

The results showed that the subjective workload rating of material A was significantly higher than material B. It has significant difference subjective workload rating between material A and B, subscales include mental demands ($P < 0.05$), physical demands ($P < 0.05$), temporal demands ($P < 0.05$), performance ($P < 0.05$), effort ($P < 0.05$) and frustration ($P < 0.05$), as shown in Table 1 and Fig. 8.

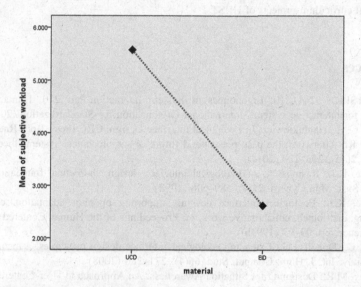

Fig. 8. The difference subjective workload between EID and UCD

4 Conclusions

Although a number of theories and principles have been developed to guide the EID and UCD, it is not always apparent how to apply the knowledge in these principles. We describe the application of EID and UCD for the analysis of the differences. General principles from EID are outlined and then applied to the analysis of the user interface design. This study provided a useful framework for analysis of the EID methods, and provided insights into the strengths and weaknesses of various aspects of EID and UCD.

The main findings of this study were as follows: (1) we found that the ecological interface design and user-centered design had significant differences in each levels; (2) the ecological interface design has a significant better effect on subjective workload compare to user-centered design in the complex electronics manufacturing systems (P < 0.05).

However, the limitations of this research should be discussed. (a) The participants: the participants were all from the same company, so they might have a partiality for this study. In would be beneficial to include a wider range of participation in future research. (b) The experimental materials: we only studied user interface in LED chip high-speed detection and sorting system; future research could use more types of user interfaces. Although this study has its limitation, we hope that it can serve as a basis for future studies.

Acknowledgments. The research financial supports from the Fundamental Research Funds for the Central Universities HUST: (2014QN017). This paper is also supported by the high-level international curriculum projects of HUST.

References

1. ISO, TSISO: 9241–210, Ergonomics of System Interaction-Part 210: Human-centered design for interactive systems. International Organization for Standardization (2010)
2. Burns, C.M., Hajdukiewicz, J.: Ecological Interface Design. CRC Press, Boca Raton (2013)
3. Eason, K.: Afterword: the past, present and future of sociotechnical systems theory. Appl. Ergon. 2(45), 213–220 (2014)
4. Vicente, K.J., Rasmussen, J.: Ecological interface design: theoretical foundations. IEEE Trans. Syst. Man Cybern. 22(4), 589–606 (1992)
5. Vicente, K.J.: Ecological interface design: supporting operator adaptation, continuous learning, distributed, collaborative work. In: Proceedings of the Human Centered Processes Conference, pp. 93–97 (1999b)
6. Upton, C., Doherty, G.: Extending ecological interface design principles: a manufacturing case study. Int. J. Hum. Comput. Stud. 66(4), 271–286 (2008)
7. Endsley, M.R.: Designing for Situation Awareness: An Approach to User-Centered Design. CRC Press, Boca Raton (2011)
8. Hajdukiewicz, J., Burns, C.: Strategies for bridging the gap between analysis and design for ecological interface design. In: Proceedings of the Human Factors and Ergonomics Society Annual Meeting, vol. 48(3), pp. 479–483. SAGE Publications (2004)
9. Maguire, M.: Methods to support human-centred design. Int. J. Hum. Comput. Stud. 55(4), 587–634 (2001)
10. Gulliksen, J., et al.: Key principles for user-centred systems design. Behav. Inf. Technol. 22(6), 397–409 (2003)
11. Carayon, P.: Human factors of complex sociotechnical systems. Appl. Ergon. 37(4), 525–535 (2006)
12. Vicente, K.J.: Ecological interface design: progress and challenges. Hum. Factors: J. Hum. Factors Ergon. Soc. 44(1), 62–78 (2002)

Cognition in Aviation

Scaling the Aircrew Risk-Taking Behavior in Aviation Accidents: The Moderating Role of Phase of Flight

Muhammad Aftab Alam[(✉)]

Iqra University Islamabad, Sector H/9, Islamabad, Pakistan
alamgemex@yahoo.com

Abstract. This study linked aircrew risk-taking behavior to aviation loss, and in this relationship it examined the moderating role of phase-of-flight. First, it developed a measurement model in view of prior accident causation theories and findings of 715 general aviation accidents in Pakistan over a period spanning 2000–2014. Later, it espoused this model for hypotheses testing using original data from 224 randomly chosen accidents and assessed the model through structural path analysis. Results indicated a positive relationship between aircrew risk-taking behavior and aviation loss, and significant moderating role of phase-of-flight.

Keywords: Accident · Risk-taking · Aircrew · Flight · Injury · Aviation-loss

1 Introduction

Why do we have accidents? This query has concerned aviation safety managers for a longtime. Numerous accident causation theories have evolved to explain their occurrence. Starting with "Heinrich's domino theory", the first scientific approach to accident causation in 1920s, several other theories were coined e.g. Human Factors Theory, Accident/Incident Theory, Epidemiological Theory, Systems Theory and Behavior Theory. They were all founded on the ontological position that accidents are "caused", they do not "happen" by chance. Nevertheless, risk-taking is fundamental to every theory of accident causation. While all such theory have merits in explaining aircraft accident per se, none offers empirical measures for estimating aircrew risk-taking behavior (ARTB) and its influence on aviation loss (AL) in accidents.

Aviation history is full of mishaps. Since the advent, when first aircraft crashed after few moments it took off in Kitty Hawk, there is a long trail of mishaps. Many of these accidents were avoidable particularly the more frequent ones. A large number of studies focused on analyzing multi-year accident data have been published e.g., [1, 2]. Notably, these efforts have widely focused on risk as a decision variable but tended to neglect its interaction [3]. In fact, very little is known about how the phase-of-flight, might have affected the ARTB in ensuing AL during accidents.

This study attempted to model the influence of ARTB on AL. Specifically, it addressed two queries: (a) what determines the amount of ARTB and its resulting AL in an accident? And (b) what influence does phase-of-flight have on relationship

© Springer International Publishing Switzerland 2016
D. Harris (Ed.): EPCE 2016, LNAI 9736, pp. 365–376, 2016.
DOI: 10.1007/978-3-319-40030-3_36

between ARTB and AL? The answers to these queries addressed in this study may contribute to the existing body of knowledge advance the present empirical research on risk and aviation safety.

2 Theory and Model Development

In line with the prior researchers [e.g., 4–6] this study approached accident causation through metaphysical presumption of determinism i.e. events (accidents) does not happen by subjective chance, all events have causes, and whatever event (accident) occurs can be connected to other events by general laws [7]. The trade-offs between theory development in social sciences and applying it for developing methods in ergonomics and human factors was dealt with by the work of prior researchers [8]. In developing the method for risk assessment and narrowing the gap of research and practice, simplicity and generality was given more importance than accuracy [9]. A concise outline of the accident causation theories provided foundation for model development.

2.1 Accident Causation Theories

Numerous theories have been developed to describe accident etiology. Starting with industrial safety axioms of Heinrich [4], to the "Domino theory" of Bird [5] and human errors "Swiss cheese model" of Reason [6], have been consistently embraced in aviation scholarship [10]. 'Domino Theory' radically traced the root cause of all mishaps to malfunctions in organizational control. Admittedly, the most significant one has been the narrative of latent and active failures described by Reason [6], in his "Swiss cheese model" of accident causation. It described four stages of crew failure, and suggested that each one triggers the next: (a) organizational influence leading to instance of; (b) unsafe supervision that sets; (c) precondition for; (d) unsafe act of aircrew. Mostly aircraft accident investigations have focused on the last level i.e. the unsafe act. Reason's study changed the course of accident investigation but it lacked necessary details for its application in real world scenario [10]. Unfolding the Reason's design into practical application, Shappell and Wiegmann [11, 12], developed "Human Factors Analysis and Classification System" (HFACS), which is widely being used today for accident investigations. Reason alleged that in complex system, a mishap is the result of unpredictable combinations of organizational and human factors [13].

2.2 Aircrew Risk Taking Behavior

Risk is the probability of mishap and severity of expected loss including damage of property and injury to people that may result from exposure to hazards [14]. Investigations discovered that accidents generally result from wrong decision of aircrew in the face of risky situation [15]. Wiegmann and Shappell [16] argued that aircrafts are reliable, but humans progressively play significant causal role in aircraft accidents. Aircrew has unfitting cockpit culture [17], and suffers from plan-continuation error, whereby they continue with their flight plan despite clear indications in the cockpit, instructions from air traffic controller and dicey weather [18]. Risky attitudes lead to accidents [19]. Mishaps do not occur in isolation, rather it is a chain of events that usually culminate into aircrew risk-taking and unsafe act. Drawing on HFACS, the findings of 715 aircraft accidents investigations in Pakistan over the period spanning 2000–2014 illustrated certain perennial causal factors (hazards) across accidents: (a) Material failure; (b) Bird hit; (c) Weather; (d) Technical failure; (e) Training hazard; (f) Foreign object damage or FOD; (g) Maintenance error; (h) Human error: and (i) Pilot error. The study found that these factors (hazards) pervasively played primary, secondary and (or) contributory role in accident causation. Accepting the avoidable hazards (risk) determine the risk-taking behavior (RTB) of aircrew in an accident. Hence, the ARTB can be measured as:

ARTB = [Risk] x [Avoidability]

or ARTB = [Causal Factors] x [Avoidability]

or ARTB = [Primary + Secondary + Contributory factor] x [Avoidable/Unavoidable]

The operational definition of ARTB is provided in Fig. 1.

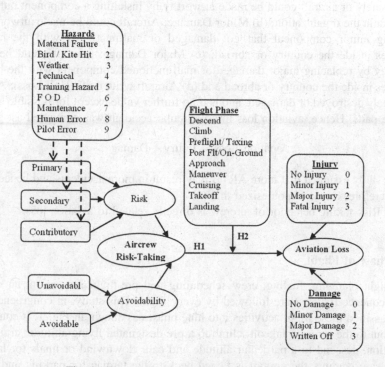

Fig. 1. The ARTBAL model and study hypotheses

2.3   Aviation Loss

Accident can be minor or major, depending upon its resulting loss, which is determined by severity of injuries and extant of damage. The study measured aviation loss of an accident by adding up aircrew injuries and material damage. Previously, several probabilistic models have been proposed for investigating the injury severity that based on various characteristics, allocate occupant in various injury severity segment [20]. In the present study injuries were scaled in a continuum on the basis of their severity (from less to more severe), and classified in four categories: (a) No injury- when there is no injury to aircrew, or the injury is so minor that it does not require medical treatment resulting in absence from normal duty for more than one day; (b) Minor injury: Injury that require proper medical treatment resulting in aircrew absence from duty up to one week; (c) Serious injury: Injury which require medical treatment resulting in aircrew absence more than one week, and may involve trauma to some internal organ, extensive laceration, bone fracture, burn involving more than 5 % of the body and any other condition declared serious by medical authorities; and (d) Fatal injury: Injury which results in the death of occupant. The operational definition of aviation loss is depicted in Fig. 1.

Damage to aircraft was also scaled in a continuum (from less to more severe) in four categories: (a) No damage: when there was no recordable damage and the aircraft landed safely or aircraft could be made airworthy by installing a component out of the shelf within the organization; (b) Minor Damage: Aircraft could be made airworthy by replacing minor component that got damaged or malfunctioned with the help of resources inside the country or abroad; (c) Major Damage: Aircraft could be made airworthy by replacing major damaged or malfunctioned component with the help of resources inside the country or abroad and (d) Aircraft written off (Hull Loss): Aircraft completely destroyed or damaged, and had no further value except for possible salvage of some parts. Hence, aviation loss in a particular accident was computed as:

$$\text{Aviation Loss} = \text{Injury} + \text{Damage}.$$

The study assumed that more ARTB may result in more accidents and hence, more AL. Therefore, it was hypothesized that:

H1: Risk taking behavior of aircrew is directly related to aviation loss.

2.4   Phase of Flight

After flight planning, fueling, crew scheduling and pre-flight inspection, an orchestrated sequence (phases) are followed by every flight. This study, in congruence with [21], classified these flight activities into nine phases as shown in Fig. 1. It comprised taxing out to the runway, takeoff, climb to a pre designated flying altitude; cruising to destination, descend to a particular altitude and calls downwind or finals for landing. After a safe landing, the aircraft is taxied back to the tarmac for parking and a post flight inspection is carried out. Various studies [e.g., 2], disclosed significant involvement of phases-of-flight in accidents. General aviation statistics revealed that majority of these mishaps occurred during landings (24.1 %) and takeoffs (23.4 %).

Also, 3.5 % accidents occur during preflight and taxing, 3.3 % during climb, 15.7 % while cruising, 2.6 % at descent, 13 % while maneuver, 9.7 % at approach and 4.7 % after landing or post flight [21]. Also, [22] found a significant positive effect of psychological function of driving (and presumably, flying) on risk taking behavior. Keeping statistics of prior accidents in view, the study assumed that certain phases such as landing, takeoff etc. have a psychological effect and provide aircrew with more chances to err and take risk, hence, it was hypothesized that:

H2:   The phase-of-flight strengthens the relationship between aircrew risk-taking behavior and aviation loss.

3   Method

The study collected data of 715 general aviation accidents investigations in Pakistan over the fifteen years 2000–2014 for model development in view of HFACS. The model was espoused as precursor for hypotheses testing using data from 224 randomly chosen accidents. The sample satisfied the representativeness and adequacy criteria for parametric tests [23–25]. It also fulfilled the sample-size requirement for modeling crash severity proposed by Ye and Lord [20]. The aircrew and accident profile is provided (Tables 1 and 2). The variables were mean centered to reduce multicollinearity issues [37], and two hypotheses were tested at $\alpha = .05$ significance level using hierarchical multiple regression analysis (Fig. 1). The moderation significance was tested through coefficient's t and F test [26].

Table 1. Accidents profile

Risk				Aircrew Total Flight Hours			
Causal Factors	*Freq*	*%*	*C%*	*Experience*	*Freq*	*%*	*C%*
Bird hit / Kite Hit	18	8.0	8.0	Up to 1000	43	19.2	19.2
Material Failure	83	37.0	45.0	1000- 2000	45	20.1	39.3
Weather	13	5.8	50.8	2000- 3000	47	21.0	60.3
Technical Failure	11	4.9	55.7	3000 - 4000	47	21.0	81.3
Training Hazard	19	8.5	64.2	5000- 6000	34	15.2	96.4
FOD	15	6.7	70.9	6000 +	8	3.6	100
Maintenance Error	8	3.6	74.5	Total	224	100	
Human Error	20	9.0	86.5				
Pilot Error	37	16.5	100				
Total	224	100					

Not. FW - Fixed Wing Aircraft;   HEL - Helicopter;   C% - Cumulative Percentage

Table 2. Accidents profile

Damage To Aircraft				Crew Injuries			
Extant	*Freq*	*%*	*C%*	*Type*	*Freq*	*%*	*C%*
No Damage	19	8.5	8.5	No Injury	169	75.4	75.4
Minor Damage	160	71.4	79.9	Minor Injuries	22	9.8	84.3
Major Damage	27	12.1	92.0	Major Injuries	16	7.1	91.4
Written off	18	8.0	100.0	Fatal	17	7.6	100.0
Total	224	100.0		Total	224	100.0	

Not. C% - Cumulative Percentage

3.1   Independent Variable

Aircrew risk-taking behavior (ARTB) was computed by multiplying risk and avoid-ability. The "Risk" was scaled in nine categories of hazards in a continuum from lesser to more severe depending upon the degree to which they can be avoided by the aircrew. The ranking (provided in Fig. 1) was based on concordance between 18 raters (comprising pilots of varying aircraft type and experience, flying instructors, a flight surgeon, and an aviation psychologist). They rank ordered these factors in a linear continuum from least avoidable to easily avoidable risk, and their ranking consistency was assessed through Kendall's W coefficient (Kendall W = 0.8792, chi-squared = 126.5981, df = 8, p < 0.0001), which indicated a strong degree of agreement [27]. For example, they agreed that avoiding a stray bullet or a small bird becomes very difficult (though a good lookout is always advisable in low level visual meteorological condition-VMC flying); hence, it was assigned the least score.

In case of engine failure, aircrew can land safely if landing ground is available and they follow a standard procedure of emergency landing i.e. "SFO"(simulated flameout) for FW and "Autorotation" for helicopters [28]. Similarly, FOD can be avoided if various procedures in civil aviation and FOD drills in military aviation are religiously followed i.e. if tarmac, taxi-links, holding areas and runway are scanned on weekly basis for debris, loose pebbles and other hazardous material, and their record is maintained. Hence, they are in the middle of the continuum. But, pilot-error depicts aircrew negligence [11, 29]. It represents hazards that could have been avoided easily by adhering to standard procedures, and therefore, it was assigned the maximum score. However, "Avoidability" was scaled nominally i.e. Unavoidable = 1, avoidable = 2.

3.2   Dependent Variable

In a particular accident, AL was computed by adding up severity of injuries and extant of damages. They were scaled using the Fisher's exact test [30], and injury severity (i.e., 0 = No Injury; 1 = Minor Injury; 3 = Serious Injury; and 4 = Fatal Injury), and extant of damage (i.e., 0 = No Damage; 1 = Minor Damage; 3 = Major Damage; and 4 = Aircraft Written off or Hull Loss) was employed.

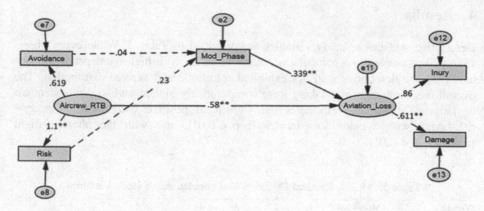

Fig. 2. Latent structure of the ARTBAL model with moderating variables

3.3 Moderating Variable

In line with FAA [21], accident statistics, the phase-of-flight was classified into nine categories in a continuum from less to most probable as: Descend, Climb, Preflight/Taxing, Post Flight/On-Ground, Approach, Maneuver, Cruising, Takeoff and Landing.

3.4 Model Fit

The ARTBAL model along with the moderating variables was evaluated through structural path analysis with renowned model-fit indices. The standard criteria were: Chi-squared/df $\leq$ 5 [31], goodness-of-fit index GFI $\geq$ .90 [32], comparative fit index CFI $\geq$ .90 [33], normed fit index NFI $\geq$ 0.8 and root-mean-square-error of approximation RMSEA $\leq$ .10, through a confidence interval CI of 90 % [34].

The path model (as shown in Fig. 2) converged without iterations and agreeable indices were attained. Since the model had lesser degree of freedom, therefore the absolute fit index with fitted covariance matrix (Chi-squared/df) at 0.05 thresholds was 5.2, and the RMSEA was .105. While these two values were slightly above the upper threshold [31, 34], researchers argued that accidents' data with independent residuals, higher kurtosis values, and small degree of freedom, usually generate inflated Chi-squared values, but the comparative model fit indices are not affected much [35, 36]. Hence, all comparative fit indices of ARTBAL model were well within agreed limits. For example, variance accounted for through anticipated population covariance, the GFI was .941 [23]. Likewise, the NFI .925 indicated that based on the Chi-squared the ARTBAL model enhanced the fit by 92.5 % relative to null model. And, ensuring the least effect of sample size, the CFI of .935 was found. With these parameters, Chi-squared (11, N = 224) = 57.6, p > .05; RMSEA = .105 with 90 % CI {.079, .132}; and CFI = .935, the model provided a reasonable good fit to the data.

4 Results

Descriptive statistics of study variables are provided in Table 3. While every observation corresponded to a particular accidents situation with higher independent residuals [35], the descriptive statistics exhibited a kurtotic and skewed distribution. The overall mean values of risk-taking were comparatively higher, and so do its standard deviation. Table 3 also elucidates the significant positive correlation of aircrew risk-taking with aviation loss ($r = .567$; $p < 0.01$), and with the phase-of-flight ($r = .251$; $p < 0.01$).

Table 3. Means, Standard Deviation and correlations of study Variables

Variables	Mean	S.D.	1	2	3	4	5	6	7	8
1. Aircraft type	3.66	2.331								
2. Phase of flight	5.03	4.174	−.010							
3. Loss	.05	.383	−.010	−.021						
4. Damage	.99	.507	.001	.023	.526**					
5. Experience (Hours)	2.86	1.629	.161*	−.252**	.140	.082				
6. Risk	4.228	5.864	−.042	.287**	.480**	.490**	.045			
7. Risk taking	7.212	11.92	−.050	.251**	.487**	.511**	.053	.988**		
8. Aviation loss	1.052	.8573	−.002	.001	.854**	.876**	.128	.551**	.567**	
9. Avoidability	1.25	.458	−.150*	.256**	.228**	.334**	−.054	.721**	.767**	.320**

Note. * $p \leq .05$. ** $p \leq .01$. (2-Tailed).

Hypotheses were tested systematically while controlling for the effect of previous exogenous and moderating variable in hierarchical regression analysis. Hypothesis 1 proposed the main effect of ARTB. The model accounted for 34.3 % explained variance in AL ($F3, 220 = 32.02$, $R2 = .343$, $p < .001$), and a positive correlation between ARTB and AL was found ($R = .586$, $\beta = .044$, $t = 9.80$, $p < .01$). These results duly supported Hypothesis 1 stating that ARTB is directly related to AL. The addition of moderator "phase-of-flight" in the model demonstrated a significant F change from ($F3, 220 = 32.02$, $p < .001$) to ($F4, 219 = 34.75$, $p < .01$). Moderator phase-of-flight significantly enhanced the positive relationship between ARTB and AL, and increased the explained variance in AL by 5.1 % ($\Delta R2 = .051$, $\beta = .048$, $t = 10.80$, $p > .01$). These results sufficiently supported Hypothesis 2 asserting that the phase-of-flight strengthens the positive relationship between ARTB and AL. The results of all three hypotheses are provided in Table 4.

Table 4. Hierarchical regression analysis

Hypotheses	R	R^2	SE	Change statistics			Coefficients		Decision
				ΔR^2	ΔF	df_{1-2}	B	t	
H1	.586	.343	.70	.343**	32.02	3-220	.044	9.801	Supported
H2	.628	.394	.67	.051**	15.39	4-219	.048	10.809	Supported

Note. ** $p \leq .01$. (2-Tailed),

To probe further, the interaction patterns were plotted through significant change in the slope and intercept of the regression line in accordance with Aiken and West [37], approach as shown in Fig. 3.

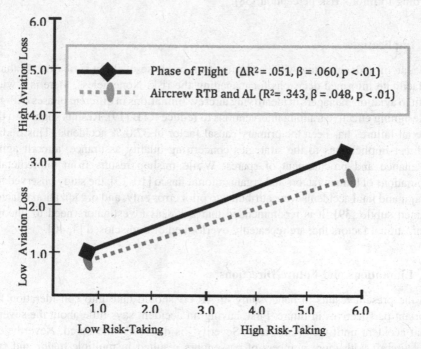

Fig. 3. Interaction Effect depicted through change in the slope and intercept of Regression

5 Discussion

Present study developed a practical model for scaling the ARTB and AL, and analyzed the aircrew behavioral aspect towards risk-taking that led to AL. Results demonstrated a positive relationship between RTB and AL (R = .586, p < .001), and significant moderation effect of phase-of-flight in this relationship. It supported the assertion of Moller and Gregersen [22], regarding a positive psychological function of driving (and presumably, flying) on risk taking behavior. Moreover, accident profile (Table 1) indicated that maximum accidents (25.4 %) occurred during the landing phase, which is slightly higher than accident rate (24.1 %) provided by FAA [21]. Also, phase-of-flight significantly augmented the relationship between RTB and AL by 5.1 % (ΔR2 = .051, p < .01). These results supported the earlier viewpoint that majority of accidents occurred during the critical stage of flight (such as landing) owing to aircrew improper decisions [15]. Present results, though, are in slight variation to the findings of Shaoa et al. [2], who found that maximum accidents in Taiwan occurred during takeoff instead of landing phase. Similarly, it was also noticed that bulk of accidents occurred during a flight phases that demand superior handling (e.g., landings and takeoffs). This finding presumes that alongside ARTB, presence of skill-based errors cannot be ruled out. These findings strengthen the need for enhancing aircrew personal-skills through risk management coaching programs aimed at transforming risk perception and attitudes towards risky flying, and designing aviation infrastructure according to pilot's risk perception [38].

5.1 Implications

The value of understanding ARTB as a function of phase-of-flight is obvious in that it will facilitate informed decisions for managing the risk. Nonetheless, there is a wider benefit to aviation managers in identifying aircrew limitations in different phases of flight, and designing effective training interventions to reduce RTB [19]. Results suggested that "material failure" has been the primary causal factor in 37.0 % accidents. This finding has direct implications to the strategies concerning quality assurance, aircraft aging, maintenance and procurement of spares. While mishap results from unpredictable combinations of human factors and organizational fiasco [10, 13], the study observed that all major and fatal accidents were attributed to pilot error only, and organizational factors remained subtle [39]. It is recommended that accident investigators need to uncover organizational factors that are repeatedly overlooked or undisclosed [4, 40].

5.2 Limitations and Future Directions

With the present results in hand, study in ARTB should take into consideration few important perspectives in future. First, having an accident says little about the severity of that accident until the "Rate" and "Severity" is discretely measured. Nevertheless, larger aircraft with more numbers of passengers resulted in multiple major and fatal injuries, and in many accidents damages were more expensive to be fixed. If these variables are measured precisely, the present results can be replicated with greater confidence in future studies. Second, more experienced pilots are less likely to be involved in air accident than less experienced pilots [1]. More flight experience also provides aircrew with more chances to err. Hence, future study in ARTB should also take aircrew flight experience in consideration. And last, as do others [e.g., 35], this study also recognized the inbuilt limitation of frequentist approach in dealing with aircraft accidents data, and recommends trying a Bayesian approach in future study.

5.3 Conclusion

In conclusion, this study presented a practical model for measuring aircrew risk-taking behavior and aviation loss, and provided empirical evidence that they are directly related in general aviation accidents. The relationship gets stronger when aircrew faces diverse situations in varying phases of flight. Numerous factors limit the generalization of these findings. Nevertheless, the results are noteworthy in their own domain and warrants ex-ante measures for measuring potential risks associated with every phase of flight. If it were assumed that aircrew is driven by complacency and obsolescence, the cause of their risk-taking propensity at different phases of flight would clearly be more essential and justifiable for further study.

References

1. Rebok, G., Qiang, Y., Baker, S., McCarthy, M., Li, G.: Age, flight experience, and violation risk in mature commuter and air taxi pilots. Int. J. Aviat. Psychol. 15(4), 363–374 (2005)
2. Shaoa, P., Changa, Y., Chenb, H.J.: Analysis of an aircraft accident model in taiwan. J. Air Transp. Manage. 27, 34–38 (2013). doi:10.1016/j.jairtraman.2012.11.004
3. Ross, D.G.: Taking a chance: a formal model of how firms use risk in strategic interaction with other firms. Acad. Manage. Rev. 39(2), 202–226 (2014). doi:10.5465/amr.2012.0107
4. Heinrich, H., Petersen, D., Roos, N.: Industrial Accident Prevention: A Safety Management Approach, 5th edn. McGraw Hill, New York (1980)
5. Bird, F.: Management Guide to Loss Control. Institute Press, Atlanta (1974)
6. Reason, J.: Human Error. Cambridge University Press, New York (1990)
7. Abel, R.: Man is the Measure: A Cordial Invitation to the Central Problems in Philosophy. The Free Press, New York (1976)
8. Weick, K.: The Social Psychology of Organizing. Addison-Wesley, Reading (1979). Weick, K.E., Roberts, K.H.: Collective Mind in organizations: heedful interrelating on flight decks. Adm. Sci. Q. 38, 357–381 (1993)
9. Waterson, P., Clegg, C., Robinson, M.: Trade-offs between reliability, validity and utility in the development of human factors methods Human Factors In: Organizational Design And Management – XI, Nordic Ergonomics Society Annual Conference-46 (2014). doi:10.4122/dtu:2406
10. Underwood, P., Waterson, P.: Systems thinking, the swiss cheese model and accident analysis: a comparative systemic analysis of the grayrigg train derailment using the ATSB, AcciMap and STAMP models. Accid. Anal. Prev. 68, 75–94 (2014)
11. Shappell, S., Wiegmann, D.: The Human Factors Analysis and Classification System (HFACS). Federal Aviation Administration, Office of Aviation Medicine Report No. DOT/FAA/AM-00/7. Office of Aviation Medicine: Washington, DC (2000)
12. Shappell, S., Wiegmann, D.: Applying Reason: the Human Factors Analysis and Classification System (HFACS). Hum. Factors Aerosp. Saf. 1, 59–86 (2001)
13. Fajer, M., Almeida, I.M., Fischer, F.M.: Contributive factors to aviation accidents. Rev. Saude Publica 45(2), 432–435 (2011)
14. FAA: Aviation Instructor's Handbook. FAA-H-8083-9A. Skyhorse Publishing Inc., New York (2008)
15. Bourgeon, L., Valot, Ç., Navarro, C.: Communication and flexibility in aircrews facing unexpected and risky situations. Int. J. Aviat. Psychol. 23(4), 289–305 (2013)
16. Wiegmann, D.A., Shappell, S.A.: Human error perspectives in aviation. Int. J. Aviat. Psychol. 11(4), 341–357 (2001b). doi:10.1207/S15327108IJAP1104_2
17. Alam, M.A.: Cockpit learning in power distant cockpits: the interaction effect of Pilot's interdependence and inclination to teamwork in airline industry. J. Air Transp. Manage. 42, 192–202 (2015)
18. Orasanu, J., Martin, L., Davison, J.: Cognitive and Contextual Factors in Aviation Accidents: Decision Errors. In: Salas, E., Klein, G.A. (eds.) Linking Expertise and Naturalistic Decision Making, pp. 209–225. Erlbaum, Mahwah (2001)
19. David, R., Hunter, D.R.: Measurement of hazardous attitudes among pilots. Int. J. Aviat. Psychol. 15(1), 23–43 (2005). doi:10.1207/s15327108ijap1501_2
20. Ye, F., Lord, D.: Comparing three commonly used crash severity models on sample size requirements: multinomial logit, ordered probit and mixed logit models. Analytic Methods Accid. Res. 1, 72–85 (2014)

21. FAA: Pilot's Handbook of Aeronautical Knowledge. Aeronautical Decision-Making: FAA-H-8083-25A. Skyhorse Publishing Inc., New York (2009)

22. Moller, M., Gregersen, P.: Psychosocial function of driving as predictor of risk-taking behavior. Accid. Anal. Prev. **40**(1), 209–215 (2008)

23. Tabachnick, B.G., Fidell, L.S.: Using Multivariate Statistics, 3rd edn. Harper Collins, New York (1996)

24. Hair, J.F., Black, W.C., Babin, B.J., Anderson, R.E., Tatham, R.L.: Multivariate Data Analysis, 6th edn. Prentice Hall, Upper Saddle River (2005)

25. Sekaran, U.: Research Methods for Business: A Skill Building Approach, 4th edn. Wiley India Pvt, Limited (2006)

26. Bedeian, A.G., Mossholder, K.W.: Simple question, not so simple answer: interpreting interaction terms in moderated multiple regression. J. Manage. **20**, 159–165 (1994)

27. Siegel, S., Castellan, N.J.: Nonparametric Statistics for the Behavioural Sciences. McGraw-Hill, New York (1988)

28. FAA: Air Traffic Organization Policy. Order JO7110.65 V. U.S. Department of Transportation (2014)

29. Wiegmann, D.A., Shappell, S.A.: Human error analysis of commercial aviation accidents: application of the human factors analysis and classification system (HFACS). Aviat. Space Environ. Med. **72**(11), 1006–1016 (2001a)

30. Hinkelbein, J., Spelten, O., Neuhaus, C., Hinkelbein, M., Özgür, E., Wetsch, W.: Injury severity and seating position in accidents with german EMS helicopters. Accid. Anal. Prev. **59**, 283–288 (2013)

31. Marsh, H.W., Hocevar, D.: Application of confirmatory factor analysis to the study of self-concept: first- and higher order factor models and their invariance across groups. Psychol. Bull. **97**, 562–582 (1985)

32. Byrne, B.M.: Structural Equation Modeling With EQS and EQS/Windows. Sage, Thousand Oaks (1994)

33. Hu, L., Bentler, P.M.: Fit indices in covariance structure modeling: sensitivity to underparameterized model misspecification. Psychol. Methods **3**, 424–453 (1998)

34. Kline, R.B.: Principles and Practice of Structural Equation Modeling, 3rd edn. Guilford Press, New York (2010)

35. Huang, H., Abdel-Aty, M.: Multilevel data and Bayesian analysis in traffic safety. Accid. Anal. Prev. **42**(6), 1556–1565 (2010). doi:10.1016/j.aap.2010.03.013

36. Kenny, D.A., Kaniskan, B., McCoach, D.B.: The performance of RMSEA in models with small degrees of freedom. Sociol. Methods Res. **44**, 486–507 (2015)

37. Aiken, L.S., West, S.G.: Multiple Regression: Testing and Interpreting Interactions. Sage, Thousand Oaks (1991)

38. Joseph, C., Reddy, S.: Risk perception and safety attitudes in Indian Army aviators. Int. J. Aviat. Psychol. **23**(1), 49–62 (2013). doi:10.1080/10508414.2013.746531

39. Dismukes, K., Young, G., Sumwalt, R.: Cockpit interruptions and distractions: effective management requires a careful balancing act. Airline Pilot **68**(5), 18–21 (1999)

40. Thaden, T.L., Wiegmann, D.A., Shappell, S.A.: Organizational factors in commercial aviation accidents. Int. J. Aviat. Psychol. **16**(3), 239–261 (2006). doi:10.1207/s15327108ijap1603_1

Research of Image Recognition Training Method on Manual Rendezvous and Docking

Jiayi Cai[1(✉)], Bin Wu[1], Xiang Zhang[1], Jie Li[1], and Weifen Huang[1,2]

[1] China Astronaut Research and Training Center, Beijing 100094, China
abstemious_cjy@163.com
[2] National Key Laboratory of Human Factors Engineering, China Astronaut
Research and Training Center, Beijing 100094, China

Abstract. Astronauts may need to face a lot of complex operations and the emergency in the future space station mission. The manual rendezvous and docking image recognition training method was established based on meta-cognition in this study.

In this research, they were analyzed about the cognitive task and the image recognition process of rendezvous and docking mission. The meta-cognitive question list which help subjects to monitor their own cognitive process was designed depending on the difficulty of image recognition, then establish the meta-cognitive auxiliary training method.

By implementing metacognitive training, the following research conclusions were obtained: Metacognitive levels and self-learning results of the RVD Pictorial Handbook Test were positively correlated: Metacognitive training could effectively enhance participants' metacognitive levels and Metacognitive training could effectively enhance participants' image recognition abilities.

Keywords: Metacognition · RVD · Training · Image recognition

1 Introduction

In future space station missions, manual rendezvous and docking (RVD) operations will be one of the basic operational skills required by astronauts. Throughout this process, astronauts will need to continuously alternate between image perception and decision-making activities, and the results of each decision will provide new status information for subsequent image perception, until docking between the spacecraft and the target aerospace vehicle (AV) is complete [1, 2]. Therefore, under such cognitively demanding operational conditions, it is necessary to further build on the foundations of currently established manual RVD training to explore and establish training methods for image perception and decision-making based on metacognitive theories. This will further enhance the outcomes of manual RVD training, thus adapting to the needs of future space missions.

D. Harris (Ed.): EPCE 2016, LNAI 9736, pp. 377–388, 2016.
DOI: 10.1007/978-3-319-40030-3_37

2 Analysis of Manual Rendezvous and Docking Missions

The operational activities of astronauts during manual RVD missions include three components: perception of image information, decision-making on control strategy, and implementation of operational actions [5].

2.1 Perception of Image Information

The images received by the astronauts come directly from the TV camera installed on the spacecraft, which photographs the target AV from the perspective of the spacecraft [6]. The image information is then transmitted to the display on the spacecraft. As the display presents the information in the form of 2D images, the astronauts are required to reconstruct the spatial relationship between the two AVs based on the images. In other words, they need to visualize the relative positional and attitudinal relationships in 3D based on the 2D image information [4]. However, during actual operations, astronauts often make mistakes during image perception, such as judgment errors in attitudinal and directional relationships, and in spatial position relationships, which might lead to decisions to operate the wrong control levers, thus increasing fuel consumption and failures in smooth docking.

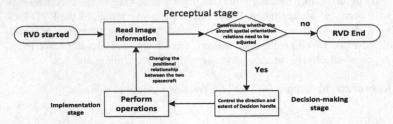

Fig. 1. The three processes of perception, decision-making, and implementation in manual rendezvous and docking [10]

2.2 Decision-Making on Control Strategies

Once the astronauts have perceived the image information, they make control decisions, which determine the selection of the control levers, as well as the direction and magnitude of the operations. The basis for decision-making stems from the spatial cognitive model formed during the perception stage, and the rules for lever control. Correct decision-making is a prerequisite and foundation of implementing operations.

2.3 Operation Implementation

The astronauts implement operational actions based on their decisions. During this process, they will perform actual operations on the control levers in order to control the spacecraft by adjusting its relative attitude and position. This process directly influences RVD outcomes (Fig. 1).

3   Training Design

Current training for manual RVD is mainly implemented through instructor teaching with excessive emphasis on the operations and operational strategies, and no in-depth coverage of the cognitive aspects. The primary focus of this study is the accuracy of image perception and operational decisions, combined with metacognitive strategies, in order to create an RVD pictorial handbook for use as training material. The RVD pictorial handbook comprises typical images acquired during the manual RVD process, and is a breakdown of the RVD process. This enables the targeted training of astronauts for missions with greater difficulty and larger deviations, as well as to improve on their weaker cognitive aspects.

3.1   Classification of Task Difficulty

Typical tasks performed during RVD operations were identified through expert interviews. Cognitive task decomposition was then used to analyze the process of perceptual judgment by the participants in order to ascertain the difficult and easy aspects of cognition. Next, the difficulty levels of the images in the RVD pictorial handbook were classified by combining the positional deviations between the AVs and the magnitude of the spacecraft yaw attitude.

3.2   Metacognitive Training Strategy

The focus of metacognitive strategies is on the participants' monitoring of their cognitive status and regulation of cognitive processes, thereby allowing them to achieve cognitive goals [3]. The two processes undertaken by astronauts when learning the pictorial handbooks (image perception and determination of operational decisions) were divided into five steps based on Gick's model of problem solving: viewing the images, re-stating the images, model placement, operation planning and implementation, and operation evaluation [9]. Metacognitive questions were designed for each step to guide the participants in planning their own problem-solving methods [8]. The participants searched for appropriate image recognition features and recognition strategies independently in order to complete judgments on the positions of the two AVs and the attitude of their own spacecraft in the images. Guidance was also provided for the monitoring of their cognitive processes (Fig. 2).

Fig. 2. Images of three different initial deviations

4 Experiment

4.1 Experimental Aims

Our aim was to investigate the effects of metacognitive training on RVD training outcomes in operators. Volunteers were recruited and assigned to either the control group, where they underwent training through independent learning, or the experimental group, where they underwent supplementary metacognitive training. Experimental research was employed to investigate the effectiveness of our training method.

A between-group design was adopted for the experiment. The independent variable was the two different training methods, and the dependent variables were the RVD image perception and decision-making abilities, and level of metacognitive ability. Perceptual and decision-making abilities were evaluated using the results of the RVD Pictorial Handbook Test.

4.2 Experimental Setup and Materials

The experimental materials required included: the Metacognition Scale, RVD Pictorial Handbook, RVD Pictorial Handbook Test, and Manual of Metacognitive Training Procedures.

(1) Manual of Metacognitive Training Procedures. By summarizing the operators' perceptions and judgment procedures during the RVD process, we developed a set of metacognitive training procedures. The metacognition group followed the related questions listed in the procedures to report their learning processes during training, including learning methods and judgment criteria, as well as their thought processes (see the Appendix for detailed procedures).

(2) Metacognition Scale. This scale was designed with reference to the Metacognitive Awareness Inventory (MAI) developed by Schraw in order to test the participants' levels of metacognition [11]. The three main dimensions included metacognitive knowledge, metacognitive awareness, and metacognitive strategies, which were intended to measure the participants' levels of metacognition.

(3) RVD Pictorial Handbook. The RVD Pictorial Handbook was used as the training material. It comprises images of the target AV acquired by the spacecraft camera at specific orbital positions during the RVD process. The participants were required to judge the positional and attitudinal information of both AVs based on the handbook (i.e., to identify whether there were translational or yaw deviations, and provide a rough judgment on the magnitude of the deviations).

(4) RVD Pictorial Handbook Test. Two sets of test papers with comparable difficulty were developed according to the knowledge of the RVD image recognition taught during training. One set was randomly selected for the pre-test and the other for the post-test.

(5) Desktop RVD Training Platform. This platform could be used to accomplish the design and development of functional modules, such as Guidance, Navigation and Control (GNC) modeling and simulation, TV image simulation, docking mechanism simulation, data storage and playback, and so forth. The platform strived for similarity between the simulated and real-world environments, and realistic modeling and simulation were performed for GNC and dynamics, docking mechanism, instruments, TV images, and other factors. The results were approved and confirmed by the project developers. The platform also took into account the flexibility requirements during experimental application; hence, the platform was equipped with functions, such as configurable experimental protocol and initial information, real-time recording of various performance data during the experiment, and complete recording and playback of experimental data and image information. This platform produced good simulation results and design, while also providing flexible configuration of experimental protocol, and accurate and complete records of experimental data. Thus, it established an excellent foundation for our experiment.

4.3   Experimental Methods

The duration of the entire experimental process lasted 60 days, and included three stages: participant selection and grouping, theoretical training, and operation implementation.

(1) Participant Selection and Grouping. Before the experiment commenced, participants were selected and asked to sign the informed consent form. Measurements of basic cognitive abilities related to RVD, metacognitive ability, and personality were then performed. Next, the participants received a general theoretical and operational explanation, and then performed a practical RVD operation. The test results were then used to evenly divide the participants into Groups A and B (i.e., experimental and control groups, respectively) according to their ability levels. Measurement of basic cognitive ability was based on the discussions of the instructors and experts with rich experience in RVD; a total of eight items were tested including: scale comparison, visual interference avoidance, judgment of spatial position, speed estimation, instrument comprehension, mental rotation, and visual changes. The Big Five Personality Test was used to measure the participants' personality traits, and screening was performed. Metacognitive ability was measured using the Metacognition Scale, which was modified from the MAI developed by Schraw. The participants were randomly divided into two groups based on their metacognitive ability and individual items of cognitive ability.

(2) Theoretical Training. Before implementing the experiment, the chief astronaut instructor provided theoretical training on RVD techniques and operational strategies to beginner-level participants. Next, the participants performed three practical operational exercises on the RVD training platform under the real-time supervision of the main experimenter. Through the practical exercises, participants were able to master basic image recognition skills, as well as operational methods and strategies. They had essentially achieved the skill requirements of manual RVD operations (Fig. 3).

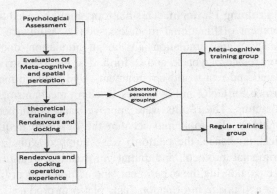

Fig. 3. Workflow of experimental preparations

(3) Experimental Implementation. The RVD training experiment formally began at the end of theoretical training. In this stage, participants in the experimental and control groups received five rounds of RVD training; each round involved 30 min of RVD Pictorial Handbook self-learning, and six sessions of manual RVD operations. During the 30 min training with the RVD Pictorial Handbook, the experimental group use the Manual of Metacognitive Training Procedures during learning, whereas the control group only undertook self-learning. After the completion of the training experiment, post-testing of metacognitive levels, as well as manual RVD image perception and decision-making abilities were performed in both groups (Fig. 4).

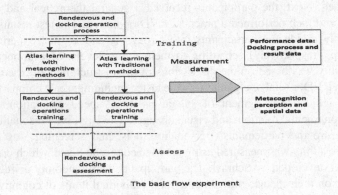

Fig. 4. Basic experimental flow

5   Experiment Results and Analysis

5.1   Pre-test Descriptive Statistics of Relevant Variables

In the experimental design, the control group learned the materials of the RVD Pictorial Handbook through independent learning. Next, they undertook the RVD Pictorial

Handbook Test, and obtained their results. The metacognitive levels were also measured before and after training using the Metacognition Scale. Correlational analysis was then performed on the results.

As shown in Tables 1 and 2, participants' metacognitive levels and self-learning outcomes of the RVD Pictorial Handbook showed a significantly positive correlation ($P < 0.01$). This indicates that after independent learning, participants' self-learning results and their existing levels of metacognition were closely related. Participants with higher levels of metacognition were able to obtain better results on the RVD Pictorial Handbook test after independent learning; participants with lower levels of metacognition scored less well on the test after independent learning of the RVD Pictorial Handbook.

Table 1. Participants' existing metacognitive levels and self-learning results

Variable	Mean	SD	Minimum	Maximum	Kurtosis
Metacognitive level	57.20	7.73	44.86	70.93	−0.744
Test results	27.63	13.72	9.09	55.68	−0.738

Table 2. Correlational analysis of participants' metacognitive levels and test results

	Pictorial handbook test results
Metacognitive level	0.700**

5.2 Difference Testing of Pre- and Post-Test Metacognitive Levels and RVD Pictorial Handbook Test Scores in the Experimental and Control Groups

(1) Difference testing of pre- and post-test metacognitive levels and self-learning results in the control group

During the experiment, the control group undertook independent learning when the experimental group was undergoing metacognitive training. Difference testing of pre- and post-test metacognitive levels and self-learning results of the control group can be found in the tables below (Fig. 5).

As shown in Tables 3 and 4, when $t = -1.96$, $P = 0.847$ ($P > 0.05$); hence, there was no significant difference between the pre- and post-test results for the participants' metacognitive levels in the control group. Furthermore, when $t = -1.831$, $P = 0.082$ ($P > 0.05$); hence, the difference between the pre- and post-test results of the RVD Pictorial Handbook self-learning was not significant in the control group (Fig. 6).

(2) Difference testing of pre- and post-test metacognitive levels and self-learning results in the experimental group

As shown in Tables 5 and 6, when $t = -2.994$, $P = 0.009$ ($P < 0.05$); hence, there was a significant difference between the pre- and post-test results of the metacognitive levels in the experimental group. Furthermore, when $t = -3.798$, $P = 0.02$ ($P < 0.05$);

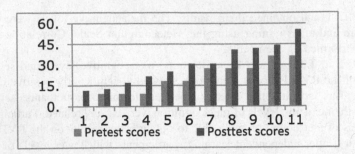

Fig. 5. Pre- and post-test results of the RVD Pictorial Handbook self-learning in the control group

Table 3. Difference testing of pre- and post-test self-learning results in the control group

	Group	Mean score	SD	t	P
Test results	Pre-test results	19	12.07	−1.831	0.082
	Post-test results	30	14.30		

Table 4. Difference testing of pre- and post-test metacognitive levels in the control group

	Group	Mean score	SD	t	P
Metacognitive level	Pre-test results	57.50	8.09	−1.96	0. 847
	Post-test results	58.18	7.90		

hence, the difference between the pre- and post-test results of the RVD Pictorial Handbook Test was significant in the experimental group. This indicates that after the participants in the experimental group undertook metacognitive training, their metacognition and self-learning results of the RVD Pictorial Handbook improved significantly.

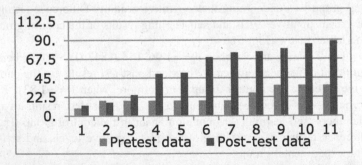

Fig. 6. Pre- and post-test results of the RVD Pictorial Handbook self-learning in the experimental group

Table 5. Difference testing of pre- and post-test self-learning results in the experimental group

	Group	Mean score	SD	t	P
Test results	Pre-test results	23.14	9.41	−3.798	0.02
	Post-test results	57.13	28.15		

Table 6. Difference testing of pre- and post-test metacognitive levels in the experimental group

	Group	Mean score	SD	t	P
Metacognitive level	Pre-test results	59.21	7.16	−2.994	0.009
	Post-test results	72.66	13.05		

5.3 Analysis of Post-Test Metacognitive Levels and the RVD Pictorial Handbook Test Results

(1) Difference testing of the post-test metacognitive levels

The metacognitive levels of participants in the experimental and control groups were measured again after training, and difference testing was performed on the post-test results (Table 7).

Table 7. Difference testing of post-test metacognitive levels

	Group	Mean score	SD	t	P
Metacognitive level	Experimental group	72.66	13.05	2.93	0.011
	Control group	60.14	5.46		

As shown in Table 7, for the post-test metacognitive levels, when t = 2.93, P = 0.011 (P < 0.05); this indicates that the metacognitive levels after training in the experimental group were significantly higher than that of the control group. Targeted training of metacognitive skills was performed during the training process, such as guiding the participants in formulating plans for image recognition, regulating learning strategies, monitoring their own cognitive status, and reflecting on the shortcomings in their own cognition. These skills also formed the basic content of the Metacognition Scale. Hence, after a period of training, the experimental group showed significantly better performance than the control group (Fig. 7).

(2) Difference testing of the post-test RVD Pictorial Handbook test results

The RVD Pictorial Handbook Test was performed in the experimental and control groups after training, and difference testing was performed on the post-test results (Table 8).

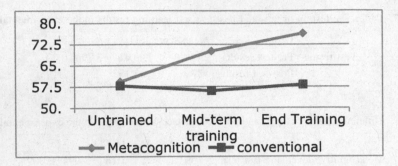

Fig. 7. Plot of changes in the metacognitive ability in both groups

Table 8. Difference testing of the post-test RVD Pictorial Handbook self-learning results

	Group	Mean score	SD	T	P
Results	Experimental group	72.66	13.05	2.93	0.011
	Control group	60.14	5.46		

As shown in Table 8, when t = 2.93, P = 0.011 (P < 0.05). After metacognitive training, the RVD self-learning results of the experimental group were significantly higher than those of the control group. This indicates that metacognitive training could effectively enhance the results of the RVD Pictorial Handbook Test. During RVD perceptual and operational training combined with the RVD Pictorial Handbook, targeted participant training was achieved. This included cultivating independent thinking, image analysis, self-reporting on the processes during image perception to operational decision-making, spatial imagination, and self-learning ability (Fig. 8).

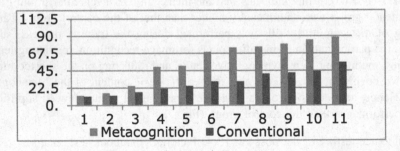

Fig. 8. Post-test learning results of the experimental and control groups

6 Conclusions and Discussion

By implementing metacognitive training, the following research conclusions were obtained:

6.1 Metacognitive Levels and Self-Learning Results of the RVD Pictorial Handbook Test Were Positively Correlated

Participants with high metacognitive levels had a better grasp of the knowledge of interpreting the images in the RVE Pictorial Handbook, and their success rates for the test questions were also higher. This implies that their self-learning outcomes were better. Therefore, increasing metacognitive levels could increase their self-learning outcomes.

6.2 Metacognitive Training Could Effectively Enhance Participants' Metacognitive Levels

After a period of metacognitive training in the experimental group, their metacognitive levels were significantly higher than those of the control group. This also indicates that the metacognitive levels of the experimental group had improved significantly, which once again verifies that performing metacognitive training during the learning process of the RVD Pictorial Handbook was effective.

6.3 Metacognitive Training Could Effectively Enhance Participants' Image Recognition Abilities

The self-learning results for the RVD Pictorial Handbook Test were performed on both groups before the experiment; the between-group difference in the test results was not significant. However, after a period of RVD training, the post-test determined that the test results of the experimental group were significantly higher than those of the control group, and the between-group difference was significant. This implies that metacognitive training significantly enhanced the RVD image interpretation abilities of the experimental group.

Acknowledgement. This research was financially supported by the Fund of Chinese Manned Spaceflight (2014SY54A0001).

References

1. Jianping, Z.: Rendezvous and docking technology of manned space flight. Manned Spacefl. **17**(2), 1–8 (2011)
2. Weifen, H.: Review and outlook of china's astronaut selection and training. Space Med. Med. Eng. **03**, 175–181 (2008)
3. Flavell, J.H.: Metacognitive aspects of problem solving. Nat. Intell. **12**, 231–235 (1976)
4. Bin, W., Meng, W., Yijing, Z., et al.: Investigation on operator's situation awareness and mental workload during manually controlled rendezvous and docking. Manned Spacefl. **20** (4), 378–385 (2014)
5. Dehan, W., Weifen, H.: Astrounat task analysis. Space Med. Med. Eng. **9**(4), 454–459 (1996)

6. Chunhui, W., Ting, J.: Study on ergonomics design of displays - control system in manual-control rendezvous and docking. Manned Spacefl. **17**(2), 50–53 (2011)
7. Frith, C.D.: The role of metacognition in human social interactions. Philos. Trans. R. Soc. B Biol. Sci. **367**(1599), 2213–2223 (2012)
8. Yeung, N., Summerfield, C.: Metacognition in human decision-making: confidence and error monitoring. Philos. Trans. R. Soc. B Biol. Sci. **367**(1594), 1310–1321 (2012)
9. Gick, M.L., Lockhart, R.S.: Cognitive and affective components of insight. In: The Nature of Insight, p. 618. The MIT Press, Cambridge (1995)
10. Yu, T.: Research on the key characteristics of cognitive manual rendezvous and docking tasks. Chinese astronaut center (2012)
11. Schraw, G., Dennison, R.S.: Assessing metacognitive awareness. Contemp. Educ. Psychol. **19**(4), 460–475 (1994)

Pilots' Latency of First Fixation and Dwell Among Regions of Interest on the Flight Deck

Hong-Fa Ho[1(✉)], Hui-Sheng Su[1], Wen-Chin Li[2], Chung-San Yu[2], and Graham Braithwaite[2]

[1] Department of Electrical Engineering,
National Taiwan Normal University, Taipei, Taiwan
jackho@ntnu.edu.tw

[2] Safety and Accident Investigation Centre, Cranfield University, Cranfield, UK

Abstract. The purpose of this pilot study is to investigate the differences of eye movements among three different flight backgrounds. There were eleven participants (2 military pilots with average 2,250 flying hours, 6 commercial pilots with average 5,360 flying hours, and 3 novices). All participants wear a mobile eye tracker during the experiment operating a Boeing 747 flight simulator for landing. The eye tracker recorded all participants' eye movement data automatically. The average values of the latency of first fixation (LFF) and the total contact time (TCT) for five regions of interest (ROIs) are used to examine proposed hypotheses. The findings include: (1) participants of different flight backgrounds have different sequences of viewing ROIs; (2) participants of military pilots and novices spent most of time viewing the outside of cockpit (ROI-3); however, participants of commercial pilots spent most of time viewing the Primary Flight Display (ROI-1). Current research findings might be applied for developing conversion training for military pilots conversed to civil airlines pilots. The fundamental reasons of why pilots viewing ROIs in different sequence and spending significant different time on the ROIs needed to be studied further in the future.

Keywords: Attention distribution · Eye movement · Fixation duration · Flight deck design

1 Introduction

Landing is one of the most dangerous stage related to high accident rate (56 %), followed by take-off (27 %) and approach (15 %) phases [1]. With such huge number of accidents occurring during landing, it is important to enhance training methods for pilots. Pilots operate aircraft mainly by visual perception to process symbols, number, texts and flashing warning signals present on interface displays on the flight deck. Pilots process information through vision, eyesight is often more directed and attracted to texts, pictures, and animation [2]. Therefore, eye-tracking technology has been used to conduct various studies, such as visual and content design [3], reading strategy [4] and dashboard design [5]. In this study, researchers used eye gaze data to analyze

© Springer International Publishing Switzerland 2016
D. Harris (Ed.): EPCE 2016, LNAI 9736, pp. 389–396, 2016.
DOI: 10.1007/978-3-319-40030-3_38

participants' eye movements in order to find out whether or not there are differences between the novice and expert viewing the flight deck during the airplane landing.

Eye movements consist of a series of fixations and saccades [6]. When a pilot performs visual search, the eyes move rapidly from one gaze point to another. Most visual information is obtained through fixations which are formed when a pause exists between gaze points. The previous study indicated that eye movements can be useful cues to indicate a pilot's current cognitive state and to explore their operational behaviour [7]. The eye movement pattern and cognitive process are closely related to interface design and the development of training syllabus [8], e.g., it was found that expert pilots had significantly shorter fixation duration and more total fixations [9] than novice. Also, experts had more fixations on airspeed and fewer fixations on altimeter than novices. Experts were also found to have better defined eye-scanning patterns [10]. However, due to the limited capacity of a human's working memory, it is necessary to distribute attention on the most critical task at hand when selecting the visual channel to be attentive to [11, 12]. Two of eye movement variables, the latency of first fixation (LFF) and total contact time (TCT), are usually used to assess participants' attention distribution. For examples, the shorter the LFF paid on a region of interest (ROI), the more attractive it is to the participant; the longer the TCT, the more attractive the ROI is to the participant [13].

Previous research indicated that operator's performance is impacted by the tools, tasks and environments in which they operate [14]. Pilots' attention distribution could be influenced by the types of aircraft, the features of operational context, and the specific organization where they come from. Hence, to investigate visual scan patterns not only benefits the understandings of pilots' attention distribution, but also can be applied to improve the safety and efficiency of pilot's conversion training. Based on the literature review, two null hypotheses were generated as followings.

H_1: There are no differences of viewing sequences among pilots.
H_2: There are no differences of the total contact time of eye movements among pilots.

2 Methodology

2.1 Participants

There were eleven participants (2 military pilots with average 2,250 flying-hours, 6 commercial pilots with average 5,360 flying-hours, and 3 novices). Due to the number of participants in this pilot study was small, the arithmetic mean was chosen instead of the statistics analysis.

2.2 Apparatuses

All participants operated the landing procedure by using a Boeing-747 flight simulator following visual flight rules (VFR) scenario. The eye movement data was recorded by a headed mounted eye tracker (ASL-4000) (Fig. 1).

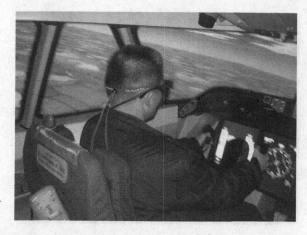

Fig. 1. Research apparatus including eye tracker and Boeing 747 flight simulator

Boeing 747 simulator is a high fidelity and fixed-base type for the purpose of routine flight training. It utilizes a simplified cockpit with identical display panels, layout and controls to those in the actual aircraft. The instructor sat at right seat and installed experimental scenarios in advance via a normal operation procedures. Participants can get the required information from the cockpit instruments, such as Altimeter, Attitude, Airspeed, and etc. In addition, the sampling rate of the mobile eye tracker ASL 4000 is 30 Hz. It recorded the position and radius of participants' pupil, the view from the angle of participants, and the spot point in the scene.

For the eye movement analysis, EyeNTNU-120p analysis system was applied in this study. Researcher not only define those ROIs with frame by frame, but also analyze more than twenty-three variables of eye movement provided, e.g., LFF, TCT, First Fixation before First Arrival, and etc.

2.3 Experimental Design

The present study is a single independent variable experiment. The independent variable is the backgrounds of participants (military pilot, commercial pilot, and trained novices) and it is a between-subject variable. Dependent variables include the latency of first fixation and the total contact time of fixations of eye movement for each region of interest (ROI). In the definition of ROIs, ROI-1 indictaes the region of Primary Flight Display (PFD); ROI-2, Engine and Alert Display (EAD); ROI-3, Outside of Cockpit; ROI-4 Navigation Display (ND), and ROI-0, the region of others (Fig. 2).

2.4 Procedures

All participants undertook the following procedures; (1) the participant completed the demographical data including gender, working backgrounds, type ratings and total flight hours (3 min to complete); (2) a short briefing explained the purposes of the

Fig. 2. The definition of ROIs: ROI-1(PFD-Primary Flight Display); ROI-2 (EAD-Engine and Alert Display); ROI-3 (Outside of Cockpit); ROI-4 (ND-Navigation Display), and ROI-0 (Other regions).

study and introduced the landing scenario (5 min); (3) the participant was seated at left seat in the simulator and the eye tracker was put on for calibration by using three points distributed over the cockpit instrument panels and outer screen (5-10 min); (4) the participant performed the landing task and simultaneously the instructor pilot sitting at the right seat (6 min). The eye tracker recorded both the scene video and corresponding eye movement data during the flight operations.

After the experiment, two types of data would be observed. One was participants' eye movement data; and the other was the scene video. EyeNTNU-120p analysis system only supported eye movement data saved in txt format. The eye movement in ASL 4000 was saved in csv format. Hence, the format of data should be transformed first. Secondly, using the ROI define tool in EyeNTNU-120p analysis system to define ROIs for each scene videos. After the analysis, the results (LFF and TCT) would be saved in txt format.

3   Results and Discussions

The results show that different background pilots' have different sequences of viewing ROIs; military pilots and novices spent more time viewing outside of cockpit compared with commercial pilots spent more time viewing the Primary Flight Display (ROI-1). The viewing sequences of military pilots is ROI-0, ROI-3, ROI-2, ROI-1, and ROI-4, the viewing sequence of commercial pilots is ROI-1, ROI-0, ROI-3, ROI-4, and ROI-2, and the viewing sequence of novices is ROI-0, ROI-4, ROI-1, ROI-3, and ROI-2. Therefore, the first null hypothesis (H_1) was rejected due to the significant differences of viewing sequences among different background pilots (Table 1).

The percentage of total contact time of pilots' first fixation indicated significant differences that military pilots spent most of time on ROI-3 (Outside of Cockpit),

Table 1. The latency of first fixation for all ROIs (milliseconds)

Participant code	ROI-0	ROI-1	ROI-2	ROI-3	ROI-4
1	456	7180	4123	0	16388
2	2388	0	36508	22360	9238
3	3862	0	*	44146	4027
4	236	0	*	7759	89255
5	0	1789	*	297	9194
6	0	759	9581	7923	7395
7	3254	0	*	18491	2043
8	0	*	*	3828	*
9	1039	7320	*	15285	0
10	100	1899	*	7353	0
Military	278	4540	4123	3677	8194
Commercial	1948	358	36508	18611	22751
Novices	346	4040	9581	9012	3698
Mean	1134	2105	16737	12744	34643

* denotes the ROI never been fixated.

0 denotes the ROI had been fixated at the very beginning.

commercial pilots on ROI-1(PFD), and novice pilots focus on ROI-0 (Others). The result rejected the second null hypothesis (H_2). Hence, there are differences of the total contact time of eye movements among different background pilots (Table 2).

Table 2. The percentage of total contact time of fixations for all ROIs

Participant code	ROI-0	ROI-1	ROI-2	ROI-3	ROI-4
1	34.42 %	.2.64 %	0.35 %	61.74 %	0.84 %
2	36.60 %	42.87 %	0.65 %	3.72 %	16.15 %
3	7.09 %	79.05 %	0.00 %	5.13 %	8.73 %
4	61.90 %	31.48 %	0.00 %	6.33 %	0.29 %
5	44.91 %	9.69 %	0.00 %	16.78 %	28.62 %
6	59.19 %	2.41 %	2.85 %	26.10 %	9.45 %
7	3.93 %	83.20 %	0.00 %	0.23 %	12.64 %
8	70.16 %	0.00 %	0.00 %	29.84 %	0.00 %
9	39.17 %	3.07 %	0.00 %	37.73 %	20.04 %
10	18.25 %	4.95 %	0.00 %	59.73 %	17.07 %
Military	26.34 %	3.80 %	0.18 %	60.73 %	8.96 %
Commercial	30.88 %	49.26 %	0.13 %	6.44 %	13.29 %
Novices	56.17 %	1.83 %	0.95 %	31.22 %	9.83 %
Mean	37.80 %	18.30 %	0.42 %	32.80 %	10.69 %

Flying an aircraft is comprised of a series of cognitive processes. Visual scan sequence and time could outline pilots' patterns of attention distribution in the cockpit which relate to pilot's situational awareness and decision-making process [11]. The results of present study indicate the flight background, e.g., experience and training, impacts pilots' visual scan patterns. Table 1 shows the first two ROIs where military pilots viewed are Others and Outside of Cockpit; commercial pilots' sequence is PFD and then Others. Table 2 demonstrated the scan sequences and the time distribution by the military and commercial groups are compatible, for both of military and commercial pilots relied on what they learned from previous training experiences to acquire necessary information supporting their task in hand. Furthermore, novices' attention sequence and visual time distribution do not match each other. However, it seems to be rational that novice pilots scanned ROI-0 (Others) as the first priority with the highest percentage time (56.17 %) due to the unfamiliar of cockpit instruments. After knowing where he/she could acquire the necessary information, novices shifted attention to the secondary ROI (Outside of Cockpit). However, even the latency of first fixation is meaningful, it is necessary to interpret pilots' cognitive process combined with the total dwell time distributed on those ROIs.

In addition, at the very beginning phase during fundamental training, military pilot was required to control the aircraft by scanning the horizon only, not by using the instruments while flying with VFR condition, for military pilots have to pay more attention on tactical manoeuvres and engagement. This might be the reason why the participants with military background spent the highest percentage of visual time (60.73 %) viewing outside of cockpit (ROI-3). In contrast with military pilots, the participants having commercial flight experience distributed most time (49.26 %) on the instrument, PFD. In fact, the total percentage of time that commercial pilots distributed on PFD and ND summed up as 62.55 %, which is very equivalent to the time on outside cockpit distributed by military pilots. It is reasonable that the information provided by PDF an ND can be acquired from outside of cockpit, such as runway direction and terrain features. On the other side, the ROI where novices spent most time is the other regions. This phenomenon could tell novice pilots' scanning strategy during the landing task is not well organized and even unfamiliar with the functions of PFD and ND, they might not be able to control the aircraft by using the horizon which military pilots were familiar with (Table 2).

Pilots' visual scans patterns among ROIs are related with selective attention. It is a critical skill for improving situational awareness and decision-making in the cockpit [15]. The findings of current research indicate the factors impacting pilots' cognitive processes of selective attention are reinforced by pilot's previous training background, e.g., knowledge and experience, which also could be observed and identified by specific LFF and TCT patterns. Therefore, with real-time visual scan patterns distributed on the control panel, the performance level of trainee's attention distribution can be understood at very early training phase. It should be able to apply for improving the effectiveness of conversion training.

4   Conclusion and Future Work

Flying an aircraft is comprised of a series of cognitive processes. Visual scan sequence and time could outline pilots' patterns of attention distribution in the cockpit relate to pilot's situational awareness. The results of present study indicate the flight background, e.g., experience and training, impacts pilots' visual scan patterns. The fundamental reasons of why pilots viewing ROIs in different sequence and spending significant different time on the ROIs needed to be studied further in the future. However, the findings might be applied for developing conversion training for military pilots conversed to civil airlines pilots. The application of eye tracking devices could be a suitable tool for investigating pilot's fixation distributions between the surrounding operational environments. Pilots with different flight experience have different strategies of viewing ROIs and pay attention on different interface displays. According to the findings of current small scale of piloting, a formal experiment why pilots were viewing ROIs in different sequence and pay attention in different ROIs are critical issues to aviation training and flight deck design, and needed to be studied further in the future for improving aviation safety.

Acknowledgements. This research is partially supported by the "Aim for the Top University Project" and "Center of Learning Technology for Chinese" of National Taiwan Normal University (NTNU), sponsored by the Ministry of Education, Taiwan, R.O.C. and the "International Research-Intensive Center of Excellence Program" of NTNU and Ministry of Science and Technology, Taiwan, R.O.C.

References

1. Statistical Summary – Aviation Occurrences (2014). (Transportation Safety Board of Canada)
2. Jaušovec, N.: Differences in cognitive processes between gifted, intelligent, creative, and average individuals while solving complex problems: an EEG study. Intelligence **28**, 213–237 (2000)
3. Chwo, G.S.M., Ho, H.F., Liu, B.C.Y., Chiu Lin, S.W.: Using eye-tracking as a means to evaluate visual and content design choices in web 2.0-An initial finding from Livemocha. Uhamka press (2013)
4. Thang, S.M., Jaffar, N.M., Soh, O.K., Ho, H.F., Chen, G.A.: Eye movements and reading strategies: Second language learners reading of a biology text with diagram. In: SoLLs. INTEC 2015 Theme: Language Studies Evolution and Revolution: The Past, Present, Future (2015)
5. Kim, S., Dey, A.K., Lee, J., Forlizzi, J.: Usability of car dashboard displays for elder drivers. In: Proceedings of the SIGCHI Conference on Human Factors in Computing Systems, pp. 493–502. ACM, Vancouver (2011)
6. Vernet, M., Kapoula, Z.: Binocular motor coordination during saccades and fixations while reading: a magnitude and time analysis. J. Vision **9**, 2 (2009)
7. Henderson, J.M.: Human gaze control during real-world scene perception. TRENDS Cogn. Sci. **7**(11), 498–504 (2003)

8. Yu, C.S., Wang, E.M., Li, W.C., Braithwaite, G., Greaves, M.: Pilots' visual scan pattern and attention distribution during the pursuit of a dynamic target. Aerosp. Med. Hum. Perform. **87**(1), 40–47 (2016)

9. Kasarskis, P., Stehwien, J., Hickox, J., Aretz, A., Wickens, C.: Comparison of expert and novice scan behaviors during VFR flight. In: Proceedings of the 11th International Symposium on Aviation Psychology, pp. 1–6, Citeseer (2001)

10. Li, W.-C., Chiu, F.-C., Kuo, Y.-S., Wu, K.-J.: The investigation of visual attention and workload by experts and novices in the cockpit. In: Harris, D. (ed.) EPCE 2013, Part II. LNCS, vol. 8020, pp. 167–176. Springer, Heidelberg (2013)

11. Johnson, A., Proctor, R.W.: Attention: Theory and Practice. Sage Publications, Inc, London (2004)

12. Morelli, F., Burton, P.A.: The impact of induced stress upon selective attention in multiple object tracking. Military Psychol. **21**, 81–97 (2009)

13. Ho, H.F.: The effects of controlling visual attention to handbags for women in online shops: evidence from eye movements. Comput. Hum. Behav. **30**, 146–152 (2014)

14. Dekker, S.: Disinheriting Fitts and Jones '47. Int. J. Aviat. Res. Develop. **1**, 7–18 (2001)

15. Yu, C.S., Wang, E.M., Li, W.C., Braithwaite, G.: Pilots' visual scan pattern and situation awareness in flight operations. Aviat. Space Environ. Med. **85**(7), 708–714 (2014)

Trajectory Recovery System: Angle of Attack Guidance for Inflight Loss of Control

Nicholas Kasdaglis[1(✉)], Tiziano Bernard[2], and Kimberly Stowers[3]

[1] Human Centered Design Institute,
Florida Institute of Technology, Melbourne, FL, USA
nkasdaglis@my.fit.edu
[2] Florida Institute of Technology, Melbourne, FL, USA
tbernard2011@my.fit.edu
[3] University of Central Florida, Orlando, FL, USA
kstowers@ist.ucf.edu

Abstract. This paper describes the design and development of an ecological display to aid pilots in the recovery of an In-Flight Loss of Control event due to a Stall (ILOC-S). The Trajectory Recovery System (TRS) provides a stimulus → response interaction between the pilot and the primary flight display. This display is intended to provide directly perceivable and actionable information of the aerodynamic performance state information and the requisite recovery guidance representation. In an effort to reduce cognitive tunneling, TRS mediates the interaction between pilot and aircraft display systems by deploying *cognitive countermeasures* that remove display representations unnecessary to the recovery task. Reported here, are the development and initial human centered design activities of a functional and integrated TRS display in a 737 flight-training device.

Keywords: Trajectory recovery system · In-Flight loss of control · Angle of attack · Affordance · Stall · Human-Centered design · ILOC · ILOC-S · AOA · HCD · TRS

1 Introduction

The Trajectory Recovery Systems (TRS) is a joint cognitive system [17] proposed as a mitigation tool to reduce In-Flight Loss of Control (ILOC) accidents by facilitating appropriate human-computer interaction. As there is no single intervention strategy to prevent ILOC, TRS may fit into NASA's framework for a Future Integrated Systems Concept to prevent ILOC accidents [5] —specifically providing flight safety assurance and resilience as a part of Flight Safety Management & Resilient Control and Crew Interface Management. This paper addresses ILOC due to stall conditions, how the notion of JCS relates to the TRS concept, state of art technologies, TRS system features, and efforts that resulted in a functional prototype of the TRS system.

D. Harris (Ed.): EPCE 2016, LNAI 9736, pp. 397–408, 2016.
DOI: 10.1007/978-3-319-40030-3_39

2   In-Flight Loss of Control Involving a Stall (ILOC- S)

ILOC has been defined qualitatively by a characterization of observed flight behaviors [11, 28] such as: (a) flight outside of normal operating envelope; (b) ineffective or unpredictable response to pilot control inputs; (c) nonlinearities, to include kinematic/inertial coupling; divergent or oscillatory flight behavior; and (d) high sensitivity to small variable changes. The leading causal factors of ILOC accidents are human induced. Over 80 % of ILOC accidents happened close to the ground—thus demanding accurate and timely recovery. However, ILOC accidents frequently involve inappropriate crew response, and a stalled condition [10]. An examination of 126 ILOC accidents elicited seven generalized sequences of events [10]; crew response, inappropriate control inputs, and aerodynamic stalls were major contributors.

A stall occurs when an airfoil exceeds its critical angle of attack, resulting in a loss of lift. A stall will result in a rapid increase in drag, and rapid decrease in lift, which can propagate to a dangerous loss of control situation [1]. However, ILOC is not synonymous with a stall. There are various situations in which ILOC can occur; for instance, mechanical failure of an aircraft system. Yet an analysis of 126 ILOC accidents occurring over a 30 year period found that 42.8 % involved inappropriate crew response to an off-nominal event; moreover 77.8 % of accidents involved a vehicle upset (i.e. abnormal attitude, airspeed, stall), and specifically 38.9 % of the accident set analyzed involved a stall [4]. This work is concerned specifically with mitigation as it relates to ILOC that involves a stall.

3   ILOC-S Cognitive Functions and Aircraft Control Displays

3.1   Cognitive Cues for ILOC-S

The crash of Air France 447 was an ILOC accident. All three pilot static systems became inoperative and unreliable due to an accumulation of ice crystals. This off-nominal event disrupted the collaborative information processing between pilot and technological agents of the aircraft—the aircraft automated system entered a state of reversion; excess angle of attack protection was lost. The pilot flying inexplicably introduced inappropriate nose back on the side stick controller, causing the aircraft to enter a stalled condition. The accident report [3] explicates the failure of the pilots to understand the situation leading to "the de- structuring of crew cooperation [that] fed on each other until the total loss of cognitive control of the situation" (p. 199).

A system such as the one discussed here is composed of a tightly coupled complex relationship between *task, operator, and artifact* [7–9]. Seeking to parse the impact one element has on the system is nearly impossible due to the impact each element has on the other. With the loss of all airspeed indications, the pilots *(operator)* had to develop new *task* to control the aircraft *(artifact)*. Clearly the requisite information processing in this is context is what Rasmussen envisioned as *knowledge level* [24]. However, pilots most often work at a *skill level*— and generally aircraft displays are built around nominal processes [5]. The report finds the crew response lacking because of a failure to respond with the right action arising from the complexity of the situation. In keeping with Rasmussen's constructs, the crew was suddenly thrust into a context that required the highest information processing level, yet the report suggests a failure to transition to this level. Instead inappropriate controls meant for nominal events were applied.

The final report of AF 447 suggests that if *cognitive control* were maintained or regained, appropriate crew response would follow, and thereby a return of the aircraft to controlled flight would subsequently follow [3]. This is not a matter of simply appropriate task fulfillment by an individual pilot, but appropriate cognitive functions being fulfilled to produce context appropriate activity. Boy [8] contends that *Cognitive Functions* (CF) transform a generic task into an appropriate activity; as a function *resources* brought to bear, *roles* of multiple agents (human and artificial) in a system, and that which is environmentally persistent (*context*). Inherent in transformation are mental models, which give rise to an abstract construction of the state, structures, processes of the system and its environment. Accordingly, cognitive processes that occur at Rasmussen's skill level are based upon training and mental models [23]. Yet situations such as that which faced the AF 447 pilots required an adaptive response due to erroneous aerodynamic performance information that had arisen from the blocked pitot tubes. In other words, the situation demanded an adaptive response— first and foremost, an update to the mental model. This *knowledge* response presupposes cognition that is resilient and goal orientated.

Given a task, certain information requirements exist [19, 27] based upon the hierarchical level of human involvement in the task. A framework has been proposed as a convention of cueing representations for appropriate information processing levels (Table 1) [24]. Therefore, the information requirements are not only related to the task at hand, but the required level of cognition for a given context. For AF 447, in order for the requisite identification and subsequent action to occur, appropriate symbols must have been made available. Thus, for knowledge-based behavior to occur, signs or signals were less than adequate, as those correspond to rules and skill respectively; a symbol is required for adaptive behavior. Remarkably, the final accident document reports that no symbols for adaptive action were available [3]; a less than adequate cognitive function existed to transform the recovering task into an effective activity.

The Bureau d'Enquêtes et d'Analyses made the following recommendation in the wake of the AF 447 accident [3]:

The crew never formally identified the stall situation. Information on **angle of attack is not directly accessible to pilots** [emphasis mine]…It is essential in order to ensure flight safety to reduce the angle of attack when a stall is imminent. Only a direct readout of the angle of attack could enable crews to…take the actions that may be required. Consequently, the BEA recommends: that EASA and the FAA evaluate the relevance of requiring the presence of an angle of attack indicator directly accessible to pilots on aeroplanes (p. 205).

Appropriate action, as stated in the accident report, was a reduction of the angle of attack, yet the final report suggests that outside of signals indicating a stall, no provision for such adaptation was available. Such adaptation required technological as well as temporal resources time that the crew did not have.

Table 1. Examples for appropriate information processing. adapted from Rasmussen [24]

Information Processing Level	Representation	Example	Description
Knowledge	Symbol	**STOP**	Holds and imparts semantic qualities for information assimilation, planning, and goal directed behavior
Rules	Signs		Cues for recognition for a rule based response
Skill	Signal		Introduces a binary stimulus to elicits a preconditioned response

3.2 Aerodynamic Control for ILOC Recovery

Early in initial training, pilots experience and learn how to recover from stalls. Stalls may feel different from aircraft to aircraft, yet the aerodynamics and recovery procedures and similar. Recovery from a stall involves, at the highest level of abstraction, a reduction of the angle of attack. This is instantiated by advancing the throttles, and applying the appropriate amount of forward control yoke input to effect a downward elevator control deflection—the result is a reduction of angle of attack [16].

Control responsiveness is a function of dynamic pressure and flow adhesion on the suction surface of the wing (or elevator). During a stall, both elements are in jeopardy—dynamic pressure as airspeed decreases, and airflow over the wing as it becomes prone to flow separation at high angles of attack. A loss in an aircraft's responsiveness to control stick movement occurs—the controls become "sluggish." Dynamic pressure and flow separation change in strength during a stall; it is important to begin the recovering maneuver expeditiously and accurately to avoid losing too much altitude. Additionally, during high angles of attack greater thrust is required [2].

3.3 Synthesis of Control Paradigms: Cognitive Functions for ILOC Recovery

Given that there exists an objective aerodynamic reality and constraints that imposes environmental constraints on the aircraft, automation, and crew; and there also exist requisite cognitive control—the use of CFs provide offer a means to balance the two demands [8]. The state of the world as it is must be available to the pilot; yet it must be provided in a form to facilitate its use [19, 20]. Vicente offers a similar sentiment in proposing that the appropriate display paradigm required for control of a system that has external constraints for goal directed behavior is a *correspondence* rather *coherence* model [26]. Norman describes HCI design display challenges by identifying the gap between an operator's intention and required action, and the effect of that input and the operator's perception as the *gulf of execution* and the *gulf of evaluation* respectively [22]. Thus ILOC recovery requires a display that closes the gap between execution and control, and the state of the word and evaluation.

Practically, a pilot's desire and intent may not be directly related to an appropriate action to attain the desired aircraft state—for example, a pilot's intent to stop the approach of the ground by pulling the control yoke of a stalled aircraft. The intention is to immediately make the aircraft go up; yet in a stalled condition, this intention is aerodynamically impossible! Angle of attack (AOA) must first be reduced for generation of lift to fly away from the ground. Thus, there exist two requisite CFs for ILOC recovery, control inputs that: a) return the aircraft to the intended flight path; and b) restore the aerodynamic functioning of the wings.

Remarkably, little is offered in most cockpits to explicitly support these CFs [3]. This may be because traditional models of situation awareness (SA) that inform display design may be insufficient to support appropriate analysis of CFs. Implicit here, is that design must include cognition of CFs (macro-cognition) and their potential conflicts to overall system behavior. System State Awareness has been proposed to transcend the archetype linear SA construct [14]; this concept may better supports pilot-aircraft coupling.

Important here is that effective pilot-aircraft coupling is accomplished between efferent and afferent channels mediated by aircraft control systems and displays organized around a pilot's accurate mental model. Nominal aircraft control task are built upon the supposition that this coupling exists. Therefore, restoring an aircraft to control entails restoring or modifying the relationship between pilot and aircraft.

To manipulate AOA, complex relationships composed of aircraft configuration, thrust, speed, flight path, altitude, and load factors must be mentally modeled by the pilot. Here, AOA is not an abstract topic, but a parameter that is directly influenced by, and influences these other parameters. Therefore, recovery from a novel stall may catapult a pilot into a problem-solving task—Rasmussen's knowledge level. Yet in time critical situations, inciting a stimulus-response pilot behavior may be most appropriate. It is in this sense that adaption of pilot-aircraft coupling must occur, as restoring the pilot to attain an appropriate mental model may not be practical as they be constrained by time available for recovery.

4   State of the Art for ILOC-S

Industry has developed, and installed, various instrumentation and systems that aim to mitigate the risk of an aircraft entering a stall; Fig. 1 depicts one such display. Experimental displays have been designed and developed to incorporate physical flight parameter representations as well as higher order flight function representations; one such display offers the pilot directly perceivable insight into their aircraft's aerodynamic performance [25].

4.1   Pitch Limit Indicator, PLI

The pitch limit indicator, labeled "A" in 1, shows the limit in terms of pitch angle, that the aircraft can increase before stalling. The PLI is automatically engaged by the system when the aircraft is at higher than normal angles of attack [21]. This PLI provides a higher level of situational awareness, and aids the observer up to an angle of 30 degrees.

Fig. 1. The display on the B737-800's primary flight display

4.2 Boeing Angle of Attack Indicator

The angle of attack indicator, labeled "C", is a pure indicator, giving a dial reading and a numerical value of angle of attack. The dial on the round gauge rescales depending on the change in angle of attack [21]. It becomes clear that both instruments have a preventive nature, and if the airplane exceeds a critical angle of attack, there technically is no optimized tool to safely guide a pilot away from LOC-S back into controlled flight.

4.3 Airbus Flight Laws

The Airbus *Flight Laws* [10] are designed on three levels to monitor the situation, and activate when necessary. The three levels are normal, alternate, and direct. These are a group of flight laws that are designed to automatically adjust for unusual situations. For example, in the event of a stall, the first law is designed to automatically pitch the nose down and increase airspeed.

4.4 LOC-S and Need for New Innovation

Although the various state of the art systems described above are indeed operational and useful to pilots, LOC-S is still a threat to aviation safety [4, 6]. Often aviation safety enhancement is not a direct need, but a need that should be taken into consideration in order to predict future accidents. In order to do this, there is a need to redefine a new set of requirements for a "system" that will be able to exist during LOC-S, where conventional flight laws are definitely different.

5 TRS Design Process and Features

5.1 TRS Functions

The Trajectory Recovery System (TRS) guides a pilot to reduce AOA and avoid terrain by following a salient bull's-eye; it also informs necessary thrust settings for recovery

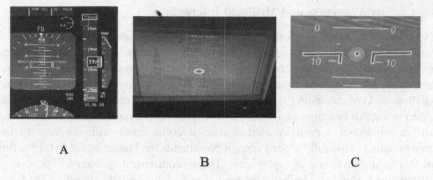

A   B   C

Fig. 2. TRS not displayed (A); TRS displayed directing pitch and power (B); TRS pitch and power targets attained (C)

(Fig. 2). TRS is context dependent; an aerodynamic algorithm drives the appearance, movements, and removal of TRS representations.

5.2   Human Centered Design

TRS has been proposed as a Human Design Centered (HCD) solution as part of an overall integrated effort towards ILOC mitigation [5]. HCD attempts to analyze, design, and evaluate life critical systems for optimum safety, efficiency, and comfort [9].

Insights into ILOC-S suggest that is not simply a human operator failure, but instead a joint cognitive system (JCS) [17] behavioral outcome that arises from complex interactions between technological artifacts, organizations elements, and human action. A JCS perspective embraces the totality of cognitive interactions that precede an ILOC accident—(CF) are no longer isolated to the human. CFs are emergent system properties that are shared amongst elements of the entire socio-technical system [7, 8]. In addition to roles and resources of the JCS, cognition for ILOC recovery is embodied in context. Thus, the concomitant interplay of all elements affords the pilot information of "what is possible" and "what can be done" [22]. It follows that mitigation efforts to ILOC be supported by formative design efforts that account for these; namely HCD development process is discussed elsewhere.

5.3   Direct Perception for ILOC-S Recovery

TRS leverages environmental cues in order to provide a pilot with affordances for action [15, 18, 22]. It incorporates an ecological display that reduces the distance between interpretation of aircraft AOA and the required AOA for recovery. Additionally, the danger of cognitive tunneling is addressed through cognitive countermeasures [12, 13]; removal of non-recovery pertinent representations.

5.4   Context Awareness and Mediated Interaction

TRS is ubiquitous—always active, monitoring and facilitating appropriate cognitive control based on aerodynamic and environmental constraints and context. TRS captures live aerodynamic data, analyzes it and mediates appropriate human computer interactions. Interaction with automation can occur at various levels: supervision, mediation, and collaboration [9]. For example, the Traffic Collision Avoidance System (TCAS) in aircraft functions at all three levels. That is, at a non-alerting state, it simply identifies targets; at a partially alerted state it collaborates with the user to issue warnings; while at the fully alerted state, it commands the human agent to take actions; thus, this final state is one of supervision. These requirements presume logic— robust algorithms to facilitate assimilation of new data and appropriate action.

5.5   Target Design

TRS is depicted in Fig. 2. Information is eliminated and a target is displayed on the screen [12, 13]; "TRS MODE" is annunciated on the display. Magenta *Bull's-eyes Target* appears and directs an optimized pitch for expeditious and accurate recovery when the aircraft's critical angle of attack is exceeded. Upon reaching the target pitch, the magenta center will turn to green. An outer unfilled ring indicates the necessary to increase thrust; upon advancement of throttles the outer ring will progressively fill yellow, and then green when the appropriate power setting for recovery is set. Upon a safe trajectory TRS will then disengage and return the PFD to the nominal display.

5.6   Target Engagement and Disengagement

TRS is animated by an aerodynamic algorithm. It engages only when required for a recovering maneuver, then disengages when the event is resolved. TRS continuously calculates the stall speed and AOA of the aircraft. Therefore, exceeding critical angle of attack and slowing down to below stall speed are considered as the triggering elements for the trajectory recovery system, as shown in Eq. 1.

$$\alpha_{indicated} > \alpha_{critical} = 15° \tag{1}$$

Another criterion that engages the TRS is the airspeed dropping below the stall speed. The second criterion is shown in Eq. 2.

$$V < V_{stall} \tag{2}$$

Providing two independent triggering points for TRS increases safety by assuring more aspects of the incipient stall are acknowledged by the system. Disengagement criteria are defined by the triggering airspeed, a safe angle of attack (8°), and a safe vertical speed (100 feet per minute) demonstrating a gain in altitude. Initial testing demonstrated that these values were excellent and provided a successful recovery.

6   Target Dynamics

The TRS target will present itself at the point where the aircraft would experience zero angle of attack. This angle will constantly move, as the pitch attitude will decrease with the angle of attack shown in Eq. 3.

$$\theta_{TRS} = \theta - \alpha \tag{3}$$

The pitch attitude that the target displays on TRS, as shown in Eq. 3, calculates the flight path angle of the aircraft. In order for the target to start increasing in pitch, a triggering airspeed has been decided to act as a criterion. The value for V2, (1.2Vs) was determined to be appropriate, as shown in Eq. 4. If the triggering velocity as well as the flight path angle criteria are achieved, TRS target begins its ascent.

$$V_{trigger,recovery} = 1.2V_{stall} \tag{4}$$

TRS also provides bank-leveling guidance. The algorithm for this situation instructs the pilot to level the wings, not to bank in the opposite direction. A simple mirror equation was used to obtain the shifting of the target horizontally as shown in Eq. 5.

$$\phi_{TRS} = -\phi \tag{5}$$

6.1   Usability

To validate the design of TRS, an online survey was given to 35 professional pilots with an average of 9474 total flight hours. It was found that offering access to information does not necessarily mean that it will be used. For example, 8 out of the 32 (25 %) professional pilots indicated weakness or neutrality in their ability to use an AOA indicator. This finding suggests that attention must be paid to the use of information to be effective [19]. Specifically, does the information provided afford and signify the use [22]? When queried, 87.5 % survey participants supported the desirability of a display for command guidance from ILOC recovery. Such a device would provide access to and use of information necessary for recovery from an ILOC event.

6.2   Iterative Usability Validation

Although our algorithmic approach allows the aircraft to recover, the angle of attack is much slower to decrease compared to the pitch attitude of the aircraft, causing the aircraft to accelerate to very high values. A constant, or buffer, was therefore applied to the equation governing the location of the TRS target as demonstrated in Eq. 6.

$$\theta_{TRS} = \gamma + 5^{\circ} \tag{6}$$

Different constants were used on different computers, due to the CPU available from each. An optimal value of 5 degrees was deemed appropriate by the expert pilot during testing of the TRS on the simulator. The second equation in need of manipulation was the trigger airspeed for recovery. Just like the TRS target pitch position, a buffer was put in place Eq. 7 to allow for a more rapid recovery, given the fact that the target will begin to increase in pitch as the airplane reaches its position.

$$V_{trigger,recovery} = 1.2V_{stall} - 15knots \qquad (7)$$

This buffer value of 15 knots was chosen after various other values were tested. The last thoroughly tested value is the rate of ascent, which was decided to be 7 degrees per second. This was determined to be an aggressive enough pull up to allow a small loss in altitude.

7   Conclusion

Analysis of ILOC cognitive and aerodynamic control suggests that one strategy for accident mitigation is to mediate human computer interaction for optimal aircraft performance. Conceptual development TRS has been developed with the intention to mitigate LOC-S. Specifically, TRS provides recovery guidance is provided for a return to controlled flight. Other use applications include training prompts and guidance for scaffolded learning.

The development of TRS is presently at an evaluation phase, as it has already functional as a prototyped and has been integrated into a 737 FTD. Evaluation and iterative design will be conducted as a part of the HCD design process. Future TRS functionality could support commanded optimal terrain avoidance while respecting aerodynamic constraints, and an enhanced commanded recovery maneuvers—for a banking and "slicing" to the horizon maneuver in order decrease load factor and expeditiously return to the horizon.

Acknowledgements. We would like to thank the people of Florida Tech's Human Centered Design Institute, including Delilah Caballero, Dr. Guy Boy and Dr. Lucas Stephane. Additionally, we would like to thank Presagis for the use of VAPS XT software and Disti Corporation for the use of GL Studio. Finally, we wish to acknowledge Ben Remy for his work in usability and Alexander Troshchenko for his integration of TRS into the 737 FTD.

References

1. Anderson Jr, J.D.: Fundamentals of Aerodynamics. Mcgraw-Hill Education, Boston (1985)
2. Anderson Jr, J.D.: Aircraft Performance and Design. Mcgraw-Hill, Boston (1999)
3. BEA.: Final Report on the Accident on 1st June 2009 to the Airbus A330-203 Registered F-Gzcp Operated By Air France Flight Af 447 Rio De Janeiro – Paris (2012)

4. Belcastro, C.M., Foster, J.: Aircraft loss-of-control accident analysis. In: Proceedings of AIAA Guidance, Navigation and Control Conference, Paper No. AIAA-2010-8004, Toronto (2010)
5. Belcastro, C.M., Jacobson, S.R.: Future integrated systems concept for preventing aircraft loss-of-control accidents. In: AIAA Guidance, Navigation, and Control Conference, pp. 2–5 (2010)
6. Boeing Commercial Airplanes. Statistical Summary of Commercial Jet Airplane Accidents, Worldwide Operations, 1959–2011. Worldwide Operations (2011)
7. Boy, G.A.: The Making of Complex Systems. Orchestrating Human-Centered Design, pp. 89–115. Springer, London (2013)
8. Boy, G.A.: Cognitive Function Analysis. In: vol. 2. Greenwood Publishing Group. Westport (1998.)
9. Boy, G.A.: The Handbook of Human-Machine Interaction: A Human-Centered Design Approach. Ashgate Publishing, Ltd., Farnham (2012)
10. Briere, D., Traverse, P.: Airbus A320/A330/A340 electrical flight controls-a family of fault-tolerant systems. In: 23rd IEEE International Symposium on Fault-Tolerant Computing, pp. 616–623. IEEE (1993)
11. CICTT.: Aviation Occurrence Categories: Definitions and Usage Notes. 4.2 (2011)
12. Dehais, F., Tessier, C., Chaudron, L.: Ghost: experimenting countermeasures for conflicts in the pilot's activity. In: Proceedings of the Eighteen International Joint Conference on Artificial Intelligence, Acapulco, Mexico, pp. 163–168 (2003)
13. Dehais, F., Tessier, C., Christophe, L., Reuzeau, F.: The perseveration syndrome in the pilot's activity: guidelines and cognitive countermeasures. In: Palanque, P., Vanderdonckt, J., Winckler, M. (eds.) HESSD 2009. LNCS, vol. 5962, pp. 68–80. Springer, Heidelberg (2010)
14. Endsley, M.R.: Toward a theory of situation awareness in dynamic systems. Hum. Factors J. Hum. Factors Ergonomics Soc. 37, 32–64 (1995)
15. Gibson, J.: The theory of affordances. In: Shaw, R.E., Bransford, J. (eds.) Perceiving, Acting, and Knowing. Lawrence Erlbaum Associates, Hillsdale (1977)
16. Handbook, A.F. US Department of Transportation, Federal Aviation Administration–Flight Standards Service (2004)
17. Hollnagel, E., Woods, D.D.: Joint Cognitive Systems: Foundations of Cognitive Systems Engineering. CRC Press, Boca Raton (2005)
18. Hutchins, E.L., Hollan, J.D., Norman, D.A.: Direct manipulation interfaces. Hum.-Comput. Interact. 1, 311–338 (1985)
19. Kasdaglis, N., Deaton, J.: The art of managing information in the national airspace architecture. In: Strother, J.B., Ulijn, J.M., Fazal, Z. (eds.) Information Overload, An International Challenge For Professional Engineers and Technical Communicators, p. 195. Wiley, Hoboken (2012)
20. Kasdaglis, N., Newton, O., Lakhmani, S.: System state awareness: a human centered design approach to awareness in a complex world. In: Proceedings of the Human Factors and Ergonomics Society 58th Annual Meeting, pp. 305–309 (2014)
21. Kelly, B.D., Veitengruber, J.E., Mulally, A.R.: Apparatus and Methods for Generating a Stall Warning Margin on an Aircraft Attitude Indicator Display. US Patent No. 4,910,513, 20 Mar 1990
22. Norman, D.A.: The Design of Everyday Things. Basic Books, NewYork (2002)
23. Rasmussen, J., Vicente, K.J.: Coping with human errors through system design: implications for ecological interface design. Int. J. Man Mach. Stud. 31, 517–534 (1989)

24. Rasmussen, J.: Skills, rules, and knowledge; signals, signs, and symbols, and other distinctions in human performance models. IEEE Trans. Syst. Man Cybern. **13**, 257–266 (1983)
25. Temme, L.A., Still, D., Acromite, M.: OZ: a human-centered computing cockpit display. In: 45th Annual Conference of the International Military Testing Association, pp. 70–90 (2003)
26. Vicente, K.J.: Coherence-and correspondence-driven work domains: implications for systems design. Behav. Inform. Technol. **9**, 493–502 (1990)
27. Wickens, C.D., Lee, J.D., Liu, Y., Gordon-Becker, S.: Introduction to Human Factors Engineering, 2nd edn. (2004)
28. Wilborn, J.E., Foster, J.V.: Defining commercial transport loss-of-control: a quantitative approach. In: Proceedings of the AIAA Atmospheric Flight Mechanics Conference and Exhibit, Providence (2004)

The Evaluation of Pilot's Situational Awareness During Mode Changes on Flight Mode Annunciators

Wen-Chin Li[1](✉), James White[1], Graham Braithwaite[1],
Matt Greaves[1], and Jr-Hung Lin[2]

[1] Safety and Accident Investigation Center, Cranfield University,
Bedfordshire, UK
wenchin.li@cranfield.ac.uk
[2] Humanities and Technology Lab, Lund University,
Helgonabacken 12, Lund, Sweden

Abstract. Current research investigates automation feedback design compared with a potential design solution that may increase pilot's situation awareness of the Flight Mode Annunciators (FMAs) to reduce pilot workload and improve human-automation coordination. The research tools include an Eye Tracker and B747 flight simulator. This research evaluated two types of FMAs; a proposed glareshield mounted FMAs against the baseline FMA design mounted on the Primary Flight Display using an objective eye tracker. There are 19 participants including professional and private pilots and aerospace engineers. The results suggest that proposed glareshield design is the better design compared with the baseline design which demonstrated larger mean pupil sizes related to the higher workload. A design solution was proposed that moved the FMAs to a MCP position, taking into account EASA and FAA design guidance, as well as several design principles including positioning to increase salience and the proximity compatibility principle. The results of the experiment found that FMAs on the MCP could increase pilot SA and reduced the mean fixation duration compared to the PFD position. Although the study used a small sample size, it demonstrates the value of further research to evaluate the proposed design.

Keywords: Attention distribution · Eye movement · Flight deck design · Mode confusion · Proximity compatibility principle

1 Introduction

Eye tracking provides scientific evidence on the underlying causal relations between independent variables and dependent variables. In other words, eye-trackers offer not only what causes the results, but also how the results are caused (Mayer 2010). The application of eye-tracking in the study of flight simulation is promising as it provides direct feedback, which could diagnose potential factors that impact upon pilot attention and situation awareness on the flight deck (Robinski and Stein 2013). Military aviation studies suggest analysing eye movements is beneficial for fighter pilots to increase their

© Springer International Publishing Switzerland 2016
D. Harris (Ed.): EPCE 2016, LNAI 9736, pp. 409–418, 2016.
DOI: 10.1007/978-3-319-40030-3_40

tactical performance (Wetzel et al. 1998; Yu et al. 2014). Eye tracking methodology is based on two assumptions: eye-mind and immediacy assumptions. The immediacy assumption proposed the location of a fixation coincides with the cognitive processing of concurrent visual stimuli (e.g., words) at that location. The eye-mind assumption indicated eye movement is correlated to concurrent perceptual and cognitive processes which coincides with, and is bounded by, the position fixated at the point in time, and that this processing starts at the point of fixation and continues until all possible analyses were completed (Just and Carpenter 1980). Furthermore, eye tracking studies focus on two aspects: "When" and "What" (van Gompel 2007). The temporal aspect of eye movement control (when) primarily concerns the question as to when a given saccade is executed or, more precisely, the time course of cognitive processing events and control decisions occurring during a fixation. In contrast, "What" concerns what information is extracted concurrently to guide the eyes. With the development of technologies, more research has adopted eye-tracking in various contexts, such as cognitive processes in reading (Rayner 1998), learning (van Gog and Scheiter 2010), problem solving (Hegarty et al. 1995; Lin and Lin 2014), information processing (Lu et al. 2011), and flight deck design (Li et al. 2015). It provides researchers a promising way to study what people think when they see something, such as text or graphics (Renshaw et al. 2004).

The formal authority of the automation status is communicated within the cockpit via the FMAs situated at the top of the cockpit PFD. Monitoring these FMAs, and calling out mode transitions seen via the FMAs is considered important for obtaining and maintaining mode awareness on the flight deck. The 'call-out' is when one member of the flight deck team aurally announces a mode change to highlight the change to the other crew member; intending to ensure effective crew communication and SA (Airbus 2006). However, an experiment using eye tracking techniques investigating mode awareness by Björklund et al. (2006) found that flight crews used a variety of strategies to keep track of the autopilot status, and relied little on the PFD FMAs. Lack of SA is a primary reason for pilot error, even among experienced pilots, and pilot SA can be assessed by monitoring visual behavior (van Dijk et al. 2011). Eye movement patterns can be used as an objective measure of cognitive workload and thus the efficiency of a HMI design; where inefficient designs lead to an increase in relative cognitive workload. An eye tracking device can be used to measure various metrics related to a pilots' attention (Zelinsky 2008).

Breakdowns in human-machine coordination have been a repetitive problem in automated aircraft (Dekker 2000; Woods and Sarter 2000), and recent reports captured via the Aviation Safety Reporting System (ASRS) administered by NASA (National Aeronautics and Space Administration) show that this continues to be the case (NASA 2015). To avoid human-machine coordination breakdown in the cockpit, pilots have to maintain situation awareness (SA) of the automatic system's status. 'Mode awareness' is a critical ingredient for avoiding automation-related problems (Funk et al. 1997). The introduction of autopilot and auto-thrust functions on aircraft was designed to reduce flight crew workload and therefore reduce the number of accidents and incidents that occur due to high workload conditions as a contributing factor, among other reasons such as more efficient trajectory flying. Particularly on long flights, use of an autopilot can reduce pilot fatigue by maintaining a set course and steady, level flight for long periods of time without needing the human pilot to concentrate on this task (Harris 2011). However, while the original aim of this was to reduce crew workload in terms of manually flying the aircraft, it shifted the pilot's role from hands-on flying to a systems managing role while the autopilot is in operation. Rather than reducing workload, this changed the workload; relieving the pilot of perceptual motor load ('doing') with an increase in cognitive workload ('thinking'). Humans are not ideally suited to monitoring roles. Combined with inadequate feedback from automation systems, this creates a recipe for mode awareness to be reduced (Endsley 1996). The aims of current research are to investigate the design aspect of FMAs with a potential for improvement to Human-Computer Interactions (HCI) on the flight desk to improve pilot SA performance.

2 Method

2.1 Participants

The study involved twenty-five participants consisting of three qualified commercial pilots with flight experience between 1,242 and 2,400 h (M = 1722.3, SD = 603.7); eight private pilot license holders with flight experience between 50 and 185 h (M = 108.1, SD = 41.67) defined as experienced participants; and 14 avionics engineers with limited flight experience consisting of between 0 and 10 h (M = 3.64, SD = 5.84) defined as non-experienced participants. As data were gathered from human participants a research proposal was created and submitted to the Cranfield University Research Ethics System (CURES) for ethical approval of the research and experiment. Ethical approval was granted for the research prior to starting the experiment by the CURES team, and informed consent secured by all participants prior to commencement of the experiment. All signed forms are available upon request.

2.2 Apparatus

B747-400 Flight Simulator. The experiment was run on Cranfield University's high-fidelity B747-400 Flight Simulator. This simulator comprises a realistic mock-up of a cockpit of Boeing commercial aircraft with functioning flight controls, stick-shaker stall warning, and overspeed alerts (Fig. 1a).

Eye Tracking Device. To capture objective eye metrics a Pupil Labs "Pupil Pro" eye tracking device was applied. The device carries the following specifications, Eye Camera Maximum Resolution – 640 × 480 at 30fps; World Camera Maximum Resolution – 1920 × 1080 at 30fps; Headset Weight 44 g plus Cable Weight – 60 g. The Pupil Pro eye tracking device is worn like a pair of glasses and connected via cable to a data recorder. This device has a 'World Camera' mounted in the centre of the glasses showing the orientation and view of the wearer's head. A second camera, the Eye Camera, is mounted offset right and low. This part of the device tracks a participant's pupil on the right eye (Fig. 1b).

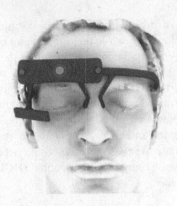

Fig. 1a. Cranfield B747-400 flight simulator.   **Fig. 1b.** Pupil pro eye tracker

2.3   Research Design

To test ability of participants in noticing, monitoring, and responding to mode changes during flight a scenario was prescribed that would induce some workload to keep the participants on a primary task of flying the aircraft. The participants were set a workload-inducing scenario consisting of flying the B747 down a 3° ILS beam while on approach to land; starting at 3,200ft, 8 miles from the runway. Due to some participants having little or no experience of the cockpit, aircraft configuration settings were set at gear down, flaps 20°, and a power setting to achieve 170–190 knots for all flights. To accommodate limited access to the flight simulator and increase the number of participants, a short flight was devised of 2.5 min, stopping approximately 1 mile before final touchdown on the runway. The vertical and horizontal deviation from the ILS beam was displayed to the researchers during the experiment. The flight simulator had the lights and switches in the correct places on the MCP for a realistic setting. A bespoke FMAs panel was created which was convenient to relocate around the cockpit instruments, connected to a switch held by the researchers to turn the mode annunciations on and off. Automatic-unexpected mode changes would be simulated and require the participants to callout the mode change when noticed; introduced as another task for the participants to be aware of, and to test data-driven monitoring performance from the FMAs design.

Two different positions of FMAs were evaluated for the efficiency of increasing pilot's SA on the changing modes of automation. The FMAs on the position A is situated above the attitude indicator on the PFD, where FMAs are traditionally placed (Fig. 2a); and the FMAs on the position B is situated on the far left of the MCP (Fig. 2b). Position B was so designated as to keep within the pilot's primary field of view, and in a position that could accommodate the FMAs panel without significant disruption or redesign of current MCPs. The participants were split into two groups: The control group was assigned to fly the scenario with the FMAs panel on the PFD and the experimental group was assigned to fly the mission with the FMAs panel on the MCP. There are four defined AOIs for the current experiment design, namely the airspeed, attitude, altitude indicators, and the FMAs panel.

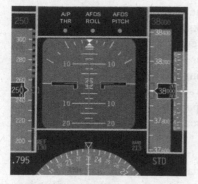
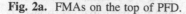

Fig. 2a. FMAs on the top of PFD.   **Fig. 2b.** FMAs on the left of MCP

2.4 Data Collection Process

Once the participant's consent form was signed, participant were given a briefing sheet for the experiment, followed by calibration process to the left seat of the B747 simulator and fitted with the eye-tracking device. The laptop displays the Pupil Labs 'Pupil Player' showing the World View camera and the Eye Viewer feed. Adjustments are made on the Eye Viewer camera to find the optimal position with the participant looking towards the PFD screens. Optimal position was deemed to be found when the Confidence bar was consistently above 70 %.

The calibration process consisted of moving a black and white circle marker around the viewing area with the participant tracking the centre of the marker with their eye, as depicted in Fig. 3. The marker is held still at a location on the viewing area while the eye-tracker fixes the position. Within a few seconds an aural beep is heard once the marker position is fixed by eye-tracker. The marker is then moved onto another

Fig. 3. The calibration process of Pupil Pro is searching for the marker held adjacent to Navigation Display

location and so on, until the approximate area of the viewing area has been covered. This process is repeated for a minimum of nine 'marks'. Once the calibration process is finished the participant is instructed to look at the centre of the PFD, ND, and FMAs Panel. At each fixation, the tracking of the eye-tracker is verified by visually confirming the feedback of the tracking via red dots, representing fixations, shown on the World View camera. The calibration process ensured accuracy for the specific viewing areas calibrated, but accuracy was found to drop off when participants looked at areas beyond the calibration marks. If participants looked at an area beyond the calibrated areas the data was recorded as 'Undefined'.

Recording began to capture at least 5–10 s of participant 'at rest' data for baseline capture, then a signal to the flight simulator technician is given that the experiment is ready to start. The technician commences the flight with a 3 s countdown. 50 s into each flight an FMAs is switched on by the researcher and the participant response, if any, is noted. At 1 min 30 s into the flight, the FMAs mode is changed via a switch by the researcher and again response is recorded. Mode changes are made at the same time for each participant. At 2 min 30 s the simulation is stopped and the participant told to

Table 1. Mean (SD) of eye movement measures for FMAs between PFD and FCP in 4 AOIs

AOIs	FMA Positions	Fixation Count	Total Fixation Duration	Total Sequence Fixations (%)	Mean Fix Duration (ms)
FMAs	PFD	16.44	6.80	48.28	337.44
		(9.62)	(5.05)	(32.32)	(158.85)
	MCP	17.30	5.39	38.40	278.80
		(10.34)	(3.59)	(24.24)	(133.27)
	Total	16.89	6.06	43.08	306.58
		(9.74)	(4.28)	(27.99)	(144.91)
Attitude	PFD	13.44	7.25	45.67	477.00
		(7.97)	(6.84)	(35.18)	(311.91)
	MCP	19.90	7.83	52.30	379.00
		(8.17)	(4.60)	(24.94)	(151.59)
	Total	16.84	7.55	49.16	425.42
		(8.52)	(5.61)	(29.54)	(239.29)
Airspeed	PFD	1.78	0.57	3.99	170.78
		(1.99)	(0.66)	(4.97)	(163.71)
	MCP	3.10	0.83	6.34	280.30
		(2.28)	(0.55)	(4.53)	(224.34)
	Total	2.47	0.70	5.23	228.42
		(2.20)	(0.60)	(4.76)	(200.58)
Altitude	PFD	1.44	0.33	2.06	105.44
		(2.60)	(0.57)	(3.57)	(161.46)
	MCP	1.00	0.38	2.96	109.70
		(1.63)	(0.67)	(4.81)	(183.17)
	Total	1.21	0.36	2.54	107.68
		(2.10)	(0.61)	(4.18)	(168.43)

relax for a few moments. The mode display is switched off, and calibration is checked by having the participant focus on the PFD, ND and mode panel. If calibration is still considered acceptable, by the red dot tracking fixation point within one inch on the World View, the second flight commences with the same format as the first. If calibration been found inaccurate, usually resulting from excessive head movement, the calibration process is repeated and the participant advised not to make large head movements.

3 Result

Six out of 25 participants were discounted due to incomprehensible data expressed as excessive amounts of undefined fixations and low data confidence (below 70 % confidence). Reasons for the incomprehensible data included: excessive head movement by the participant upsetting calibration (3); participant wearing mascara upsetting the eye tracking algorithm and data confidence (1); participant requiring eye correction and unable to wear glasses while wearing the eye-tracker, leading to difficulties reading the flight displays accurately (1); improper fit of tracker due to physical size of participant with very large head, leading to low data confidence (x1). This left 19 validated participants in total for the position design of FMAs on the flight deck, 9 for the PFD, 10 for the MCP position (Table 1).

4 Discussion

Previous research found mode changes are often missed on the flight deck, and low salience of FMAs – small alphanumeric displays against a dynamic background on the PFD produced in the form of cryptic abbreviations – may be a significant contributor to this. Pilots were familiar with using the MCP to track automation, despite the MCP not being designed for this purpose. A design solution was proposed that moved the FMAs to a glareshield position, taking into account design guidance from EASA and the FAA, as well as several design principles including positioning to increase salience and the PCP. Therefore, current research planned to evaluate this design using objective eye tracking and subjective feedback methods. The results of the experiment found that there were no significance in the fixation counts of FMAs situated on PFD (M = 16.44, SD = 9.62) compared with the MCP (M = 17.30, SD = 10.34). However, a significant difference was found in the mean fixation duration on the FMAs with pilots spending a longer duration on the PFD (M = 337.44, SD = 158.85) than on the MCP (M = 278.80, SD = 133.27). The greater attention allocated to the PFD by the experienced participants through Mean Fixation Duration (MFD) is mirrored in the percentage of total fixations allocated to the PFD (M = 48.28, SD = 32.32), which was also found to be significant larger than MCP (M = 43.08, SD = 27.99).

Based on the observation, the non-experienced participants did not value the information on the PFD as much as the experienced participants when completing the ILS-following task. During the briefing for the experiment participants were instructed to follow the ND lateral and vertical guidance bugs to guide them down the ILS beam, and the PFD was introduced as the display to which they can find their flight parameters such as attitude, airspeed, and altitude. It is likely that the non-experienced participants did not appreciate the importance of monitoring basic flight parameters, and even if they did, they may not have had the background knowledge to understand appropriate airspeeds, descent attitude etc. without specific briefing on these elements. This may have been exacerbated by having the power settings fixed. The lower MFD on the PFD from the non-experienced participants was not correlated with improved ILS beam tracking (deviations noted informally during the experiment), and can be explained by these participants extracting less meaning from the parameters presented. The experienced participants, with a greater resource of knowledge, will have spent many hours maintaining awareness of their flight parameters using the PFD, and so could be expected to give more importance to these parameters, with 'flying the beam' as a secondary priority; quite rightly. This reflects previous research where experienced pilots were found to visit more important instruments more often (Bellenkes et al. 1997).

There are two aspects of the cockpit instrument panel to illustrate proximity compatibility principle. The first aspect relates to the layout of the pilots' most important cockpit instruments. The second aspect of the instrument panel demonstrates how display proximity can be achieved through the actual integration of related information rather than spatial proximity. While the proximity compatibility principle dictates display closeness for information that needs to be integrated, it also dictates that for information channels that do not need to be integrated but should be the sole focus of attention, close proximity (to other information) should be avoided, since such proximity produces unwanted clutter (Wickens and Carswell 1995). Based on current research, the FMAs position had no significant difference on PFD and MCP, however a trend showing an increase of approximately 70 ms duration can be seen for the PFD FMAs position. This is supported by percentage of fixation that showed a trend for increased attention allocation to the PFD (48.28 %) for the than MCP position 38.40 %). Greater time allocated to the PFD may be due to the proximity of relevant instruments, including the distinguishing the modes of FMAs task for the current flight status. The proximity compatibility principle can therefore be used to help reduce attentional demands when comparing information. However, closely-spaced irrelevant information might distract the focus of attention. The Attitude (AOI-2) indicator shown no significant differences of total fixation duration, but pilots demonstrated a trend towards shorter mean fixation duration on the MCP (M = 379, SD = 151.59) position than on the PFD (M = 477, SD = 311.91) position.

Interestingly some participants who had hardly recorded visits to the FMAs panel still correctly called out mode changes. These individuals may have relied on peripheral vision and memory of the three possible modes that could present. There also appears to be a trend towards reduced MFD on the FMAs panel for the MCP position. It was thought MFD would be lower for the MCP FMAs position, on the assumption that a more salient FMAs position would require less time to interpret. Reduced salience of the PFD position may be drawing attention away faster. Participants viewing MCP FMAs are slightly fast on the FMAs due to lower background dynamic activity and the increased salience, this may increase their mode awareness as they afford more time for information extraction. It has been found in a previous study that this position did not have a more detrimental effect on the performance of other concurrent visual tasks (Nikolic and Sarter 2001).

5   Conclusion

With the increase of automation complexity on the flight deck, there has been a corresponding rise in 'automation surprise' related incidents and accidents. Lack of mode awareness is a contributing factor to automation surprise. The aviation industry has responded to this through improved training and procedures for operators in order to solve this problem. However, mode related incidents and accidents are still prevalent. Long and costly certification procedures inherent to the safety-critical nature of aviation, dictating an evolutionary rather than revolutionary design process, may explain why an effective, targeted design solution has not yet been introduced. The current design method of FMAs with a green box to highlight mode changes is well recognised in the literature as an imperfect design. Reinforcement of the status quo by certification guidance enables manufacturers to design for airworthiness approval at minimal cost, but given the prevalence of mode-related incidents and accidents, the design guidance may require a critical review. Simply acknowledging in the guidance that the problem is known, while specifically encouraging the known flawed-design solution of current FMAs has not led to more effective designs. Current research has found mode changes are often missed on the flight deck, and pilots prefer using the MCP to track automation, despite the MCP not being designed for this purpose. A design solution was proposed that moved the FMAs to a glareshield position, taking into account design guidance from EASA and the FAA, as well as several design principles including positioning to increase salience and the proximity compatibility principle. The results of the experiment found that FMAs on the MCP did not adversely affect pilot performance and could increase pilot's SA and reduced the mean fixation duration compared on the PFD position.

References

Airbus: Flight crew operating manual A320. Airbus Industrie, Toulouse (2006)

Arnold, D.C., Tinker, M.A.: The fixational pause of the eyes. J. Exp. Psychol. **25**, 271–280 (1939)

Bellenkes, A.H., Wickens, C.D., Kramer, A.F.: Visual scanning and pilot expertise: the role of attentional flexibility and mental model development. Aviat. Space Environ. Med. **68**, 569–579 (1997)

Björklund, C.M., Alfredson, J., Dekker, S.W.: Mode monitoring and call-outs: an eye-tracking study of two-crew automated flight deck operations. Int. J. Aviat. Psychol. **16**, 263–275 (2006)

Dekker, S.W.: Crew situation awareness in high-tech settings: tactics for research into an ill-defined phenomenon. Transp. Hum. Factors **2**, 49–62 (2000)

Endsley, M.R.: Automation and situation awareness. In: Parasuraman, R., Mouloua, M. (eds.) Automation and Human Performance: Theory and Applications, pp. 163–181. Lawrence Erlbaum, Mahwah, NJ (1996)

Funk, K.H., Lyall, E.A., Niemczyk, M.C.: Flightdeck automation problems: perceptions and reality. In: Mouloua, M., Koonce, J.M. (eds.) Human-Automation Interaction: Research and Practice. Lawrence Erlbaum Associates Inc, Mahwah, NJ (1997)

Harris, D.: Human Performance on the Flight Deck. Ashgate Publishing Ltd, Burlington (2011)

Hegarty, M., Mayer, R.E., Monk, C.A.: Comprehension of arithmetic word problems: a comparison of successful and unsuccessful problem solvers. J. Educ. Psychol. **87**, 18–32 (1995). doi:10.1037/0022-0663.87.1.18

Just, M.A., Carpenter, P.A.: A theory of reading: from eye fixations to comprehension. Psychol. Rev. **87**, 329–354 (1980). doi:10.1037/0033-295X.87.4.329

Li, W.-C., Yu, C.-S., Braithwaite, G., Greaves, M.: Interface design and pilot's attention distribution during pursuing a dynamic target. In: 17th International Conference on Human Computer Interaction, Los Angeles, USA (2015)

Lin, J.H., Lin, S.J.: Tracking eye movements when solving geometry problems with handwriting devices. J. Eye Mov. Res. **7**(1), 1–15 (2014)

Lu, W., Li, M., Lu, S., Song, Y., Yin, J., Zhong, N.: Visual search strategy and information processing mode: an eye-tracking study on web pages under information overload. In: Qi, L. (ed.) ISIA 2010. CCIS, vol. 86, pp. 153–159. Springer, Heidelberg (2011)

Mayer, R.E.: Unique contributions of eye-tracking research to the study of learning with graphics. Learn. Instr. **20**(2), 167–171 (2010). doi:10.1016/j.learninstruc.2009.02.012

NASA ASRS. Autothrottle speed control issues (2015). Accessed http://asrs.arc.nasa.gov/docs/cb/cb_423.pdf

Nikolic, M.I., Sarter, N.B.: Peripheral visual feedback: a powerful means of supporting effective attention allocation in event-driven, data-rich environments. Hum. Factors: J. Hum. Factors Ergon. Soc. **43**, 30–38 (2001)

Rayner, K.: Eye movements in reading and information processing: 20 years of research. Psychol. Bull. **124**(3), 372–422 (1998). doi:10.1037/0033-2909.124.3.372

Renshaw, J.A., Finlay, J.E., Tyfa, D., Ward, R.D.: Understanding visual influence in graph design through temporal and spatial eye movement characteristics. Interact. Comput. **16**(3), 557–578 (2004). doi:10.1016/j.intcom.2004.03.001

Robinski, M., Stein, M.: Tracking visual scanning techniques in training simulation for helicopter landing. J. Eye Mov. Res. **6**(2), 1–17 (2013)

van Dijk, H., van de Merwe, K., Zon, R.: A coherent impression of the pilots' situation awareness: Studying relevant human factors tools. Int. J. Aviat. Psychol. **21**, 343–356 (2011)

van Gog, T., Scheiter, K.: Eye tracking as a tool to study and enhance multimedia learning. Learn. Instr. **20**(2), 95–99 (2010). doi:10.1016/j.learninstruc.2009.02.009

van Gompel, R.: Eye Movements: A Window on Mind and Brain. Elsevier Science Ltd, London (2007)

Wetzel, P.A., Anderson, G.M., Barelka, B.A.: Instructor use of eye position based feedback for pilot training. In: Proceedings of the Human Factors and Ergonomics Society Annual Meeting, vol. 42, pp. 1388–1392 (1998). doi: 10.1177/154193129804202005

Wickens, C.D., Carswell, C.M.: The proximity compatibility principle: its psychological foundation and relevance to display design. Hum. Factors: J. Hum. Factors Ergon. Soc. **37**, 473–494 (1995)

Woods, D.D., Sarter, N.B.: Learning from automation surprises and going sour accidents. In: Sarter, N.B., Amalberti, R. (eds.) Cognitive Engineering in the Aviation Domain, pp. 327–353. Lawrence Erlbaum Associates Inc, Mahwah, NJ (2000)

Yu, C.S., Wang, E.M., Li, W.C., Braithwaite, G.: Pilots' visual scan pattern and situation awareness in flight operations. Aviat. Space Environ. Med. **85**(7), 708–714 (2014). doi:10.3357/ASEM.3847.2014

Zelinsky, G.J.: A theory of eye movements during target acquisition. Psychol. Rev. **115**, 787–835 (2008)

Seeing the Big Picture: Pilot Assessments of Cockpit System Interactions Contribution to Situation Awareness

David R. Meyer, Christina F. Rusnock[✉], and Michael E. Miller

Department of Systems Engineering and Management, Air Force Institute of Technology, Wright-Patterson AFB, OH 45433, USA
christina.rusnock@afit.edu

Abstract. Pilots build and maintain situation awareness based on their interaction with the world around them. This interaction includes a complex and dynamic series of tasks including running checklists, reading instruments and displays, looking out of the window, or listening to the radios. However, since the quality and quantity of information derived from each interaction is not well known, cockpit designers can only have an abstract understanding of how much situation awareness their system imparts to the human operators. This paper examines the opinions of pilots regarding how performing cockpit tasks contribute towards gaining situation awareness. Twenty-one military aviators were asked to rate 19 generic cockpit tasks based on how they contribute to or degrade situation awareness. This research shows that modern avionics, such as the Heads-Up Display, Multi-Function Display, and other sensors can provide strong positive situation awareness, but depending on the mission phase and other factors, they may not be significantly more advantageous than their analog counterparts.

Keywords: Situation awareness · Aircrew · Pilot · Cockpit design · Human-machine interaction

1 Introduction

The ability to conceive of the aircraft's whereabouts, status, weather, fuel state, terrain, and, in combat, enemy disposition is critical to effective aircraft operation. In critical phases of flight, in poor weather, or in the face of systems malfunctions, this ability can mean the difference between mission success and failure or even aircrew survivability [1]. Operator performance in complex or dynamic environments is often a function of situation awareness (SA) [2]. Aircrews spend considerable portions of time and effort developing and maintaining SA, especially in evolving environments [3]. Indeed the military has had a keen interest in SA in the cockpit dating back to World War I and especially more so in the information age of the late 20th century [4–6]. In tactical situations, this includes knowledge about the locations, actions, and capabilities of both friendly and enemy forces [3]. A leading cause of military and 88 % of commercial aviation accidents have been attributed to poor SA [7, 8]. If SA is essential to mission

© US Government (outside the US) 2016
D. Harris (Ed.): EPCE 2016, LNAI 9736, pp. 419–428, 2016.
DOI: 10.1007/978-3-319-40030-3_41

accomplishment, then harnessing the pilot interaction with the cockpit controls and displays which aid the collection of key information is a driving goal in both engineering design and operator training. This paper explores the operator's perspective on how cockpit tasks affect SA.

2 Background

Situation awareness (SA) is the knowledge of environmental factors that influence decisions and depends on the operator's internal perceptual model of the world [9]. More specifically, SA has been defined as the operator's perception (or mental model) of elements in the environment around them within a volume of space and time, the comprehension of their meaning, and the projection of their status into the future [3, 10]. Non-routine and unpredictable situations, such as those that can occur during emergency situations or combat, demand effective integration of large quantities of information to be processed with limited cognitive capacity [2, 4]. Situation awareness drives decision making based on the operator's mental model of the environment. The process of gaining situation awareness, while independent from the process of decision making, forms a basis for this mental model [4, 11]. The performance of a pilot is highly related to their ability to fuse information to augment SA and drive decision-making [12]. The resulting decision leads to an action, which alters the environment and situation and the cycle begins again.

No current criteria exist to determine the required level of SA needed to obtain a desired level of performance [13]. Less than perfect SA causes the operator to assume a level of risk for error as they must make a decision without complete information. Good SA increases the probability of good performance, but does not guarantee high performance as factors, such as excessive workload, poor decision making, or poor task execution can degrade performance in the presence of good SA [11]. Because of the critical effects situation awareness has on mission outcome and survivability, designers have a vested interest in providing the operator with appropriate resources, and operators have a vested interest in maintaining a high level of SA [1].

Designers can incorporate heads-up displays (HUD), multi-function displays (MFD), automation, expert systems, advanced avionics, and sensors to provide more information in a more useful manner [10]. In this regard, for a given task, all cockpits are not created equal. Cockpit design affects the number of required tasks the operator must perform, the workload of those tasks, and the information provided to the operator during their completion [4]. Automation and intelligent cockpits can tailor information to match the operator's needs or perform support functions based on the required situation [2]. Operators develop procedures to scan information sources and train to maximize the use of all available tools and observations to increase SA.

Traditional methods for measuring SA often probe the operator's awareness of critical facts within an environment or require the operator or an observer to rate the operator's SA when using a system or simulator [14]. However, these methods do not readily provide insight into the utility of any single device in the cockpit for improving SA. Evaluations of the impact of individual display or display formats on SA are limited within the human factors research, but often include evaluating a system in which a single display is modified within the cockpit [15].

It might be reasonable to assume that by increasing the availability of information in the cockpit, SA will be improved. However, the literature and experience demonstrate that this assumption is not true. For example:

- Cues in the normal field of view can be missed if they are too subtle or if the operator is not paying sufficient attention [16], yet most pilots would immediately perceive a flashing "Master Warning" light, especially if it was accompanied by an audible warning tone. However, frequent or nuisance warnings desensitize operators, thus negating the effectiveness of those warnings [17, 18].
- As cockpits evolve, new "black boxes" are added: autopilot, radar, weapons systems, mission sensors, navigational aids, computers, etc. While many of the additions undeniably present more information to the aircrew and have the potential to solve specific problems, they each present another interface to the human operator, increasing workload and decreasing the time available to scan each device.
- Information overload is a significant concern in modern cockpits [2, 19]. SA is inherently a function of the quantity and quality of data, however the format of image presentation determines the availability and the likelihood of use of that data. Poorly designed and integrated interfaces increase workload and time needed to synthesize information and open opportunities for confusion and errors [2]. Conversely, well-designed interfaces can reduce workload. However, even the best cockpit displays and controls cannot overcome human performance limits [20], including the human operator's capacity for attention of 2−40 bits per second; far lower than the presentation rate of the environment and modern cockpit systems [21].
- Because glass cockpits rely much more on integrating display layers and inputs, primarily through a Flight Management System (FMS). These systems provide more data in a richer format. However, they also require paging through multiple display layers. As such, interaction now requires a keyboard for instrument manipulation, therefore, accessing a function that once required twisting a dial or a couple of switches is more complex—with an associated increase in workload and time delay.
- By reducing the number of places a pilot is required to scan within the cockpit, attention resources available to the remaining scan areas can be increased. However, if the pilot neglects to maintain a scan elsewhere and becomes dependent or fixated on certain information sources (e.g., the HUD), his or her SA will remain limited [22–24]. Dependency on automation elements may cause fixation to the neglect of other duties.
- Automation can increase feedback or provide new methods of communicating feedback, which may alter how an operator must assimilate that data [25]. If performed well, this can aid the operator in comprehending the meaning of items in the environment and projecting future states; however, if performed poorly, critical information may be obscured.

Each of these examples illustrates that each information source in the cockpit may have a significant influence (positive or negative) on SA. Therefore, there is a need for a method to allow one to understand the effect of each of these information sources on the operator's SA, allowing one to assess the importance of each display and perhaps each information representation. As indicated before, however, the presence of a display does not aid SA. Instead SA is gained as the operator actively interacts with the system, gaining information through this interaction. Since the cockpit and situation awareness are inextricably linked, this paper seeks to answer the question "how do various cockpit tasks contribute to aircrew SA?"

3   Methodology

Meyer [1] distilled over 1200 different cockpit tasks found in typical C-130 airlift missions into 19 generic cockpit tasks representing human-machine interaction and non-machine interaction tasks. This list of tasks is provided in Table 1. These generic tasks can easily be applied as an analogy to the majority of cockpit tasks found in any aircraft. These generic tasks can then be classified as machine or non-machine interaction tasks; where the human either interacts with the machine or with other humans. Some generic tasks, specifically talking and listening tasks were difficult to classify. For instance, if these tasks were conducted via radio or aircraft but the communication was human-human interaction with electronic transmission means, the tasks were classified as non-machine interaction tasks. However, aircraft generated advisories (listening, simple) and monitoring the Radar Warning Receiver (RWR), which permit interaction between the human and the machine could be classified as machine interaction tasks. However, they generally require natural interfaces as would be employed when interacting with another human and are therefore classified as non-machine interaction tasks.

Table 1. Generic cockpit tasks

Machine interaction tasks	Non-machine interaction tasks
Reading instrument or gauge	Looking out of window
Reading MFD/moving map/digital display	Writing (data cards, kneeboard, etc.)
Viewing Head's Up Display (HUD)	Reading charts, "sticks," approach plates
Reading raw computer data	Manual computations (flight computer, TOLD, etc.)
Radar/sensor interpretation	Talking, simple (advisory calls, responses)
Keyboard/data entry	Talking, complex (briefings, radio calls, etc.)
Simple maneuvering (maintaining parameters)	Listening, simple (alerts, advisory call)
Complex maneuvering (defensive reactions)	Listening, complex (radio, crew feedback)
Simple button/switch actuation	Background listening (monitoring RWR, radio)
Cumbersome button/switch actuation	

In order to quantify the relative contributions of each individual task to tactical SA, a survey was given to 21 aviators representing pilots and non-pilot operators of various military aircraft. The number of respondents in each aircraft type and crew position are shown in Table 2. Several of the participants had flown on multiple aircraft (hence aircraft count is greater than 21). C-130 aircrew and pilots were intentionally over-represented because Meyer [1] originally focused on the C-130 aircraft.

Table 2. Survey representation

Aircraft	n	Aircraft	n	Crew	n
AC-130 W	1	MC-130H	11	Pilot	12
C-130H	12	MC-130 J	1	Navigator	3
C-130 J	4	MH-65D	1	Electronic Warfare Officer	1
CV-22A	1	T-1	1	Flight Engineer	4
F-15E	2	U-28A	1	Special Mission Aviator	1

Respondents were asked to rate the relative impact of each task on SA. When performing this rating, participants were asked to provide a rating between −3 and 3. Participants were to provide this rating against a hypothetical baseline of flying with one's eyes closed, which was to receive a rating of 0. Note that negative numbers indicate that the tasks detract from SA, zero equals no effect of a task on SA, and positive values indicate that performing the task contributes to SA. Participants were asked to disregard the effects of workload on their SA scores and provide any remarks that they felt were appropriate. Because it is expected that SA demands change as a function of mission phase, these ratings were made for three different mission phases: cruise flight, formation airdrop, and a maximum effort landing.

4   Results

Since not every survey participant was familiar with every mission phase (i.e. F-15E pilots do not perform airdrop), or are in suitably equipped aircraft, each task did not necessarily receive 21 responses. Most notably, tasks involving the head's-up display (HUD) during the airdrop and maximum effort landing mission phases was limited to C-130 J and MC-130 J participants (n = 4). However, the standard deviation for the HUD tasks (σ = 0.52, 0.96, 0.00) was normal compared to standard deviations of other tasks with 14–21 respondents. Indeed standard deviations were relatively large due to the integer scoring and small sample size (σaverage = 1.33). Noticeably, tasks that induced positive SA tended to have lower standard deviations than negative SA tasks as shown in Table 4.

By far, the strongest sentiment in participant feedback was, "it depends." What is clearly evident from Tables 3 and 4 is that the situation itself is a strong independent variable. Objective area events, such as airdrop and airland, produced slightly stronger opinions than in cruise flight. Tasks that related to visual cues, such as looking out of the window or HUD have stronger SA scores when the aircraft was lower to the ground and when those visual cues provide richer and more detailed information. The more cognitively demanding tasks of keyboard entry, complex talking (i.e. giving a briefing), writing, and manual computations produced stronger SA penalties during objective area events. Human-machine interaction tasks that provided strong positive SA tended to receive even higher ratings during objective area events; non-machine interaction tasks that incurred strong SA penalties received lower ratings during objective area events (i.e. events near targets, drop zones, and landing zones). Conversely, human-machine interaction SA penalties did not get appreciably worse during objective area events (except keyboard entry), while non-machine interaction tasks with strong SA scores did not improve noticeably during objective area events (except for looking out of the window).

When viewing human-machine interaction tasks (Table 3), a strong preference emerges from four tasks: viewing the HUD, reading a multifunction display (MFD) or other similar moving map or digital display, reading instruments and gauges, and radar/sensor interpretation. The HUD scored moderately well during cruise flight, but the SA value increased remarkably during airdrop and airland, receiving the only scores above 2.0. Clearly the relevance of HUD information, whether by design or its relevance, increases dramatically during these two objective area events where aircraft are lower to the ground. The MFD SA averages were consistently high across all phases of flight. The quantity, quality, and relevance of this data does not seem to depend on phase of flight as much as it depends on crew position (flight engineers and some navigators consistently gave it lower SA scores, while pilots gave considerably higher SA scores to the MFD).

Table 3. SA scores, human-machine interaction tasks

Machine interaction tasks	Averages			Standard deviation		
	Cruise	Airdrop	Airland	Cruise	Airdrop	Airland
Viewing Head's Up Display (HUD)	1.33	2.25	3.00	0.52	0.96	0.00
Reading MFD/moving map	1.95	1.93	1.93	1.02	1.14	1.49
Reading instrument or gauge	1.35	1.08	1.62	0.88	1.19	1.33
Radar/sensor interpretation	1.48	1.29	1.14	0.93	1.44	1.46
Simple maneuvering	0.00	0.00	0.15	0.97	1.08	0.99
Reading raw computer data	−0.05	0.07	0.00	1.47	1.27	1.66
Simple button/switch actuation	−0.10	−0.14	−0.29	0.89	0.86	0.91
Complex maneuvering	−1.00	−0.86	−0.79	1.22	1.83	1.81
Cumbersome button/switch actuation	−0.86	−0.93	−0.93	1.39	1.54	1.77
Keyboard/data entry	−0.80	−1.00	−1.00	1.24	1.58	1.63

Surprisingly, instrument/gauge reading and radar/sensor interpretation did not exhibit clearly defined trends when viewed as averages. Reading an instrument infers reading a single component and gaining few elements of information. Compared to digital displays such as a HUD or MFD (which superimpose multiple data sources into the pilot's field of view or onto a moving map display), the gauges–by design–present far less data. However, it is surprising that in cruise flight, the SA value of raw instrument reading is nearly identical to viewing the HUD. Furthermore, raw instrument data scored lowest during airdrop and highest during airland. These trends can partially be explained when considering the non-C-130 aircrew did not answer the airdrop and airland portions. Pilots had stronger opinions of the value of instrument reading than navigators (and even some flight engineers), and pilots made up the bulk of non-C-130 participants that were represented only in the cruise flight category. This same trend was also partially evident in the radar/sensor interpretation task, but several participants indicated that it was of less value during the objective area than cruise flight. It is unclear if this is caused by radar/sensor information being degraded at low altitude, the information having less relevance during those phases, or a preference for other tasks, such as looking outside the window or HUD.

Similar to the HUD values shown in Table 3, looking out of the window increased in value during objective area events as shown in Table 4. In cruise flight, the window had similar SA values to the HUD, despite the HUD providing extra data. While pilots naturally have a strong SA value derived from looking outside, those situated farther from the cockpit windows did not feel as strongly. Naturally, the one respondent who stated, "I can barely see out the window from where I sit," rated the value of looking out of the window as marginal. Using this task as an example, one pilot emphasized that not only are phases of flight an independent variable, but specific situational elements add a host of other variables. For example, when looking out of the window, "night or low illumination will lower SA. If flying in formation through the weather, SA goes down, but looking through the window in daylight with good visibility in the mountains will greatly increase SA."

Table 4. SA scores, non-machine interaction tasks

Non-machine interaction	Averages			Standard deviation		
	Cruise	Airdrop	Airland	Cruise	Airdrop	Airland
Looking out of window	1.33	1.79	1.93	1.46	1.42	1.27
Listening, simple	0.90	0.50	0.86	1.00	1.29	1.29
Reading charts, approach plates	1.14	0.57	0.36	1.28	1.74	1.69
Listening, complex	0.81	0.14	0.14	1.33	1.75	1.83
Talking, simple	0.38	0.14	0.29	1.16	1.03	1.27
Background listening	−0.14	−0.29	−0.21	1.42	1.38	1.53
Talking, complex	−0.14	−0.64	−0.57	1.56	1.78	1.79
Writing	−0.19	−0.57	−0.93	1.12	1.28	1.21
Manual computations	−0.90	−1.15	−1.08	1.62	1.77	1.85

Naturally, reading a chart, map, or approach diagram will provide the operator with SA. Participants also showed a preference for simple listening tasks (i.e. "too low" or "5 knots fast") over more complex listening. Complex listening provided more SA during cruise flight than during objective area operations, which reinforces operational practices to conduct crew briefings during cruise portions of flight where possible. However, it is indeterminate if this trend has to do with typically lower attentional demands during cruise that allows for more complex listening, or because cruise flight grants more relevance, quantity, or quality of that data. One crew member indicated the value added depends on the information that was being conveyed: "crew feedback is good for SA, background noise is not." Naturally, listening to static, or non-relevant radio chatter might produce little or no SA, but to the electronic warfare officer, background listening through the radar warning receiver was a significant exception to that rule.

In reporting SA scores, some participants provided negative SA scores, which we hypothesize represents an opportunity cost that most likely trades off tactical and strategic SA. Performing task A (tactical task) consumes attentional resources that may have been spent on a hypothetical task B (strategic task) that would have yielded more SA. Thus, despite survey instructions, it is difficult to cognitively separate SA lost to higher workload (or to opportunity cost) from truly negative SA. In reality, a negative SA score would imply that by accomplishing a task, erroneous SA would be gained leading to an incorrect mental model.

Participant opinion appears to reflect this. One noted that the "largest loss of SA in terminal events is due to time constraints: time must be split between [being an] active participant in [the] event and other, coordination tasks." While many participants generalized anecdotal evidence that some tasks add SA and some tasks taketh away, others lament that certain cockpit tasks, such as the complex manual computations required for determining aircraft performance data "can potentially take me out of the game almost completely." Keyboard entry is considerably more complicated than simple switch actuation, and it also requires more attention devoted to ensuring that the keyboard entry is performed correctly. Furthermore, improper syntax, hitting a wrong button, and other errors create more work and perhaps distract the operator from performing other SA-generating tasks.

Perhaps what is most telling about operator opinion regarding the SA/workload tradeoff is summed up by one pilot's opinion that, "rating is a balancing act between SA gained by the task and the SA lost by time spent completing the act." Thus, the SA value of a heads-down multifunction display (MFD) was offset by the need to take the pilot's eyes out of the window or HUD to consume that information. Reading raw computer data (data displayed in number or tabular form and not integrated into an MFD, HUD, or other visual display) did not yield a positive or negative SA value, potentially because of this tradeoff.

5 Future Research

While this paper explores the concept of task-dependent SA, further research is required. This survey heavily samples C-130 and other tactical aircrew. A much larger survey should be conducted that incorporates more aircraft (with and without HUD) across the spectrum of flight. More mission sets can be added including tactical and non-tactical situations at both high and low altitudes. Within each mission phase, more resolution is needed. Many participants queried "what part of airdrop/airland are you talking about?" This infers that even within the particular mission phase, SA values could change. If, for example, viewing the HUD increases value from cruise to airland missions, how much does it increase from initial approach to the actual landing?

Furthermore, how do the SA values of specific tasks relate to the operator's dynamic priorities for SA?

Aircrews have many opinions about SA, but these may not neatly fit into current academic research into SA. For example, operators appear to conflate opportunity costs of performing a task that does not generate SA at the expense of another SA-generating task with tasks that actually reduce certainty through providing misleading information. Future studies should consider exactly what "negative SA" means and account for the difference between opportunity costs and incorrect mental models.

6 Conclusion

Capturing the effect of cockpit tasks on SA can allow for the refinement of predictive SA algorithms that incorporate both workload-dependent and task-dependent SA [1]. Clearly understanding how each task builds a pilot's mental model of his environment has clear advantages for avionics engineers when designing components, as well as for cockpit designers when incorporating those components into the aircraft's primary machine interface. This research shows that modern avionics, such as the HUD, MFD, and other sensors can provide strong positive SA, but depending on the mission phase and other factors, they may not be significantly more advantageous than analog counterparts. Furthermore, designers must not only consider the displays, but the interface required to control those displays, as well as the attention demanded by other cockpit tasks and their opportunity costs.

7 Disclaimer

The views expressed in this paper are those of the authors and do not reflect the official policy or position of the United States Air Force, the Department of Defense, or the U.S. Government.

References

1. Meyer, D.R.: Effects of Automation on Aircrew Workload and Situation Awareness in Tactical Airlift Missions. Air Force Institute of Technology, Wright-Patterson AFB (2015)
2. Secarea, J.V.: Beyond knobs and dials: towards and intentional model of man-machine interaction. In: Procedings of the IEEE Aerospace and Electronics Conference, pp. 763–783. IEEE (1990)
3. Endsley, M.R.: Situation awareness in aviation systems. In: Garland, D.J., Wise, J.A., Hopkin, V.D. (eds.) Handbook of Aviation Human Factors, pp. 257–276. Lawrence Erlbaum Associates, Mahwah (1999)
4. Endsley, M.R.: Toward a theory of situation awareness in dynamic systems. Hum. Factors 37, 32–64 (1995)
5. Press, M.: Situation awareness: Let's get serious about the clue-bird (1986)

6. 57th Figther Wing. Intraflight command, control, and communications symposium final report. United States Air Force, Nellis AFB (1986)
7. Endsley, M.R.: A taxonomy of situation awareness errors. In: 21st Conference, Western European Association of Aviation Psychology. Western European Association of Aviation Psychology, Dublin (1994)
8. Hartel, C.E., Smith, K., Prince, C.: Defining aircrew coordination: searching mishaps for meaning. In: Sixth International Symposium on Aviation Psychology, Columbus (1991)
9. Klein, G.A., Calderwood, R., Clinton-Cirocco, A.: Rapid decision making on the fire ground. In: Proceedings of the Human Factors Society - 30th Annual Meeting (1986)
10. Endsley, M.R.: Situation awareness global assessment technique. In: Proceedings of the IEEE 1988 National Aerospace and Electronics Conference: NAECON 1988, vol. 3, pp. 789–795. IEEE, Dayton (1988a)
11. Endsley, M.R.: Measurement of situation awareness in dynamic systems. Hum. Factors: J. Hum. Factors Ergon. Soc. **37**(1), 65–84 (1995)
12. Venturino, M., Hamilton, W.L., Dverchak, S.R.: Performance-based measures of merit for tactical situation awareness. In: Situation Awareness in Aerospace Operations, pp. 4/1–4/5 (1989)
13. Pew, R.W.: Defining and measuring situation awareness in the commercial aircraft cockpit. In: Proceedings of the Conference on Challenges in Aviation Human Factors: The National Plan, pp. 30–31. American Institute of Aeronautics and Astronautics, Washington, D.C. (1991)
14. Stanton, N.A., Salmon, P.M., Walker, G.H., Baber, C., Jenkins, D.P.: Human Factors Methods: A Practical Guide for Engineering and Design. Ashgate, Surrey (2005)
15. Vidulich, M.A. Hughes, E.R.: Testing a subjective metric of situation awareness. In: Proceedings of the Human Factors Society 35th Annual Meeting, pp. 1307–1311 (1991)
16. Kahneman, D.: Attention and Effort. Prentice-Hall, Englewood Cliffs (1973)
17. Billings, C.E.: Human-Centered Aircraft Automation: A Concept and Guidelines. NASA Ames Research Center, Moffett Field (1991)
18. Wiener, E.L., Curry, R.E.: Flight-Deck Automation: Promises and Problems. NASA, Washington, D.C. (1980)
19. Hart, S.G., Sheridan, T.B.: Pilot Workload, Performance, and Aircraft Control Automation. Ames Research Center. National Aeronautics and Space Administration, Moffett Field (1984)
20. Hart, S.G.: Helicopter human factors. In: Wiener, E.L., Nagel, D.C. (eds.) Human Factors in Aviation. Academic Press (1988)
21. Lovesey, J.: Information overload in the cockpit. In: IEEE Colloquium on Information Overload, pp. 5/1–5/5. IEEE, London (1995)
22. Haynes, W.: Validating the Need for a Heads up Display in the C-130 Avionics Modernization Program. Combat Aerial Delivery School, Little Rock AFB (1998)
23. Shinaberry, J.A.: (D. R. Meyer, Interviewer) (15 November 2013)
24. Kennedy, W.: (D. R. Meyer, Interviewer) (22 April 2015)
25. Endsley, M.R.: Automation and situation awareness. In: Parasuraman, R., Mouloua, M. (eds.) Automation and Human Performance: Theory and Applications, pp. 163–181. Lawrence Erlbaum, Mahwah (1996)

Potential of 3D Audio as Human-Computer Interface in Future Aircraft

Christian A. Niermann[✉]

German Aerospace Center (DLR), Institute of Flight Guidance,
Lilienthalplatz 7, 38108 Braunschweig, Germany
christian.niermann@dlr.de

Abstract. Upcoming cockpit designs will face new human-machine challenges related to an increasing number of pilot assistant and information systems. New cockpit designs aim to decreasing the visual workload to create free capacity in the human visual channel, which increases the information flow and lowers stress of the flight crews. At present time, none of them use spacial audio as an additional information channel. Current research considered mostly setups that are not applicable in state-of-the-art cockpits. The paper presents an experiment with a 3D audio system and a normal aviation like stereo headset. The localization performance of 23 participants under 4 different settings was calculated. Participants moved a digital ball with their head to mark the localized sound angle. The importance of head coupled movement become clear with a higher localization performance. The influence of sound frequency for warning sounds vs. human speech was not as high as expected.

Keywords: 3D audio · Head tracker · Localization performance · Cockpit · Assistant system

1 Introduction and Research Question

In modern cockpits, most information provided to the pilot is given visually. Large visual-display units in state-of-the-art head-down glass cockpits provide a considerable amount of information e. g., Primary Flight Display, Navigation Display, Systems Display, Engine and Warning Display. Additionally helmet-mounted displays or head-up displays on the one hand increase situational awareness but on the other hand intensely consume visual resources of the pilot (Jovanovic 2009). Audio as an interface in modern aircraft cockpits is underrepresented compared to the multitude of visual displays. It conveys no spatial information in present-day civil cockpit and is used only to bring attention to a visual display (Begault and Pittman 1996) or as intra-crew and crew to air traffic control communication. In addition to narrowed space in modern cockpits, the cognitive ability of humans is limited (Wickens 2002). With increasing number of systems that have to be used, managed or monitored by the cockpit crew, this creates new operational burdens and new kinds of failure modes in the overall human-machine system (Oving *et al.* 2004; Spence and Ho 2008).

© Springer International Publishing Switzerland 2016
D. Harris (Ed.): EPCE 2016, LNAI 9736, pp. 429–438, 2016.
DOI: 10.1007/978-3-319-40030-3_42

Audio research has been sparse in aviation and mostly covered spatial audio with a set of loudspeakers around participants head or simple left-right-volume difference in the headset (Simpson *et al.* 2007). However, several studies have suggested a multitude of applications for the use of 3D audio in the cockpit (Begault and Pittman 1996; Haas 1998; Veltman *et al.* 2004). This paper wants to fill this gap and introduces the design and results of a psychoacoustic 3D audio experiment with focus on aviation needs.

The experiment intends to test the ability of 3D audio localization presented via a standard stereo headset as it is common used in present aircraft cockpits. Three main aspects were considered: Firstly, the localization performance was evaluated i.e., the capability of positioning sound sources in 3D space at predetermined positions. This enables participants, to localize sound sources at desired positions with some uncertainty. This information is needed to decide about future possible application in the domain of aviation that could be supplemented or replaced by a 3D audio system. Secondly, the influence of linked head movement, measured by a head tracker, on the localization performance was analyzed. It is predicted, that head linking has a distinctly positive influence in the localization performance. It is important to know how strong and what kind of impact head movement has on the acceptances and performance of the participants. Thirdly, three different test sounds were presented at the same position and under the same conditions to the participants. It is mainly interested if the localization performance increase with a sound at wider frequency spectrum.

The paper is organized in three parts. Section 2 gives an overview of the used setup as well as the dependent and independent variable. In Sect. 3 the findings of the 3D audio experiment and the row data are briefly discussed. Conclusions and outline of future work are presented in the last Sect. 4.

2 Experiment Design

2.1 Procedure

The experiment was split into two parts for each participant. Firstly, every participant was introduced to the experiment and got a short summary of the following steps. After that, the pure tone audiometry test was executed. A rapid-result was shown to the experiment operator to ensure that the participant met the requirements of the experiment. Following, the main experiment part.

At the beginning, participants received a digital questionnaire. They were asked: age, gender and if the participant holds a pilot-license. In case of an existing pilot-license, participants were asked about the license-type, flight hours, medical and the use of a headset during flight. All participants were asked, if any experience with spatial audio exists. Moreover they were asked, how often and for which application they use headphones and if they play computer games or a musical instrument.

Four different sessions were created and presented to the participant mixed. They were introduced to the first experiment session and what they are going to expect. Participants were asked to rotate the whole body with the swivel chair to localize the test sound. The head tracker was calibrated, before every new test sound was played, if it was required. In every session and for every sound angle the presenting sequence was the same. First, the sound was played two times at the 0° position. Then it moved to the target position and played during the movement for three times. At the target position, the test sound played either five times (session A, D) or until the participant pressed a button (session B, C). The head tracker was enabled in session A and B and participants were asked to rotate their body as they prefer while the sound plays. In session C and D the head tracker was not active and the test sound was not played relative to the orientation of the participant's head.

During one session, 20 different angles were presented twice. Each session took around 15 – 20 min, depending on the time, the participant needed to localize and to decide the perceived position. Directly after each test session, participants replied to a questionnaire. They were asked, how they felt after the recently conducted session and what they thought about the given sound file. After a short break the next session began, again with an introduction of the now following setup.

After four sessions, the main experiment part ended and participants were asked about their overall opinion about the experiment and the 3D audio sounds.

2.2   Sound

Three test sounds *(A, B, voice)* were created as basic stimuli for the experiment, and all sounds having a length of one second. Those sounds were used to evaluate the localization performance. Sound-A is designed as a technical warning sound with a frequency of 2.000 Hz. Sound-B with a frequency of 4.000 Hz. Both sounds are similar to typical warning-sounds used in aviation context. Sound *Voice* is a synthetic English female voice, speaking out the word *position*.

2.3   Experiment Sessions

The experiment was split into four test sessions [A–D] for each participant, the order was completely mixed between the participants:

A with head tracker and five iterations at target angle
B with head tracker and looped iteration at target angle
C without head tracker and looped iteration at target angle
D without head tracker and five iterations at target angle

For the experiment 20 sound angles where defined. The first six angles always start at the positions: 90°, 30°, 270°, 330°, 150°, 210°. After these, the next 12 angles where defined randomly. Each angle was presented to the participant a second time after the first angle-sets were played completely. The presented sound angle had a distance of at least 40° to the one given before. For the test sessions four distinct angle-sets were defined. No correspondence between these sets was given. In total, 4 × 40 sound angles were presented to each participant during the experiment.

2.4   Software and Head Tracker

Audio for the right and left ear were calculated in real time by the experiment software. The head-related transfer function (HRTF) used in this experiment was non-individualized for each participant. The audio corresponded in the two *head tracker sessions* to the direction of the desired sound source position relative to the orientation of the participant's head. This was possible by combining the headset with a Carl Zeiss cinemizer head tracker, continuously sending the head positions and orientations to the experiment software. Including this information, it was able to relocate the audio in real time whenever the participant moves the head. Figure 1 shows the structure of this system. The complete real time 3D audio system including HRTF, head tracker, sound source and logging was executed on a DELL E7440 personal laptop.

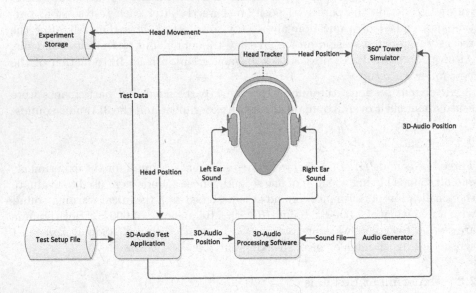

Fig. 1. Structure of the test system used in the experiment

2.5   Definition of Direction

The direction in this experiment is defined like a compass, the angle rise clockwise from 0° to 360°. An angle of 0° for the direction straight ahead and 180° in the back of the participant. Accordingly, directly to the right of the participant was 90°, on the opposite side, on the direct left 270°. Following the experiment design, the elevation angle was fixed to 0° in the horizontal plane and for all participants on the eye level.

2.6   Pointing Device

Participants had to point to the perceived position of the sound. To achieve this, they had to move a digital red ball, shown on the wall of the simulator, to their perceived position. For this, the ball-position was coupled with the head tracker attached to the participant's headset. The ball was shown after the test sound was played in the center of attention. They where instructed to rotate their whole body on the swivel chair as part of the localization task. At the perceived position, participants confirmed by clicking on a presenter button in their hand. The combination of ball and head tracker was calibrated by the participant before every new audio position was played if it was required. There is no difference whether the participant shows the position by hand, or the pointing is done by head movement (Majdak *et al.* 2010).

2.7 Location

The experiment took place in the Institute of Flight Guidance at German Aerospace Center (DLR), Braunschweig, Germany. A 360-degree round room, normally a tower simulator, was used. The wall of the simulator was in a light blue during the experiment. The positions 0°, 90°, 180° and 270° were marked by a black chessboard-line as it is shown in Fig. 2. Inside the tower simulator a constant background noise at 43 dB from the projectors is present during the whole experiment. The participant sat on a swivel chair in the center of the room, centered between the four marked positions. The cable of the headset and head tracker was attached to the chair, so that the participant could rotate on the chair without limitation. The experiment operator sad in the same room at approximately 150°, 3 meters away from the participant.

Fig. 2. 360-degree tower simulator

2.8   Participants

The experiment it targeted towards an application in aviation system. Nevertheless, in this part a wider range is aimed. Thus, participants were chosen random from scientists of the research facility. Twenty-three people, five female and eighteen male, ranging from the age of 25 to 62 (M = 36.43, SD = 10.01) participated in the experiment. Ten participants held a pilot license and experienced an average of 478 (SD = 448.06) flight hours in total.

2.9   Pure Tone Audiometry

According to the German Acoustical Society, participants in a hearing test should have a normal threshold of hearing. This can be reviewed by a sound threshold audiometry or a questionnaire (Hellbrück *et al.* 2008). For this experiment a pure tone audiometry test was built. The up-5-down-10-method, where the tone is raised by 5 dB for every *No* and lowered by 10 dB for every *Yes* was used. The presentations of the tones had no rhythmic pattern, but were played in reasonably irregular distances (Gelfand 2001). Every time participants heard a tone, they had to press a button. The hearing test was done with the same type of headset as used in the experiment. If the participants are pilots with a valid European license, they have to pass their medical intermittently. In this regard the hearing threshold gets tested. In a pure tone audiometry the hearing loss on each ear can not fall below 35 dB at 500 Hz, 1.000 Hz and 2.000 Hz and 50 dB at 3.000 Hz. (BMVI 2007).

All participants were tested and passed the pure tone audiometry test with limits for pilots in the frequency 500 Hz, 1.000 Hz, 2.000 Hz and 3.000 Hz. The average hearing threshold was at 16.03 dB (SD = 7.05) with an average left-right difference below 5 dB (M = 3.04 dB, SD = 1.84 dB).

3   Results

The localization error was calculated as the difference between the actual and estimated direction by the participant. The distribution was assumed to be a normal distribution. Mean average and standard deviation were calculated from the raw directional data.

3.1   Direction Offset

During the experiment, all participants heard in total 160 sound positions. As described before, 20 sound angles were defined for the experiment and were repeated for all sessions randomly. The average location performance under all conditions in this experiment is at M = −0.29°, SD = 16.20. The lowest localization error, except for 0°, was at the left (90°, M = 5,87°, SD = 13.63) and right position (260°, M = −1.66°, SD = 14.44) of the participant. In a range ±30° at the 0° position, the localization error was highest (M = −0.51, SD = 30.03).

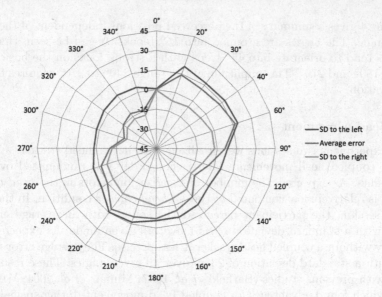

Fig. 3. Average error over all tested sessions with aberration to the left and right side

Following these results, Fig. 3 shows, that the standard deviation in the rear hemisphere is apportion for left and right. However, the deviation in the front-right-quadrant tends to be more to the left (lower angle), whereas the participant moved the localization in the front-left-quadrant more to the right (higher angle).

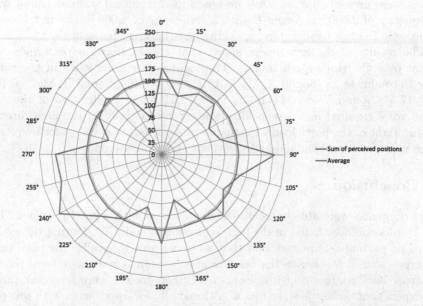

Fig. 4. Sum of all perceived positions for the whole experiment

Figure 4 gives a summary of the perceived positions independent of the given sound angle. The angles are grouped into 15° blocks. It can be seen, that participants tend to orientate into 45° steps with a strong focus on the basic angle 0°, 90°, 180° and 270°. The amplitude in the range 240° to 270° requires further consideration.

3.2   Head Movement

In the experiment two sessions were realized with active head tracker, and two without coupled head movement. The session order was randomized over the participants. As expected, the number of localization errors in the *head tracker* sessions is relatively low compared to the *no head tracker* condition. In the head tracker session, the participant perceived the sound with an average error of $-0.59°$ with a standard deviation of 8.51 over all given angle. As expected, the accuracy without a coupled head tracker is less precise. The average error rose to 1.34° with a standard deviation of 23.89 over all given angles. These results are in line with previous studies (Barfield *et al.* 1997; Minnar *et al.* 2001; Weinzierl 2008), which found advantages for coupled head movement during spacial audio sessions. A higher average error in the *no head tracker* sessions was measured at the positions front-right and back-left. Beside those findings, participants reported a more natural feeling with head coupled audio.

3.3   Different Sounds

Participants were divided into three groups. For each group a different test sounds were presented. *Sound-A* is designed as a technical warning sound with a frequency of 2.000 Hz. *Sound-B* with a frequency of 4.000 Hz. Sound *Voice* is a synthetic English female voice, speaking out the word *position*.

The results of the experiment show, that the localization performance is similar over the three given sounds. The localization error value in the range from 15 to almost 18 (Sound A: $M = -0.19°$, $SD = 15.66$; Sound B: $M = -0.13°$, $SD = 17.54$; Sound Voice: $M = 1.45°$, $SD = 15.41$). The localization of the synthetic voice resulted in a low localization error especially in the area directly left and right of the participant. Participants reported, that the wider frequency range was less disturbing and hence easier to concentrate on.

4   Conclusion

All participants were able to localize a given sound with a good precision. The best results could be found in the half between 90° and 270°. During the experiment, no participants remark that they were not able to localize the position of the given sound. Neither in the head tracker session nor without head tracker any front-back confusion or inside-the-head phenomenon were recorded during the experiment. With these results it is thinkable, for application with low precision thresholds, that a complicate head tracking inside an aircraft cockpit can be renounced.

Surely, the localization uncertainty was noticeable lower with head coupled movement during spacial audio sessions. The results of the localization performance with and without head tracker compared well to results presented by other authors. An important finding from this experiment implies, that with the programed experiment software and setup a sound object can be localized in real time with a precession that further research for future application in the domain of pilot assistant systems are thinkable.

Nevertheless the influenced of different sound was not as high as expected. It is thinkable, that the chosen sounds were too close to each other. Still a small advantage for the synthetic voice is notifiable. Further research should be done in this field.

This work opens the door for further research in the domain of aviation with the benefit of 3D audio. With the results presented in this paper, several assistant systems for pilots with 3D audio are thinkable. Ongoing research will be done in this field by the author.

References

Barfield, W., Cohen, M., Craig, R.: Visual and auditory localization as a function of azimuth and elevation (1997)

Begault, D.R., Pittman, M.T.: Three-dimensional audio versus head-down traffic alert and collision avoidance system displays. Int. J. Aviat. Psychol. **6**, 79–93 (1996)

BMVI. Neubekanntmachung der Bestimmungen über die Anforderungen andie Tauglichkeit des Luftfahrtpersonals: JAR FCL 3 deutsch (2007)

Gelfand, S.A.: Essentials of Audiology, 2nd edn. Thieme, New York (2001)

Haas, E.C.: Can 3-D auditory warnings enhance helicopter cockpit safety? In: Proceedings of the Human Factors and Ergonomics Society Annual Meeting, pp. 1117–1121 (1998)

Hellbrück, J., Ellermeier, W., Kohlrausch, A., Zeitler, A.: Kompendium zur Durchführung von Hörversuchen in Wissenschaft und industrieller Praxis (2008)

Jovanovic, M., Starcevic, D., Obrenovic, Z.: Designing aircraft cockpit displays: borrowing from multimodal user interfaces. In: Gavrilova, M.L., Tan, C.J.K. (eds.) Trans. on Comput. Sci. III. LNCS, vol. 5300, pp. 55–65. Springer, Heidelberg (2009)

Majdak, P., Goupell, M.J., Laback, B.: 3-D localization of virtual sound sources: effects of visual environment, pointing method, and training. Attention, Percept. Psychophysics **72**, 454–469 (2010)

Minnar, P., Olesen, S.K., Christensen, S.K., Moller, H.: The importance of head movements for binaural room synthesis (2001)

Oving, A.B., Veltman, J.A., Bronkhorst, A.W.: Effectiveness of 3-D audio for warnings in the cockpit. Int. J. Aviat. Psychol. **14**, 257–276 (2004)

Simpson, B.D., Brungart, D.S., Dallman, R.C., Yasky, R.J., Romigh, G.D., Raquet, J.F.: In-flight navigation using head-coupled and aircraft-coupled spatial audio cues. In: Proceedings of the Human Factors and Ergonomics Society Annual Meeting, pp. 1341–1344 (2007)

Spence, C., Ho, C.: Tactile and multisensory spatial warning signals for drivers. IEEE Trans. Haptics (2008)

Veltman, J.A., Oving, A.B., Bronkhorst, A.W.: 3-D audio in the fighter cockpit improves task performance. Int. J. Aviat. Psychol. **14**, 239–256 (2004)

Weinzierl, S. (ed.): Handbuch der Audiotechnik. Springer, Heidelberg (2008)

Wickens, C.D.: Multiple resources and performance prediction. Theor. Issues Ergon. Sci. **3**, 159–177 (2002)

Designing a Support System
to Mitigate Pilot Error While Minimizing
Out-of-the-Loop-Effects

Nikolaus Theißing[(⊠)] and Axel Schulte

Institute of Flight Systems,
Universität der Bundeswehr München, Neubiberg, Germany
{nikolaus.theissing,axel.schulte}@unibw.de

Abstract. This article describes a design pattern for human-autonomy teaming in which a human operator is supported by two cognitive agents. The first agent automates delegated tasks as a subordinate in a hierarchical relationship. The second agent serves as an assistant system. Its task is the mitigation, i.e. prevention and correction, of human erroneous behavior. Error-correcting automation can be prone to complacency effects. The assistant system is therefore specifically designed to avoid potential out-of-the-loop phenomena. The design pattern is implemented for the use case of unmanned air reconnaissance using a single-operator ground control station. The results of an experimental campaign confirm the validity of the approach.

Keywords: Human-autonomy teaming · Human error · Error mitigation · Assistant system · Cognitive agent · Complacency

1 Introduction

Complex automation in the aviation domain can improve the efficiency of flights and enable new fields of application. It does not, however, necessarily protect the human-machine-system from human erroneous behavior. Dangerous or otherwise sub-optimal commands can still cause unintended behavior of the underlying automation, especially in a supervisory-control-relationship. A high degree of automation may even increase the risk of erroneous behavior by introducing effects of automation-induced error [1, 2].

The challenge is now to employ automation in the human-machine-system that brings the desired benefits (increased effectivity and efficiency) and minimizes the amount of erroneous behavior of the pilot.

In this article, a design pattern is described that uses two distinct automation systems: A subordinate automation operated in a supervisory-control-relationship [3] is complemented by an assistant system that is designed to support the human pilot during the mission. The assistant system shall mitigate erroneous behavior of the pilot by intervening in dangerous situations or when the underlying automation is not operated properly (by harmful commands or command omissions). Alerts, messages, suggestions,

© Springer International Publishing Switzerland 2016
D. Harris (Ed.): EPCE 2016, LNAI 9736, pp. 439–451, 2016.
DOI: 10.1007/978-3-319-40030-3_43

and overrides are then used by the assistant system to help the pilot transfer the current (dangerous) situation to a normative (safe) one.

When designing an assistant system of the described kind, it is a challenge not to induce human erroneous behavior. A system that corrects errors immediately and reliably may cause complacency effects in the pilot: The pilot may put an overly high trust in the automation, therefore neglect his or her own monitoring tasks and, as a consequence, lose vigilance or situation awareness [4].

To avoid such effects, the assistant system must be designed specifically against the induction of such out-of-the-loop-effects [5]. This article proposes a technique for assisting the pilot step by step and thereby keeping him or her vigilant with respect to the task as much as possible. The assistant system described in the design pattern is supposed to mitigate erroneous behavior on the one hand and to keep the unwanted out-of-the-loop effects as low as possible on the other hand.

The design pattern will be defined in the following section. The subsequent section will describe the application of the design pattern to the domain of unmanned reconnaissance flights. After that, the results of an experimental evaluation will be shown.

2   Design Pattern "Step-by-Step Error Correction"

2.1   Separation of Two Automation Units

A key element of the design pattern is the separation of the automation used to operate the vehicle from the automation supporting the pilot.

Figure 1 shows the configuration of the work system. The work system notation [6] differentiates between the set of worker on the left-hand side and the tools on the right-hand side. Among other aspects, a worker is characterized by the access to the overall mission goal and the authority to modify that goal and use the available tools to achieve it. The tools, on the other hand, are subordinate to the worker.

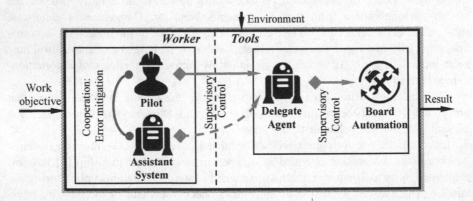

Fig. 1. The basic elements of the design pattern in the work system notation [6]

In the described design pattern the pilot, as a worker, operates the underlying automation in a supervisory-control-relationship. The underlying automation consists of a subordinate cognitive unit, referred to as the *delegate agent*, operating the conventional board automation. In addition to the human pilot, a second cognitive unit is located within the group of workers. That cognitive unit, referred to as *the assistant system*, supports the pilot during the mission management process. Onken and Schulte introduced this configuration as one which fully exploits the options of 'dual-mode cognitive automation' [7].

Each cognitive unit has a distinct purpose:

- Task of the delegate agent: Control of the conventional automation, and thereby, reduction of human taskload
- Task of the assistant system: Mitigation, i.e. prevention or correction, of erroneous behavior of the pilot

Whereas the delegate agent is subordinate to the human pilot (it does what it is told), the assistant system shall work in a cooperative way (without a hierarchical gap, on its own initiative, in pursuit of the overall mission goal). The clear separation between the underlying automation and the cooperative support system offers the following advantages:

- The aircraft is operable even with a complete assistant system shutdown. In case of malfunction the assistant system can, as a last resort, be safely deactivated.
- The board automation of an existing aircraft needs not (or only with minor changes) be modified but only complemented.
- The assistant system and the board automation may be physically detached.
- The functional separation may facilitate the development and certification process.

The pilot controls the underlying automation via a human-machine-interface (HMI) that is not explicitly depicted in the figure. Whereas the assistant system can be built to interact with the pilot in an arbitrary way, it is typically integrated into the existing interface.

2.2 The Role of the Delegate Agent

The role of the delegate agent is the control of the conventional automation of the controlled vehicle. The delegate agent is controlled by the human supervisor and, in turn, controls the underlying conventional automation in another supervisory relationship [8]. This layer of agent supervisory control enables the human pilot to delegate certain higher cognitive tasks (i.e., planning, scheduling, decision making) to the agent. This provides the pilot an automation span of control beyond that of the conventional board automation.

Delegating the control of the conventional automation to an agent can yield the following advantages:

- Independence from an active data connection: The delegate agent is usually controlled with single, discrete commands (as opposed to e.g. the immediate control exerted by flying via stick and throttle). A disruption of the data connection leaves the aircraft functional, albeit with old commands.

– Reduction of workload: The possibility to delegate even higher cognitive tasks to the machine enables the pilot to free his or her mental resources for other tasks.

The role of the delegate agent is to do what it is told without questioning its commands. Of course, depending on the design of the agent, detailed feedback to the pilot may be used to indicate abnormal situations e.g. via alerts or warnings. Also, the given commands may (implicitly) contain directives on how to react to certain situations. The agent will, however, be bound to the given commands. The rationale behind this behavior is to ensure that the pilot is always in full control of his or her vehicle. This implies that the agent will execute erroneous commands regardless of the resulting danger. The prevention and correction of such commands is the task not of the subordinate agent but of the assistant system.

2.3   The Role of the Assistant System

The delegate agent attempts to execute the given commands. It is the task of the human pilot to provide correct commands to the agent at any given time. If the given commands are erroneous, the behavior of the agent is likely to be erroneous, too.

The role of the assistant system is to mitigate erroneous behavior, i.e. to prevent it from occurring or, if that is too late, attempt to correct it and minimize its effects.

Erroneous behavior of the pilot can be classified in two types: Either the pilot gives a wrong command to the agent (error of commission) or the pilot fails to give a command to the agent although it would be necessary (error of omission) [9].

A command omission can be prevented by making sure that the right command is given to the agent in time. A wrong command can (assuming that its effects are not immediately disastrous) be corrected by giving a correcting counter-command to the agent in time. The resolution to both classes of erroneous behavior (wrong commands and omitted commands) can therefore be condensed into one principle: Ensure that a certain command is given to the agent in time.

Goal and Constraints. The assistant system shall attempt to keep up and restore, if necessary, the following goal state:

• Goal: At any given time the automation controlled by the pilot (the agent) is provided with correct commands.

That goal is constrained by the requirement that the human pilot, and not the assistant system, shall be the primary entity in charge. One reason, in addition to the legal and moral responsibility for the vehicle, is the superior knowledge of the human pilot: The pilot can be assumed to be the most valuable and reliable source of knowledge, decisions, and initiative in the system. To keep these assets available, the cognitive resources of the pilot (e.g. situation awareness, vigilance) have to be protected from negative influences such as out-of-the-loop effects.

Therefore the assistant system shall pursue its goal under the following constraints:

- Constraint 1: The given commands shall reflect the intent of the human pilot as closely as possible.
- Constraint 2: The performance of the human pilot regarding his or her cognitive resources shall be kept as high as possible.

Requirements. The constraints require the assistant system to behave in a way that will, on the one hand, eventually resolve the dangerous situation. On the other hand, the human pilot must be involved as much as possible to keep him or her in the control loop. In essence, the assistant system shall intervene if necessary, but the share of work contributed by the human pilot shall be as high as possible.

The following requirements to the behavior of the assistant system can be derived:

1. The human pilot shall be given as much time as possible to find own solutions.
2. Dangerous situations shall be resolved before damage is inflicted.
3. Interventions shall provide input that helps with the current problem.
4. The input given by an intervention shall not exceed the current problem.

The requirements call for an escalating behavior of the assistant system. Schulte demands that an assistant system behave according to an escalating scheme: The assistant system shall let the pilot do his or her tasks without intervening. Only if necessary shall the system successively guide, relieve, and – if everything fails – override the pilot [6].

This scheme will reflect in the following strategy that implements the given requirements and shall offer precise rules for the behavior of the assistant system that can be used for a practical implementation.

Strategy. At any given moment (e.g. in each computation cycle) the assistant system shall act according to the following strategy:

1. Determine if the current situation is dangerous and, if so, at what time damage (a violated threshold of certain performance parameters) will be inflicted. A situation is dangerous if the further development, without intervention by the pilot or the assistant system, leads to damage.
2. Determine what the pilot must do to resolve the dangerous situation. The resolution typically consists of giving a certain command (sequence) to the delegate agent. This action is the desired action that will be enforced by the assistant system.
3. Estimate the current cognitive state of the pilot. The cognitive state includes mental resources such as situation awareness, vigilance, workload, and focus. It also includes the state of information processing, i.e. the current task and the associated cognitive processes. This estimate should be based on a model of the pilot's information processing.
4. Compute the transitions of the pilot's cognitive state leading from the current state to the resolution of the dangerous situation, and identify the conditions for each transition: What steps will the pilot's mind have to go through to effect the desired action, beginning with its current state? These steps and estimates of their duration

(with buffers and worst-case assumptions) should be based on a model of the pilot's information processing.

5. Arrange these computed mental steps along a timeline, beginning with the rightmost one. Arrange them in a way that the final step (the desired action) takes place immediately before the moment of damage, i.e. barely in time. The position of the left end, i.e. the starting point of the sequence, will then determine the point in time at which the pilot has to begin working on the problem.

6. Determine: Is the starting point of the sequence in the future?
   (a) Yes: There is still time left for the pilot to find own solutions. Do nothing.
   (b) No: The pilot should have reacted by now. Intervene by enforcing the current transition, i.e. the first step, using any available means.

Figure 2 shows an illustration of this strategy for a simple example. New commands have to be entered in time to avoid a collision with another aircraft (1,2). The pilot is currently analyzing the tactical map (3). The sequence of thought and action leading from this current task to the desired action step (4,5) will likely not be completed in time (6a). Therefore, the assistant system intervenes (6b): It enforces the transition from the pilot's current mental state to the next state (the detection of a relevant change in the tactical environment) by alerting the pilot about an incoming other aircraft.

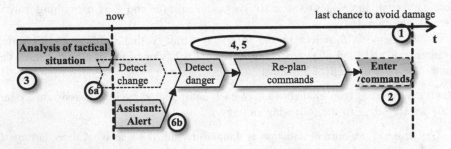

Fig. 2. The strategy of the assistant system for planning and scheduling its interventions

2.4   Functional Architecture of the Assistant System

To implement the shown intervention strategy the assistant system needs the following capabilities:

- Monitoring of the environment and detection and analysis of danger
- Monitoring of the pilot and interpretation of the observed data with respect to the pilot's cognitive state
- Planning and scheduling of interventions
- Execution of interventions, i.e. of the actual interaction with the pilot

Figure 3 shows the functional system architecture of the assistant system as a network of modules implementing the capabilities and exchanging the respective data.

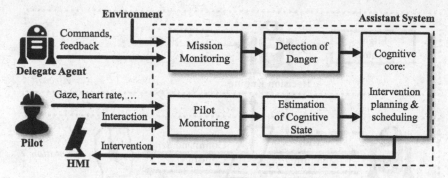

Fig. 3. The inputs, outputs and processing components of the assistant system

3   Application to Unmanned Air Reconnaissance

This section will provide an exemplary use case in which the described design pattern has been practically implemented and evaluated. The pattern has been applied to the domain of unmanned air reconnaissance conducted by a single human pilot.

3.1   Domain Description

In the given work domain it is the task of a single human pilot to gain reconnaissance information on certain objects (buildings, persons, vehicles) in an area that may possibly contain hostile forces. The information can be obtained by interpreting imagery and video data gathered by sensors that are attached to an unmanned aircraft. A single human pilot has the task to manage the flight control and sensor control of that aircraft from a ground control station.

The reconnaissance targets are given to the pilot beforehand, but may change dynamically during the mission. The execution is constrained by airspace regulations (boundaries and corridors), threats (possibly unexpected hostile air defenses), and resource limitations (fuel). The pilot has to carry out the tasks of flight management, sensor management and interpretation of the sensor data in parallel. The pilot is therefore supported by automation applied according to the described design pattern.

3.2   System Architecture

Figure 4 depicts the system architecture of the human-machine-system. In the ground control station the human pilot commands and controls the aircraft via a graphical user interface (GUI). The assistant system shares that GUI to monitor the pilot's interaction with the system and to intervene if necessary. The pilot and the assistant system exert supervisory control over the delegate agent referred to as *decision engine*. The decision engine conducts the flight and sensor control of the aircraft according to tasks received from the ground control station. The air and ground segment communicate via an air data link.

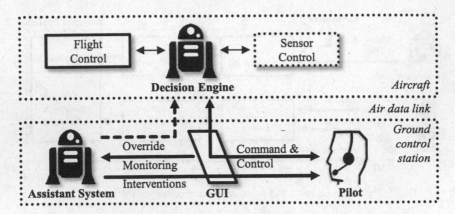

Fig. 4. The functional architecture of the unmanned reconnaissance system

3.3 Decision Engine

The decision engine implements the principle of task-based guidance [8]. Instead of detailed manual control commands, the human pilot can assign a task or a sequence of tasks to the decision engine and monitor the execution. A task is an abstract high-level command describing an action and, if necessary or desired by the pilot, parameters. Examples are "Land at the home base", "Find vehicles in area X", or "Find vehicles in area X using manual sensor guidance". A sequence of such tasks, defining the actions to be carried out, can be commanded to the decision engine.

After receiving a new or modified task sequence the decision engine plans the execution of the tasks by complementing missing steps and breaking the tasks down to elementary operations. It then executes the tasks and provides the human pilot with feedback about the currently processed task, its execution state, and the current route.

3.4 Assistant System

The assistant system shall prevent the effects of erroneous behavior of the human pilot. These effects can be, among others:

- Violation of airspace regulations by the aircraft
- Loss of aircraft by exhaustion of fuel reserves during the flight
- Loss of aircraft by entry into the threat radius of hostile air defense sites
- Ineffective reconnaissance (inadequate fulfillment of the mission objective)

To avoid these effects, the assistant system can intervene. It is integrated into the control station's systems and has access to the pilot's GUI. Depending on the conditions of the mental step the pilot shall be supported with, the assistant system can display general alerts and iconic or textual messages, highlight certain screen elements, direct the pilot's attention to other screens, or override commands.

The assistant system obtains the information necessary to plan, schedule and execute an intervention from the subsystems of the GUI. Figure 5 depicts the system architecture of the assistant system. Information about the tactical environment and the state of the decision engine is analyzed for dangerous situations according to a model of the mission domain. A model of the pilot's behavior is employed in the component inferring the pilot's gestures from the observed input and estimating the pilot's mental state. The estimation component uses a Colored Petri Net [10] as an on-line simulation of the pilot's behavior. The cognitive core plans and schedules the interventions according to the strategy described above based on another model of the pilot's behavior. The NDDL-based framework EUROPA [11] is used for the implementation of the planning and scheduling process.

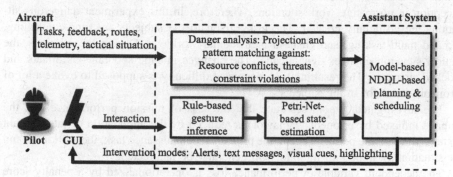

Fig. 5. Components and information flow of the implemented assistant system

4 Experimental Evaluation

To evaluate the effectiveness of the design pattern, a human-machine experimental campaign was conducted. The experiment had two goals:

- Show that the assistant system reduces the negative impact of human erroneous behavior on the overall mission performance. This is the primary system goal.
- Show that the intervention strategy fulfills its requirements. This shall justify the usage of the described strategy. After all, a system with a simpler strategy (e.g. 'override immediately upon danger') may yield the same results concerning mission performance at first, but have negative impact on the pilot's mental state.

4.1 Setup

In the experiment a group of test subjects conducts a series of reconnaissance missions with the described system in the role of the pilot. The missions are simulated (flight dynamics, tactical environment and sensor imagery are generated by a virtual environment), but the real hard- and software of the ground control station is used.

After the introduction to the system and a training mission, each subject conducts three missions. The first and third missions are carried out with a deactivated assistant system (as a baseline configuration A) whereas during the second mission, the assistant system is active (configuration B). This ABA-configuration is used to average out the influence of training effects by comparing B to the average of A measured before and after.

The missions are designed to be similar enough to be comparable to each other but sufficiently different to avoid habituation effects on the subjects. The objective of each mission is the reconnaissance of certain areas. Ancillary tasks are the monitoring of the tactical map, the detection of targets of opportunity, and the conduction of radio dialogues. These tasks are constrained by threats and resource limitations as described above.

The tasks and constraints are chosen to generate very difficult missions. The reason is that the assistant system only acts in situations of danger, which should be a rare exception in normative work situations. Therefore, in this experiment dangerous situations are artificially created. The tasks given to the subjects are time-consuming, demand multi-tasking, and create a high mental workload. During the missions, the tactical situation changes dynamically. The changes include spontaneous threats and blocked airspaces. The resulting high degree of difficulty is supposed to evoke a lot of erroneous behavior in the subjects.

The investigated hypotheses state that the loss of mission performance (i.e. the damage inflicted by erroneous behavior) is reduced by the application of the assistant system, whereas the performance in the primary reconnaissance task, the workload, and the situation awareness of the pilot will generally be unaffected.

The dependent variable of performance loss is operationalized by a penalty score for airspace violations, resource limit violations and neglected threats. The situation awareness is determined by SAGAT questionnaires [12] after each mission and an evaluation of the subjects' behavior during the missions. The workload is represented by the result of NASA-TLX questionnaires [13]. The task performance is determined by a score for the detection and classification of reconnaissance targets and targets of opportunity.

The duration of the experiment is too short to gain evidence about the influence of the assistant system on the pilot's cognitive state in the long term. The experiment does, however, allow the investigation of the behavior of the assistant system (does it do what it is supposed to?) and the reactions of the subjects.

4.2 Results

The described experiment was conducted with a group of 17 test subjects comprising officers and cadets of the German Armed Forces. Each subject had several years of military experience and either an academic background or practical experience (as a pilot or unmanned system operator) in aviation.

Figure 6 shows the measured values for the dependent variables. As the graphs suggest, the performance loss (in the upper right graph) is the only measured variable with a significant change between the configurations. With an active assistant system (mission 2) the measured performance loss is significantly lower than that observed without assistance (missions 1 and 3). The remaining investigated variables cannot be distinguished with statistical significance [14].

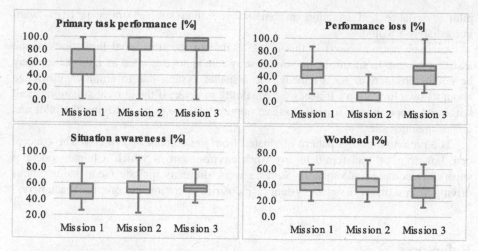

Fig. 6. Box-Whisker-plots of the measured variables comparing the configurations without assistance (missions 1 & 3) to those with an active assistant system (mission 2)

The hypotheses stated above can therefore be accepted: The application of the assistant system was shown to lower the performance loss whereas no significant effects on the remaining variables could be observed.

During the experimental campaign, 31 interventions of the assistant system were encountered. An analysis of the behavior of the assistant system and the reaction of the subjects shows that in 42 % of the cases the assistant system had to escalate to the final level of overriding the pilot to avoid damage. In the remaining cases, a lower number of interventions were necessary. 36 % of the situations only required the first two steps (general warning and highlighting of a changed element) for the pilot to find the rest of the solution on his or her own. It can be assumed that in most of those cases a static level of intervention would have been either unnecessarily explicit (giving the pilot more information than necessary) or insufficient for solving the problem.

5 Conclusion

A design pattern for human-autonomy teaming has been presented that combines the delegation of functionality to underlying automation with cooperative support by an assistant system. An experimental campaign was conducted to evaluate an implementation of the design pattern. The functionality of the assistant system has been verified regarding the desired immediate effect of error mitigation and the immediate impact of the intervention strategy on the pilot's behavior has been investigated.

Further research will have to provide evidence that the intervention strategy of the assistant system has the desired effect on the pilot's mental state in the long term. The current experiment could only monitor the immediate effects on the subjects' behavior. A long-term study will have to show that the effects of this assistant strategy sustain the pilot's vigilance and situation awareness more than simple strategies (e.g. 'warn immediately') would.

An issue not addressed in this article is that of the functional limitations of the assistant system. In situations for which the system is not designed an intervention may be counterproductive. As a remedy, the assistant system has to employ knowledge about its own limitations. It needs the capability to detect if the current situation is still within its scope. If not, it needs to react appropriately, e.g. by notifying the pilot and then remaining silent.

The presented design pattern originated from the domain of aviation. The concept can, however, be transferred to any work environment in which a human operator supervises complex automation. Suitable work domains include (semi-)autonomous driving with a driver assistant system or industrial operation of complex machinery.

References

1. Bainbridge, L.: Ironies of automation. Automatica. **19**, 775–779 (1983)
2. Sarter, N.B., Woods, D.D., Billings, C.E.: Automation surprises. In: Salvendy, G. (ed.) Handbook of Human Factors & Ergonomics, 2nd edn, pp. 1–25. Wiley (1997)
3. Sheridan, T.B.: Task analysis, task allocation and supervisory control. In: Helander, M.G., Landauer, T.K., Prabhu, P.V (eds.) Handbook of Human-Computer Interaction, pp. 87–103. Elsevier Science B. V. (1997)
4. Parasuraman, R., Molloy, R., Singh, I.L.: Performance Consequences of Automation-Induced 'Complacency'. Int. J. Aviat. Psychol. **3**, 1–23 (2009)
5. Kaber, D., Endsley, M.: Out-of-the-loop performance problems and the use of intermediate levels of automation for improved control system functioning and safety. Process Saf. Prog. **16**(3), 126–131 (1997)
6. Schulte, A., Donath, D., Lange, D.S.: Design patterns for human-cognitive agent teaming. In: Harris, D. (ed.) EPCE 2016. LNCS(LNAI), vol. 9736, pp. 231–243. Springer, Heidelberg (2016)
7. Onken, R., Schulte, A.: System-Ergonomic Design of Cognitive Automation. Springer, Heidelberg (2010)
8. Clauß, S., Schulte, A.: Task delegation in an agent supervisory control relationship capability awareness in a cognitive agent. In: 2014 IEEE International Conference on Systems, Man, and Cybernetics (SMC), pp. 825–830. IEEE (2014)
9. Hollnagel, E.: Looking for errors of omission and commission or The Hunting of the Snark revisited. Reliab. Eng. Syst. Saf. **68**, 135–145 (2000)
10. Jensen, K., Kristensen, L.M.: Coloured Petri Nets: Modelling and Validation of Concurrent Systems. Springer, Heidelberg (2009)
11. Barreiro, J., Boyce, M., Do, M., Frank, J., Iatauro, M., Kichkaylo, T., Morris, P., Ong, J., Remolina, E., Smith, T., Smith, D.: EUROPA : a platform for AI planning, scheduling, constraint programming, and optimization (2004)
12. Endsley, M.R.: Situation awareness global assessment technique (SAGAT). In: Proceedings of the National Aerospace and Electronics Conference (NAECON), New York, pp. 789–795 (1988)

13. Hart, S.G., Staveland, L.E.: Development of NASA-TLX (Task Load Index): results of empirical and theoretical research. Adv. Psychol. **52**, 139–183 (1988)
14. Theißing, N., Liegel, A., Schulte, A.: Verhindern von Pilotenfehlern durch ein zustandsadaptives Assistenzsystem. In: Grandt, M., Schmerwitz, S. (eds.) Kooperation und kooperative Systeme in der Fahrzeug- und Prozessführung, pp. 97–114. Deutsche Gesellschaft für Luft- und Raumfahrt - Lilienthal-Oberth e.V, Bonn (2015)

Analysis of Influencing Factors of Auditory Warning Signals' Perceived Urgency and Reaction Time

Lijing Wang[1(✉)], Wei Guo[1], Xianchao Ma[2], and Baofeng Li[2]

[1] Fundamental Science on Ergonomics and Environment Control Laboratory,
School of Aeronautic Science and Engineering,
Beihang University, Beijing, China
wanglijing@buaa.edu.cn, guowei0224@foxmail.com
[2] Commercial Aircraft Corporation of China Ltd, Shanghai, China
{maxianchao, libaofeng}@comac.cc

Abstract. The auditory warning is one of the most important information in cockpit. To study the effects of auditory warnings to human capability of receiving information, this paper describes the test about the effects of various warning features on the information receiving performance of the testers. Testers in the laboratory environment finish the mission for determination of 24 warning tones combined by two volumes (65 dB (A), 75 dB (A)), three frequencies (700 Hz, 1,200 Hz, 1,700 Hz), and four inter-onset intervals (100, 150, 300 and 600 ms). This test considers the perceived urgency judgment and reaction time of the tester as the study data that experiences the comparative analysis and variance analysis after being paired. The study results indicate that the sound volume influences the perceived urgency judgment significantly ($p < 0.05$) and impacts the reaction time greatly ($p < 0.01$). Sound frequencies also effect the perceived urgency judgment significantly ($p < 0.05$) and so do the inter-onset intervals in both the perceived urgency judgment and reaction time ($p < 0.01$). In conclusion, the greater the volume is, the higher the frequency is, the shorter the inter-onset interval is, and the higher the perceived urgency is while the greater the volume is, the shorter the inter-onset interval is, and the shorter the reaction time becomes.

Keywords: Auditory warning · Cockpit · Volumes · Frequencies · Inter-onset interval

1 Introduction

A great deal of researches indicate that auditory warnings can improve the alertness of operators to abnormalities and assist them in quick identification of hazards and in shortening operators' reaction time [1–3]. Auditory warning has been widely applied in many fields, especially in the field of aviation [4–6]. Cockpit audio warning system through the different auditory warning caused by the pilot's attention to quickly

D. Harris (Ed.): EPCE 2016, LNAI 9736, pp. 452–463, 2016.
DOI: 10.1007/978-3-319-40030-3_44

identify, and make the right response. However, the auditory warning tone will make it difficult for pilots to follow, resulting in information overload, and prone to human error, resulting in the occurrence of major accidents, especially in emergency situations. A lot of auditory warnings to the pilot's mental load and physiological load presents a serious challenge [6, 7]. Therefore, the optimum design of cockpit auditory warning is ergonomics concerns an important issue.

Auditory warnings of different acoustic properties will have an impact on people's alarms perception. Wogalter et al. [1] have demonstrated that voice warning signals can shorten the operators' reaction time to abnormalities through the research. United States military standard NASA-STD-3000 [8] and MIL-STD-1472F [9] only the auditory warning has developed several standards in principle, but did not address specific property requirements of the auditory warning. By now, many researchers have studied the effects of sound volume, frequency, rhythm, and inter-onset intervals, based on properties of these items, to human perceived urgency judgment and reaction time. However, there are also differences between the research content and the research results of different scholars. Suied et al. [10] have verified the effects of auditory warning properties to warning receiving and they have demonstrated the effects of sound inter-onset intervals of respective 100 ms and 300 ms and sound laws to the reaction time and perceived urgency feel. In the test, the reaction time is measured and the result indicates a quicker response from a smaller pulse separation and that the easier the attention is paid, the more irregular the signal is Haas and other researchers [3] tested and studied the perceived urgency and objective reaction time by means of pure auditory warnings with sound inter-onset intervals of 150 ms and 300 ms, sound intensities of 65 dBC and 79 dBC and with various pulse modes. Results of the perceived urgency tests show that with sound selected, the smaller the inter-onset interval is, the greater the volume is, and the higher the perceived urgency becomes while results of the response tests indicate that the volume influences the reaction time but the inter-onset interval does not. In addition, the test results show a correlation between the perceived response and reaction time, that is, the higher the perceived urgency is, the quicker the response gets. Bodendörfer [11] through the experimental study on the acoustic properties of the four (volume and frequency, pulse frequency, pulse inter-onset interval) to tone alarms perception confirm the effect. Found that reducing the frequency and pulse time of two consecutive pulses to increase workers' perception confirmed. Perception of sound frequency and number of people recognize and have no effect. Chinese scholar Li et al. [12] have studied the hearing judgment performance under different frequencies and constant volume and ordered the pure auditory warning signals of 6 frequencies under the volume of 60 dB by priority.

Aiming at the effects of properties of warning tones to perceived urgency judgment and reaction time, tests are designed in this paper to study effects of perceived urgency judgment and reaction time by selecting three different acoustic properties of sound volume, frequency and inter-onset interval, expecting to provide theoretical basis and standards for design and selection of auditory warnings in the cockpit.

2 Method

2.1 Conditions of Subjects

13 subjects are involved in the test aging from 20 to 25 years old without mental or sleep disorders. Moreover, subjects should not participate in similar tests previously.

2.2 Test Equipment and Environment

Tests should be conducted indoors and the free sound field should be selected. The sound pressure level at subjects' auricles should be 43 dB (A). The software Cool-pro 2.0 is selected to simulate the warning tones and Experiment Builder is used to program the tests. Programs automatically stimulate the subjects with sound information and record the responses.

2.3 Test Design

Tests mainly focus on the effects of different acoustic properties of auditory warnings to subjects. Therefore, for the test, the information receiving response and perceived urgency judgment serve as dependent variables while the sound volume, frequency and inter-onset interval are considered as the independent variables.

For volumes, based on the research findings and related standards [8, 9], generally the main frequency band of all main components of hearing warning signals should be at least 20 dB(A) higher than the noise level whereas in quiet environment, that of the hearing attention signal should be within 50 dB(A) $\sim$ 70 dB(A). Because the background noise level in the test field is 43 dB(A), two volumes of 65 dB(A) and 75 dB(A) are selected for the test.

For frequencies, reference standards, the fundamental tone frequency of the warnings should within 700 Hz and 1,700 Hz. For the purpose of this test and in combination with results of various preliminary tests, the test frequency has been determined to be respectively 700 Hz, 1,200 Hz, and 1,700 Hz.

For inter-onset intervals, in light of studies by Clara Suied et al. [3], human responses experience obvious differences to warning tones with inter-onset intervals of 100 ms and 300 ms ($p < 0.05$). With similar design selected, and inter-onset interval selection ranges enlarged and re-partitioned, this test considers four levels of pulse separation, which are 100 ms, 150 ms, 300 ms, and 600 ms (Table 1).

Table 1. Summary of test factors and levels

Factor	Level
Volume	65 dB, 75 dB
Frequency	700 Hz, 1,200 Hz, 1,700 Hz
Inter-onset interval	100 ms, 150 ms, 300 ms, 600 ms

2.4 Test Process

Three different levels are combined in this test, generating totally 24 simulated warning tones, among which, two of which are paired in a group randomly (sequence distinguished), creating totally 552 comparative sound groups (24×23). In order to obtain more accurate data, because subjects need to stay focused, 552 groups are divided into 24 large test teams for independent test. 23 pairs of sounds are involved in each large team and the former 12 pairs are grouped while the latter 11 pairs are grouped. It is required a ten-minute rest be set for each large team and 2 min for each small group. Therefore, the whole test may take approximately 2 h.

Specific implementations of the test are as follows:

1. Subjects sit in front of computer and adjust their sitting attitude and seat height to allow their ears to be at the desired position.
2. Start the test program and a black dot appears at the screen center to concentrate the subject. After 1 s $\sim$ 2 s random waiting, the first simulated warning tone plays. The subjects need to press the button as quickly as possible and an OK on the screen indicates the valid operation.
3. Subsequently, a circle appears on the screen center and the second simulated warning tone plays as per the identical requirement.
4. After each test, compare the perceived urgency to two simulated warning tones and proceed to the next test after the assessment.
5. Repeat steps 2 to 4 until all 522 tests are finished and test the next subject.

3 Results

3.1 Analysis on Results of Perceived Urgency Judgment

Comparison of paired data. During the tests, total 13 subjects judge each pair of simulated warning tones subjectively, select the tone of higher urgency that they consider and record it. As for no order for sound pairing, one pair of sounds is judged for twice and the test statistics are made for 26 subjects. The perceived urgency to all warning tones is determined after the pairing comparative analysis of statistic data as shown in Table 2. The smaller the perceived urgency value is, the less the urgency to the simulated warning tone is. Positive and negative marks in the results only indicate the magnitude without other meanings.

Analysis on main effect and interactive actions of influence factors. By virtue of the investigation of volume, frequency and inter-onset interval of the audio waning signal and of the effects of interactive actions among these three factors to human perceived urgency judgment, the volume, frequency and inter-onset interval as well as the variance of the interactive action are obtained following the calculation and analysis of the relative urgency parameters treated by the pairing comparative method by means of ANOVA as shown in Table 3.

Table 2. Perceived urgency value to different simulated warning tones

Volume: 65 dB	Inter-onset interval			
Frequency	100 ms	150 ms	300 ms	600 ms
700 Hz	0.0755	−0.3642	−0.9786	−2.0191
1,200 Hz	0.8452	0.2759	−0.3286	−0.8942
1,700 Hz	0.4461	0.0168	−0.5652	−1.2516
Volume: 75 dB	Inter-onset interval			
Frequency	100 ms	150 ms	300 ms	600 ms
700 Hz	0.5603	0.2111	−0.4323	−0.9991
1,200 Hz	1.4866	0.8392	0.1642	−0.2846
1,700 Hz	1.8554	1.0201	0.3463	−0.1898

Table 3. ANOVA table with F-values and significance for perceived urgency

Perceived urgency	F	P
Volume	288.943	0.000
Frequency	70.922	0.000
Inter-onset interval	236.167	0.000
Volume × frequency	0.569	0.594
Volume × inter-onset interval	2.373	0.169
Frequency × inter-onset interval	0.552	0.756

Following conclusion is obtained based on Table 2:

1. Within selected sound volume range, main effect of volumes should be significant ($F = 288.943$, $p < 0.01$) thus understanding that the volume of pure warning tones influences the perceived urgency judgment significantly.
2. Within selected frequency range, the main effect of sound frequency is obvious ($F = 70.922$, $P < 0.01$) thus knowing that the sound frequency of pure warning tone impacts perceived urgency judgment significantly.
3. Within selected inter-onset interval range, the main effect of sound inter-onset interval is obvious ($F = 236.176$, $P < 0.01$) thus knowing that the sound inter-onset interval of pure warning tone impacts perceived urgency judgment significantly.
4. Because the interactive actions between volume, frequency and inter-onset interval are not significant, it is known that the interactive actions between these factors do not impact the perceived urgency judgment significantly.

Comparison of distinctions of main effects of different influence factors. In light of the variance analysis on different levels among the three factors, it is demonstrated that the sound volume, frequency, and inter-onset interval impacts the perceived urgency judgment significantly and that the sound inter-onset interval influences the reaction time much. Figures 1, 2 and 3 show the main effect values of volume and inter-onset interval to perceived urgency judgment. As the sound volume increases, the perceived urgency judgment to sounds ascends but descends with longer sound inter-onset interval.

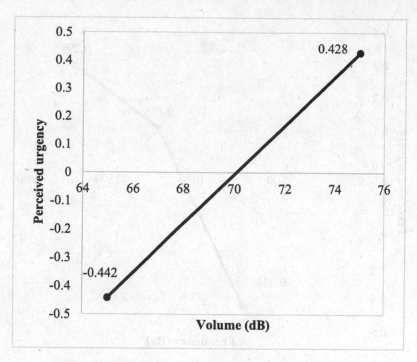

Fig. 1. Main effect value of volume to perceived urgency

3.2 Analysis on Reaction Time Results Process

Preprocessing of test data. Totally 14,352 data are acquired. To ensure correct reaction time and prevent test results from interference by limit values, abnormal data beyond ± 3 mean square deviation are eliminated under each special condition, leaving effective 13,965 data totally.

Analysis on main effects and interactive actions of influence factors. By virtue of the investigation of volume, frequency and inter-onset interval of the audio waning signal and of the effects of interactive actions among these three factors to human perceived urgency judgment, the volume, frequency and inter-onset interval as well as the variance table (Table 4) of the interactive actions are obtained following the calculation and analysis of the relative urgency parameters treated by the pairing comparative method by means of ANOVA.

Following conclusions are obtained based on Table 3:

1. Within selected sound volume range, main effects of volumes should be significant ($F = 5.597$, $0.01 < p < 0.05$) thus understanding that the volume of pure warning tones influences the perceived urgency judgment significantly.

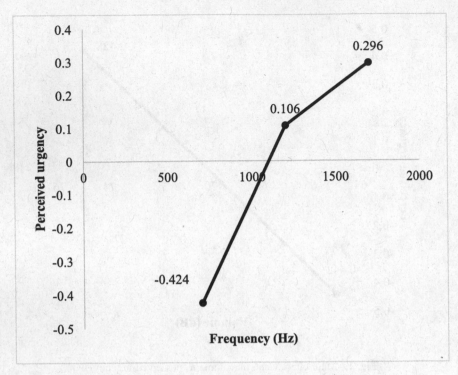

Fig. 2. Main effect value of frequency to perceived urgency

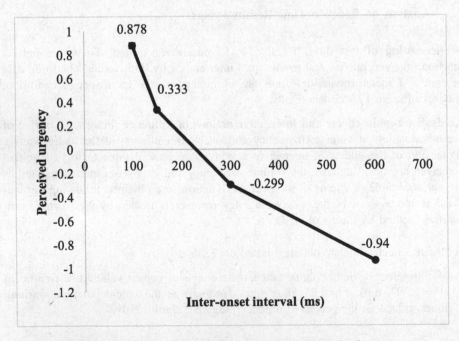

Fig. 3. Main effect value of inter-onset interval to perceived urgency

Table 4. ANOVA table with F-values and significance for reaction time

Reaction Time	F	P
Volume	5.597	0.030
Frequency	2.331	0.127
Inter-onset interval	47.573	0.000
Volume × frequency	3.443	0.101
Volume × inter-onset interval	14.240	0.004
Frequency × inter-onset interval	4.239	0.051

2. Within selected frequency range, the main effect of sound frequency is obvious (F = 2.31, P > 0.05) thus knowing that the sound frequency of pure warning tone impacts perceived urgency judgment significantly.
3. Within selected inter-onset interval range, the main effect of sound inter-onset interval is obvious (F = 47.573, P < 0.01) thus knowing that the sound inter-onset interval of pure warning tone impacts perceived urgency judgment significantly.
4. Because the interactive actions between volume and inter-onset interval are significant, it is known that the interactive actions between volume, frequency and inter-onset interval impact the perceived urgency judgment significantly.

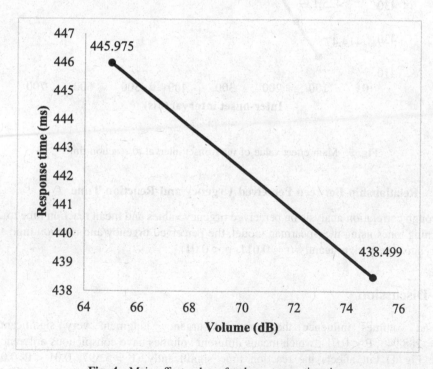

Fig. 4. Main effect value of volume to reaction time

Comparison of distinctions of main effect values of different influence factors. In accordance with variance analysis on different levels among the three factors, it is demonstrated that the sound volume impacts the reaction time significantly while the sound inter-onset interval does the reaction time more significantly. Figures 4 and 5 show the main effect values of volume and inter-onset interval to reaction time. As the sound volume increases, the response slows but quickens with longer sound inter-onset interval.

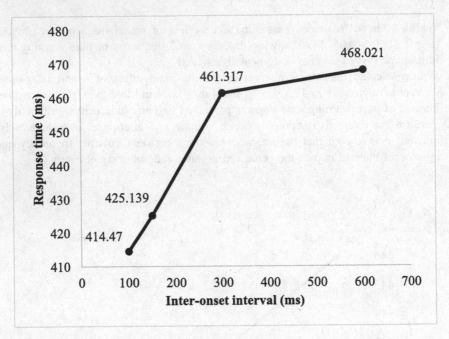

Fig. 5. Main effect value of inter-onset interval to reaction time

3.3 Relationship Between Perceived Urgency and Reaction Time

Through correlation analysis on perceived urgency values and mean reaction time to 24 warning tones using the Spearman model, the perceived urgency and reaction time are correlative very significantly ($r = 0.611$, $p < 0.01$).

4   Discussion

Sound volumes influence the perceived urgency judgment very significantly ($F = 288.943$, $P < 0.01$), which means different volumes have conspicuous differences (see Fig. 1) but affects the reaction time significantly ($F = 5.597$, $0.01 < P < 0.05$) (see Fig. 4), indicating the differences of perceived urgency judgment are small by comparison. The reason is that the perceived urgency feel is more sensitive than reaction time to the sound volume within a selected range, generating more intensive change and more significant effect.

Sound frequencies impact the perceived urgency judgment very significantly. As the frequency gets higher, the perceived urgency ascends as well yet the effect degrades gradually (see Fig. 2). On the contrary, frequencies hardly affect the reaction time significantly, which is caused by the easier change of perceived urgency due to frequency change within a selected range, thus influencing the reaction time not that much. In other words, the perceived urgency judgment is more compromising to the frequencies than the reaction time.

Hellier [13] has found that the perceived urgency judgment is subject to the consistent effect of sound inter-onset intervals. Bodendörfer [11] also proved via tests that two continuous pulse duration can improve the operators' perception affirmation. In this test, various inter-onset intervals are selected for study to prove the more significant effects of inter-onset intervals to perceived urgency judgment. In addition, with longer inter-onset intervals, the perceived urgency drops continuously and the effect extent of inter-onset intervals to perceived urgency judgment decreases (see Fig. 3).

With inter-onset interval prolongs, the perceived urgency drops continuously and the effect extent of inter-onset intervals to the perceived urgency judgment de-creases (see Fig. 3). This means the change within a short inter-onset interval impacts the perceived urgency judgment more tremendously.

For relationship between warning tone inter-onset interval and reaction time, Haas thinks that the inter-onset interval of sound pulse impacts nothing of the reaction time and Suied et al. [10] discovers that smaller pulse inter-onset interval causes quicker response. Via this test, inter-onset intervals of sound pulses impact the reaction time very significantly by observing the acquired RT data (see Fig. 5) and the RT and inter-onset intervals increase in a linear relation within an inter-onset interval between 100 ms and 300 ms. However, beyond 300 ms, the reaction time ascends obviously slowly. The reason of the difference between them may be:

1. Perceived urgency judgment is more sensitive than reaction time at an inter-onset interval between 100 ms and 300 ms, causing obvious change and more significant effect.
2. A critical point exists for the inter-onset interval effect to human response, once which is exceeded, the inter-onset interval effect to human reaction time drops. For this test, the critical point is 300 ms. Zones between 300 ms and 600 ms can be further divided for subsequent tests to search for a more accurate critical point.

In conclusion, from proceeding analysis, perceived urgency judgment is superior to the reaction time in terms of sensitivity within selected ranges for sound volume, frequency and inter-onset interval. Follow-up tests will concentrate on the relationship between the sensitivity of both objects and applicable scope in detail.

5   Conclusion

This paper describes the study of effects of various volumes, frequencies and inter-onset intervals to human perceived urgency judgment and reaction time. The test results indicate as follows:

1. Sound volumes impact perceived urgency judgment very significantly and affect the reaction time obviously. As the volume rises, the perceived urgency increases as well yet the reaction time drops.
2. Sound frequencies influence the perceived urgency judgment significantly. As the frequency gets higher, the perceived urgency rises as well; however, frequencies hardly impacts the reaction time obviously.
3. Sound inter-onset intervals affect the perceived urgency judgment and reaction time very significantly. As the inter-onset interval is prolonged, the perceived urgency drops and the reaction time increases with a greater acceleration at inter-onset interval before 300 ms and slows down at an inter-onset interval beyond 300 ms.

References

1. Wogalter, M.S., Kalsher, M.J., Rashid, R.: Effect of signal word and source attribution on judgments of warning credibility and compliance likelihood. Int. J. Ind. Ergon. **24**(2), 185–192 (1999)
2. Hellier, E., Edworthy, J.: Quantifying the perceived urgency of auditory warnings. Can. Acoust. **17**(4), 3–11 (1989)
3. Haas, E.C., Casali, J.G.: Perceived urgency of and response time to multi-tone and frequency-modulated warning signals in broadband noise. Ergonomics **38**(11), 2313–2326 (1995)
4. Zhang, T., Zheng, X., Zhu, Z.: An ergonomic study of visual and auditory alerting modes in aircraft cockpits. Chinese Journal of Applied Psychology (1995)
5. Zhang, Y., Yan, X., Yang, Z.: Discrimination of effects between directional and nondirectional information of auditory warning on driving behavior. Discrete Dyn. Nat. Soc. **2015**, 1–7 (2015)
6. Veitengruber, J.E., Boucek, G.P., Smith, W.D.: Aircraft Alerting Systems Criteria Study. Volume 1. Collation and Analysis of Aircraft Alerting Systems Data. Aircraft Alerting Systems Criteria Study (1977)
7. Arrabito, G.R.: Effects of talker sex and voice style of verbal cockpit warnings on performance. Hum. Factors J. Hum. Factors Ergon. Soc. **51**(1), 3–20 (2009)
8. NASA: Man system integration standards, NASA-STD-3000 (1995). http://msis.jsc.nasa.gov/
9. MIL-STD-1472F: Human Engineering Design Criteria for Military Systems, Equipment and Facilities, Department of Defense, July 1999
10. Suied, C., Susini, P., Mcadams, S.: Evaluating warning sound urgency with reaction times. J. Exp. Psychol. Appl. **14**(3), 201–212 (2008)
11. Bodendörfer, X., Kortekaas, R., Weingarten, M., Schlittmeier, S.: The effects of spectral and temporal parameters on perceived confirmation of an auditory non-speech signal. J. Acoust. Soc. Am. **138**(2), 127–132 (2015)

12. Li, H.-T., Ge, L.-Z., Lu, W.-H.: A study about absolute auditory discrimaination at different frequency level. Chin. J. Ergon. **11**(2), 4–6 (2005)
13. Hellier, E.J., Edworthy, J., Dennis, I.: Improving auditory warning design: quantifying and predicting the effects of different warning parameters on perceived urgency. Hum. Factors J. Hum. Factors Ergon. Soc. **35**(4), 693–706 (1993)

A Novel Approach for Comprehensive Evaluation of Flight Deck Ergonomic Design: Delphi-Order Relation Analysis (ORA) Method and Improved Radar Chart

Lijing Wang[1](✉), Yanlong Wang[1], Wenjun Dong[2],
Dayong Dong[2], and Xiuli Shu[2]

[1] Fundamental Science on Ergonomics and
Environment Control Laboratory,
School of Aeronautic Science and Engineering,
Beihang University, Beijing, China
wanglijing@buaa.edu.cn, wyllaf@sina.com
[2] Commercial Aircraft Corporation of China Ltd., Shanghai, China
{dongwenjun, dongdayong, shuxiuli}@comac.cc

Abstract. A well designed flight deck with full consideration of ergonomic aspect has a significant effect on aircraft safety. Since cockpit is a complicated system, it is necessary to have a comprehensive evaluation of flight deck ergonomic design during the design and certification process in order to grasp the overall ergonomic design quality. The determination of indicator weights and aggregation of indicator evaluation values are key steps of comprehensive evaluation. However, most of existing methods lack a sufficient consideration of uncertainty of subjective judgment and interdependence between indicators. Therefore, Delphi-order relation analysis (ORA) method and improved radar chart were proposed in this paper to address these two problems respectively. A feedback mechanism is introduced in Delphi-ORA method to control the limitation of expert's knowledge structure and experience. The correlation coefficient is incorporated in the improved radar chart to reflect the interdependence between indicators.

Keywords: Flight deck ergonomic design · Comprehensive evaluation · Delphi-ORA · Improved radar chart · Uncertainty · Interdependence

1 Introduction

1.1 The Status and the Meaning of Research About Comprehensive Evaluation on Cockpit Ergonomics Design

According to literature and accident report, about 70 % of all aviation accidents were caused by human factors [1–4]. In order to reduce human error and pilot workload, the flight deck need to be designed carefully with full consideration of ergonomics. Then the aviation safety can be enhanced. In order to ensure the design quality of man-machine interface on flight deck, the ergonomic requirements need to be integrated in design and

© Springer International Publishing Switzerland 2016
D. Harris (Ed.): EPCE 2016, LNAI 9736, pp. 464–475, 2016.
DOI: 10.1007/978-3-319-40030-3_45

the ergonomic evaluation efforts are essential. However, it is difficult to grasp the overall ergonomic design level of cockpit. There is a need for comprehensive evaluation. In the evaluation and comprehensive evaluation aspect of cockpit ergonomic design, plenty of research and application efforts have been done [5–8].

1.2   Limitations of Existing CE Methods

The process consisted of 5 steps, i.e. specify the evaluation purpose, identify the cockpit ergonomic metrics (evaluation indicator system), determine indicators' weights; rate each evaluation indicator, and select/construct comprehensive evaluation model to conduct comprehensive evaluation [9, 10].

Weight determination is a key step in the process of comprehensive evaluation. The rationality of the weight represents a correct description of the relationship of evaluation metrics and object to be evaluated, which determines the validity of the result of CE, apparently. Several methods have been proposed to determine weights Majority of them can be classified into subjective methods, objective methods and combinations of them depending on the information provided [11]. In general, objective methods assign indicator weights according to the structure or the internal mechanism of evaluation object. However, for the comprehensive evaluation problem of cockpit ergonomic design, the relationship between various indicators is complex, the effect of each individual indicator on the overall ergonomic level is not very clear. Moreover, ergonomic evaluation is greatly influenced by evaluator's subjective factors. These reasons make it difficult to determine indicator weights using objective methods. Thus, in general case, the subjective method, which is based on expert judgment, is commonly used to acquire indicator weights. However, the subjective weighting method has the following limitations:

- Strong subjective, the weighting results depend on experts' work experience, knowledge structure and their preference,
- Expert judgment is equivalent to the black box operation and the transparency of the evaluation process is poor,
- And, since the uncertainty of subjective judgment, the repeatability of results is poor.

Therefore, the same decision maker can give different weight to the same indicators under different situations. In order to achieve group consensus, Mukherjee (2014) advised the Brian Storming method [12], and Dempster–Shafer theory was used in Ju and Wang's (2012) research [13].

Comprehensive evaluation is a method using a mathematical model $(y = f(w, x))$ to aggregate individual indicator evaluation result into a composite indicator with consideration of the weight information. The comprehensive evaluation value represents the overall level of the evaluated object. Here, the mathematical model used for "aggregation" is the comprehensive evaluation model. Due to the entire cockpit is a complex system, including many subsystems, and there exist closely correlation and strong coupling between the subsystems. This makes the evaluation indicators for the comprehensive evaluation of cockpit ergonomics have significant interdependence.

Whereas the existing comprehensive evaluation models, such as fuzzy comprehensive evaluation method, principal component analysis method, andutility theory model, etc., are essentially a linear weighted method. Their results contain serious duplicated information and cannot reflect the true level of the object evaluated [14]. Although the neural network is a non-linear model, it is difficult to obtain enough high quality training samples, which greatly limits its application.

1.3   Innovation Work

The purpose of this paper is to address the limitations described above. With the feedback of the majority's opinion of experts, Delphi method can achieve group consensus through multiple rounds of consultation [15]. Inspired by Delphi method, the feedback mechanism was introduced in Order Relation Analysis (ORA) method to address the bias and uncertainty of expert subjective judgment.

The existing practice to handle the interdependence between evaluation indicators is to eliminate the overlapping information during the construction stage of the evaluation metrics [16], or to adjust the indicator weight according to the correlation between them [17], when ANP is advisable [18]. Considering the general process of comprehensive evaluation, it is apparent that another potential point to handle the redundant information between indicators lies incomprehensive evaluation model. However the related literatures are few. The improved radar chart proposed in this paper has integrated the correlation between indicators, which is a means to address the overlapping information through the development of an appropriate comprehensive evaluation model.

1.4   The Structure of the Thesis

The remainder of this paper is structured as follows. The second section introduces the process of Delphi-ORA method in detail, including the design of Loop control variable and feedback variable. The third section describes the improved Radar Chart. Finally, a conclusion and discussion is given.

2   Delphi-Order Relation Analysis Method

The order relation analysis (ORA) method proposed by Guo [19], also called G1 method, is a subjective weighting approach based on expert judgment. Compared with analytic hierarchy process (AHP), ORA method does not need consistency testing. Besides, the amount of Comparative judgment work has been reduced greatly. For these reasons, ORA method was chosen in this paper for improvement. A feedback mechanism was introduced in ORA method, which was inspired by Delphi method. The Delphi-ORA method requires organizers to do statistical processing on the data collected in previous advisory round and feedback the result to experts. Then experts are required to give their opinion again based on the feedback information. After several rounds of consultation, experts' opinion will eventually tend to be consistent.

2.1 ORA Method Process

ORA method firstly asks experts to sort the evaluation indicators according to their importance on evaluation object in a descending order. And then estimated values for the importance ratios between adjacent indicators should been given. The estimated ratios are always presented as qualitative linguistic values. During the subsequent data processing, a numerical value will be assigned to each linguistic value. Then through a simple mathematical treatment, the weight coefficient of each indicator can be calculated. The weighting process of ORA method consists of the following three steps.

Indicator Importance Sorting. For given evaluation object, if indicator u_i is more (not less) important than indicator u_j, then it can be documented as $u_i > u_j$. First, the expert need to choose the most important indicator he think among then indicators $\{u_1, u_2, \ldots, u_n\}$, and record it as u_1^*. Then select the most important indicator from the remaining n−1 indicators to be as u_2^*. Repeat the steps above, after n−1 rounds, a descending sorting according to their importance of the n indicators can be derived:

$$u_1^* > u_{n2}^* > \cdots > u_n^* \tag{1}$$

Where u_i^* is the i-th indicator after sorting (i = 1,2,...,n).

Estimate the Importance Ratio. Suppose w_i^* is the weight coefficient of indicator u_i^*. Then the importance ratio (r_i) between indicator u_{i-1}^* and u_i^* can be represented as w_{i-1}^*/w_i^* (formula 2). Through expert judgment, a qualitative linguistic value of r_i can be obtained. Then a numerical value should be assigned to each linguistic level as appropriately. The assignment can refer to Table 1.

$$w_{i-1}^*/w_i^* = r_i, \quad i = n, n-1, \ldots, 2 \tag{2}$$

Table 1. Suggested linguistic levels and corresponding numerical values for r_i

Linguistic level terms (w_{i-1}/w_i)	Numerical values (r_i)	Explanation
Equally important	1.0	u_{i-1}^* and u_i^* are equally important
Slightly important	1.2	u_{i-1}^* is slightly more important than u_i^*
Moderately important	1.4	u_{i-1}^* is moderately more important than u_i^*
Very important	1.6	u_{i-1}^* is much more important than u_i^*
Extremely important	1.8	u_{i-1}^* is extremely more important than u_i^*

Calculate Weight Coefficient w_i. Formula (3) and (4) can be used to calculate the weight coefficient of each indicator in sorting (1)

$$w_n^* = \left(1 + \sum_{k=2}^{n} \prod_{i=k}^{n} r_i\right)^{-1} \tag{3}$$

$$w_{i-1}^* = r_i w_i^*, \quad i = n, n-1, \ldots, 2 \tag{4}$$

Therefore, weight coefficients of sorted indicators can be obtained,

$$W^* = (w_1^*, w_2^*, \ldots, w_n^*) \tag{5}$$

Then adjust the order of each element in weight vector W^*, we can get the weight vector corresponding to the original indicator set $\{u_1, u_2, \ldots, u_n\}$,

$$W = (w_1, w_2, \ldots, w_n) \tag{6}$$

2.2 Information Feedback Variable

The consultation result of former round is provided to experts through information feedback variable (IFV). Assuming there are m experts participating in the indicator weight consultation of ORA method, then after the first round consultation, we can get m pairs of different sorting and corresponding estimated importance ratios (see formula 7) for indicator set $\{u_1, u_2, \ldots, u_n\}$.

$$\begin{cases} u_{i1}^* > u_{i2}^* > \ldots > u_{in}^*, \\ (r_{i2}, r_{i3}, \ldots, r_{in}) \end{cases} \quad (i = 1, 2, \ldots, m) \tag{7}$$

Thus, the weighting result for indicator set $\{u_1, u_2, \ldots, u_n\}$ of the i-th expert can be calculated using ORA method.

$$W_i = (w_{i1}, w_{i2}, \ldots, w_{in}), \quad (i = 1, 2, \ldots, m) \tag{8}$$

Where, w_{ij} denotes the weight coefficient assigned to the j-th indicator in $\{u_1, u_2, \ldots, u_n\}$ by the i-th expert.

The arithmetic mean of W_i can be calculated as formula (9), which is regarded as the ultimate weight vector of the first round consultation.

$$W = \frac{1}{m} \sum_{i=1}^{m} W_i = \left(\frac{1}{m} \sum_{i=1}^{m} w_{i1}, \ldots, \frac{1}{m} \sum_{i=1}^{m} w_{in}\right) = (w_1, w_2, \ldots, w_n) \tag{9}$$

According to the size of each element (indicator weight) in the weight vector W, the first round average sorting of the n indicators could be determined. And this average sorting is selected as the information feedback variable.

$$u_1^* > u_2^* > \ldots > u_n^* \tag{10}$$

2.3 Loop Control Variable

Loop control variable is used to test the consistency of expert judgment, upon which the weight consultation process is determined whether to be ended. In this paper, an average ordering deviation index (AODI) based on the number of reverse order is proposed to represent the consistency/divergence level of expert group ordering.

An ordered array composed of natural numbers $(1,2,\ldots,n)$ is called an-order permutation, denoted as $j_1,j_2,\ldots,j_n$. An n-order permutation can most have n! different permutations. Among them, the ascending permutation, i.e. $1,2,\ldots,n$, is defined as standard permutation or natural permutation. In a permutation, if one bigger number is in front of a smaller one, then these two numbers form a reverse order. The total number of reverse orders in a permutation is defined as the reverse order number (RON) of the permutation, denoted as $\tau(j_1,j_2,\ldots,j_n)$.

The average sorting $(u_1^* > u_2^* > \ldots > u_n^*)$ obtained from a weight consultation round is regarded as the standard permutation $(1,2,\ldots,n)$. For the i-th expert's sorting $u_{i1}^* > u_{i2}^* > \ldots > u_{in}^*$, it corresponds to a n-order permutation and its RON can be denoted as $\tau(i)$. For a n-order permutation, the maximum RON is $n(n-1)/2$. The ratio of average RON of m permutations provided by expert group and the maximum RON is used to represent the consistency/divergence level of expert group ordering, i.e. the average ordering deviation index (AODI).

$$AODI = \frac{\sum_{i=1}^{m} \tau(i)/m}{n(n-1)/2} \tag{11}$$

The smaller the ordering deviation is, the smaller AODI will be, and vice versa. If AODI < 0.1, the consistency of expert group ordering is acceptable and the weight consultation can be ended.

3 Improved Radar Chart

3.1 Radar Chart and Comprehensive Evaluation

Radar chart is also known as spider diagram, which consists of several concentric circles (or polygons) and some axes starting from the circle center. Each axis in the radar chart denotes an indicator, while each concentric circle (or polygon) represents a certain indicator level. Radar chart comprehensive evaluation model is a kind of indicator value aggregation method based on the extraction of feature variables of radar chart. Radar chart comprehensive evaluation model is a combination of graphical evaluation method and digital evaluation method, which is greatly suitable for an entire and overall evaluation of complex multi-attribute structure, and much more intuitive, as well (Fig. 1).

Huili Zheng described the general process of radar chart comprehensive evaluation [20], Liu and Chen Yong improved radar chart comprehensive evaluation respectively [21, 22]. The most commonly used feature variables in radar chart comprehensive evaluation are the area A and perimeter C of radar chart, which are calculated as:

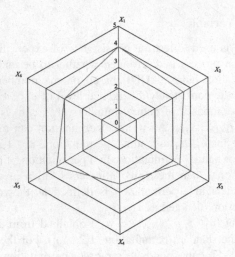

Fig. 1. The general form of traditional radar chart

$$
\begin{cases}
A = \sum_{i=1}^{n} \frac{1}{2} y_i y_{i+1} \sin \theta \\
C = \sum_{i=1}^{n} \sqrt{y_i^2 + y_{i+1}^2 - 2 y_i y_{i+1} \cos \theta}
\end{cases}
\tag{12}
$$

Where θ is angle between indicatoraxes, $\theta = 2\pi/n$. Area Arepresents the level of object being evaluated, while C reflects the balanced development of each index.

3.2 Improvement of Radar Chart

A fatal deficiency in traditional radar chart comprehensive evaluation method is that there is a lack of consideration of indicator weight and correlation between them. It is apparent in Eq. (12) that there are two factors affecting the results of radar chart comprehensive evaluation, i.e. indicator values and angles between indicator axes. Therefore, two points of improvement were conducted in this paper from the two aspects mentioned above, which will make radar chart comprehensive evaluation model more suitable for situations where strong mutual coupling exists.

Indicator Axis Value Integrated with Weight. For conventional radar chart, the evaluation value (or state value) of each indicator is used as indicator axis value immediately without consideration of indicator weight. In this paper, the indicator weight to the power of indicator evaluation value, i.e. $x_i^{w_i}$, is used as the indicator axis value. Thus the area formula in Eq. (12) will be transformed as follows.

$$
A = \sum_{i=1}^{n} \frac{1}{2} x_i^{w_i} \cdot x_{i+1}^{w_{i+1}} \sin \theta_i
\tag{13}
$$

Formula (13) is actually a combination of linear weighted model and geometric weighted model, which has certain advantages of both.

Determination of θ_i. The angles between indicator axes in a conventional radar chartare usually the same, i.e. if there are n indicators, the axis angle will be $2\pi/n$. Correlation coefficients r_i between adjacent indicators are utilized as a basis for the determination of corresponding axis angle θ_i. The calculation formula are as follows.

$$k_i = \begin{cases} \sqrt{1 - r_i^2}, & (0 \le r_i \le 1) \\ \sqrt{1 - r_i^2}, & (-1 \le r_i < 0) \end{cases} \tag{14}$$

$$\theta_i = 2\pi \cdot k_i / \sum_{j=1}^{n} k_j \tag{15}$$

Thus the angle between indicator axes will no longer be the average, but determined by correlation coefficients between adjacent indicators. Therefore, the greater the correlation between two indicators, the smaller the angle will be. As a result, their contribution to the composite indicator will be smaller, accordingly. Hence, the improved radar chart is no longer a regular polygon, but similar to the shape shown in Fig. 2. The evaluation value of indicator needs to be normalized, and the negative indicator (negatively correlated with composite indicator) should be transformed into a positive indicator (positively correlated with composite indicator) previously before determining their correlation.

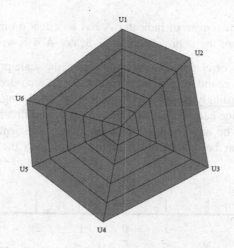

Fig. 2. Example form of improved Radar Chart

There are two methods recommended for determining the correlation coefficient r_i in this paper.

1. For the case that there exist multiple objects, supposing p objects, to be evaluated, employing the indicator set $\{u_1, u_2, \ldots, u_n\}$ to evaluate these objects respectively, then a $p \times n$-order evaluation matrix X can be obtained.

$$X = [X_1, X_2, \ldots, X_n] = \begin{bmatrix} x_{11} & x_{12} & \cdots & x_{1n} \\ x_{21} & x_{22} & \cdots & x_{2n} \\ \vdots & \vdots & \ddots & \vdots \\ x_{p1} & x_{p2} & \cdots & x_{pn} \end{bmatrix} \tag{16}$$

Where x_{ij} represents the evaluation value of the i-th object, while X_j denotes the evaluation vector of the j-th indicator on the p objects. Thus, the Pearson correlation coefficient can be calculated and used to represent the correlation between indicators.

$$r_{ij} = \frac{\mathrm{Cov}(X_i, X_j)}{\sqrt{D(X_i)}\sqrt{D(X_j)}} \tag{17}$$

Where $\mathrm{Cov}(X_i, X_j)$ is the covariance between X_i and X_j, $D(X_i)$ and $D(X_j)$ are the variance of X_i and X_j respectively.

2. For the case of only one evaluation object, such as the comprehensive evaluation of a specific alternative during the system design process, expert judgment is advisable for the acquisition of correlation coefficients. The correlation relationship between evaluation indicators may be divided into the following three conditions:

- Positive correlation: indicator B will be improved with the improvement of indicator A;
- Irrelevant: the improvement of indicator A has no effect on indicator B;
- Negative correlation: the improvement of indicator A will worsen indicator B.

When judging the correlations between indicators, the scale presented in Fig. 3 can be served as a reference, and the judgment results can be recorded in the questionnaire shown in Fig. 4 accordingly. In the subsequent data processing, an appropriate correlation coefficient value can be assigned to each level, and finally the mean of expert judgment results will be employed as the correlation coefficient between indicators. This part of work can be carried out simultaneously with the weight consultation process.

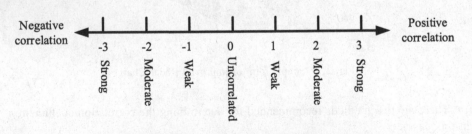

Fig. 3. The qualitative grade division of indicator correlation

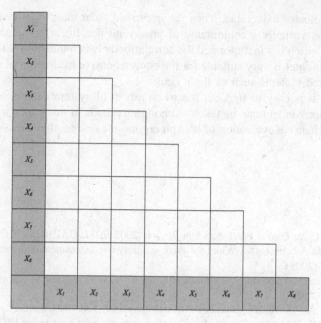

Fig. 4. A questionnaire example for correlation coefficient survey

4 Conclusion

In this paper a new approach for comprehensive evaluation of cockpit ergonomic design was proposed. Though there are plenty of researches and applications about comprehensive evaluation/multiple attribute decision making, most of them have a lack of sufficient consideration of the subjectivity of expert judgment and the interdependence between evaluation indicators. The effort of this paper is focused on these two problems.

To mitigate the limitation of individual expert's knowledge structure and experience, and handle the uncertainty and randomness of subjective judgment, a feedback mechanism was introduced into ORA method for acquiring more reasonable weight coefficients. The new proposed method, named Delphi-ORA method, can promote expert opinions to a consensus through a multi-round consultation. In the multi-round consultation, the average sorting of expert group was utilized as information feedback variable, while the average ordering deviation index based on number of reverse order was defined as loop control variable. In terms of handling the interdependence between indicators, the common method is to ensure the independence between indicators during the development stage of indicator system, or to adjust indicator weights according to their correlations. From the perspective of comprehensive evaluation model, this paper proposed the improved radar chart to incorporate the consideration of interdependence between indicators. In the improved radar chart, angles between indicator axes are determined based on the correlation coefficients of adjacent indicators, and the indicator weight to the power of indicator evaluation value, i.e. $x_i{}^{w_i}$, is used as the indicator axis value. Thus the improved radar chart comprehensive evaluation model is virtually a conjunction of linear and non-linear comprehensive evaluation model, which has incorporated the correlation between indicators. Therefore, the improved radar chart is very suitable for the comprehensive evaluation of complex and strongly coupled systems such as flight deck.

Therefore, it is easy to find out the weak aspect of system design, and then corresponding improvement can be taken. Although methods in this paper were proposed for the comprehensive evaluation of cockpit ergonomic design, they are also applicable to other areas.

References

1. Authority, C.A.: Global Fatal Accident Review 2002–2011. CAP1036 (2013)
2. Shyur, H.-J.: A quantitative model for aviation safety risk assessment. Comput. Ind. Eng. **54** (1), 34–44 (2008)
3. Boeing: Statistical Summary of Commercial Jet Airplane Accidents: Worldwide Operations 1959–2013 (2014)
4. Stanton, N.A., Harris, D., Salmon, P.M., Demagalski, J.M., Marshall, A., Young, M.S., Dekker, S.W., Waldmann, T.: Predicting design induced pilot error using HET (human error template)-A new formal human error identification method for flight decks (2006)
5. Craig, J., Burrett, G.: The design of a human factors questionnaire for cockpit assessment. In: International Conference on Human Interfaces in Control Rooms, Cockpits and Command Centres, pp. 16–20 (1999)
6. Shamo, M., Dror, R., Degani, A.: A multi-dimensional evaluation methodology for new cockpit systems. In: Proceedings of the Tenth International Symposium on Aviation Psychology, p. 120 (1999)
7. Li, Y., Yang, F., Wang, L., Yuan, X.: Study on comprehensive evaluation of cockpit ergonomics and its application. J. Beijing Univ. Aeronaut. Astronaut. **31**(6), 652–656 (2005)
8. Song, H., Sun, Y., Lu, Z.: Study on comprehensive evaluation of cockpit ergonomics. Aircraf Design **30**(4), 36–40 (2010)
9. Xu, J., Wu, W.: Multiple Attribute Decision Making Theory and Methods. Tsinghua University Press, Beijing (2006)
10. Guo, F.: Comprehensive Evaluation of Pilot Operation Procedures for Commercial Airliner. Beihang University, Beijing (2010)
11. Ma, J., Fan, Z.-P., Huang, L.-H.: A subjective and objective integrated approach to determine attribute weights. Eur. J. Oper. Res. **112**(2), 397–404 (1999)
12. Mukherjee, K.: Supplier selection criteria and methods: past, present and future (2014)
13. Ju, Y., Wang, A.: Emergency alternative evaluation under group decision makers: a method of incorporating DS/AHP with extended TOPSIS. Expert Syst. Appl. **39**(1), 1315–1323 (2012)
14. Pereira, J.M., Duckstein, L.: A multiple criteria decision-making approach to GIS-based land suitability evaluation. Int. J. Geog. Inf. Sci. **7**(5), 407–424 (1993)
15. Linstone, H.A., Turoff, M.: The Delphi Method: Techniques and Applications. Addison-Wesley, Reading (1975)
16. Li, Y., Yuan, X., Yang, C., Wang, L., Du, J.: Building of the index system for fighter cockpit ergonomics comprehensive evaluation. ACTA Aeronautica et Astronautica Sinica **2**, 148–152 (2005)

17. De Ambroggi, M., Trucco, P.: Modelling and assessment of dependent performance shaping factors through Analytic Network Process. Reliab. Eng. Syst. Saf. **96**(7), 849–860 (2011)
18. Wang, H.-J., Zeng, Z.-T.: A multi-objective decision-making process for reuse selection of historic buildings. Expert Syst. Appl. **37**(2), 1241–1249 (2010)
19. Guo, Y.: Comprehensive Evaluation: Theory and Methods. Science Press, Beijing (2002)
20. Zheng, H., Liu, C., Zhe, D.: Comprehensive evaluating method based on radar-graph. J. Nanjing Univ. Posts Telecommun. (Nat. Sci.) **21**(2), 75–79 (2001)
21. Chen, Y., Chen, X., Li, Z., Lin, Y.: Method of radar chart comprehensive evaluation with uniqueness feature. Trans. Beijing Inst. Technol. **30**(12), 1409–1412 (2010)
22. Liu, H., Liu, A., Zhang, B., Zhang, T., Zhang, X.: A fuzzy comprehensive evaluation method of maintenance quality based on improved radar chart. In: ISECS International Colloquium on Computing, Communication, Control, and Management, CCCM 2008, pp. 638–642 (2008)

Pilot Situational Awareness Modeling for Cockpit Interface Evaluation

Xu Wu[1]([⊠]), Xiaoru Wanyan[1], Damin Zhuang[1], and Shuang Liu[2]

[1] School of Aeronautics and Engineering,
Beihang University, Beijing 100191, China
{wuxu0527, wanyanxiaoru, dmzhuang}@buaa.edu.cn
[2] China Institution of Marine Technology and Economy, Beijing 100191, China
liushuangbh@163.com

Abstract. As the highly development of complexity and automation level of human-machine system in airplane cockpit, flight information shown in display and control system became diversified and complicated, which meant tremendous information was required to be simultaneously processed for pilot's sake. Therefore, great information would provide with more comprehensive data support while raise higher requirement of interface design of cockpit display. This paper concentrated on pilot situational awareness (SA) modeling based on human-machine interaction in cockpit system and developed theoretical application research in three connected parts: SA modeling based on attention resource allocation, SA modeling based on cognitive process analysis and SA modeling based on interface evaluation.

Keywords: Situational awareness · Attention allocation · Cognitive process analysis · Interface design

1 Introduction

As typical interaction system of human in the loop, airplane cockpit required the pilots to continuously monitor a large number of flight indicators on display interface and to obtain the necessary information to make immediate decisions. During the whole flight, situation awareness of the pilots had directly impact on flight safety because keeping high level of situation awareness guaranteed rapid and effective manipulation of flight control. As a result, studies on pilot's situation awareness became popular nowadays. Endsley established the original cognitive model of three levels of situation awareness and made it worldwide accepted especially in aviation ergonomics [1–3]. Then lots of scholars and researchers started their works on qualitative evaluation and quantitative measurement of situation awareness [4–6]. With great development of cognitive psychology in ergonomics researches, the interaction between situation awareness and perception, cognition, as well as attention was also investigated and analyzed aiming at human error reduction [7, 8]. Nevertheless, the exquisite definition and quantitation method of situation awareness was not perfectly ended in common conclusion. So this paper combined with cognitive analysis and mathematical modeling method in order to

© Springer International Publishing Switzerland 2016
D. Harris (Ed.): EPCE 2016, LNAI 9736, pp. 476–484, 2016.
DOI: 10.1007/978-3-319-40030-3_46

advance the study of pilot's situation awareness for ergonomics evaluation of cockpit interface design.

Based on display interface design of the new generation civil airplane, this paper carried out a series of studies on situation awareness modeling, which were involved with visual attention allocation and ACT-R (Adaptive Control of Thought- Rational) modeling. Considering the classic three levels model of situation awareness by Endsley, various qualitative analysis methods and quantitative computation models were established and developed gradually.

Firstly, this paper discussed the relationship between pilot's situation awareness and visual attention allocation [9]. Such studies could be also founded in Wickens' Attention-Situation Awareness model (A-SA). However, the cognitive status of single situation element was considered as three levels of unperceived, perceived and comprehended in this study. Thus, the probability of certain event that pilot drew attention on its situation element was equivalent to the proportion of obtained attention to the total resource. Since the higher level of situation awareness was realized on the basis of lower one, the second level of situation awareness was viewed as prerequisite conditional fact of achieving the first level. Therefore, the model of situation awareness was put forward based on attention allocation and conditional probability theory.

Furthermore, the current model of situation awareness was extended and optimized in consideration of cognitive process analysis [10]. According to ACT-R theory, pilot's cognitive process could be regarded as a progressive way of triggering rules. As long as the obtained cognitive status of situation element reached certain level, perception was triggered. And after the filtration of information processing, further comprehension and prediction was also triggered and realized only if the related valid information exceeded the certain threshold value. Based on the optimal rules of cognition mechanism, matching and triggering might lead into either the second level of situation awareness reached by understanding the current status or the third level of well-prepared to the further. Hence, the situation awareness model was evolved based on the triggering rules in ACT-R theory.

In addition, the situation awareness model was advanced and adopted to develop ergonomics method for interface evaluation of cockpit display. The fuzziness and randomness of pilot's cognition of situation element importance was taken into account as well as the maintaining memory of various format design of cockpit display interface. And the relationship between each situation element and the current situation awareness level was furthered to provide a quantitative method of interface evaluation based on cognitive process analysis.

2 SA Modeling Based on Attention Allocation

Facing to tremendous information, the pilots were required to obtain the most effective information through the data flow immediately. In the perspective of information processing, some information attributes were processed in parallel during the pre-attention period and then registered to form cognition. Attention resource was considered to affect pilots' SA because it constrained the number of situational elements to be correctly understood during the cognition procedure.

Assuming the current scenario related to flight task was composed of several situational element i under certain circumstance in airplane cockpit. Therefore, each situational element was contributed to pilot's performance to complete flight task.

According to Man–machine Integration Design and Analysis System (MIDAS) proposed by Hooey [8], SA was defined as the ratio of actual status to optimal SA:

$$SA = \frac{SA(actual)}{SA(optimal)} = \sum_{i=1}^{n} u_i p_i \tag{1}$$

Where p_i represented for three cognitive status of situational element and u_i was its coefficient. In case $p_i = 0$, the situational element was unperceived. In case $p_i = 0.5$, the situational element was perceived which indicated SA1. In case $p_i = 1$, the situational element was fully understood which indicated SA2.

Then, assuming the event a_i was attention resource allocated on situational element i, so the occurring probability of event a_i was equal to the percentage attention allocation of situational element i:

$$p(a_i) = f_i. \tag{2}$$

According to Eq. (2), SA1 was acquired when event a_i occurred. Because the acquisition of SA1 was a sufficient condition for realizing SA2, situational element being fully understood was also considered as a probability event that event b_i for failure and c_i for success respectively with probability of k_i and $(1 - k_i)$. Therefore, the expectancy of possible cognitive level for situational element i was $\bar{p}_i$:

$$\bar{p}_i = p(a_i c_i) \times 1 + p(a_i b_i) \times 0.5 + (1 - p(a_i)) \times 0 \tag{3}$$

So the current situational awareness was quantified by each situational element:

$$SA = \sum_{i=1}^{n} u_i \bar{p}_i = \sum_{i=1}^{n} (1 - 0.5 k_i) u_i f_i \tag{4}$$

Where u_i represented for the priority of situational element involved in current flight task and f_i represented for attention allocation ratio according to multiple factors model [11]. Because u_i was influenced and determined by task, the pilots was required to reach perfect cognitive status of essential situational element when they need to keep high level of SA.

Notably, this model concerned with only the first and second level of SA, which was mainly affected by attention resource allocation. And the model output value was relatively comparable rather than an absolute value because the actual SA was manipulated by more factors such as mental workload, short term memory and time pressure. Furthermore, the model predicted immediate value of SA based on attention allocation which could be considered as equal to the average value during certain task phase. For example, the pilot was required to monitor the display interface and the flight information was task-related situational element. Therefore, SA of such interface was different as attention allocation changed during different task phases.

3   SA Modeling Based on Cognitive Process Analysis

To further the current SA model, cognitive process analysis was acquired to explain the internal forming procedure of SA according to the basic theories of ACT-R. ACT-R was a popular cognitive architecture proposed by Anderson. It provided an effective method to illustrate cognitive process mechanism and explore mental activities of the pilots.

Three main parts were included in ACT-R: basic module, buffer and production rule. The basis module contained perception movement module and memory module. The front one involved with visual attention transform while the latter one covered both declarative and procedural (if, then) memory knowledge. The buffer was in charge of interaction between modules where information was exchanged. The production rule was the essence of ACT-R that continuously triggering of the rules was considered as the fact of cognitive process. The production was triggered only when consistency matched with the present status of buffer. As a result, the buffer was updated to change cognitive status. To be noticed, one production was allowed to be triggered simultaneously.

The pilots were required to filter flight information from display interface and then selected certain part into short-term memory through sensory register, which was referred to selective attention of situational element in visual module. The buffer module obtained situational information from visual module and accessed declarative memory module to withdraw the corresponding declarative knowledge. Situational element was perceived when its activating quantity reached certain level of threshold. This process coincided with the function of attention module in A-SA model and realized the first level of SA. The content of buffer represented for the current status of ACT-R. When the "if" part of the procedural knowledge matched it, the production was selected or the "then" part was realized according to the production rule.

According to Wickens, there were no obvious boundaries between SA2 and SA3 in the dynamic system, because the comprehension of current status had direct influence on the prediction of the future and both were equally important for the current flight task. Therefore, the distinction between comprehension and prediction of cognitive status of certain fact was still ambiguous in ACT-R model that what production rules was matched and trigger to occur might lead to awareness of the current status or the forehead status. In fact, human errors such as incorrect operation and reaction delay would induce potential aviation accidents. It is necessary to keep fluent and skilled ability of the basic level of SA in order to improve the ability of higher level. The comprehension of situational element was formed by gradually completed information chunk in real solutions rather than accomplish at one stroke. So it was much easier for the experienced pilot to keep higher level of SA than the novice one (Fig. 1).

According to Eq. (2), event a_i occurred and attention resource was allocated to situational element i. Meanwhile, the buffer accessed the visual module to acquire situational information, and then accessed the memory module to retrieve related declarative knowledge, which led to cognitive activation of situational element i. The level of such activation AC_i was determined by the addition of baseline activation AC_{0i} and relative activation $\sum_j W_j S_{ij}$:

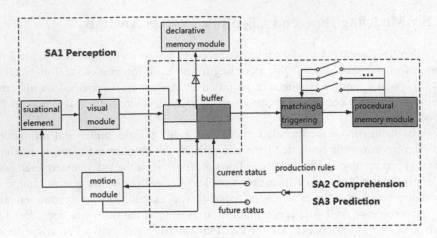

Fig. 1. Three Levels of SA based on ACT-R

$$AC_i = AC_{0i} + \sum_j W_j S_{ij} \tag{5}$$

Where $AC_{0i} = 0.5\ln t$ indicated the fact that recognizing situational element had been presented for times. W_j represented for the attention weighting of situational element j due to the current fact i and S_{ij} represented for the strength of association from the current fact i to the related situational element j:

$$S_{ij} = S - \ln(fan_j) \tag{6}$$

Where fan_j was the number of facts associated to situational element j, and S was defined as 2.

When AC_i reached certain level of threshold τ (normally $\tau = 1$), the relevant declarative knowledge was considered to be successfully acquired, which indicated the situational element was perceived (event b_i) according to ACT-R:

$$p(b_i/a_i) = \left(1 + e^{-(AC_i - \tau)/s}\right)^{-1} \tag{7}$$

Where s controlled the noise in the activation levels and was typically set as 0.4, and τ was set as 1.0.

According to ACT-R theory, multiple production rules were expected to be matched at any time, but only one production with the highest utility U_i was chosen to be executed. When declarative knowledge was successfully retrieved by the buffer, the current situational element was fully comprehended if the perfect production rule was executed, which was considered as event c_i:

$$p(b_i/a_i) = e^{U_i/\theta} / \sum e^{U_i/\theta} \tag{8}$$

In specific cognitive activities, the width of cognition was limited to a certain level due to the continuously triggering of procedural knowledge. Besides, the information chunk related to the current goal module was so large in the declarative knowledge warehouse that it was difficult for cognition system to choose the correct knowledge. Based on the former SA modeling, the expectancy of certain situational element was revised as:

$$\bar{p}_i = \left(e^{U_i/\theta} / \sum e^{U_i/\theta} + 0.5\right) \times \frac{f_i}{1 + e^{-(AC_i - \tau)/s}} \tag{9}$$

In addition, the current situational awareness was revised accordingly:

$$SA = \sum_{i=1}^{n} \left(e^{U_i/\theta} / \sum e^{U_i/\theta} + 0.5\right) \times \frac{s_i u_i f_i}{1 + e^{-(AC_i - \tau)/s}} \tag{10}$$

Where the sensitive coefficient of each situational element was determined by both salient s_i and importance u_i.

4 SA Modeling for Ergonomics Evaluation of Cockpit Display Interface

Situational awareness was a complicated conception by which the pilot capability, training, experience, interface design, flight performance, automatic level, as well as their relationship could be organically connected and put together. The influencing factor involved with SA was shown in Table 1.

According to Table 1, there were numbers of influencing factors of SA, including the inside factors and the outside ones. During the forming procedure of the three levels of SA, each inside factor had direct impact on establishment and maintenance of SA while outside factors affected SA level through manipulating the inside ones to the pilots. In addition, the comprehension of situational element required knowledge and goal to integrate the outside information, which led to prediction of the change of the following situational element. Because the acquisition of higher level of SA relied on the achievement of the lower SA, the perception of related situational element was considered as the foundation of forming SA, and also the phase when most SA errors took place.

The information communication by perception was conducted through kinds of coding method. Moreover, reasonable visual coding of display information helped the transition of visual storage to both short-term memory and long-term memory, which largely improved the accuracy and efficiency of information identification. Therefore, optimal information coding (e.g. color, character, graph, etc.) of visual stimulus could enhance the humanity and utility of display interface, and also improve the capability

Table 1. Influencing factos of SA

Conditions	SA Level	Factors
Inside	SA1	Visual perception: spatial perception, depth perception, color perception
		Object identification: pattern detection, target identification
		Cognition: top-down and bottom-up channels
		Attention: attention allocation, focus, vigilance
	SA2	Memory: working memory, recall and forget
		Schema: knowledge experience organization
	SA3	Reasoning: diagnosis cognition by cueing
Outside	SA1, 2 and 3	Pressure: cognitive tunnel
		Workload: task-related performance
		System: system design, system complexity
		Interface: human-computer interaction, information acquisition and comprehension

of the pilots including memory ability, attention allocation ability, superior cognition ability and decision ability, which resulted in perfect level of SA.

Usually, memory in human brain might either further in process and storage, or vanish as time went by. If the memory of situational element was kept well, then it was good for the maintenance of SA. Assuming memory retention of situational element was defined as r_i, so the sensitive coefficient was positively correlated to r_i. Besides, such memory retention was affected by visual identification of situational element that various physical characteristics caused different effect on memory retention during the bottom-up processing. Assuming comprehensive performance of visual identification of situational element was defined as d_i, so the sensitive coefficient was positively correlated to d_i:

$$d_i = \frac{1}{m} \sum\nolimits_{\lambda=1}^{m} \varepsilon_\lambda l_{i\lambda} \tag{11}$$

Where $l_{i\lambda}$ indicated the readability of visual coding λ, and ε_λ was its weighting coefficient.

Therefore, Eq. (10) was revised and SA based on interface design was determined as:

$$SA = \sum\nolimits_{i=1}^{n} \left(e^{U_i/\theta} / \sum e^{U_i/\theta} + 0.5 \right) \times \frac{\frac{r_i u_i f_i}{m} \sum_{\lambda=1}^{m} \varepsilon_\lambda l_{i\lambda}}{1 + e^{-(AC_i - \tau)/s}} \tag{12}$$

It was most significant for the pilots to monitor cockpit display and keep ideal SA during flight task. However, the pilots were prone to overly rely on automatic-pilot so that they might ignore the real-time change of flight information due to high technology used in the modern aviation. Moreover, excessive attention resource was drawn when ordinary fault suddenly occurred so that the real fatal information was failed to obtain, which induced potential flight accident with the lack of SA. Therefore, the interface design should be evaluated using ergonomics method whether it was appropriate for SA maintenance and how it would affect SA.

5 Discussion

This paper concentrated on the forming procedure and mechanism of pilot SA. Combined with visual and cognitive characteristics of pilot, SA modeling was established for interface evaluation based on comprehensive researches in the multiple fields of cognitive engineering, ergonomics, probability and informative theory. Qualitative analysis model and quantitative calculation model of pilot SA were concluded and discussed to investigate the complex connection between cockpit display interface and pilot SA. Then, a framework of ergonomics evaluation system of interface design was put forward according to SA modeling, which was valuable for theoretic and application researches involved with optimal design of display interface and human-machine function allocation.

However, it was necessary to further this explorative study with improvement and extension in consideration of flight task, flight environment as well as complexity of cognitive activity. The relation between display interface and cognitive characteristics during human-machine interaction was mainly discussed in SA modeling. Therefore, the pilots in these models were considered as perfect human so that certain parameters were set as constant value, which was blind to cognitive variance caused by individual difference. Moreover, the capability of SA acquisition and maintenance was also influenced by time pressure and mental workload related to current task, which was not concluded in this study. Besides, the calculation value of SA modeling was discrete result of comparable meaning. And the cognitive analysis of SA was just macroscopic description of forming procedures than continuous functions varied with time. Simulation and deduction of SA generating and forming procedures would be analyzed and discussed in the future.

Acknowledgement. This study was financially supported by Foundation of Key Laboratory of Science and Technology for National Defense (Program Grant No. 9140C770102140C77313).

References

1. Endsley, M.R.: Measurement of situation awareness in dynamic systems. Hum. Factors **37**, 65–84 (1995)
2. Endsley, M.R.: Situation awareness in aviation systems. Handbook of Aviation Human Factors, pp. 257–276 (1999)
3. Endsley, M.R., Garland, D.J.: Situation Awareness Analysis and Measurement. Erlbaum, Mahwah (2000)
4. Wei, H.Y., Zhuang, D.M., Wanyan, X.R., et al.: An experimental analysis of situation awareness for cockpit display interface evaluation based on flight simulation. Chin. J. Aeronaut. **26**, 884–889 (2013)

5. Kirlik, A., Strauss, R.: Situation awareness as judgment I: statistical modeling and quantitative measurement. Int. J. Ind. Ergon. **36**, 463–474 (2006)
6. Wickens, C.D.: Situation awareness and workload in aviation. Curr. Dir. Psychol. Sci. **11**, 128–133 (2002)
7. Wickens, C.D., Jason, M.C., Thomas, L.: Attention–Situation Awareness (A-SA) Model. In: NASA Aviation Safety Program Conference on Human Performance Modeling of Approach and Landing with Augmented Displays, pp. 189–205. NASA (2003)
8. Hooey, B.L., Gore, B.F., Wickens, C.D.: Modeling pilot situation awareness. In: Cacciabue, P.C., Hjälmdahl, M., Luedtke, A., Riccioli, C. (eds.) Human Modeling in Assisted Transportation, pp. 207–213. Springer, Milan (2012)
9. Liu, S., Wanyan, X.R., Zhuang, D.M.: A quantitative situational awareness model of pilot. In: Proceedings of the International Symposium of Human Factors and Ergonomics in Healthcare, pp. 117–122 (2014)
10. Liu, S., Wanyan, X.R., Zhuang, D.M.: Modeling the situation awareness by the analysis of cognitive process. J. Bio-Med. Mater. Eng. **24**, 2311–2318 (2014)
11. Wu, X., Wanyan, X., Zhuang, D.: Pilot attention allocation modeling under multiple factors condition. In: Harris, D. (ed.) EPCE 2013, Part II. LNCS, vol. 8020, pp. 212–221. Springer, Heidelberg (2013)

The Research of Eye Movement Behavior of Expert and Novice in Flight Simulation of Landing

Wei Xiong[1], Yu Wang[2], Qianxiang Zhou[2], Zhongqi Liu[2],
and Xin Zhang[3(✉)]

[1] Science and Technology on Complex Electronic
System Simulation Laboratory, Beijing 101416, China
[2] Key Laboratory for Biomechanics and Mechanobiology of the Ministry
of Education, School of Biological Science and Medical Engineering,
Beihang University, Beijing 100191, China
[3] China National Institute of Standardization, Beijing 100191, China
zhangx@cnis.gov.cn

Abstract. The objective of this research is to study the eye movement patterns of pilots in landing process by analyzing and comparing the eye movement data of experts and novices so as to reveal their cognitive process of information processing in the final landing stage. Ten experts who have flown above 1000 h and fourteen novices whose flight hours were between 200 to 400 participated the experiment. All subjects' task was to implement a landing task according visual flight rules in no wind and shinning day and the landing task was completed with a high fidelity flight simulator. Eye movement data and flight parameters data were recorded during the experiment. The result showed that there was obvious difference of flight performance between experts and novices. The course deviation, roll angel and pitch angel of experts were better compared to that of novices. And the land course of experts was also better than that of novices. It could be found by the comparison of eye movement index between experts and novices that there were obvious differences of six eye movement index. Expert showed shorter fixation time, smaller pupil size changes, lager scanning range, faster scan velocity, greater scan frequency and greater fixation frequency. So the conclusion can be made that there is obvious differences between experts and novices not only in flight performance but also in eye movement pattern; the scanning pattern is related to flight performance and effective scanning pattern is related to better flight performance; so the measurement of eye movement pattern can be used to evaluate and forecast flight performance and thus to guide the training.

Keywords: Eye movement · Expert · Novice · Flight simulation · Ergonomics

1 Introduction

The research of eye movement is the most effective means of Visual information processing. The expert-novice paradigm has often been applied by the eye movement researchers in the past more 30 years and it is widely used in sports, traffic, medical,

D. Harris (Ed.): EPCE 2016, LNAI 9736, pp. 485–493, 2016.
DOI: 10.1007/978-3-319-40030-3_47

text reading, aviation environments, etc. [1–7] In this paradigm the subjects would be divided into experts and novices, and their eye movement data which include the fixation time, fixation count, scanning range and so on were recorded and the comparison was made between the two groups of their eye movement data, so as to find the difference of the eye movement pattern of the two groups. With this comparison, the efficient and practical eye movement mode of experts and the scanning defects of novices could be found which is of great practical significance to guides novices for their skills training.

As early as the late 1940s, Fitts found the scan difference between expert and novice, and noted the scan difference between skilled pilots and novice [8]. He found that experts have shorter fixation time than novices on each instruments and suggested this difference could be used to distinguish the degree of operational maturity of the expert and novice. Eye movement is also used to evaluate the usability of newly developed electric map. Simulated flight according to visual flight rules, Ottati et al. compared the scanning mode of expert and novice in different terrain conditions [5]. It was found that experts have shorter time to search the sign of navigation and fixate to it, while novices are difficult to search navigation signs and have longer time to fixate it. Bellenkes et al. (1997) found that expert pilots make more frequent scanning on speed instrument than novices when the height is in variation [6]. Kasarskis Peter et al. (2001) recorded the eye movements data of 10 novice and 6 expert pilots in the approach and landing phase [9]. It is could be found that experts have shorter fixation time, more fixation count than novices, less attention to the speed meter, more simple and regular sweep mode. In order to improve the novices training efficiency, Sajay et al. recorded the fixation points and scanning path of the experts observation to the cargo in the cockpit, and used the recorded eye movement data as a feed forward to train the novices [7]. They divided the novices into two control groups, one was trained with the experts' search pattern, and the other did not. The results showed that the performance of providing the experts' search mode group was higher than the other. So they think that experts' scanning mode could be used to guide novices to scanning. Through systematic study, the military of American found that eye movement measurement system could significantly improve the effect of training when the system was applied to the air force training and it was obvious when it was particularly used in the initial training phase, and in that condition, it can correct the wrong scan habits at an early stage. In the training course for F16B, there exists 10 courses that use eye movement measurement systems [10].

As could be seen, professional experience and knowledge in the field affects not only the performance also the scanning behavior. In the field of aviation research, as the task situation varies, the choice of performance and eye movement indicators are also different. The manipulation of the landing stage is complex and the information changes rapidly, so the accident rate is higher, but the current research of visual scanning to this phase is still little, lack of detailed and comprehensive studies. So as to further learn the scanning pattern of expert pilots and novice, this paper simulate the final landing phase of the mission to makes an overall comparison based on records of eye movement data between expert and novice glance to obtain quantitative differences in the two scanning mode. The results will provide support for pilot training and for the evaluation of flight performance.

2   Method

2.1   Participants

Twenty-four subjects who are flight simulation amateurs participated the experiment, and their skill came from the PC (personal computer) on the flight simulator games and flight simulators. NASA found that training skills in the PC can be actively transferred to the actual flight, so the choice of subjects is reasonable [11].

After the observation to the performance in the simulator operation and also the interview, it could be found that 10 individuals' simulation flight time is longer and their operation was more skilled, so they were defined as experts. The flight hours of the others were shorter, and their proficiency in operating was poorer, so they were defined as novices. Subjects ages ranged from 20 to 30 years old who all of them were of normal vision or corrected vision with no other eye diseases. All subjects could implement all courses of basic simulation tasks.

2.2   Apparatus

Experimental measurement systems included flight simulators and eye movement measurement system. The prototype of the simulator was a fighter that has been tested with high validity. The simulator could measure and record the flight parameters during the flight. Eye movement measurement system was Eyelink II measurement system which was made by Canada SR Research company. It worked with a way of pupil and corneal reflex and its sampling frequency was 250 Hz, average gaze error was less than $0.5°$.

Eye movement measurement system could not only measure eyes numerical data, also could record the video data. The position of the subjects' fixation and the sequence to scan instrument of subjects could be known bye the playback of video. The measured data by Eyelink II system was processed by the software of DataViewer and then many eye-movement indices could be obtained, such as the fixation duration, pupil size, scanning amplitude, blink count and so on.

2.3   Experiment Task

Experiments required subjects to complete the approaching and landing task with simulator according an visual flight rules (VFR, Visual Flight Rule) on a cloudless and sunny day. The diagram of landing task was shown in Fig. 1. When the subjects landing, they were asked to keep a good attitude, and make a smooth land on the runway as accurately as possible. The landing point was near the position of 5400 m from the starting point of landing. Each subject completed 4 landing missions.

2.4   Procedure

Before the subjects made the flight, the background of the experiment task was introduced to them and then they worn the head mounted eye tracking system to make

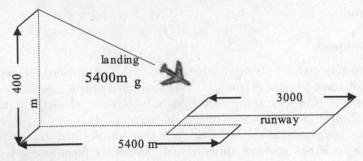

Fig. 1. Experiment pictures

a calibration. After the calibration, the subjects entered the cockpit of the simulator and exercised about 5 to 10 headgear to minutes to adapt simulator and get familiar to the task. Then the experiment started. Each subject would calibrate again before the starting of the task, and performed the same procedure. The experiment scene was shown as Fig. 2.

Fig. 2. Experimental scenario

3   Results

The performance of plane landing at last stage could be evaluated by four indexes, flight gliding angle, yaw angle, tilt angle and falling rate. The first three indicators evaluated the pilots' capabilities of controlling the aircraft attitude while the gliding rate accessed the stability of the aircraft flight. The stability of landing is the key to the safe landing of plane. The "t" test of performance indices of the expert and novice has been carried on and results showed the significant differences (see Table 1). It could be seen that the experts' performance of controlling the attitude in three flight axes was better than that of novices. It was particularly in aircraft directional controlling and tilt angle controlling, there existed significant difference between expert and novice. Moreover expert performed better than novices in landing stability.

Table 1. Comparison of the flight performance between expert and novice ($n = 24$, $\bar{x} \pm s$)

Subject	Pitch angle (°)	Yaw angle (°)	Roll angle (°)	Gliding rate (m/s)
Expert	2.5 ± 1.5	1.4 ± 1.4	3.5 ± 2.8	11.8 ± 1.6
Novice	3.9 ± 2.9	6.5 ± 3.4	16.3 ± 12.1	15.6 ± 3.0
"t" test	*	***	***	***

Note: *$P < 0.05$, ***$P < 0.001$, as compared with expert group

After the processing of the eye movement data, it was found that s there exist obvious differences in six eye movements indices, including average fixation time, average scan amplitude, the average pupil change rate, average scanning velocity, fixation frequency and scanning frequency, the "t" test results were shown in Table 2. Expert have shorter fixation time, smaller average pupil changes, lager scanning amplitude, faster scanning velocity, greater scan frequency and greater fixation frequency. Ottati found that novices pay more attention to out view of cockpit compared with the experts [5] and the similar results were obtained in this experiment. From the video playback, it could be found that the distribution of attention between experts and novices was significantly different. Experts not only paid attention to the external visual, but also intermittently glanced at cockpit instrument. The experts regularly switched vision between cockpit instruments and external scene. The novices just scanned external view of cockpit and particularly focused on the narrow runway. The novices almost didn't pay any attention to the instrumentation.

Table 2. Comparison of eye movement indices between expert and novice ($n = 24$, $\bar{x} \pm s$)

Subject	Fixation Time (ms)	Saccade amplitude (°)	Pupil Variance (%)	Saccade Velocity (°/s)	Fixation Frequency (min-1)	Saccade frequency (min-1)
Expert	591 ± 43	7 ± 1.3	0.32 ± 0.05	133 ± 21.7	104 ± 6.1	95 ± 19.2
Novice	730 ± 35	5 ± 0.3	0.38 ± 0.01	79 ± 8.4	77 ± 6	65 ± 11
"t" test	**	*	***	***	***	***

Note: *$P < 0.05$, **$P < 0.001$, ***$P < 0.001$, as compared with expert group

4 Discussion

4.1 The Analysis of Differences in Scanning Mode

Seen from the video playback, novice was almost paid all their attention on the runway, while expert not only concentrated on the runway and the horizon but also regularly scanned the speedometer, the altimeter and the attitude instrument in the cockpit. For this reason, more information sources were obtained by experts, and range of the scanning was relatively wide. Expert could more accurately grasp flight parameters information, land more accurately and smoothly and make better flight performance by contrasting the information obtained from visual reference of exterior scenes with instrument information in cockpit. In conclusion, one important reason of different flight performances between novice and expert was that the way they distributed their attention. So the feature of expert's attention distribution should be studied more deeply which could guide novice distribute their attention more reasonably in actual flight training.

The time of landing process was very short. So as to acquire information from more sources within limited time, high-speed and flexibility of experts' eye movement were required. Experts must reasonably allocate time on each information source. They also need to transfer and switch attention quickly. So the scanning speed of expert was faster, and the scanning frequency was greater. Relevant expert held the opinion that the defect of acquisition or processing of information could be remedied by frequent and rapid scanning activity [12]. It was a necessary condition that driver scanned instrument and exterior scenes fast and frequently in the process of training novice to become a skilled pilot. So at the beginning of flight training, novice should be guided to make quick and frequent scanning consciously to develop correct scanning habits.

Relevant research found that expert spent less time on all instruments and had more fixation point compared with novice in flight [13]. Although this experiment task was VFR flight, the same result was obtained. There were two main reasons for this difference between experts and novices. For the first reason, because trained for a long time, Expert had more developed peripheral vision than novice, and expert could use the surrounding visual to access information preferably. In this way, expert did not require to stare at instrument to obtain information, they reduced the time spent on fixating at instrument [3]. The second reason is that expert had more knowledge and experience. Because of long time flight, the information processing and cognition of expert tended to programmed and automation. They processed information with a way of high efficiency of Top-Down that can process information with modularization. They did faster than novice in the process of extracting and encoding information and in decision, so they had the advantage of time [14]. Because of lacking of training, the scanning pattern of Bottom-Up was more used by novice which made novice spend more time on information searching and locating. It was difficult for novice to extracting information and they need fixate on information longer time to perceive it. As the result, expert had the ability to extract information at a shorter fixation time, which provided them plenty of time to adjust the deviation in time when aircraft was flying and made plane landing accurately and stably. Thus, enlightenment was acquired. There were two factors needed to make the driver faster in accessing the target location information in the complex cockpit environment. The first was the well training that automated scanning of top-down was developed. The second was the good design. For example, the alarm display system captured operator's attention in the way of Bottom-Up which cause the efficient distribution of attention.

Changes of the pupil reflected the changes of pilot's mental workload in the information processing. High pupil change rate reflected the heavy information processing task and the high mental workload. Conversely, mental workload was low. A fact could be found from the result that the higher frequency and greater scanning amplitude of scanning of expert haven't raised the mental workload which showed that the improvement of the flight performance is not at the expense of mental workload and efficient and good eye movement pattern not only can improve performance but also release mental workload. Relevant person also made the same opinion [15].

Shapiro found that the performance of subjects adopting high efficient pattern of eye movement was significantly better than that didn't use and after a period of time, the subjects who did not use the high effective eye movement pattern would automatically adopt the effective scanning method when they played video game [16]. The eye movement pattern of the expert pilots should be recorded by the eye movement measuring system when they are training to provide mode that the novice could imitate. The imitating effect should be checked by eye movement system, so as to help novices develop correct scanning habits in the early stage of training, and help them to improve their training efficiency and shorten the training period.

Two characteristics could be found from the above discussion. One was that the flight performance of expert was better than novice; the other was that the scanning mode of expert was different from novice. Analyzing from the aspect of information processed, eye movement reflected the input and processing of information. Flight performance was the result of output information. Although eye movement behavior was not the single factor that produced performance differences, the flight performance could be reflected from the eye movement pattern. A continuous, active and efficient scanning pattern corresponded to a perfect flight performance. Therefore, performance analysis could be judged by analyzing the pattern of eye movement.

4.2   The Relationship Between Scan Pattern and Training

Usually, instructional training could promote the speed of learning. Therefore for the training of instrument scanning in cockpit, instructors generally used the language to guide trainee the method used to read instruments which showed the flight status under specific tasks, the optimal time to read instruments, the type of instrument they should read and the order of scanning. After repeated such training, trainee can master the relationship between instrument and task, they could also extract relevant information when they manipulate flight. For example, in the initial stage of training trainee was required to begin to check the instrument from the level flight indicator and came back to the level flight indicator in the end. I.e. the level flight indicator to climb meter to the level flight indicator; the level flight indicator to speedometer to the level flight indicator; the level flight indicator to heading device (radio compass) to the level flight indicator; and so on. In the middle period of the training, trainee must learn to assign and shift attention to the instrument cluster and do instrument inspection work in an "8" shaped way. The sequence was the level flight indicator-speedometer-altimeter-turn and sideslip indicator. Then the sequence is the level flight indicator-automatic wireless electronic compass-climb meter. Relevant experts believed that this guidance was helpful to the formation of a stable and flexible instrument scanning skill, and it could make trainee gradually raise a good scanning instrument habit [17].

The question whether scanning guidance of expert was effective, whether novice carried out the intention of the instructor was not validated. It was a effective way to use eye movement to check it. Mission in Shapiro's video game belonged to simple mission compared to aircraft manipulation [16]. The environment of cockpit was complex and the flight was difficult to control. The conclusion about pattern of expert scanning hadn't formed. From the perspective of cognition theory, someone held the opinion that the scanning technology of expert would not be formed in a accelerate way, it would only be obtained gradually by practice. In this opinion, the guidance of the scanning strategy was based on expert's knowledge and experience of the Top-Down training strategy. This kind of scanning strategy which was efficient strategy was obtained by the experts after a long time of practice, training and continuous optimization. At the beginning of the training, expert practiced in the Bottom-Up way. With the addition of exercise time, the scanning components of Top-Down way gradually increased, until it was dominant [18]. The report recognized that the guidance of expert scanning patterns may be more effective in the case of relatively simple procedural tasks such as task which need to monitor instrument but didn't need to make control action. In the case of complex operation task in which trainee needed the coordinate eye and hand and make more decision, scanning strategy perhaps mostly relied on trainee daily practice and gradual development. For example, the mental workload of pilot was small in cruising flight when trainee needed to check the instrument according to the procedure, while in stunt training and tactical training, the task was more difficult, and trainee may not scan the instrument according to the intention of the instructor. Since the initial stage of the novice pilot flight training was generally start with a simple primary task. The eye movement measurement equipment could be used to record the expert pilot's scanning mode which was provided to novice to imitate. This can help novice develop a correct scanning habit, improve training efficiency, shorten the training period in initial stage of training.

5   Conclusion

Through the comparative study of expert and novice, the characteristics of the scanning mode of expert and novice were obtained, the relationship between the scanning mode and flight performance was determined. Quantitative differences between expert and novices in the 6 eye movement indexes were obtained. The specific conclusions are as follow:

1. Expert and novice not only have obvious differences in flight performance, but also have significant differences in eye movement patterns.
2. Performance of expert is better than novice. Expert has the shorter fixation time, more fixation point, faster scanning velocity, greater scan frequency and wider scan area than novice. It is also found that eye movement pattern of expert bring lower mental workload than novice.
3. The eye movement patterns relate to the flight performance. High efficiency eye movement patterns relate to better flight performance. Therefore, contrasted with the mode of expert's eye movement, the eye movement measuring instrument could be used in the training to inspect the novice's scanning defect, track and evaluate the training progress, and provide the reference for the flight training plan adjustment and the formulation.

Acknowledgement. This research was funded by National science and technology support plan "User evaluation technology and standard research of display and control interface ergonomics" (2014BAK01B04).

References

1. Falkmer, T., Gregersen, N.P.: A comparison of eye movement behavior of inexperienced and experienced drivers in real traffic environments. Optom. Vis. Sci. **82**(8), 732–739 (2005)
2. Chapman, P.R., Underwood, G.: Visual search of driving situations: danger and experience. Perception **27**, 951–964 (1998)
3. Mourant, R.R., Rockwell, T.H.: Strategies of visual search by novice and experienced drivers. Hum. Factors **14**, 325–335 (1972)
4. Benjamin, L.M., Stella, A.A.E., et al.: Eye gaze patterns differentiate novice and experts in a virtual laparoscopic surgery training environment. In: Proceedings ETRA 2004 - Eye Tracking Research and Applications Symposium, pp. 41–47 (2004)
5. Ottati, W.L., Hickox, J.C., Richter, J.: Eye scan patterns of experienced and novice pilots during visual flight rules (VFR) navigation. In: Proceedings of the Human Factors and Ergonomics Society, 43rd Annual Meeting, Minneapolis, MN (1999)
6. Bellenkes, A.H., Wickens, C.D., Kramer, A.F.: Visual scanning and pilot expertise: their role of attention flexibility and mental model development. Aviat. Space Environ. Med. **68** (7), 569–579 (1997)
7. Sajay, S., Joel, S., Greenstein, A.K., et al.: Use of eye movements as feedforward training for a synthetic aircraft inspection task. Eyes Interact. **4**(2), 140–149 (2005)
8. Fitts, P.M., Jones, R.E.: Eye fixation of aircraft pilots, III. Frequency, duration, and sequence fixations when flying air force ground controlled approach system. AF-5967 (1949)
9. Kasarskis, P., Stehwien, J., Hickox, J., et al.: Comparison of expert and novice scan behaviors during VFR flight. In: The 11th International Symposium on Aviation Psychology (2001)
10. Wetzel, P.A., Anderson, K., Gretchen, M., et al.: Instructor use of eye position based feedback for pilot training. Hum. Factors Ergon. Soc. **2**, 5–9 (1998)
11. Henry, L., Taylor, D.A., Talleur, T.W., et al.: Incremental Training Effectiveness of Personal Computers Used for Instrument Training: Basic Instruments. ARL-02-4/NASA-02-2 (2002)
12. Ding, B.X.: Aircraft Driving. The Blue Sky Press, Beijing (2004). (in Chinese)
13. Kramer, A., Tham, M., Wichkens, C., et al.: Instrument scan and pilot expertise. In: Proceedings of the Human Factors and Ergonomics Society 38th Annual Meeting, pp. 36–40 (2004)
14. McConkie, G., Kramer, A.: Information extraction during instrument flight: an evaluation of the validity of the eye-mind hypothesis. In: Proceedings of the Human Factors and Ergonomics Society 40th Annual Meeting, pp. 77–81 (1996)
15. Ahern, S., Beatty, J.: Pupillary responses during information processing vary with scholastic aptitude test scores. Science **205**, 1289–1292 (1979)
16. Shapiro, K.L., Raymond, J.E.: Training of efficiency oculomotor strategies enhances skill acquisition. Acta Psychol. **71**, 217–242 (1989)
17. E, Z.M.: Flight Training Psychology. Aviation Industry Press, Beijing (1991). (in Chinese)
18. Bellenkes, A.H.: the use of expert pilot performance models to facilitate cockpit visual scan training. College of the University of Illisnois at Urbana-Chamaign (1976)

Author Index

Printed in the United States
By Bookmasters